To the Memory of Distinguished Professor David Syrett

PUBLICATIONS

OF THE

NAVY RECORDS SOCIETY

VOL. 148

THE RODNEY PAPERS, VOLUME I

The NAVY RECORDS SOCIETY was established in 1893 for the purpose of printing unpublished manuscripts and rare works of naval interest. The Society is open to all who are interested in naval history, and any person wishing to become a member should apply to the Hon. Secretary, Department of War Studies, King's College London, Strand, London WC2R 3LS. The annual subscription is £30, which entitles the member to receive one free copy of each work issued by the Society in that year, and to buy earlier issues at much reduced prices.

SUBSCRIPTIONS and orders for back volumes should be sent to the Membership Secretary, 1 Avon Close, Petersfield, Hants GU31 4LG.

THE COUNCIL OF THE NAVY RECORDS SOCIETY wish it to be clearly understood that they are not answerable for any opinions and observations which may appear in the Society's publications. For these the editors of the several works are entirely responsible.

THE RODNEY PAPERS

Selections from the Correspondence
of Admiral Lord Rodney

VOLUME I

1742–1763

Edited by

DAVID SYRETT

*Distinguished Professor of History, Queen's College,
City University of New York*

PUBLISHED BY ASHGATE
FOR THE NAVY RECORDS SOCIETY
2005

© The Navy Records Society, 2005

All rights reserved. No part of this publication may be reproduced, stored in a retrieval system, or transmitted in any form or by any means, electronic, mechanical, photocopied, recorded, or otherwise without the prior permission of the publisher.

Crown copyright material is reproduced by permission of The Stationery Office.

Published by
Ashgate Publishing Limited
Gower House
Croft Road
Aldershot
Hants GU11 3HR
England

Ashgate Publishing Company
Suite 420
101 Cherry Street
Burlington, VT 05401-4405
USA

Ashgate website: http://www.ashgate.com

British Library Cataloguing in Publication Data

Rodney, George Brydges
  The Rodney papers : selections from the correspondence of Admiral Lord Rodney
  Vol. 1: 1742–1763. – (Publications of the Navy Records Society ; no. 148)
  1.Rodney, George Brydges – Correspondence 2.Admirals – Great Britain – Correspondence
  I.Title II.Syrett, David
  359.3'31'092

Library of Congress Cataloging-in-Publication Data

Rodney, George Brydges Rodney, Baron, 1718–1792.
  The Rodney papers : selections from the correspondence of Admiral Lord Rodney / edited by David Syrett.
    p. cm. – (Navy Records Society publications ; 148)
  Contents: v. 1. 1742–1763
  ISBN 0-7546-5179-7 (alk. paper)
  1. Rodney, George Brydges Rodney, Baron, 1718–1792 – Correspondence. 2. Great Britain – History, Naval – 18th century – Sources. 3. Admirals – Great Britain – Correspondence.
  I. Syrett, David. II. Title. III. Publications of the Navy Records Society ; vol. 148.

DA87.1.R6A4 2005
359'.0092–dc22
[B]
                                                                    2004047680

ISBN 0 7546 5179 7

Printed on acid-free paper

Typeset in Times by Manton Typesetters, Louth, Lincolnshire, UK.
Printed and bound in Great Britain by MPG Books Ltd, Bodmin, Cornwall.

THE COUNCIL OF THE NAVY RECORDS SOCIETY 2005

PATRON
H.R.H. THE PRINCE PHILIP, DUKE OF EDINBURGH,
K.G., O.M., F.R.S.

PRESIDENT
Admiral of the Fleet SIR BENJAMIN BATHURST, G.C.B., D.L.

VICE-PRESIDENTS
M.A. SIMPSON, M.A., F.R.Hist.S.
Professor R.J.B. KNIGHT, M.A., D.Phil., F.R.Hist.S.
Dr M. DUFFY, M.A., D.Phil., F.R.Hist.S.
Lt-Commander F.L. PHILLIPS, R.D., T.D., R.N.R.

COUNCILLORS

Captain C.H.H. OWEN, R.N.
Professor R. HARDING
R.W.A. SUDDABY, M.A.
Captain C.J. PARRY, M.A., R.N.
Professor J.B. HATTENDORF
Professor C. DANDEKER
Captain S.C. JERMY, B.Sc., M.Phil., R.N.
Dr C.S. KNIGHTON, M.A., Ph.D., D.Phil., F.S.A., F.R.Hist.S.
Dr C. WILKINSON
Rear Admiral J.R. HILL
Dr C.I. HAMILTON, M.A., Ph.D.
C. White
Dr S.P. ROSE, M.A., Ph.D.

A. MCGOWAN
Professor D.A. BAUGH
J. WRAIGHT
R.H.A. BRODHURST
Dr J.D. DAVIES, M.A., B.Phil.
Commander M. MASON, RN
Captain P. HORE
Dr J. MAIOLO
Dr T. BENBOW
Professor D. LOADES, F.R.Hist.S.
Dr T. WAREHAM
P. K. CRIMMIN, M.Phil., F.R.Hist.S., F.S.A.

HON. SECRETARY
Professor A.D. LAMBERT, M.A., Ph.D., F.R.Hist.S.

HON. TREASURER
J.V. TYLER, F.C.C.A.

GENERAL EDITOR
R.A. MORRISS, B.A., Ph.D.

MEMBERSHIP SECRETARY
Mrs A. GOULD

CONTENTS

	PAGE
Preface	xi
Editorial Policies	xiii
Abbreviations for Repositories of Manuscript Sources	xiii
EARLY YEARS, 1742–1748	1
POST CAPTAIN, 1749–1759	123
FLAG OFFICER, 1759–1763	259
Appendix: List of Documents and Sources	493
Index	515

PREFACE

George Brydges Rodney is one of the great British admirals of the Age of Sail. A participant, and in many instances a major player, in some of the great naval events of the 18th century, Rodney's career as a navy officer spans the three great naval conflicts of his time – the War of Austrian Succession, the Seven Years War, and the American War. Rodney, even though a towering figure in the Royal Navy of the 18th century, has attracted comparatively little attention. For he is, as are most other navy officers of the period, eclipsed in the imagination of both historians and the public by Nelson. Additionally, being in many respects almost a caricature of the age in which he lived, Rodney is a most difficult personality for many in the early 21st century to sympathise with or even understand. For many, due to the way in which Parliamentary elections and patronage were conducted during the 18th century, and due to Rodney's perceived life style, there is an aroma of political corruption and personal dissipation that seems to emanate from the admiral. At the same time he is seen as larger than life: Rodney appears to many as an overbearing man, carrying himself with aristocratic hauteur, at loggerheads with everybody and always questing for and squandering money. Though Rodney, especially during the American War, may well have been overbearing, avaricious, difficult and uncongenial, he was nevertheless a great admiral as well as an original thinker of considerable importance in naval affairs.

Historians, in the more than two hundred years that have lapsed since the admiral's death, have not paused long to study Rodney. There are only two biographies of Rodney worth any notice. At the beginning of the third decade of the 19th century G. B. M. Mundy published *Life and Correspondence of the Late Admiral Lord Rodney* (London, 1830). Modern historians of Hanoverian England and of the Royal Navy, usually with some reason, have dismissed Mundy's work as an inaccurate attempt to rehabilitate Rodney in the eyes of pre-Victorians. It was not until 1969 that a satisfactory biography of Rodney appeared with the publication of David Spinney's *Rodney* (London, 1969). While some people have taken exception to some of Spinney's judgements, it is difficult to disagree with the facts in Spinney's biography, for the work is based on extensive research in manuscript sources. The later work thus goes a certain way to filling the gap in the historiography concerning Rodney's life and career.

The selection of documents in this volume of the *Rodney Papers*, the first of a projected three volume edition of the admiral's papers, deals with Rodney's early career from 1742, when he was promoted to post captain, through to the end of the Seven Years War. It is an attempt to elucidate the role of Rodney in the events of the 18th century and to present his views on naval affairs of his time. The materials for this volume came from the National Archives of the United Kingdom with a leavening of manuscripts from the British Library. While these documents overwhelmingly concern Rodney's career as a navy officer, they also present the reader with interesting glimpses of his political and personal life. The picture that emerges from the documents is one of a very talented and extremely ambitious navy officer who is pushing himself, with all the means at his command, ahead in the world.

This volume would never have been possible without the assistance and co-operation given to the editor by a number of people and institutions in Great Britian and the United States. Crown copyright material from The National Archives of the United Kingdom appears with permission of the Controller of HM Stationery Office. I wish to thank the staffs of the National Archives of the United Kingdom, Kew; the British Library, London; the Institute of Historical Research, University of London; and the Rosenthal Library of Queens College, City University of New York. I also wish to thank Dr K. E. Evans and in particular Dr. Roger Morriss, General Editor of the Navy Records Society, for all his good care and concern. The research for this book was supported, in part, by the City University of New York PSC-CUNY Research Award Program and the completion of this volume was assisted by a Queens College, City University of New York Scholar Incentive Award.

EDITORIAL POLICIES

In general, the hand-written originals of the documents which appear in this volume have been transcribed literally although, in accordance with the policy of the Society, spelling and punctuation have been modernised. Words supplied by the editor for clarity of meaning appear within square brackets. Mis-spelled or erratically spelled geographical place names have also been standardised using the *Columbia Gazetteer* and *The Times Atlas*.

In providing factual annotation, the editor has assumed that his readers will be naval historians with a fairly high level of expert knowledge. Thus such notes have been limited, for the most part, to providing the following data:

1. When an important person is first mentioned, a complete indentification is given with full name, title and position. For figures of lesser importance, the editor has, whenever possible, provided full names and ranks within square brackets within the text of the document.
2. References made in the documents to military, naval and political events are also explained in footnotes.
3. Some technical naval and maritime words have also been explained in footnotes.

Cross-references are provided to information which appears in more than one document. In addition, in many cases the phrase 'Enclosed is the state and condition of the ship under my command', which appears at the end of many documents, has been omitted. Equally, the signature of the author and the complimentary close at the end of the letters have also been omitted.

Abbreviations used in the citations

BL British Library
Add. MSS Additional Manuscripts
TNA The National Archives of the United Kingdom
ADM Admiralty

PRO   Private collections, Rodney Papers

PART I

EARLY YEARS, 1742–1748

Admiral Lord Rodney, who was born at the end of 1717, or at the beginning of 1718 and baptised on 13 February 1718 in London at the church of St Giles-in-the-Field, Marylebone, was a member of a younger branch of a good Somerset family. The future admiral was the second son of Henry Rodney of Walton-on-Thames and Mary Newton, the daughter of a diplomat and Admiralty Judge.[1] Information on his early years is rather sketchy. His father, Henry Rodney, was an ex-captain of marines who had lost the family fortune speculating in South Sea Company stock,[2] and according to one authority, George Rodney was brought up by and under the protection of George Rodney Brydges of Avington and Keinsham.[3] There can be little doubt, however, that Rodney did also receive the support and protection of another relative, James Brydges, 1st Duke of Chandos. For it must have been on the recommendation and sponsorship of the duke that Rodney may have attended the prestigious Harrow School. His name does not appear in the school register.[4] Nevertheless, it has been suggested he may have attended the school; if he did, his stay at that educational institution was of a short duration for he was destined for a career as an officer in the Royal Navy.

In 18th-century England there were very few careers which a person, such as George Brydges Rodney, coming from a poor but respectable family with a military background,[5] could pursue without loss of status. Business and trade were not suitable, and besides they required capital; moreover before the rise of the modern professional classes careers such as one in medicine were also frowned upon. To be a surgeon was to be one step removed from being a barber. That left the civil service, the church, and the armed forces of the Crown as suitable alternative

---

[1] Romney Sedgwick, *History of Parliament: The House of Commons, 1715–1754* (London, 1970), vol. II, p. 390.
[2] David Spinney, *Rodney* (London, 1969), p. 20.
[3] R. Egerton Brydges, *Collin's Peerage of England* (London, 1812), vol. VII, p. 562n.
[4] W. T. J. Gun, *The Harrow School Register, 1571–1800* (London, 1934), p. 22.
[5] Rodney's father, grandfather and great uncle held commissions in the marines. Spinney, *Rodney*, p. 22.

careers. The government, especially the Royal Navy, was a career in which the sons of the impoverished middle classes could not only enter but, with a certain amount of skill, luck and no little determination, even gain fame and fortune.

George Rodney's career in the Royal Navy began on 7 May 1732 when his name was entered in the muster books of HMS *Sunderland*, a fourth rate 'hulked' at Chatham, as a volunter per order.[1] He was probably one of the last to do so, for in the first decades of the 18th century there were two ways in which a young man, who aspired to be an navy officer, could enter the Royal Navy. One route to becoming an officer was to be sponsored by a captain of a warship. These young men were known as captain's servants and this was the way in which a majority of the officers of the Georgian Royal Navy began their careers. An alternative method of becoming a naval officer in the early 18th century was to become a volunteer per order, by being issued a warrant by the Admiralty. Colloquially one was then known as a King's Letter Boy because of the warrant from the Admiralty. This warrant assigned a young man to a particular ship in order for him to be prepared to qualify as a lieutenant.[2] However, by the third decade of the 18th century, this method of entry into the Royal Navy was being phased out. So that when Rodney became a volunteer per order, he was one of the last persons to have entered the Royal Navy in this way.[3]

Almost no information has survived concerning Rodney's first years of service in the Royal Navy and what little does remain consists of items such as cryptic entries in muster books. For instance, it is not known who decided that Rodney should pursue a career as an officer in the Royal Navy. Nor is it known what influence was deployed at the Admiralty to obtain for Rodney, the son of an obscure ex-captain of marines, a warrant assigning him to a warship as a King's Letter Boy. Further, it is not even known for sure if Rodney ever actually stepped on to the decks of HMS *Sunderland* for false entries in ships' books and notarial attendance at duty in such circumstances were not uncommon.[4] For all anybody knows, while being carried on the books of HMS *Sunderland* Rodney could have remained behind a school desk at Harrow. Either way, it is of little consequence since Rodney's stay, whether

---

[1] TNA, ADM 36/4052, ff. 99.
[2] Cf. Michael Lewis, *A Social History of the Navy, 1793–1815* (London, 1960), pp. 143–4.
[3] Cf. C. F. Walker, *Young Gentlemen: The Story of Midshipmen from the XVIIth Century to the Present Day* (London, 1938), p. 23.
[4] Horatio Nelson, for example, was carried notarially for 14 months on the muster books of HMS *Triumph*.

notarial or not, in HMS *Sunderland*, was brief: on 7 August 1732, three months after being entered as a volunteer per order in the ship's muster books, Rodney was, in the records at least, discharged from the ship.[1]

Rodney's career in the Royal Navy only began in earnest on 1 January 1734. It was on this day at Spithead, that his name was entered into the muster book, as an able seaman, on HMS *Dreadnought*, a 60-gun ship commanded by Captain Alexander Geddes.[2] Altering Rodney's rating from volunteer per order to able seaman was not a change of status, but rather a means to permit him to draw wages. Volunteers were unpaid while able seamen were paid at the rate of 24 shillings per month less deductions for the Chatham Chest and Greenwich Hospital. Apparently Geddes took almost no interest in Rodney during his period of command of HMS *Dreadnought*. However, in November of 1734, Geddes was replaced in command of the ship by Captain Henry Medley who soon advanced Rodney to midshipman ordinary.[3] This was the first step on a promotional ladder which would lead, 44 years later, to Rodney becoming an admiral of the white squadron. Being rated as a midshipman was a prerequisite for entering the ranks of the commissioned officers of the Royal Navy.[4] Besides receiving the same pay as an able seaman, the responsibilities and status of a midshipman ordinary were exactly the same as a midshipman.[5] However, there was a distinction between the two ranks. Should the number of midshipmen on a ship be superior to what was permitted by the establishment, and authorised by the Admiralty, then all additional young men would be entered in the vessel's muster books as midshipmen ordinary. A midshipman was considered neither a commissioned officer nor a warrant officer, but rather a rating in which a young gentleman learnt the duties of and the skills necesary to subsequently become a comissioned officer in the Royal Navy. Rodney would become a midshipman and cease being a midshipman ordinary on 13 August 1737.[6]

HMS *Dreadnought* would provide Rodney in some respects with easy duty with which to begin his career. A month-and-a-half after he had joined HMS *Dreadnought*, the ship sailed from Spithead for the Downes where she would lay at anchor for the next four months before returning to Spithead on 8 August 1734. Then HMS *Dreadnought*

[1] TNA, ADM 36/4052, f. 122.
[2] TNA, ADM 36/814, f. 12.
[3] TNA, ADM 36/814, ff. 90, 132.
[4] *Regulations and Instructions Relating to His Majesty's Service at Sea* (London, 1746), p. 15.
[5] N. A. M. Rodger, *The Wooden World: An Anatomy of the Georgian Navy* (London, 1986), pp. 24–5.
[6] TNA, ADM 36/814, f. 132.

remained for a further ten months at either Portsmouth or at anchor at Spithead. On 27 May 1735, in company with a number of other British warships, HMS *Dreadnought*, with Midshipman Rodney on board, sailed from Spithead for Lisbon arriving in that port on 10 June. For the next two years HMS *Dreadnought*, based at Lisbon, would cruise up and down the coast of Portugal and into the Mediterranean calling at Cadiz, Gibraltar, and on one occasion reaching as far to the eastward as Genoa. On 3 September 1737 HMS *Dreadnought* returned to Spithead.[1] Service on HMS *Dreadnought* must have indeed been comparatively easy, with no fighting or great long voyages, in which Rodney could adapt to life in the Royal Navy.

The next ship in which Rodney served was HMS *Berwick*. Rodney's name first appears in the ship's muster book on 1 January 1738. One authority believes that there is a possibility that Rodney's service in this ship might have been notional.[2] There is no evidence other than entries in the muster book of HMS *Berwick*[3] that Rodney ever appeared on board the vessel. Moreover, the ship, during the time that Rodney was supposed to be on board, never left Portsmouth.[4] On 1 May 1738 Rodney was discharged from HMS *Berwick*, at least as far as the records show, and the next day he entered HMS *Romney*.[5] Shortly after Rodney joined HMS *Romney*, the ship sailed for Newfoundland where she remained during the summer and early autumn, before returning to England by way of Lisbon. On 26 December HMS *Romney* anchored at Spithead and then proceeded to Woolwich where the ship was paid off before entering the dockyard for repairs and a refit.[6]

In the Georgian Royal Navy for a young man such as Rodney to have a successful career required not only skill and perseverance but also patronage or, in the parlance of the time, the interest of a senior officer or some other powerful personage. In the case of Rodney interest would be provided by the Duke of Chandos. It was the Duke's support which obtained Rodney promotion from midshipman to lieutenant. In April of 1739 Chandos 'commanded young Rodney to Admiral [Nicholas] Haddock's care in the Mediterranean'.[7] After returning from Newfoundland, Rodney most likely obtained a berth in HMS *Falkland*, which was sailing from England, to join Haddock's squadron in the

[1] TNA, ADM 51/237, 1 Jan. 1734–3 Sept. 1737.
[2] Spinney, *Rodney*, p. 36.
[3] TNA, ADM 36/287, f. 9.
[4] TNA, ADM 51/105, 1 Jan.–1 May 1738.
[5] TNA, ADM 36/2985, f. 39.
[6] TNA, ADM 51/797, 26 June 1738–15 Feb. 1739.
[7] C. H. Collins Baker and Muriel Baker, *The Life and Circumstances of James Brydges First Duke of Chandos: Patron of the Liberal Arts* (Oxford, 1949), p. 219.

Mediterranean.[1] On 24 July 1739, the day HMS *Falkland*[2] actually joined Haddock's squadron, Rodney's name first appears in the muster book of the admiral's flag ship, HMS *Somerset*.[3]

On 30 October 1739 Rodney was transferred out of HMS *Somerset* into HMS *Dolphin*, a 24-gun ship, commanded by Captain Lord Aubrey who was an uncle of Rodney's.[4] While on board HMS *Dolphin* Rodney, by means which are not entirely clear, was promoted to the rank of lieutenant. When Rodney's name first appeared in the muster book of HMS *Dolphin* it was accompanied by the notation 'Supernum. Borne as an acting officer by order of Nicholas Haddock Esq. Rear Admiral of the Red and Commander in Chief.'[5] Then on 15 February 1740 Rodney was commissioned a lieutenant.[6] To be commissioned a lieutenant in the Royal Navy a midshipman was required to pass an oral examination on seamanship and navigation and to produce certificates showing that he was 'not under twenty-years of age' as well as that he had served at sea for at least six years.[7] Rodney's lieutenant's passing certificate is missing[8] and there is no record of his ever having taken the examination required in order to be commissioned a lieutenant. Two days after being commissioned a lieutenant, on 17 February 1740, Rodney was discharged from HMS *Dolphin* and the next day his name re-appeared in the ship's muster book as a lieutenant.[9]

Rodney would serve as a lieutenant in the Royal Navy for two months short of three years before being promoted to the rank of post captain. It was a swift promotion, and given the manner it was achieved, a rather exceptional one. HMS *Dolphin*, with Rodney serving on board, sailed from Gibraltar on 9 December 1739. Five days before Rodney's departure, Britain's declaration of war against Spain had been proclaimed at Gibraltar. HMS *Dolphin*, escorting a convoy of 23 merchant ships, arrived at Falmouth on 23 February 1740 and then proceeded up the Channel to Spithead.[10] After being refitted at Sheerness Dockyard, HMS *Dolphin* from May 1740 onwards operated for ten months, initially in the Western Approaches to the English Channel, the Bay of

[1]HMS *Falkland's* muster books for this period are missing from TNA.
[2]TNA, ADM 51/338, 24 July 1739.
[3]TNA, ADM 36/3850, f. 191.
[4]Spinney, *Rodney*, p. 17.
[5]TNA, ADM 36/862, f. 17.
[6]TNA, ADM 6/15, p. 248.
[7]*Regulations and Instructions Relating to His Majesty's Service at Sea*, pp. 14–15.
[8]Cf. Bruno Pappalardo, *Royal Navy Lieutenant's Passing Certificates, 1691–1902* (Chippenham, Wiltshire, 2001), part 2, p. 435.
[9]TNA, ADM 36/862, ff. 17, 33, 53, 78.
[10]TNA, ADM 51/255, Dec. 1739–Feb. 1740.

Biscay and subsequently in the North Sea along the east coast of Britain, protecting British trade from enemy attack.[1] On 21 February 1741, at Edinburgh Firth, Rodney was discharged from HMS *Dolphin* and placed into HMS *Essex*.[2]

Rodney's transfer out of HMS *Dolphin* and into HMS *Essex* was the first step in a series of transfers and manoeuvres which would lead to his promotion to the rank of post captain. Rodney's patron, the Duke of Chandos, believed that it would be very difficult for Rodney to be promoted in Britain, but that in the Mediterranean, with Rear Admiral Thomas Mathews serving as commander in chief, promotion would be almost certain.[3] Rodney's transfer into HMS *Essex* was apparently an attempt to get Rodney out to the Mediterranean. When Rodney had departed from HMS *Dolphin* in Scotland and began to make his way south, to England, HMS *Essex* was moored alongside a hulk at Woolwich; however, the ship was soon to be fitted for service. On 20 June 1741 HMS *Essex*, with Rodney serving as a lieutenant, was ready and in the Downes, en route to Portugal. After conducting several short cruises along the coast of Portugal, in the Bay of Biscay, as well as in the Western Approaches of the English Channel, the ship returned to Spithead.[4] On 3 October 1741, having served as third lieutenant of the ship, Rodney was discharged from HMS *Essex*.[5]

On 5 March 1742, Rodney was appointed, apparently at the request of Mathews, fifth lieutenant of his flagship HMS *Namur* which was being fitted for service in the Mediterranean at Portsmouth.[6] HMS *Namur* sailed for the Mediterranean and after a brief stop-over at Gibraltar, arrived at the British anchorage at Villa Franca, off the south coast of France, where the ship would remain at anchor serving as Mathews's flagship.[7] With great rapidity Rodney advanced up through the ranks of lieutenants on Mathews's flagship to become, on 25 July 1742, first lieutenant of HMS *Namur*.[8] Three months later, on 9 November 1742, at Villa Franca, Rodney was discharged from HMS *Namur*[9] and, on that very same day, he was appointed by Mathews to be captain of the 60-gun ship HMS *Plymouth*.[10] In one promotion Rodney had

[1]TNA, ADM 51/256, Feb. 1740–Feb. 1741.
[2]TNA, ADM 36/862, f. 159.
[3]Baker and Baker, *James Brydges, First Duke of Chandos*, p. 220.
[4]TNA, ADM 51/319, 26 Feb.–1 Oct. 1741.
[5]TNA, ADM 36/1049, f. 201.
[6]Spinney, *Rodney*, p. 48.
[7]TNA, ADM 51/620.
[8]TNA, ADM 36/2100, ff. 66, 115.
[9]TNA, ADM 36/2100, f. 158.
[10]TNA, ADM 51/699, 9 Nov. 1742.

progressed from being a lieutenant to acquiring the rank of post captain.

Rodney's promotion to the rank of post captain, which was confirmed by the Admiralty on 4 April 1743,[1] was not only wholly exceptional, but also a supreme act of patronage and contrary to Admiralty regulations. Indeed, Rodney is one of the very few, if not the only person, to obtain the rank of post captain without first serving as a master and commander.[2] For Admiralty regulations clearly state that 'None are to have the Rank of Captain, who have not commanded a Frigate of Twenty Guns, or more'.[3] By being appointed to command HMS *Plymouth*, a 60-gun ship, Rodney had in essence jumped over the head of scores of senior lieutenants and of all the masters and commanders in the Royal Navy.

When Rodney was appointed captain of HMS *Plymouth* he became a post captain. Attaining the position of post captain was an important step in the career of a navy officer for not only did post captains command ships of the line but, unlike the ranks of lieutenant, master and commander, a person holding the rank of post captain could, by seniority alone, advance to flag rank. And then, if he lived long enough, an officer could, again by seniority, advance through all the grades of admiral to obtain, at a very old age, the rank of admiral of the fleet – the highest rank of all![4] When Rodney obtained the rank of post captain, he was only 24 years old and had been a commissioned officer in the Royal Navy for little under two years. This rapid promotion was certainly not unheard of in the Georgian Royal Navy. We have the example of Hon. Augustus Keppel who, being on an even faster track for promotion, spent less than a year as a lieutenant, master and commander! Nevertheless, Rodney's promotion to post captain still stands out for speed. It took Hon. Samuel Barrington, Philip Affleck and Charles Middleton two, four and five years respectively to achieve the rank of post captain, while Maurice Suckling did not reach post captain until ten years after being commissioned a lieutenant. And Richard Hughes spent eleven years as a commissioned officer before being promoted to post captain.[5] It is, of course, difficult to generalise about promotion to post captain in the 18th-century Royal Navy. In many instances it depended not only on interest and family connections, but also on ability as well as on being in the right

---

[1]TNA, ADM 6/16, p. 166.
[2]Cf. David Syrett and R. L. DiNardo, *The Commissioned Sea Officers of the Royal Navy, 1660–1815* (Aldershot, Hants. for the Navy Records Society, 1994).
[3]*Regulations and Instructions Relating to His Majesty's Service at Sea*, p. 8.
[4]Cf. Lewis, *A Social History of the Navy*, pp. 186–9.
[5]Syrett and DiNardo, *Commissioned Sea Officers*, pp. 2, 20, 223, 231, 252, 255, 427.

place at the right time. Taking into account all these factors, in the case of Rodney, it is clear that interest and family connections were decisive. They are also representative of the way the social elite functioned in the 18th century. For rapid promotion to the rank of post captain was one of the benefits of being even distantly related to a duke in the England of George II.

On 9 January 1743 Rodney, in command of the 60-gun HMS *Plymouth*, which was greatly in need of repairs,[1] sailed from Villa Franca.[2] After a stop-over at Gibraltar HMS *Plymouth* made her way to Lisbon arriving at that port on 11 February.[3] Rodney remained at Lisbon until 7 March when HMS *Plymouth* sailed for England escorting a convoy of nine merchant ships.[4] After a passage of 25 days, during the course of which heavy gales were encountered, which forced all but two of the merchant ships of the convoy to part company, HMS *Plymouth* arrived at Plymouth.[5] On 24 April Rodney paid off and decommissioned HMS *Plymouth*.[6]

On 10 August 1743 the Admiralty ordered Rodney to take command of HMS *Sheerness* which was being built at Rotherhithe on the River Thames.[7] HMS *Sheerness*, which was launched on 8 October 1743, was a 24-gun sixth-rate warship manned by 160 men.[8] This was the type of ship which was usually commanded by a junior post captain. No doubt Rodney was placed in command because the Admiralty believed he had to gain experience before progressing to a larger class of warship. HMS *Sheerness* had her masts stepped, rigging fitted and was stored at Deptford before dropping down to Longreach where she took on board additional stores as well as her guns. On 10 December HMS *Sheerness*, which had by then been fully fitted, stored and armed, although not completely manned, arrived at the Nore.[9] Rodney would discover in the course of his career that the speed and ease with which the ships of the Royal Navy could be readied for sea depended ultimately upon the ability to obtain the necessary seamen to man the vessels. Manning a ship was a complicated and often time-comsuming

---

[1] TNA, SP 42/91, Condition and Disposition of His Majesty's Ships in the Mediterranean, 24 Oct. [1742].
[2] TNA, ADM 51/699, 9 Jan. 1743.
[3] Document No. 2.
[4] TNA, ADM 51/699, 7 March 1743.
[5] Document No. 3.
[6] TNA, ADM 51/699, 24 April 1743.
[7] Document No. 7.
[8] David Lyon, *The Sailing Navy List. All the Ships of the Royal Navy – built, purchased and captured – 1688–1860* (London, 1993), pp. 49, 51, 52.
[9] TNA, ADM 51/899, 23 Sept.–10 Dec. 1743.

operation. For instance, in the case of HMS *Sheerness* the Admiralty had ordered, in August 1743, that 80 seamen be transferred from HMS *Ruby* into Rodney's ship. However, as late as 12 October, 58 of these men had not yet appeared on board HMS *Sheerness*. As a result a tender had to be sent to Shields to raise seamen for the ship. Nevertheless, when HMS *Sheerness* went to Longreach to take in her guns, in order to navigate the ship Rodney had to be assisted by 40 seamen supplied by other ships. And later, 20 seamen would be lent to Rodney by HMS *Princess Royal* to assist in sailing HMS *Sheerness* to the Nore.[1] The problems caused by the shortage of seamen were eventually overcome by Rodney, and on 14 December, the Admiralty ordered HMS *Sheerness* to proceed with 'any trade bound that way' to Spithead.[2]

Small warships, such as HMS *Sheerness*, were primarily employed to escort convoys of merchant ships and to cruise in search of enemy ships. Rodney, while in command of HMS *Sheerness*, would serve off the coasts of Ireland, in the English Channel and the North Sea either cruising to intercept enemy ships or escorting British trade convoys. On 27 December 1743 Rodney and HMS *Sheerness* sailed from Spithead to cruise in search of a Spanish privateer thought to be operating off the southern coast of Ireland.[3] Arriving off Cape Clear, on the south coast of Ireland, on 29 December, Rodney cruised for almost a month. In the course of this operation he intercepted a number of British merchant ships and sent into a British port a French merchant ship on suspicion of carrying contraband, but did not encounter any Spanish privateers before putting into Cork on 23 January 1744. After a stay of several days in the Irish port Rodney proceeded onto Dublin arriving at the Irish capital on 10 February.[4]

At first the Admiralty intended that HMS *Sheerness* would escort, from Dublin to Holland, a ship carrying the Duke of Devonshire's baggage. This plan was soon altered, probably owing to a French fleet having been sighted in the Western Approaches of the English Channel, and HMS *Sheerness* was instead employed to escort transports carrying troops from Ireland to the west coast of England.[5] After seeing the transports with the troops from Ireland safely across St George's Channel, Rodney passed on to Plymouth and then to the eastward arriving on 27 March at Spithead.[6] On 2 April HMS *Sheerness* entered Portsmouth

[1] Nos. 7, 11, 14, 16, 20.
[2] No. 26.
[3] No. 31.
[4] TNA, ADM 51/899, 17 Dec. 1743–10 Feb. 1744.
[5] Nos. 31, 36, 37, 39, 41.
[6] TNA, ADM 51/899, 13 March–27 March 1744.

Dockyard to have her bottom 'cleaned, graved, tallowed' as well as to be refitted and restored.[1] After a short stay in Portsmouth Dockyard HMS *Sheerness* sailed from Spithead and arrived at the Nore on 26 April 1744. Rodney, for the remainder of his time in command of HMS *Sheerness*, would be employed in the North Sea. Based at the Nore, HMS *Sheerness* escorted trade convoys up and down the east coast of Britain and back and forth to the Netherlands. At the end of June, of the same year, in company with HMS *Anglesea*, Rodney escorted a convoy across the North Sea to Norway and then proceeded back to Britain, to cruise off Scotland, before returning, on 23 September, to the Nore. On 13 June HMS *Sheerness* recaptured a British collier manned by a French prize crew. On 6 September the East Indiaman *Montfort*, which was 'very much distressed' having lost her masts, was intercepted by Rodney who subsequently saw the battered British merchant ship into Yarmouth Roads.[2] Nevertheless, these voyages in the North Sea, primarily for the purpose of escorting convoys were, for the most part, routine and uneventful even when they were accomplished successfully.

On 6 August 1744 Rodney was appointed to command HMS *Ludlow Castle*.[3] Being fitted out at Deptford, HMS *Ludlow Castle* was a new design of two-decked warship. It represented an attempt to place a great amount of firepower – twenty 18-pounder guns on the lower deck and twenty 9-pounder guns on the upper deck – on a small hull.[4] This type of vessel was not a success and had a number of problems. The vessels were crowded and lower deck gun ports could not be opened even in a moderate sea. And the ships were top heavy because of the weight of the guns on the upper deck. Indeed, two-decked 40-gun ships were thought by some authorities to be among the most ill-designed ships ever to serve in the Royal Navy.[5] When Rodney arrived at the Nore he was discharged from HMS *Sheerness*[6] and on 29 September 1744 his name was entered in the muster book of HMS *Ludlow Castle*.[7] Seventeen men, including two master's mates, and a quartermaster as well as the ship's clerk, transferred out of HMS *Sheerness* and followed Rodney to HMS *Ludlow Castle*.[8] Among the men who transferred out of HMS *Sheerness*, in order

---

[1] No. 45.
[2] TNA, ADM 51/899, 14 April–25 Sept. 1744.
[3] No. 64.
[4] Lyon, *The Sailing Navy List*, pp. 48, 49.
[5] Cf. John Charnock, *A History of Marine Architecture* (London, 1802), vol. III, p. 158.
[6] TNA, ADM 36/3599, f. 26.
[7] TNA, ADM 36/1865, f. 109.
[8] TNA, ADM 36/3599, *passim*.

to follow Rodney to the *Ludlow Castle*, was a midshipman called Samuel Hood. A close relative, James Rodney, who was in fact Captain Rodney's brother, would also serve in HMS *Ludlow Castle*, firstly as a midshipman and then as a master's mate.[1]

After being fitted and stored at Deptford and embarking her guns at Longreach, HMS *Ludlow Castle* operated during the first months of Rodney's command in the North Sea in escorting convoys up and down the east coast of England and across to the Netherlands.[2] On a return passage to England, from the Netherlands, after having escorted a convoy to Holland and Germany, which had included a ship carrying six horses that were being sent by George II to the Prince Royal of Denmark, HMS *Ludlow Castle*, owing to pilot error, 'struck several times' on the Standford Shoal with such force that the vessel required a dockyard repair.[3] Entering Sheerness Dockyard, during the last days of December 1744, HMS *Ludlow Castle* was repaired and restored.[4] Sailing from the Nore at the end of January 1745 HMS *Ludlow Castle* arrived at Spithead on 6 February.[5] On 9 February the Admiralty issued orders to Rodney to escort the trade of Lisbon.[6] Rodney with HMS *Ludlow Castle* and escorting a convoy of merchant ships, in company with a squadron of warships under the command of Rear Admiral Henry Medley, sailed from Spithead on 24 February. After a long and slow passage Rodney and the convoy arrived on 29 April at Lisbon.[7] At the request of the British consul, at Lisbon, Rodney cruised for ten days off the coast of Portugal 'for the protection of the trade'. Then, after a passage of 26 days from Lisbon, and escorting a convoy of merchant ships bound to Ireland and England, Rodney arrived on 5 July in the Downes.[8] It was a successful mission for Rodney. On the voyage from Portugal to England he earned £441 16s. 6d., as freight money, which was one per cent of the value of a consignment of money embarked on HMS *Ludlow Castle* for transport to England.[9]

Rodney and HMS *Ludlow Castle*, after returning from Portugal in July of 1745, operated this time in support of British and Allied military forces at Ostend, in Belgium. Though present at the French siege of Ostend, Rodney's duties mainly consisted of escorting military con-

[1] TNA, ADM 36/1865, ff. 110, 117.
[2] TNA, ADM 51/534, 29 Aug.–11 Dec. 1744.
[3] Nos. 83, 86, 88, 92, 94.
[4] Nos. 98, 99, 102.
[5] TNA, ADM 51/534, 19 Jan.–6 Feb. 1745.
[6] No. 114.
[7] TNA, ADM 51/534, 24 Feb.–29 April 1745.
[8] Nos. 120, 121, 122.
[9] TNA, 30/20/26/7, ff. 130–1.

voys back and forth between England and Ostend.[1] During the last days of August and in the first days of September 1745, HMS *Ludlow Castle* escorted several trade and military convoys to Holland and then back to England before entering the dockyard once again at Sheerness.[2] After being refitted, on 21 December in 'thick hazy weather', while running south along the coast of England HMS *Ludlow Castle* ran on to the Whiting Sand off Orfordness. According to the log of HMS *Ludlow Castle*:

> the ship struck upon the eastward most part of the Whiting Sand, fired 3 shots at some vessels to bring to for our assistance, finding the ship too stuck fast. Hoisted out the boats and sounded round the ship and found but 2 fathoms water. Stove 34 butts of beer; all the gang casks and several butts of water in order to lighten the ship. ½ past 2 sent the barge with 3 hawsers on board a sloop in order to carry out an anchor, cut away the main topmast with the running and standing rigging thereto belonging and lightened the ship as much as possible. ½ past 4 we beat over the Whiting (after several severe strokes) with the loss of the rudder and anchored with the best bower in 6 fathoms water.[3]

On 28 December Rodney, and a much damaged *Ludlow Castle*, arrived at Sheerness and began to prepare the ship to enter the dockyard.[4] At another time and in different circumstances the running of HMS *Ludlow Castle* on to the Whiting Sands might have resulted in a court martial; but instead Rodney, on 3 December, was appointed to command HMS *Eagle*.[5]

On 8 January 1746 Rodney took command of HMS *Eagle* at Harwich.[6] The ship, a 60-gun fourth-rate ship of the line, was a new vessel having been launched on 2 December 1745[7] and had to be fitted out, stored and manned before entering service. With considerable speed, and no little skill, Rodney readied HMS *Eagle* for service in less than two months by fitting and storing the ship as well as obtaining the neccessary seamen to man the vessel.[8] On 26 February 1746 HMS *Eagle* sailed from Harwich ready for service.[9]

---

[1] Nos. 123–30.
[2] TNA, ADM 51/534, 23 Aug.–22 Sept. 1745.
[3] TNA, ADM 51/534, 22 Dec. 1745. See also Nos. 159, 165.
[4] No. 160.
[5] No. 162.
[6] TNA, ADM 36/971, f. 25.
[7] Lyon, *The Sailing Navy List*, p. 45.
[8] Nos. 164, 166, 170, 173–6.
[9] TNA, ADM 51/326, 26 Feb. 1746.

On 4 March in the Downes, Rodney and HMS *Eagle* joined the squadron, under the command of Commodore Matthew Michell, which was blockading Ostend in order to prevent the French from sending supplies and reinforcements to the Rebels in Scotland. From 18 March to 24 April HMS *Eagle* was off Ostend; she then returned to the Downes from whence Rodney sailed westward, along the south coast of England, escorting a convoy of merchant ships to Plymouth, where HMS *Eagle* entered the dockyard to be refitted.[1]

On 15 May 1746 the Admiralty ordered Rodney in HMS *Eagle* to cruise, with several other British warships, off southern Ireland in the Western Approaches to the English Channel.[2] This was the first of a number of cruises conducted by HMS *Eagle*, during the last years of the War of Austrian Succession. In the course of these operations Rodney, by the capture of enemy ships, would not only lay the foundations of a personal fortune with prize money, but would also show that he was a sea officer of considerable skill and who, moreover, was endowed with luck in almost equal measure. Having sailed from Plymouth on 21 May, and after only three days at sea, Rodney captured and carried into Kinsale, in Ireland the Spanish privateer *Experience* of 16 guns and 136 men.[3] Departing from Kinsale on 7 June, in company with HMS *Nottingham* and HM Sloop *Falcon*, Rodney captured next, on 8 June, the French brigantine *Joseph Louis*. Three days later, on 14 June, still in company with HMS *Nottingham* and HM Sloop *Falcon*, he captured a French privateer of 12 guns and 138 men called the *Ponte Quarré*.[4] Continuing on their series of successful captures, on 17 July, HMS *Eagle*, HMS *Nottingham*, and HM Sloop *Falcon* took the Spanish privateer *Nuestra Señora del Carmen*, armed with 26 guns and a crew of 148 men, from San Sebastian. On 23 July Rodney and HMS *Eagle* put into Kinsale before proceeding on to Plymouth where HMS *Eagle* went into the dockyard once more for a refit. Sailing from Plymouth on 31 August, Rodney and HMS *Eagle* captured, on 15 October, a Spanish merchant ship with an English name, the *Prudent Sarah*; and on 30 October, after a long chase, the French privateer *Shoreham* of 22 guns and 260 men, from Morlaix was also taken.[5]

Cruises in the Western Approaches of the English Channel and in the Bay of Biscay in search of enemy ships continued relentlessly into 1747. On 2 January 1747 Rodney captured the *Grand Comte*, a

[1]TNA, ADM 51/326, 4 March–11 May 1746.
[2]No. 185.
[3]No. 187.
[4]Probably the name of this ship was *Pont Carré*.
[5]TNA, ADM 51/326, 21 May–15 Oct. 1746.

French ship of 20 guns with a crew of 77 men. And on 3 February, in company with HMS *Nottingham* and HMS *Edinburgh*, HMS *Eagle* took the French privateer *Bellona* of 36 guns and 310 men.[1] This ship was a French vessel, well-known for having made a number of voyages to Scotland in support of the Rebels and for having conveyed a number of the adherents of the Pretender to safety in France after the Battle of Culloden. Rodney and Captain Philip Saumarez, would later accuse the captain and officers of the *Bellona* of committing an atrocity by consigning the crew and passengers of an English merchant vessel to their deaths in a sinking ship.[2] On 11 April the French privateer *Mary Magdalene*, mounting 22 guns and 170 men, was taken. Three weeks later and a hundred leagues to the west of the Scilly Islands Rodney captured, on 1 May, a small French privateer called the *Marshal de Saxe* which, too, was carried into Kinsale.[3] Rodney and HMS *Eagle*, in the course of operating for a year in the Western Approaches of the English Channel and the Bay of Biscay had either captured, or participated in the capture, of no less than ten enemy ships of which all but two were armed vessels. It was certainly a lucrative accomplishment.

On 1 June Rodney in HMS *Eagle* joined a small squadron,[4] at this time under the command of Commodore Thomas Fox, in conducting offensive sweeps in the Bay of Biscay in order to continue the search for enemy ships.[5] At daylight on 20 June the British squadron, proceeding northwest, discovered that to the northward of them there was a French fleet, of over a hundred ships, proceeding to the southeastwards towards the French Biscay ports. Fox's ships immediately turned towards the enemy and began to chase the French ships which were soon seen to be a large number of merchantmen escorted by four warships. The wind was out of the northwest. For the remainder of the daylight hours as well as throughout the night the British warships persisted in their attempts to overtake the French. At daylight, on 21 June, with overcast skies, occasional showers and the wind still from the northwest, the French warships were not to be seen. By contrast, over a hundred French merchant ships, in two groups, were in sight of the British warships! Most of the French merchant ships were to the northeast and east of the British while another smaller group of French merchant ships were on the other tack to the northwest. The British warships, at daylight on 21 June, were slowly

[1] TNA, ADM 51/326, 2 Jan.–3 Feb. 1747.
[2] Nos. 205–206.
[3] TNA, ADM 51/326, 17 April–2 May 1747.
[4] *Kent, Hampton Court, Lion, Chester*, and the fireships *Pluto* and *Dolphin*.
[5] TNA, ADM 1/1782, Fox to Corbett, 1 June 1747.

overtaking the main body of the French. However, with the exception of HMS *Eagle*, the British ships were sluggish sailors owing to the foulness of their bottoms and, in the face of a northwest wind, they were only very slowly overhauling the French merchant ships. At 5 am Rodney decided to make his move by tacking to windward towards the French merchant ships, to the northwest of the British squadron. As HMS *Eagle* tacked to the northwest, Fox made a signal for Rodney to rejoin the squadron.[1] Rodney ignored this command. As a result, at about 2 pm, HMS *Eagle* was among the French merchant ships. When the first enemy vessel was captured the British discovered that they had intercepted a French convoy from St. Domingo. Altogether Rodney captured from this convoy six French merchant ships,[2] laden with sugar, coffee and indigo, which were then carried to England, arriving in the Downes on 30 June.[3]

Rodney, during the autumn of 1747, continued to serve in the Western Approaches of the English Channel and the Bay of Biscay, with HMS *Eagle*, as a member of a squadron commanded by Rear Admiral Edward Hawke. This squadron consisted of 12 ships of the line, two 50-gun ships,[4] and several frigates. At 7 am, on 14 October, west of Cape Finisterre, Hawke's ships sighted 'a great number of ships, so crowded together that we could not count them'. It was soon perceived by the British that they had intercepted a large French convoy, escorted by eight French ships of the line,[5] and several lesser warships. When Hawke first sighted the French, he made the signal for a chase; however, at 8 am, seeing the great number of enemy ships the British admiral formed his squadron into a line ahead formation. The French, upon sighting the British, also formed seven of their ships of the line into a line ahead formation; at the same time they detached, under the escort of the 64-gun *Content*, the convoy to leeward. Hawke, seeing that his squadron now out-numbered the French warships, hauled down the signal for a line ahead formation and ordered a general chase. He then followed it with the signal to engage the enemy. As the rear of the French line was overhauled by the British warships a running battle resulted in which the French line was overpowered by the weight of British firepower and numbers.[6] Rodney, because his ship was at the rear of the British line, did not begin to engage the French until noon,

[1]TNA, ADM 1/1782, Fox to Corbett, 28 June 1747.
[2]*St Malo, Europa, Charlotta, Espérance, Marshal de Saxe, St Claire.*
[3]TNA, ADM 51/326, 20–30 June 1747.
[4]*Devonshire, Kent, Edinburgh, Yarmouth, Monmouth, Princess Louisa, Windsor, Lion, Tilbury, Nottingham, Defiance, Eagle*, and the 50-gun ships *Gloucester* and *Portland*.
[5]*Tonnant, Intrépide, Trident, Monarque, Severn, Fougeux, Neptune, Content.*
[6]Ruddock F. Mackay, ed., *The Hawke Papers: A Selection, 1743–1771* (Aldershot, Hants.: Scolar Press for the Navy Records Society, 1990), pp. 51–5.

when HMS *Eagle* overtook, and began to engage to port, the French 70-gun ship *Neptune*. As HMS *Eagle* fought the *Neptune*, the French 64-gun ship *Fougeux* approached and engaged Rodney's ship from the starboard side. Fortunately for Rodney, the *Fougeux* was soon disabled by gunfire and dropped astern of HMS *Eagle*, which continued to battle the *Neptune* for more than an hour, before drifting astern and clear of the French ship. HMS *Eagle* was badly damaged and by the time Rodney could, in the late afternoon, manoeuvre the ship once more, the battle was over.[1]

The Battle of Cape Finisterre was a great, though marred, British victory. Out of the eight French ships of the line that had been engaged only two[2] escaped capture. However, on the British side, the conduct of Captain Thomas Fox, of HMS *Kent*, did not meet with the approval of Hawke. As Rodney was engaging the *Neptune* and the *Fougueux*, Fox in HMS *Kent*, who had begun the battle ahead of HMS *Eagle* in the British line, fell astern of Rodney and failed to support HMS *Eagle* when she was engaged by the two enemy ships. Fox also failed to respond to a signal from Hawke calling for HMS *Kent* to engage the French ship of the line *Tonnant*. Later Rodney would be a prosecution witness at a court martial in which Fox was found guilty of disobeying Hawke's order to attack the *Tonnant*.[3]

When the War of Austrian Succession ended Rodney, and HMS *Eagle*, were part of a small squadron that had been undertaking a cruise, this time to Portugal. Returning to England on 13 August 1748, Rodney decommissioned HMS *Eagle* at Plymouth.[4] When he left HMS *Eagle* in the Plymouth naval base in the summer of 1748, Rodney was a man of rank and fortune. He had a pocket full of prize money and had become a successful post captain with almost six years of seniority in the Royal Navy. In the course of 16 years of service Rodney had risen from behind a school desk to the command of a ship of the line in which he had demonstrated considerable skill in naval warfare.

[1] TNA, ADM 51/326, 14–15 Oct. 1747.
[2] *Intrépide, Tonnant*.
[3] Mackay, *Hawke Papers*, pp. 61–5.
[4] TNA, ADM 51/326, 13 Aug. 1748.

1. From Vice Admiral Thomas Mathews[1]

[TNA, ADM 1/2380]

Namur
31 December 1742

You are hereby directed and required to receive all such invalids[2] as shall be put on board His Majesty's ship under your command from the squadron at this place or the hospitals of Mahon and Gibraltar and give them passage to England. Where on your arrival you are to put them on shore bearing them as supernumeraries for victuals only.

2. To Thomas Corbett[3]

[TNA, ADM 1/2380]

Plymouth
Lisbon Harbour
15 February 1743

Sir,

Please to acquaint their Lordships that I am arrived at this port with His Majesty's ship under my command in thirty six days from the Bay of Hyères and four from Gibraltar. My orders are to wait here for the convoy and then proceed to Spithead and wait there for further orders. Nothing remarkable occurred in my passage, but had information by a French ship I spoke with that two very rich ships were arrived from New Spain, the one at Cadiz, the other at Lagos, and another shortly expected. They are computed to be worth three millions of dollars, but as Captain [Charles] Powlett in the *Oxford* was to sail very soon, the Spanish were in great fear for the third.

3. To Corbett

[TNA, ADM 1/2380]

Spithead
31 March 1743

Sir,

Please to acquaint their Lordships that this day I arrived at Spithead with His Majesty's ship *Plymouth* under my command, in twenty five days from Lisbon, having nine sail of merchant ships under convoy,

---

[1]Commander-in-chief in the Mediterranean and minister to Sardinia and the Italian states.
[2]Enclosed is a list of four men and the names of hospital or their ship.
[3]Secretary to the Lords Commissioners of the Admiralty, 1741–51.

most of whom lost company by excessive bad weather which laid us under a reefed main sail fourteen days, and was succeeded by a hard gale at SW which brought us into the Channel under a reefed foresail, with two sail of the convoy. But it proving such bad weather could not press their hands. The ship is in very bad condition, most of the rigging and sails being quite unfit for service, besides the main and orlop beams being sprung and the checks of the head and bows very rotten. The rudder likewise is very loose and works ponderously at sea. As their Lordships might be glad to hear news concerning Commodore Anson,[1] I have brought home his cook who was taken prisoner in the South Seas, and came to Lagos in the *Princessa* galleon, lately arrived in that place. I shall send him up to London forthwith in order for their Lordships' examination, meantime refer them to the enclosed.[2]

4. *To Corbett*

[TNA, ADM 1/2380]
Plymouth
Spithead
2 April 1743

Sir,
Enclosed[3] I send my commission for His Majesty's ship *Plymouth*, granted me by Vice Admiral Mathews, which I hope their Lordships will be so good to confirm.[4] I should be glad to know their Lordships' pleasure concerning [James] Hall, a prisoner, who was put on board me by Captain [Samuel] Loftin of His Majesty's sloop *Wolf*, from whom he deserted, and by whom he was taken on board a Spanish privateer, having entered into the King of Spain's service. Captain Loftin informed me he had sent affidavits concerning him.

---

[1]Captain George Anson commanded an expedition to the west coast of South America which then sailed around the world. Anson was promoted Rear Admiral 23 June 1744; Vice Admiral 14 July 1746; Admiral 15 July 1748. During the years 1746–48 Anson was Commander-in-chief of the Channel Fleet. MP Hendon, 1744–1747. On 15 July 1747 he was created Lord Anson and served as a Lord of the Admiralty, 27 Dec. 1744–22 June 1751; First Lord of the Admiralty, 1751–17 Nov. 1756 and 2 July 1757–6 June 1762.
[2]Enclosed is an account by Lewis Ledger of Anson's voyage around Cape Horn into the Pacific. Ledger was Anson's cook, who, after being captured by the Spanish off Acapulco on the west coast of Mexico, made his way to Europe.
[3]Not enclosed.
[4]The Admiralty on 4 April 1743 confirmed Rodney's promotion to the rank of post captain with seniority dating from 9 November 1742.

5. From the Lords of the Admiralty

[TNA, ADM 2/59, p. 419] 2 April 1743

Whereas we have ordered His Majesty's ship under your command to be laid up and paid off at Plymouth, you are hereby required and directed to proceed with her thither for that purpose, taking under your convoy such trade bound to the westward as shall be ready and desirous to accompany you. And whereas we have ordered her petty officers and foremast men to be paid the wages to them to the 31st December 1741 on board the ship, as soon as she is cleared for the dock and fit to be delivered into the hand of the officers of the yard, you are to make out and transmit to the Navy Board the proper pay books for that purpose. And as soon as the said payment is made, you are to give the said petty officers and foremast men fourteen days' leave of absence, strictly charging them to repair at the expiration of that time, one half as they stand first on your books on board the *Jersey* and the other half on board the *Superb*, at Plymouth, where they will be paid the remainder of their wages and two months' wages advance before those ships proceed to sea. And you are to let the petty officers know, that if they cannot be provided for in those ships in the same or equal stations they now possess in the *Plymouth*, the captains of those ships will give them certificates thereof and discharge them. Upon producing which certificates at the Pay Office in Broadstreet, they will be paid the remainder of their wages for the *Plymouth*. And you are to take care to transmit to Captains [Henry] Harrison and [Harry] Norris lists of the names of the petty officers and men whom you order to repair on board their respective ships and how rated.

6. To Corbett

[TNA, ADM 1/2380] Plymouth
Plymouth
22 April 1743

Sir,
In obedience to their Lordships' commands, I herewith send them a list of what supernumeraries[1] I brought home with me as likewise my orders from Vice Admiral Mathews [No. 1] concerning them. On my

---

[1] Enclosed is a list of 36 invalids conveyed to England by HMS *Plymouth*.

arrival at Portsmouth I applied to Sir Charles Hardy[1] about them, who ordered me to follow the directions I received from Admiral Mathews which I accordingly executed and put them all on shore. As His Majesty's ship under my command is cleared and fit to be delivered into the hands of the officers of the yard, the commissioner proposes putting her out of commission tomorrow morning.

7. *From the Lords of the Admiralty*

[TNA, ADM 2/60, pp. 270–1] 10 August 1743

Whereas we have appointed you captain of His Majesty's ship the *Sheerness*, in the river Thames, which ship we have ordered to be fitted and stored for foreign service, manned with her highest complement of men, which is 160, victualled with three months provisions of all species, except beer, in lieu of half the allowance of which, she is to be furnished with a proportion of English malt spirits. You are hereby required and directed to repair on board the said ship and cause all possible diligence to be used in fitting her for sea, and when she shall be in a readiness you are to repair with her to Longreach, and having there taken in her guns, and gunner's stores, proceed with her to the Nore, and remain there till further order; taking care to keep your provisions, stores, and water always complete till you proceed to sea…

And whereas we have directed the Navy Board to turn over into the ship you command eighty of the men lately belonging to the *Ruby*, as they stand first in her books, and to send you a list of their names and how rated. You are hereby required and directed to receive and enter the said men as part of your complement, and not rate them worse than in their former ship, and to take care that they be paid the wages due to them in the *Ruby*, and two months' wages advance before your ship proceeds to sea.

You are to procure what seamen you can for the service, either by pressing or entering volunteers and to bear such as you get…

---

[1]Rear Admiral Sir Charles Hardy (c.1680–17 Nov. 1744), Vice-Admiral, 7 Dec. 1743; Lord of the Admiralty, 13 Dec. 1743–27 Nov. 1744. Early in 1744 Hardy suspended his attendance at the Admiralty to command a squadron which escorted a convoy of victuallers and storeships to Lisbon. Upon his return to England, Hardy resumed his duties as a member of the Board of Admiralty.

8. To Corbett

[TNA, ADM 1/2380]

London
1 October 1743

Sir,
Whereas their Lordships were pleased to order the Navy Board to turn eighty men lately belonging to the *Ruby* into His Majesty's ship under my command and to send me a list of them, I find by examining some of the seamen that five of the said list are either dead, entered on board another ship with their Lordships' leave, or absent for some time with the same. Enclosed I send a list of them and hope their Lordships will order my number to be completed.[1]

9. To Corbett

[TNA, ADM 1/2380]

Sheerness
In the River
5 October 1743

Sir,
As His Majesty's ship under my command has been commissioned these twelve days I must beg leave to acquaint their Lordships that only the boatswain, carpenter and purser have yet made their appearance. As it is impossible to keep the men together without their respective officers, [I] hope their Lordships will order them to repair forthwith to their duty. I have not been able to attend myself having been ill for some time of a fever but am now pretty well recovered. I must likewise desire you to let their Lordships know that only six men of the eighty from the *Ruby* have as yet appeared.

10. To Corbett

[TNA, ADM 1/2380]

Sheerness
Deptford
9 October 1743

Sir,
Please to acquaint their Lordships that yesterday in the evening His Majesty's ship under my command was launched and warped down to

---

[1]Enclosed is a list of five men, three of which are listed as belonging to HM Sloop *Grampus*, plus 1 which is dead, and a fifth with 'six months leave to go to Ireland'.

her moorings at Deptford. In obedience to their Lordships' commands I shall use the utmost dispatch in fitting her out and the first forty men that appear will send them out in the tender in order to complete my complement.

11. To Corbett

[TNA, ADM 1/2380] *Sheerness* at Deptford
12 October 1743

Sir,

His Majesty's ship under my command has got her lower masts in, and what men have as yet appeared are employed in getting in the ballast. For fear their Lordships should think me negligent, I beg leave to acquaint them in what condition the ship is in at present. Not so much as one cabin is as yet finished, likewise the cook room will not be ready to dress the provisions till the latter end of this week and but yesterday the painters began upon the inside works, all [of] which makes it impossible for either the officers or men to lie on board. To remedy which I have ordered the tender to haul along side and victual the men on board of her. When the carpenters and joiners have finished, their Lordships may be sure I will use the utmost expedition in fitting her for the sea. Fifty eight men of the *Ruby* have as yet absented themselves from their duty.

12. To Corbett

[TNA, ADM 1/2380] *Sheerness*
Deptford
19 October [1743]

Sir,

Enclosed[1] I send their Lordships a weekly account for His Majesty's ship under my command and must beg leave to acquaint them that none of the cabins are as yet furnished nor [is] the ship in a condition to receive men which is the reason I have retained the tender so long, but on Monday next I intend to send her to the northward in order to complete my complement. In the meantime [I] shall get the rigging as forward as possible. Fifty five men of the *Ruby* are as yet absent.

[1] Not enclosed.

13. To Corbett

[TNA, ADM 1/2380] *Sheerness* at Deptford
29 October 1743

Sir,
I received yours with their Lordships' directions to know my reasons for detaining the tender so long at Deptford.

I have never had as yet a competent number of men to send in the tender, and what have appeared have been wholly employed in rigging the ship which is now completed and all that can possibly be got together shall go on board the tender which sails this day for Hull and to cruise on the adjacent coast. I hope their Lordships have given directions to Captain [Christopher] O'Brien of the *Princess Royal* to deliver what men he has belonging to the *Sheerness*, to my lieutenant, to enable him to raise more men.

I must likewise acquaint their Lordships that I shall be obliged to lie idle unless they please to order some men to assist in getting my provisions in.

14. To Corbett

[TNA, ADM 1/2380] *Sheerness* at Deptford
2 November 1743

Sir,
Enclosed[1] I send the weekly account for His Majesty's ship under my command, and at the same time must acquaint you that I have stationed the *Rich Charlot* tender at Shields, and have given my lieutenant orders to call at every port in his way, and acquaint you with what men he raises at each of them.

15. To Corbett

[TNA. ADM 1/2380] *Sheerness* at Deptford
9 November 1743

Sir,
Enclosed[2] is the weekly account for His Majesty's ship under my command. The marines are come on board, whose lieutenant's name is

[1] Not enclosed.
[2] Not enclosed.

[Thomas] Achmuty. We are now making all the dispatch possible in getting our anchors, cables, and the remainder of the stores on board and hope to be ready to go to Longreach the latter end of this week or the beginning of next, tho' I have not seaman enough on board to carry the ship there, most of the men that are mustered being officers and servants, besides the marines.

16. *From the Lords of the Admiralty*

[TNA, ADM 2/60, p. 381] 16 November 1743

Having ordered the captains of His Majesty's yachts named in the margin[1] to lend twenty men each to the ship you command, to assist in sailing her to Longreach, when you apply to them for that purpose, you are hereby required and directed to receive and victual the said men as your ship's company. And when she is anchored in Longreach you are to send the men back again to their respective yachts.

17. *To Corbett*

[TNA, ADM 1/2380] *Sheerness* at Deptford
18 November 1743

Sir,
His Majesty's ship under my command being ready to fall down to Longreach, but having very few seamen on board hope their Lordships will order some of the yacht's men to assist in carrying there. I have wrote to my lieutenant to return in the tender with what men he has raised and hope he will meet me soon at the Nore.

18. *To Corbett*

[TNA, ADM 1/2380] *Sheerness* at Deptford
Friday noon

Sir,
Please to acquaint their Lordships that this morning the wind being fair I got everything ready to fall down to Longreach, but the pilot not coming till the tide was far spent, would not take charge of the ship till tomorrow morning.

[1]*Mary, Tubbs.*

19. To Corbett

[TNA, ADM 1/2380] *Sheerness* at Longreach
19 November 1743

Sir,
Please to acquaint their Lordships that His Majesty's ship under my command is safe moored in Longreach. If their Lordships will please to order Captain O'Brien to send what men he has belonging to the *Sheerness* up in the next tender it will contribute to my dispatch in getting my guns and other stores in, which I shall do as soon as possible, having already wrote to have them sent down.

20. To Corbett

[TNA, ADM 1/2380] *Sheerness* at Longreach
23 November 1743

Sir,
I received yours of the 21st instant and shall take care to acquaint Lieutenant [William] Leaver on his arrival here, that he is appointed second lieutenant of the *Burford*, and that their Lordships desire him to make what haste he can down to his ship. As the storeship was getting under sail on Monday morning there being very little wind and the tide of flood running pretty quick, she fell athwart our hawse but has done us very little damages; only the jib boom and spritsail yard being sprung. I have sent the carpenter to Deptford to make a demand for others which I hope will be down next tide. We are now getting the guns and gunners stores in and I hope by the time the tender arrives, to be ready to go to the Nore.

21. From the Lords of the Admiralty

[TNA, ADM 2/60, pp. 414–15] 2 December 1743

Having ordered the captain of the *Royal Caroline* to lend you twenty men, to help sail the ship under your command to the Nore, you are hereby required and directed to apply to Sir Charles Molloy[1] for them accordingly, and to receive and victual them as your ship's company. And then you are to proceed without loss of time to the Nore, and

---

[1] The commander of HM Yacht *Royal Caroline*.

remain there [un]til further order; sending the *Royal Caroline's* men back again, as soon as you are anchored at that place.

22. To Corbett

[TNA, ADM 1/2380] *Sheerness* at Longreach
4 December 1743

Sir,

I received their Lordships' orders [No. 21] to proceed with His Majesty's ship under my command to the Nore, as likewise your letter concerning the three men belonging to the *Princess Royal* who petitioned their Lordships to serve under my command. I have sent to Sir Charles Molloy for the twenty yacht's men and [with] the first spirit of wind will proceed to the Nore. I can't help taking notice to their Lordships that I am afraid some accident has befallen the tender, the lieutenant having acknowledged the receipt of my orders above three weeks ago. He was then in Yarmouth Roads, and intended to sail the first easterly wind, but is not as yet arrived.

23. To Corbett

[TNA, ADM 1/2380] *Sheerness* in Longreach
9 December 1743

Sir,

This morning Lieutenant Leaver arrived here in the *Rich Charlot* tender with my men having left the impressed men on board the *Princess Royal* at the Nore. I acquainted him it was their Lordships' directions [No. 20] he should make the best of his way to the *Burford* at Portsmouth who is under sailing orders.

As my own people are returned I shall send the *Royal Caroline's* on board again. The weather has been so foggy for several days that the pilot would not take charge of the ship, but will lose no opportunity in proceeding to the Nore. I should be glad to know their Lordships' directions concerning the *Ruby's* men that have not as yet appeared.

24. To Corbett

[TNA, ADM 1/2380] *Sheerness* at the Nore
11 December 1743

Sir,
　Yesterday in the evening I arrived with His Majesty's ship under my command at this place where I received your letters of the 8th and 9th instant with their Lordships' orders to discharge Robert Grange if what was alleged in the enclosed letter was true. I have examined both him and Moses Wood and find by his own account that he was idling on shore and had no protection about him when Lieutenant Leaver pressed him. Moses Wood is a very lusty man about twenty five years old, [and] was pressed out of the ship's boat as he was going on board, but owns he had no protection with him. It is a common custom with the masters of colliers to get their best men bound apprentice to them for two or three years, and by that means protect them from being impressed. I shall discharge neither of them till I know their Lordships' pleasure. I hope their Lordships will permit me to keep the supernumeraries till I know whether the *Ruby's* men will repair to their duty.

25. To Corbett

[TNA, ADM 1/2380] *Sheerness* at the Nore
11 December 1743

Sir,
　Since writing my former letter [No. 24] I have been informed by several of the captains here, that their Lordships was pleased to give orders that the malt spirits should not be served till the beer was expended. I should be glad to know if it is their Lordships' pleasure that I should do the same by my ship's company.

26. From the Lords of the Admiralty

[TNA, ADM 2/60, p. 437] 14 December 1743

　You are hereby required and directed to proceed without loss of time, with His Majesty's ship under your command to Spithead, and remain there [un]til further order; giving convoy to any trade bound that way, that shall be ready and willing to accompany you.

27. To Corbett

[TNA, ADM 1/2380]
Sheerness at the Nore
15 December 1743

Sir,

I received their Lordships' orders [No. 26] to proceed with His Majesty's ship under my command to Spithead, as likewise your letter of the same date, and shall without loss of time (when the pilot comes down) immediately put them in execution.

28. To Corbett

[TNA, ADM 1/2380]
Sheerness in the Downes
18 December 1743

Sir,

Yesterday in the evening I arrived with His Majesty's ship under my command in the Downes where I was obliged to come to an anchor the wind being westerly. It blows now very hard at WNW but the first opportunity that offers I shall proceed according to their Lordships' directions [No. 26]. The surgeon of His Majesty's ship under my command having represented to me that the gunner was dangerously ill of a mortification in one of his legs, which must be cut off, and that if immediate assistance was not had he must likewise lose his life, I thought proper to send him to the hospital at Chatham and take the first opportunity to acquaint their Lordships of it, that another gunner might be appointed. This officer on board a twenty gun ship always having the command of [the] watch in case the lieutenant or master are sick, and having one Mr. Richard Adams who is master's mate on board this ship and has served in the same station on board several others, who has passed for gunner, been many years in the service, and is both a good artist[1] and able seaman, I should be much obliged to their Lordships if they would be so good to favour me with him as I know him to be a very fit person for that station.

---

[1] A name formerly applied to those seamen who were expert navigators.

29. To Corbett

[TNA, ADM 1/2380]
Sheerness in the Downes
19 December 1743

Sir,

Enclosed is the weekly account for His Majesty's ship under my command. The wind still continues westerly and blows so hard that most of the outward bound ships which sailed lately under the convoy of the *Greyhound* are putting back. I forgot in my last [No. 28] to acquaint their Lordships that the purser who went to Chatham upon duty and the marine officer to whom I gave leave for a day to go to his regiment were both left behind when I sailed from the Nore and are not as yet returned.

30. To Corbett

[TNA, ADM 1/2380]
Sheerness at Spithead
23 December 1743

Sir,

Yesterday in the evening I arrived here with His Majesty's ship under my command. I should be glad to know if their Lordships think proper to have the *Ruby's* men paid their wages, as likewise two months' advance, before I proceed to sea.

31. From the Lords of the Admiralty

[TNA, ADM 2/60, pp. 458–9]
23 December 1743

Whereas we have received intelligence of a Spanish privateer which is cruising on the coast of Ireland, and lately took a merchant ship off of Cape Clear, you are hereby required and directed to proceed without loss of time, with His Majesty's ship under your command, and cruise on the coast of Ireland between Cape Clear and Cork, using your best endeavours to come up with and take or destroy the aforesaid or any other privateer of the enemy, and to protect the trade of His Majesty's subjects.

And whereas Lord Duncannon,[1] secretary to His Grace the Duke of Devonshire,[2] has informed us that a ship with his Grace's baggage on

---

[1] William Ponsonby, Lord Duncannon of Fort Duncannon, County Wexford, 2nd Earl of Bessborough and secretary to the Lord Lieutenant of Ireland, 1741–44.
[2] William Cavendish, 3rd Duke of Devonshire, Lord Lieutenant of Ireland, 1737–44.

board will be ready to sail from the port of Dublin, the first fair wind after the 25th of January next, and requested that a ship of war may be appointed to convoy her from thence to England, you are to cruise on the aforementioned station no longer than the 23rd January, and then make the best of your way to Dublin, where you are to enquire for the said ship laden with the Duke of Devonshire's baggage, and to take her under your convoy, and see her in safety as far as the Downes, where you are to remain with the ship you command [un]til further orders; sending us an account of your arrival and proceedings and a journal of your cruise.

32. *From the Lords of the Admiralty*

[TNA, ADM 2/60, p. 469] 26 December 1743

Whereas we think it reasonable that seamen removed from their ships, which are under orders of being paid off, into ships fitting out for the sea, should be entered for wages on board the latter ship, from the day after the former is paid off, you are hereby required and directed to enter the men removed into the ship you command from the *Ruby*, from the 10th of September for wages, being the day after their discharge from the *Ruby*, provided they appeared on board when their leave of absence expired, or within a reasonable time after it. But if they delayed coming on board for any considerable time, so as the fitting out of the ship was retarded by reason of their not attending at their duty, you are then to enter them only from the day of their appearance. But in case any of the said men have not yet appeared on board, now that the ship you command is sailed from the port she was fitted out, you are to run them.

33. *To Corbett*

[TNA, ADM 1/2380] *Sheerness* at Spithead
26 December 1743

Sir,

I received their Lordships' orders of the 23 instant [No. 31] as likewise your letters of the 24th. The wind being easterly I am getting under sail as soon as possible and shall use my best endeavours to execute my orders to their Lordships satisfaction.

34. *From the Lords of the Admiralty*

[TNA, ADM 2/60, p. 492] 2 January 1744

You are hereby required and directed, if you get to Dublin before the vessel laden with the Duke of Devonshire's baggage is ready to sail for England, to use your utmost endeavours to procure seamen for the fleet, during your stay there, and to do the same upon all occasions.

35. *To Corbett*

[TNA, ADM 1/2380] *Sheerness* at sea
Cape Clear NE 8 leagues
5 January 1744

Sir,
I take the opportunity (by His Majesty's sloop the *Hawke* who I spoke with today) to acquaint their Lordships of my proceedings since I left England. On the 29th of December I made the coast of Ireland and got upon my station and have since constantly had very hard gales at ESE which has obliged me to keep a little to the westward of the Cape to avoid being upon a lee shore. I have spoke only with one vessel (who came from Dublin) since I have been out, and as yet have had no intelligence of the enemy. My people continue healthy, but [I] am afraid if we have any more bad weather they will fall down, the ship making a great deal of water in her upper works and bow ports. I shall proceed to execute the remainder of my orders when my cruise is expired and miss no opportunity of letting their Lordships know of my proceedings.

36. *From the Lords of the Admiralty*

[TNA, ADM 2/60, pp. 522–3] 13 January 1744

Whereas His Majesty has been pleased to direct an embarkation of 1,400 men, to be transported from Dublin to Ostend, which will probably be ready to sail from that place by the first day of next month, you are hereby required and directed, notwithstanding former orders, to remain with the ship you command at Dublin [un]til the said troops are embarked, wherein you are to assist all you can by your boats or otherwise, and then take them under your convoy and proceed with them to Ostend, and give the best assistance you can in landing the troops there, according as the commanding officer shall desire. And you are to see the vessel which has the Duke of Devonshire's baggage on board, safe as near to the Downes as your way lies together.

And whereas we have ordered his Majesty's sloop the *Ferret* to proceed to Dublin, in order to strengthen the convoy for the said troops, you are to take her under your command accordingly, her captain being directed to follow your orders.

We send you herewith a copy of the letter from Captain Conway, who was appointed to attend the late embarkations of soldiers to Flanders, giving his thoughts of the nature of the navigation on that coast, to which you are to have due regard.

You are to be cautious not to be imposed on by French pilots instead of Flemish, upon the coast of Flanders, and you are to anchor in the road of Ostend, and not go into the harbour.

When the troops are disembarked, you are to quicken the transports in coming out to join you, and then see them in safety into St. George's Channel, if their masters desire it, and then return with the ship under your command and the *Ferret* to Spithead and remain there [un]til further orders.

37. *To Corbett*

[TNA, ADM 1/2380] *Sheerness* in Cork Harbour
24 January 1744

Sir,

As my cruize was expired on the 23rd instant at which time I had orders [Nos. 31] to repair to Dublin to take under my convoy a ship laden with the Duke of Devonshire's baggage, but the wind being contrary and not having any person on board that was acquainted with St. George's Channel, I thought it was for the safety of His Majesty's ship under my command to put into this port for a pilot for that channel. I have already got one and the first fair wind that offers shall proceed according to their Lordships directions, taking under convoy all vessels bound my way. I hope their Lordships received my letters [No. 35] by the two vessels I sent to Portsmouth. Both of them having false clearances and bills of lading. On my arrival here I had upwards of thirty seamen ill of fevers occasioned by the continual dampness between decks, which was owing to the bad caulking of the bow ports. During my stay here my carpenters shall be constantly employed to make them tight and hope it will make the ship much more healthy. I have pressed as yet only eleven men, most of the vessels at this port having protections, but shall do my best endeavours to raise as many as I possibly can.

38. *To Corbett*

[TNA, ADM 1/2380] *Sheerness* Dublin Bay
11 February 1744

Sir,

Yesterday in the evening I arrived here with His Majesty's ship under my command and received their Lordships' orders [No. 36] to convoy the troops to Ostend as likewise two press warrants with the orders concerning them and shall use my utmost endeavours to raise as many seamen as possible. I waited on his Grace the Duke of Devonshire to receive his commands concerning the troops that are embarked. He is pleased to detain them till he receives further instructions from England and will acquaint me when they may proceed.

I sailed from Cork the 9th instant, His Majesty's ship *Squirrel* having arrived there the 7th. Captain [John] Moore reports he saw the French fleet the day after he left Plymouth off the Lizard. He counted twenty one sail with three flags, but believes by their not chasing him they could not discern him being in shore and they in the offing. He put into Cork in order to get a pilot for Dublin. I shall sail the first fair wind after his Grace will permit the transport to proceed and strictly observe the instructions given by Captain Conway in relation to the coast of Flanders and the manner the transport must go into the harbour of Ostend.[1]

39. *From the Duke of Devonshire*

[TNA, ADM 1/2380] 16 February 1744

Whereas His Majesty hath signified to us His Royal pleasure that the men drafted from His Majesty's foot regiments in this kingdom, which are now embarked on transports in Dublin harbour, and were to have been sent under your convoy to Ostend, should be landed at Bristol or Chester. These are to authorize and require you to take the said transports under your convoy and to sail with the same and to see them over the bar at Chester or in King Road at Bristol, as the wind may best serve, notwithstanding your former orders. And when this service is

---

[1] See also No. 36.

performed you are to repair to Spithead and there deliver, according to such orders as you shall receive from the Lords Commissioners of the Admiralty, ten pilots, which will be delivered to you by Captain John Weller of His Majesty's yacht *Dublin* and for doing this shall be your warrant.

40. *To Corbett*

[TNA, ADM 1/2380] *Sheerness* in Wild Road near Chester
19 February 1744

Sir,
Enclosed is a copy of the order [No. 39] I received from His Grace the Duke of Devonshire to take the transports with the foot soldiers under my convoy, either to Bristol or Chester as the wind would best serve. We sailed from Dublin the 18th instant and arrived this morning at Hoyle Road, it blowing so excessive hard at southwest the pilots would not take charge of the ship into Hoyle Lake. This seems to be the best road and in case a fair wind should offer, would be easier to get to sea from, though whenever its moderate I shall not wait for a fair wind but make the utmost dispatch with His Majesty's ship under my command to Spithead. I endeavoured at Dublin to impress seamen but found every ship in the harbour was either protected by their Lordships or hired for transports to carry the troops to England. Captain Moore in the *Squirrel* is likewise arrived with the convoy of Horse.

41. *To Corbett*

[TNA, ADM 1/2380] *Sheerness* in Hoyle Lake
8 March 1744

Sir,
Since my last [No. 40] acquainting their Lordships of my arrival with His Majesty's ship under my command with the transports of foot soldiers, I have been ever since detained here by contrary winds which have blown excessive hard and prevented my putting to sea, but as the weather is at present moderate I shall take the first opportunity to proceed to Spithead and in my passage use all my best endeavours to procure what seamen fall in my way. Since the late very hard gale of wind I thought it for the safety of His Majesty's ship to remove into Hoyle Lake having made but indifferent weather of it in Wild Road. Since being here I have impressed twenty two seamen.

42. To Corbett

[TNA, ADM 1/2380]

Sheerness
Plymouth Sound
18 March 1744

Sir,

This acquaints their Lordships of my arrival with His Majesty's ship under my command in Plymouth Sound being obliged to put in here by a strong easterly wind which prevented my getting to Spithead, but whenever it is moderate I shall proceed there according to their Lordships' directions.

43. To Corbett

[TNA, ADM 1/2380]

Sheerness in Plymouth Sound
23 March 1744

Sir,

Enclosed[1] is my weekly account for His Majesty's ship under my command. The wind continues still easterly which detains me here, but [I] shall proceed the first opportunity that presents to Spithead, unless I receive other orders from their Lordships. I must likewise acquaint them of the death of my boatswain and hope their Lordships will please to appoint another.

44. To Corbett

[TNA, ADM 1/2381]

Sheerness at Spithead
26 March 1744

Sir,

This day I arrived with His Majesty's ship under my command at Spithead, and applied to Sir Charles Hardy concerning the ten pilots I brought from Dublin (by order of His Grace the Duke of Devonshire) who informed me he had no orders concerning them. As the admiral has given me orders to sail with him I should be glad to know their Lordships' directions how to dispose of them.

---

[1] Not enclosed.

45. From the Lords of the Admiralty

[TNA, ADM 2/61, pp. 116–17] 27 March 1744

Having ordered His Majesty's ship under your command to be cleaned, graved, tallowed, and refitted at Portsmouth, stored for foreign service, and her provisions completed to three months' of all species, except beer, of which she is to have but one months only, and to be furnished with a proportion of English malt spirits in lieu of the other two months. You are hereby required and directed to repair with her into Portsmouth Harbour.

When the ship is ready again in all respects for the sea, you are to repair with her out to Spithead, and remain there [un]til further order, taking care to keep your provisions, stores, and water always complete until you proceed to sea.

46. To Corbett

[TNA, ADM 1/2381] *Sheerness* in Portsmouth Harbour
30th March 1744

Sir,

This acknowledges the receipt of their Lordships' orders of the 17th instant. I am now in Portsmouth harbour and shall use the utmost diligence in clearing the ship for the dock, and afterwards in refitting her. I must take notice to their Lordships that I have no boatswain or gunner and hope they will be pleased to appoint them.

47. To Corbett

[TNA, ADM 1/2381] *Sheerness* in Portsmouth Dock
3 April 1744

Sir,

His Majesty's ship under my command being [ready] to go out of the dock this day I shall use my utmost diligence in getting her to Spithead, where I hope their Lordships will give orders for the payment of the *Ruby's* men that were turned over into this ship.

48. *From the Lords of the Admiralty*

[TNA, ADM 2/61, p. 151]   4 April 1744

You are hereby required and directed, as soon as His Majesty's ship under your command is ready for the sea, to repair with her without a moment's loss of time to the Nore, and remain there till further order. And whereas application has been made to us for a convoy for some salt ships, now lying at Spithead, bound to the eastward, you are to take them under your care, as also any other trade bound your way, and see them in safety as far as your way lies together.

You are not to stay at Spithead till the *Ruby's* men removed into your ship are paid, unless the same can be done without delaying your sailing.

49. *To Corbett*

[TNA, ADM 1/2381]   *Sheerness* in Portsmouth Harbour
6 April 1744

Sir,

This acknowledges the receipt of their Lordships' orders of the 4th instant [No. 48] as likewise the copy of the letter from Mr. [Walter] Titley, His Majesty's minister at Copenhagen. I have waited these four days for ballast the hoys having been sunk in the late bad weather, and am afraid I shall not be ready to sail till Monday or Tuesday next. I must take notice to their Lordships that the boatswain has not as yet made his appearance.

50. *To Corbett*

[TNA, ADM 1/2381]   *Sheerness* in Portsmouth Harbour
7 April 1744

Sir,

Conformable to yours of the 5th instant I shall put to sea the moment the ship is ready and the wind will permit. I should be glad to know their Lordships' pleasure concerning the ten pilots I brought from Dublin. My boatswain has not as yet appeared [and] as he is a very necessary officer I hope their Lordships will order him immediately to repair to his duty.

51. *To Corbett*

[TNA, ADM 1/2381]

Sheerness in Portsmouth Harbour
9 April 1744

Sir,

I received both yours of the 7th April instant and must acquaint their Lordships that what superunumeraries I had were put on board the *Hampshire* by Sir Charles Hardy's orders. I shall sail conformable to their Lordships orders [No. 48] the first wind that will permit me to get out of the harbour.

52. *To Corbett*

[TNA, ADM 1/2381]

Sheerness in Portsmouth Harbour
13 April 1744

Sir,

I received yours of the 10th instant and conformable to their Lordships' directions have discharged the ten pilots. I have been ready for sea ever since Monday but am detained in harbour by contrary winds. The first fair one that offers I shall make the utmost dispatch to the Nore taking all the trade bound to the eastward under convoy.

53. *From the Lords of the Admiralty*

[TNA, ADM 2/61, pp. 187–9]   13 April 1744

You are hereby required and directed to collect together all the trade lying at the Nore or thereabouts, bound to the several ports of this Kingdom to the northward of the River Thames, as also those bound to Greenland, and to Iceland, and proceed with all the said trade to sea with the first fair wind and weather, and see those bound to the several ports, in safety off of the respective ports they are bound to.

And whereas His Majesty's sloop the *Wolf* is at the Nore, you are to take her along with you, her captain being hereby directed to follow and obey your orders.

And whereas the *Richard & Thomas* tender, belonging to the *Eltham*, is ordered to the Nore, you are to take her along with you, or any other tender that is at hand, if she is not in the way.

And whereas His Majesty's ship the *Harwich* is now cruising off the coast of Tynemouth you are diligently to look out for that ship, and deliver the enclosed order to her captain, which (among other things) contains instructions to him to take care of all the trade with you bound to the northward of Newcastle, as well as those bound to Greenland and Iceland, all which trade you are to consign over to his care, as also the tender which you carry with you.

When you have done what is above directed, you are to proceed as high as Leith Road, and to send letters ashore there, as also to all the principal sea port towns from thence to Yarmouth, letting the chief magistrates know, that you are appointed to take care of their trade bound to Holland and London, and by what time you shall call off their ports for the same; and accordingly, taking with you such trade as you shall find ready at Leith, you are to return from thence along the coast, calling off of the several trading ports in your way as far as Yarmouth, to collect all the said trade together.

When you shall be joined in Yarmouth Road by the trade from that place, you are to order the commander of the *Wolf* sloop to proceed directly to the Nore with all the trade bound to London. And you are to take under your own care all the trade bound to Holland, and see them safely into the mouth of the Meuse, and then proceed to Hellevoetsluis, where you are to remain ten days for such merchant ships bound to London as may be ready to sail in that time, giving notice thereof to the trade in the Meuse. And you are accordingly at the expiration of that time, to proceed to the Nore, with such trade under your convoy, as shall be ready to come with you.

You are always to endeavour to procure what men you can for the service, without interrupting the particular service you are employed upon, and to bear such as you get above the allowed complement of the ship you command as supernumeraries for victuals only till further order. And you are to give the like orders to the captain of the *Wolf* sloop.

54. *To Corbett*

[TNA, ADM 1/2381] *Sheerness* at the Nore
21 April 1744

Sir,

This day I arrived here with His Majesty's ship under my command and received their Lordships orders to convoy the trade to the northward as likewise a pacquet enclosed for Captain [Philip] Carteret which I shall take care to deliver. In coming over the flats yesterday it falling calm and the tide of ebb being made before the ship could possibly be towed into deep water she grounded. But on the flood got off without receiving any damages. I shall sail conformable to their Lordships' orders [No. 53] the first fair wind.

55. *From the Lords of the Admiralty*

[TNA, ADM 2/61, pp. 210–11] 23 April 1744

Notwithstanding our order to you of the 13th instant [No. 53] you are hereby required and directed to proceed up no higher than Newcastle with His Majesty's ship under your command, and to send letters on shore there and at all the other principal sea port towns from thence to Yarmouth, letting the chief magistrates know, that you are appointed to take care of their trade bound to Holland and London, and by what time you shall call off their ports for the same, and accordingly taking such trade as you find ready at Newcastle, you are to return from thence along the coast, calling off of the several trading ports in your way as far as Yarmouth, to collect all the said trade.

And whereas His Majesty's ship the *Squirrel* is ordered to cruise on a station between Aldeburgh, Yarmouth, and Lowestoft [un]til she joins the ships under your command and the trade under her convoy, you are when you meet with the said ship, to consign the trade bound to London to the care of her and the *Wolf* sloop, to be convoyed by them to the Nore. And then you are to proceed with the trade bound to Holland as you was before directed.

But if you should not meet with the *Squirrel* on the station abovementioned, you are then to pursue our said order of the 13th instant and follow the instructions therein contained for your proceedings in this service.

56. *To Corbett*

[TNA, ADM 1/2381] *Sheerness* at the Nore
 23 April 1744

Sir,

This acknowledges the receipt of yours of the 22nd instant wherein their Lordships order me to discharge my gunner, he being appointed lieutenant of the *Hind* sloop in the River. I hope their Lordships will give me leave to recommend Mr. Richard Adams [No. 28] who acted in the station of gunner during my cruise to the coast of Ireland. I would not presume to recommend him if he was not a very good man, has served nineteen years in the navy, and is qualified for that station.

Enclosed is the weekly account for His Majesty's ship under my command. The Iceland trade is not as yet arrived. When they do I shall take the first opportunity of wind and weather and proceed with the convoy to the northward.

57. *From the Lords of the Admiralty*

[TNA, ADM 2/61, pp. 211–12] 23 April 1744

Whereas the Commissioners of the Navy have represented to us, that Messrs Ambrose and John Crowley, who are under contract with them for supplying His Majesty with anchors &c. have represented to them, that they have now two ships lying at Shields, viz. the *Mary* and *Theodosia*, laden with anchors and iron work for His Majesty's immediate service, and also a great many other stores which are immediately wanted for His Majesty's service, and praying that a convoy may be appointed to take care of the aforesaid vessels, or any others laden with stores for His Majesty's service, as far as the Nore. You are hereby required and directed, when you call off Shields in your return from Newcastle, to make particular enquiry for the aforesaid ships, or any others belonging to Messrs Crowley, laden with stores for His Majesty's service, and convoy them, along with the other trade, down the coast, consigning them to the care of the captain of the *Squirrel* when you join her, directing her commander to take care of them as far as the Nore.

58. *From the Lords of the Admiralty*

[TNA, ADM 2/61, p. 227] 26 April 1744

Having ordered the captain of His Majesty's sloop the *Furnace*, to come from Leith to Tynemouth, and cruise there [un]til he joins you, and then put himself under your command, you are hereby required and directed, when you join the said sloop, to take her under your command accordingly, and when you arrive off Yarmouth, you are to order her captain to put himself under the command of the captain of the *Squirrel*, and proceed with her and the *Wolf* sloop and the trade bound to the Nore, and remain there [un]til further order.

59. To Corbett

[TNA, ADM 1/2381] *Sheerness* in Burlington Bay
3 May 1744

Sir,
Enclosed[1] is the weekly account for His Majesty's ship under my Command and the *Wolf* sloop.

The wind coming northerly obliged me (for the safety of the convoy) to anchor in this bay till a fair wind presented.

60. To Corbett

[TNA, ADM 1/2381] *Sheerness* in Tynemouth Haven
11 May 1744

Sir,
This day I arrived here with His Majesty's ship under my command and the *Wolf* sloop; having delivered their Lordships' orders to Captain Carteret off Tynemouth. As there were near two hundred ships ready, I propose sailing with the trade the first wind that offers.

On my arrival here I received their Lordships orders [No. 58] of the 26th April as likewise their enclosed petition from Mr. Ezekiel Hall and other merchants concerning the *Prudent* a French ship taken by me on the coast of Ireland. I am conscious my proceedings are just and will soon be determined in the High Court of Admiralty.

I have applied to the mayor of Newcastle and Tynemouth for any able bodied seamen or landmen they may have taken up in pursuance of a late Act of Parliament,[2] and shall receive them on board my ship according to their Lordships' directions.

61. To Corbett

[TNA, ADM 1/2381] *Sheerness* in Hellevoetsluis Road
23 May 1744

Sir,
Yesterday I arrived here with His Majesty's ship under my command with the convoy of one hundred and three merchant ships.

[1] Not enclosed.
[2] 17 Geo. II, c. 34. An Act for the better Encouragement of Seamen in His Majesty's Service, and Privateers to annoy the enemy.

About twelve leagues ESE of Lowestoft a small privateer endeavoured to cut off the rear of the convoy, but a fresh breeze springing up I tacked and disappointed him, but could not pursue him far, for fear of exposing the convoy to other privateers that might have been lurking about. And as several strange ships were in sight I rejoined the convoy and kept them as close together as possible.

The privateer is a Folkestone cutter of about forty ton. His station has been for some time about twelve or fourteen leagues off the land between Aldeburgh and Lowestoft. He has taken one small prize which now lies at The Brill,[1] but has done no other damage.

In compliance with their Lordships orders [No. 53] I have given notice to the trade in the Meuse that I shall sail the 2nd of June and take all that are ready and willing under convoy.

62. To Corbett

[TNA, ADM 1/2381] *Sheerness* at the Nore
6 June 1744

Sir,
Enclosed is a list of all the ships that have taken convoy since my departure from the Nore, by which their Lordships will perceive I had no opportunity of procuring men, all of them being coasters and properly protected, but I shall at all times use my utmost endeavours to get as many as possible.

As their Lordships' orders to me were always to keep my ship completely victualled to three months, on my arrival here I applied to the Commissioners of the Victualling for that purpose, but received for answer that they had no orders concerning it.

63. To Corbett

[TNA, ADM 1/2381] *Sheerness* at the Nore
20 June 1744

Sir,
This acknowledges the receipt of their Lordships' orders of the 18th instant directing me to put myself under the command of Captain [Jacob] Elton of His Majesty's ship *Anglesea* and to follow his orders for my further proceedings.

[1] Brielle in the Netherlands.

As I am in want of twenty two men to complete my complement of marines, I applied to the commanding officer of Colonel [James] Cockran's Regiment, who was pleased to inform me he could not comply with my request without orders from their Lordships which I hope they will please to give.

64. *From the Lords of the Admiralty*

[TNA, ADM 2/62, pp. 54–5] 6 August 1744

Whereas we have appointed you captain of His Majesty's ship the *Ludlow Castle* at Deptford, which ship we have ordered to be fitted for the sea, and stored for foreign service, manned with her highest complement of men, and victualled with three months provisions of all species except beer, of which she is to have but one month, and to be furnished with a proportion of English malt spirits in lieu of the other two months. You are hereby required and directed to repair without loss of time on board her, and cause all possible diligence to be used in fitting her for the sea, and when she shall be in a proper forwardness, you are to fall down with her to Longreach, and there get on board her guns, and gunners stores, and such other stores and provisions as may remain to be got on board. And as soon as she shall be completely ready, you are to proceed with her to the Nore, and remain there [un]til farther order; taking care to keep your provisions, stores, and water always complete, till the ship proceeds to sea.

65. *To Corbett*

[TNA, ADM 1/2381] *Sheerness* in Yarmouth Roads
12 September 1744

Sir,
Please to acquaint their Lordships that I am arrived with His Majesty's ship under my command at this place having parted company with the *Aldborough* on the 24th of last month off Shetland in a gale of wind.

On the 5th instant I fell in with the *Montfort* East Indiaman who was in great distress having lost her masts off Shetland and buried the greatest part of her men. I assisted her with men, sails, rigging, and yards (an account of which I shall send to the Navy Board) and have brought her safe into this road. I could impress but thirteen men out of the whole ship's company, the rest being either dead or sick. I shall take the first opportunity of wind and weather to see her safe to the Nore.

66. To Corbett

[TNA, ADM 1/2381] *Sheerness* off Orford Ness
17 September 1744

Sir,

Please to acquaint their Lordships that I am now at an anchor under Orford Ness with His Majesty's ship under my command in company with the *Gibraltar* and two East India ships.

On the 15th instant the *Salisbury* East Indiaman coming into Yarmouth Roads, I sent my boats and those belonging to the *Gibraltar* and *Hawke* sloop to impress his men, but all absolutely refused to be impressed and would not suffer the boats to go on board. I was therefore obliged to unmoor my ship and fall down along side of him. I went myself on board and told them the consequence that might happen by my boarding them with my ship and that it would be much better for them to enter voluntarily as His Majesty had such an urgent occasion for men. Whereupon they unanimously agreed to enter, hoping their Lordships would permit them to stay some little time on shore to see their friends having been three years out of England.

There are about fifty good men. I not having above twenty that I could trust to send in lieu, have ordered Captain Collins[1] to take the rest, he having men sufficient to send in their stead.

I shall make all the dispatch I can to the Nore.

67. To Corbett

[TNA, ADM 1/2381] *Sheerness* at the Nore
20 September 1744

Sir,

Please to acquaint their Lordships that I am arrived with His Majesty's ship under my command at the Nore, having put my lieutenant and forty men on board the two East India ships [Nos. 65, 66] to carry them safe up the River. As I had no tickets of leave to give the men I ordered the lieutenant to stay on board them till a tender should call for them and as it is likely some of them may desert I hope their Lordships will please to give orders for a tender to bring them to their duty.

I received your letter of yesterday's date informing me it is their Lordships' order to put the men I impressed out of the two East India

---

[1] Captain Richard Collins of HMS *Gibraltar*.

ships on board the *Royal Sovereign* and shall immediately comply with it.

68. From the Lords of the Admiralty

[TNA, ADM 2/62, p. 205] 22 September 1744

Notwithstanding former orders, you are hereby required and directed, so soon as His Majesty's ship under your command is ready for the sea, to proceed with her to St. Helens or Spithead, where you are to apply to Vice Admiral [Thomas] Davers,[1] and put yourself under his command.

69. To Corbett

[TNA, ADM 1/2381] *Sheerness* at the Nore
23 September 1744

Sir,

This acknowledges the receipt of both your letters of the 21st instant with their Lordships' order of the same date requiring me to repair with His Majesty's ship under my command into this harbour in order to clear her for the dock, which shall be done with the utmost expedition.

I shall take care to give the necessary orders until Captain [William] Gordon relieves me, and beg leave to return their Lordships thanks for appointing [No. 64] me to command the *Ludlow Castle*.

70. To Corbett

[TNA, ADM 1/2381] *Sheerness*
25 September 1744

Sir,

Please to acquaint their Lordships that His Majesty's ship *Sheerness* is in the harbour, and shall use the utmost diligence to clear her for the dock. The powder is all out, and the guns now are getting out as fast as possible tho' out of all the men that went up in the two India ships, only four are returned with the lieutenant, the rest having got on shore before the tender arrived. They are the men of the longest standing in the ship and [I] believe will not desert. I have but few men to do the

---

[1] Appointed to be Commander-in-chief at Jamaica.

duty of [the] ship, most of them being put on board the *Royal Sovereign*, not caring to trust them least they should desert.

71. *From the Lords of the Admiralty*

[TNA, ADM 2/62, p. 211]   25 September 1744

Whereas we directed you by our order of the *22nd instant* [No. 68] to proceed with His Majesty's ship under your command to St. Helens, to join Vice Admiral Davers, we do hereby revoke the said order, and require and direct you to act with His Majesty's ship under your command, according to the orders [No. 64] you were under, prior to the same.

72. *To Corbett*

[TNA, ADM 1/2381]   *Sheerness*
                                                         28 September 1744

Sir,

Please to acquaint their Lordships that Captain Gordon having relieved me in His Majesty's ship the *Sheerness*, I shall make the utmost dispatch to take upon me the command of the *Ludlow Castle*.

As I am informed that many of the men that their Lordships were pleased to turn over on board the *Ludlow Castle* are very desirous to go with Captain Gordon and at the same time many men belonging to the *Sheerness* are willing to take their fortunes with me, I must take the liberty to beg their Lordships will permit us to change man for man.

Upon the *Sheerness* coming into the dock I put all the men on board the *Defiance* with orders not to permit any of them to go on shore, but last night many of them took the liberty to go on shore without leave notwithstanding I ordered the lieutenant and master with all the petty officers to take their proper watches. They are the longest standers in the ship and I believe will not desert His Majesty's service.

73. To Corbett

[TNA, ADM 1/2381] *Ludlow Castle* Deptford
4 October 1744

Sir,

This acknowledges the receipt of their Lordships' order of yesterday's date in regard to the marines that are to serve in His Majesty's ship under my command as likewise your letter of the same date wherein you let me know it is their Lordships' directions that I hasten with [His][1] Majesty's ship under my command to Longreach in order to get ready for sea as soon as possible. In answer to which I beg leave to inform their Lordships that I am ready to fall down to Longreach and have already a pilot on board but he does not care to take charge of the ship unless there is thirty more men ordered to assist in carrying her down the River.

74. From the Lords of the Admiralty

[TNA, ADM 2/62, p. 252] 5 October 1744

Having ordered the captains of the ship and yacht named in the margin[2] to send twenty men each with a discreet officer, on board the ship you command, to assist in sailing her to Longreach, and from thence to the Nore, you are hereby required and directed to receive and victual the said men as your ship's company, taking care to return them again on your arrival at the Nore.

75. To Corbett

[TNA, ADM 1/2381] *Ludlow Castle* at Deptford
8 October 1744

Sir,

Please to acquaint their Lordships that the yacht's men are repaired on board His Majesty's ship under my command according to their Lordships' orders [No. 74], and that I wait for nothing but a wind to proceed to Longreach. At present it [is] calm, but if a fair wind should spring up before noon, I shall fall down today, if not, I beg leave to assure their Lordships that I shall take the first opportunity and use the utmost dispatch in getting ready for the sea.

---

[1] Manuscript torn.
[2] *Royal Caroline, William and Mary.*

76. From the Lords of the Admiralty

[TNA, ADM 2/62, p. 265] 9 October 1744

Whereas the Navy Board have represented to us that the master attendant at Deptford has not a sufficient number of riggers to attend the launching and transporting to the moorings there, His Majesty's ships the *Defiance* and *Maidstone* which are ordered to be launched the 12th instant, you are hereby required and directed to send thirty of the yacht's men whom you have on board, under the care of a discreet officer, on Friday morning next at six o'clock, to attend the master attendant, and assist him in performing that service, and then to order them to return to your ship.

77. To Corbett

[TNA, ADM 1/2381] *Ludlow Castle* Longreach
17 October 1744

Sir,
I received your letter of yesterday's date.
I beg leave to acquaint their Lordships that I expect the guns and powder down tomorrow, when all possible dispatch shall be used in getting them on board. As also to proceed to the Nore after that service is performed which I hope will be by Saturday morning if the wind and weather permits.

78. To Corbett

[TNA, ADM 1/2381] *Ludlow Castle* at the Nore
22 October 1744

Sir,
Please to acquaint their Lordships that I am arrived here with His Majesty's ship under my command.
Enclosed[1] is my weekly account, but have not as yet had time to rate the men, but hope their Lordships will order my complement to be completed.
I must likewise beg their Lordships will comply with my request in granting one John Carr, late boatswain mate of the *Kent*, but now a

---
[1] Not enclosed.

supernumerary aboard the *Royal Sovereign*, to be turned over on board my ship, he having petitioned me on that head.

79. *From the Lords of the Admiralty*

[TNA, ADM 2/62, pp. 318–19] 23 October 1744

Having ordered your complement to be completed out of the supernumeraries on board the *Royal Sovereign*, as they stand first on the list, in this proportion, viz. to make your whole company consist of 2/3rds seamen, including officers and servants, 1/3rd landmen including marines, you are hereby required and directed to receive and enter them from the days they were first raised for the service according to the list you will receive with them.

80. *To Corbett*

[TNA, ADM 1/2381] *Ludlow Castle* at the Nore
25 October 1744

Sir,

This acknowledges the receipt of their Lordships' orders of the 23rd instant [No. 79.] where in they are pleased to order my complement to be completed from the supernumeraries on board the *Royal Sovereign*. I must take notice to their Lordships that the carpenter of His Majesty's ship under my command has absented himself from his duty several days and neglected to get his stores on board, though he had informed me they were all complete. As a carpenter is a very necessary officer I must beg their Lordships will either command him to his duty or appoint another.

81. *To Corbett*

[TNA, ADM 1/2381] *Ludlow Castle* at the Nore
26 October 1744

Sir,

In answer to your letter of the 24th instant wherein I am commanded by their Lordships to return the yacht's men to their respective yachts, I am to acquaint you that on my arrival here they were all discharged for that purpose.

82. To Corbett

[TNA, ADM 1/2381] *Ludlow Castle* at the Nore
28 October 1744

Sir,
Enclosed[1] I send their Lordship a weekly account of His Majesty's ship under my command.

I with pleasure submitted to their Lordships' regulation in having one third landmen and two thirds seamen [No. 79]. But out of fifty six men that came from the *Royal Sovereign*, many of them were landmen, and the greater part far from being seamen. It has always been my endeavour to avoid troubling their Lordships in regard to men, but as the safety of His Majesty's ship under my command and the honour and reputation of those that serve in her might suffer by her being so ill manned, I beg their Lordships will be so good to indulge me with a few of the *Kent's* men that were turned into the *Colchester* and now on board the *Royal Sovereign*, to enable me to procure more men for the service, having at present but very few I can trust in lieu of impressed men.

83. From the Lords of the Admiralty

[TNA, ADM 2/62, pp. 334–5] 29 October 1744

His Majesty having ordered six horses to be sent over to Hamburg, as a present to his Royal Highness the Prince Royal of Denmark, and the Navy Board being directed to take up a transport for that purpose, and send her (when the horses are embarked) to the Nore, you are hereby required and directed, if the said transport arrives at the Nore before you are ready to sail, to take her under your convoy and see her in safety into the Elbe.

84. To Corbett

[TNA, ADM 1/2381] *Ludow Castle* at the Nore
31 October 1744

Sir,
This acknowledges the receipt of their Lordships' orders [No. 83] and your letter of the 29th instant requiring me to take under my

---

[1] Not enclosed.

convoy the transport with six horses as a present from His Majesty to His Royal Highness the Prince Royal of Denmark and see her in safety into the Elbe. I beg leave to return their Lordships thanks for granting my request in regard to the *Kent's* men.

85. *From the Lords of the Admiralty*

[TNA, ADM 2/62, p. 352] 31 October 1744

You are hereby required and directed to receive on board His Majesty's ship under your command Lieutenant Henry Angel with his servant and baggage and give them a passage to Hamburg, when you proceed thither victualling them as your ship's company during their passage.

86. *From the Lords of the Admiralty*

[TNA, ADM 2/62, pp. 345–7] 1 November 1744

Whereas the merchants trading to Amsterdam have represented to us, that they have several ships fully loaded and ready to sail for that place, and the merchants trading to Bremen and Hamburg have likewise represented to us, that they have now on board sundry ships bound for the said ports, large quantities of goods to a considerable value, which are wanted for those markets and for others in Germany at this season, a list of which ships is set down in the annexed list[1] and they having also represented, that they have several ships laden at Hamburg and Bremen with linens and other goods for consumption here, and for exportation to the West Indies. You are hereby required and directed to use your utmost diligence in getting the ship you command ready in all respects for the sea, and then to make enquiry for all the said trade, and having collected them all together, to proceed with them to sea the first fair wind after the 4th instant, giving convoy also to any other trade bound to the northward that shall be ready and desirous of accompanying you, as far as their way and yours lies together.

You are in the first place to proceed off of the Texel, and having seen the Amsterdam trade safe into that road, without going in yourself, to proceed to the mouth of the Weser, and when you have seen the trade bound to Bremen in safety into that river, you are then to go on with the rest to Hamburg.

---

[1] Enclosed a list of eight merchant ships bound to Amsterdam, four merchant ships bound to Bremen, and seven other merchant ships bound to Hamburg.

When you arrive in the Elbe you are to send immediate notice of your arrival to Mr. [James] Cope, His Majesty's minister at Hamburg, and if he sends any English or foreign seamen to you, whom he has procured to enter into His Majesty's service, you are to receive them on board and enter them as supernumeraries in your ship's books for wages and victuals. And whereas we have promised that every seamen, who shall enter voluntarily into His Majesty's service at Hamburg, shall receive an advance of two months' wages so soon as they come on board His Majesty's ships, you are in case any seamen do enlist upon that encouragement, to pay them accordingly as soon as they come on board you, drawing bills for the value upon the Navy Board, and sending them a list of their names and money paid, in order to their charging the same against their growing wages in the ship under your command.

You are to make no longer stay than ten days in the Elbe, and then, having collected together all the trade homeward bound from Hamburg and Bremen or sooner if the merchants desire it, to proceed with them to England, seeing the said trade in safety off of their respective ports they are bound to from which ports also you are to take any trade bound your way that is ready to join you, and proceed with them to the Nore, where you are to remain until further order, sending us an account of your arrival and proceedings.

You are to be very careful to inform yourself at all foreign ports, that you shall touch at, whether there be any English seamen prisoners of war there, and to use your best endeavours to get them on board, giving receipt to the French consul, or who ever has them in his custody, with a promise to endeavour to procure the releasement of as many French prisoners in England, and you are to let us and the Commissioners for Sick and Wounded know your proceedings therein.

You are to use your utmost endeavours to procure seamen or able bodied landmen for the service, and to bear all such as you get above the allowed complement of the ship you command as supernumeraries for victuals until further order, and when you return again to the Nore, you are to send us an account of the number of men you have procured, distinguishing how many of them are seamen and how many landmen.

And whereas we have appointed His Majesty's ship the *Gibraltar* to convoy the trade bound from the Nore to Rotterdam, as also His Majesty's yacht the *Charlotte*, and directed the captain of the *Gibraltar* to sail when you do, for the better security of the said trade, and to put himself under your command while you are together, you are to take the said ship under your command accordingly, and to give protection to the said trade, and also to the *Charlotte* yacht, while you are together, and when you come to a proper station for parting, you are to make the signal for that purpose, and pursue the other part of your instructions of this date.

87. To Corbett

[TNA, ADM 1/2381]
Ludlow Castle at the Nore
4 November 1744

Sir,

One George Martin, a midshipman on board His Majesty's ship *Ludlow Castle* under my command, having been sent upon duty on the 1st instant deserted from the service, I thought it proper to acquaint their Lordships thereof in order for his being apprehended.

He is about five foot eight inches, of a fair complexion, thirty years old, wears a wig and generally lives at Biddiford, but may be heard of at the Standard near the Lower Watergate at Deptford.

I believe his being refused his discharge (he having passed for a master) was the occasion of his desertion. He was one of the men turned over from the *Hound* sloop into this ship.

88. From the Lords of the Admiralty

[TNA, ADM 2/62, pp. 367–8]
7 November 1744

Whereas upon the petition of the merchants concerned in the trade bound to Rotterdam, we have appointed His Majesty's ship under your command to convoy the said trade thither, as also the *Charlotte* yacht which is bound to Rotterdam, you are hereby required and directed notwithstanding former orders [No. 87], to enquire diligently for the said trade, and proceed with them and the yacht the first fair wind and weather off of the Meuse, and after having seen them in safety, you are to make the best of your way to Ostend Road, and take the *Gosport* under your command, if you meet with her there; and you are to send notice on shore to General Wade,[1] that you are appointed to convoy him, with the two yachts and transport vessel, over to England, which you are accordingly to do, as also any trade that shall be ready to proceed with you, and make the best of your way with them, if you have no other man of war with you, to the Nore, and remain there until further order, sending us an account of your arrival and proceedings.

[1] Major General George Wade, Commander-in-chief of the British forces in Flanders.

And whereas we have appointed His Majesty's ship the *Gibraltar* and *Furnace* sloop, to convoy the trade bound from the Nore to Amsterdam, Bremen, and Hamburg, and directed their captains to sail when you do, for the better security of the said trade, and to put themselves under your command while you are together, you are to take the said ship and sloop under your command accordingly, and to give protection to the said trade while you are together, and when you come to a proper station for parting, you are to make the signal for that purpose, and pursue the other part of your instructions of this date.

89. *From the Lords of the Admiralty*

[TNA, ADM 2/62, p. 368]   7 November 1744

Whereas Rear Admiral [Isaac] Townsend[1] has transmitted to us a list of sick men belonging to the ship under your command, you are hereby required and directed to put such of them ashore whose cases do absolutely require it, and to apply to Captain [Thomas] Hanway of the *Royal Sovereign* for the like number. We having directed him to supply you therewith, and you are to victual them as supernumeraries while they are on board and to return them when you come back to the Nore.

90. *To Corbett*

[TNA, ADM 1/2381]   *Ludlow Castle* at the Nore
8 November 1744

Sir,
This acknowledges the receipt of their Lordships' orders [Nos. 89, 90], as likewise your letter of yesterday's date, and beg leave to assure them that His Majesty's ship under my command has been several days ready for sea, and only waits till Captain [Coningsby] Norbury in His Majesty's sloop *Furnace* gets a pilot and joins me at the Nore.

91. *From the Lords of the Admiralty*

[TNA, ADM 2/62, p. 370]   8 November 1744

Notwithstanding former orders [No. 88], you are hereby required and directed to remain with His Majesty's ship under your command at

[1] The Admiral in command at the Nore.

the Nore [un]til further order, holding yourself ready to sail in a moment after receiving your orders, which you may expect by another express which will be sent this evening.

92. *From the Lords of the Admiralty*

[TNA, ADM 2/62, pp. 378–9] 8 November 1744

Sir,

You are hereby required and directed immediately to proceed to sea, with the *Charlotte* yacht and trade bound to Rotterdam, without staying for the *Gibraltar* and *Furnace* sloop if they are not ready, and see them in safety off of the Meuse, pursuant to the orders you have already received [No. 88].

And whereas His Majesty's ship the *Wager* is on her passage from the Sound with a large number of homeward bound merchant ships under her convoy, the *Dover* and *Jamaica* sloop, which were to have come along with her, having been disabled from doing so by the damages they have received; and the Russia merchants having requested that three of His Majesty's ships may be appointed to cruise, in order to meet with the said convoy, for their better security, and that one of them may be appointed to cruise between 20 and 30 leagues off at sea, Flamborough Head bearing from her WSW or west, and to make the land once in every five or six days for intelligence. You are hereby required and directed, as soon as you have seen the yacht and trade off of the Meuse, as aforesaid immediately to make the best of your way to the aforementioned station off Flamborough Head, and cruise there in the manner requested by the merchants; and in case you meet with the *Wager* and the trade under her convoy, you are to take Captain Loftin under your command, and to see such of the merchant ships as shall be bound to Hull, safe into the Humber, and the rest into their respective ports between that place and the Nore, where you are to remain till further order. But if you do not meet with the *Wager*, but should fall in with any merchant ships separated from her, you are to see them into the ports they are bound to, as aforesaid. If you should neither meet with the *Wager*, nor any merchant ships separated from her, you are to continue cruising till you receive certain intelligence of the convoy's being passed by, and then return with the ship you command to the Nore, sending us an account of your arrival and proceedings.

93. To Corbett

[TNA, ADM 1/2381] *Ludlow Castle* at the Nore
10 November 1744

Sir,
This acknowledges the receipt of both their Lordships' orders of the 8th instant [Nos. 91, 92]. The one I received by express at five o'clock on Friday morning, the other in the evening. Upon receipt of the first, I immediately unmoored and got ready to sail at a moment's warning, but not receiving the other till late in the evening, I could not proceed to sea last night. At day light this morning I made the signal to weigh the wind being WNW, but it flying about to the north and blowing very hard, the pilot would not take charge down [the] Swynn until the weather proves more moderate. I beg leave to assure their Lordships that nothing shall be wanting on my part to put their orders in execution as soon as possible.

94. To Corbett

[TNA, ADM 1/2381] *Ludlow Castle* in Yarmouth Road
24 November 1744

Sir,
Having received their Lordships' orders of the 8th instant [Nos. 91, 92] by express, commanding me immediately to sail with His Majesty's ship under my command and see the *Charlotte* yacht and the trade bound to Rotterdam in safety off of Goree. In compliance with the same, I made the best of my way with the said yacht and trade, leaving them in safety off Goree the 13th instant, but upon ordering my pilot (which I had out of the *Gibraltar*) to shape his course for Flamborough Head, he absolutely refused to take charge of the ship, not being a pilot for the North Sea, but proposed to carry her to Yarmouth or Orford Ness, at either of which places I could get a pilot to enable me to execute the remainder of my orders, which I thought was better than returning to the Nore, but the wind blowing very hard at west and WSW forced us into the latitude of Flamborough Head, at which place likewise [I] intended to have touched at for a pilot; but was disappointed by an excessive hard gale of wind at NNW and NNE accompanied with a great quantity of snow and hail, which put us by our topsails for seven or eight days, great part of my ship's company being rendered unfit for service by severity of the weather,

having at present upwards of eighty men sick on board, the ship being so very leaky in her upper works and decks that makes it impossible for men to lie dry in their hammocks and not having seen the land in this narrow sea for ten days and the strong northerly winds having drove us to the southward, I thought it for the safety of His Majesty's ship to put into this road, in order to refit our shattered rigging and get another pilot, but in coming over the Standford [Shoal] this morning the ship struck several times with such violence that I was afraid all her masts would have been carried by the board, but after striking for some time together, I got her safely into this road though I am afraid not without receiving some damage by the violence of her striking. I shall remain here until I know how I am to proceed.

95. To Corbett

[TNA, ADM 1/2381] *Ludlow Castle* in Yarmouth Roads
27 November 1744

Sir,

Please to acquaint their Lordships that this day His Majesty's ship *Wager* with the convoy from the Sound arrived here. But it blows so fresh I cannot send on board him, as my orders [No. 93] were to return to the Nore upon meeting the said ship and trade. I shall proceed with them accordingly.

96. From the Lords of the Admiralty

[TNA, ADM 2/62, p. 441] 27 November 1744

You are hereby required and directed to proceed with His Majesty's ship under your command to Sheerness, (*taking under your convoy any trade bound your way that are desirous of accompanying you,*) where we have ordered her to be cleaned, graved, tallowed, and refitted, stored for foreign service, and her provisions completed to three months of all species, except beer, of which she is to have but one month, and to be furnished with a proportion of English malt spirits in lieu of the other two months.

97. To Corbett

[TNA, ADM 1/2381] *Ludlow Castle* in Yarmouth Road
1 December 1744

Sir,

This acknowledges the receipt of their Lordships' orders of the 27th of November [No. 96] and shall proceed with the trade for London the first opportunity of wind and weather, but am afraid I shall not be able to get over the Standford [Shoal] till the spring tides come on.

98. To Corbett

[TNA, ADM 1/2381] *Ludlow Castle* in Sheerness
10 December 1744

Sir,

Please to acquaint their Lordships that I am arrived with His Majesty's ship under my command at this place, and shall use the utmost expedition in order to get her ready for the dock. I must likewise acquaint them that George Martin, a midshipman who I had acquainted [No. 87] their Lordships had deserted from my ship, returned to his duty the day before I sailed from the Nore.

Enclosed[1] is a list of the ships that came under my convoy and my weekly account.

99. To Corbett

[TNA, ADM 1/2381] *Ludlow Castle* in Sheerness
10 December 1744

Sir,

As His Majesty's ship under my command has been very sickly during the last cruise, I beg leave to give their Lordships my sentiments upon the occasion; which I am apt to think is by the men being so very much exposed upon the quarter deck, not having the least shelter to protect them from the severity of the weather, having at present near sixty sick on board, most of whom belong to the after guard.[2]

---

[1] A list of six merchant ships.
[2] The seamen whose station is on the poop or quarter deck to work the gear of the ship.

As an awning would be of very great use to protect the men from the weather. And the taffarell[1] high enough to allow two cabins to to be built on the quarter deck for the first lieutenant and master, which would make more room, to stow the men, the ship being deficient in that point by the officers having births betwixt decks. I think it my duty to inform their Lordships of it and hope they will please to take it into consideration.

100. *To Corbett*

[TNA, ADM 1/2381] *Ludlow Castle* at Sheerness
18 December 1744

Sir,

Whereas Lieutenant [Bowles] Seymour of His Majesty's ship *Royal Sovereign* has represented to me that Captain Smith[2] had ordered him in their ship's tender to repair to Standgate Creek to impress the men out of the ships there at the expiration of their quarantine, and that the ships mentioned in the enclosed list[3] would have pratique granted them on the 22nd and 27th instant, but that their numbers being upwards of two hundred he was afraid he should not be able to perform that service unless a small man of war was ordered to assist him. As such a number of men would be so beneficial to His Majesty's service I thought it my indispensable duty to send their Lordships an express of it, as likewise to acquaint them that as His Majesty's ship under my command will be ready for the dock on Wednesday next, I shall be able to spare upwards of fifty men to perform the said service and believe the *Princess Mary* can send one hundred.

101. *To Corbett*

[TNA, ADM 1/2381] *Ludlow Castle* in Sheerness Harbour
29 December 1744

Sir,

Whereas I acquainted their Lordships in my last that the boatswain of His Majesty's ship under my command had wrote to me that he was

---

[1] Upper part of the flat portion of a ship's stern above the transom.
[2] Commodore Thomas Smith, Captain, 5 May 1730; Rear Admiral 15 July 1747; Vice-Admiral 12 May 1748; Admiral 1757. Governor of Newfoundland, 1741–44; Commander-in-chief, Downes, Nov. 1744; Commander-in-chief, Nore, Sept. 1745; Commander-in-chief, Leith, 1747.
[3] Not enclosed.

rendered incapable of doing his duty by reason of sickness and desired to be put on shore which letter I imagined miscarried, made me trouble them with this, as the boatswain is a very necessary officer I hope their Lordships will not permit me to go to sea without one, and shall be much obliged to them if they will comply with my request in removing William Mossom, boatswain of the *Sheerness* into my ship. I shall make what dispatch I can in getting ready for sea, but at present wait for water, provisions, and cables.

102. To Corbett

[TNA, ADM 1/2381] *Ludlow Castle* in Sheerness Harbour
4 January 1745

Sir,
Please to acquaint their Lordships that His Majesty's ship under my command will be ready to sail for the Nore on Monday next, unless prevented by the cables not being sent down, which have been demanded these three weeks. I must likewise take notice to their Lordships that I have fifty five of my best men now sick on shore, and am afraid none of them will be fit to go to sea in the ship. As they were most of them men that lately belonged to the *Kent*, I hope their Lordships will please to order me some of the same ship's men in lieu of those sent sick on shore before I proceed to sea being at present very ill manned.

103. To Corbett

[TNA, ADM 1/2381] *Ludlow Castle* in Sheerness Harbour
7 January 1744

Sir,
Please to acquaint their Lordships that His Majesty's ship under my command is in all respects ready to sail to the Nore, and if the wind had permitted would have been there today. On my arrival there, I shall send their Lordships a particular state of my ship's company, but am sorry to acquaint them that the sickness still rages among them, three or four being taken ill with fevers daily, notwithstanding all the precaution possible has been to prevent it, the ship having been washed several times with vinegar and thoroughly dried during the time the men continued on board the *Defiance*.

104. From the Lords of the Admiralty

[TNA, ADM 2/63, pp. 81–2]   11 January 1745

Having ordered the captain of His Majesty's ship the *Royal Sovereign* to complete your complement (*when you come to the Nore*) out of his supernumeraries as they stand first on the list, without favour or partiality, and to send a list of their names, and the days they were first raised for the service along with them observing this proportion viz. to make the whole complement consist of two thirds seamen including officers and servants, and one third landmen including marines, you are hereby required and directed to receive and enter the said men, as part of your complement for wages from the days they were first raised and for victuals from the day of their appearance. And you are to hold yourself in constant readiness for sailing for which you may expect speedy orders.

And whereas we have directed the said captain to send no men to you but who are in perfect health, to prevent their carrying sickness along with them into your ship, you are to receive none but who are in good health.

105. From the Lords of the Admiralty

[TNA, ADM 2/63, p. 82]   11 January 1745

You are hereby required and directed, as soon as your complement is completed from the *Royal Sovereign*, to proceed with His Majesty's ship under your command to Spithead, and remain there until further order, taking all the trade from the Nore and the Downes under your convoy that shall be ready and desirous to accompany you.

106. From the Lords of the Admiralty

[TNA, ADM 2/63, p. 95]   14 January 1745

Whereas a considerable number of merchant ships bound to Portugal are expected to arrive every day in the Downes, you are hereby required and directed to repair with His Majesty's ship under your command, with all possible dispatch, to the Downes, and to remain there till the 20th instant and then collecting together all the trade bound westward to proceed with the first fair wind to Spithead, seeing the trade in safety as far as your way and theirs lies together.

107. *From the Lords of the Admiralty*

[TNA, ADM 2/63, p. 97]   14 January 1744

Having ordered the commanding officer of the *Royal Sovereign* to send on board the ship you command several men late belonging to the *Colchester* in order to their being carried to Spithead to serve on board His Majesty's ship the *Ipswich*, you are hereby required and directed to receive the said men on board your ship and carry them to the *Ipswich* at Spithead, and you are to victual the said men as your ship's company while they remain on board.

108. *To Corbett*

[TNA, ADM 1/2381]   *Ludlow Castle* at the Nore
16 January 1745

Sir,

This acknowledges the receipt of their Lordships' orders of the 14th instant [Nos. 106, 107] as likewise your letter of yesterday's date, and shall immediately send the petty officers and imprest men under a sufficient guard to Chatham. I must likewise acquaint their Lordships that His Majesty's ship under my command is in all respects ready to sail and will only wait the return of the men.

109. *From the Lords of the Admiralty*

[TNA, ADM 2/63, p. 104]   16 January 1745

Whereas it is represented to us that the ship *Levant* bound to Turkey, is now at the Nore, waiting for convoy, you are hereby required and directed to make enquiry for the said ship, and take her under your convoy, as also all other trade bound your way, and see them in safety to the Downes, and from thence to Spithead in pursuance of our orders of the 11th and 14th instant [Nos. 105, 106].

110. *To Corbett*

[TNA, ADM 1/2381] *Ludlow Castle* at the Nore
18 January 1745

Sir,
This acknowledges the receipt of their Lordships' orders [No. 109] of the 16th instant requiring me to take under convoy the ship *Levant* bound to Turkey.

As there are several young gentlemen on board His Majesty's ship under my command, I must desire their Lordships will be pleased to warrant a schoolmaster to instruct them in the art of navigation.

111. *From the Lords of the Admiralty*

[TNA, ADM 2/63, p. 113] 21 January 1745

Having ordered the provisions of His Majesty's ship under your command to be completed to four months of all species except beer, of which she is to have but six weeks, and to be furnished with a proportion of English malt spirits in lieu of the other ten weeks, you are hereby required and directed to use all possible dispatch in getting the same on board, and keep them complete till you proceed to sea, for which you are to hold yourself in constant readiness.

112. *To Corbett*

[TNA, ADM 1/2381] *Ludlow Castle* in the Downes
22 January 1745

Sir,
Please to acquaint their Lordships that His Majesty's ship under my command is arrived in the Downes, and shall take the first opportunity of wind and weather to proceed to Spithead taking all the ships bound my way under convoy.

113. To Corbett

[TNA, ADM 1/2381] Ludlow Castle at Spithead
5 February 1744

Sir,

Please to acquaint their Lordships that I am arrived at Spithead with His Majesty's ship under my command and the trade bound there. As there was not marines at Maidstone to complete my complement I hope their Lordships will please to order Admiral [James] Stewart[1] to complete them here.

Enclosed is a list of ships that came under my convoy and a weekly account.[2]

114. From the Lords of the Admiralty

[TNA, ADM 2/63, pp. 184–5] 9 February 1745

Whereas the merchants trading to Portugal have represented to us, that they have a considerable number of ships laden and ready to sail for the ports of the said kingdom, you are hereby required and directed to use all possible diligence in completing the provisions, stores and water of the ship under your command, and when you have collected all the trade aforesaid (for which you are to make diligent enquiry, and to give timely notice to them of your sailing), you are to proceed to sea. And when you come off of Oporto, you are to see the trade bound to that port in safety over the bar, unless you shall happen to meet with any of His Majesty's ships cruising there, and in that case you are to consign over the said trade to their care.

Having so done you are to proceed on with the trade bound to Lisbon, where you are to give notice to the consul and factory, that you are ordered to stay ten days for any trade bound from thence to Great Britain, and accordingly at the expiration thereof, to come out of Lisbon River with the said trade. And as you are during your stay at Lisbon, to send timely notice overland to the consul and factory at Oporto, of the day you shall sail from Lisbon, so are you to advise with intelligent persons [of] the best methods of making it easy for the trade from Oporto to come out and join you, when you appear off of that place, and to proceed accordingly, and when the said trade is come out to you, to give the whole trade safe convoy to Great Britain, accompa-

---

[1]Commander-in-chief at Portsmouth.
[2]Enclosed is a list of 33 merchant ships.

nying the trade bound into St. George's Channel as far as you judge proper towards the entrance into it, and then proceed with the rest up the British Channel as far as the Downes, where you are to remain till further order, sending our secretary an account of your arrival and proceedings for our information.

And whereas Rear Admiral Medley[1] is under orders to proceed with the ships named in the margin[2] to the Mediterranean, you are to go to sea along with him, if he is not sailed before you are ready, putting yourself under his command. And when the said Rear Admiral thinks proper to give you orders for separating from him, you are to proceed and put in[to] execution the aforesaid instructions.

And whereas we have received advices of the French having a large squadron of ships on this side of the Strait's mouth divided sometimes into two or three divisions, part of them riding sometimes in the Bay of Cadiz, and the rest cruising off of the coasts of Spain and Portugal between the Strait's mouth and Lisbon and particularly that on the 23rd of the last month ten French ships of war from 50 to 60 guns were steering ESE in the latitude of 39° north and longitude 10° 14' west from the Lizard. We give you this notice thereof to the end that you may steer such a course in your passage to Lisbon as may be most likely to avoid them, if they should be still at sea.

115. *To Corbett*

[TNA, ADM 1/2381]

Ludlow Castle at Spithead
9 February 1745

Sir,

This acknowledges their Lordships' orders of the 21st January [No. 111] which I received yesterday from Admiral Stewart, and shall use the utmost dispatch in completing my provisions to four months.

I must beg leave to take notice to their Lordships that the three men mentioned in the margin[3] belonged to the *Kent* and were absent when the rest of the men on board my ship were paid their wages.

---

[1] Rear Admiral Henry Medley, appointed to be Commander-in-chief in the Mediterranean.
[2] *Ipswich, Jersey, Torrington.*
[3] [Manuscript torn] Tarrell, Richard Burne, John Buchanan.

116. To Corbett

[TNA, ADM 1/2381]
Ludlow Castle at Spithead
14 February 1745

Sir,

Agreeable to their Lordships orders of the 9th instant [No. 114] I have let the trade bound to Portugal know that I am appointed convoy to them and am now in all respects ready to sail except in regard to my officers, the first and second lieutenants being so ill as to be incapable to perform their duty and have desired leave to go to sick quarters. I have applied to Vice Admiral Stewart who has ordered me to let the first lieutenant go on shore. I hope their Lordships will not let me go to sea without officers in their room.

117. From the Lords of the Admiralty

[TNA, ADM 2/63, p. 217]
15 February 1744

Whereas we have ordered His Majesty's ship the *Torrington* to keep you company as far as Oporto, you are hereby required and directed in addition to our instructions to you of the 9th instant [No. 114], when you come off of Oporto, to consign the trade bound to that port to the care of the captain of the *Torrington*, and proceed yourself with the trade bound to Lisbon.

You are to stay at Lisbon for the homeward bound trade as long as the consul and factory shall desire, not exceeding forty days, and then put in execution our aforesaid instructions.

118. To Corbett

[TNA, ADM 1/2381]
Ludlow Castle at Spithead
16th February 1745

Sir,

Please to acquaint their Lordships that the first and second lieutenants of His Majesty's ship under my command are both put sick on shore with the leave of Vice Admiral Stewart and I believe neither of them will be able to perform their duty before the ship proceeds to sea, and hope their Lordships will appoint others before I sail.

119. *To Corbett*

[TNA, ADM 1/2381] *Ludlow Castle* in Plymouth Sound
2 April 1745

Sir,

I had the favour of yours of the 22nd February in regard to the character of Mr. Boswell Lyon.[1] Please to acquaint their Lordships that he has behaved so well ever since he has been with me, that if His Majesty's ship under my command should be deficient of an officer [I] would be very glad to have him made one of my lieutenants.

120. *To Corbett*

[TNA, ADM 1/2381] *Ludlow Castle* in Lisbon River
29 April 1745

Sir,

Please to acquaint their Lordships that since my arrival at this place, the consul has acquainted me that the trade could not be ready until the first of June, and as my orders expire the second, I propose sailing with the convoy that day for England. He has likewise applied to me to cruise for a fortnight off the Rock of Lisbon for the protection of the trade, the *Alderney* being disabled by springing her foremast and the *Blandford* not having been heard of for some time. As I imagine their Lordships will approve of it, I intend to sail tomorrow and cruise till such time as one of the ships return to their stations.

Yesterday six French men of war appeared off this port, and made a signal for a Spanish ship that lay in the river to get out. Upon her joining them they made sail to the southward and by all accounts are gone for Cadiz, but as this days post from Lagos brought advice that Captain [Henry] Osborn[2] with thirteen sail was off that port, it is to be hoped he will fall in with them. These are the six French ships that have so long cruised off Cape St. Vincent.

---

[1] Boswell Lyon was commissioned a lieutenant on 25 January 1746.
[2] Rear Admiral, 1747; Vice Admiral, 1755; Admiral, 1757; MP Bedfordshire, 1761–62.

121. To Corbett

[TNA, ADM 1/2381] *Ludlow Castle* Lisbon
28 May 1745

Sir,

Please acquaint their Lordships that I am returned with His Majesty's ship under my command to this port having cruised off the bar for the protection of the trade bound here till Captain [Edward] Dodd, in one of the station ships relieved me.

As the homeward bound trade is almost ready and the ships from Oporto [are] to join me the first of June, I propose sailing for England on the 2nd and take this opportunity to inform their Lordships thereof.

122. To Corbett

[TNA, ADM 1/2381] *Ludlow Castle* in the Downes
5 July 1745

Sir,

Please to acquaint their Lordships that I am arrived with His Majesty's ship under my command with the Portugal trade in twenty six days from Lisbon, having seen those bound to Ireland and St. Georges Channel safe as far as our way lay together.

Nothing remarkable has happened in my passage worth relating to their Lordships. Enclosed I send a list of the convoy as likewise the state and condition of the ship.[1]

123. To Corbett

[TNA, ADM 1/2381] *Ludlow Castle* in Ostend Road
16 July 1745

Sir,

Please to acquaint their Lordships that I arrived this day in Ostend Road with the convoy who are got safe into the harbour, the place not being invested by the French though they daily expect it as the French King is to make his entry tomorrow into Bruges with thirty thousand men.[2] I have waited upon the commanding officer of the British forces

---

[1] Enclosed a list of the convoy, but not an account of the state and condition of the ship.

[2] French strategy in the Low Countries during 1745 was in part one of cutting off the

as likewise the consul to know if they had any dispatches for England. They informed me the packet was to sail this evening and chose to send them by her, preferable to the *Mediator* who has joined me again after seeing the trade to Middlesborough. I was applied to by the commanding officer, the governor, and the consul to let the *Mediator* carry a messenger to Flushing with dispatches of the utmost consequence for His Highness the Duke of Cumberland,[1] the communication between this place and the army being cut off. As I imagined their Lordships would approve of it I have accordingly sent Captain Brown and upon his return will dispatch him for England agreeable to their Lordships' directions.

124. *To Corbett*

[TNA, ADM 1/2381] *Ludlow Castle* in Ostend Road
18 July 1745

Sir,

This morning the *Mediator* returned having conveyed the King's messenger to Flushing and according to their Lordships' directions I send him immediately for England.

Nothing material has happened since I wrote last, the enemy as yet not having invested the town, although it is daily expected.

The dykes are cut in four different places, it is thought the next tide will lay the country under water, except the sand hills to the eastward and westward of the town.

125. *To Corbett*

[TNA, ADM 1/2381] *Ludlow Castle* in Ostend Road
25 July 1745

Sir,

As it was their Lordships' commands that I should endeavour to get the best intelligence I could concerning the affairs in these parts in order to communicate it to them, I am sorry now to inform them that all

---

communications of the Allied forces with the sea. In pursuit of this end the French laid siege in August of 1745 to Ostend. Even though the defenders of Ostend were assisted by British naval forces, including ships drawn from the Downes squadron, the city was soon forced to surrender.

[1] William Augustus, Duke of Cumberland, Captain General of the British army and Commander-in-chief of the British forces in the Low Countries.

our hopes are frustrated in regard to Ostend. Twenty four battalions of foot and eighteen or twenty squadrons of horse being now actually in full march from Ghent in order to invest it.

Yesterday the French seized all the beer in Bruges and have ordered the brewers of that place to supply them immediately with two thousand cask of water, and eight thousand of beer, the springs about this place being poisoned with salt water. But I am sorry to inform them that none of the meadows near the town are over flowed tho' the last spring tides were four or five foot higher than the surfaces of the canals but as the new sluice towards Bruges was not finished, I believe that was the occasion they do not lay the country under water, and am now afraid (as it is neap tides) it will be impossible to be done.

The governor has settled a proper signal in case he should want to speak with me when the town is invested. But as it will be impossible to have any communication with the harbour in case the enemy get possession of the sand hills to the eastward which entirely command the entrance and are much higher than the bulwarks of the town. I shall be obliged to land at the strand which is not always practicable as there generally runs a great surf upon it, but their Lordships may be sure I shall take all opportunities to keep open the correspondence with the town.

As there was but six gunners in the garrison (three of which deserted today) the governor has applied to me to lend him some from His Majesty's ship under my command promising to return them when demanded. I should be glad to know their Lordships' pleasure therein and in what manner I may supply the garrison with ammunition, men or stores in case the governor demands it.

I have taken a pilot of this port on board and have consulted with many others concerning how near they can carry the ship to the shore in order to annoy the enemy in their approaches to the town. But they all inform me that the ship is of too great a draught of water to go even within random shot, but that smaller vessels may go within point blank, not without running great risk should the wind come from the sea.

Whenever the enemy make their approaches to the town, I will annoy them as much as lays in my power, and anchor as near the shore as any pilot will take charge. All the transports are come out of the harbour and Captain [Thomas] Stanhope in His Majesty's ship the *Bridgewater* is arrived here.

126. To Corbett

[TNA, ADM 1/2381]
Ludlow Castle Ostend Road
30 July 1745

Sir,

In answer to your letter of the 10th instant I must acquaint their Lordships that I impressed thirty four men out of the merchant ships under my convoy, being then that number short of complement, but not having more men to send in lieu, I brought them too on my arrival in the Downes in order for the tenders belonging to His Majesty's ship the *Duke* to impress the rest.

According to their Lordships' directions I have examined Court Myer and find that he has been a long time in English service. He is neither married in England or Holland and I am inclinable to believe that he is no Dutchman, he speaking exceedingly good English.

127. From Commodore Thomas Smith

[TNA, ADM 1/2381]
Ostend Road, 31 July 1745

You are hereby required and directed to proceed with His Majesty's ship under your command, and take the transports and all ships bound to England under your convoy, seeing them in safety to Dover, and afterwards proceed yourself to the Downes where you are to apply to the commanding officer to complete His Majesty's ship under your command to three months provisions of all species, and as much water as you can stow taking care from Dover to acquaint their Lordships of your arrival and proceedings and when you are completed you are to join me with all possible dispatch in this road.

128. To Corbett

[TNA, ADM 1/2381]
Ludlow Castle in Dover Road
1 August 1745

Sir,

Please to acquaint their Lordships that I am arrived with His Majesty's ship under my command with all the transports from Ostend having left that road about twelve o'clock last night.

As I suppose Commodore Smith has informed their Lordships concerning the news of the place, I shall only let them know that the

French works are advanced within half a musket shot of the glacis, and they have likewise erected batteries upon the sand hills to the eastward and westward of the town fronting the sea, which I am afraid will cut off all communication with the harbour.

Yesterday about three o'clock in the afternoon a French officer deserted and came into Ostend. He reports that the enemy were thirty thousand strong and that it was the common conversation of the camp that they daily expected the Brest fleet in Ostend Road.

Enclosed I send copy of Commodore Smith's order [No. 117] which I shall immediately put in execution and likewise the state and condition of the ship.[1]

129. To Corbett

[TNA, ADM 1/2381] *Ludlow Castle* in Dover Road
4 August 1745

Sir,

This acknowledges the receipt of their Lordships' orders of the 2nd instant by express, as likewise the letter enclosed to Captain Smith. In compliance therewith I am now in Dover Road, and only wait for a fair wind to proceed with the empty transports to Ostend.

On my arrival here Mr. Benjamin Lotherington, master of the *Hope* transport, complained to me that two of his men had been severely beat by the officers and men of the *St. George* privateer while they were upon His Majesty's service in assisting to load the transports. Upon my examining into the affair, I found the men had been very ill used, and beat in a most barbarous manner.

As I presume their Lordships do not protect any privateer to insult and beat people in His Majesty's service, I have taken five men out of her, that being the number employed in beating and abusing the transport's people. I shall keep the men until I know their Lordships' pleasure therein, and hope they will approve of it.

Mr. Lotherington intends to send his complaint, as likewise the mens' affidavits by this post.

---

[1] State and condition of ship not enclosed.

130. To Corbett

[TNA, ADM 1/2381]
Ludlow Castle in Dover Road
8 o'clock at night 4th August 1745

Sir,

Please to acquaint their Lordships that it proving calm this last twenty four hours is the reason I have not proceeded with the empty transports, but I beg leave to assure them that I shall make the utmost dispatch whenever the weather will permit, and am in hopes it will be the next tide, tho' what wind there is, proves contrary.

Captain [Bradshaw] Thompson of His Majesty's ship the *Poole* having communicated to me the contents of an express he just now received, and the *Bird in Hand* cutter in which Lieutenant [Mark] Milbank came express from Ostend being sailed for the Nore, as Captain Thompson informs me, I thought as their Lordships orders were so pressing it was proper to send Lieutenant James Allan belonging to His Majesty's ship the *Duke* (who was here in the *May Flower* cutter) to Ostend and hope their Lordships will approve of it. I have likewise delivered to the officer a packet that I received three hours ago which came by express to Deal.

131. From the Lords of the Admiralty

[TNA, ADM 2/65, p. 1]
12 August 1745

Notwithstanding former orders, you are hereby required and directed to put yourself under the command of George Anson Esq., Rear Admiral of the white squadron of His Majesty's fleet, and follow his orders for your further proceedings.

132. From the Lords of the Admiralty

[TNA, ADM 2/65, p. 48]
22 August 1745

You are hereby required and directed immediately to proceed with His Majesty's ship under your command, in company with such of the ships named in the margin[1] as are in the Downes, or if none of them are there, alone, over to Hellevoetsluis, and there put yourself under the command of Rear Admiral Anson and follow his orders for your further proceedings.

---

[1] *Sheerness, Bridgewater, Kinsale.*

133. To Corbett

[TNA, ADM 1/2381] *Ludlow Castle* at anchor off Orford Ness
15 September 1745

Sir,

Please to acquaint their Lordships that I am arrived here with His Majesty's ship under my command and the *Prince of Wales* East India ship, and shall proceed forthwith to the Nore. I have impressed thirty men out of her the others being foreigners and sick, and put the like number on board with a lieutenant. I should be glad their Lordships would please to order the regulating captains to send a tender to Gravesend to bring my men down to the Nore as very few of them can be trusted on shore and my lieutenant having orders to remain on board the Indiaman until a tender arrives.

134. To Corbett

[TNA, ADM 1/2381] *Ludlow Castle* at the Nore
17 September 1745

Sir,

Please to acquaint their Lordships that I am arrived with His Majesty's ship under my command at the Nore with the *Prince of Wales* East India ship under my convoy. As a great many of the men I have put on board her are not to be trusted, I have ordered the lieutenant to keep them on board until a tender arrives to take them out.

135. To Corbett

[TNA, ADM 1/2381] *Ludlow Castle* at the Nore
17 September 1745

Sir,

Agreeable to your orders I have convoyed the *Prince of Wales* East India ship to the Nore having impressed all her hands. I must likewise take the liberty to acquaint you that His Majesty's ship under my command has been off the ground ever since the 24th of December last and is so very foul that all the loaded ship[s] out sail her.

136. To Corbett

[TNA, ADM 1/2381] *Ludlow Castle* at the Nore
18 September 1745

Sir,

Whereas the complement of men allowed to His Majesty's ship under my command is not sufficient to man the great guns without taking part of those men that should be employed at small arms, and as I have raised between twenty and thirty supernumeraries, I hope their Lordships will indulge me with them as the weight of metal is equal to that of the old fifty gun ships.

137. *From the Lords of the Admiralty*

[TNA, ADM 2/65, p. 156] 18 September 1745

You are hereby required and directed to proceed with His Majesty's ship under your command into Sheerness, where we have ordered her to be cleaned, tallowed, and refitted, stored for foreign service, and her provisions completed to three months', of all species, except beer, of which she is to have but two months', or as much as you can conveniently stow, and to be furnished with a proportion of English malt spirits for one month…

When the ship is ready again in all respects for the sea, you are to repair with her out to the Nore, and remain there till further order, keeping your provisions, stores, and water always complete till you proceed to sea.

138. *From the Lords of the Admiralty*

[TNA, ADM 2/65, pp. 205–06] 1 October 1745

Whereas the city of Edinburgh is fallen into the possession of the Rebels, and it may happen that other sea port towns may have the same fate, and His Majesty's service requiring that all means that tend to support and encourage this present rebellion, should be defeated, and prevented as much as possible, you are hereby required and directed, whenever you meet with any ships or vessels, whether belonging to His Majesty's subjects or foreigners, either in any river, road, or harbour whose principal port town, or any of the said port towns, are in the power of the Rebels, to bring them away from thence with their ladening and conduct them either to Berwick or Newcastle, or some port of England, that shall be most convenient to you, leaving them there under the custody of the proper officers of the customs, without embezzlement, or taking anything from them as you will answer the contrary at your peril.

You are also to examine all ships, vessels, or boats you meet with at sea, whether belonging to His Majesty's subjects or foreigners, and if you find or suspect them to be bound to any sea port in possession of the rebels, to conduct them to Berwick or Newcastle as aforesaid, leaving them under the care of the proper officers of the customs.

But if you meet with any ships, vessels, or boats, whether in port, or at sea, and whether belonging to His Majesty's subjects or to any foreign nation in amity with His Majesty that are laden with men, arms, ammunition, or provisions for the use of the rebels, you are to seize them and bring them into Berwick or Newcastle in order to their condemnation. And if you meet with resistance to endeavour to take or destroy them.

139. *To Corbett*

[TNA, ADM 1/2381] *Ludlow Castle* at Sheerness
2 October 1745

Sir,

Please to acquaint their Lordships I am repaired to my duty here. Sir Chal[oner] Ogle[1] having dispensed with my absence from the court martial as my ship is docked and fitting for sea.

The bad weather has not permitted the ship to be transported alongside the old *Defiance* w[h]ere all her stores are so that nothing has been done as yet but as I am very sensible how necessary it is the ship should be ready for the sea, I assure their Lordships I shall use the utmost dispatch and wait now for the provisions, water, and cables which I am informed will not be down till the latter end of the week.

---

[1] Admiral Sir Chaloner Ogle was president of the court martial which tried all officers other than those of flag rank for misconduct during the action off Toulon on 22 February 1744.

140. To Corbett

[TNA, ADM 1/2381] *Ludlow Castle* in Sheerness Harbour
3 October 1745

Sir,

This acknowledges the receipt of your letter of the 1st instant, and beg leave to assure their Lordships that I will use my utmost diligence in getting the ship to the Nore. At present I wait for the water, provisions, cables, none of which is yet come down.

I beg leave to take notice to their Lordships that the marines belonging to His Majesty's ship under my command of Colonel Cotterell's Regiment[1] have not been clothed for this year, tho' I have ordered the lieutenant of marines to apply for that purpose several times. As the men are almost naked and the winter season coming on, it will be impossible for the men to do their duty unless they are properly clothed.

If there be a master at arms attending at the Admiralty, I shall be very glad that their Lordships would appoint one for His Majesty's ship under my command, the former being dead.

141. To Corbett

[TNA, ADM 1/2381] *Ludlow Castle* in Sheerness Harbour
8 October 1745

Sir,

This acknowledges the receipt of your letter of the 7th instant. Yesterday in the evening all the provisions came down, which I am stowing away with the utmost dispatch. Tomorrow I shall take in the guns and hope to be at the Nore on Thursday or Friday morning at furtherest.

142. From the Lords of the Admiralty

[TNA, ADM 2/65, pp. 224–5] 8 October 1745

Whereas the Board of Ordnance are sending 1,500 stand of arms with a quantity of powder and other ordnance stores, to Inverness in North Britain, part of which are now on board the *Betsey* tender at the Nore, and the rest on board the *Saltash* sloop, and are also sending 1,500 stand of arms to Newcastle, which are put on board the *Robert &*

---

[1] Colonel John Cotterell's regiment of marines.

Jane, Robert Punton, master, which will fall down this day to the Nore. You are hereby required and directed to make all possible dispatch in getting His Majesty's ship under your command ready for the sea, and then to take the *Saltash* sloop and *Betsey* tender under your command, and the said vessel laden with arms for Newcastle (as well as any other ordnance vessel, or any trade bound to the northward that shall be ready and willing to accompany you) under your convoy, and proceed with them to Newcastle, and having seen the *Robert & Jane* safe into that port, to proceed on with the *Saltash* sloop and the *Betsey* tender off of the Firth of Cromarty, sending them up to Inverness, and directing Captain [John] Pitman to cause the said arms and ammunition to be delivered into the care of Duncan Forbes Esq., Lord President of the Session, who is to give a receipt of the same, and then to return with the tender to you in the Firth of Edinburgh, or on such other station as you judge proper. But you are to send the tender back to the Nore by the first opportunity of convoy.

But if you shall meet with any of the ships or sloops named in the margin,[1] you are then not to go off of Cromarty, but to send a ship or sloop to strengthen the *Saltash* sloop and tender to Inverness, and afterwards to return together and join you.

And whereas His Majesty's said ships and vessels are now cruising in the Firth of Edinburgh, or elsewhere on the coast of Scotland, you are to repair to the Firth of Edinburgh, and take the said ships and vessels under your command, as fast as they join you, and to employ yourself and them cruising in such detachments as you think proper, not being less than two together, for guarding the coast of Scotland, and for preventing the enemy from landing any arms, provisions, or other supplies, according to such intelligence as you shall procure of their motions. And you are to keep diligently at sea in execution of these orders.

And whereas we have received undoubted intelligence that the French at Dunkirk and the neighbouring ports have shipped and are shipping arms, ammunition and soldiers on board transport vessels, to be convoyed by privateers, which are themselves likewise laden with men and arms for the use of the Rebels in Scotland, you are to endeavour to get information of them, and if you get certain intelligence of any such ships or vessels being upon any part of that coast, you are to go immediately in quest of them, and use your utmost endeavours to take or destroy them.

You are also to correspond with the generals of His Majesty's forces in North Britain, and to follow and obey such orders as you may

---

[1] *Fox, Glasgow, Hazard, Raven, Happy Janet, Ursula.*

receive from them, from time to time, for the annoying the enemy, and for the good of His Majesty's service.

143. *To Corbett*

[TNA, ADM 1/2381] *Ludlow Castle* in Sheerness
9 October 1745

Sir,
This acknowledges the receipt of their Lordships' orders of the 8th instant which I this day received by express, and shall put them in execution with the utmost dispatch. I have already got everything on board except the guns, the tide not being high enough to permit the hoy to come off that had them on board, but I have sent a sufficient number of men to get her through the mud, and shall proceed to the Nore early on Friday morning.

I am sorry I am obliged to complain to their Lordships of Mr. [Alexander] Philips, my purser, who tho' he had leave to be absent as a witness at the court martial at Chatham, came down to the ship in order to supply her with proper necessaries which he has so greatly neglected that I am now obliged to order my clerk to supply her with coals and other necessaries, the purser having been absent seven days, and none yet arrived. The master at arms their Lordships were pleased to appoint for His Majesty's ship under my command is not yet arrived.

144. *To Corbett*

[TNA, ADM 1/2381] *Ludlow Castle* in Sheerness
10 October 1745

Sir,
I am now to acquaint their Lordships that I have got all the guns and gunners stores in and propose sailing to the Nore tomorrow, at which place I shall make as short a stay as possible only waiting for the purser's necessaries as coals, candles &c. As it is every man's business at this critical juncture to do his duty to the utmost of his power in the service of his King and country and to detect and punish those under his command who are dilatory, I think it my duty to lay before their Lordships the behaviour of Mr. Philips, my purser, who had leave to be absent in order to attend as a witness at the court martial held on board His Majesty's ship the *London* at Chatham, but, as he was not wanted for some time he repaired to his duty, and would not permit his deputy

to supply the ship with proper necessaries, intending (as he said) to supply them himself.

On my arrival here from the court martial which was eight days ago, I ordered Mr. Philips to Chatham to send down the necessaries with the utmost dispatch and have several times ordered my clerk to remind him of it. But I have not seen him since and only a small quantity of wood (not sufficient to stow the cask) is come on board, and I am credibly informed he is gone to London about private affairs. I have wrote to Commodore Smith to desire that he will give orders to the purser of the *Royal Sovereign* to supply me with what is necessary and as soon as the pilot is come down, which I have wrote for, I shall instantly proceed according to their Lordships' directions.

145. To Corbett

[TNA, ADM 1/2381] *Ludlow Castle* in Sheerness Harbour
11 October 1745

Sir,

Please to acquaint their Lordships that I shall sail this evening to the Nore and shall proceed from thence with the utmost dispatch according to their orders.

The two marines undermentioned[1] are run from His Majesty's ship under my command. I shall be glad if their Lordships will please to give orders for their being apprehended and tried as deserters.

146. To Corbett

[TNA, ADM 1/2381] *Ludlow Castle* of Tynemouth
18 October 1745

Sir,

Please to acquaint their Lordships I am arrived off here with His Majesty's ship under my command as likewise the *Saltash* sloop and *Betsey* tender. The *Robert and Jane* laden with ordnance stores having got safe into the harbour, I shall make the utmost dispatch with the other vessels for Inverness.

---

[1]Thomas Gray and John Oakley of Colonel Cotterell's and Colonel Byng's Regiments respectively.

147. *To Corbett*

[TNA, ADM 1/2381]

Ludlow Castle in Yarmouth Road
November 1745

Sir,

Please to acquaint their Lordships that I am arrived with His Majesty's ship under my command in this road, having received orders from Rear Admiral Byng[1] dated November the 1st in Leith Road to take under my command His Majesty's ship *Milford* and cruise for the space of fourteen days, between Montrose and Buchan Ness. I kept my station until the 15th instant having ever since had excessive hard storms of wind northerly which drove me to the southward of the Humber. The wind then blowing hard at NW, my beer and brandy expended, the rigging in a very shattered condition, the long boat and another boat stove, and the ship's company very much harassed with the continual and excessive bad weather, obliged me to bear up for this place in order to complete the provisions, recruit the ship's company, and repair the shattered condition of the ship.

I am sorry to acquaint their Lordships that on the 20th instant in the morning it then blowing an excessive hard gale of wind at NNE laying to under a reefed mizen. I observed a ship about half a mile to windward with her mainmast gone by the board. A short time after which she foundered by the bearings.[2] I am very much afraid it was the *Milford*, she being the only ship in sight when the gale of wind came on.

I must acquaint their Lordships that when I arrived in the Firth of Edinburgh, the *Fox* being very short of provisions, I supplied her with a month of all species which occasioned the beer and brandies being so soon expended. Enclosed I send a journal of my cruise[3] for their Lordships' information, as likewise the state and condition of the ship.

P.S. Next post I shall send their Lordships a more exact account of the condition of the hull, masts, and rigging of the ship.

---

[1] Rear Admiral Hon. John Byng, second in command to Admiral Edward Vernon in the North Sea.
[2] To sink on an even keel.
[3] Not enclosed.

148. To Corbett

[TNA, ADM 1/2381]
Ludlow Castle in Yarmouth Road
25 November 1745

Sir,

I must acquaint their Lordships that on the 9th instant I spoke with a brigantine from Dundee bound to Virginia who gave me information that a few days before several boats belonging to a small fishing town called John's Haven had towed a French dogger with ammunition into Montrose. Being at that time within two mile of John's Haven, I hoisted French colours, causing the brigantine to do the same and made a signal for a boat, upon which one came on board with fifteen men, not finding their mistake until they got into the ship. I shall be glad to receive their Lordships' directions concerning them, as likewise a rebel who was put on board by order of Admiral Byng.

149. From the Lords of the Admiralty

[TNA, ADM 2/65, pp. 431–2]
26 November 1745

Whereas you have acquainted us, by your letter [No. 147] of 25th instant, that you have been forced into Yarmouth by bad weather, and are in want of provisions and water, we do hereby require and direct you to get some provisions and water on board with the utmost dispatch, and then repair, with all trade bound your way that shall be ready and desirous of accompanying you (for which you are to make diligent enquiry and timely signals) to the Downes, and there put yourself under the command of Admiral Vernon,[1] and follow his order for your further proceedings.

150. To Corbett

[TNA, ADM 1/2381]
Ludlow Castle in Yarmouth Roads
30 November 1745

Sir,

This acknowledges the receipt of their Lordships' orders [No. 149] of the 26th instant which I shall execute as soon as possible.

I have had a survey upon the masts, rigging, and hull of the ship, and find very little damage except the standing rigging, which I have refit-

---

[1] Admiral Edward Vernon, commander of a squadron serving in the North Sea.

ted, and shall sail as soon as the water, beer and provisions can be got on board, my cask being all on shore for that purpose. But I am afraid the continual surf that runs upon the beach will make it some what tedious, but their Lordships may depend upon my using the utmost dispatch.

151. *From the Lords of the Admiralty*

[TNA, ADM 2/65, p. 445]　　　　　　　　　　　　　　2 December 1745

Notwithstanding any former orders [No. 149], you are hereby required and directed to complete your provisions and water with all possible dispatch and to remain in Yarmouth Road with his Majesty's ship under your command until further order, holding yourself in a constant readiness to proceed to sea at a moment's warning.

152. *To Corbett*

[TNA, ADM 1/2381]　　　　　　　　　　*Ludlow Castle* in Yarmouth Road
　　　　　　　　　　　　　　　　　　　　　　　　　3 December 1745

Sir,

This acknowledges the receipt of your letter of the 29th November with one enclosed from the armourer of His Majesty's ship under my command complaining of the ill usage he lately received from the master. Agreeable to their Lordships' orders I have enquired into it, and find that he did beat and abuse the said armourer. I have had several such complaints about him, and should have formerly complained to their Lordships of his ill behaviour, (he being a man of a very bad character) had not the Commissioners of the Navy promised to appoint another master for His Majesty's ship under my command.

The weather has been so bad for several days past that no provisions could be got on board. When it moderates I shall make the utmost dispatch and sail as soon as possible. Enclosed[1] I send the armourer's letter.

---

[1]Not enclosed.

153. *From the Lords of the Admiralty*

[TNA, ADM 2/65, p. 449] 3 December 1745

Sir,

You are hereby required and directed to put yourself under the command of Thomas Smith Esq. and follow his orders for your further proceedings.

154. *To Corbett*

[TNA, ADM 1/2381] *Ludlow Castle* in Yarmouth Roads
5 December 1745

Sir,

This acknowledges the receipt of their Lordships' orders [No. 151] of the 2nd instant. My provisions and water have been ready several days, but the continual easterly winds having made a great surf upon the beach, it has been impossible to get them on board. Whenever the weather moderates I shall make the utmost dispatch and be ready to sail at a moment's warning.

155. *To Corbett*

[TNA, ADM 1/2381] *Ludlow Castle* at Yarmouth
7 December 1745

Sir,

I received their Lordships' orders [No. 153] of the 3rd instant to put myself under the command of Commodore Smith as likewise his order to join him at the buoy of the Gunfleet.

I must acquaint their Lordships that the wind having been easterly which occasions a very great surf at this place I have not been able to get the provisions on board these eight days though it is all ready to be shipped but whenever it [is] moderate I shall use the utmost dispatch and join Commodore Smith as soon as possible.

156. To Corbett

[TNA, ADM 1/2381]

Ludlow Castle at Yarmouth
11 December 1745

Sir,

Whereas I have received certain intelligence that two Dutch vessels are now in Yarmouth Pier loaded with a great number of fat oxen, hogs and a large quantity of butter, which I have reason to think are designed for Ostend, several gentlemen at this place being of the said opinion, I thought it my duty to acquaint their Lordships therewith to know if I must suffer them to proceed.

157. To Corbett

[TNA, ADM 1/2381]

Ludlow Castle Yarmouth Roads
14 December 1745

Sir,

I must acquaint their Lordships that all my provisions are now on board and the first wind that offers I shall sail for the Gunfleet. It blows hard now at SE and as the Standford [shoal] is a very dangerous shoal the pilot will not take charge of the ship until the wind comes westerly. About ten this morning ten sail of ships passed without the sands to the northward which I took to be a convoy from the Nore as there seemed to be two men of war with them. I thought proper to acquaint their Lordships therewith.

P.S. It blew hard at SE or I would have ordered one of the sloops to have reconnoitred them, but they were soon out of sight.

158. To Corbett

[TNA, ADM 1/2381]

Ludlow Castle at Yarmouth
15 December 1745

Sir,

Agreeable to their Lordships' directions I have made enquiry concerning the two Dutch ships now in the Haven and loading with bullocks, hogs and butter. I am informed the masters buy up the cattle themselves paying ready money for them and clear at the custom house for Rotterdam, but as they are consigned to no particular person I suppose when they get to sea they make no scruple to carry them to the French ports, which has been too often practised during this war to the great prejudice of His Majesty's service. This collusive war of trading being very difficult to detect unless the people themselves betray it, and as in all probability the embarkations carrying on are in want of provisions I thought it my duty to acquaint their Lordships with any thing that I imagined might conduce to put a stop to them, but since my former letter the mob of this place have obliged the vessels to be unloaded and will not permit them to be shipped again. I hope that their Lordships will approve my acquainting them with this affair as I should be glad at all time to distress His Majesty's enemies and do my utmost endeavours for the good of His service.

159. *To Corbett*

[TNA, ADM 1/2381] *Ludlow Castle* near Orford Ness
22 December 1745

Sir,

I am sorry to acquaint their Lordships that yesterday about one o'clock in the afternoon being then under double reef topsails, hazy weather, and the wind at SbW, the pilot through mistake ran His Majesty's ship under my command upon the weather part of the Whiting [Sand]. She continued there about three hours striking violently during which we started the beer and water, cut the topmasts by the board and was preparing to do the same by the main mast when after many excessive hard strokes she beat over the sand with the loss of the rudder and I am afraid part of the keel. She is now safe moored between the sand and the shore making about four foot water a watch.

This morning Lieutenant [John] Rowzier brought several vessels from Harwich to my assistance and as all the pintles of the rudder are broke short off [I] am afraid it cannot be hung again. However I have sent the old ones to the naval officer at Harwich to have others of the same dimensions and shall get the ship ready to proceed to the Nore as soon as possible. I have sent Commodore Smith advice of this misfortune.

160. *To Corbett*

[TNA, ADM 1/2381]　　　　　　　　　　Ludlow Castle at Sheerness
　　　　　　　　　　　　　　　　　　　　28 December 1745

Sir,

Please to acquaint their Lordships that I am arrived with His Majesty's ship *Ludlow Castle*, in this harbour and shall clear her for the dock as soon as possible.

I have received your letter of the 25th instant and agreeable thereto have put the pilot under confinement.

161. *To Corbett*

[TNA, ADM 1/2381]　　　　　　　　　　Ludlow Castle at Sheerness
　　　　　　　　　　　　　　　　　　　　29 December 1745

Sir,

Captain [William] Bulley having superceded me in the command of His Majesty's ship *Ludlow Castle* I should be glad you would let me know what ship their Lordships have been pleased to appoint me.

162. *From the Lords of the Admiralty*

[TNA, ADM 2/65, pp. 566–7]　　　　　　　　　31 December 1745

Sir,

Whereas we have appointed you captain of His Majesty's ship the *Eagle* at Harwich, which ship we have ordered to be fitted for the sea and stored for foreign service, manned with her highest complement of men, and victualled with three months provisions of all species except beer, of which she is to have but two months, or as much as she can conveniently stow, and to be furnished with a proportion of English malt spirits for one month, and to be floored with water, you are hereby required and directed to repair without loss of time on board her, and cause all possible diligence to be used in fitting her for the sea, and when she shall be ready in all respects, you are to proceed with her to the Nore, and remain there till further order, taking care to keep your provisions, stores, and water always complete until the ship proceeds to sea.

163. To Corbett

[TNA, ADM 1/2381]

Sheerness
1 January 1746

Sir,
Yesterday I received your letter as likewise a commission to command the *Eagle* at Harwich for which I beg leave to return their Lordships my humble thanks. When I have settled the ship's books with Captain Bulley I repair with the utmost dispatch to Harwich.

164. To Corbett

[TNA, ADM 1/2381]

Harwich
7 January 1746

Sir,
This acknowledges the receipt of their Lordships' order [No. 162] of the 31st of December, as likewise the three impress warrants and their instructions.

All the standing masts are rigged and shall complete the rest as soon as possible. But I must acquaint their Lordships that neither lieutenant, master, or surgeon are as yet repaired to their duty and if none should be appointed, hope they will be so good to indulge me with the first and third lieutenants that were in the *Ludlow Castle* with me. The boatswain is likewise very dangerously ill on shore with a fever, who is a material man in rigging the ship.

I must beg leave to represent to their Lordships that the poop of His Majesty's ship under my command, not coming so far forward as the mizen mast, is so very short as not to be able to contain the proper number of marines usually quartered there, which, if lengthened with an awning to come six foot before the mizen mast, will be of great service to the ship, as likewise a shelter to the afterguard in bad weather, there being none at present. I shall use the utmost dispatch in fitting the ship for sea.

165. *To Corbett*

[TNA, ADM 1/2381]
Harwich
9 January 1746

Sir,
I received yours of the 7th instant with a petition enclosed from Cuthbert Wake, late pilot of His Majesty's ship *Ludlow Castle*, representing that he had several times taken charge of His Majesty's ships and piloted them in safety, and that the late misfortune in running the *Ludlow Castle* on the Whiting Sand[1] was occasioned by thick hazy weather and the man's mistake at the...[2] I must beg leave to acquaint their Lordships that he has many times been my pilot, always behaved well, and conducted the ship in safety, and I look upon him to be the best pilot for the North Sea in England. The misfortune that lately happened I believe was occasioned by thick hazy weather, the wind being at SbW and the leadsman's calling seven fathom a moment before the ship struck. I must likewise represent to their Lordships that if a buoy was placed upon the east part of the Sand,[3] it would be of great service to His Majesty's ships that go north as it is generally well known that the North Sea traders some time or other strike upon the Whiting, the Channel between that and the shore being very narrow. If their Lordships would be pleased to take the opinion of the pilots I believe they will concur with me. Enclosed I return the petition.[4]

166. *To Corbett*

[TNA, ADM 1/2381]
Harwich
11 January 1746

Sir,
I must acquaint their Lordships that I hope in a day or two to complete the rigging of His Majesty's ship under my command and have applied to the Commissioners of the Victualling to hasten down the ground tier, and the rest of the provisions as soon as possible. I am informed there are about sixty marines of Colonel Pawlett's Regiment,[5] employed in the tenders and armed vessels under the command of

---
[1] See No. 159.
[2] Page torn.
[3] Whiting Sand.
[4] Not enclosed.
[5] Colonel Charles Pawlett's regiment of marines.

Commodore Smith, which I should be glad might serve as part of the detachment for the *Eagle*, and if their Lordships would be so good to indulge me with some of the seamen lately belonging to the *Prince of Orange*, I should be ready for the sea in a fortnight or three weeks at farthest. At present I muster but thirty two, officers and servants included.

167. To Corbett

[TNA, ADM 1/2381] *Eagle* at Harwich
18 January 1746

Sir,

I have received yours of the 15th instant, relating to the five petty officers lately belonging to the *Dragon*, but now on board the *Royal Sovereign* at the Nore, signifying that it is their Lordships' directions that I let them know if I have room to rate them in the same stations they had in the[ir] former ships and must acquaint them I have a vacancy for one of the mates and all the midshipmen and should be glad their Lordships would please to order them on board the *Eagle*.

168. To Corbett

[TNA, ADM 1/2381] Harwich
20 January 1746

Sir,

I must acquaint their Lordships that Commodore Smith left with me one hundred and fifty men, officers, marines and servants included, of which fifty are sick ashore.

All the ground tier, the beer and part of the provisions are on board. And I only wait for the guns and men to be ready for the sea in a few days. In my former letter [No. 164] I acquainted their Lordships of the boatswain of His Majesty's ship under my command, who is a very good man, being ill ashore. As he still continues so with a nervous fever and no probability of his being able to do his duty before the ship proceeds to sea, if their Lordships please to appoint another boatswain, I hope they will indulge me with Mr Henry Massom boatswain of the *Ludlow Castle*.

169. *From the Lords of the Admiralty*

[TNA, ADM 2/66, p. 44] 20 January 1746

Whereas we have ordered all the petty officers and men late belonging to His Majesty's ship the *Sapphire* to be turned over into the ship you command, and having directed Captain [Thorpe] Fowke to send them to you in a vessel, Commodore Smith is ordered to provide for that purpose, with a list of their names and qualifications. You are hereby required and directed to receive the said men, and enter them as part of your complement taking care that they be paid their wages for the *Sapphire* on board the *Eagle* before she proceeds to sea. And you are to rate the petty officers in the same stations or equal to what they possessed in their former ship.

170. *To Corbett*

[TNA, ADM 1/2381] *Eagle* at Harwich
23 January 1746

Sir,

This acknowledges the receipt of their Lordships order of the 20th instant [No. 169] wherein they have been pleased to order all the men lately belonging to the *Sapphire* to be turned over into His Majesty's ship under my command. I shall take care to rate them in the same or equal stations agreeable to their directions.

I must again acquaint their Lordships that the boatswain of His Majesty's ship under my command, who has been sick ashore above a month and still continues very ill of a nervous fever, attended with a paralytic disorder. As he has never yet taken charge of any stores, and will not be able to perform his duty before the ship proceeds to sea, I should be glad their Lordships would be pleased to appoint another boatswain having no proper person on board to take charge of the stores. I should likewise be glad their Lordships would be pleased to appoint a master at arms.

171. *To Corbett*

[TNA, ADM 1/2381]
Eagle at Harwich
29 January 1746

Sir,

This acknowledges the receipt of their Lordships' orders of the 28th instant, as likewise your letter of the same date concerning the boatswain of His Majesty's ship under my command who still continues very ill, and as the *Dragon* lies in ordinary, should be glad their Lordships would please to grant a change of warrants between the boatswains.

I beg leave to acquaint their Lordships that during my command of the *Ludlow Castle* I permitted Mr. [Richard] Carter my clerk to act as deputy purser in the absence of Mr. Philips who was ordered to attend the court martial at Chatham. On my being appointed for the *Eagle*, I left him at Sheerness to settle the *Ludlow Castle's* books and then repair to me at Harwich, but I have received a letter from him wherein he informs me that Captain Bulley, at the request of Mr. Philips, still detains him to act as deputy purser, contrary to his own inclination. As he is my clerk and has all my accounts in his hands, I must beg they will please direct Captain Bulley to grant him his discharge.

I shall use the utmost dispatch in getting in the guns and stores and proceed to the Downs.

The third lieutenant has not made his appearance and as Commodore Smith has appointed Mr. Daniel Rainier, one of the lieutenants of the *Prince of Orange*, to act in his room, hope their Lordships will please to confirm him so.

172. *To Corbett*

[TNA, ADM 1/2381]
Eagle at Harwich
1 February 1746

Sir,

Whereas the long boat belonging to His Majesty's ship under my command is fitted with eight stocks for swivel guns, I should be glad their Lordships would please to give directions to supply guns for them.

173. *To Corbett*

[TNA, ADM 1/2381] *Eagle* at Harwich
2 February 1746

Sir,

I must inform their Lordships that all the lower tiers and quarter deck guns are on board and I only wait for the upper ones and the remainder of the *Sapphire's* men (who are kept at the Nore by the easterly wind) to be ready for sea.

174. *To Corbett*

[TNA, ADM 1/2381] *Eagle* at Harwich
4 February 1746

Sir,

This acknowledges the receipt of your letter of the first instant, concerning the forty men belonging to the *Royal Caroline* that are on board His Majesty's ship under my command. And must beg leave to acquaint their Lordships that Lieutenant [Henry] Rose of the *Convenor* tender is this morning arrived with the remainder of the *Sapphire's* men, which does not complete my complement by upwards of seventy. And as he has fifty men in the tender, if their Lordships will permit me to take them out I shall be able to discharge the *Royal Caroline's* people.

I must likewise acquaint them that my upper tier of guns is arrived, which I shall get in with the utmost dispatch.

175. *To Corbett*

[TNA, ADM 1/2381] *Eagle* at Harwich
15 February 1746

Sir,

I must acquaint their Lordships that His Majesty's ship under my command is in all respects ready to proceed to the Downes as soon as the caulkers have done with her and the relieving chains for the [illegible][1] are made none having been sent with her stores.

The boatswain is excessive ill on shore and no hopes of his being able to perform his duty for many months, so hope their Lordships will

---

[1] Possibly rother or rudder.

please to order the boatswain of the *Dragon*, who you informed me was appointed to my ship, to be hastened to his duty. I shall take the first opportunity of wind and weather to obey their Lordships' orders.

176. *To Corbett*

[TNA, ADM 1/2381] *Eagle* at Harwich
20 February [1746]

Sir,

This acknowledges the receipt of your letter of the 18th instant in regard to three servants belonging to tenants of Lord Fitzwalter[1] having been pressed on board His Majesty's ship under my command. In answer thereto I must acquaint their Lordships that I have constantly kept a cutter with a lieutenant at sea in order to complete the complement of the ship, and give their Lordships as little trouble as possible therein. The officers that have been so employed have done their duty very diligently and raised upwards of thirty men among which are three the men represented to be servants who have all been at sea three years and were taken idling on shore so hope their Lordships will permit me to keep them as they are able bodied men and fit to serve His Majesty.

His Majesty's ship under my command is now ready to proceed to the Downes and will take the first opportunity of wind and weather to proceed there, but am sorry to acquaint their Lordships that I shall want upwards of eighty men to complete the complement besides sixty sick on shore and many of the *Sapphire's* men not repaired on board and half of those that have appeared are landmen lately brought from Ireland. So hope their Lordships on my arrival in the Downes will be pleased to give directions to the commanding officer there to complete the complement.

177. *To Corbett*

[TNA, ADM 1/2381] *Eagle* at Harwich
22 February 1746

Sir,

Mr. William Bell surgeon of His Majesty's ship under my command being reduced to a necessity of petitioning their Lordships for the pay due to him in the several ships he hath served in.

[1] Benjamin Mildmay, 19th Lord Fitzwalter.

I must beg leave to acquaint their Lordships that during my command of the *Sheerness* and the *Ludlow Castle*, he was my surgeon and always diligently and strictly performed his duty and believed in his petition which I have seen to be true.

I am now ready to sail at a moment's warning and shall take the advantage of the first fair wind to proceed to the Downes.

178. To Corbett

[TNA, ADM 1/2381] *Eagle* off Ostend
21 March 1746

Sir,

This acknowledges the receipt of your letter of the 15th instant wherein you are pleased to inform me that Commodore Boscawen[1] is ordered to assemble a court martial for trying William Harsel, sergeant of marines, who deserted from His Majesty's ship under my command.

Agreeable to their Lordships' directions I shall take the first opportunity to send proper evidence to the Nore to support the charge against him.

179. To Corbett

[TNA, 1/2381] *Eagle* off Ostend
23 March 1746

Sir,

This acknowledges the receipt of their Lordships' order of the 20th instant, the contents thereof I have communicated to Commodore [Matthew] Michell,[2] who has his broad pendant on board His Majesty's ship under my command, and when he is pleased to send me to the Downes, I shall use the utmost dispatch in proceeding to Plymouth.

As several of the men lately belonging to the *Sapphire*, who were left sick on shore at Chatham, are now on board the *Royal Sovereign* at the

---

[1] Commodore Hon. Edward Boscawen, commanding a small detached squadron operating in the Sounding. Captain, May 1742; Rear Admiral, 15 July 1747; Vice Admiral, 6 February 1755; Admiral, 17 February 1758. MP Truro, 1742–61; Lord of the Admiralty, 22 June 1751–10 January 1761. During the Seven Years War Boscawen, after serving as second in command of the Channel Fleet, commanded the British naval forces in 1758 during the capture of Louisburg and then in 1759 became Commander-in-chief in the Mediterranean.

[2] Sometimes spelled Mitchell. Commander of a squadron in the Downes, 1745–46; Captain, 30 June 1740, MP Westbury, 1748–52.

Nore, I should be glad their Lordships would give directions to Commodore Boscawen to send them by the first opportunity to the *Eagle* in the Downes.

180. *From the Lords of the Admiralty*

[TNA, ADM 2/66, pp. 402–03] 24 March 1746

You are hereby required and directed to proceed with His Majesty's ship under your command, into Hamoaze, where we have ordered her to be cleaned, tallowed, and refitted, stored for foreign service, and her provisions completed to three months, of all species except beer, of which she is to have but two months, or as much as she can conveniently stow, and to be furnished with a proportion of English malt spirits for one month, and to be floored with water...

When the ship is ready again in all respects for the sea you are to repair with her between the island and the main or into Plymouth Sound, and remain there till further order, keeping your provisions, stores, and water always complete till you proceed to sea.

181. *From the Lords of the Admiralty*

[TNA, ADM 2/66, pp. 451–2] 1 April 1746

Sir,
Whereas it has been represented to us by the mayor of Rye, that there are lying in that harbour two ships whose names are in the margin,[1] laden with wool for Exeter and Topsham and the *Robert and Mary* laden with the same commodity for Southampton, you are hereby required and directed to call off Rye, in your way to Plymouth for the said three ships, and take them under your care and protection and see them in safety, as far as their way and yours lies together.

---

[1]*Providence, Mary & Martha.*

182. To Corbett

[TNA, ADM 1/2381]
Eagle off Ostend
19 April 1746

Sir,

This acknowledges receipt of their Lordships' orders [No. 181] of the first instant wherein I am directed to call off Rye in my way to Plymouth, and to take under my protection three vessels laden with wool bound to Exeter, Topsham, and Southampton, and see them in safety as far as their way and mine lies together, which I shall take care to execute.

As I shall want twenty marines to complete the complement of His Majesty's ship under my command, I should be glad their Lordships would please to give directions to the commanding officer of Brigadier General Pawlett's regiment at Canterbury to send twenty men to Deal against I arrive in the Downes.

183. To Corbett

[TNA, ADM 1/2381]
Eagle in Hamoaze
6 May 1746

Sir,

Please to acquaint their Lordships that I am arrived with His Majesty's ship under my command at this place, and shall use the utmost dispatch in refitting the ship for the sea.

In regard to the enclosed petition[1] of Robert and John Mearns I must beg leave to inform their Lordships that the boats of the village they belonged to (which is situated between Montrose and Stonehaven) were employed to look out for French transports expected on the coast, in order to pilot them into port. A convincing proof of their disaffection was their coming on board me when I hoisted French colours, and always endeavouring to avoid me when I hoisted English colours.

My duty to my King and country obliged me to distress people so notoriously disaffected to His Majesty's government and was the cause of my destroying all the boats I met with that they might be of no service to the enemy and keeping all those men I thought fit for His Majesty's service. I know nothing of their being turned on board of

---

[1] Not enclosed.

other ships having left them all on board when Captain Bulley took command of the *Ludlow Castle*.

184. *To Corbett*

[TNA, ADM 1/2381] *Eagle* in Hamoaze
10 May 1746

Sir,

I must acquaint their Lordships that on Sunday last His Majesty's ship under my command came out of the dock, has now all the ground tier of water in, and will be completely ready for the sea in three or four days. Captain [Henry] Harrison of the *Monmouth* informs me he has orders to have his complement completed from my ship, which I suppose proceeded from their Lordships not imagining the *Eagle* could be docked this spring, but as she will now be the first ship ready hope they will countermand those orders.

185. *From the Lords of the Admiralty*

[TNA, ADM 2/67, pp. 140–1] 15 May 1746

You are hereby required and directed to use all possible dispatch in getting His Majesty's ship under your command ready in all respects for the sea, and so soon as she is so, you are to proceed and join [Captain] Lord George Graham, who is cruising with His Majesty's ships and sloop named in the margin,[1] off of Cape Clear, extending their cruise 50 or 60 leagues to the westward of [the] Soundings, and upon joining them, you are to deliver the enclosed pacquet to Lord George Graham, and put yourself under his command, and follow his orders for your further proceedings.

If you do not find Lord George Graham in a week after your arrival upon the aforesaid station, you are to repair off of Kinsale and send in your boat to know if he is there, and if so to apply to him for orders. But if he is not there, you are then to cruise off of Cape Clear in quest of his lordship. And if the *Maidstone* or *Portland's Prize* shall join you, you are then to extend your cruise together as far as 50 or 60 leagues to the westward of [the] Soundings, and to continue to do so until you join him, or as long as your provisions and water will last, and then return to Kinsale for further orders.

[1] *Nottingham, Sunderland, Falcon* sloop.

186. *From the Lords of the Admiralty*

[TNA, ADM 2/67, p. 158]   19 May 1746

Notwithstanding any former orders [No. 185] you are hereby required and directed, if Captain Harrison in His Majesty's ship the *Monmouth* is not sailed from Plymouth to put yourself under his command and follow his orders for your further proceedings.

But if he is sailed you are then to proceed to sea in quest of him, who is cruising with the ships named in the margin[1] off Scilly, and when you join him to put yourself under his command as aforesaid.

187. *To Corbett*

[TNA, ADM 1/2381]   *Eagle* at Kinsale
27 May 1746

Sir,

Agreeable to their Lordships' orders [No. 186] I made the utmost dispatch with His Majesty's ship under my command to the appointed station, and on the 24th instant had the good fortune to fall in with and take in the latitude of 49° 30' the *Esperance*, a Spanish privateer from San Sebastian, mounted with 16 guns, 136 men and commanded by Don Francisco Bonocile. This vessel has cruised since the commencement of the war and taken thirty four prizes. I shall send the prisoners on shore as soon as possible and repair again to my station.

188. *To Corbett*

[TNA, ADM 1/2381]   *Eagle* in Kinsale
14 July 1746

Sir,

This acknowledges the receipt of their Lordships' orders of the 24th and 28th June, as likewise your letter of the 19th in regard to Mr. Charles Gardner who has set forth that he was [the] pilot on board the *Ludlow Castle*, under my command, on the coast of Flanders, but that he has been refused payment in regard that another pilot was in her at the same time who has been paid.

---

[1] *Monmouth, Advice, Windsor, Mermaid.*

I must acquaint their Lordships that this was during the siege of Ostend at which time Commodore Smith (who commanded there) gave directions to bear two pilots in each ship.

189. *From the Lords of the Admiralty*

[TNA, ADM 2/67, p. 495] 21 July 1746

You are hereby required and directed to proceed with His Majesty's ship under your command into Hamoaze where we have ordered her to be cleaned, tallowed and refitted for Channel service, and her provisions completed to three months of all species except beer, of which she is to have but two months or as much as you can conveniently stow, and to be furnished with a proportion of English malt spirits for one month. And to be floored with water...

When the ship is ready again in all respects for the sea, you are to repair with her between the Island and the Main, or into Plymouth Sound, and remain there till further order, keeping your provisions, stores, and water always complete till you proceed to sea.

190. *To Corbett*

[TNA, ADM 1/2381] *Eagle* in Plymouth
8 August 1746

Sir,
I must acquaint their Lordships of my arrival here with His Majesty's ship under my command in company with the *Maidstone* and *Falcon* sloop, and likewise acknowledge the receipt of their orders of the 21st July [No. 189] for cleaning and refitting the *Eagle* which I shall execute with the utmost dispatch.

191. *To Corbett*

[TNA, ADM 1/2381] *Eagle* in Plymouth
10 August 1746

Sir,
Mr. [John] Bispham, master of His Majesty's ship under my command, having represented to me that being on shore at Kinsale, one John Norgate, seaman on board His Majesty's ship under my command, insulted and struck him. I have confined the said John Norgate

and desire their Lordships will be pleased to order a court martial to be held upon him.

192. *To Corbett*

[TNA, ADM 1/2381] *Eagle* in Crookhaven
3 November 1746

Sir,

Please to acquaint their Lordships that I am arrived with His Majesty's ship under my command at this port, having on the 29th day of October taken the *Shoreham de Nantz*, a French privateer of twenty two guns and two hundred and sixty men, after a chase of sixteen hours. The wind continuing easterly, the prize much shattered, and being short of provisions obliged me to put into this port where I shall make but little stay, having sent a messenger to Kinsale to desire provisions may be sent me as soon as possible when I shall use the utmost dispatch to join Admiral Anson at Plymouth.

193. *From Vice Admiral George Anson*

[TNA, ADM 1/87] *Yarmouth* in Plymouth Sound
8 November 1746

Sir,

You are hereby required and directed forthwith to proceed between the Island and the Main with His Majesty's ship under your command and to make all possible dispatch in giving her boot hose tops[1] and completing her provisions to three months of all species except beer, of which you are to have as much as you can take in. And when she is ready in all respects for the sea you are to proceed and cruise from three to twenty leagues southwest from Scilly for three days. Then make Cape Clear and cruise southwest from thence between five and twenty five leagues for seven days, and then stretch into the latitude of 48°30' and cruise between that latitude and 49°30' from ten to eighty leagues to the westward of Scilly till the tenth day of December after which you are to proceed immediately off Cape Finisterre

---

[1] To heel the ship and to clean and then cover her bottom with a mixture of tallow, sulphur, or lime, and rosin.

and cruise till you join me from ten to thirty leagues west of the said cape.

And whereas the *Nottingham* is directed to cruise upon the same station, you are, upon joining her there, to deliver the enclosed packet to Captain [Philip] Saumarez which contains orders for him to put himself under your command and you are to take him under your command accordingly.

But notwithstanding your station is limited, as aforesaid, you are at liberty to go yourself, or send the *Nottingham*, in quest of any ship or privateer of the enemy, you may gain certain intelligence of, without the bounds of your station, and endeavour to take or destroy them, returning to your proper station as soon as the service you left it for is over.

194. *To Corbett*

[TNA, ADM 1/2381] *Eagle* at Kinsale
10 November 1746

Sir,

I must acquaint their Lordships of my arrival here where I shall only stay to put the prisoners on shore and take in some provisions and then make the utmost dispatch for Plymouth.

195. *To Corbett*

[TNA, ADM 1/2381] *Eagle* in Kinsale Harbour
16 November 1746

Sir,

I must acquaint their Lordships that I have landed the prisoners and taken in what provisions and stores they can spare me, and shall proceed to Plymouth with the utmost dispatch.

As His Majesty's ship under my command has been continually cruising since her being commissioned, by which her complement has been diminished by death and sickness without having an opportunity of procuring others, I hope their Lordships will so far indulge me as to give orders to the commanding officer at Plymouth to supply me with twenty or thirty able seamen by which means I hope to be enabled to keep my complement complete without troubling their Lordships any further upon that head.

196. *From Corbett*

[TNA, ADM 2/689, p. 59]   21 November 1746

I have received and communicated to the Lords Commissioners of the Admiralty your letter of the 3rd instant [No. 192] giving an account of your arrival in Crookhaven with His Majesty's ship under your command and a French privateer you had taken the 29th past.

197. *From Corbett*

[TNA, ADM 2/689, p. 76]   25 November 1746

Sir,
I have laid before the Lords Commissioners of the Admiralty your letter of the 16th instant [No. 195], giving an account of your having the prisoners taken on board your prize at Kinsale and have taken in what provisions and stores they can spare, and that you shall proceed to Plymouth with the utmost dispatch, and desiring orders may be given to the commanding officer there to supply you with twenty or thirty able seamen to enable you to keep your complement complete, which has been much decreased in your late cruise by death and sickness. And in return thereto, I am commanded by their Lordships to acquaint you that they hope you used your utmost endeavours to procure men, while you was in Ireland, and that you continue to do so, for there are no men at Plymouth to spare you.

198. *To Corbett*

[TNA, ADM 1/2381]   *Eagle* in Kinsale Harbour
                                                        7 December 1746

Sir,
I must beg leave to acquaint their Lordships that hard gales and contrary winds have still detained me at this port. I endeavoured to get out this morning, but the wind shifting obliged me to anchor again. Their Lordships may depend upon my taking the first opportunity to proceed to Plymouth. Captain [Edward] Legg[e] with his convoy are still here.

199. *From Corbett*

[TNA, ADM 2/693, p. 206]　　　　　　　　　　11 December 1746

Sir,

In my letter of 15 August last, I acquainted you that Thomas Cobey, late belonging to His Majesty's ship under your command, had been discharged from St. Thomas's Hospital not cured, and that the regulating captains had certified that he was unserviceable and signified the direction of the Lords Commissioners of the Admiralty to you to make out a ticket for the time of his service in the *Nottingham*, noting him therein to be discharged unserviceable, and to send the same forthwith to the Navy Board. And you not having complied therewith, nor made any answer to their Lordships, I am commanded by their Lordships to signify their direction to you to let them know the reason thereof.

200. *To Corbett*

[TNA, ADM 1/2381]　　　　　　　　　*Eagle* in Plymouth Sound
　　　　　　　　　　　　　　　　　　　　16 December 1746

Sir,

I must acquaint their Lordships with the arrival of His Majesty's ship under my command at this place where I have received Admiral Anson's orders to join him with the utmost dispatch which I shall execute as soon as possible.

201. *To Corbett*

[TNA, ADM 1/2381]　　　　　　　　　*Eagle* in Plymouth Sound
　　　　　　　　　　　　　　　　　　　　20 December 1746

Sir,

I must acquaint their Lordships that His Majesty's ship under my command is in all respects ready for the sea, and if the wind and weather will permit I shall sail tomorrow morning and use the utmost dispatch in joining Admiral Anson.

202. *From Corbett*

[TNA, ADM 2/693, p. 339] 9 January 1747

Sir,

In my letters to you of the 15th August and 11th December [No. 199] last I signified to you the directions of my Lords Commissioners of the Admiralty to send Thomas Cobey's ticket for the time of his service in the *Eagle* to the Navy Office, he being discharged unserviceable. And you not having sent the ticket to the Navy Office, or made any answer to their Lordships thereupon, I am commanded by their Lordships to signify their direction to you to let them know the reason thereof.

203. *To Corbett*

[TNA, ADM 1/2382] *Eagle* in the Hamoaze
19 January 1747

Sir,

Agreeable to the Lords Commissioners directions signified to me by your letter of the 9th instant [No. 202], I have transmitted the ticket for the service Thomas Cobey hath performed on board His Majesty's ship under my command to be deposited in the Navy Office.

204. *From John Clevland*[1]

[TNA, ADM 2/693, p. 443] 30 January 1747

Sir,

The Lords Commissioners of the Admiralty having by their order to you of 5 November directed you to discharge Peter Madson late belonging to His Majesty's ship under your command, I am to signify their direction to you to make out his ticket for the time of his service on board your ship and send it forthwith to the Navy Board.

---

[1] Second Secretary to the Lords Commissioners of the Admiralty, 1746–51; Secretary, 1751–59; First Secretary, 1759–63.

205. To Corbett

[TNA, ADM 1/2381] *Eagle* in Plymouth Sound
5 February 1747

Sir,

Please to acquaint their Lordship of my arrival here with His Majesty's ship under my command having brought in with me three hundred and forty prisoners taken on the 2nd instant (being in company with the *Edinburgh* and *Nottingham*) in the *Bellona* of Nantz, commanded by Monsieur Claude Lory, mounts thirty six carriage and twelve swivel guns, is about two years old and little inferior to the *Ambuscade*. She has been out forty days, during which time she had taken only one brig from Boston. The prize parted company with me in a fog the fourth instant off [the] Eddystone and believed has bore up for Spithead.

This is the privateer that made so many trips to the west part of Scotland during the late rebellion, and engaged the *Greyhound* and several small frigates, and after the battle of Culloden[1] brought off Lord Elcho,[2] Lochiel,[3] and several of the Pretender's[4] adherents. Among the prisoners was one Peter Kenny born in the county of Tyrone in the Kingdom of Ireland, who says he was taken about a year ago in the *Rover* privateer belonging to Bristol, that his long confinement obliged him to enter in the *Bellona* in hopes of regaining his liberty. He acknowledged this voluntarily at his coming on board the *Eagle* or among such a number of prisoners he might have escaped notice, but he is a subject of Great Britain, and was found in arms on board an enemy ship of war, I have confined him till I know their Lordships' directions.

---

[1] At Culloden Moor, on 16 April 1746, an army under the command of the Duke of Cumberland defeated the Highlanders under the command of Charles Stuart, the Pretender, thus ending the Jacobite Rebellion of 1745.

[2] David Wemyss, Lord Elcho, a supporter and member of the Pretender's council.

[3] Donald Cameron, known as Gentle Lochiel. He was the first Scottish clan chieftain to join with and to support the Pretender.

[4] Charles Edward Stuart, also know as the Young Pretender.

110 THE RODNEY PAPERS

206. *To Corbett*[1]

[TNA, ADM 1/2382] *Eagle* in Plymouth Sound
7 April 1747

Sir,

His Majesty's ships, the *Eagle* and *Nottingham* under our commands, in company with the *Edinburgh*, having on our last cruise taken a privateer of 36 guns called the *Bellona*,[2] whose officers and men are now in this port, have lately heard of such an act of inhumanity committed by her captain, as we cannot without a breach of our duty, omit acquainting their Lordships with. That in the course of their cruise an English merchant ship bound to Barbados called the *Elenor*, from London, whose cargo chiefly consisted of mules and horses, having sprung a leak and almost foundering were obliged to have recourse for relief to the first ship they saw, which proved to be this privateer in company with another, and having surrendered fondly flattered themselves with the hopes of having saved their lives, at the expense of their libertys. But the captain of the *Bellona*, on sending his boat on board, probably incensed at the disappointment, equally in the value of the cargo, as the situation of the ship, instead of the generous enemy acted the rapacious pirate, and having plundered them refused admitting them on board, and even forcibly turned [them] back into the merchant ship, where they perished, some of the people who had taken shelter in his privateer, after having ill treated them. One of whom favoured by the obscurity of the night and the humanity of the boat's crew returned concealed on board where he remained till taken by us, and is now on board the *Eagle* who attests this fact, as likewise a master of a merchant ship who was a prisoner on board at that time. What still if possible aggravates this tragical accident were the entreaties of a gentleman and his lady who with their servants were passengers in the ship and earnestly implored him, to receive them on board, but were with the like barbarity refused and perished in the ship. The other privateer behaved some what better having taken some of the men on board and was reprimanded by the *Bellona's* captain for so doing. As all the officers are at Tavistock, it has prevented our making such an enquiry into this affair as the seriousness of it requires and can only give their Lordships this general relation, but we are informed some of them when taxed with it, have confessed the fact, but lay the guilt on the captain. As there appears to us strong presumptions that this unnatural treatment of His

[1]This letter is signed by both Rodney and Captain Philip Saumarez.
[2]See No. 205.

Majesty's subjects will on a proper examination be fully proved, we have taken the liberty to lay it before their Lordships whom we are persuaded will punish such a flagrant violation of the laws of nations and arms as the heinousness of crime deserves.

207. *From Clevland*

[TNA, ADM 2/690, pp. 354–5] 11 April 1747

Sir,

I have received and read to the Lords Commissioners of the Admiralty the letter [No. 206] signed by yourself and Captain Saumerez of the 7th instant giving an account of an act of inhumanity committed by the captain of the *Bellona* French privateer against the crew of the *Elenor* English merchant ship. And I am commanded by their Lordships to signify their direction to you to cause the information you have received relating thereto to be verified by oath and transmitted hither.

208. *From Anson*

[TNA, ADM 1/87] 20 April 1747

Sir,

Whereas I have received information that there is a large privateer of 44 guns belonging to St. Malo now at sea upon a cruise, you are therefore hereby required and directed forthwith to proceed with His Majesty's ship under your command, and cruise between Scilly and 120 leagues to the westward of it within the latitudes of 48° 00' and 49° 30', making Scilly once every four or five days, carefully looking out for, and using your utmost endeavours to take, or destroy the said privateer. As also any other ships, privateers, or trade of the enemy that you may meet with or get intelligence of.

You are to continue upon this service for the space of 14 days, and then make the best of your way to join me according to the sealed rendezvous which you have already received from me. But altho' your station is limited as above, if you get any certain intelligence of the said privateer or any others being without the bounds of your station, you are at liberty to go in pursuit of her, or them, returning to your proper station as soon as the service you left it for is accomplished. And if in the time of your cruise you should gain any intelligence that you shall judge necessary for me to be acquainted with, you are to quit your station immediately and join me without a moment's loss of time.

209. To Corbett

[TNA, ADM 1/2382]
Eagle at Kinsale
5 May 1747

Sir,

I must desire you will acquaint their Lordships that I was dispatched with His Majesty's ship under my command from Vice Admiral Anson on the 21st April with orders [No. 208] to cruise for the space of fourteen days between the latitudes of 48° 00' and 49° 30', extending my cruise 120 leagues to the westward of Scilly or wherever I had certain intelligence of the privateers of the enemy and at the expiration of this service to rejoin the said Vice Admiral.

On 1 May about 100 leagues to the westward of Scilly I fell in with and took a small privateer belonging to Bayonne, called the *Marshal de Saxe*, mounted with 4 guns and eighty men, had been out a month, and taken a snow from the West Indies. She gave me intelligence of several other privateers cruising off Cape Clear, but I have not had the good fortune to meet with any of them. As soon as I have landed the prisoners, I shall proceed again immediately to sea.

210. From Anson

[TNA, ADM 1/87]
15 May 1747

Sir,

Notwithstanding any former orders, you are hereby required and directed with His Majesty's ship under your command, to return forthwith to your cruising station between the latitudes of 48°30' and 49° 30' from Scilly to one hundred and twenty leagues to the westward, and continue to cruise there as long as your provisions and water will hold out, for the protection of His Majesty's subjects and the annoyance of the ships, privateers, and trade of the enemy, using your utmost endeavours to take or destroy all such as you shall meet with, or get intelligence of. After which you are to return to Plymouth and continue there until further orders.

Memo.

Instead of making Scilly once every four or five days (as your cruising orders direct), you are to make Scilly, Ushant and Cape Clear once every fourteen days.

211. To Corbett

[TNA, ADM 1/2382]
Eagle in the Downes
30 June 1747

Sir,

I must desire you will acquaint their Lordships with the arrival of His Majesty's ship under my command in the Downes and six prizes from St. Domingo of considerable value.[1] As I hear the *Kent* and *Hampton Court* are arrived at Spithead, I must refer their Lordships to their account of our falling in with the St. Domingo fleet on the 20th instant and the men of war escaping under favour of the night.

As I was obliged to put a number of men on board the prizes, I hope their Lordships will approve of my coming to the Downes, by which the people will sooner return to their duty, and hope they will be pleased to direct the regulating captains to supply my lieutenant with a tender to bring the men down to the Downes.

212. From the Lords of the Admiralty

[TNA, ADM 2/70, p. 70]
1 July 1747

Having ordered the regulating captains to furnish a tender to bring back to the Downes the men you have brought up,[2] we do hereby require and direct you, when they are all returned on board again to proceed without loss of time to Plymouth where you will find orders to clean and refit.

You are to make enquiry, before you sail for all trade bound to the westward, and taking under your convoy all such as are ready and willing to accompany you to see them in safety as far as your way and theirs lies together.

---

[1] On 20 June 1747 a British squadron, including HMS *Eagle*, intercepted a French convoy from St. Domingo. Out of 48 French merchant ships captured by the British from this convoy Rodney in HMS *Eagle* took six French ships. The value of HMS *Eagle's* prizes taken from this convoy were £37,798 8s 2d.

[2] See No. 211.

213. *From Corbett*

[TNA, ADM 2/691, p. 334] 1 July 1747

Sir,

I have received and read to the Lords Commissioners of the Admiralty your letter [No. 211] of yesterday's date giving an account of your arrival in the Downes with His Majesty's ship under your command and six prizes from St. Domingo.

Their Lordships have directed the regulating captains to supply your lieutenant with a tender to bring your men you put on board the prizes back to your ship as you desire.

214. *From Corbett*

[TNA, ADM 2/691, p. 334] 1 July 1747

Sir,

I am commanded by the Lords Commissioners of the Admiralty to signify their direction to you to send hither a list of the French ships taken from the St. Domingo fleet[1] brought into the Downes either by the *Hector* or yourself with their names, tonnage, number of men and lading.

215. *To Corbett*

[TNA, ADM 1/2382] *Eagle* in the Downes
 3 July 1747

Sir,

Agreeable to their Lordships' directions [No. 214] I send enclosed,[2] the account of the ships taken by His Majesty's ship under my command, with their tonnage, number of men, and laden. As it blows hard I cannot get Captain Stanhope's account in time enough to save this post.

---

[1]See Nos. 211, 215.

[2]The enclosure consists of a list of six French merchant ships whose cargoes consisted of 1,030 hogsheads of white sugar, 25,000 pounds of indigo, and 22,200 pounds of coffee.

216. From Clevland

[TNA, ADM 2/692, p. 1] 4 July 1747

Sir,
I have laid before the Lords Commissioners of the Admiralty your letter of yesterday's date [No. 215] enclosing the account of ships taken by His Majesty's ship under your command, with their tonnage, number of men, and ladings.

217. To Corbett

[TNA, ADM 1/2382] *Eagle* in the Downes
4 July 1747

Sir,
I must acknowledge the receipt of their Lordships' order of the 1st instant [No. 212], and agreeable thereto shall proceed to Plymouth with His Majesty's ship under my command, when my lieutenant returns with the men from London.

218. To Corbett

[TNA, ADM 1/2382] *Eagle* in the Downes
4 July 1747

Sir,
The enclosed[1] is a list of the French ships taken by His Majesty's ship *Hector* with their tonnage, number of men and laden. The others were taken by the *Hampton Court* and came under convoy of the said ship into the Downs, of which Captain Stanhope cannot give any account as to the above particulars.

---

[1] A list of four French merchant ships loaded with sugar, coffee, indigo and leather taken by HMS *Hector* as well as a list of six French merchant ships taken by HMS *Hampton Court* without an indication of their cargoes.

219. *From Corbett*

[TNA, ADM 2/692, p. 7] 6 July 1747

Sir,

I have received and read to the Lords Commissioners of the Admiralty your letter [No. 218] of the 4th instant enclosing a list of the French ships taken by His Majesty's ships the *Hector* and *Hampton Court*.

220. *To Corbett*

[TNA, ADM 1/2382] *Eagle* in the Downes
11 July 1747

Sir,

I must beg leave to acquaint their Lordships that one of our prizes, called the *Saint Esprit* of five hundred tons, and computed to be worth seventy thousand pounds, had the misfortune to be wrecked on the Goodwin Sands, by the carelessness of the pilot. And as several boats and vessels belonging to Ramsgate has stolen a great quantity of indigo out of her, upon information thereof, I sent several boats with officers and men, to detect them in their villainy, and last night impressed forty men who were plundering the said prize. As it will be an endless trouble to sue them all at common law, and most of them being able bodied men and fit to serve His Majesty, I hope their Lordships will approve of my keeping them on board the *Eagle* to deter others from the like practices for the future.

221. *From Corbett*

[TNA, ADM 2/692, p. 28] 13 July 1747

Sir,

I have received and read to the Lords Commissioners of the Admiralty your letter [No. 220] of the 11th instant, giving an account of your having pressed forty men who were plundering the wreck of the *Saint Esprit* prize. And I send this to acquaint you Captain [Richard] Spry of the *Chester* is directed to carry the said men to Spithead and dispose of them as Vice Admiral Stewart shall direct.

222. To Corbett

[TNA, ADM 1/2382] *Eagle* in Hamoaze
17 July 1747

Sir,
Please to acquaint their Lordships that I am arrived with His Majesty's ship under my command in Hamoaze and shall make the utmost dispatch in clearing her for the dock.

223. From Clevland

[TNA, ADM 2/692, p. 60] 20 July 1747

Sir,
I have received and read to the Lords Commissioners of the Admiralty your letter [No. 222] of the 17th instant giving an account of your arrival in Hamoaze with His Majesty's ship under your command.

224. To Corbett

[TNA, ADM 1/2382] *Eagle* in Hamoaze
24 July 1747

Sir,
Whereas Mr Lewis Joyce carpenter of His Majesty's ship under my command has through age, sickness, and infirmities been obliged to stay on shore two cruises, in particular the last, and his being now unfit to go in a cruizing ship, he has solicited me to beg their Lordships to take his long services into consideration, and give him some ship in ordinary, and whereas Mr John Lorema, carpenter of the *Kennington*, has been acting carpenter of the *Eagle* these four months past by order of Commissioner Vanbrugh,[1] and executed his duty in that station with diligence, care, and sobriety, I must beg leave to recommend him to their Lordships to grant him a warrant for the *Eagle*.

---

[1] Captain Philip Vanbrugh, Commissioner of Plymouth Dockyard, 1739–53.

225. *To Corbett*

[TNA, ADM 1/2382]
Eagle in Hamoaze
28 July 1747

Sir,

Whereas I have constantly given directions to the officers of His Majesty's ship under my command to take their proper watches to prevent desertion or disturbance, and in the absence of any commission officers (by leave or sickness) that the gunner should take charge of a watch in harbour.

I must desire you will acquaint their Lordships that on Saturday last, some of the officers being on shore by my leave, my first lieutenant Mr. [John] Harrison ordered the gunner to take charge of the first watch which he refused, alleging it was not his duty and behaved in a most insolent manner, daring the said lieutenant to confine him and offering his warrant to him, saying he had rather be out of the ship than in her. I believe the prizes we have taken have somewhat contributed to this insolent behaviour, which is the more unpardonable as it ought to be a spur to every officer strictly to do his duty but as this is not the first time of his insolence and neglect of duty, and my first lieutenant being a very sober, good and diligent officer, I thought it my duty to acquaint their Lordships with this affair, as inferior officers disputing the authority of their superiors and disobeying their orders would entirely ruin the discipline of the navy, and be greatly prejudicial to His Majesty's service, so humbly hope their Lordships will be pleased to remove the said gunner, otherwise his insolent behaviour will oblige me to trouble them for a court martial.

I beg you will acquaint them the *Eagle* was docked yesterday and the beginning of next week will be ready to put in execution any orders their Lordships are pleased to give.

226. *From Clevland*

[TNA, ADM 2/692, p. 181]
15 August 1747

Sir,

Thomas Cobey,[1] late belonging to His Majesty's ship under your command, having been discharged from St. Thomas's Hospital not cured and the regulating captains having certified that he is unservice-

---
[1] See also Nos. 199, 202, 203.

able, I am commanded by the Lords Commissioners of the Admiralty to signify their direction to you, to make out a ticket for the time of his service in your ship, noting him therein to be discharged unserviceable, and to send it forthwith to the Navy Board.

227. To Corbett

[TNA, ADM 1/2382]

Eagle at Plymouth
30 August 1747

Sir,

I must desire you will acquaint their Lordships that I am arrived here with His Majesty's ship under my command having had the misfortune to spring the boltsprit[1] in so dangerous a manner that prevented my keeping the sea any longer during my cruise which extended one hundred and fifty leagues to the westward of Scilly. I have not seen one privateer which makes me imagine very few are now at sea as I continually made a traverse between the latitudes of 48°00' and 49°50' and in all probability should have fell in with them.

I have applied to the commanding officer here to give orders for a new boltsprit and by the return of the post shall be ready to put in execution whatever orders their Lordships shall please to give me.

228. From Anson

[TNA, PRO 30/20/20/4, pp. 1–3]

Admiralty
10 November 1747

Dear Sir,

I find you have dropped me as a correspondent because I have not been punctual in answering your letters; don't ascribe it to any thing but the real cause, indolence and an aversion to writing, for nobody can esteem you more than I do, nor has felt a more sensible satisfaction in the share of honour which you have gained in the late action,[2] which has raised the reputation of our fleet to the highest pitch. May the same success attend your attack on shore, which I find was the reason I had not the satisfaction of seeing [you] at Portsmouth, where it was intended your ship should have cleared.

---

[1] An obsolete version of the word bowsprit.
[2] Second Battle of Cape Finisterre, 14 October 1747, in which a British squadron, including HMS *Eagle*, captured six French warships escorting a West India convoy.

I was extremely flattered by the remembrance of the Western Squadron in appointing my secretary agent for their prizes. I should be glad of any opportunity of showing them how much I think myself obliged by it, as it was done unasked and beg you will make my compliments to them upon the occasion, as I cannot write to them all by this post. I have just parted with your friend Keppel[1] who perseveres in your old scheme and I suppose will come off no better than usual before he leaves town, your example may make a sober discreet man of him.

229. To Corbett

[TNA, ADM 1/2382]　　　　　　　　　　　　　　　　　Portsmouth
19 November 1747

Sir,
Whereas Mr. [John] Goodwin purser of His Majesty's ship under my command and Mr. [John] M[a]ckay, purser of the *Nottingham*, have informed me, they have applied to their Lordships for an exchange of warrants.

I humbly hope their Lordships will indulge their request.

230. To Corbett

[TNA, ADM 1/2382]　　　　　　　　　　　　　*Eagle* in Plymouth Sound
1 July 1748

Sir,
I must desire you will acquaint their Lordships with the arrival of His Majesty's ship under my command with the homeward bound trade from Lisbon.

Enclosed I send the state and condition of the ship as likewise a list of the convoy.[2]

---

[1] Captain Hon. Augustus Keppel. Rear Admiral, 21 Oct. 1762; MP Chichester, 1755–61; MP New Windsor, 1761–80. Keppel in 1758 commanded the naval forces during the capture of Goree and in 1761 at the reduction of Belle Isle. In 1762 Keppel served as second in command of the squadron at Havana and then after the capture of the city became Commander-in-chief of the squadron at Havana and Jamaica.

[2] A list of two merchant ships.

231. From the Lords of the Admiralty

[TNA, ADM 2/72, p. 119]
12 July 1748

Sir,

Having ordered His Majesty's ship under your command to be paid off and laid up at Plymouth, you are hereby required and directed to cause all possible dispatch to be used in clearing her of her guns, stores, provisions, and ballast, and leave her in a proper condition under the care of the officers of the yard.

You are to make out pay books from the last time the ship was last paid and transmit them without delay to the Navy Board.

232. To Corbett

[TNA, ADM 1/2382]
Bath
1 October 1748

Sir,

Whereas my accounts for His Majesty's ships *Sheerness* and *Ludlow Castle* have been passed a considerable time, and general certificates granted me accordingly.

I hope their Lordships will please to give directions that I may receive the pay due to me for the time I have the honour to command the said ships.

233. From Corbett

[TNA, ADM 2/695, pp. 452–3]
3 October 1748

Sir,

I have received and read to my Lords Commissioners of the Admiralty your letter [No. 232] of the 1st instant, desiring an order for the payment of your wages for the time you commanded His Majesty's ships the *Sheerness* and *Ludlow Castle* and in return I am commanded to acquaint you that an order is sent to the Navy Board accordingly.

234. *To Corbett*

[TNA, ADM 1/2382]

Soho Square
23 November 1748

Sir,

I desire you will please to acquaint their Lordships that Mr. Richard Carter[1] who was my clerk on board the *Ludlow Castle*, and acted for some time on board the said ship as deputy purser. When I was commissioned for the *Eagle* he could not prevail upon the purser to send down another deputy, tho' he had given notice several times of his having my books and agreed to go along with me in the *Eagle*. He was ill at that time at Sheerness and Captain Bulley sailed without him. When he was recovered he came down to Harwich to the *Eagle* and continued with me. He was run[2] upon the *Ludlow Castle's* books about fifteen days after his appearance on board the *Eagle*. His R has not yet been taken off occasioned (as I believe) upon some dispute between him and Mr. Philips, the purser, tho' I don't know that Mr. Philips wanted any books or papers from him, I having signed every thing he required of me relating to the passing his accounts. Mr Carter is a man that has a wife and two small children and is in very low circumstances therefore [I] hope their Lordships will take his case into consideration and will please to order his R to be taken off.

[1] See No. 177.
[2] Run or R against a man's name in a ship's books means that he deserted.

PART II

POST CAPTAIN, 1749–1759

When Captain George Rodney came ashore from HMS *Eagle*, at the end of the War of Austrian Succession, he had ambitions which went far beyond the confines of the Royal Navy. Described by Horace Walpole as 'a young seaman, who has made a fortune by very gallant behaviour during the war',[1] Rodney not only desired further advancement within the Royal Navy, but moreover he sought to become a landholder as well as a political personage.

Within a year of coming ashore Rodney was made, probably on the recommendation of the Duke of Bedford, captain of HMS *Rainbow* and governor of Newfoundland.[2] This was a plum appointment, indeed, for a navy officer in peacetime for, with the coming of peace in 1748, the Royal Navy had been demobilised and greatly reduced in force. From a wartime strength in April of 1748, of 62,185 men manning 247 ships and vessels, by December of 1752, the Royal Navy would be reduced to a peacetime establishment of only 7,287 men.[3] To be able to obtain command of a fifth rate warship, as well as the governorship of Newfoundland, both in peacetime, not only was a testament to Rodney's standing within the ranks of the Royal Navy's post captains, but also to his political connections.

The main objectives of the government of Newfoundland were to preserve the colony as a source of cod fish as well as a nursery of seamen for the Royal Navy. Under the terms of the 1698 statute, entitled 'An Act to Increase the Trade of Newfoundland',[4] permanent settlement within the colony was to be prevented, if at all possible, and the cod fishery activities be conducted by fishing fleets, which were to arrive from England each year in order to catch cod fish on the Grand Banks of Newfoundland. After being caught, the fish would first be

---

[1]Paget Toynbee, ed., *The Letters of Horace Walpole Fourth Earl of Orford* (Oxford, 1903), vol. II, p. 358.
[2]*Journal of the Commissioners for Trade and Plantations from January 1741–42 to December 1749 preserved in the Public Record Office* (Liechtenstein, 1970 reprint), p. 406.
[3]TNA, ADM 8/26, April 1748; ADM 8/28, Dec. 1752.
[4]10 William III. c.14.

salted, and then dried on racks along the shores of Newfoundland, before being transported to the Iberian Peninsula for sale. After landing and selling the salted cod fish, in Spain or Portugal, the British fishing fleet would then return to England. British fishermen were thus not permitted at all to settle in Newfoundland in order that in time of war their services could be co-opted by the Royal Navy. Each year the governor of Newfoundland, who was usually a post captain in the Royal Navy, would accompany the fishing fleets in a warship to Newfoundland; he would remain at the island, during the fishing season on the Grand Banks, and then sail with the fishing fleet to the Iberian Peninsula before returning to England. It was the task of the governor of Newfoundland to maintain law and order at such times among the British fishermen, to protect Newfoundland and the cod fishery from encroachments by foreigners, as well as to ensure that no fishermen remained in Newfoundland during the winter so that they would be available for future service in the Royal Navy.

On 1 March 1749 Rodney assumed command of HMS *Rainbow* at Woolwich.[1] The ship was being repaired and refitted for service and it would not be until 5 May when Rodney sailed from Woolwich for Spithead where he arrived on 30 May. In 1749, besides HMS *Rainbow*, the Newfoundland squadron consisted of the sloops HMS *Mercury* and HMS *Saltash*. On 3 June Rodney sailed from Spithead and proceeded directly to Plymouth while HMS *Mercury* went from port to port along the south coast of England picking up and escorting to Plymouth fishing boats. Sailing from Plymouth on 1 July Rodney arrived at St. John's, Newfoundland on 4 August. He would remain on board HMS *Rainbow*, at anchor in St. John's Harbour, during his stay at Newfoundland[2] while HMS *Mercury* and HMS *Saltash* ranged along the coasts of the island overseeing the activities of the British fishermen. For reasons that are unclear, Rodney was certainly not taken by the Newfoundlanders. During his governorships, Rodney seemed to have disliked almost all those inhabitants of Newfoundland that he came into contact with and declared that they were 'mostly Irish Papists' who were 'disaffected with the present royal family'.[3] Indeed, it would appear that the impressions of Newfoundlanders, that he obtained when he was governor, would colour and influence Rodney's opinion of all Americans for the rest of his life. After a stay of several weeks Rodney sailed from St. John's for Lisbon where he arrived on 5 November. After a month-long

---

[1] TNA, ADM 36/2811, f. 11.
[2] TNA, ADM 51/786, 3 March–7 Oct. 1749.
[3] No. 248.

stay at the Portuguese capital Rodney left for England and arrived back at Woolwich on 23 December.[1] And on 20 January 1750 Rodney, performing his last duties as governor of Newfoundland for that year, would send to the Board of Trade a report on the 'Scheme of the Fishery of Newfoundland for the year 1749' along with returns of the garrison and the ordnance stores at Newfoundland.[2]

During the summers of 1750 and 1751 Rodney served again as governor of Newfoundland. As in the 1749 season, so during his governorships of 1750 and 1751, Rodney passed the summers in St. John's Harbour on board of HMS *Rainbow* and then returned to England by way of the Iberian Peninsula. On the outward voyage to Newfoundland in 1751, on orders from the Admiralty, Rodney searched for a month without result for an island that was supposed to be a hundred miles west of the Scilly Isles at 50°N.[3] The island did not exist and in the end the reports of sighting an island were put down to what 'sailors call fog banks'.[4] Also during the 1751 voyage to Newfoundland, Rodney, again on orders of the Admiralty, tested a new type of compass, which had been invented by Dr. Gowin Knight.[5] Employing warships, in peacetime, to conduct acts of exploration and to test new equipment which might be of use to the Royal Navy was a common practice at the time.

Owing to prize money – more than fifteen thousand pounds – that he had earned during the last years of the War of Austrian Succession, Rodney was now a wealthy man.[6] In fact immediately upon his return to England, in 1748, Rodney had already begun to convert his monetary wealth into landed wealth by purchasing an estate at Old Alresford in Hampshire.[7] Over the years Rodney would expend money, not only on improving the property at Old Alresford,[8] but also on the purchase of additional land.[9] It was a tactical move. By purchasing a landed estate Rodney had passed a milestone on the traditional road to respectability and status travelled by the upwardly-mobile and newly wealthy in

---

[1] TNA, ADM 51/786, 7 Oct.–23 Dec. 1749.
[2] *Journal of the Commissioners of Trade and Plantations, from January 1749–1750 to December 1753 preserved in the Public Record Office* (Liechtenstein, 1970 reprint), p. 37.
[3] No. 301.
[4] John Charnock, *Biographia Navalis; or Impartial Memoirs of the Lives and Characters of the Officers of the Navy of Great Britain* (London, 1797), vol. V, pp. 206–07.
[5] Nos. 292, 293.
[6] David Spinney, *Rodney*, pp. 86,89.
[7] William Page, ed., *The Victoria History of the Counties of England: Hampshire and the Isle of Wight* (London, 1900–12), vol. III, p. 306; vol. IV, p. 190.
[8] TNA, TNA 30/20/16, Receipt Book for money paid at Greenwich, 1767, 1768, 1769.
[9] Eg., No. 413.

England. The next stage on this journey for Rodney, not surprisingly, would be obtaining a seat in the House of Commons.

As was the case with many ambitious men in Hanoverian England, Rodney sought to become a Member of Parliament, for a seat in the House of Commons placed a person at the very centre of the political world of Britain. For Rodney, who would be absent from Westminster for long periods of time while at sea and who was for the most part without a political agenda other than to support the King and his governments, being in the House of Commons was a means to 'make a figure' and to be in close proximity to that greatest of all elixirs – political power![1] It would not be an easy process.

As early as the beginning of 1749 Rodney began manoeuvring to obtain a seat in the House of Commons.[2] His political career began in earnest in 1750 when, with the support of the Duke of Bedford he, ultimately unsuccessfully, contested a seat in a by-election to represent the Borough of Launceston. Rodney's hopes of winning this seat were soon dashed however, when it was discovered that the Duke of Bedford's electoral interest in the Corporation of Launceston was, at best, limited. Nevertheless, within a year, on 15 May 1751, again supported by the patronage of Bedford, Rodney was elected to the House of Commons to represent the Borough of Saltash in Cornwall.[3] Saltash, being adjacent to the Royal Navy's dockyard at Plymouth, was totally under the political control of the Admiralty and as such appeared to be a safe seat for a government supporter such as Rodney. In spite of all this, Rodney was subsequently deselected and did not stand for a seat from Saltash during the general elections of 1754. That year the government had decided, because of 'certain difficulties', to permit instead Henry Pelham to select men for both of the seats of the Borough of Saltash in the House of Commons. Disappointed in his hopes of being reselected as a government candidate at Saltash, Rodney decided, in one of the few if not the only act of opposition to a sitting government during his life, to stand against the ministerial interest and he ran for a seat, this time to represent the Borough of Camelford in Cornwall in the House of Commons. Even though he was willing to spend £3,000, it became apparent to Rodney that he could not win at Camelford and he dropped out of the election without a poll.[4]

[1] Cf. Sir Lewis Namier, *The Structure of Politics at the Accession of George III* (London, 1957), pp. 1–61.
[2] No. 235.
[3] Romney Sedgwick, *The History of Parliament: The House of Commons, 1717–1754* (London, 1970), vol. I, pp. 213, 219.
[4] Sir Lewis Namier and John Brooke, *The History of Parliament: The House of Commons, 1754–1790* (London, 1964), vol. I, 239–40; vol. III, p. 327.

On 16 January 1753 Rodney took command of HMS *Kent* at Portsmouth.[1] HMS *Kent* was the very same ship that Thomas Fox had commanded at the Battle of Cape Finisterre during the War of Austrian Succession. During Rodney's period of command the vessel was a guard ship which never left Portsmouth Harbour. Fifteen days after taking command of HMS *Kent* Rodney, on 31 January 1753, married Jane Compton in the Oxford Chapel on Vere Street, Marylebone. There has been speculation that Rodney first met Jane Compton in Lisbon.[2] However, there is no foundation for this other than the fact that when Rodney had visited Lisbon Jane Compton's father, Hon. Charles Compton, was the British consul there and then envoy extraordinary to the Portuguese court.[3] Rodney married well for Jane Compton's grandfather was the 4th Earl of Northampton; her two uncles were the 5th and 6th Earls of Northampton and her brothers, Charles and Spencer, would become, respectively, the 7th and 8th Earls of Northampton.[4] And of Jane Compton's sisters, one had married Captain Richard Haddock, the controller of the navy, 1743–49; another, the 2nd Earl of Egmont; and the third would marry Henry Drummond, the banker.[5] There would later be talk among some contemporaries,[6] and subsequently from a few historians,[7] that Rodney was a womaniser. There is no evidence to support this notion during the period of his marriage to Jane Rodney. In fact all the evidence, especially his letters to Jane Rodney,[8] point to the conclusion that Rodney was deeply in love with his wife. Jane Rodney bore him, in rapid succession, three children. The oldest, George, was born in 1753 and would out-live his father to become, in 1792, the 2nd Baron Rodney of Rodney Stoke.[9] A second son, James, was born in 1754 and would be lost at sea in 1776.[10] And a daughter, who would die in infancy, was born in 1756.[11] At the end of 1756 tragedy hit Rodney when both his wife and himself fell ill.[12]

[1]TNA, ADM 51/502, 16 Jan. 1753.
[2]Spinney, *Rodney*, pp. 35–6, 110.
[3]Namier and Brooke, *History of Parliament*, vol. II, p. 241.
[4]Geoffrey H. White, *The Complete Peerage* (Gloucester, 1987 reprint), vol. 4, p. 44.
[5]Spinney, *Rodney*, p. 123.
[6]Eg., Henry B. Wheatly, ed., *The Historical and Posthumous Memoirs of Sir Nathanial William Wraxall, 1772–1784* (London, 1884), vol. 1, p. 224.
[7]Eg., William Edward Hartpole Lecky, *A History of England in the Eighteenth Century* (London, 1905 reprint), vol. V, p. 59.
[8]Nos. 339, 340, 342, 344, 347, 350, 370, 371, 374–5, 401, 405, 413, 416, 419, 421, 432, 435.
[9]White, *Complete Peerage*, vol. 5, p. 66.
[10]David Syrett and R. L. DiNardo, *The Commissioned Sea Officers of the Royal Navy, 1660–1815* (Aldershot, Hants: Scolar Press for the Navy Records Society, 1994), p. 384.
[11]Spinney, *Rodney*, p. 123.
[12]Nos. 435, 438.

Rodney would discribe his illness as 'a violent billious colic'.[1] Rodney recovered his health, but Jane Rodney, probably weakened by the rigours of the birth of their daughter, died on 29 January 1757.[2]

On 6 April 1754 Rodney was placed in command of HMS *Fougueux*,[3] one of the ships that had been captured in 1747 at the Battle of Cape Finisterre. HMS *Fougeux* was a guard ship and during Rodney's period of command, like HMS *Kent* previously, she, too, never left Portsmouth Harbour.[4] While Rodney was in command of HMS *Fougeux* Britain and France began to slip towards war with each other. Such tensions, added to the fact that fighting had already begun in North America, led the Royal Navy to start mobilising for war. As HMS *Fougeux* was being manned and otherwise readied for active service Rodney, desirous to remain close to his wife and children, sought to avoid going to sea, and requested that Lord Anson, the First Lord of the Admiralty, transfer him to another ship.[5] Influence worked once more for, on 14 February 1755, Rodney wrote to his wife that he would be placed in command of HMS *Prince George* which was a brand new 90-gun ship with no 'likelihood that she will ever go to sea'.[6]

During the first months of 1755 Rodney prepared HMS *Prince George* for sea. The main problem in this endeavour was, as it had been the case before, the raising of the men required to man the ship. Even though a lieutenant, with money, was sent to London to open a rendezvous[7] to recruit men for HMS *Prince George,* the process of obtaining seamen dragged on into the early summer. On 16 July Rodney was placed in a squadron under the command of Vice Admiral Edward Hawke[8] and several days later, 22 July, HMS *Prince George* sailed from Spithead. For 48 days HMS *Prince George* and the other ships of Hawke's squadron cruised in the Bay of Biscay ranging as far south as Cape Finisterre.[9] Rodney could not see much point to this cruise[10] for war had not yet been declared with France and it was not until the end of August that Hawke received orders to capture and detain French ships.[11] On 29 September Rodney and HMS *Prince George* returned to Spithead.

[1]No. 436.
[2]Spinney, *Rodney*, pp. 127–9.
[3]No. 331.
[4]TNA, ADM 51/4194, 16 April 1754–18 Feb. 1755.
[5]No. 340.
[6]No. 347.
[7]Nos. 352, 358, 363.
[8]No. 369.
[9]TNA, ADM 51/726, 22 July–29 Sept. 1755.
[10]Nos. 370, 371.
[11]TNA, ADM 1/89, Hawke to Clevland, 30 Aug. 1755.

On 20 November 1755 Rodney's father-in-law, Hon. Charles Compton, died and Rodney was named executor of his will and guardian of his two sons Charles and Spencer Compton. The settling of his father-in-law's affairs required Rodney's attendance in London for a longer period of time than the Admiralty was prepared to grant him leave.[1] To obtain additional leave from the command of HMS *Prince George* Rodney successfully appealed to the Duke of Newcastle, who was to replace Bedford as his patron.[2] Apparently Newcastle not only arranged for Rodney to obtain the necessary leave to settle his father-in-law's estate, but also his transfer out of HMS *Prince George* into the command of HMS *Monarch*. HMS *Prince George* was under orders to go to the Mediterranean,[3] and Rodney, because of the birth of a third child, and other family responsibilities, did not desire at this time to leave England.

On 5 May 1756 Rodney took command of HMS *Monarch* at Plymouth and began to fit and man the ship for service.[4] In the absence of a senior officer at Plymouth Rodney, while fitting HMS *Monarch*, acted as the Royal Navy's commander at that port.[5] At the beginning of July, HMS *Monarch* was ready to put to sea, and on 4 July, Rodney received orders to join a squadron in the Bay of Biscay under the command of Vice Admiral Hon. Edward Boscawen.[6] Sailing from Plymouth on 10 July, Rodney and HMS *Monarch* joined Boscawen's squadron on 28 July, some nine leagues west of Ushant. However, eight days later Rodney left Boscawen and the Bay of Biscay and on 13 August HMS *Monarch* anchored at Spithead.[7] Boscawen had been forced to order HMS *Monarch* to England when it was discovered that, owing to structural defects, the vessel was in an almost sinking condition and thus in urgent need of repairs.[8] Rodney would never go to sea again in HMS *Monarch*. As the ship was undergoing repairs, at Portsmouth, Rodney was firstly subjected to a prolonged illness,[9] and then he was caught up in the nightmare of Jane Rodney's death.

On 4 April 1757 Rodney took command of the new 74-gun ship of the line, HMS *Dublin*, which was nearing completion at Deptford. The ship was not yet in the water and Rodney had a pendant hoisted on

[1] Nos. 378–80, 384, 385, 388.
[2] Nos. 389, 390.
[3] No. 397.
[4] TNA, ADM 51/3914, 5 May 1756.
[5] Eg., Nos. 402, 404, 405.
[6] No. 420.
[7] TNA, ADM 51/3914, 10 July–13 Aug. 1756.
[8] TNA, ADM 1/90, ff. 57, 58.
[9] Nos. 436–8.

HMS *Dublin* commissioning her while she was still in the stocks.[1] On 6 May HMS *Dublin* was launched and Rodney began fitting the vessel for sea and raising the seamen required to man her.[2] During the course of making HMS *Dublin* ready for the sea Rodney refused to accept seventy tons of iron ballast on board the vessel, as ordered by the Surveyor of the Navy, claiming that 'it always made ships laboursome' and that it was an 'option' of a captain, in such circumstances, to refuse to take on board extra ballast. By return letter Rodney was over-ruled by the Admiralty who believed that, because HMS *Dublin* was a new ship, the Surveyor of the Navy was 'the proper judge of what ballast should be put in her'.[3] At the beginning of June HMS *Dublin* was ready to proceed to Longreach to take in her guns[4] and by 5 September the ship was at Spithead waiting orders and completely fitted, stored, and manned.[5]

On 8 September Rodney and HMS *Dublin* sailed from Spithead with a squadron under the command of Hawke for the Bay of Biscay arriving on 24 September at Basque Road on the west coast of France.[6] HMS *Dublin* and Rodney did not play a major role in the abortive operations before Rochfort other than voting in a council of war, on 28 September, 'to attack the forts leading to and upon the mouth of the River Charente'.[7] Soon thereafter he returned to England and on 6 October HMS *Dublin* anchored at Spithead.[8] Rodney in HMS *Dublin* undertook, during the autumn 1757 and the first weeks of 1758, two uneventful cruises, with no encounters with the enemy, in the Western Approaches of the English Channel and the English Channel.[9]

On 2 March 1758 Rodney was ordered to convey Major General Jeffery Amherst to Halifax, Nova Scotia.[10] Sailing from Spithead on 17 March Rodney headed southwest into the Atlantic to follow a southern great circle route to Nova Scotia. On 21 March 'in the Latitude 49° off Ushant' Rodney captured the French East Indiaman *Montmartel*, which he carried into Vigo, on the northwest corner of Spain, because the 'violent scurvy and sickness which I found raging among the prisoners

---

[1] TNA, ADM 51/278, 4 April 1757.
[2] Nos. 439, 440–42, 446.
[3] Nos. 444, 445.
[4] No. 449.
[5] TNA, ADM 51/278, 5 Sept. 1757.
[6] TNA, ADM 51/278, 8–24 Sept. 1757.
[7] Ruddock F. Mackay, ed., *The Hawke Papers: A Selection, 1743–1771* (Aldershot, Hants: Scolar Press for the Navy Records Society, 1990), pp. 181–2.
[8] TNA, ADM 51/278, 6 Oct. 1757.
[9] TNA, ADM 51/278, 22 Oct. 1757, 22 Oct. 1757–17 Feb. 1758; Mackay, *Hawke Papers*, pp. 186–8.
[10] No. 502.

obliged me to put in here in order to preserve the health of my own ship's company'.[1] After a stay of a little less than four days at Vigo, prolonged owing to 'a calm',[2] Rodney sailed from the Spanish port and arrived on 8 May at Halifax, Nova Scotia.[3] There are a number of misconceptions concerning this voyage to North America. For instance, one historian says that it took Rodney 72 days to sail from England to Nova Scotia[4] and Julian S. Corbett accuses Rodney of dilly-dallying at Vigo for a fortnight because of the capture of the *Montmartel*.[5] The passage to North America in fact only took 51 days, which was not abnormal for a westward Atlantic crossing in the 18th century, while Rodney's stay at Vigo, it would appear, was brief. Whilst in Nova Scotia Rodney did not take part in the reduction of Louisburg probably owing to sickness among the crew of HMS *Dublin*. On 15 August, carrying French naval prisoners of war, HMS *Dublin* sailed from Halifax and arrived on 18 September at Spithead.[6] HMS *Dublin* would be the last ship in which Rodney would serve as a captain for he would soon be promoted to flag rank.

---

[1] No. 507.
[2] No. 508.
[3] TNA, ADM 51/278, 17 March–8 May 1758.
[4] Brian Tunstall, *William Pitt: Earl of Chatham* (London, 1938), p. 211.
[5] Julian S. Corbett, *England in the Seven Years War: A Study in Combined Strategy* (London, 1907), vol. I, p. 315.
[6] TNA, ADM 51/278, 15 Aug.–18 Sept. 1758.

235. *To Corbett*

[TNA, ADM 1/2382]
London
18 January 1749

Sir,

Whereas I have a prospect of getting a seat in Parliament which is inconsistent with the government of Newfoundland,[1] I therefore hope their Lordships will represent this to His Majesty that he may be graciously pleased to grant me leave to resign the said government.

236. *To Corbett*

[TNA, ADM 1/2382]
London
9 February 1749

Sir,

As I have lately been very ill, and my health still continuing to be bad being confined to my house, I must desire you will apply to their Lordships that they will be pleased to grant me liberty to be absent from His Majesty's ship under my command[2] for a fortnight or three weeks, in order to restore my health.

237. *To Corbett*

[TNA, ADM 1/2382]
Woolwich
17 March 1749

Sir,

His Majesty's ships *Rainbow* under my command being in the dock, and Captain [Patrick] Baird her late commander having informed me that the ship was very leewardly, he had intended to have applied to their Lordships in order to remedy it had not the ship been paid off. And consulting since with Mr. Allen,[3] the Surveyor, he is of opinion that if an addition of six or eight inches be added to the false keel to angle to nothing at the gripe it would make her hold a better wind and likewise fore reach. If their Lordships approve of this addition Mr.

---

[1] Rodney did not become a member of Parliament at this time and was appointed governor of Newfoundland on 20 April 1749.

[2] Rodney was slated to be captain of HMS *Rainbow*, but did not take command of the ship until 3 March 1749.

[3] Joseph Allen, Surveyor of the Navy.

Allen assures me it can be done in a proper time so that the ship may come out of the dock this spring.

As a few additions to the inside of the ship are necessary, and what I shall request being a very little expense to the government, I hope their Lordships will indulge me with them. viz:

A steerage before the great cabin at the bulkhead of which a small office for my clerk to keep my books and accounts in.

A cabin on the quarter deck for the officers, the tafferell being of a sufficient height to admit it, and a slight awning to the mizzen mast, as the voyage to Newfoundland will require the peoples being sheltered from the fogs and bad weather incident to those parts.

238. *To Clevland*

[TNA, ADM 1/2382] 15 April 1749

Sir,

Whereas His Majesty's ship *Rainbow* under my command is in want of a school master, and Mr. Robert Graham being recommended to me, as a person properly qualified, I must beg their Lordships will be so good to grant him a warrant to be school master of the ship.

239. *To Corbett*

[TNA, ADM 1/2382] *Rainbow* at Longreach
4 May 1749

Sir,

I desire you will please to acquaint their Lordships that His Majesty's ship under my command is fallen down to Longreach, where I shall use the utmost dispatch in getting the guns and gunner's stores on board, and proceed to the Nore as soon as the men repair on board, a great number having absented themselves (as their Lordships will see by the weekly account) many of which, I am informed, have entered on board His Majesty's ship the *Success* at Deptford. I should be glad their Lordships will please to give directions to the captains of the ships fitting out at Deptford, to secure and send on board the deserters from His Majesty's ship under my command, who offer themselves to enter on board their ships.

240. *To Corbett*

[TNA, ADM 1/2382] *Rainbow* at the Nore
21 May 1749

Sir,
I desire you will please to acquaint their Lordships that I am fallen down to the Nore with the *Rainbow*, and have agreeable to their directions taken the *Mercury* under my command.

I must acknowledge the receipt of their Lordships' orders of the 12th and 16th instant, and shall proceed as soon as possible to put them in execution.

241. *To Corbett*

[TNA, ADM 1/2382] *Rainbow* at Spithead
30 May 1749

Sir,
I must acquaint their Lordships with the arrival of His Majesty's ship under my command and the *Mercury* at Spithead.

242. *From the Lords of the Admiralty*

[TNA, ADM 2/73, p. 10] 30 May 1749

You are hereby required and directed to receive on board His Majesty's ship under your command the bearer Mr. Christopher Glass and give him a passage to Newfoundland victualling him as one of your ship's company while he is on board.

243. *From the Lords of the Admiralty*

[TNA, ADM 2/73, p. 12] 2 June 1749

The Secretary at War having acquainted us that twelve deserters and recruits belonging to General Philips'[1] regiment at Newfoundland, who were to have a passage in His Majesty's sloop the *Albany* are left behind at Portsmouth. You are hereby required and directed to receive the said deserters and recruits on board His Majesty's ship under your

---
[1] Lieutenant General Richard Philips, colonel of the 40th Regiment of Foot.

command and deliver them to the said regiment upon your arrival at Newfoundland, victualling them as your ship's company during their passage, taking care the agent of the regiment accounts with your purser for what provisions they may expend.

244. *To Clevland*

[TNA, ADM 1/2382] *Rainbow* at Spithead
2 June 1749

Sir,

Whereas the men belonging to His Majesty's ship under my command are very bare in cloths and necessaries, I should be glad their Lordships will please to give directions to Commissioner Vanburgh at Plymouth to pay them two months advance before the ship proceeds to sea as proper pay books are made out for that purpose.

245. *To Clevland*

[TNA, ADM 1/2382] *Rainbow* Plymouth Sound
5 June 1749

Sir,

I must beg you will please to acquaint their Lordships of my arrival here, where I shall only remain till I am joined by Captain [Francis William] Drake who I have ordered to call off Poole, Weymouth, Topsham, and Dartmouth to collect the trade of those ports. On his arrival here I shall proceed to put their Lordships' orders in execution.

246. *To Corbett*

[TNA, ADM 1/2382] Plymouth Dock
6 June 1749

Sir,

I beg leave to acquaint you that at the time I commanded His Majesty's ship the *Eagle* Mr. Lewis Joyce, Carpenter, being taken ill was sent to sick quarters the 1st May 1747 and was not able to get to the said ship until the 31st day of July following.[1] In the meantime I had the

---

[1] See No. 224.

carpenter of His Majesty's ship *Kennington* to act in his room, born on my books for victuals only.

My clerk out of a mistake put a D[1] on the said Mr. Joyce and when he returned reentered him again. By that means it seems he can't obtain any wages for that time, notwithstanding he did duty for the carpenter of the *Kennington*. Therefore desire you will please to move the case to their Lordships that they may take it into consideration and give an order for his being paid for that time.

247. *To Clevland*

[TNA, ADM 1/2382] *Rainbow* Saint John's Harbour
Newfoundland
4 August 1749

Sir,

I must desire you will please to acquaint their Lordships with the arrival of His Majesty's ships *Rainbow* and *Mercury* under my command at this place.

248. *To Clevland*

[TNA, ADM 1/2382] *Rainbow* Saint John's Harbour
7 September 1749

Sir,

I acquainted their Lordships in my letter of the 4th of last month [No. 247], with the arrival here of His Majesty's ships *Rainbow* and *Mercury* under my command. Since which agreeable to their directions to me on that head, I have employed the *Mercury* in protecting the fishery, on the coast between Saint John's and Cape Bonavista in the north, and the *Saltash*, between the Bay of Bulls and Placentia in the south, and at the expiration of their cruise to call in at the several ports, and to determine all differences that may have happened concerning the fishery.

But as many and great complaints have been made to me from almost all the ports in the island of many illegal practices committed therein, which if not timely prevented, may lend to the destruction of the fishery, I have been necessitated to hire two small vessels, in each of which I have put a lieutenant and a sufficient number of men, with orders, one to repair to the northern ports, the other to the southern,

---

[1] A D entered in a ship's books against a man's name means that he is dead.

there to administer justice, settle and determine all disputes that may have arisen, agreeable to the instructions I have give them on that head, which are conformable to the Act of Parliament[1] made for encouraging the trade to Newfoundland, and the custom of the country.

I am sorry to acquaint their Lordships that much the greater part of the inhabitants of this island, are men disaffected to the present royal family, being mostly Irish Papists. The majority even of the inhabitants of this place, are of that profession, being upwards of three hundred, only six of which would take the oaths of allegiance when tended to them.

However as I have given directions to tender the oaths to all His Majesty's subjects residing in this island, I shall at my arrival in England, give their Lordships a more particular account of this affair, but unless some stop is put to the notorious practice of the fishing ships &c. bringing yearly such great numbers of Irish Papists, to lend the fishery contrary to the salutary meaning of the Act for Encouragement of the Trade to Newfoundland, which ordains, that every master of a fishing ship or bye-boat[2] keeper, shall carry over with him yearly, one fresh man out of five, which it is to be supposed, was in order to bring up seamen, for the better manning the Royal Navy, in cases of necessity. But as the practice of bringing nothing but Irish Papist, prevails throughout all the ports in this island, I think it my duty to acquaint their Lordships, that numbers of the merchants of this place agree with me that the trade of Newfoundland, as it is at present carried on, is far from being a nursery for British seaman, the great number of Papists employed in it being most notoriously disaffected to His Majesty, and the present happy establishment.

249. *To Clevland*

[TNA, ADM 1/2382] *Rainbow* at Lisbon
7 November 1749

Sir,

I must desire you will please to acquaint their Lordships that on the 6th of October I sailed from Saint John's, with His Majesty's ship under my command, in company with the *Mercury* who separated from me the next day in a hard gale of wind.

I arrived at this place the 4th instant, and found riding here His Majesty's ships the *Mermaid* and *Lyme*, who still remain here.

---

[1] An Act to Increase the Trade of Newfoundland. 10 William III. c.14.
[2] A supplementary or extra boat.

250. *To Clevland*

[TNA, ADM 1/2382] *Rainbow* at Downes
14 December 1749

Sir,
Please to acquaint their Lordships with the arrival here of His Majesty's ship under my command in nine days from Lisbon. Sometime before I left that place Mr. [Abraham] Castres, His Majesty's envoy at that court, applied to me as commanding officer of His Majesty's ships there, that one of them might immediately proceed to Cadiz with a very considerable sum of money, agreeable to a petition he had received from many merchants of that factory.

As Captain [John] Montagu of His Majesty's ship *Mermaid* informed me that his ship was ready to proceed to sea, and as it would be but a few days difference, I gave him orders to take the money on board accordingly, and after landing it, immediately to put his former orders in execution, without a moment's loss of time.

I hope their Lordships will not disapprove of my complying with the envoy's request, as it will be the means of remitting a very considerable sum of money to Great Britain.

251. *From the Lords of the Admiralty*

[TNA, ADM 2/73, p. 139] 15 December 1749

You are hereby required and directed to proceed with His Majesty's ship under your command into Longreach, and there put out your guns and gunners stores, and having so done repair to Woolwich where you will find orders to clean and refit.

252. *To Clevland*

[TNA, ADM 1/2382] *Rainbow* at Longreach
21 December 1749

Sir,
I must acknowledge the receipt of their Lordship's order [No. 251] of the 15th instant, directing me to proceed with His Majesty's ship *Rainbow*, under my command, to Longreach where I anchored this afternoon.

I shall use all possible dispatch in getting out the guns and gunners stores, and then proceed to Woolwich. On the ship's arrival there I hope their Lordships will grant me liberty to come to town.

253. To Clevland

[TNA, ADM 1/2382] *Rainbow* at Woolwich
23 December 1749

Sir,

I must desire you will please to acquaint their Lordships with the arrival of His Majesty's ship under my command at this place.

254. To Clevland

[TNA, ADM 1/2382] *Rainbow* at Woolwich
24 December 1749

Sir,

Whereas John Harper, quarter gunner, has deserted from His Majesty's ship under my command, and as this is the third time of his so doing, I hope their Lordships will please to give directions to the marshal of the Admiralty for apprehending him, in order to his being brought to justice.

He is about five feet eight inches high, much pock broken, and of a black complexion, wears his own black shock hair, has a scar under his chin, is a married man, and may be heard of at a public house kept by a Welshman near Bearl's Wharf, Southwark.

255. From Clevland

[TNA, ADM 2/697, p. 289] 27 March 1750

Sir,

His Majesty's ship under your command being wanted on immediate service I am ordered by my Lords Commissioners of the Admiralty to signify their direction to you to get her ready for the sea with all possible dispatch, it being absolutely necessary she should sail from the Nore by the 10th of next month at the farthest.

256. From the Lords of the Admiralty

[TNA, ADM 2/73, p. 235] 30 March 1750

You are hereby required and directed to put yourself under the command of the Right Honorable Lord Anson, Vice Admiral of Great Britain and Admiral of the blue squadron of His Majesty's fleet, and follow his orders for your further proceedings.

257. To Clevland

[TNA, ADM 1/2382]
Rainbow at Woolwich
1 April 1750

Sir,

I must acknowledge the receipt of their Lordships' order [No. 256] of the 30th of March, wherein I am directed to put myself under the command of the Right Honorable Lord Anson, Vice Admiral of Great Britain, and Admiral of the blue squadron of His Majesty's fleet, and to follow his orders for my further proceedings.

258. From the Lords of the Admiralty

[TNA, ADM 2/73, pp. 251–2]
19 April 1750

Whereas the Secretary at War has represented to us that there are now in the *Savoy* twelve men, who were deserters and turned over to the regiment of foot now commanded by Colonel [Edward] Cornwallis, and desired that directions might be given to the captain of the first man of war going to Newfoundland or Nova Scotia to take them on board and deliver them to the said regiment upon his arrival at Newfoundland or Nova Scotia, you are hereby required and directed to receive the said twelve deserters on board His Majesty's ship under your command, and on your arrival at Newfoundland you are to take care that they are delivered to the commanding officer of the aforesaid regiment. And you are to order your purser to keep an exact account of the expense of their provisions which will be paid by the agent of the regiment.

259. To Clevland

[TNA, ADM 1/2382]
Rainbow in the Downes
22 April 1750

Sir,

I must desire you will acquaint their Lordships with the arrival of His Majesty's ship under my command in the Downes from convoying His Majesty to Holland.[1]

I shall proceed to Spithead as soon as possible, agreeable to the orders I have received from the Right Honourable Lord Anson.

---

[1] Rodney and HMS *Rainbow* was a member of a squadron which escorted George II to the Netherlands.

As the *Rainbow* is not victualled or completed for sea service, I beg their Lordships will indulge me so far as to let it be done at Plymouth.

260. *From the Lords of the Admiralty*

[TNA, ADM 2/73, pp. 254–5] 24 April 1750

Having ordered His Majesty's ship under your command to be stored for a foreign voyage at Plymouth and her provisions to be completed to 8 months of all species except beer, of which she is to have as much as she can conveniently stow, you are hereby required and directed to proceed with her to Plymouth, and there take on board the said stores and provisions, and get the ship ready in all respects for the sea, and then you are to repair with her between the Island and the Main, and wait there for our further orders.

261. *To Clevland*

[TNA, ADM 1/2382] *Rainbow* at Spithead
26 April 1750

Sir,

I must desire you will acquaint their Lordships with my arrival at Spithead and enclosed is the state and condition of His Majesty's ship under my command.[1]

262. *From the Lords of the Admiralty*

[TNA, ADM 2/73, p. 261] 30 April 1750

Whereas the Navy Board have represented to us that the[y] intend to send money to Portsmouth, to be sent from thence to Plymouth, for paying off His Majesty's ships *Chester* and *Eltham*, and desired a ship of war may be appointed to receive the said money at Portsmouth and carry it to Plymouth, you are hereby required and directed to receive the said money on board His Majesty's ship under your command, with such clerks as shall attend the same, and carry them to Plymouth, and you are to victual the clerks as part of your ship's company while they are on board.

[1] Not enclosed.

263. To Clevland

[TNA, ADM 1/2382]　　　　　　　　　　　　　　*Rainbow* at Spithead
　　　　　　　　　　　　　　　　　　　　　　　　　4 May 1750

Sir,
I must acknowledge the receipt of their Lordships' orders [Nos. 260, 262] to proceed with His Majesty's ship under my command to Plymouth, as likewise to receive the money on board for the payment of His Majesty's ships the *Chester* and *Eltham*. I shall make the utmost dispatch to put the said orders into execution.

264.　From the Duke of Bedford[1]

[TNA, PRO 30/20/20/4, p. 5]　　　　　　　　　　　　　　　London
　　　　　　　　　　　　　　　　　　　　　　　　　　　5 May 1750

Sir,
I cannot omit returning you my thanks for your obliging letter by the first opportunity, and am glad to find you still continue in the intention of making a visit to Launceston,[2] before your departure for Newfoundland. I fear Mr. [John] Butcher will hardly be able to be in time in that country, to meet you at Launceston. However, I will direct my agent at Tavistock, Mr. Wynne, to attend you there whenever you shall please to appoint him. I have the satisfaction to be able to inform you that the high bailiff returned this morning Lord Trentham[3] upon a majority of one hundred and seventy.

265.　From the Lords of the Admiralty

[TNA, ADM 2/73, pp. 272–8]　　　　　　　　　　　　　　　11 May 1750

Whereas we have appointed His Majesty's ship under your command together with the *Mercury* and *Saltash* sloop to protect the fishing ships

---

[1]John Russell, 4th Duke of Bedford, First Lord of the Admiralty, 27 Dec. 1744–26 Feb. 1748; Secretary of State (south), 13 Feb. 1748–14 June 1751.
[2]The Duke of Bedford at this time proposed that Rodney become a member of Parliament for Launceston in Cornwall. However, the idea was abandoned when it was found to be impossible to obtain the votes necessary for election.
[3]Grenville Leveson Gower, Viscount Trentham. In 1750 Trentham, on the interest of his brother-in-law, the Duke of Bedford, fought and won, in the midst of acts of corruption and violence, a hugely expensive election, to become a member of Parliament for Westminster.

during the ensuing season at Newfoundland, you are hereby required and directed to make all possible dispatch in getting your ship ready in all respects for the sea, and as soon as she is so, you are to make enquiry at Plymouth for all [the] trade bound to Newfoundland, and taking them under your care and protection, you are to proceed with them to sea, calling off Falmouth for any trade that may be there bound your way, and then make the best of your way to Newfoundland, and there use your best endeavours to settle and guard the fishery, and to prevent all illegal trade, during your continuance on the coast.

And whereas His Majesty' ship the *Mercury* is intended to be sent after you to Newfoundland, you are, when she joins you, to take her under your command and employ her as may best answer the purport of these instructions.

And whereas His Majesty's sloop the *Saltash* is also intended to follow you, and to protect the fishery this season, between Placentia and Trepassey, you are to take her under your command when you meet with her, and employ her agreeable to the instructions her captain is under from us, which he is to communicate to you.

And in regard it has been represented to us, that pirate ships and vessels did formerly lurk about the Banks of Newfoundland, and infest the ships fishing upon that coast, you are never to make any unnecessary stay in port, but keep diligently cruising at sea, and so employ the ship under your command as may most effectually keep the pirates from those parts, and protect the trade of His Majesty's subjects.

You are to be aiding and assisting to the admirals, vice admirals, and rear admirals of the respective ports and harbours of Newfoundland, from time to time, as need shall require, in preserving the peace and good government amongst the seamen and fishermen, and in apprehending offenders.

And whereas the Lords Commissioners for Trade and Plantations have represented to us that it is very prejudicial to this kingdom, that the fishing ships do not bring home from Newfoundland, the complement of men they carry out, many of them being enticed away to New England, and others left in the country, for which reason they have desired that we should give you directions to signify to the masters of all British ships at Newfoundland, that they take care to bring home the number of men they carry out (except in case of death) for that otherwise they will be prosecuted at their return. You are to let the masters know the same accordingly, and to use your best endeavours to oblige them thereto as far as in you lies.

And whereas it is His Majesty's pleasure that if any foreign ships or vessels shall be fitted out for Newfoundland, on pretence that they have a liberty to fish there, the commanders of His Majesty's ships bound as convoy thither, shall not allow of their fishing in those parts. You are to take care that His Majesty's pleasure therein be strictly complied with, and that if you do meet with any foreign ships fishing at or about Newfoundland, you do oblige them to desist, and depart from off the coast. But as you will receive herewith a copy of the 13th article of the treaty of peace, concluded with France at Utrecht in the year 1713, which relates to their right of fishing on that part of the coast of Newfoundland, you are to have a particular regard thereto.[1]

And whereas Vice Admiral [Thomas] Smith when he was at Newfoundland, built a house at the watering place in St. John's, for lodging the men employed in trimming the casks for beer and water, and to preserve the sails and other stores yearly made use of for tents, you are to take care that the said house be kept in proper repair, as the same may be done at a very small charge, by employing thereon the carpenters of His Majesty's ships.

You are to be careful that there be not taken into the ship under your command, to be transported to Newfoundland, any seamen, or others, than such as do belong to her. And as you are not to lend any of the ship's company to any of the fishing ships, so neither are you to suffer to be taken on board her any sort of fish, either by way of merchandise, freight, or otherwise, excepting what shall be necessary for use and spending of the ship's company.

You are to give such sailing instructions to the masters of the merchant ships, which shall from time to time be under your convoy, as shall be fitting for the better keeping you company, and meeting again in case of separation, or which shall be necessary for their security and defence, and you are to convoy any other ships of His Majesty's subjects which you shall meet with, and shall desire it, as far as your way shall lie together.

In case you shall meet with any ships or vessels upon your going out of, or coming into the Channel, which you shall have reason to suspect are carrying on any clandestine trade, you are strictly to search them and upon finding wool, or any uncustomed goods on board, to seize and bring them into the nearest port, delivering them into the charge of the custom house officers there, in order to their being proceeded against according to law.

---

[1] Under the terms of the 13th article of the Treaty of Utrecht the island of Newfoundland was ceded to Great Britain and French fishermen were granted the right to catch fish off Newfoundland and then to land and dry them on the coast of that island between Cape Bonavista and Ponte Riche.

You are, when you come from Newfoundland, or before, if the merchant ships bound for Portugal shall be ready, to order the captain of the *Mercury* to take that trade under his convoy, and see such of them as are designed for Oporto safe thither, and then proceed to Lisbon with those bound to that port, where he is to stay ten or twelve days, and then repair to Great Britain with such trade as shall desire to accompany him, calling at the Downes in expectation of our orders, and sending us an account from thence of his arrival and proceedings. And you are to give the like directions to the commander of the *Saltash* sloop, with regard to such merchant ships bound to Portugal as may be under his protection.

You are to continue on the coast of Newfoundland till the first week in October next, if the trade shall not be sooner ready, and then you are to take under your care and protection all such merchant ships as shall be bound up the Mediterranean, and proceed to Cadiz with such of them as may be bound thither, where you are not to stay above ten or twelve days, and then repair with your convoys to the ports where they shall be bound, as high as Livorno, where you are not to stay longer than twenty days, and then take under your care and protection such ships of His Majesty's subjects, as shall be homeward bound, and ready to accompany you, calling in at Barcelona, Majorca, Minorca, Alicante, and Cadiz, and from thence, after staying not above ten or twelve days for such merchant ships as shall be ready to accompany you, you are to make the best of your way with them to Great Britain, calling in the Downes for further orders, and sending us from thence an account of your arrival and proceedings. But if you shall not have any merchant ships under your convoy when you return down the Mediterranean, you are to call at Lisbon, for such trade as may be ready to sail with you from thence homeward in ten days after your arrival, and proceed to the Downes as aforesaid giving an account by all opportunities of your proceedings.

266. *From the Lords of the Admiralty*

[TNA, ADM 2/73, p. 278] 11 May 1750

In addition to our order of this date [No. 265] for your proceeding to Newfoundland, you are hereby required and directed to make enquiry into the state of the fishery at that place and to transmit to us an account thereof in the same form that was prescribed to you last year by the instructions which were annexed to your commission as governor of that island.

267. To Clevland

[TNA, ADM 1/2382] *Rainbow* Plymouth Sound
18 May 1750

Sir,

I must acknowledge the receipt of their Lordships' orders [Nos. 265, 266] of the 11th instant, and shall proceed agreeable thereto as soon as His Majesty's ship under my command is fitted for the sea.

In regard to one article of my instructions concerning the house built by Vice Admiral Smith at the watering place at Saint John's, for lodging the men employed in brewing beer and trimming the cask. I must beg leave to take notice to their Lordships, that on my arrival last year at Saint John's, the said house was entirely decayed and fell down, which obliged me to lodge the men employed as aforesaid in tents, to the great prejudice of their health, as well as expense to His Majesty in destroying sails &c.

I hope their Lordships will therefore permit me to build a new house for that purpose, as I will answer the sum required shall not amount to upwards of one hundred and fifty pounds sterling, which sum is now yearly expended in sails made use of for tents &c.

I humbly submit this to their Lordships' consideration, begging leave to remind them of the inclemency of the weather in Newfoundland.

268. To Clevland

[TNA, ADM 1/2382] *Rainbow* Plymouth
22 May 1750

Sir,

As I spoke to Mr. Clevland when I was in town about some Mediterranean passes[1] that would be proper to carry to Newfoundland, (as many requests were made to me last year for some), he promised they should be sent me with proper instructions how to dispose of them. But as none are as yet come to my hands I must take the liberty to remind you about them as I shall soon sail, and as several ships are now building in that country and will stand in need of passes.

---

[1] A document issued by the British government to British flag merchant ships to ensure freedom from attack by Barbary Corsairs.

269. *From the Lords of the Admiralty*

[TNA, ADM 2/73, pp. 297–8] 24 May 1750

Whereas you have acquainted us in your letter [No. 267] of the 18th instant that the house built by Vice Admiral Smith at the watering place at St. John's for lodging men employed in brewing beer and trimming the cask was entirely decayed and fallen down when you arrived there last year, which obliged you to lodge the men employed as aforesaid in tents, to the great prejudice of their healths as well as expense in destroying sails &c.; and therefore desiring you may be permitted to build a new house for that purpose, as you will answer the charge shall not exceed £150, which you represent is now yearly expended in sails made use of for tents &c. We do hereby signify to you our permission for building a house accordingly, but you are to take care not to exceed the said sum of one hundred and fifty pounds.

270. *From the Duke of Bedford*

[TNA, PRO 30/20/20/4, p. 9] Woburn Abbey
26 May 1750

Sir,
I promised Sir Danvers Osborn,[1] who called upon me two or three days before I set out for this place, to write to you, to let you know how very much he was my friend and acquaintance, and how much obliged I should be to you for any civilities he might receive from you in his voyage to Newfoundland. I can assure you, I shall esteem myself much obliged to you for any attentions he may receive from you, and will detain you no longer than to wish you a successful voyage.

271. *From Lord Mount Edgecumbe*[2]

[TNA, PRO 30/20/20/4, p. 11] 27 May 1750

Dear Rodney,
Being obliged to go back again to London, I think I am in conscience bound to make you some acknowledgement for the 130 guineas I took

---

[1] Member of Parliament for Bedfordshire, 1747–53. Appointed governor of New York in 1763 and then committed suicide within days of his arrival at New York City.
[2] George Edgecumbe, 3rd Lord Mount Edgecumbe.

of yours on board the *Rainbow*. And accordingly I write you this as a receipt, and promise to repay it [to] you on your return.

I am very sorry I can't stay to do the honours of the mount to Sir Danvers,[1] whom I saw this morning. And I beg you will take upon you to order the gunner to salute him when he goes ashore. I don't despair of seeing you again before you sail, for, if my Lord is better, I will return immediately. If not, I wish you a good voyage.

272. *To Clevland*

[TNA, ADM 1/2382]

Rainbow Plymouth Sound
6 June 1750

Sir,

I must acquaint you that I have received the twenty Mediterranean passes,[2] and shall take care to dispose of them agreeable to the instructions I have received therewith.

His Majesty's ship under my command being now completed for the sea, I must desire you will please to acquaint their Lordships that I shall forthwith proceed to Newfoundland.

273. *To Clevland*

[TNA, ADM 1/2382]

Rainbow at St. John's
Newfoundland
25 July 1750

Sir,

I must desire you will please to acquaint their Lordships that I arrived here with His Majesty's ship under my command on the 21st instant, and find that the fishery proceeds with great success, without any disturbance.

---

[1] Sir Danvers Osborn.
[2] See No. 268.

274. To Clevland

[TNA, ADM 1/2382]

Rainbow at St. John's
Newfoundland
7 August 1750

Sir,

I must desire you will please to acquaint their Lordships that I have arrived with his Majesty's ship under my command on the 21st of July, the *Mercury* having joined me here on the 3rd instant.

As there is no likelihood of any vessels proceeding from hence to Nova Scotia, I hope their Lordships will approve of my sending the *Saltash* with the Admiralty packets of the 25th May, directed for Governor [Edward] Cornwallis and Captain [John] Rous, which were put on board me by Commissioner Vanbrugh at Plymouth, and by the directions were intended to have been sent by the *Saltash*.

275. To Clevland

[TNA, ADM 1/2382]

Rainbow at St. John's
Newfoundland
25 September 1750

Sir,

By a vessel bound to England I take the opportunity of acquainting their Lordships that on the 16th of August I dispatched His Majesty's sloop the *Saltash* to Halifax with the Admiralty packets directed to Governor Cornwallis and Captain Rous of the *Albany*.

Captain [John] Knight had directions to land the crew of a French ship that was cast away on this coast at Louisburg in his way to Nova Scotia where he was to remain till the middle of October in case Governor Cornwallis should desire his assistance, and from thence proceed with the trade to Lisbon.

And whereas Captain Knight returned Mr. Sidney Breeze, purser of His Majesty's sloop under his command, absent without leave, and their Lordships having given directions to the Commissioners of the Victualling for indenting with Mr Robert Palmer the deputy purser of the said sloop, and as I thought it would meet with their Lordships' approbation I gave Mr. Palmer an order to continue as purser, till their pleasure should be known.

I must beg leave to acquaint their Lordships that agreeable to their order [No. 269] of the 24th of May last, I have caused to be built a house at the watering place at St. John's for lodging the men employed in brewing beer and trimming the cask which will likewise serve for an hospital and storehouse. The whole charge of the building comes within the sum of one hundred and fifty pounds which before was yearly expended in sails made use of for tents &c. I hope their Lordships will please to give directions to the Navy Board to answer the bill I shall draw on them for that purpose.

276. *To Clevland*

[TNA, ADM 1/2382]

Rainbow Cadiz Bay
27 October 1750

Sir,

I must desire you will please to acquaint their Lordships that on the 22nd instant I arrived here with His Majesty's ship under my command having been eighteen days on my passage from Newfoundland. The *Mercury* parted company with me the 18th instant off Lisbon, in order to take the trade homeward bound under her convoy from that place, agreeable to their Lordships' directions to me on that head.

The Spaniards have at this port four ships of seventy four guns ready to sail, two of which are destined to cruise off Cape Finisterre, the other two off Cape St. Vincent, in order to cruise against the Algerians, who infest this coast. They have no other ships at present in commission here.

Since my arrival I have made enquiry if any ships are bound up the Mediterranean, but finding that none are desirous or willing to take convoy for Italy, but that several masters of ships from North America have requested of me that I would take them under convoy and see them safe one hundred leagues off this coast, they not being supplied with Mediterranean passes, and His Majesty's consul at this place not having any in his possession, I presume their Lordships will approve of my complying with their request.

277. *To Anson*

[BL, Add. MSS 15956, ff. 323–4]

Cadiz
27 October 1750

My Lord,

I take the first opportunity of paying my respects to your Lordship and to acquaint you with my arrival here in eighteen days from St. John's, from whence I sailed on the 11th in company with the *Mercury* who had nigh foundered in the passage.

Since my arrival here I have seen the governor and the First Admiral Don Navarro. They received me with much politeness and have ever since endeavoured to convince me, of the great regard they have for the English nation, but on the last visit Don Navarro could not help with some warmth to express his dislike to the behaviour of some of our men of war who lately sailed from hence; and as he said insulted the Spanish nation, contrary as he imagined to the intention of the British court. The fault laid to their charge, was that they not only answered the salutes of English ships, but likewise those of all other nations. As I imagine it is not the intention of the Admiralty we should answer the salutes in a foreign port but those of English ships, I assured him nothing of that nature should happen during my stay and that I imagined the former proceeded from mistake. I hope I spoke their Lordships' sentiments on that head as the dislike the Spaniards have generally expressed to English officers has proceeded from these sort of things. For my part I perceive nothing but the greatest civility in all sorts of people and if other gentlemen have met with different usage I cannot help thinking it has proceeded from their not appearing in a proper character.

As your Lordship's kind intention in permitting [me] to proceed this year to Italy, is frustrated by there being neither money or ships bound up the Mediterranean, I hope it will not be construed amiss if I proceed from hence to England, especially as several masters of ships bound to America have solicited me to convoy them off this coast, they not being supplied with Mediterranean passes and the consul having none.

As I have acquainted the Board with the ships ready to sail from this port, I shall not trouble your Lordship further.

278. *To Clevland*

[TNA, ADM 1/2382] *Rainbow* Plymouth Sound
28 December 1750

Sir,
I must desire you will please to acquaint their Lordships with the arrival here of His Majesty's ship under my command in twelve days from Cadiz, from whence I shall immediately proceed to the Downes, to wait their Lordships' further directions.

I must likewise acquaint you that I have brought home with me the men that were discharged by their Lordships' orders from the Mediterranean squadron.

279. *From the Lords of the Admiralty*

[TNA, ADM 2/73, pp. 403–04] 3 January 1751

You are hereby required and directed to repair with His Majesty's ship under your command to Longreach, where you are to put out your guns and gunner's stores and then proceed to Woolwich, where we have ordered her to be cleaned, graved, and refitted, stored for Channel service, and her provisions completed to four months of all species except beer, of which she is to have as much as she can conveniently stow.

If you have any men who you suspect will run away, you are to secure them on board some ship in ordinary, till your ship is ready to receive them.

When the ship is ready again in all respects for the sea, you are to proceed to Longreach, and there take in your guns and gunner's stores, and then repair to the Nore where you are to remain till further order.

280. *To Corbett*

[TNA, ADM 1/2382] *Rainbow* at Downes
8 January 1751

Sir,

I must desire you will please to account their Lordships, that this day I arrived here with His Majesty's ship under my command, and received their orders [No. 279] of the 3rd instant, which I shall immediately put in execution.

281. *To Corbett*

[TNA, ADM 1/2382] *Rainbow* at the Nore
13 January 1751

Sir,

I must acquaint you with the arrival of His Majesty's ship under my command at the Nore in her way to Woolwich, and on her arrival there I hope their Lordships will permit me to come to town.

282. To Corbett

[TNA, ADM 1/2382] *Rainbow* at Longreach
15 January 1751

Sir,

I must desire you will please to acquaint their Lordships with the arrival of His Majesty's ship under my command at this place. I shall use the utmost dispatch in getting the guns and gunner's stores out, in order to proceed to Woolwich.

Agreeable to their Lordships' order I transmit them to the scheme of the fishery of Newfoundland for the year 1750.[1]

283. From the Lords of the Admiralty

[TNA, ADM 2/73, p. 410] 16 January 1751

Whereas the Navy Board have represented to us that the ship under your command cannot be taken into a dock at Woolwich, in order to be refitted, without putting the *Essex* out which is now repairing at that place. You are hereby required and directed, notwithstanding former orders [No. 279], to repair with the ship under your command to Blackstake, and there put out her guns and gunner's stores, and then proceed with her to Chatham for her being cleaned and refitted there, agreeable to the enclosed order.[2]

284. To Corbett

[TNA, ADM 1/2382] Woolwich
18 January 1751

Sir,

Yesterday I received their Lordships' orders [No. 283] of the 16th instant, at which time His Majesty's ship under my command was arrived at Woolwich and dismantled, but I should be glad to know if their Lordships would have me proceed agreeable to their direction.

I should likewise be glad to know their Lordships' pleasure in regard to the supernumeraries I brought home from the squadron under the

---

[1]Enclosed is a detailed abstract compiled by Rodney showing the activities of the men and vessels employed in the Newfoundland fishery during the year 1750, entitled 'A general scheme of the Fishery and inhabitants of the Newfoundland for the year 1750.'
[2]Not enclosed.

command of Captain Keppel,[1] they still continuing on board, the pay list having been transmitted to the Navy Board.

285. From the Lords of the Admiralty

[TNA, ADM 2/73, pp. 415–16]   18 January 1751

Whereas you have acquainted us [No. 284] that the ship under your command was arrived at Woolwich and dismantled when you received our orders [No. 283] to proceed to Chatham, you are hereby required and directed to remain with her at Woolwich and put in execution the order you have received for her cleaning there.

286. To Corbett

[TNA, ADM 1/2383]   *Rainbow* at Woolwich
                                                               27 March 1751

Sir,

There being at present a vacancy for master at arms, on board His Majesty's ship under my command, I beg leave to recommend to their Lordships Mr. Jeremiah Smith as a person properly qualified for that office.

287. To Corbett

[TNA, ADM 1/2383]   *Rainbow* at Woolwich
                                                                5 April 1751

Sir,

His Majesty's ship under my command being now in readiness for taking in her ground tier of water, and the Commissioners of the Victualling having acquainted me by letter of yesterday's date that they can only supply me with the usual quantity for Channel service, which is not near sufficient for the ground tier, [I] therefore hope their Lordships will give directions that I may be supplied with the quantity which I have already demanded.

---

[1]Commodore Hon. Augustus Keppel was in command of a small squadron sent into the Mediterranean to persuade, either by negotiation or by force, the Dey of Algiers to cease attacking British shipping.

288. From the Lords of the Admiralty

[TNA, ADM 2/73, p. 443] 6 April 1751

Whereas we have ordered His Majesty's ship under your command to be victualled to eight months of all species of provisions except beer, of which she is to have as much as she can conveniently stow, and to be stored for a voyage to Newfoundland, you are hereby required and directed to cause all possible dispatch to be used in getting the same on board and making the ship ready in all respects for the sea.

289. To Corbett

[TNA, ADM 1/2383] *Rainbow* at Woolwich
10 April 1751

Sir,

As it was necessary to leave one of the company of His Majesty's ship under my command to look after the house built at Newfoundland last season for use of His Majesty's ships on that station, Thomas Smith was left there for that service and victualled by the purser for eight months, which I hope their Lordships will approve of, and give directions to the clerk of the cheque at Woolwich to muster him as he has been checked ever since our arrival here.

As the ship has been in extra petty warrant victualling[1] since her coming to Woolwich I beg their Lordships will be pleased at the same time to direct the clerk of the cheque to put her into sea victualling, as the provisions are now completed to eight months, and the people will then of course have the advantage of fresh meat with greens, and better provisions for the short time they may continue at Longreach.

290. From Corbett

[TNA, ADM 2/697, p. 529] 11 April 1751

Sir,

I have read to the Lords Commissioners of the Admiralty your letter [No. 284] of yesterday's date representing that Thomas Smith one of the company of His Majesty's ship under your command was left

---

[1] A reduction in the amount of provisions issued to seamen when a ship is in port to about two thirds of the amount received at sea.

behind at Newfoundland to look after the house built there last season for the use of the ships on that station. And desiring, as he has been victualled by the purser for eight months, that the clerk of the cheque at Woolwich may be ordered to mustered him [*sic*]. And I send this to acquaint you that directions are given to the Navy Board accordingly.

As to that part of your letter desiring that the ship you command may be put into sea victualling, their Lordships command me to acquaint you that it cannot be done till she departs from Woolwich.

291. *From the Lords of the Admiralty*

[TNA, ADM 2/73, p. 449] 11 April 1751

Sir,

Having ordered the Commissioners of the Victualling to supply His Majesty's ship under your command with *two months* brandy, or rum, in lieu of beer, (they having informed us that there is a sufficient quantity thereof in the victualling stores for that purpose) you are hereby required and directed to receive the same on board in lieu of beer accordingly.

292. *To Corbett*

[TNA, ADM 1/2383] *Rainbow* at Woolwich
12 April 1751

Sir,

I must acknowledge the receipt of their Lordships' orders [No. 289] of the 10th instant, with the copy of the memorial of Doctor Knight,[1] and shall take care to made the proper observations agreeable to their Lordships' directions.

293. *From the Lords of the Admiralty*

[TNA, ADM 2/73, pp. 450–1] 16 April 1751

Sir,

In addition to our orders to you of the 4th instant for making an experiment of Doctor Knight's improvement of the compass, and a

---

[1] Dr Gowin Knight was the inventor of an improved azimuth compass as well as artifical bar magnets for use in a compass.

copy of the memorial of the said doctor sent you therewith,[1] you are hereby required and directed to take an opportunity of seeing the said doctor before you sail, in order to your being thoroughly instructed by him in the use of his magnetical bars to prevent any mistake and also informed of the improvements made in the compass that you may be the better enabled to make your observations thereon, and when you shall report to us your observations agreeable to the aforementioned order you are also to report your opinion whether it will be advisable to bring them into general use in His Majesty's navy.

294. *From Clevland*

[TNA, ADM 2/697, p. 539]   22 April 1751

Sir,

I am commanded by my Lords Commissioners of the Admiralty to signify their direction to you to attend them at this office next Thursday at twelve o'clock.

295. *From the Lords of the Admiralty*

[TNA, ADM 2/73, p. 461]   24 April 1751

Sir,

You are hereby required and directed to use all possible dispatch in getting His Majesty's ship under your command ready in all respects for the sea, and as soon as she is so, you are to repair with her to Spithead, and remain there till further order.

296. *To Corbett*

[TNA, ADM 1/2383]   *Rainbow* at Woolwich
28 April 1751

Sir,

I must acknowledge the receipt of their Lordships' orders [No. 295] of the 24th instant, as likewise your letter of the 25th, with a box enclosing thirty Mediterranean passes for the use of His Majesty's subjects trading to Newfoundland, which shall be issued according the rules prescribed in your letter of 25th of May last.

[1] Not enclosed.

I must desire you will please to acquaint their Lordships that His Majesty's ship under my command has been in all respects ready to fall down to Longreach since the 21st, but is still detained here by contrary winds. I shall take the first opportunity to proceed according to their directions.

297. *To Clevland*

[TNA, ADM 1/2383] *Rainbow* at Longreach
2 May 1751

Sir,

I must desire you will please to acquaint their Lordships that this morning His Majesty's ship under my command fell down to Longreach.

I shall use the utmost dispatch in getting in her guns and gunners stores on board, and then proceed agreeable to their Lordships' directions.

298. *From Lord Egremont*[1]

[TNA, PRO 30/20/20/4, p. 15] Whitehall
20 May 1751

Sir,

As I am obliged to go into Sussex today, and possibly may not return till you may be sailed and so miss the honour of seeing you, I hope you will excuse my troubling you with this; to enclose a letter[2] I received from one of my leading men at Taunton relating to a Newfoundland cause. I feel myself much ashamed to be forced to importune you upon such a subject, but rely upon your goodness to pardon me when you consider that to an important man in a corporation almost nothing can be refused. If I do not find you here when I come back I take this opportunity to wish you health, pleasure, and success in your voyage.

---

[1] Charles Wyndham, 2nd Earl Egremont, Secretary of State (Southern), 9 Oct. 1761–21 Aug. 1763.
[2] Not enclosed.

299. To Clevland

[TNA, ADM 1/2383]
Rainbow at Plymouth Sound
8 June 1751

Sir,

I must desire you will please to acquaint their Lordships with the arrival here of His Majesty's ship under my command.

I sailed yesterday in the evening from Spithead in company with His Majesty's ship the *Boston*, and gave Captain Drake orders to call off the different ports (as mentioned in their Lordships orders to me) to collect the trade bound to Newfoundland, and then to rejoin me at Plymouth.

300. To Clevland

[TNA, ADM 1/2383]
Rainbow at Plymouth Sound
16 June 1751

Sir,

I must desire you will please to acquaint their Lordships that His Majesty's ship under my command has been ready in all respects for the sea since the 11th instant but has been detained by hard gales westerly.

The weather seems now more moderate, I therefore will not lose the first opportunity of proceeding and hope in a few days to be out of the Channel.

301. To Clevland

[TNA, ADM 1/2383]
Rainbow at St. John's, Newfoundland
14 August 1751

Sir,

I must desire you will please to acquaint their Lordships that His Majesty's ship under my command in company with the *Boston* arrived at Agua Fort[1] on the 3rd instant having been six weeks on our passage from Plymouth.

We endeavoured for a month to discover the island as mentioned in their Lordships' orders to me of the 26th of May last, but without success, occasioned by the continual fogs and westerly winds which

---

[1] Newfoundland.

generally prevail in that latitude and longitude during the summer months, which their Lordships may perceive by a copy of my journal, which I send enclosed herewith,[1] and to which I refer them for further particulars. I have likewise heard from Captain Knight of the *Saltash*, who informs me he did not find the said island on his passage.

I am to acquaint their Lordships that I have employed His Majesty's ship the *Boston* between Trepassey and St. John's, and shall take care of that to the northward myself. Everything is very quiet in the island, but it's likely to prove a very bad fishery this season.

302. *From Count William Bentinck*[2]

[TNA, PRO 30/20/20/4, pp. 17–20]

The Hague
24 September 1751

Sir,

I hope this will find you and all those under your command in the best state you can wish. I am very impatient to hear news from you. And you may easily judge that it will be a great satisfaction to me to have some account of my son,[3] which I shall be infinitely obliged to you for, if you can find leisure to send me. I hope he will have shown himself worthy of the goodness you were disposed to have for him. And I doubt not but he will go on upon the principles and in the road traced out to him by you. If you consign him to Commodore Keppel, I hope you will be so good as to recommend him at the same time to his particular care, so as that he may become an officer and a gentleman: and beg that Mr. Keppel will keep a strict eye on him as to his conduct and morals, which I shall ever be obliged to Mr. Keppel for. I have written to my son without having determined with him anything as to the part he is to take, either to come back with you, or to remain in the Mediterranean because I will not force him directly or indirectly. But I hope he will of himself take and stick to the resolution of continuing, rather than coming home. And in that case, I hope that you will be so good as to act my part to my son. I shall approve of everything you shall be pleased to order, and take immediate care for the repayment of whatever you shall have advanced. I shall also beg to know of you how I must do at this distance with Commodore Keppel, and whether he

---

[1] Not enclosed.

[2] Count William Bentinck. A son of the 1st Earl of Portland, a count of the Holy Roman Empire, and a resident of the Netherlands.

[3] John Albert Bentinck, lieutenant, 21 July 1757; Master and Commander, 18 May 1758; Captain, 17 Oct. 1758; MP Rye, 1761–68.

will not take it amiss, if I desire him to furnish what money shall be necessary for my son. I beg you to settle this affair, and to let me know how you have done it.

I shall be very glad to know from yourself the success of your intended discovery, and if anything remarkable happened in your voyage.

303. *From Lieutenant John Harrison*

[TNA, ADM 1/2383] *Boston* at Lisbon
12 October 1751

Sir,

I beg leave to represent to you that I have for a considerable time been in a very bad state of health, which the surgeons inform me is consumptive, and give it as their opinions I ought to remain some time in this climate, as the approaching winter in England would be very detrimental to my health. I therefore beg you will favour me with leave (if the service will permit) to remain some time in this country, as I am informed this climate is the most likely to effect my recovery.

304. *To Clevland*

[TNA, ADM 1/2383] *Rainbow* at Lisbon River
15 October 1751

Sir,

Since I acquainted you last with the arrival here of His Majesty's ship under my command, we have been detained by contrary winds and the necessary repairs that were wanted to the ship she proving very leaky in her upper works.

The *Saltash* Captain Knight arrived here the 10th instant from Placentia.

I must acquaint their Lordships that Mr. John Harrison lieutenant of His Majesty's ship the *Boston*, having by letter [No. 303] of the 12th instant represented to me that he had been for some time in a bad state of health, which the surgeons informed him was consumptive, and had given it as their opinion he ought to remain in this climate, as the approaching winter in England might be fatal to him, and desiring I would favour him with leave (if the service would permit it) to remain in this country until the spring, in order to restore his health.

As I found upon inquiry the representation to be true, I complied with his request, and have appointed Mr. Thomas Adams to be lieutenant of the *Boston* in his room, until their Lordship's pleasure shall be known.

Enclosed I transmit a copy of Mr. Harrison's letter [No. 303], with the state and condition of His Majesty's ships in this River.[1]

305. To Clevland

[TNA, ADM 1/2383] *Rainbow* at Lisbon River
9 November 1751

Sir,

I must desire you will please to acquaint their Lordships that tomorrow I propose sailing with His Majesty's ship under my command for Cadiz, having been detained here so long by contrary winds and a bad state of health.

His Majesty's ship the *Garland* sailed a few days since for Italy. The ships now in the river are the *Rainbow*, *Boston*, and *Saltash* sloop, but as the *Boston* sails for England tomorrow, enclosed I transmit by her the state and condition of His Majesty's ships under my command as likewise the scheme of the fishery of Newfoundland for this present year.[2]

306. To Clevland

[TNA, ADM 1/2383] *Rainbow* at Lisbon River
13 January 1752

Sir,

I must desire you will please to acquaint their Lordships with the arrival here of His Majesty's ship under my command in eleven days from Cadiz. Sometime before I left that port the *Dragon* and *America*, two Spanish men of war of sixty four guns (commanded by Don Pedro Steuart), took in their cruise off Cape St. Vincent an Algerian ship of fifty four guns and six hundred men after an action of four days, the Algerian sinking soon after she struck. Among the prisoners is the renegade Israel, the person who was the occasion of the Lisbon's packet being carried into Algiers.[3] Nothing else has occurred worth mentioning to their Lordships.

[1] Both are enclosed.
[2] Enclosed is an abstract compiled by Rodney showing the activities of the men and vessels engaged in the Newfoundland fishery during the year 1751.
[3] On 6 March 1746 the Algerians captured the post office packet *Prince Frederick* off the coast of Portugal. On board the Algerian ship was a renegade Englishman, David

307. To Clevland

[TNA, ADM 1/2383]　　　　　　　　　　*Rainbow* at Lisbon River
　　　　　　　　　　　　　　　　　　　　22 January 1752

Sir,

In addition to my letter [No. 306] of the 13th instant, I must acquaint you that an express arrived here from Cadiz giving an account that on the 3rd of this month, a violent storm of wind at SE had drove upwards of thirty sail of ships on shore, and many to sea, very few riding it out that were then in the Bay. I am sorry to acquaint their Lordships that the same express takes notice of all the peoples perishing in the ships that drove on shore.

We have likewise had here, for these ten days past, excessive hard gales of wind which have done considerable damage, and drove several ships on shore in this river.

My ship's company for some time past have been very sickly with the small pox, and fevers, which still continues.

308. From Clevland

[TNA, ADM 2/698, p. 225]　　　　　　　　　　20 February 1752

Sir,

I have received and communicated to my Lords Commissioners of the Admiralty, your letters of the 13th and 22nd instant [Nos. 306, 307], and I am commanded by their Lordships to acquaint you that His Majesty having ordered the Lord Tyrawley[1] to repair forthwith to the Court of Lisbon, it is their direction that you do not lose a moment's time after his arrival in returning to England with the ship under your command to prevent the growing expense of keeping her in commission.

Israel, who, within ear shot of the master of the *Prince Frederick*, informed the Algerians that the packet, even though a vessel owned by the British government, was a lawful prize for not having a Mediterranean Pass. The *Prince Frederick* was carried into Algiers and 'plundered' of bullion and diamonds valued at £25,000 before the vessel was released.

[1] James O'Hara, Baron Tyrawley, minister plenipotentiary to Portugal, April–July 1752.

309. *To Clevland*

[TNA, ADM 1/2383] *Rainbow* at Spithead
18 March 1752

Sir,
I must desire you will please to acquaint their Lordships with the arrival here of His Majesty's ship under my command in fourteen days from Lisbon, at which place I left His Majesty's ships the *Nightingale* and *Unicorn*.

310. *From Clevland*

[TNA, ADM 2/698, p. 247] 20 March 1752

Sir,
I have received and read to the Lords Commissioners of the Admiralty your two letters of the 18th instant [No. 309], one of them giving an account of the observations you have made upon Doctor Knight's magnetical bars and box compass.

311. *From the Lords of the Admiralty*

[TNA, ADM 2/74, p. 89] 20 March 1752

Sir,
Having ordered His Majesty's ship under your command to be paid off at Woolwich, you are hereby required and directed to make the best of your way with her to Longreach, where you are to put out her guns and gunners stores, and then proceed to Woolwich, and clear of her provisions and the remainder of her stores, and cause her to be unrigged and properly delivered into the care of the officers of the yard, which they are to certify to the Navy Board, who are not to pay you till you produce such certificates to them, without our particular order.

You are to cause proper pay books to be immediately made out and transmitted to the Navy Board.

312. To Clevland

[TNA, ADM 1/2383]
Rainbow at Spithead
23 March 1752

Sir,

I must acknowledge the receipt of their Lordships' orders [No. 311] of the 20th instant, which I shall put in execution as soon as the weather will permit, the beer and bread I have demanded to come on board not having more than two days of each specie.

313. To Clevland

[TNA, ADM 1/2383]
Rainbow at Spithead
25 March 1752

Sir,

We have had these two days past an excessive hard gale between the north and NNW which obliged us to strike yards and topmast and rendered it impossible to get under sail without leaving our anchors behind. The moment the weather moderates their Lordships may depend upon my making the utmost dispatch to Woolwich.

314. To Clevland

[TNA, ADM 1/2383]
Portsmouth
26 March 1752

Sir,

I am sorry my ill health forces me to be so troublesome to their Lordships as to request the favour of them, to suffer the *Rainbow* to be carried round by the first lieutenant.

I was in hopes to have been able (if the weather had permitted) to have proceeded agreeable to their orders, but finding myself much worse, being confined to my bed and attended by a physician, obliges me to acquaint their Lordships therewith, and if not better by the return of the post, I flatter myself they will grant my request.

315. *From Clevland*

[TNA, ADM 2/698, p. 252]　　　　　　　　　　　　27 March 1752

Sir,

I have received and read to the Lords Commissioners of the Admiralty your letter [No. 314] of yesterday's date, setting forth that you are so very ill as not to be able to proceed to Woolwich with His Majesty's ship under your command. Their Lordships command me to acquaint you that they are sorry for your indisposition, and that you may send your ship round under the command of the first lieutenant.

316. *To Clevland*

[TNA, ADM 1/2383]　　　　　　　　　　　　Conduit Street [London]
　　　　　　　　　　　　　　　　　　　　　　　　23 April 1752

Sir,

The bearer Mr. [John] Wareham was school master of His Majesty's ship *Rainbow* under my command. Mr Cotes[1] desired me to recommend him to you, in order to be appointed school master of the *Severn*.

317. *To Clevland*

[TNA, ADM 1/2383]

　　　　　　　　　　　　　　　　　　　　　　　　23 April 1752

Sir,

I must desire you will please to acquaint their Lordships that on my arrival at St. John's in Newfoundland in 1749, great complaints were made to me from all the out ports, both to the northward and southward, that no officer had been for many years to adjust the differences between the inhabitants and settle the fishery at the said ports; that they laid under great hardships and begged I would appoint a proper person to decide all their disputes.

And as their Lordships' instructions to me as likewise those I received from His Majesty commanded me to collect the schemes of the fishery in the exactest manner, which it is impossible to do without hiring a small vessel for that purpose: (most of the ports to the north-

---

[1] Captain Thomas Cotes.

ward being incapable of receiving a man of war) I thought my duty in obedience to their Lordships' orders, and in compliance to the merchants' and inhabitants' request to hire a sloop of sixty tons, in which I sent my first lieutenant in order to collect the schemes of the fishery and to adjust all the differences between the merchants and inhabitants.

In my letter to their Lordships of August 1749 I acquainted them with my proceedings, as likewise the Navy Board, that I had drawn on them for the sum of twenty five pounds for the hire of the said sloop, which account the Navy Board have not thought proper to pass, though proper vouchers were laid before them. I therefore hope their Lordships will please to give directions that the said account be passed at the Navy Office; and I must beg leave to assure them that the schemes of the fishery cannot be collected in an exact manner without the hire of a small coaster being allowed; complaints will likewise arise from the inhabitants and fishery (who are greatly increased within these few years) unless a proper officer yearly attends to settle all their disputes.

318. *To Clevland*

[TNA, ADM 1/2383]   Conduit Street
24 April 1752

Sir,

I must acquaint you that I have issued seventeen Mediterranean passes of those committed to my charge, and enclosed transmit to you the remainder of the passes, together with what has been delivered up to me.[1]

I am ready to pay the fees to whom you are pleased to order.

319. *To Clevland*

[TNA, ADM 1/2383]   London
7 May 1752

Sir,

Their Lordships having approved of my leaving Thomas Smith [Nos. 289, 290] (one of the company of His Majesty's ship the *Rainbow*) at Newfoundland to look after the storehouse &c. built there for the use of His Majesty's ships on that station, by their letter [No. 290] of 11th April 1751; and having at the same time given the Navy Board direc-

---

[1] Not enclosed.

tions to order the clerk of the cheque at Woolwich to muster him, as he was victualled by the purser for eight months from the time of our leaving Newfoundland, agreeable to my order to him. I beg you will acquaint their Lordships that the purser has again victualled him from the 18th September last for eight months, agreeable to the enclosed order and receipts,[1] and as he has been checked since our arrival in England, I hope their Lordships will be pleased to give orders to the Navy Board that he may be mustered whilst the ship was in commission, as even that will not within 15 days, complete the time he has been victualled for.

320. *To Clevland*

[TNA, ADM 1/2383] London
31 May 1752

Sir,

It appearing by the purser of His Majesty's ship the *Rainbow's* accounts at the Victualling Office that in his first there was 193 men for one day borne short of the allowed complement, and in his succeeding and final account for the said ship, one hundred and three men for a day overborne. As we were under the allowed complement 620 men for a day upon the whole, and that the small number overborne now, was entirely owing to a mistake of my clerk's, I beg you will move their Lordships to give the Victualling Board directions to dispense with it.

321. *To Clevland*

[TNA, ADM 1/2383] London
28 December 1752

Sir,

Upon the 20th of May last I applied to their Lordships for the mustering of George Smith[2] on the books of His Majesty's ship the *Rainbow* having left him at Newfoundland to look after the brew house built for the use of His Majesty's ships on that station, the purser having supplied him with provisions, which they were pleased to order. But finding since that the said George Smith left Newfoundland the 8th of January last, I beg their Lordships will give directions for the dis-

---

[1]Not enclosed.
[2]This name appears as Thomas Smith in documents Nos. 289, 290 and 319.

charging him accordingly, and taking off the charge against me for bearing over complement, which was owing to my not knowing this at the payment of the ship and bearing him open upon the books.

322. *From the Lords of the Admiralty*

[TNA, ADM 2/74, p. 209] 16 January 1753

Sir,

Having appointed you captain of His Majesty's ship the *Kent*, at Portsmouth, which we intend for the service of a guardship at that port, and having fixed her complement at *one hundred men*, agreeable to the scheme on the other side hereof, and ordered her to be stored and victualled in the manner usual for a guardship, you are hereby required and directed to repair on board the said ship, and to use the best dispatch in fitting her accordingly; taking particular care not to enter any foremastmen but such as are able seamen.[1]

323. *To Clevland*

[TNA, ADM 1/2383] 19 January 1753

Sir,

I must acknowledge the receipt of their Lordships' orders of the 16th instant [No. 322] which I shall take care shall be duly executed.

324. *To Clevland*

[TNA, ADM 1/2383] *Kent* Portsmouth Harbour
2 May 1753

Sir,

I must desire you will please to acquaint their Lordships that I have taken upon me the command of His Majesty's ship *Kent* at this port, and am now at my duty here.

---

[1] The last paragraph of this document has been omitted.

325. To Clevland

[TNA, ADM 1/2383] *Kent* Portsmouth Harbour
30 June 1753

Sir,
I must desire you will please to lay this letter before their Lordships, which is to beg their permission to be absent from His Majesty's ship under my command for a fortnight, having some business of consequence to transact in town, which requires my presence.

326. To Clevland

[TNA, ADM 1/2383] London
10 July 1753

Sir,
My state of health being such that I am ordered by my physician to drink the waters of Tunbridge in hopes of restoring it.

I must desire you will acquaint their Lordships therewith and make it my humble request that they will be pleased to lengthen my leave of absence for a month longer, at the expiration of which time I hope my health will be perfectly restored when I shall forthwith repair to my duty.

327. To Clevland

[TNA, ADM 1/2383] *Kent* at Portsmouth
3 November 1753

Sir,
The meeting of the Parliament drawing near, if their Lordships have no particular commands for me at Portsmouth, I would beg their permission to attend the House.[1]

---

[1] Rodney, on 13 May 1751, had been elected with the support of the government to be an MP for Saltash.

328. *From the Lords of the Admiralty*

[TNA, ADM 2/74, p. 367]　　　　　　　　　　3 January 1754

Having ordered His Majesty's ship under your command to be sheathed and filled, cleaned, graved, refitted, and stored for service in the East Indies, her complement of men to be increased to *four hundred and eighty*, and to be victualled with eight months' provisions for the said complement, of all species except beer, of which she is to have only so much as she can conveniently stow, and to be floored with water, you are hereby required and directed to use all possible expedition in preparing her accordingly, and repair with her *out to Spithead* where you are to remain for further orders.

329. *To Clevland*

[TNA, ADM 1/2384]　　　　　　　　　　　　　London
　　　　　　　　　　　　　　　　　　22 January 1754

Sir,

My accounts for His Majesty's ship the *Kent*, during the little more than twelve months I commanded her, being by this time passed, I beg you will move their Lordships to order that I may be paid my wages.

330. *From Clevland*

[TNA, ADM 2/699, p. 383]　　　　　　　28 February 1754

Sir,

In return to your letter of the 22nd instant [No. 329], I am commanded by my Lords Commissioners of the Admiralty to acquaint you that they have ordered your wages to be paid.

331. *From Clevland*

[TNA, ADM 2/699, p. 432]　　　　　　　　　6 April 1754

Sir,

My Lords Commissioners of the Admiralty having appointed you commander of His Majesty's ship the *Fougeux*, I send this to acquaint you therewith that you may come to this office and take out your commission.

332. To Clevland

[TNA, ADM 1/2384] *Fougeux* Portsmorth Harbour
6 May 1754

Sir,
I must desire you will please to acquaint their Lordships that I have taken upon me the command of His Majesty's ship the *Fougeux*, and am now at my duty on board her.

333. To Clevland

[TNA, ADM 1/2384] *Fougeux* Portsmouth Harbour
25 October 1754

Sir,
Having some business to transact that requires my presence in London, I must beg the favour of you, to make it my request to their Lordships that I may obtain two months leave of absence.

334. To Clevland

[TNA, ADM 1/2384] 3 December 1754

Sir,
The time allowed by their Lordships not being sufficient to transact the business I came to town about, if they have no immediate service for His Majesty's ship under my command I must desire you will please to make it my request that they will grant me a months' longer leave of absence.

335. From the Lords of the Admiralty

[TNA, ADM 2/75, p. 16] 16 January 1755

Having ordered His Majesty's ship under your command to be *cleaned*, graved, and refitted for the service she at present performs, and to be floored with water, you are hereby required and directed to clear her for the dock as soon as possible, and as soon as she shall be *cleaned* to use the best dispatch in refitting and flooring her accordingly.

336. *From the Lords of the Admiralty*

[TNA, ADM 2/75, p. 21] 18 January 1755

You are hereby required and directed to increase the present complement of His Majesty's ship under your command to her highest complement which is *six hundred* men, and for that purpose you are to enter all such seamen and able bodied land men as shall offer.

And having ordered the ship to be stored for Channel service, floored with water; and victualled to four months of all species of provisions, except beer, of which she is to have only as much as she can conveniently stow, you are to make the best dispatch in getting on board stores, water, and provisions accordingly.

337. *To Clevland*

[TNA, ADM 1/2384] *Fougeux* Portsmouth Harbour
28 January 1755

Sir,

The leave their Lordships were pleased to grant me being near expired I must beg the favour of their indulging me with a months' longer leave of absence.

338. *To Clevland*

[TNA, ADM 1/2384] *Fougeux* Portsmouth Harbour
28 January 1755

Sir,

I must acknowledge the receipt of their Lordships' order of the 25th instant with four of His Majesty's proclamations for procuring seamen.

I shall use every method in my power to man His Majesty's ships under my command with the utmost expedition.

339. *To Jane Rodney*[1]

[TNA, PRO 30/20/20/2, pp. 9–10] Portsmouth
30 January 1755

My dearest Jenny,

I was made happy by the receipt of yours last night. Believe me my love, the greatest pleasure I have in this world, (next to seeing you), is to hear from you. That happiness let me often enjoy since at present cruel necessity parts us. I sincerely wish I had quitted before this bustle came on. However, I will be wiser for the future and learn to live without a guardship. It is but staying so much longer in the country to make up the difference in expense. I now learn when it is too late, that ambition has lost its charms to me, and that to have a wife and children engrosses all our attention and that where one's heart is, there the mind is also, for whatever I am about or doing, I think of nothing but Hill Street[2] and the dear pledges I left there with you.

I hope by this time you have followed Doctor Hunter's advice. I am certain it is the best method that can be taken in your complaint and there is no doubt if you use it you will soon be well. For God's sake keep up your spirits. Remember my happiness depends upon your health and that nothing in this world can give me pleasure without you.

I have caught cold but today it is much better and my spirits pretty well. Adieu my love, kiss the little ones for me and in remembering me to all in Grosvenor Street[3] believe that I am ever yours.

340. *To Jane Rodney*

[TNA, PRO 30/20/20/2, pp. 13–14] Portsmouth
1 February 1755

The want of franks is the occasion my dearest love that I enclose this letter to your father, who I hope will send it to you immediately on his receipt of it. Pray desire Kitty[4] to enclose me a dozen franks in two covers that I may always direct to you as I know you had rather receive my letters at first hand. I have had all your letters the receipt

---

[1] On 31 January 1753 Rodney, at the Oxford Chapel on Vere Street in London, married Jane Compton. Jane Rodney, who died on 29 January 1757 after an illness brought about in part from child birth, was the daughter of Hon. Charles Compton of Eastbourne in Sussex.
[2] Rodney's residence in London.
[3] The Compton residence in London.
[4] Jane Rodney's sister Catherine Compton.

of which always makes me happy as thereby I learn that my dear girl and our little ones are in good health, may you ever continue so. For God sake my dearest, don't grieve at what is unavoidable. Our separation cannot be long and it shall be my care not to put it in fortune's power to divide us again till we part for ever. To convince you that I don't intend going abroad in case the *Fougeux* should be ordered to sea, I have this day desired my Lord Anson to remove me into a ship of ninety guns that is in this harbour and which it will be impossible to be ready for the sea at least in a year long before which I hope all this storm will blow over.

As I have many letters to write this post my Jenny must pardon me if I conclude…

341. *To Clevland*

[TNA, ADM 1/2384] *Fougeux* Portsmouth Harbour
5 February 1755

Sir,

I must desire you will please to acquaint their Lordships that His Majesty's ship under my command will be at Spithead by Friday or Saturday next. Had the Victualling Office given greater dispatch, we should have now been ready to sail out of the harbour.

342. *To Jane Rodney*

[TNA, PRO 30/20/20/2, pp. 25–6] 8 Febuary 1755

This morn[ing] I had my dearest Jenny's letter concerning the masquerade and sincerely regret I had not the pleasure of seeing Kitty in her dress. If mankind saw her with my eyes she would not be long without a husband, but I would by no means recommend a sailor to her as every little bustle must deprive her of him for a time, but (may be) that she would approve of as the impertinent would be out of the way.

I give my consent that Mrs Walter takes Jamy[1] provided she can make her husband believe he is his son and that his estate will descend to him.

The letter you sent me came from a lady if you had seen the contents you would certainly have been jealous. Tho' from an old woman –

---

[1] Rodney's second son James.

Lady Carbery[1] – in France. I only wait till Sir Edward Hawke[2] or Mr. West[3] come to hoist their flag, when I will set out for Alresford[4] and from thence to see my dear girl. Take care of yourself and my boys as you tender the welfare of him who ever is with the utmost affection, ever yours.

343. To Clevland

[TNA, ADM 1/2384] *Fougeux* Portsmouth Harbour
9 February 1755

Sir,

As most of the men belonging to His Majesty's ship under my command are in great want of slops, and as their being exposed to the severity of this weather may be very detrimental to their health, I should be glad their Lordships would approve of my giving orders to the purser to supply them with proper necessaries, provided the pay due to them will answer the same. I shall likewise be glad to know how far their Lordships would approve of my giving directions for supplying the new entered men with slops as most of them are excessive ragged and scarce clothes to cover them.

344. To Jane Rodney

[TNA, PRO 30/20/20/2, pp. 29–30] 9 February 1755

I had yours my dearest love and am glad to find that you follow Doctor Duncan's advice, as I have heard that the bark is a very great strengthener, tho' I hope you do not find yourself weaker than when I left town. If so for God sake don't let the child suck too much but rather feed him more. I long to see both yourself and my dear boys and will certainly be with you some time this week, tho' I believe it will be the latter end – because I must call at Alresford in my way to town.

---

[1]Anne Evans, Baroness Carbery.
[2]Vice Admiral Sir Edward Hawke; Admiral, 24 Feb. 1757; Admiral of the Fleet, 15 Jan. 1768; First Lord of the Admiralty, 11 Dec. 1766–12 Jan. 1771; created Baron Hawke, 20 May 1776. Hawke for most of the Seven Years' War was in command of the Western Squadron.
[3]Rear Admiral Temple West; Vice-admiral, 8 Dec. 1756; Lord of the Admiralty, 17 Nov. 1756–6 April 1757, 2 July–9 Aug. 1757.
[4]Old Alresford near Winchester, Rodney's country residence.

I am glad Georgy[1] grows and should be glad I heard that he walked alone. We have had terrible cold weather here which still continues and I can assure you that my clothing is much warmer than when I left town.

Adieu my dearest Jenny and with my love to my boys and all in Grosvenor Street...

345. To Clevland

[TNA, ADM 1/2384] *Fougeux* Portsmouth Harbour
10 February 1755

Sir,

I must desire you will please to acquaint their Lordships that His Majesty's ship under my command would have proceeded to Spithead this morning had not my people been employed in sailing His Majesty's ship *Terrible* to that place. But I hope to get her there tomorrow morning.

346. To Clevland

[TNA, ADM 1/2384] *Fougeux* Spithead
11 February 1755

Sir,

I must desire you will please to acquaint their Lordships that His Majesty's ship under my command is moored at Spithead. If their Lordships will please to allow a tender, I make no doubt but soon to complete her complement.

347. To Jane Rodney

[TNA, PRO 30/20/20/2, pp. 37–8] Portsmouth
14 February 1755

My dear girl will be surprised to receive this letter instead of seeing me but she will find thereby, that love will get the better of interest and that her influence has induced me to change the best sailing ship in the world for the *Prince George* of ninety guns of which there is not the least likelihood that she will ever go to sea, but I beg you will not let

---

[1] Rodney's oldest son.

your father know it as he certainly will laugh at me. Last night (after I had bespoke four horses to be in my chaise at day light) I had a letter from the Admiralty to acquaint me that I might have the *Prince George* if I pleased and that they must have an answer by the return of the post. So that it was lucky I had not left this place in the morning. I have by this post accepted the ship and suppose that my commission will be down on Tuesday – so that my dear girl may now be easy in her mind and depend upon seeing me some day next week and has not now the least occasion to dread my going abroad. I expect this will raise your spirits and make you seem livelier than you have been lately, but don't betray me hussy. I must stay to deliver the *Fougeux* to the new captain and make up my books as Mr. Mackay can let you know I am obliged to do and I look upon it as a very lucky incident that I was not on my journey for I must have left you again immediately. Now my dearest I will bring you down with me and if we can but prevail with one of your sisters to accompany you I shall be happy.

348. *To Clevland*

[TNA, ADM 1/2384]

Portsmouth
16 February 1755

Sir,

I received your letter of the 14th instant acquainting me that their Lordships have been pleased to honour me with the command of His Majesty's ship *Prince George* for which I beg leave to return them my thanks.

If their Lordships will please to indulge me with the seven men named in the margin[1] to be discharged from the *Fougeux* into the *Prince George*, I will be answerable soon to rig her with the assistance of the men I may raise. It will not be distressing the *Fougeux*, but will greatly enable me to forward the fitting the *Prince George* and raising more men. I must beg leave to take notice that if their Lordships comply with my request, that there will be still two good boatswain mates remaining on board the *Fougeux*.

---

[1] William Wells, boatswain mate; and the able seamen James Jacobs, Thomas Potter, John Doran, John Wesledge, John Guy, James Meather.

349. *From Clevland*

[TNA, ADM 2/700, p. 245]　　　　　　　　　　　18 February 1755

Sir,

I have received and read to my Lords Commissioners of the Admiralty, your letter of the 16th instant [No. 318] desiring to have the seven men named in the margin[1] discharged out of His Majesty's ship the *Fougeux* into the *Prince George* and am commanded by their Lordships to acquaint you that when Captain [James] Douglas arrives at Portsmouth you may settle it with him, as their Lordships do not doubt but he will discharge them agreeable to your desire.

350. *To Jane Rodney*

[TNA, PRO 30/20/20/2, pp. 41–2]　　　　　　　18 February 1755

My dearest Jenny perceives I cannot pass a post without letting her hear from me. I hope my last gave her no uneasiness as it is owing to a demur whether the *Royal George* shall be commissioned or not. However, I hope soon to hear they are come to a resolution that I may make haste to see my dear girl and her boys for I really think it an age since I had that happiness. You must if possible only conclude that I have been thus long absent on a visit to my uncle as you have heard all young married people should sometimes pay that visit in order to make their company the more agreeable when they meet again. If you will only ask your father he will tell you it is sometimes necessary.

Tell my dear Kitty I have desired George Medley[2] to give her a kiss for me the next time he sees her, but I suppose she won't thank him for a brother's kiss which wants something of the warmth with which a lover bestows his, and he will be a silly dog if he don't kiss for himself when he has it in his power. Tell her that next to yourself I wish her happier than all the world besides and to see her so will greatly contribute to my own. Kiss my dear little boys and be sure don't let Georgy forget me, and let him know I shall be very angry if he don't rejoice and clap his hand when he sees me.

---

[1] See No. 348.
[2] George Medley of Buxted Place, Sussex; a wine merchant in Portugal and then MP for Seaford, 1768–80.

351. *To Clevland*

[TNA, ADM 1/2384] *Prince George*
25 February 1755

Sir,
As there is no master of arms as yet appointed for His Majesty's ship under my command I must beg leave to recommend Mr. John Allen for that office who has been many years a corporal in the guards.

352. *To Clevland*

[TNA, ADM 1/2384] *Prince George* Portsmouth Harbour
20 March 1755

Sir,
Whereas Lieutenant [James] Allan of His Majesty's ship under my command who attends the rendezvous in town has acquainted me that he has expended all the impress money allowed for His Majesty's ship *Prince George*, I must therefore desire you will please to acquaint their Lordships therewith, and hope they will please to grant an order for a further supply.

353. *From Clevland*

[TNA, ADM 2/700, pp. 516–17] 21 March 1755

I have communicated to my Lords Commissioners of the Admiralty your letter of the 20th instant [No. 352] acquainting them that the money impressed to Lieutenant Allan for the service of raising men is all expended, and desiring that he may be supplied with a farther sum. In return to which I am commanded by their Lordships to acquaint you they have directed the Navy Board to impress £20 more to him for carrying on the said service which will be also charged to you.

354. *To Clevland*

[TNA, ADM 1/2384] *Prince George* Portsmouth Harbour
27 March 1755

Sir,
I received a letter from Lieutenant Allan of His Majesty's ship under my command who attends the rendezvous in town, complaining that

the money for that service has been some time expended, and that upon his inquiry at the Navy Office for the twenty pounds their Lordships were pleased to order him last [No. 353], he cannot find that order has been as yet sent to the Navy Office.

I must desire you will please to acquaint their Lordships that we are now getting in our guns, and hope His Majesty's ship under my command will be ready by Saturday or Sunday to proceed to Spithead.

355. *From Clevland*

[TNA, ADM 2/701, p. 41] 29 March 1755

Sir,

In return to your letter of the 27th instant [No. 354] I send you this to acquaint you that my Lords Commissioners of the Admiralty have been pleased to order you an imprest of £20 for the better carrying on the service of raising men, which upon Lieutenant Allan's application to the Navy Board will be paid to him.

356. *To Clevland*

[TNA, ADM 1/2384] *Prince George* Portsmouth Harbour
31 March 1755

Sir,

As there has no master at arms as yet appeared[1] for His Majesty's ship under my command, and as their Lordships are no strangers to the usefulness of that officer to instruct the men in the use of the small arms, I hope they will please to appoint one.

357. *From Clevland*

[TNA, ADM 2/701, p. 56] 1 April 1755

Sir,

Lieutenant Allan of His Majesty's ship under your command, having applied to my Lords Commissioners of the Admiralty to grant him a further sum of money for the better carrying on the service of raising men, I am commanded by their Lordships to acquaint you therewith

---

[1] See No. 351.

and that they have ordered £20 more to be imprested to you for that service.[1]

358. To Clevland

[TNA, ADM 1/2384] *Prince George* Spithead
8 April 1755

Sir,

I must desire you will please to acquaint their Lordships that His Majesty's ship under my command sailed out of the harbour this morning and is now moored at Spithead.

359. From Clevland

[TNA, ADM 2/701, p. 151] 19 April 1755

Sir,

I have received and read to my Lords Commissioners of the Admiralty your letter of the 17th instant, desiring that you may have leave to enter the twelve men therein named on your ship's books, and am commanded by their Lordships to acquaint you that the said men are wanted for ships designed on immediate service.

360. From Clevland

[TNA, ADM 2/701, p. 157] 21 April 1755

Sir,

Mr. Joseph Arrowsmith, a supernumerary on board His Majesty's ship under your command, turned over from the *Jason*, having applied to my Lords Commissioners of the Admiralty to be entered on your ship's books for preferment,[2] it is their Lordships' direction that you do enter him on her books provided you can make him mate.

---

[1] See Nos. 352–5.
[2] Joseph Arrowsmith was commissioned a lieutenant on 6 May 1757.

361. To Clevland

[TNA, ADM 1/2384]

Prince George at Spithead
28 April 1755

Sir,
I must acknowledge the receipt of seven press warrants of the 22nd instant.

362. To Clevland

[TNA, ADM 1/2384]

Prince George
30 April 1755

Sir,
Having been educated under Mr. Ichabod Harding in the different branches of the mathematics, I cannot refuse his earnest request in giving him a testimomal to their Lordships of the character I have known him bear, for sixteen years past, part of which time I have sailed in the same ship with him.

I must beg leave to assure their Lordships that Mr. Harding was remarkable for his diligence, sobriety, and keeping a proper discipline among the young gentlemen entrusted to his care, being himself an example to them of morality, patience, and even temper, and has always been so happy as to gain the esteem of every officer under whom he has served.

363. From Clevland

[TNA, ADM 2/701, p. 302]

22 May 1755

Sir,
Lieutenant Allan of His Majesty's ship under your command, having applied to my Lords Commissioners of the Admiralty for a further supply of money to enable him to raise men in town. And, their Lordships having directed the Navy Board to imprest £20 more to you for that purpose, I am commanded to acquaint you therewith.

364. *To Clevland*

[TNA, ADM 1/2384] *Prince George* at Spithead
26 May 1755

Sir,

I am to own receipt of your letter of the 24th instant acquainting me that Lieutenant Allan of His Majesty's ship *Prince George* under my command has applied to their Lordships for a farther supply of money. I must desire you will represent to their Lordships that Lieutenant Allan is now of but little use to His Majesty's ship under my command, as but few men for this month past are come to the ship. And if their Lordships have no objection, I shall be glad they will give me leave to order him with the gang down to the ship, as I can employ them here more efficaciously.

I must beg leave to take notice to their Lordships, that I bear on my books upwards of 600 men, but the reason of mustering so few at present, they were taken from me to complete the squadrons that are lately sailed, but am in hopes that by the assistance of my two tenders to be manned soon.

365. *From Clevland*

[TNA, ADM 2/701, p. 347] 3 June 1755

Sir,

I have received and read to my Lords Commissioners of the Admiralty your letter [No. 264] of the 26th instant, desiring that your lieutenant employed at the rendezvous in town may be ordered on board His Majesty's ship under your command, and send this to acquaint you the regulating captains are directed to order him to break up his rendezvous and repair with his gang on board her.

366. *To Clevland*

[TNA, ADM 1/2384] *Prince George* at Spithead
7 July 1755

Sir,

Whereas my accounts for His Majesty's ship *Fougeux* have passed the proper offices and a general certificate has been granted by the Navy Board, I must desire you will move their Lordships that they will be pleased to grant an order for the payment of my wages for the time I commanded the said ship.

367. *To Clevland*

[TNA, ADM 1/2384]   10 July 1755

Sir,

In case my first Lieutenant Mr. [John] Hatch should be removed into some other ship, I shall take it as a particular favour if you can procure Mr. John Hawford to be appointed second Lieutenant of the *Prince George*. He is now upon half pay and if commissioned will come in agreeable to his rank.

Memorandum

Captain Rodney begs it as the greatest favour that Mr. Hatch his first lieutenant may be put into some other ship and Lieutenant Edward Clark appointed his first lieutenant.

NB Lieutenant Clark is second lieutenant of the *Prince George*.

368. *From Clevland*

[TNA, ADM 2/701, p. 496]   15 July 1755

Sir,

I have communicated to my Lords Commissioners of the Admiralty your letter of the 7th instant, desiring that your wages for the *Fougeux* may be paid, and am to acquaint you that your request cannot be complied with at present.

369. *From the Lords of the Admiralty*

[TNA, ADM 2/75, p. 287]   16 July 1755

You are hereby required and directed to put yourself under the command of Sir Edward Hawke, Vice Admiral of the White, and follow his orders for your farther proceedings.

370. *To Jane Rodney*

[TNA, PRO 30/20/20/2, pp. 65–8] Off Cape Finisterre on the
coast of Spain
3 August 1755

I take the opportunity by one of our small ships that goes for Plymouth tomorrow morning to tell my dearest Jenny that thank God I am very well, but not in the least satisfied with being at sea, as to my great mortification I have seen several French ships which politely put themselves in our possession but it seems our orders would not allow us to detain them. For my part I don't understand this method of proceeding for I imagine the people of England expect that this noble fleet has sailed with an intention of distressing France, but they will find themselves deceived in their imagination when they hear that we let the French trade pass by us unmolested. What could the French possibly desire more of us, for certainly they will not be such fools to let their ships of war come near us, especially as they must certainly know our great superiority and that that superiority is not employed to distress them in the most sensitive part viz. their trade. However now I am at sea I hope they will send us proper orders for I desire not to have been sent of a fool's errand – so much for sea news. I must now enquire about what more nearly and tenderly concerns myself which is of the welfare of my dear girl and dear little ones. I was a stranger even to myself in what I should feel in being absent from them, but I can most sincerely assure you, both waking and sleeping you are ever in my mind and present yourselves to my imagination as the dearest blessings heaven could bestow upon me. Supremely happy should I be if I could be assured you was in health and bear my absence with that resignation which your virtue and education should indicate to you. Trust, my Jenny, in providence and depend upon that being who has so often conducted me with safety through so many perils and brought me to the highest pitch of human happiness by bestowing on me a women of virtue and one that I love preferable to the whole world besides. Kiss my dear babies and pray take care that Georgy don't forget to know me when I arrive which I think cannot be long as I certainly think they will not keep these great ships out above a month longer. Make yourself easy in regard to the French fleet for you may depend they will take care to avoid us by keeping in port and not run the risk of their six ships to our sixteen. I send this to Bourne[1] in hopes you are there but have

---

[1] The residence of Jane Rodney's father, Compton House, Eastbourne.

sent another to Alresford for fear this might miscarry. Remember me to all friends...

371. *To Jane Rodney*

PRO, PRO 30/20/20/2, pp. 69–71]

Off Cape Finisterre on the coast of Spain
3 August 1755

As you promised me my dearest Jenny to go to Bourne I have enclosed my letters to your father,[1] but in case any thing has prevented your going there, that you may sooner hear from me I send this letter to Alresford as a duplicate [No. 370] of that [I] wrote to Bourne. I flatter myself that you and my dear little ones are well and what makes me more solicitous in thinking you are so, is that my thoughts sleeping and waking are continually employed in flattering myself that I see and hear you, which to me is supreme happiness. Take care of yourself and my dear boys and remember that I expect not only yourself but that they are more than ordinarily pleased when they see me, which I think cannot be long as our orders are not to touch the French merchant ships, several of whom have passed through our fleet unmolested. And as for their men of war I think there is not the least probability that they will be so foolish to put themselves in our way especially when we have sixteen ships to their six. So that I am likely to have gone to sea to pretty purpose and lose the pleasantest month of the year at Alresford. Though I must say it is very hot w[h]ere I am at present but you know I love sunshine weather and Spain or Portugal was always my favourite country. I hope you received my letter that I wrote to you off Plymouth and I shall long to hear that you are easy in mind and find yourself happy at Bourne and that Georgy does not take the liberty of doing his occasions in every room of the house to your great disgrace and to the offence of the good company. Tell the young rogue if I hear any complaints I shall certainly exert my authority and confine him to his nursery when he longs to [go] abroad. I know when you read this you will call me [an] old fool and say to yourself that it is I spoil him most and am most foolishly fond of him and that I have no business to trouble my head about him till he is ten years old.

My love to Kitty and all at Bourne and tell her I shall be very angry if I don't hear she is on the brink of matrimony. Adieu my dearest.

[1] Rodney's father in law, Hon. Charles Compton (1698–1755), MP for Nottingham, 9 Dec. 1754–20 Nov. 1755.

372. From Hawke

[TNA, PRO 30/20/6]

St. George at sea
4 August 1755

You are hereby required and directed in case of separation to endeavour by all means in your power to seize and take, as well all French ships of war you shall be able to cope with, as privateers and merchant vessels that you may meet with during your absence from me, and with them make the best of your way to join me on the station prescribed in the sealed rendezvous you receive herewith taking particular care that the stores and effects on board such ships and vessels as you may take be put under the charge of a discreet officer and that no plunder or embezzlement be made of them and that their officers and crews be treated with all possible civility for which this shall be your orders.

373. To Jane Rodney

[TNA, PRO 30/20/20/2, pp. 73–4]

Prince George at sea
28 August 1755

I see an English merchant ship near the fleet and while my ship is giving chase to her, I am writing to my dearest Jenny, in hopes the ship may be bound to England that you may hear I am well and much better since I have received orders to take all ships belonging to France. Had we had these orders sooner we should have been in possession of fifty sail at least. But now we have only a few but am in hopes of having many to bring in with us which I believe will be the later end of September. When if you are at Bourne I will come over to you immediately, but in case your father goes into Northamptonshire in September I should think my dear Jenny would do well to prevail upon him to spend the remainder of the winter at Alresford especially as he loves hunting and as now you can accommodate him with stabling and every convenience for servants &c.

I long to see my dearest love and her little ones and flatter myself Georgy will be able to call papa when he sees me. My Lieutenant informs me the ship is bound to England and as the admiral has made my signal I must conclude with assuring my Jenny that I am in good health and to be assured that she and my little ones was the same would be supreme happiness to him who can never be otherways than most tenderly and affectionately ever yours.

PS Pray tell your father I have not time to write as the ship goes this moment. Since I wrote last we have received orders to take all the French ships we meet with. I cannot stay out more than three weeks or a month at most.

Remember me to dear Kitty and all at Bourne and kiss my dear boys for me.

374. *To Jane Rodney*

[TNA, PRO 30/20/20/2, pp. 77–9]   *Prince George* at sea
8 September 1755

I have wrote my dear Jenny a long letter to Bourne and send this as a duplicate in case you should be returned to Alresford that you may hear from me sooner than you otherway could. Thank God I am pretty well and hope to have the happiness of seeing you so the latter end of this month as by that time I expect to be at Spithead.

We have taken several prizes of considerable value and hope we shall bring more in with us tho' many have escaped our hands in a hard gale of wind we lately had. But now the weather seems set in for fair which I hope will continue for nothing in nature is so disagreeable as bad weather at sea.

To hear my dear girl and her little ones were well would be the most charming news that could possibly come to me as I shall never think myself happy till I can for a certainty spend all my days with her undisturbed and unmolested with warships or any other thing that make the world so busy being but too certain that happiness can never be found but in company with those who love so dearly as we do. That providence may bestow this blessing upon me is my constant and daily wish which I hope will be accomplished when this bustle is abated. Adieu my dearest love and rest assured that you are ever in the thoughts and heart of him who can never be otherways than your most tender and affectionate husband and lover.

[PS] Kiss my dear little ones and take care of your own health.

375. *To Jane Rodney*

[TNA, PRO 30/20/20/2, pp. 81–4]

Prince George
14 September 1755

I take the opportunity by some more prizes that we send in to return my dearest Jenny thanks for her kind letters, which came to me about two days ago, as it is very seldom we have ships join us from England. And indeed it is no easy matter for them to find us, in case they are sent on that errand, as we are never in the same station for any time. Your letters gave me the greatest and sincerest pleasure as by them I was assured my dear girl and my dear *little ones* were well. I wish you had dwelt longer upon the subject concerning *them* as you know I dearly love to hear every thing about them. It gives me great pleasure to find that Georgy can be so entertaining and don't fear their spoiling him, especially as you are with him. Tho' I shall be angry with the young rogue if he don't speak soon. By the time you receive this you may be daily expecting my arrival for in eight or ten days at farthest we shall certainly be for making our best way to Spithead. So I wish my dear girl you would contrive to go to Alresford as soon as you can after the receipt of this letter. It would be but charitable if some of the good people of Bourne would attend you there. I should think your father might take up his residence there in order to hunt till the Parliament meets. As I suppose you expect to hear some news of the transactions of our fleet since we have received orders to make reprisals I must acquaint you that we have taken about thirty ships and daily I hope shall make captures of more if they are so obliging to come in our way. They are all sent to England and I suppose by this time war is declared that we may make our captures legal prizes.

I hope you have continued your exercise and that you have had no return of the pain in your side for to find you otherways than well will be the greatest grief that I can possibly feel. Take care therefore my dearest Jenny of yourself and be assured that the greatest blessing I can possibly know is that of meeting you and yours in health and spirits. Thank God I am perfectly well and can be never otherways than most tenderly and affectionately ever yours.

PS Remember me to dear Kitty and all at Bourne.

376. To Clevland

[TNA, ADM 1/2384]

Prince George Portsmouth Harbour
20 October 1755

Sir,
I must desire you will be pleased to acquaint their Lordships of the desertion of Mr. William Russell, a midshipman on board His Majesty's ship the *Prince George* under my command, who was put on board the *L'Austrée* a French ship at sea, to take care in bringing the said ship into harbour, which service he deserted from on the on the 4th instant. I hope their Lordships will be pleased to direct his being apprehended and tried as a deserter.[1]

PS Enclosed I have sent you a description of Mr. William Russell.[2]

377. From Clevland

[TNA, ADM 2/702, p. 333]

21 October 1755

Sir,
I have read to my Lords Commissioners of the Admiralty your letter of yesterday's date [No. 376] informing them that William Russell hath deserted from His Majesty's ship under your command. And I am to acquaint you that the marshal of the Admiralty is directed to apprehend him.

378. To Clevland

[TNA, ADM 1/2384]

Prince George
13 November 1755

Sir,
I must desire that you will please to move their Lordships to grant me a months' leave of absence in order to go to Bath. They may depend upon my being ready at a moment's warning to return to my duty.

---

[1] See also No. 399.
[2] Mr. William Russell is a thick well set man of a dark brown complexion (inclinable to be swarthy), about 5' 4" high, wears a black wig, is about 30 years of age, and lives somewhere in Shoreditch.

379. *To Clevland*

[TNA, ADM 1/2384] [London] Grosvenor Street
1 December 1755

Sir,

I must desire you will please to make it my request to their Lordships that they will be pleased to grant me a renewal of leave to be absent from my duty for some time longer, the being appointed guardian to two young gentlemen of considerable fortunes makes this request necessary, in order to have time to settle their affairs.[1]

380. *To Clevland*

[TNA, ADM 1/2385] [London] Grosvenor Street
2 January 1756

Sir,

As the business that brought me to town is of great consequence to two young gentlemen, and will take up some time longer before it can be finished, I hope their Lordships will be so good to take it into their consideration, and in case it will not be detrimental to His Majesty's service that they will be pleased to grant me a longer leave of absence from the ship I command.

381. *From Clevland*

[TNA, ADM 2/703, p. 153] 7 January 1756

Sir,

Having read to my Lords Commissioners of the Admiralty your letter [No. 380] of the 2nd instant desiring longer leave to be absent from your duty on your private affairs, I am commanded to acquaint you that their Lordships are pleased to give you ten days further leave.

---

[1] On 20 November 1755 Rodney's father-in-law, Hon. Charles Compton, died and Rodney was the sole executor of his will as well as the guardian of Charles and Spencer Compton, two under age brothers-in-law.

382. *To Clevland*

[TNA, ADM 1/2385] [13 January 1756]

Sir,

As I constantly correspond with the officers on board His Majesty's ship under my command, that I may the better be acquainted with her state and condition – and as Captain [Claud] Hamilton had made it his request that I would consent to his being absent a few days on business of consequence, good nature induced me to comply with his request as I imagined he might be at his duty again within the limited time. However, as I find it does not meet with their Lordships' approbation, I am very sorry I complied with his request and shall take care for the future not to grant any officer to be absent without leave from their Lordships.

383. *To Clevland*

[TNA, ADM 1/2385] London
13 January 1756

Sir,

As my accounts for His Majesty's ship the *Fougeux* have been passed a long time and the general certificates been granted I therefore pray you will move their Lordships to grant an order that I may be paid my own and servant's wages for the said ship.

384. *To Clevland*

[TNA, ADM 1/2385] London
16 January 1756

Sir,

As the only motive that induced me to apply to their Lordships to be absent from my duty at this critical conjuncture was the being appointed sole executor, by the last will and testament of the late Hon. Charles Compton and likewise guardian to his sons, which trust I have endeavoured to execute with all the dispatch the nature of such an affair would admit, but finding it impossible to finish these sort of affairs so soon as I could wish and that some time longer will be necessary before I can so dispose of the personal effects as to enable me to pay the fortunes left by Mr. Compton to his younger children, I hope their

Lordships upon these considerations, and that His Majesty's ship under my command (from her want of men) is in no immediate readiness for the sea, will be pleased to lengthen my leave of absence, if His Majesty's service will admit thereof.

385. *From Clevland*

PRO, ADM 2/703, p. 206] 16 January 1756

Sir,

Having read to my Lords Commissioners of the Admiralty your letter of this date [No. 384], desiring longer leave to be absent from your duty on your private affairs, I am commanded to acquaint you, that their Lordships are pleased to extend the same for 14 days longer.

386. *From Clevland*

[TNA, ADM 2/703, p. 272] 30 January 1756

Sir,

I am commanded by my Lords Commissioners of the Admiralty to signify their direction to you to give Mr. Thomas Hayward on board His Majesty's ship under your command 14 days leave to come to town in order to pass his examination for a lieutenant.[1]

387. *From Clevland*

[TNA, ADM 2/703, p. 276] 31 January 1756

Sir,

I am commanded by my Lords Commissioners of the Admiralty to acquaint you that they are pleased to extend your leave of absence from your duty for 14 days longer.

---

[1] See also Nos. 399 and 424.

388. From Clevland

[TNA, ADM 2/703, p. 306]   7 February 1756

Sir,

I am commanded by my Lords Commissioners of the Admiralty to signify their directions to you forthwith to repair to your duty on board the *Prince George*, notwithstanding the leave given you may not be expired.

389. To the Duke of Newcastle[1]

[TNA, ADM 1/2385]   *Prince George* at Portsmouth
                                                         12 February 1756

My Lord,

Having repaired to my duty conformable to the order I received to that purpose [No. 388], and not having as yet completed the trust reposed in me by the late Mr Compton, obliges me to trouble your grace, and to beg your influence with the Board of Admiralty, that in case His Majesty's service will permit, I may be granted leave of absence till the 8th of March, by which time I shall have completed the affairs relative to my trust, and likewise have removed the young gentleman[2] entrusted to my care from the council of those, whose advice can only tend to delude his mind and make him prove a bad subject and troublesome neighbour.

I must beg leave to refer your Grace to Mr. [Robert] Andrews[3] for further particulars, and that you will permit me to assure you of my firm and sincere attachment to your Grace's interests.

390. From Newcastle

[TNA, PRO 30/20/20/4, p. 23]   Newcastle House
                                                         13 February 1756

Dear Sir,

I have the favour of your letter [No. 384]. I have this morning desired Mr. Clevland to explain the affair so to my Lord Anson that I dare say

---

[1]Thomas Pelham-Holles, 1st Duke of Newcastle, First Lord of the Treasury, 18 March 1745–15 Nov. 1756; 2 July 1757–28 May 1762.
[2]Charles Compton.
[3]The Compton family lawyer.

you will immediately receive leave to come to town for the purposes you propose, and which are so well designed for the service of the King and His Majesty's government. I am extremely sensible of your goodness to me and of the constant zeal for the King's service. I most sincerely wish you success in your endeavour but the sooner that Mr. [Charles] Compton can be prevailed upon to go abroad the better.

391. From Clevland

[TNA, ADM 2/703, pp. 330–1] 14 February 1756

Sir,

It being represented to my Lords Commissioners of the Admiralty that you have some private affairs of consequence to transact in town which requires your attendance, I am commanded by their Lordships to acquaint you that if they are so very pressing they will dispense with your being absent from your duty for 14 days longer, which leave Sir Edward Hawke is directed to give you on your application to him for the same.

392. To Clevland

[TNA, ADM 1/2385] *Prince George*
14 March 1756

Sir,

You may remember when I spoke to you to get Mr. [James] Logie appointed first lieutenant of the *Prince George*, you informed me that my Lord Anson intended providing better for him shortly, but as the *Lancaster* of which his is first lieutenant is now under orders for the Mediterranean, I hope and entreat you will be so obliging to remind Lord Anson that Mr. Logie has been many years a lieutenant of unblemished character and had once the honour to command the *Nottingham* for three months upon Captain Saumarez[1] being killed in the battle of October 1747. As the going into the Mediterranean in a private ship may be detrimental to the preferment Lord Anson has given him hopes of obtaining, and being sensible of the regard you must have for a good officer, [I] hope you will contrive that Mr. Logie may not be sent to a place far from the hopes of obtaining that preferment which his merits deserves. At the same time that I take the liberty of reminding you how happy I should

---

[1] Captain Philip Saumarez, killed in action 14 October 1747.

have thought myself in having so good a first officer, I must acquaint you that Mr. Logie is far from declining to go where ever their Lordships are pleased to command him.[1]

393. To Clevland

[TNA, ADM 1/2385] *Prince George* at Spithead
3 April 1756

Sir,

Enclosed[2] I have sent you a description of John Bridgar Allen coxswain of His Majesty's ship *Prince George* under my command lately deserted. I hope their Lordships will be pleased to direct his being apprehended as a deserter.

394. From Clevland

[TNA, ADM 2/704, p. 126] 6 April 1756

Sir,

I have communicated to my Lords Commissioners of the Admiralty your letter of the 3rd instant [No. 393] enclosing the description of John Bridgar Allen, your coxswain, who is a deserter. I am commanded by their Lordships to acquaint you that they have sent the same to Rear Admiral Holburne[3] and directed him to cause him to be searched for and apprehended.

395. From Clevland

[TNA, ADM 2/704, p. 128] 6 April 1756

Sir,

I have communicated to my Lords Commissioners of the Admiralty your letter [No. 376] of the 2nd instant representing that William Russell,

---

[1] This appeal was successful for on 23 March 1756 James Logie was promoted to master and commander.
[2] Not enclosed.
[3] Rear Admiral Francis Holburne, Vice Admiral, 24 Feb. 1757; Admiral, 5 Aug. 1767. In 1756 Holburne was third in command of the Western Squadron and then in 1757 he commanded the naval forces on the expedition intended to attack Louisburg and which was diverted instead to Halifax, Nova Scotia. Returning to England Holburne was appointed Commander-in-chief at Portsmouth, a position he held, with several breaks, for the next eight years.

a deserter from His Majesty's ship under your command, had been apprehended and sent back on board your ship and desiring that he may be tried for the same at a court martial. And I am commanded by their Lordships to acquaint you that [Vice] Admiral [Henry] Osborn is directed to try him accordingly.

396. *From Anson*

[TNA, PRO 30/20/4, pp. 27–8]   Admiralty
30 April 1756

Dear Sir,
I was favoured with your letter giving me an account of your arrival at Spithead. As I had no opportunity of seeing you I gave Captain [John] Campbell a commission to execute for me at Boulogne, so that I shall have no occasion for the favour you offer me and for which I am very much obliged. I heartily wish you health and all kinds of prosperity in your voyage. If any vacancy in Parliament happens in your absence, I will not fail to remind your friends of you.[1]

397. *To Clevland*

[TNA, ADM 1/2385]   *Prince George* Spithead
3 May 1756

Sir,
I must desire you will please to make it my request to their Lordships that they will be so good to indulge me with the discharge of the men namely in the enclosed list,[2] to be removed with me into the *Monarch*. I flatter myself when their Lordships recollect that the *Prince George* was manned without any assistance from any admiral and by my officers only, they will comply with this request and as it will likewise be the means of my getting the *Monarch* sooner manned.

---

[1] Rodney in the general election of 1754 unsuccessfully stood for election, supported by the Bedford interest, for a seat in the House of Commons to represent Camelford. He would not again be in the House of Commons until 1759.

[2] Enclosed is a list of 20 mostly petty officers and midshipmen.

398. From Clevland

[TNA, ADM 2/704, pp. 331–2]　　　　　　　　　　　　　　8 May 1756

Sir,

My Lords Commissioners of the Admiralty directed Captain Knight of the *Wolf* sloop to proceed to Spithead, and take upon him the command of the *Prince George* and carry her to Plymouth from whence she is to proceed to the Mediterranean. I am commanded by their Lordships to signify their directions to you to use all possible dispatch in fitting and getting her ready to proceed to Plymouth the moment Captain Knight arrives.

399. To Clevland

[TNA, ADM 1/2385]　　　　　　　　　　　　　　　　　　Portsmouth
　　　　　　　　　　　　　　　　　　　　　　　　　　　17 May 1756

Sir,

Whereas Mr. Thomas Haywood,[1] master's mate of the *Prince George* late under my command, has made application to be removed with me into the *Monarch*, I hope their Lordships will please to comply with his request.

400. To Clevland

[TNA, ADM 1/2385]　　　　　　　　　　　　　　　　*Monarch* at Hamoaze
　　　　　　　　　　　　　　　　　　　　　　　　　　　26 May 1756

Sir,

I must desire you will please to acquaint their Lordships that this day I have got in the masts of His Majesty's ship under my command and in case I could procure men she should be ready for sea in a very short time. However, their Lordships may depend upon my using my utmost endeavours to procure as many as I possibly can, and as several men that belonged to the *Prince George*, which were lent to the *Northumberland* last cruise, are now here, I hope their Lordships, in consideration that the said men were raised by me and are very desirous to serve under my command, that they will be so good to indulge me with them as it will greatly enable me to raise others and sooner get the *Monarch*

---

[1] See also Nos. 386 and 424.

fit for sea. I must beg leave to take notice that many of them are at sick quarters here.

401. *To Jane Rodney*

[TNA, PRO 30/20/20/2, pp. 99–101] 1 June 1756

My Dearest love,

As Admiral Mostyn[1] is sailed and the whole business of this port is fallen upon me as commanding officer, it is as much as I can possibly do, to find time to write this short letter to my dearest Jenny, who is ever upper most in my thoughts and nearest my heart. I hope you have had my two letters that I have wrote since being here and that my two dear babies are in health and spirits.

I have this day received a most polite letter from Mr. Blunt about Alresford pond. As it is so very much for my interest to have the pond I cannot answer it to myself or children not to purchase it, especially as the reeds only will pay me the interest of money and I may never again have such an opportunity. Besides when we have [it] we may have frequent opportunities of showing our mercy, in not suffering the poor birds to be shot at – not to mention the opportunity of always having what fish we please.

Pray send the letters to Mr. Duthy and order him to make the agreement immediately.

Let me hear from you my Jenny when time will permit and be assured of the affection of him who is ever most tenderly yours.

PS Remember me to all with you.

PS Send me some franks.

402. *To Clevland*

[TNA, ADM 1/2385] *Monarch* at Hamoaze
1 June 1756

Sir,

Being the senior officer at present in this port, I think it my duty to acquaint their Lordships that Rear Admiral Mostyn with the squadron under his command sailed this morning, with a southerly wind and

---

[1]Rear Admiral Savage Mostyn, second in command of the Western Squadron.

moderate weather. At eleven this evening the wind veered to the westward about which time the Admiral was seen off the Sound standing to the southward. I am sorry to acquaint their Lordships that a snow from Antigua is this moment arrived, the master of whom reports that the *Warwick*[1] is certainly taken, the packet he brought for their Lordships is sent by this post.

I shall use the utmost dispatch in getting His Majesty's ship under my command ready for sea, and will take every opportunity of raising men for that purpose.

403. *From Thomas Angel*

[TNA, ADM 1/2385] *Monarch* in Hamoaze
3 June 1756

Sir,
I beg leave to inform you that I have been thirty five years in the service, twenty two of which I have been a boatswain, and am now sixty seven years of age and I find my memory and eye sight much impaired besides I am sometimes six weeks together afflicted with the gout, all which renders me quite incapable of going through the present necessary fatigue of a boatswain. I therefore humbly beg you will be pleased to get me superannuated.

404. *To Clevland*

[TNA, ADM 1/2385] *Monarch* in Hamoaze
4 June 1756

Sir,
I am to acquaint you that last night I received a packet, with your letter of 20th past to Rear Admiral Mostyn, to send Mr Edward Powell, chaplain of the *Rochester*, to Portsmouth for his warrant for the *Medway*, but she being sailed the 1st instant, the same could not be complied with. I am likewise to own the receipt of their Lordships' orders of the 31st May, wherein His Majesty has been pleased to direct, that any English vessels seized and detained in consequence of their order of the 3rd March past should be released and agreeable thereto have this day signified His Majesty's pleasure to the respective captains of His Majesty's ships and vessels in this port. I have also their Lordships' order to

---

[1] HMS *Warwick* was captured by the French *L'Atlante* off Martinique.

Captain [Alexander] Innes of the *Otter* sloop concerning the release of the *John* of Cork, Thomas MacDonald master from Rochford, detained by him, but as he is not on the spot, shall make enquiry and release the said vessel if I find her to be here. I have delivered their Lordships' orders and rendezvous to Captain [Thomas] Hanway of the *Weymouth* who is now under sail and turning out of the Sound. You will please also to signify that in obedience to their Lordships' commands I have made enquiry into the complaint alleged by Captain Webb, commanding the detachment of marines on board his Majesty's ship *Vanguard*, that they were very ill, for want of the common necessaries of life, and the reason he gives for such complaint being made by him to Colonel [James] Patterson,[1] the commanding officer of marines, is that the men could not be supplied with slops as there were none in store, and if there had, he presumes four shillings per month would have been insufficient for that purpose, as it would not find them in shoes alone. Therefore, he thought by his acquainting Colonel Patterson therewith the marines might be better supplied for the future, but that such which are now come from the store are supplied, and that Captain [Hon. John] Byron always complied with the instructions relative to the slopping the marines when application was made to him for that purpose.

I have received your letter of the 1st addressed to Admiral Mostyn, relating to John Pole, a deserter from the marines, and that to George Duncan belonging to the *Northumberland* who is sailed from this place.

Yesterday noon arrived in the Sound His Majesty's ship *Eagle* with a prize from the westward and this morning came in His Majesty's ship *Falmouth* who is now come up into Hamoaze.

I herewith send you the state and condition of His Majesty's ships and vessels in this place and the Sound where remain His Majesty's ships *Eagle* and *Windsor*.[2]

405. *To Jane Rodney*

[TNA, PRO 30/20/20/2, pp. 103–04]

Monarch
6 June 1756

Express upon express give me but just time to acknowledge the receipt of my dearest Jenny's kind letters. Some gave me great uneasiness as you had not received my letters notwithstanding I had wrote

---

[1] A major general in the army.
[2] Enclosed is a list of 13 ships showing the number of men and the amount of provisions on each vessel.

every post since I came here. However, yours today made me easy on that score. I have much on my head as the whole fitting of the fleet at this port depends upon me at present as commanding officer. The *Monarch* is almost ready but I want four hundred men. I hope tomorrow to be able to write a long letter. At present I can only say that I am in good health. Kiss my dear boys, give my love to all with you, take care of yourself and believe me to be ever most affectionately my dearest Jenny ever yours.

PS I don't believe a word of the French news concerning Mr. Byng.[1]

406. *To Clevland*

[TNA, ADM 1/2385] *Monarch* in Hamoaze
6 June 1756

Sir,

I am to acquaint you that I have received your several letters dated the 2nd and 3rd of this instant to Rear Admiral Mostyn and to the commanding officer here. I find it is their Lordships' directions, that the one hundred and twenty five men, which Vice Admiral Osborn has put on board the *Duke*, to sail her to this place, belonging to the *Prince*, must be returned back, together with such other of her men which are lent to the *Vanguard*, *Northumberland* and *Falmouth* by the first opportunity, and in consequence thereof, I have given orders to the *Vanguard* to leave as many of her men behind, as they can conveniently spare without detriment to His Majesty's service, by hindering her proceeding immediately to sea. And also given orders to the *Lyme* to discharge those six she has on board before she goes from hence.

I am to desire that you will please to signify to their Lordships, that as several of the frigates in this port have no marines, and there being a great want of seamen to carry on the service, I have given directions that proper detachments may be embarked on board them agreeable to the regulations and instructions I have received on that head, by which means these frigates will go to sea with their full complement of men. And in the number of seamen they discharge in lieu of the marines will

---

[1] Vice Admiral Hon. John Byng was sent to the Mediterranean with a squadron to defend Gibraltar and Minorca. On 20 May 1756, he fought a tactically inconclusive action with the French after which he withdrew to Gibraltar to repair his damaged ships. Blamed for the subsequent loss of Minorca, Byng was court martialled and found guilty of negligence. Although recommended to mercy, Byng was shot, on 14 March 1757, on the quarter deck of HMS *Monarch* in Portsmouth Harbour.

be included those they have lent, and such which they have put sick on shore, all which are to return to the *Monarch* there to remain until their Lordships' pleasure shall be known.

Captain Byron of the *Vanguard* having acquainted me that the surgeon's first and third mates of the said ship are dead, the second dangerously ill on shore, I have ordered Captain [William] Brett of the *Falmouth* who is come to clean, to lend him a surgeon's mate which I hope will not be disapproved.

His Majesty's ship under my command being without a carpenter, in case their Lordships should not have appointed one, I beg leave to recommend Mr Joseph Fabin of the *Newcastle* to be removed into her, and as I have no master at arms, should be glad to have Mr. Robert Caster now corporal on board the *Monarch* to be appointed in that station.

I must desire you will acquaint their Lordships that this day the *Vanguard* and *Arundel* sailed into the Sound and remain there with the *Eagle* and *Windsor*, the former of which has not as yet had a wind to bring her into the Hamoaze.

With the few men their Lordships was pleased to grant me from the *Prince George*, and what I have raised since being here, the *Monarch* is now completely rigged, and (men excepted) is in all respects as ready for the sea as any ship in this port, and I shall use my best endeavours to get her manned as soon as possible.

Their Lordships may depend upon my using the utmost dispatch, while I am commanding officer, in getting the ships ready for the sea, and by the time they receive this letter, I hope the *Lyme*, *Ludlow Castle*, and *Sheerness* will be in the Sound.

I hope their Lordships will approve of my completing the frigates with marines as thereby a number of seamen will accrue to the service.

407. *To Hon. Richard Edgcumbe*[1]

[TNA, ADM 1/2385]

Monarch
6 June 1756

Dear Sir,

Having application made to me by Cannon Snow to take his nephew Mr. John Snow as chaplain to the *Monarch*, be so good to get him appointed.

[1]MP for Penryn, 1745–22 Nov. 1758; Lord of the Admiralty, 29 Dec. 1755–17 Nov. 1758; created 2nd Baron Edgcumbe 22 November 1758.

We are all under the utmost astonishment on account of Mr. Byng's squadron, but I hope by the time this reaches you, the French account will be contradicted and that he has returned to the charge and defeated the French fleet.

408. *To Clevland*

[TNA, ADM 1/2385]

Monarch in Hamoaze
8 June 1756

Sir,

I am to beg you will be pleased to lay before their Lordships, the enclosed letter [No. 403] from the boatswain of His Majesty's ship under my command. I must assure their Lordships I have enquired into the matter and find the facts he alleges to be true, and that he appears to be incapable of doing his duty. I must also observe that he has been a good officer in his station, which I hope will recommend him to their Lordships' consideration.

I must desire you will please to inform their Lordships, that yesterday Sergeant Priest of Colonel Anstruther's[1] Regiment, apprehended two seamen belonging to the *Sheerness*, who had left the boatswain upon duty, and having secured and delivered the men to me, I granted a certificate to the said serjeant for obtaining the customary reward, and although he presented it twice to the clerk of the cheque at this port, who notwithstanding he knew I was the commanding officer, absolutely refused paying the said reward, unless he had a certificate from the captain of the ship with their numbers as inserted on the books. I must beg leave to infer that if persons who take up deserters meet with these obstacles for want of such a form being complied with, it may be a great hindrance to the service, as the captains of the ships may be in the Sound, sailed, or otherwise absent upon duty, and yesterday it blowing so very hard, it was improbable he could get to Captain [Thomas] Graves for a certificate, and was thereby hindered from returning to his duty.

Yesterday morning arrived here His Majesty's sloop *Otter* from Ireland, and came into the Sound. For these last forty eight hours, it has blown very hard with thick weather, and still continues. Remains in the Sound His Majesty's ships *Eagle*, *Vanguard*, and *Arundel*.

---

[1] Lieutenant General Philip Anstruther, colonel of the 26th Regiment of Foot.

409. To Clevland

[TNA, ADM 1/2385]
Monarch in Hamoaze
11 June 1756

Sir,
I have received your letter of the 7th instant wherein it is their Lordships' directions that His Majesty's ships *Eagle*, *Falmouth*, and *Sheerness* be cleaned and refitted with all possible dispatch. I am to desire you will please to signify to them that the *Eagle* for want of a wind, is not yet come into Hamoaze, the *Falmouth* is now out of the dock and will be ready in a few days, the *Lyme* sails tomorrow to join Vice Admiral Boscawen, and the *Sheerness* on Monday.

I have received their Lordships' orders with respect to the putting men sick on shore which I shall strictly adhere to. I herewith enclose[1] for their observation the state and condition of His Majesty's ships and vessels in this port and the Sound. Yesterday afternoon sailed to the westward the *Vanguard*. Remaining in the Sound the *Windsor*, *Eagle*, *Arundel*, and *Lyme*.

Their Lordships may depend upon my using the utmost dispatch in fitting the ships for sea while I am commanding officer.

410. To Clevland

[TNA, ADM 1/2385]
Monarch in Hamoaze
13 June 1756

Sir,
Yesterday in the afternoon about 4 o'clock I received your letter of the 10th instant express, signifying to me their Lordships' directions to hasten the cleaning of His Majesty's ship *Falmouth* and get her ready with the *Ludlow Castle* as fast as possible. I am to desire you will please to inform their Lordships that agreeable thereto, I have given directions to their respective commanders to get ready with all possible dispatch. The *Falmouth* who is out of the dock will be fit in every respect by Thursday and the *Ludlow Castle* will, (the weather permitting), be in the Sound tomorrow where so soon as she arrives, I shall immediately complete her complement of men, that she may be in every respect in a constant readiness for sailing.

---

[1]Enclosed is a list of 12 ships showing the number of men and the amount of provisons on each vessel.

His Majesty's ship the *York* is now cleaned and out of the dock, but the weather has been so rainy, with winds at S and SSW, that it has in great degree retarded the fitting the several ships in this port. But you may assure their Lordships not a moment's time has been lost in the forwarding of them.

I have also your letter of the 9th by post, relating to the sending the twenty Alsatian women to Ostend, for which purpose a tender shall be in readiness for them, on the first application.

This day remains in the Sound His Majesty's ships *Windsor, Eagle, Lyme,* and *Arundel*. The *Ludlow Castle, Sheerness* and *Raven* sloop [are] ready to sail from Hamoaze when the wind will permit. Where are fitting the *Monarch, York, Falmouth,* and *Otter* sloop.

411. *To Jane Rodney*

[TNA, PRO 30/20/20/2, pp. 107–09]

Plymouth
15 June 1756

My Dearest Jenny,

The post between this place and Alresford is very perverse for on the Sunday, Monday, and Tuesday I never receive a letter from my dear girl, as I find you receive two from me at a time tho' they are wrote at two days' distance of time. I fancy they go round about to some distant place on those days which makes the letters longer a coming.

I now hope soon to go a cruise or come to Portsmouth as Lord Anson has ordered me some men by the *Duke* the moment she arrives which will be the first easterly wind as I hear she has been at St. Helens this week past. We had most terrible weather for some time past, more like November than June. But it is now more moderate tho' the wind still continues at south.

I am sorry to hear that Mr. Byng's retreat causes such confusion, hatred, and uneasiness among the great men in London. Why did they not send him with a superior force, then there would have been no doubt, but he would have obliged the enemy to retire and would have relieved Port Mahon. However, there is now a sufficient force but I am afraid the island will be entirely in the enemy's hands before they can get there.

I hope to hear in your next that my dear boys and yourself are perfectly well and that Georgy has got the better of his cold. Pray my love don't let them be out after sunset upon any account, as that is the time all children contract disorders. I hear that there are very bad sore throats going about London. When it blows cold put something about their necks. You will call me an old fool, but consider how infinitely dear yourself and they are to me.

I hope your companions are well and that Alresford is agreeable to them. Suppose after all this rain every thing will look very pleasant.

Take care of your health, keep up your spirits, and continue to love him who is with inexpressible affection ever yours.

412. *To Clevland*

[TNA, ADM 1/2385] *Monarch* in Hamoaze
15 June 1756

Sir,

Your letter of the 11th instant enclosing to me their Lordships' order for Captain Innes of the *Otter*, appointed to command the *Ludlow Castle*, to put himself under the command of Rear Admiral Brett,[1] I have received. But no order for his proceeding with her off the islands of Guernsey and Jersey. I have therefore in consequence of their Lordships' direction, signified to me, given Captain Innes an order to take upon him the command of that ship for the cruise. As also given him my direction to proceed with her, without loss of a moment's time, and join Rear Admiral Brett off the islands of Guernsey and Jersey, and to put himself under his command agreeable to their Lordships' order of the 10th instant delivered him for that purpose.

I have by this day's post received your letter of the 12th wherein it is their Lordships' direction that I should enter on board the *Monarch*, as part of her complement, the one hundred and twenty five men on board the *Duke* belonging to the *Prince*. They may be assured I shall lose no opportunity of sending to Spithead what men belonging to the *Prince* I may collect, which were on board the ships here, and you will please to acquaint them that the greatest regard was had to the *Vanguard*, going to sea with her full complement of men, which I am certain was complete before she sailed hence. I am glad their Lordships have been pleased to approve of my causing those frigates to be completed with marines which had none before as it will enable me to man the *Ludlow Castle* who is many short of complement, besides a great number put sick on shore. The winds have still continued southerly which has prevented not only the *Ludlow Castle* sailing, but likewise the rest of the ships, who have been some time in a readiness.

[1] Captain John Brett. On 4 June 1756 Brett, according to seniority, was promoted to Rear Admiral, but he refused to take up the commission and left the Royal Navy.

Their Lordships may depend the moment the weather permits, they shall be hurried away with the utmost dispatch.

Yesterday arrived in the Sound His Majesty's ship *Greyhound* where remains the *Windsor*, *Eagle*, *Arundel*, and *Lyme*.

Herewith I send you Captain [Nicholas] Vincent's account of what ships he has spoke with.[1]

413. To Jane Rodney

[TNA, PRO 30/20/20/2, pp. 111–14] Plymouth
18 June 1756

I am just now made happy by two of my dearest Jenny's letters, notwithstanding they are of different dates, which assures me there is some unaccountable contradiction in this post for I never hear from you on Monday, Tuesday or Wedesday and Thursday, as you receive two letters from me on the Wednesday when one of them ought to be with you on the Sunday.

I have the greatest satisfaction to hear that my dear Georgy has got over the rash so well. Pray my love take particular care he does not eat the green gooseberries. I could wish you would order the gardener to gather them all and forbid the maids letting him go into the kitchen garden for they are certainly very detrimental to children and will fill him full of humours.[2] I am glad my other dear boy keeps so well, and that he is likely to be so drole, but you don't tell me how they go on with their speech and whether George can say anything besides yes and no. As for Jamey I am sure he will soon get whatever the other utters. Kiss them both dearly for me and tell them I am never happy but when I am with their mother.

Nothing but rain still continues in this country. A fine day would be a great rarity, which I am not to expect while I am here, and am much grieved to think you have such bad weather at Alresford, even tho' I know it will contribute to the growth of my trees. Pray ask Betty[3] if she thinks the leaves could now be counted or whether they grow thick enough to screen any person from being seen that would steal a kiss in the wood work.

As for the wood my dear pray let all the beech be cut up for firewood, and the oak be laid all in a heap upon each other that the field

---

[1] Not enclosed.
[2] Rodney is referring to the four bodily humours (blood, phlegm, choler and melancholy).
[3] Elizabeth Compton.

may not be lumbered. In case the faggots are brought home don't let the horses go any more to the wood till the fall of the leaf as it will hurt the underwood.

I entirely approve of the purchase of the farm beyond Lanham[1] and always was told it would amount to upwards of 1,500 pounds. However, I would have you acquaint Mr. [Robert] Andrews that it is the bargain that I was so very desirous of because it joined to our estate and will bring in more interest than the stocks. The lawyer that wrote the letter is a cunning fellow and endeavoured to persuade me that he might have the advantage of drawing the writings, and then he would take care that no person should purchase the estate over my head. Therefore I would advise you not to stick out for a few pounds as the bargain will be very advantageous for us. The purchase my dear must be made in your name, therefore refer Mr. Duthy to Mr. Andrews to give him an account of it, and if possible let him secure it while he can, but in case the money is not to be paid down I will give security to pay it or interest for it, which is the same thing. Let me my dear know as soon as possible as it will make us masters of all that wood and not subject to encroachments.

I hope Betty will stay with you and Lady Egmont[2] go[ing] into Somersetshire. PS Our ministry are very quick in their superceding admirals before they know what Mr. Byng has done.

414. *To Clevland*

[TNA, ADM 1/2385] *Monarch* in Hamoaze
18 June 1756

Sir,

I have received both your letters of the 14th and 15th instant, the former of which signifies their Lordships' direction to give three weeks' leave to the surgeon's mate of the *Rupert* hospital ship which I have this day complied with.

I must desire you will please to inform their Lordships that the day before yesterday His Majesty's ships *Windsor*, *Lyme*, and *Arundel* with the trade sailed out of the Sound – and the *Eagle* and *Greyhound* came into Hamoaze. Yesterday the *Sheerness* went into the Sound, and this morning sailed from thence to the westward. The wind veering to the

---

[1]In 1756 Rodney purchased two properties, known as Pingleton and Lanham Farms, which were adjacent to his estate at Alresford.
[2]On 26 January 1756 Catherine Compton married John Perceval, 2nd Earl of Egmont.

southward prevented my getting out the *Ludlow Castle*, who is in every respect ready for sailing. And I must beg leave to observe to their Lordships, that from what she was short of complement and the number she has put sick on shore, she has taken me up sixty one men, besides forty four marines, to complete her in order for going to sea, in which number I was obliged to send fourteen men, being supernumerary belonging to other ships, having no others to put on board. The *Falmouth* and *Raven* sloop are also ready for sea, and will sail so soon as the wind will permit.

Yesterday came in here a cutter, belonging to the *Rochester*, Captain [Robert] Duff, who brings an account that he spoke with a brig from Gibraltar on the 14th, who reports he met Commodore [Robert] Brodnick[1] the ninth off the Burlings,[2] with a fresh gale of wind at north. No ships in the Sound. Herewith I send you the state and condition[3] of His Majesty's ships and vessels in this port.

[PS] Wind at SSE blows and rains hard.

415. To Clevland

[TNA, ADM 1/2385] *Monarch* in Hamoaze
20 June 1756

Sir,

I have received both your letters of the 17th instant and I find it is their Lordships' direction that the forty men belonging to the *Chichester* put sick on shore at this place, should as fast as they recover and amount to any number be sent to their ship by the first opportunity which you will please to inform them the same shall be punctually executed together with the *Somerset* and *Prince's* men, as heretofore directed to be sent around.

I must beg you will please to signify to their Lordships, that there is now borne upon the *Monarch's* books as part of her complement, twenty one men which were lent in December last, to His Majesty's ship *Tilbury* and *Sea Nymph* press tender, and no account having been give of them since, I beg to know how their Lordships would be pleased to have me act with respect to them.

This afternoon sailed from Hamoaze His Majesty's ships *Falmouth*, *Ludlow Castle*, *Raven*, and *Otter* sloop. The *Ludlow Castle* is pro-

---

[1] In command of a small squadron sent to reinforce Byng in the Mediterranean.
[2] Berlenga on the coast of Portugal.
[3] Enclosed a list of nine ships giving their state and condition.

ceeded to sea, as will the *Falmouth* and *Raven* tomorrow morning. But as Captain Brett has many men short of complement, I hope their Lordships will approve of my completing him from the supernumeraries I have on board belonging to other ships, the *Chichester's*, *Somerset's*, and *Prince's* men excepted.

This day a merchant ship came into the Sound, whose master informs me that the *Sterling Castle* with her convoy anchored yesterday in Torbay.

Remains in Hamoaze the *Monarch*, *York*, *Eagle*, *Greyhound*, and *Lightning* fireship.

416. To Jane Rodney

[TNA, PRO 30/20/20/2, pp. 115–18] 22 June 1756

I have just time to acquaint my dear girl that I am now very busy and have been so all this day upon account that the men of war and transports are arrived, that are to carry two regiments to strengthen the garrison of Gibraltar and I am to dispatch them as soon as possible and hope to send them away by tomorrow night. The *Duke* has likewise brought my men but I have not had time yet to see them, but hope I shall tomorrow.

There is as yet no certain account from our friend Mr. Byng, and [I] have great reason to hope that the vile reports that have been propagated concerning him are without the least foundation. If they should prove so what can our great men say, for their precipitate measure in sending Sir Edward Hawke to supercede him, I hope when Sir Edward gets to the Mediterranean he will find Mr Byng a conqueror.

Our Alresford post is a very provoking one as I never receive any letters from you on the Monday, Tuesday or Wednesday. You must know the post comes in here every day but one in the week and goes out from here on Tuesday, Friday and Sunday.

I find Lord Harry Powlett[1] is made an Admiral but I hear is not to be employed. They had at first superceded him but his friends have got him restored.

I long for the next post that I may hear how my dearest Jenny and her boys does, and hope to find that Alresford is in high beauty and that you enjoy the fine weather that is now set in here. What is surprising, is

---

[1] Harry Powlett, Duke of Bolton. MP for Lymington, 1755–61. Powlett was promoted from captain to Rear Admiral of the white, on 4 June 1756, after the Duke of Newcastle intervened on his behalf with the First Lord of the Admiralty.

that a man of war that came in here yesterday, reports that for these three weeks past they have had the finest weather possible without a drop of rain, when he has not been above one hundred miles from this port.

417. To Clevland

[TNA, ADM 1/2385]
Monarch in Hamoaze
22 June 1756

Sir,

At the desire of Mr. Harrison,[1] who you will please to signify to their Lordships arrived here yesterday, in His Majesty's ship *Monmouth* from the westwards. I am to acknowledge the receipt of your letters of the 18th and 19th instant enclosing to me orders for Captain Innes of the *Otter* sloop, to proceed with the *Ludlow Castle*, and put himself under the command of Captain [Hon. Richard] Howe, who is appointed in the room of Captain Brett for going upon the service off Guernsey and Jersey. But as the *Ludlow Castle* sailed hence the 20th, the same came too late to be delivered for that purpose.

I have likewise received a warrant appointing Robert Carter, master at arms of His Majesty's ship *Monarch* under my command. Together with an account that the warrant for the removal of the carpenter of the *Newcastle* into her was sent to Commissioner Hughes[2] at Portsmouth. And if their Lordships should think proper to superannuate or remove the present boatswain of the *Monarch* who is gone to London to be reviewed by their Lordships agreeable to their order to me; I must beg leave to recommend to their favour one Henry Wright, who is at present boatswain of the *Anglesea* in this port to be appointed in his room.

I beg leave to enclose for their Lordships' inspection a petition I received this day from the Alsatian women on their being ordered to embark on board the tender appointed to carry them to Ostend wherein they beg they may be permitted to remain with their husbands, and will subsist upon the allowance granted them by the French king.

You will please to inform them, at about noon arrived here His Majesty's ships *Duke*, *Jersey*, *Gosport* and *Peregrine* sloop with the transports from the eastward, and at the same time sailed hence the *Falmouth* whose complement I completed from the supernumeraries borne on board the *Monarch* belonging to other ships, amounting in

---

[1] Captain John Harrison.
[2] Captain Richard Hughes, commissioner of Portsmouth Dockyard, 1754–73.

number to fifty men, which I hope will meet with their Lordships' approbation.

418. To Clevland

[TNA, ADM 1/2385]

Monarch in Hamoaze
25 June 1756

Sir,

I beg you will please to signify to their Lordships, that as many of the company of His Majesty's ship under my command, are very bare and in want of clothes and necessaries, and as two months' advance will greatly contribute towards their clothing and preservation of their healths, I hope their Lordships will be pleased to give directions that the same may be paid them before the ship proceeds to sea.

419. To Jane Rodney

[TNA, PRO 30/20/20/2, pp. 119–22]   29 June 1756

I can now acquaint my dearest girl that the *Monarch* is now completely manned and I hope that in a few days Lord Anson will order me to join Mr Boscawen[1] as I shall then certainly return before my dearest Jenny brings me a dear little girl. Tho' I shall not be uneasy if it should prove a boy, but let it prove what it will I would fain be with her at the time.

You shall certainly know when I shall sail and as we shall frequently have ships sent in from the fleet I will constantly let you hear from me, but my dear Jenny must not be uneasy if she reads in the papers of ships arriving from Boscawen's fleet because they are oftener false than true, and you may depend upon hearing when ever I can possibly write.

We have had our old weather here again, almost a constant rain, but I hope you have enjoyed quite different weather at Alresford and that my dear boys are still obliged to play in the shade. I would fain have you know nothing but joy, and when this bustle is once over, will endeavor

---

[1]Vice Admiral Hon. Edward Boscawen, Vice Admiral, 6 Feb. 1755; Admiral 7 Feb. 1758; Admiralty Commissioner 1751–61, MP for Truro, 1742–61. Boscawen in 1755 commanded the British ships in the Gulf of St. Lawrence which fired the first shot of the Seven Years War at sea. Returning to England Boscawen then at frequent intervals commanded squadrons in the Channel, off Brest, or in the Bay of Biscay. Serving as a second in command to Hawke in 1757, Boscawen in 1758 commanded the squadron during the capture of Louisburg, and then in 1759 became Commander-in-chief in the Mediterranean.

all in my power to make the remainder of our days pass serenely on in peace and happiness. My dear girl will do me the justice to think that all my happiness is comprised in her and her little ones and that to see them pleased would be to me the most supreme delight.

Pray how does Jocky Poll's[1] &c. do? Give my love to them all, and tell little green Poll that Mrs Hanway has got a brother of his the prettiest creature that I ever saw with the purple ring just come round his neck and he speaks extraordinary well so pray don't despair but he will talk. Mrs Hanway never keeps him in a cage or ever covers him up in the coldest night of the winter so pray my dear endeavour to harden yours by degrees. I have sent an order to my agent to send you bills to the amount of £100 and in case you want more always draw upon Magnus.[2]

Kiss my dear boys and tell them how foolishly fond I am of them and of some body else, they won't guess who, however you won't believe (any more than I do) that there is any foolishness in it. May I ever continue to think so, which I am certain that I shall, for I never can or shall believe but our dear ones will prove a comfort to us in our age as well as in our youth. Take care of yourself my dear Jenny as you value the happiness of him whose fondest delights is to be with you and when absent ever to think of you.

[PS] My love to all with you.

420. *To Clevland*

[TNA, ADM 1/2385]

Monarch in Hamoaze
4 July 1756

Sir,

I have received your letter of the 29th past enclosing a petition of John Ahlgren's with the protection annexed and have agreeable to their Lordships' direction enquired into what he therein alleges. And find that the man is now at the hospital in a weak and sickly state and not well enough to be discharged, and was impressed by one of His Majesty's sloops.

I have this day received their Lordships' orders to proceed to sea and put myself under the command of Vice Admiral Boscawen, and you will please to inform them, I shall use the utmost dispatch in putting them same in execution.

[1] A pet parrot.
[2] Francis Magnus, Rodney's agent.

421. *To Jane Rodney*

[TNA, PRO 30/20/20/2, pp. 123–6]

Plymouth
6 July 1756

Yesterday I was made happy by my dearest Jenny's letter of the 1st July, and beg my love will not make herself uneasy about Mr. Boscawen's staying out so long, for tho' he has been so long all his ships have been shifted and the *Royal George* is now gone in the room of the *Invincible*. I make no doubts but I shall be with you by the time you are in the straw, but beg my Jenny will well consider before she determines whether she will lye in town or country, and for my sake follow that advice which will most contribute to your peace of mind and safety. If you should choose to be in town I shall certainly have leave to come to you on my arrival, but in case they should deny I certainly shall take leave.

I hope you have received my letter concerning the intended purchase and am much obliged to you for being so considerate, gold may be bought too dear, I beg my dear you will insist upon Mr. Duthy's sending the deed to Mr. Blunt, if he has not done it I shall get some other person to do it, tho' don't tell him so at once, in case you find Mr. Duthy is slack in that matter write to Mr Blunt and let him know it is not my fault. And that if he will send a deed the money shall be paid immediately.

I am glad Charles[1] is so good. I wrote to him last post and should be glad time allowed me to say much more but my ship is under sail to join Mr. Boscawen.

422. *To Clevland*

[TNA, ADM 1/2385]

Monarch in Plymouth Sound
8 July 1756

Sir,

Having put the accounts of His Majesty's ship the *Prince George* into the proper office to be passed during the time I commanded her between the 19th February 1755 and the 5th May 1756 and there appearing as I can learn no objection, I beg their Lordships will be pleased to give directions that my own and servants' wages may be accordingly paid me.

---

[1] Rodney's brother-in-law Charles Compton.

423. *To Jane Rodney*

[TNA, PRO 30/20/20/2, pp. 127–30]

At sea
30 July 1756

Captain Keppel has this moment sent me word that I may have an opportunity of writing to my dearest Jenny as he has received orders to go for Portsmouth tomorrow morning, and will take particular care that my letter is sent to you immediately on his arrival.

We are now prodigiously strong having been joined this morning by another first rate which makes us sufficient strong to cope with the whole naval power of France, should even the ships in the Mediterranean be joined with those at Brest. There is now very little probability of taking many ships as the French will never be weak enough to run the risk of losing their navy when there is not the least probability of their success. All the chance we have is to intercept their homeward bound trade.

The songs upon Mr. Byng occasion some mirth to those who are glad to trip up his heels, but I hope he will be able to give sufficient reasons for his conduct when he comes home, tho' I must own I cannot perceive the least glimpse in his favour. His not landing the troops after the battle is inexcusable, as likewise his not sending a boat on shore to Saint Philips to acquaint them with the occasion of his retreat. I suppose I shall be plagued with being one of his judges next winter. You know I abhor court martials.

I hope my dear girl and our little ones enjoy fine weather and that Alresford daily improves in beauty and that Georgy and Jamy can play all day long without doors. Georgy certainly knows the place and I suppose the other would after being absent some time. Kiss them both most tenderly and tell them how very dear themselves and their mother are to their papa. If you have gained their hearts from me I will certainly be revenged on you for you know Georgy has sense sufficient to know that I can protect him against anybody, notwithstanding somebody scolds him.

I hope you will receive my letter which I sent two days since by the *Bedford* Captain [James] Douglas. And assure my Jenny I will never lose any opportunity of letting her hear from me.

Mackay[1] promises to call upon you in his way to town. Pray make him welcome. I hope he will find Alresford much improved since he was there.

---

[1] Lieutenant Hugh Mackay.

424. From Lord Sandwich[1]

[TNA, PRO 30/20/20/5, pp. 1–3]

Hinchingbrook
1 August 1756

Dear Sir,

After returning you many thanks for the favours you have shown to my friend Mr. Hayward,[2] give me leave to consult you as to the method of getting him appointed a lieutenant, which however I shall not apply for any where without your testimonial as to his character and ability in his profession.

I have been so often troublesome to Lord Anson that I don't choose upon this occasion to apply through his channel tho' I know it would be the most expeditious method; but I have some reason to imagine an application from me to Sir Edward Hawke would gain him preferment as if (as I believe is the case) he deserves it. The favour therefore I have to beg of you is that you would be so good as to put me in a way of getting him as soon as possible into the Mediterranean, and if you would write me an ostensible letter as to his character (in case he deserves a good one and I don't desire it otherwise) it would be an additional obligation.

I believe you know I wish you success wherever you are concerned so that it must be unnecessary to tell you it will be a pleasure to me to hear of any good fortune that may attend you, but as a friend to this country I may very sincerely add, that I wish such men as you may fight for us whenever a future opportunity shall happen, I believe they are not plenty and therefore are the more to be esteemed.

425. To Clevland

[TNA, ADM 1/2385]

Monarch at Spithead
12 August 1756

Sir,

I must desire you will please to acquaint their Lordships with the arrival of His Majesty's ship under my command at Spithead. She being in so bad a condition that Vice Admiral Boscawen was pleased to

---

[1]John Montagu, 4th Earl of Sandwich, Lord of the Admiralty, 27 Dec. 1744–26 Feb. 1748; First Lord of the Admiralty, 26 Feb. 1748–22 June 1751, 20 April–16 Sept. 1763; Secretary of State (North), 9 Sept. 1763–11 July 1765; First Lord of the Admiralty, 12 Jan. 1771–1 April 1782.

[2]Thomas Hayward was not promoted to the rank of lieutenant until 26 March 1758. See also Nos. 386 and 399.

order her into this port. Enclosed I transmit you a copy of the report of the survey taken by order of Vice Admiral Boscawen at sea as likewise the state and condition of the ship.[1]

426. To Clevland

[TNA, ADM 1/2385] *Monarch* at Spithead
16 August 1756

Sir,
I have this day received your letter of the 14th instant. And I am to desire you will please to acquaint their Lordships that I shall use the utmost dispatch in proceeding with His Majesty's ship *Monarch* into Portsmouth Harbour.

427. To Clevland

[TNA, ADM 1/2385] *Monarch* Portsmouth Harbour
26 August 1756

Sir,
I desire you will please to inform their Lordships that the purser of His Majesty's ship *Monarch* under my command, having represented to me that there is upwards of eighteen days' wine for her complement now remaining on board her, exclusive of seven days' beer, and that the said wine cannot be expended, as the men are all lent into other ships, beg they will be pleased to give directions, that the said wine may be put on board such of the ships as are fitting for sea at this port.

And he having also informed me that there is near three months' provisions, which are now put on board an old ship. The Commissioners of the Victualling having refused to be received into store for want of their Lordships' orders for that purpose, and as the ship it is on board may be wanted to receive the stores of the first ship of war which comes in to clean, beg their Lordships may be pleased to give directions, that a clerk from the Victualling Office may be directed to deliver the said provisions into one of the men of war now fitting for sea, as it cannot be returned into store from the *Monarch* for want of men to do it.

---

[1] The state and condition of the ship or the report of the survey are is enclosed. Only the survey is enclosed.

428. To Clevland

[TNA, ADM 1/2385]

Monarch Portsmouth Harbour
27 August 1756

I beg you will pleased to inform their Lordships that His Majesty's ship *Monarch* under my command is in all respects clear and ready to be surveyed and the men distributed into His Majesty's ships *Terrible* and *Berwick*, agreeable to their Lordships' order. All that are now remaining being officers, servants, and petty officers of different denominations.

429. From Henry Fox[1]

[TNA, PRO, 30/20/20/4, pp. 31–2]

2 September 1756

Sir,

I have received the honour of a letter from Mr. [Charles] Compton and in part obeyed his commands. But he bids me direct to him at Lausanne; and you say I must send his letters to Lord Bristol[2] at Turin. I shall be able to furnish him with as many and as good letters as he can wish from the foreign ministers here, and I am heartily glad he is so well disposed to make use of them. I hope you will not cramp him in time but encourage his stay in Italy as long as he can make it agreeable to himself.

I hardly know how to wish you in Parliament where I foresee too great fatigue for so tender a constitution as yours is. But this should not make me omit any opportunity of bringing you there should that offer.

Lady Caroline[3] desires hers and I beg my best respects to Mrs. Rodney. I have had a sore throat of which I am now quite well and the rest of my family have been so all this summer. We are much obliged by your very kind enquiries and good wishes.

---

[1] MP for New Windsor, 1742–61; Secretary of State (South), 14 Nov. 1755–13 Nov. 1756; Paymaster General, June 1757–May 1765.

[2] George William Hervey, 2nd Earl of Bristol; Envoy Extraordinary at Turin, 1755–58; Ambassador to Spain, 1758–61.

[3] Lady Georgiana Caroline Lennox Fox (created Baroness Holland of Holland, 3 May 1762).

430. From Lord Ilchester[1]

[TNA, PRO 30/20/20/4, pp. 35–7]

Redlynch
5 September 1756

Dear Sir,

I beg leave to return you many thanks for your kind letter which I yesterday received. I wrote three months ago to Lord Bristol and had a very obliging answer from him that he should think himself very happy in having an opportunity on Mr. [Charles] Compton's arrival at Turin to show him all possible civilities and I make no doubt what time he passes in that place he will spend very agreeably. I am extremely glad to hear the account you give of the turn he is taking. I am sure hereafter he will think himself under great obligations to you for delivering him out of the hands he was falling into, and at present all his friends and relations (when I say all I believe I may except 2 ladies) must be of the same opinion.

I heartily congratulate you on the prospect you have of coming soon into Parliament[2] and I am sure I may wish my brother[3] joy of having there so sincere and valuable a friend.

Lord Digby[4] is still at Bristol and by the accounts I have of him I am afraid recovers but slowly. I don't expect to see him soon. I wish I could hear of your coming into this part of the West. I should think myself very happy in having the pleasure of waiting upon you at this place.

I beg you will be so kind as to make my compliments acceptable to Mrs. Rodney &c.

[PS] If you choose I should write another letter to Lord Bristol pray let me know and I will with a great deal of pleasure.

---

[1] Stephen Fox, 1st Earl Ilchester.
[2] Rodney did not enter Parliament at this time.
[3] Henry Fox.
[4] Edward Digby, 6th Baron Digby, the grandson of Lord Ilchester.

431. To Clevland

[TNA, ADM 1/2385] *Monarch* Portsmouth Harbour
10 September 1756

Sir,

Enclosed[1] I return back the petition of Philip Hull belonging to His Majesty's ship under my command, and you will please to inform their Lordships that I think him very fit still to serve in His Majesty's ships. His being a pensioner to the Chest at Chatham[2] was the reason I gave him leave upon his application to go there to obtain his pension.

With regard to the facts he alleges, I am entirely a stranger to them as he was a healthy able man during the time he served with me in the *Prince George* and *Monarch*.

432. To Clevland

[TNA, ADM 1/2385] Portsmouth
13 September 1756

Sir,

As the seven men mentioned in the margin[3] have been so simple as to come to Portsmouth, without first obtaining the consent of the Admiralty, depending upon the petition which they delivered into my Lord Anson's hands. Upon finding they were turned over into a sloop in the River, I acquainted Mr. Osborn[4] with it, who advised me to apply to the Board concerning them, before which application could be made an order came down, to send them prisoners on board the *Royal Ann*.

As the men have served many years under my command and always behaved remarkably well I cannot help concerning myself in their behalf and shall take it as a particular favour if you will solicit their Lordships that their present crime be forgiven, as they have erred more through their regard for their old captain than any premeditated intention of deserting. I cannot expect to have the men myself though I would willingly give ten of the best men of my ship's company for them. My friend Keppel would be made very happy could he get them and I will answer for the men that for the future they will never deserve

---

[1] Not enclosed.

[2] A contributory fund to which seamen paid six pence a month from their wages for the benefit of the wounded and the widows of those killed in action.

[3] John Miller, Thomas Carter, Edward Wilson, Robert Grey, John Browne, Timothy Sulivan, Andrew Patton.

[4] Vice Admiral Henry Osborn, Commander-in-chief at Portsmouth.

punishment. You will oblige me much if you can possibly prevent their punishment which must give me great uneasiness as it was through their regard for me they have offended.

PS I have wrote to Lord Anson in that favour.

433. *To Newcastle*

[BL, Add. MSS 32867, f. 343] Portsmouth
19 September 1756

My Lord,
 I beg leave to return your Grace many thanks for the honour of your letter, and the recommendatory ones for Mr. Compton which I have forwarded to him obeying your Grace's command, which I shall ever with the utmost assiduity execute.

434. *To Clevland*

[TNA, ADM 1/2385] *Monarch* Portsmouth Harbour
29 October 1756

Sir,
 If His Majesty's service will permit it, I must desire you will please to make it my request to their Lordships to grant me ten days' leave of absence to transact some business of consequence to me.

435. *To Jane Rodney*

[TNA, PRO 30/20/20/2, pp. 131–3] 4 November 1756

 Yesterday I had my dearest Jenny's letters, which tho' to hear from her always gives me pleasure, yet to hear that you do not gather strength faster gives me some pain, and has carried me this day to Duncan who, not being at home, I have left word for him to call on me tomorrow. I have wrote for the candles and hope he will send them ready to go down with me, which I propose doing the beginning of the week as I must go to Woburn[1] tomorrow to try what my rhetoric will do with the Duke of B - d - d[2] to make him take upon

---
[1] Woburn Abbey, the seat of the Dukes of Bedford.
[2] Duke of Bedford.

himself the care of naval affairs as I hear Lord A – n[1] must certainly go out.

There never was such confusion as at present and it seems almost impossible for the great to agree among themselves. However tomorrow or next day I hear it will certainly be settled. I hope it will as I should be glad to make my interest with the First Lord now I am in town which will save me a second jaunt.

Your account of my dear boys and girl gives me unspeakable pleasure. I hope to God their mother will soon be as well as the children and that I shall find you perfectly recovered.

Poor Betty is prodigiously bloated and I am afraid will require a great deal of physick to get her into proper order.

Take care of yourself and [the] little ones as you value the happiness of him who will ever be with the utmost tenderness my dearest Jenny's most affectionate husband.

[PS] Your house is in excellent order and a good house maid in it if you choose to keep her.

436. To Clevland

[TNA, ADM 1/2385] 8 November 1756

Sir,

If it will not be detrimental to His Majesty's service, I must desire you will please to make it my request to their Lordships to grant me ten days leave of absence longer.

437. To Clevland

[TNA, ADM 1/2385] Hill Street
12 December 1756

Sir,

Being afflicted with a violent bilious colic I desire you will please to represent the same to their Lordships' and hope they will indulge me with as long a time as the nature of the service I am ordered on will admit, and hope a short time will enable me to execute any commands they are pleased to honour me with.

[1] Lord Anson.

438. To Clevland

[TNA, ADM 1/2385]

Hill Street [London]
24 December 1756

Dear Sir,

I beg you will acquaint Lord Temple[1] that I am under the greatest concern that my health still continues so bad as to render it impossible for me to set out for Portsmouth, not having been out of doors since I had the honour to see his Lordship last, and constantly attended by a physician as Mrs Rodney is by three.[2]

I beg you will acquaint his Lordship that if he thinks it necessary he will dispose of the *Monarch* as he pleases and I hope by the time the new ships are launched, I shall be able to execute any orders he pleases to honour me with.

439. From the Lords of the Admiralty

[TNA, ADM 2/78, pp. 280–1]

6 April 1757

Having appointed you captain of His Majesty's ship *Dublin* in the *River Thames* which we have ordered to be fitted and stored for Channel service, manned with *600* men, and victualled to *four* months of all species of provisions except beer of which she is to have as much as she can conveniently stow, you are hereby required and directed to get her ready for service accordingly, with the utmost expedition and then falling down to *Longreach* take in her guns and gunners stores and proceed to the Nore for further order.

440. To Clevland

[TNA, ADM 1/2385]

Dublin at Deptford
27 April 1757

Sir,

His Majesty's ship under my command being fitting out in the River, I hope their Lordships will please to give directions that an impress bill be made out in order to the procuring seamen at a rendezvous.

---

[1] Richard Temple, 2nd Earl Temple, First Lord of the Admiralty, 17 Nov. 1756–6 April 1757.
[2] Jane Rodney did not recover from her illness and died on 29 January 1757.

441. *From John Milnes*[1]

[TNA, ADM 2/707, p. 259] 27 April 1757

Sir,

I am commanded by my Lords Commissioners of the Admiralty to signify their direction to you to send a lieutenant with two petty officers and six men to town to open a rendezvous and procure men. The Navy Board being directed to impress £35 to you to enable you to carry on this service.

442. *From Clevland*

[TNA, ADM 2/707, p. 323] 10 May 1757

Sir,

Having read to my Lords Commissioners of the Admiralty your letter of yesterday's date desiring them to order you the yacht's men to assist in fitting and getting the ship you command ready for sea, I am commanded to acquaint you that you cannot have the yacht's men, but must procure landmen and enter them as part of your ship's complement, who you will find of great use in taking in the stores.

443. *To Boscawen*

[TNA, ADM 1/2385] [13 May 1757]

Captain Rodney presents his complements to Mr Boscawen and begs leave to inform him that he has an answer from Portsmouth and that there are several tenders there. Hopes he will be so good to procure him an order for one to bring round his petty officers &c that he may employ them in raising men for the *Dublin*.

---

[1] Deputy Secretary to the Lords Commissioners of the Admiralty, 15 June 1756–16 Oct. 1759.

444. To Clevland

[TNA, ADM 1/2385]

Dublin at Deptford
13 May 1757

Sir,

Mr. [William] Slade, the Surveyor of the Navy, having enforced his directions to the master attendant at Deptford to send seventy tons of iron ballast on board the *Dublin*, notwithstanding I had acquainted the said master attendant with my objections to the receiving the same as it always made ships very laboursome, and the receipt or refusal of such ballast being usually left as the option of the captain, I hope their Lordships will not be offended at my refusing to take the said ballast on board till I receive their directions therein.

445. From Clevland

[TNA, ADM 2/707, p. 339]

13 May 1757

Sir,

I have communicated to my Lords Commissioners of the Admiralty your letter [No. 444] of this date informing them that you have refused to receive seventy tons of iron ballast which was ordered to be sent on board the ship you command by the surveyor of the navy. And I am commanded to acquaint you that as the *Dublin* is a new ship their Lordships look upon the surveyor of the navy to be the proper judge of what ballast should be put in her, and therefore they expect that you should conform thereto.

446. From Clevland

[TNA, ADM 2/707, p. 364]

18 May 1757

Sir,

I have read to my Lords Commissioners of the Admiralty your letter of this date informing them of the arrival of the tender with your men from Portsmouth. And I am commanded by their Lordships to signify their direction to you to order her to the Nore.

447. *From the Lords of the Admiralty*

[TNA, ADM 2/78, p. 458] 26 May 1757

You are hereby required and directed to send *thirty* men from His Majesty's ship under your command (half of which to be seamen), including as many petty officers as you can furnish, on board the *Preston* in Longreach, taking care to send their chests and bedding along with them, as they are to be in the first place employed in carrying that ship to the Nore. And then to be put on board tenders to raise men for the fleet.

448. *To Clevland*

[TNA, ADM 1/2385] *Dublin* at Deptford
27 May 1757

Sir,

This morning I received their Lordships' order of yesterday's date [No. 447] commanding me to send thirty men from His Majesty's ship under my command, on board the *Preston* in Longreach with their chests and bedding, as they are not only to be employed in carrying the said ship to the Nore, but to be put on board tenders to raise men for His Majesty's fleet.

I must desire you will please to acquaint them that I have complied with their order as far as was in my powers, having sent fifteen petty officers and fifteen landmen on board the *Preston*, there being no able seamen (foremast men) as yet belonging to His Majesty's ship under my command. I must likewise desire you will please to represent to their Lordships that had not the public service required the lending these petty officers and men, with their assistance the *Dublin* would have been ready to have fallen down to Longreach in ten or twelve days, her rigging being almost completed, ballast in, and the greatest part of the ground tier on board and stowed. The loss of so much strength as thirty men will disable me from getting on board the anchors and cables until some others are entered, unless their Lordships are pleased to order me the assistance of the yacht's men or the labourers of this yard.

449. *To Clevland*

[TNA, ADM 1/2385] *Dublin* at Deptford
3 June 1757

Sir,

His Majesty's ship under my command being in every respect ready to fall down to Longreach, except getting the cables on board and bending the sails, and having applied to the Navy Board to suffer the riggers to assist in performing that service, they have acquainted me that I must apply to their Lordships on that head which I hope they will permit, as the *Dublin* will then be ready to fall down to Longreach when ever their Lordships are pleased to order a sufficient number of men to assist in carrying her there.

450. *From Clevland*

[TNA, ADM 2/707, p. 452] 6 June 1756

Sir,

I have read to my Lords Commissioners of the Admiralty your letter [No. 449] of the 3rd instant representing that you are ready to fall down to Longreach if you had men to navigate the ship. And I am to acquaint you that the Navy Board are ordered to assist you with men.

451. *To Clevland*

[TNA, ADM 1/2385] *Dublin* at Deptford
8 June 1757

Sir,

As my accounts are passed for the time that I commanded His Majesty's ship *Monarch*, I hope that their Lordships will please to order that I may be paid my own and servant's pay for the said ship.

452. *To Clevland*

[TNA, ADM 1/2385] *Dublin* at Deptford
10 June 1757

Sir,

There being no master at arms appointed at present to His Majesty's ship *Dublin* under my command, and one John Simpson, a person duly qualified for that station having applied to me, I hope their Lordships will be pleased to grant him a warrant for her.

453. *From Clevland*

[TNA, ADM 2/707, p. 476]   10 June 1757

Sir,

In return to your letters of the 8th [No. 451] and 10th [No. 452] instant desiring the payment of your wages for the *Monarch* and that John Simpson may be appointed master at arms to the *Dublin*, I am to acquaint you that directions have been given to the Navy Board for the payment of your said wages, and that a master at arms is already appointed to the *Dublin*.

454. *To Clevland*

[TNA, ADM 1/2385]   *Dublin* at Deptford
16 June 1757

Sir,

Lieutenant Robert Haswell of His Majesty's ship under my command who is employed to impress seamen at London having represented to me that the impress money is expended, I hope their Lordships will please to give directions for a further supply.

455. *To Clevland*

[TNA, ADM 1/2385]   *Dublin* at Deptford
19 June 1757

Sir,

I must desire you will please to represent to their Lordships that His Majesty's ship *Dublin* under my command is ready to proceed to Longreach. The wind now offers but the pilot refuses to take charge unless there are at least one hundred seamen on board more than at present. As the *America* will probably fall down this day and has her complement near complete, [I] hope their Lordships will please to order an officer with a sufficient number of men to assist in navigating the *Dublin* to Longreach. I must beg leave to represent to them if this opportunity is lost, the ship may remain here a long time as there [are] only four points of the compass on which the wind can favour us.

456. *From Clevland*

[TNA, ADM 2/707, p. 520] 20 June 1757

Sir,

Herewith you will receive an order to Captain Byron of the *America* to lend you 100 men to assist in carrying the ship you command to Longreach. And it is the direction of my Lords Commissioners of the Admiralty you receive them and proceed without loss of time to that place.

457. *To Clevland*

[TNA, ADM 1/2385] *Dublin* at Deptford
21 June 1757

Sir,

It is with great concern I am under the necessity to desire you will acquaint their Lordships that the pilot has refused to carry His Majesty's ship under my command down to Longreach as this day.

The reasons he alleges are the wind being too scant and the tides having fallen off, which renders it too dangerous to take charge of such a ship as the consequence of her touching the ground would be her remaining in that situation till the next spring tides. I shall forthwith return the hundred men to the *America* that the service may not suffer by their absence.

458. *From Clevland*

[TNA, ADM 2/707, p. 533] 22 June 1757

Sir,

I have read to my Lords Commissioners of the Admiralty your letter [No. 457] of yesterday's date informing them the pilot has refused taking charge of the ship you command down to Longreach the wind being too scant and the tide having fallen off. And I am to acquaint you that their Lordships approve of your proceedings herein.

459. *To Clevland*

[TNA, ADM 1/2385] 28 June 1757

Sir,

The pilot has given me to understand that he will take charge of the ship down to Longreach tomorrow if the wind offers and their Lordships will please to order a sufficient number of men to assist in carrying her there. As the riggers and ordinary[1] of Woolwich and Deptford will be sufficient, and a few hours will carry her there, I hope they will be so good to oblige me with an order for their assistance, and I promise their Lordships I will not make the signal for their assistance till the pilot assures me he will carry the ship down that tide.

460. *From Clevland*

[TNA, ADM 2/708, p. 6] 28 June 1757

Sir,

I have read to my Lords Commissioners of the Admiralty your letter of this date [No. 459] desiring that the riggers and ordinary of Woolwich and Deptford yards may be ordered to assist in carrying the ship you command to Longreach. I am to acquaint you that orders are given for the riggers and labourers going on board on your making the signal.

461. *To Clevland*

[TNA, ADM 1/2385] *Dublin* Longreach
7 July 1757

Sir,

Lieutenant Robert Haswell of His Majesty's ship *Dublin* under my command who is employed to impress seamen at London having represented to me that the impress money is expended, I hope their Lordships will please to give directions for a further supply.

---

[1] Men serving on board ships laid up in ordinary.

462. From Clevland

[TNA, ADM 2/708, p. 37] 7 July 1757

Sir,
In return to your letter of this date [No. 461] desiring a supply of money for the service of raising me[n], I am to acquaint you that an imprest of £20 is ordered [for] you.

463. From Clevland

[TNA, ADM 2/708, p. 52] 11 July 1757

Sir,
His Majesty's sloop the *Firedrake* being ordered to be reduced to a bomb vessel, I am commanded by my Lords Commissioners of the Admiralty to acquaint you that her additional number of men as a sloop are ordered to be discharged into His Majesty's ship under your command, and to signify their Lordships' direction to you to receive and enter them as part of your complement.

464. To Clevland

[TNA, ADM 1/2385] *Dublin* in Longreach
13 July 1757

Sir,
I have received your letter [No. 463] of the 11th instant acquainting me that as the *Firedrake* is ordered to be reduced to a bomb vessel their Lordships have been pleased to direct that her additional number of men as a sloop are to be discharged into His Majesty's ship under my command, which so soon as they appear shall be entered agreeable to their order as part of the complement.

465. To Clevland

[TNA, ADM 1/2385] *Dublin* in Longreach
14 July 1757

Sir,
I must beg you will please to represent to their Lordships that upon settling accounts with my agent I find he has neglected to receive my

pay due to me as lieutenant of the *Essex* in the year 1741 the journals for which he has lost. I therefore hope their Lordships will please to dispense with the same and give orders for payment.

466. *From Clevland*

[TNA, ADM 2/708, p. 83] 18 July 1757

Sir,

In return to your letter [No. 465] of the 14th instant desiring that your journals for the time you was lieutenant [in] the *Essex* may be dispensed with and that you may be paid your wages for her, I am to acquaint you that orders are given for that purpose.

467. *From John Kennedy and George Surtes*[1]

[TNA, ADM 1/2385] *New Britain* tender Sheerness
18 July 1757

Sir,

As we have the honour of belonging to the ship under your command we think it our duty to acquaint you of our proceedings since we left her at Deptford. We was ordered on board the *Preston* to assist in carrying her to the Nore. Then was ordered on board the *New Britain* tender, commanded by Joseph Norwood, lieutenant of the *Richmond*, to go the northward to raise men. On our passage and in Shields we raised eighty eight men. Nineteen of them Captain [James] Smith in the *Strombolo* took from us in Shields. The remainder we brought up to Sheerness and delivered all of them on board the *Princess Amelia* except the six men entered for the *Richmond*. There is ten entered for the *Dublin* which are very desirous of being on board under so good a commander.[2] We should be glad to have an order for us and them.

468. *From the Lords of the Admiralty*

[TNA, ADM 2/79, p. 81] 19 July 1757

Having ordered His Majesty's sloop *Hazards Prize* in Galleons Reach to be paid off at Woolwich and her petty officers and foremastmen to be

---
[1]Enclosed with No. 473.
[2]At the bottom of this letter is a list of ten seamen entitled 'Entered for the *Dublin*'.

turned over into His Majesty's ship under your command to serve as part of her complement, you are hereby required and directed to receive and enter them as part of her complement accordingly.

469. To Clevland

[TNA, ADM 1/2385]   *Dublin* in Longreach
19 July 1757

Sir,

Lieutenant Robert Haswell of His Majesty's ship *Dublin* under my command, who is employed to impress seamen at London, having represented to me that the impress money is expended, I hope their Lordships will please to give directions for a further supply.

470. To Clevland

[TNA, ADM 1/2385]   *Dublin* in Longreach
20 July 1757

Sir,

I must desire you will please to represent to their Lordships that Mr. John Wareham late midshipman and schoolmaster on board His Majesty's ship *Monarch*, under my command, who was made run upon the ships books, has made it appear to me by sufficient and undoubted evidence that he was really confined by a long and dangerous sickness from returning to his duty, which occasioned his being run. I therefore hope their Lordships will be so good to order his R to be taken off, and that he may be appointed school master of His Majesty's ship *Dublin*.

471. From Clevland

[TNA, ADM 2/708, p. 90]   20 July 1757

Sir,

The commanding officer at the Nore having informed my Lords Commissioners of the Admiralty that the four men named in the margin,[1] belonging to the *Catherine* yacht, have behaved in a very insolent manner to the commanding officer of the *New Britannia* tender and the captain of the yacht being directed to discharge them to the ship you

---

[1] Edward Carpenter, John Bradley, Richard Leonard and Moses Castill.

command and to send their tickets to you. It is their Lordships' direction you enter them as part of your complement.

472. *From Clevland*

[TNA, ADM 2/708, 91] 20 July 1757

Sir,

In return to your letter of yesterday's date [No. 468] desiring a further imprest of money for the service of raising men, I am to acquaint you that the Navy Board are directed to imprest £20 more to you on that account.

473. *To Clevland*

[TNA, ADM 1/2385] *Dublin* in Longreach
20 July 1757

Sir,

I must desire you will please to lay before their Lordships the enclosed letter [No. 467] which I this day received from three of my petty officers who were some time since lent by an order of the Admiralty to assist in raising men. As they are now returned to Sheerness I hope their Lordships will please to give directions that they may be ordered to their duty on board the *Dublin*, as likewise the ten men as mentioned in their letter to have entered for her.

I must likewise desire you will please to acquaint their Lordships that the *Dublin* is now ready to fall down to the Nore, provided there were but one hundred seamen on board to assist in carrying her there.

474. *From the Lords of the Admiralty*

[TNA, ADM 2/79, p. 86] 21 July 1757

Captain [John] Lindsay of the *Pluto* frigate being directed to reduce her complement to forty five men, and to discharge all above that number into His Majesty's ship under your command, you are hereby required and directed to receive and enter them as part of your complement.

475. *From the Lords of the Admiralty*

[TNA, ADM 2/79, p. 87] 21 July 1757

You are hereby required and directed immediately to lend thirty men from His Majesty's ship under your command to the *Salamander* in Galleons Reach, to assist in carrying her off lee and to enable her to press men from a fleet of colliers expected in the River.

476. *From Clevland*

[TNA, ADM 2/708, p. 97] 22 July 1757

Sir,

I have read to my Lords Commissioners of the Admiralty your letter of the 20th instant desiring that the three midshipmen named in the margin[1] belonging to the ship you command who have been employed in raising men in the *New Britannia* tender may be ordered to return to their ship, and that you may have ten men who entered with them for the *Dublin*, and in return I am commanded to acquaint you that the commanding officer at the Nore is directed to order the midshipmen on board your ship, but you can't have the ten men.

477. *To Clevland*

[TNA, ADM 1/2385] *Dublin* in Longreach
24 July 1757

Sir,

Whereas His Majesty's ship under my command will fall down to the Nore tomorrow morning, I hope their Lordships will please to give directions to the regulating captains, that the rendezvous in town be broke up, and the lieutenant, petty officers, and men be ordered to repair to their duty on board the ship at the Nore.

I have this moment received their Lordships' order concerning Alexander Patterson, boatswain of the *Reynolds*, but as the man chooses to stay, and has since entered voluntarily as a boatswain's mate I presume their Lordships don't expect he should be discharged.

I must likewise acknowledge the receipt of their Lordships' orders to the twenty third instant.

---

[1] William Grime, John Kennedy and George Surtes.

478. From Clevland

[TNA, ADM 2/708, p. 115] 25 July 1757

Sir,
I have communicated to my Lords Commissioners of the Admiralty your letter [No. 476] of yesterday's date desiring, as His Majesty's ship under your command will fall down to the Nore this day, that your lieutenant, petty officers and gang in town may be ordered to repair on board to their duty. And I am to acquaint you that the regulating captains are directed to order the lieutenant to break up his rendezvous and repair on board with his gang.

Their Lordships also direct me to acquaint you that they expect you should forthwith transmit to them the state and condition of the ship.

479. To Clevland

[TNA, ADM 1/2385] *Dublin* at the Nore
27 July 1757

Sir,
I must desire you will please to acquaint their Lordships that His Majesty's ship under my command is arrived at the Nore.

Enclosed I transmit to them an exact state and condition of the ship,[1] and do most solemnly assure them upon the word of an officer that the ratings expressed in this return are exact, and will bear the strictest examination.

Since I received their Lordships' orders to impress from protections we have boarded upwards of sixty sail, but without success they having been visited before by the ships in the Downes, at the Nore, and other stations.

480. To Clevland

[TNA, ADM 1/2385] *Dublin* at the Nore
28 July 1757

Sir,
I have received your letter concerning William Heard, and have made the strictest enquiry about him, find that he is a freeholder in

---
[1] Not enclosed.

Hertfordshire, lives at Ware, is about fifty years old, seems much older, has been a very stout man in his time. But I think he can not be of much service as his health seems to be declined.

481. To Clevland

[TNA, ADM 1/2385] *Dublin* at the Nore
29 July 1757

Sir,

I have received your letter of the 28th instant enclosing two petitions concerning the persons mentioned in the margin.[1] The allegations concerning them are true, they being impressed into His Majesty's service the night of the general impress.

I have likewise discharged agreeable to their Lordships' order, the three foreigners as mentioned in the margin.[2]

Enclosed I return the two petitions.

482. To Clevland

[TNA, ADM 1/2385] *Dublin* at the Nore
30 July 1757

Sir,

I return you the enclosed petitions,[3] and find upon enquiry that the two Danes as mentioned in the margin[4] were pressed in Yarmouth Roads by the captain of the *Firedrake* from their protections.

William Johnson has been discharged into the *Adventure* armed vessel by order of Lord Harry Powlett.

I have likewise enquired into the petitions concerning Richard Johnson and William Marshall, belonging to the *Greyhound* of Whitby, and find what is therein alleged to be true.

---

[1] Samuel Pain, John Brooks and Robert Burnside.
[2] John Fredrick Wellhalm, John G. Moss and David Prust.
[3] Not enclosed.
[4] Jacob Shute and Anders Floers.

483. *To Clevland*

[TNA, ADM 1/2385] Dublin at the Nore
3 August 1757

Sir,

Herewith I return to you the petition of Samuel Saul, and having enquired into the matter therein alleged, he has produced to me the enclosed paper[1] which you will please to lay before their Lordships for their inspection having nothing more to observe but that he appears to be a very good seaman.

484. *From the Lords of the Admiralty*

[TNA, ADM 2/79, p. 138] 5 August 1757

You are hereby required and directed to put yourself under the command of Sir Edward Hawke, Vice Admiral of the blue squadron of His Majesty's fleet, and follow his orders for your further proceedings.

485. *To Clevland*

[TNA, ADM 1/2385] Dublin at Spithead
28 November 1757

Sir,

I desire you will please to acquaint their Lordships that I am arrived in His Majesty's ship *Dublin* under my command at Spithead, in company with the *Alcide*, having left Sir Edward Hawke with the fleet under his command on the 25th instant in the latitude of 48° 15' about seventy leagues to the westward of Ushant.

The *Alcide* making a signal that he could not keep company, hoisting his colours and bearing away for England, the Admiral, who knew the sickly condition of the *Dublin*, and had sent me word by an officer a few days before that he intended to send me into port the first opportunity, made my signal to bear up after the *Alcide* it then blowing too hard to have any communications with boats.

We have had excessive hard gales of wind for these three weeks past. The *Dublin* having carried away three tillers in the rudder head, owing as the carpenter imagines, to some defect of the rudder and

[1] Not enclosed.

being prevented at the same time from opening the lower deck ports, it has contributed to the sickness (an epidemic fever) increasing on board the ship, there being at present one hundred and sixty five down in it, exclusive of those who have recovered from it and remain very weak.

I think it my duty to acquaint their Lordships that the distemper was brought on board by the detachment of troops belonging to Lord Effingham's Regiment,[1] few of whom have been able to do any duty the greatest part of the cruise, and are composed of such wretches as must cause a sickness in any ship whose misfortune it is to have them on board; being either very old men or mere boys, unacquainted with the use of arms and without spirit or discipline. As most of the detachment must be sent to the hospital, I hope their Lordships will be pleased to give directions that marines be ordered on board in their room.

486. *From the Lords of the Admiralty*

[TNA, ADM 2/79, pp. 448–9]　　　　　　　　　　30 November 1757

You are hereby required and directed to repair with His Majesty's ship under your command into Portsmouth Harbour where we have ordered her to be cleaned, graved, tallowed over it, and refitted, stored for Channel service, and her provisions completed to four months' of all species except beer, of which she is to have as much as she can conveniently stow.

And you are strictly to observe the following instructions:

You are to give a constant attendance at the ship, and to keep your officers and men together during the whole time that she is in harbour.

You are to use your utmost diligence in getting out your guns and powder, and if necessary your stores and provisions and ballast, or so much thereof as shall be necessary, and no more, and to leave no part thereof to be done by the officers of the yard.

You are to use the like diligence in getting in your guns, powder, stores, and provisions (as also your ballast if you found it necessary to put it out) when the ship is ready for it, and in putting her into a condition to proceed on service.

If you have any men who you suspect will run away, you are to apply to Vice Admiral [Charles] Knowles[2] for their security.

---

[1] Thomas Howard, 2nd Earl of Effingham, colonel of the 34th Regiment of Foot.
[2] Second in command of the Western Squadron.

When the ship is ready again in all respects for the sea, you are to repair to Spithead for further orders.

You are always to keep your provisions, stores, and water complete until you proceed to sea.

487. *From Clevland*

[TNA, ADM 2/709, p. 77] 6 December 1757

Sir,

Herewith I transmit you a letter from the Judge Advocate of His Majesty's forces, and am commanded by my Lords Commissioners of the Admiralty to acquaint you that you have their leave to be absent for so long as may be necessary on this occasion.

488. *To Clevland*

[TNA, ADM 1/2385] *Dublin* in Portsmouth Harbour
9 December 1757

Sir,

I have received your letter of the 7th instant, signifying to me, their Lordships' direction to send them immediately the qualities of His Majesty's ship under my command. I beg you will please in consequence thereof, to lay before their Lordships the enclosed[1] account which are the best observations I could make during the small trial I have already had of her.

489. *From Clevland*

[TNA, ADM 2/709, p. 148] 28 December 1757

Sir,

Richard Leonard late belonging to the ship you command, who was discharged from the Hospital at Haslar unserviceable, having represented to my Lords Commissioners of the Admiralty that you have got his ticket for the *Catherine* yacht in your possession, and that he is in great distress for want of his money, I am commanded by their Lordships to signify their direction that you immediately send the said ticket to the Navy Board.

[1] Not enclosed.

490. *To Clevland*

[TNA, ADM 1/2385]

Dublin at Portsmouth
30 December 1757

Sir,

I have received your letter of the 28th [No. 489] and have sent to the Navy Board the ticket belonging to Richard Leonard who was discharged unserviceable from Haslar Hospital.

491. *To Clevland*

[TNA, ADM 1/2386]

Dublin in Portsmouth Harbour
9 January 1758

Sir,

I herewith transmit to you a list of the men,[1] with an account of their pay tickets, which were turned over from His Majesty's ship *Roebuck* and the *Firedrake* bomb into the *Dublin*. And beg you will be pleased to move their Lordships, that before the ship proceeds to sea the said men may be paid the wages due thereon for the time they have served in the several ships; being absolutely induced to make this application to their Lordships from the great discount the men will suffer from if they dispose of them.

I must also beg their Lordships will be pleased to order two months' advance to be paid to the ship's company as they are bare of necessaries and no money of that sort having as yet been paid to them since I have commanded the ship.

492. *From Clevland*

[TNA, ADM 2/709, pp. 186–7]

10 January 1758

Sir,

I have read to my Lord Commissioners of the Admiralty your letter [No. 491] of the 9th instant enclosing a list of ten pay tickets belonging to men turned over from the *Roebuck* and *Firedrake* into the *Dublin* which you desire may be paid their wages. And I am to acquaint you that the Navy Board are directed to do it if they have no objection.

---

[1] Enclosed is a list of 64 seamen and details concerning their pay.

With regard to the men who you desire may be paid two months advances, I am to acquaint you that you should deliver your lists agreeable to your instructions to the commissioner.

493. *To Clevland*

[TNA, ADM 1/2386] *Dublin* at Spithead
14 January 1758

Sir,
I must desire you will please to acquaint their Lordships that His Majesty's ship under my command went out of the harbour this day.

494. *To Clevland*

[TNA, ADM 1/2386] *Dublin* at Spithead
26 January 1758

Sir,
Rear Admiral [Thomas] Broderick having this day informed me that it was their Lordships' direction, a pay ticket should be made out for James Horn, late belonging to His Majesty's ship under my command, said to be discharged unserviceable from her the 13th of October last.

I beg you will be pleased to acquaint their Lordships, that the said James Horn was turned over with several others into His Majesty's ship *Anson* on the 1st of last August at the Nore and that five regular pay list[s] were made out for the men so turned over, and transmitted to the Navy Board agreeable to their Lordships' order upon that head.

495. *From the Lords of the Admiralty*

[TNA, ADM 2/80, p. 66] 27 January 1758

You are hereby required and directed to accompany His Majesty's ships *Prince Frederick* and *Juno* two hundred leagues to the westward of Scilly and then make the best of your way back to Spithead and remain there till further order.

496. To Clevland

[TNA, ADM 1/2386]

Dublin at Spithead
18 February 1758

Sir,

I must desire you will please to acquaint their Lordships that I am returned to Spithead with His Majesty's ship under my command having accompanied the *Prince Frederick* and *Juno* with their convoy of transports into the latitude of 42° 20' 200 leagues SW from Scilly, where I left them on the 9th instant with moderate weather, and their whole convoy in company.

Enclosed I transmit to you the state and condition of the ships as likewise a journal of my proceedings.[1]

497. From the Lords of the Admiralty

[TNA, ADM 2/80, p. 142]

23 February 1758

You are hereby required and directed to use the utmost dispatch in completing the beef and pork of His Majesty's ship under your command to six months, and all other species of provisions to as much as she can conveniently stow, and her stores to a proper proportion for foreign service. And having so done you are in pursuance of the King's pleasure signified to us by Mr. Pitt,[2] one of His principal secretaries of state, to proceed without a moment's loss of time to join Admiral Boscawen, agreeable to the rendezvous you will receive from Captain [Sir John] Bentley late of the *Invincible*, and Captain [Robert] Swanton of the *Vanguard*. And you are to put yourself under the command of the said Admiral and follow his orders for your farther proceedings.

498. From Clevland

[TNA, ADM 2/709, p. 377]

27 February 1758

Sir,

I am commanded by my Lords Commissioners of the Admiralty to signify their direction to you to receive on board His Majesty's ship under your command Mr. Bray and Mr. Mace, two of the hospital mates who are going to North America in the *Invincible* and are now on

---

[1] Not enclosed.
[2] William Pitt, Secretary of State(South), 6 Dec. 1756–5 Oct. 1761.

board the *Royal Sovereign*, and give them passage to North America when you proceed thither, taking care that they account with your purser for what provisions they may expend during their passage.

499. *To Clevland*

[TNA, ADM 1/2386] *Dublin* at Spithead
27 February 1758

Sir,

I have this moment received their Lordships' orders [No. 497] of the 23rd, by express and shall use the utmost dispatch in putting them into execution, and hope in a few days to be ready to sail.

I must beg leave to take notice to their Lordships that His Majesty's ship under my command is many men short of complement; hope they will be pleased to order her to be completed from the *Invincible*, as the *Dublin* goes in her place.

I must likewise take notice that the boatswain, through sickness, is incapable of duty and obliged to be sent to sick quarters. I should be glad their Lordships would be pleased to let either the boatswain of the *Invincible* or *Tilbury* do duty on board the *Dublin* in his absence.

500. *From Clevland*

[TNA, ADM 2/709, p. 383] 28 February 1758

Sir,

I have read to my Lords Commissioners of the Admiralty your letter of the 24th instant informing them that the ship you command is many men short of complement, and I am to acquaint you that Sir Edward Hawke is directed to make up the deficiency, but their Lordships hope more care will be taken of your men it appearing the *Dublin* lost near fifty men by desertion the last time she came into harbour.

I am also to inform you that the boatswain of the *Tilbury* is appointed to the ship you command.

501. To Clevland

[TNA, ADM 1/2386]
Dublin at Spithead
1 March 1758

Sir,

I have received your letter [No. 498] of the 27th past, signifying to me their Lordships' directions to receive on board the ship I command Mr. Bray and W. Mace, two of the hospital mates and give them a passage to North America.

You will please to inform their Lordships that so soon as the wind offers, His Majesty's ship under my command will be ready to proceed to sea.

502. From the Lords of the Admiralty

[TNA, ADM 2/80, p. 160]
2 March 1758

Major General Amherst[1] who may be expected daily to arrive at Portsmouth being under orders to proceed to North America, you are hereby required and directed to wait till he arrives and then receive him together with his retinue and baggage on board His Majesty's ship under your command and give them a passage to Halifax, victualling them whilst on board as the ship's company.

503. To Clevland

[TNA, ADM 1/2386]
Dublin at Spithead
5 March 1758

Sir,

I have received their Lordships' order [No. 502] of the 2nd instant directing me to receive on board His Majesty's ship under my command, Major General Amherst, together with his retinue &c. and give them a passage to Halifax. You will please to inform their Lordships that agreeable to their orders I shall wait his arrival at this place and receive him on board accordingly. You will please likewise to acquaint them that His Majesty's ship *Dublin* is in every respect ready for the sea.

---

[1] Major General Jeffery Amherst, commander of the land forces during the British attack on Louisburg.

504. To Clevland

[TNA, ADM 1/2386] *Dublin* at Spithead
6 March 1758

Sir,

Having received orders from Sir Edward Hawke to take the *Elizabeth* transport under convoy to Halifax, and since that directions [No. 502] from their Lordships to receive on board Major General Amherst, I hope their Lordships will not think me impertinent if I take the liberty to remind them that the *Vanguard* who will soon be ready, has already orders from Mr. Boscawen to take the convoy with him to Halifax, and as this single transport may make the passage considerably longer than it would otherways be, I hope their Lordships will please to permit me to sail when the General arrives without the said transport.

505. From Clevland

[TNA, ADM 2/709, p. 405] 6 March 1758

Sir,

I have received and read to my Lords Commissioners of the Admiralty your letter [No. 502] of the 5th instant giving an account that the ship you command is ready for the sea. And I am to acquaint you that Mr. Pitt, His Majesty's principal secretary of state is informed thereof.

506. From Clevland

[TNA, ADM 2/709, p. 411] 7 March 1758

Sir,

I have read to my Lords Commissioners of the Admiralty your letter [No. 504] of the 6th instant relating to the *Elizabeth* transport which you were ordered to take under your convoy to Halifax. And I am commanded to acquaint you that this transport is ordered to be discharged out of the service.

507. To Clevland

[TNA, ADM 1/2386]

Dublin at Vigo
29 March 1758

Sir,

I desire that you will please to inform their Lordships that I am this day put into this port with His Majesty's ship *Dublin* under my command having on the 21st instant taken in latitude of 49° off Ushant a French East Indiaman called *Le Montmartel* who sailed from the Islands of Bourbon[1] 20th November last.

A violent scurvy and sickness which I found raging among the prisoners, obliged me to put in here, in order to preserve the health of my own ship's company, where my stay shall be as short as possible, proposing to sail from hence as tomorrow morning.

I flatter myself their Lordships when opportunity offers will be so obliging as to grant her convoy to England.

His Majesty's sloop *Peregrine*, Captain Logie, arrived here this day and brought in with him a retaken ship.

508. To Clevland

[TNA, ADM 1/2386]

Dublin at Vigo
31 March 1758

Sir,

Since my writing to their Lordships yesterday [No. 507], a calm has prevented my getting out, but I am ready and shall sail at a moment's warning, having completed my water.

On my arrival here I immediately applied to the English consul to acquaint the French consul at this port, that I was willing to land the prisoners belonging to his nation, provided he would give me proper security that none of them should serve against His Britannic Majesty until exchanged.

He accordingly came on board this day, gave me all the security I could desire, and took the prisoners on shore in the boat with him.

But having learned since that this has given great offence to the inhabitants of Vigo, on account of the bad state of health of the French

[1] Reunion.

prisoners, notwithstanding they had visited and granted pratique[1] to both ships.

As false representations may be made to the Court of Madrid on this head, and as I am certainly informed that two hundred seamen went from this place to Ferrol this morning, that all the seamen in the ports of Galicia are ordered forthwith to repair on board their fleet fitting out there, and to prevent any disputes arising between the two courts from the detention of the Indiaman, taken by His Majesty's ship under my command, I hope their Lordships will approve of my having given Captain Logie of His Majesty's sloop *Peregrine* an order to convoy her in safety to England.

509. To Clevland

[TNA, ADM 1/2386] *Dublin* at sea
7 May 1758

Sir,

I take the opportunity by a merchant ship I this day spoke with, to acquaint their Lordships that His Majesty's ship under my command is now in the latitude of 40°00', Cape Sambrough[2] bearing NNW 81 leagues.

I have been detained several hours, in taking out the crew belonging to the *Mars* privateer of Bristol, which ship foundered this morning and part of her men perished.

It blows hard at south and I hope to be at Halifax in a day or two.

My ship's company have proved very sickly, many died and one hundred and thirty men ill of the scurvy and fever.

The poor wretches I have saved are all in a terrible condition.

510. To Clevland

[TNA, ADM 1/2386] *Dublin* off the Start
14 September 1758

Sir,

Please to acquaint their Lordships that I sailed from Louisburg on the 15th August with His Majesty's ships and transports (named in the

---

[1] A licence to have dealings with a port after quarantine or upon showing a clean bill of health.
[2] Cape Sable.

margin[1]) under my command, having on board the governor and garrison of the said place as likewise all the officers and seamen of the men of war taken or destroyed, in or off that port.

As the wind continues easterly and the transports who are very sickly losing ground, I thought it prudent to harbour them as soon as possible, more especially since I have detected a design formed by the officers and prisoners on board one of them to carry her to France, had an opportunity of a dark night and bad weather offered.

Some even of the principal officers who are prisoners on board the men of war, approved of their intentions notwithstanding the capitulation expressly declared they should be carried to England.

As the commodore and all sea officers in general are on board the *Dublin*, and the governor and principal officers of the troops and the garrison on board the *Terrible*, I shall endeavour to get with them to Portsmouth as soon as possible.

I spoke to my Lord Anson on the 11th instant off Ushant and enclosed I transmit the state and condition of the ships under my command.[2]

511. To Clevland

[TNA, ADM 1/2386]

Dublin at Spithead
17 September 1758

Sir,

I beg you will please to acquaint their Lordships of my arrival at Spithead with His Majesty's ship under my command, in company with His Majesty's ships *Northumberland* and *Terrible*.

I hope you have received my express [No. 510] sent by Captain [William] Parry from Plymouth, acquainting you with the reason of my sending the transports under the care of His Majesty's ship *Kingston* and *Burford* into that port.

---

[1]*Northumberland, Terrible, Kingston, Burford*. Transports *Samuel and Robert, Samuel and Mary, Lark, Wallington, Mary, Dolphin, Maria Theresa, Juno, Hopeful Success* and *Two Brothers*.
[2]Enclosed a list of four ships showing the number of men and the amount of provisions on board each vessel.

512. *From Clevland*

[TNA, ADM 2/710, p. 374] 18 September 1758

Sir,

I have communicated to my Lords Commissioners of the Admiralty your letter [No. 510] of the 14th instant, giving an account of your arrival off the Start with His Majesty's ships and transports therein named, from Louisburg, and of your having detected a design formed by the officers and prisoners on board one of the transports to carry her to France. And I am commanded by their Lordships to signify their direction to you to send them the names of those officers, and what proof there is, of their acting in this manner.

513. *To Clevland*

[TNA, ADM 1/2386] *Dublin* at Spithead
18 September 1758

Sir,

As I have the misfortune to be much afflicted with the scurvy, I must desire you will please to make it my request to their Lordships that they will give me leave to go into the country for a month for the recovery of my health.

514. *From the Lords of the Admiralty*

[TNA, ADM 2/81, pp. 112–13] 19 September 1758

You are hereby required and directed to repair with His Majesty's ship under your command into Portsmouth Harbour, where we have ordered her to be cleaned, tallowed, and refitted, stored for Channel service, and her provisions completed to three months' of all species except beer of which she is to have as much as she can conveniently stow.

If you have any men who you suspect will run away, you are to apply to Vice Admiral Holburne for their security.

When the ship is ready again in all respects for the sea you are to repair to Spithead for further orders.

515. *From Clevland*

[TNA, ADM 2/710, p. 381] 19 September 1758

Sir,

I have received and read to my Lords Commissioners of the Admiralty your letter [No. 512] of yesterday's date desiring a months' leave to go into the country for the recovery of your health. And I am to acquaint you that Admiral Holburne is directed to give you the said leave as soon as the ship is clear for the dock.

516. *To Clevland*

[TNA, ADM 1/2386] *Dublin* at Spithead
21 September 1758

Sir,

I received your letter [No. 511] of the 18th instant ordering me to send the names of the French officers &c who I mentioned [No. 510] had formed a design to carry the transport to France.

I must beg you will please to acquaint their Lordships the time would not permit my making so strict an enquiry as I would have done, it being near night, and discovering a strange fleet in the SW quarter, which proved to be my Lord Anson, but Captain Parry of His Majesty's ship *Kingston* will be able to give their Lordships a very distinct account of the same, to whom I must beg leave to refer their Lordships; as I ordered all the officers concerned in the attempt on board his ship.

517. *To Clevland*

[TNA, ADM 1/2386] *Dublin* at Spithead
25 September 1758

Sir,

I have received your answer [No. 514] informing me of their Lordships' leave to go into the country, as soon as His Majesty's ship under my command is come into the harbour and cleared for the dock. But as the wind has continued northerly and at present no appearance of a change, and my health being very much impaired, I beg you will be pleased to move their Lordships that I may have immediate leave to be absent for the recovery thereof.

518. *From Clevland*

[TNA, ADM 2/710, p. 397] 26 September 1758

Sir,
Having read to my Lords Commissioners of the Admiralty your letter [No. 517] of the 25th instant desiring that your leave may commence directly, and that you may not wait till the ship is cleared for the dock, I am to acquaint you that Admiral Holburne is directed to give you leave directly.

519. *To Clevland*

[TNA, ADM 1/2386] 27 September 1758

Sir,
As Lieutenant Joseph Hunt who was sent home in the *Montmartel*,[1] a prize taken by His Majesty's ship under my command, is now returned to the said ship, I beg you will [be] pleased to move their Lordships that he may be reinstated in his former station of third lieutenant from which he was superseded in America.

520. *From Clevland*

[TNA, ADM 2/710, p. 404] 28 September 1758

Sir,
In return to your letter of the 27th instant [No. 519] desiring that Lieutenant Hunt, who was sent home in a prize you took, may be reinstated in the ship you command, I am to acquaint you that it was done before your application.

521. *To Clevland*

[TNA, ADM 1/2386] Alresford
1 October 1758

Sir,
The captains of the French ships of war, who were taken prisoners at Louisburg and are now at Alresford, have desired me to make it my

---

[1] See also No. 507.

humble request to their Lordships that they may be granted more liberty than one mile from their quarters. They are ready to give their parole of honour or any other security that may be demanded that they will comply with whatever directions [that] are given concerning them. As they came to England in the *Dublin*[1] and behaved remarkably well during their continuance on board her, I take the liberty to represent their case to their Lordships, which at present is the same as the meanest of the officers who were in their merchant service, and are allott Alresford for their place of residence as there is no considerable town within less than seven mile of this place. If their lordships would be pleased to let their liberty extend to four of [*sic*]five mile, I could answer for their not exceeding that distance.

522. *To Clevland*

[TNA, ADM 1/2386]   19 October 1758

Sir,

His Majesty's ship *Dublin* under my command being in want of a school master, and one Mr John Harrison being recommended as a person properly qualified, I hope their Lordships will be pleased to grant him a warrant.

523. *To Clevland*

[TNA, ADM 1/2386]   21 October 1758

Sir,

Having returned from America in a very ill state of health and being much afflicted with the scurvy, which I am told must return with greater violence should I immediately go to sea again.

I hope their Lordships will be so good as to permit me to remain on shore during the *Dublin's* next cruise, who is now out of the dock and refitting.

I hope in six weeks or two months I shall be able to do my duty again.

---

[1] See also No. 510.

524. *From Clevland*

[TNA, ADM 2/710, p. 493]　　　　　　　　　　　　21 October 1758

Sir,

Having read to my Lords Commissioners of the Admiralty your letter [No. 523] of this date, desiring leave to remain ashore during the next cruise of His Majesty's ship under your command, on account of your ill state of health. I am to acquaint you that their Lordships are pleased to comply with your request.

525. *To the Duke of Newcastle*

[BL, Add. MSS 32890, f. 330]　　　　　　　　　　Hill Street [London]
　　　　　　　　　　　　　　　　　　　　　　　　　24 April 1759

Captain Rodney presents his most humble respects to the Duke of Newcastle, and begs leave to acquaint his Grace that Lord Northampton[1] is this evening arrived in town from his travels and intends waiting upon his Grace tomorrow in the forenoon.

Upon some conversation with his Lordship he finds him truly sensible of his Grace's favours and he likewise added he should think himself happy to be introduced to His Majesty by your Grace. This I thought proper to make you acquainted with and hope your Grace will take it as a sincere token of my attachment to your service.

---

[1] On 6 December 1758 George 6th Earl of Northampton died without issue and the earldom descended to his nephew Charles Compton who became the 7th Earl of Northampton.

PART III

FLAG OFFICER, 1759–1763

The Channel

On 19 May 1759 George Rodney, after having served in the Royal Navy for 27 years, was promoted to the rank of rear admiral of the blue squadron.[1] Rodney's first assignment, upon being promoted to flag rank, was to act, in the absence of Vice Admiral Francis Holburne, as commander-in-chief at Portsmouth.[2] The position of commander-in-chief at Portsmouth was one in which the occupant in essence served as a conduit through which reports on the activities of naval forces in the Portsmouth region passed to the Admiralty and orders from that body were sent to various ships and vessels at Portsmouth and Spithead.[3] Rodney would serve as acting commander-in-chief at Portsmouth for only a few weeks before being placed in command of a squadron assigned to operate along the French Channel coast in the Bay of Seine.

Intelligence reports, during the first months of 1759, arrived in London telling of the assembling of French troops in the coastal areas of Normandy and Brittany, across the English Channel from the southern coast of Britain, as well as the construction of flat-bottomed boats and other naval activities in French Channel ports. These measures, which pointed to a French attempt to invade England, could not be hidden for long and soon came to the notice of the British government.[4] On 30 May 1759 William Pitt, Secretary of State, communicated to Parliament in the form of a message from George II the government's belief that the French were making preparations to invade England.[5]

The British government was certainly not going to wait for the arrival of the French invasion forces on the shores of England; it

---

[1]David Syrett and R. L. DiNardo, eds, *The Commissioned Sea Officers of the Royal Navy, 1660–1815* (Aldershot, Hants.: Scolar Press for the Navy Records Society, 1994), p. 384.
[2]No. 526.
[3]Eg., Nos. 528–30, 539.
[4]Lawrence Henry Gipson, *The Great War for the Empire: The Culmination, 1760–1763* (New York, 1953), vol. VIII, pp. 4–7.
[5]*The Parliamentary History of England From the Earliest Period to the Year 1803* (London, 1813), vol. XV, col. 940.

intended instead that the first line of Britain's defence against a French invasion were to be the coasts and ports of France. The plan, which emerged in the spring of 1759, was one in which the Western Squadron under Admiral Sir Edward Hawke would blockade the French battle fleet in Brest while further British naval forces disrupted the enemy's invasion plans by blockading the northern coast of France. Dunkirk and Le Havre were obviously to be the main ports of embarkation for the intended French invasion of England. A small naval force, supported by the British squadron in the Downes, would blockade Dunkirk; at the same time another squadron would firstly disrupt with gunfire the French invador's preparations at Le Havre and then blockade that port.[1] Lord Anson, the First Lord of the Admiralty, who was apparently the intellectual force behind the formation of these plans to counter the threat of French invasion in 1759, selected Rodney to command the squadron designed to operate in the Bay of Seine against the French naval forces in Le Havre.[2]

On 5 June Rodney was informed of the government's intentions that he should lead an attack on Le Havre. The whole matter was supposed to be secret. In an attempt to deceive the French as to the objective of Rodney's assembled force, orders were issued calling for Rodney to command a squadron proceeding to the Mediterranean. The captains of a number of ships at Portsmouth were also informed that they were to go to the Mediterranean with Rodney.[3] In spite of these measures, such attempts at deception were not very successful. For not only did Rodney have to find pilots with a knowledge of the Bay of Seine, but the fitting of bomb vessels at Portsmouth easily led to speculation among navy officers that an attack against a French Channel port was soon to be undertaken.[4]

On 26 June the Admiralty issued secret orders to Rodney to take command of a squadron of twelve warships,[5] five bomb vessels[6] as well as a number of cutters and flat-bottomed boats. Rodney, at the head of this force, was directed to attack and destroy 'by bombardment as well as all other means' any boats being built at, together with any warlike or naval stores found in Le Havre as well as 'any boats, stores, provi-

---

[1]Gipson, *The Great War for the Empire*, vol. VIII, p. 8.
[2]Julian S. Corbett, *England in the Seven Years War: A Study in Combined Strategy* (London, 1907), vol. II, p. 24n.
[3]Nos. 544–6.
[4]No. 543.
[5]*Achilles, Norwich, Isis, Chatham, Deptford, Chesterfield, Brilliant, Vestal, Juno, Boreas, Fly* and *Wolf.*
[6]*Basilisk, Mortar, Furnace, Blast* and *Carcass.* Later the *Firedrake* would also join Rodney's squadron.

sions and materials' that were located near the city. Rodney was further ordered 'not to permit any ships or vessels whatsoever to enter the said Port.'[1] The ships and vessels of Rodney's squadron were prepared, during the month of June, to undertake this attack on Le Havre. On 28 June Rodney reported to the Admiralty from Portsmouth that the force assigned to attack Le Havre was ready to begin operations. However, the ships would have to wait at St Helens until the conditions of wind and weather on the French coast were favourable for the deployment and operation of bomb vessels.[2]

On 2 July the weather turned favourable and Rodney's squadron sailed from St Helens for the coast of France. Arriving, on 3 July, in the road of the French port Rodney deployed the bomb vessels of his squadron to bombard 'the flat bottomed boats, and the enemy magazines, stores &c. that were in the town of Le Havre.'[3] For 52 hours the city of Le Havre was bombarded by the 10 and 13 inch mortars of the five British bomb vessels. In his report to the Admiralty Rodney states 'that the town was several times in flames and their magazine of stores for the flat bottomed boats burnt with a great fury for upwards of six hours.'[4] The bomb vessel *Basilisk*, in the course of the bombardment, fired a total of 182 carcasses and shells into Le Havre.[5] According to a French account the British bomb vessels destroyed some 30 houses, 3 rope works, several boats, and a great quantity of wooden planking.[6] The bombardment ended only when the mortar beds in the British bomb vessels were rendered, owing to repeated firing, unservicable.[7] On 8 July Rodney with most of his squadron, including the bomb vessels, returned to Spithead while five ships[8] remained in the Bay of Seine to blockade Le Havre to prevent any vessels with the materials necessary for the construction of flat bottomed boats from entering the port.[9]

On 17 August Rodney was ordered to return to Le Havre with his squadron, including four bomb vessels, in order to renew the bombardment of the city.[10] Arriving off Le Havre on 28 August Rodney discovered

[1] No. 560.
[2] Nos. 563–6.
[3] No. 567.
[4] No. 569.
[5] TNA, ADM 51/83, 6 July 1759.
[6] Richard Waddington, *La Guerre de Sept Ans: histoire diplomatique et militaire* (Paris, 1905), vol. III, p. 366.
[7] No. 569.
[8] *Isis, Chatham, Unicorn, Boreas, Fly* sloop.
[9] No. 571.
[10] No. 577.

that owing to a combination of unfavourable weather conditions and new French defensive measures it would be impossible to subject the city with any results to a second bombardment. In a letter to Pitt, Rodney explained that another bombardment of Le Havre 'would be attended with unsurmountable difficulties' because the French had placed two floating batteries and two 'flat bottomed vessels' so as to be able to 'rake' the bomb vessels. Further, there were now four French gallies, armed with heavy cannon and protected by shoals and sand banks, which were placed in such a position so as to attack with cannon any bomb vessels attempting to bombard Le Havre. At the same time Rodney reported that the French had almost completed the construction of some 30 flat bottomed boats on the beach near Le Havre and furthermore that he had intelligence that there were an additional 120 flat bottomed boats in the Seine River and at Rouen.[1] Because of these circumstances it was decided not to continue the attempt to renew the bombardment of Le Havre, but rather to blockade the place.[2] One consequence of Rodney's operations against Le Havre was to force the French to conclude that before an invasion of England could be mounted from ports on the north coast of France some method, however fleeting, of winning naval control of the English Channel must first be discovered.[3]

The British blockade of Le Havre, which began in September of 1759, was to be a continuous and prolonged effort. Rodney would remain in command of the squadron deployed in the Bay of Seine for the blockade of Le Havre throughout the autumn of 1759 into January of 1760. It was a difficult and trying duty, especially as the weather became worse with the onset of autumn and winter gales that prevailed that time of year in the English Channel. There was always the danger that the blockading ships would be forced onto a lee shore in the course of northwest or northeast gales. Indeed as a result of the adverse weather, Rodney's ships had to seek shelter, on many occasions, at Spithead.[4] At other times ships fell into a state of disrepair requiring them to be sent in the dockyard at Portsmouth,[5] while the shortage of provisions amongst Rodney's force, during its stay in the Bay of Seine was also always a problem.[6] Nevertheless, week after week, Rodney's squadron, in the face of deteriorating weather conditions in the area, continued to

---

[1](W. S. Taylor and J. H. Pringle, eds), *The Correspondence of William Pitt, Earl of Chatham* (London, 1838), vol. III, pp. 420–2.
[2]Nos. 601 and 602.
[3]Gipson, *The Great War for the Empire*, vol. VIII, p. 10.
[4]Eg., Nos. 638, 644 and 646.
[5]Eg., Nos. 641 and 666.
[6]Eg., No. 616.

blockade Le Havre. In January 1760 Rodney, due to the 'severity of the weather', and believing that there was little possibility of any French ships putting to sea, suggested that only two frigates and a few cutters be stationed off Le Havre and that the bulk of his squadron should be stationed at St Helens 'ready to relieve those before Le Havre every eight or ten days'.[1] However, before this suggestion could be acted upon Rodney became ill and was replaced, temporarily, in command of the blockading squadron by Captain George Darby.[2]

While on blockade duty off the French coast, Rodney was on 24 November 1759 elected unopposed as an administration candidate to Parliament for the Borough of Okehampton in Devon.[3] His successful election to a seat in the House of Commons for Okehampton was brought about through the interest of the Duke of Newcastle.[4] While his political career did not exactly take off as a result of his election to Parliament, it did show that he remained the recipient of political patronage. Rodney's attendance at the House of Commons would, at best, be irregular owing to his service at sea. As it had been the case in Saltash, although for different reasons, in the election of 1761, he was not reselected to stand, once more, for Okehampton. Moreover, Newcastle had neglected to inform Rodney before the event of this change of circumstance. This brought forth a panicky letter[5] from Rodney, who had concluded that he had fallen from favour. Matters were soon put to right when Newcastle arranged for Rodney's election to the House of Commons from the Borough of Penryn in Cornwall.[6] Rodney would remain a Member of Parliament for Penryn until 1768. However, his duties as commander of the squadron blockading Le Havre and then commander-in-chief in the Leeward Islands would prevent regular attendance at the House.[7]

On 20 May 1760 Rodney was ordered to resume command of the squadron blockading the port of Le Havre and the French coast of the Bay of Seine.[8] Seven days later Rodney hoisted his flag on board the 50-gun ship HMS *Deptford* at Spithead.[9] The duty was much the same

[1] Nos. 678 and 684.
[2] No. 688.
[3] Sir Lewis Namier and John Brooke, *The History of Parliament: The House of Commons, 1754–1790* (London, 1964), vol. III, p. 369.
[4] No. 659.
[5] No. 836.
[6] No. 841.
[7] Namier and Brooke, *History of Parliament*, vol. III, p. 369.
[8] Rodney's squadron consisted of *Deptford, Tweed, Aquilon, Rose, Albany* sloop, as well as *Firedrake* and *Furnace* bombs. No. 689.
[9] TNA, ADM 51/241, 27 May 1760.

as before: day after day the ships of Rodney's command blockaded the harbour of Le Havre, ranged along the French coast, and patrolled the Bay of Seine and the English Channel searching out any French ships which might be attempting to run the British blockade. It was a difficult, and in some respects, a dull assignment, for contacts with the enemy were few. What looms large in Rodney's correspondence during this period are problems, such as, the difficulties of keeping station along the French channel coast during adverse weather,[1] the problems of ships falling into disrepair,[2] and the logistics of supplying provisions and other stores required to sustain ships at sea.[3] A major task of Rodney, and of the ships under his command, was to obtain and send to the Admiralty all the intelligence possible on enemy activities. For instance, on 12 July 1760 Rodney reported that the French were fitting out a 32-gun frigate, called the *Félicité*, at Le Havre. Over the next several months additional reports were dispatched to the Admiralty, concerning the state and condition of this French vessel, until 1 November, when the admiral reported that the *Félicité* had been lost, after breaking out through the blockade of Le Havre. She would eventually be chased up the English Channel, by British warships, and driven ashore while attempting to enter Dunkirk.[4] What contact there actually was between Rodney's ships and the enemy consisted, for the most part, in small-scale actions with French coasters attempting to run the blockade. For example, on 18 July Rodney reported to the Admiralty that HMS *Albany* and HM Bomb *Furnace*, in what was probably the largest action fought during this period by ships under his command, had driven on shore, and destroyed, five French 'flat bottomed boats'.[5] Rodney continued in command of the British squadron in the Bay of Seine charged with the blockade of Le Havre until the end of January 1761.[6]

The Leeward Isles

On 5 October 1761 Rodney was informed that he had been appointed Commander-in-chief of the squadron in the Leeward Islands.[7] It was Lord Anson, the First Lord of the Admiralty, who had 'brought for-

---

[1]Eg., Nos. 743 and 745.
[2]Eg., Nos. 735 and 739.
[3]Eg., Nos. 746 and 777.
[4]Nos. 711, 730, 736, 749, 759 and 763.
[5]No. 716.
[6]No. 802.
[7]No. 846.

ward' Rodney[1] and had selected him to command the squadron in the Leeward Islands in preference to a number of more senior officers. This appointment was a vote of confidence by Anson in the professional abilities of Rodney for the new commander-in-chief in the Leeward Islands would be charged with the task of capturing the French colony of Martinique. Following the British conquest of Canada, the island of Martinique was one of the last major French strongholds in the Western Hemisphere. Its securing by British forces would be a major step towards the complete destruction of the French overseas empire. There was a lot at stake here. Martinique, the bastion of French power in the Lesser Antilles, was not only a major producer of sugar, but also a centre of extensive privateering activity. With the eventual capture of Martinique the French position in the entire region of the Leeward Islands would collapse; all that would remain of the French empire in the Western Hemisphere would be the island of St. Domingo and the province of Louisiana on the North American mainland.[2]

Planning and preparing for the British assault on Martinique began in December of 1760, when orders were issued to ready British troops, in North America, for service in the West Indies. However, the attack on Martinique would not be undertaken until the hurricane season of 1761 had ended.[3] The British plan for the conquest of the island after it had been fully formulated was, indeed, formidable. It called for the deployment of almost 14,000 troops and a powerful naval force of 13 ships of the line, supported by numerous other vessels and manned by some 11,000 men of the Royal Navy. This force, assembled from places as far distant as New York and England would, when the time came, mount the assault on Martinique from Carlisle Bay on the island of Barbados.[4] Rodney's orders, issued on 7 October 1761, called for him to sail from England with six ships of the line and two bomb vessels,[5] which would be escorting transports carrying the 61st, 69th, 76th and 90th Regiments of Foot, and to proceed to the Leeward Islands. Upon arrival at Barbados, Rodney was directed to take command of the ships of the Royal Navy in the Leeward Islands and then,

[1] Cf. Philip C. Yorke, *The Life and Correspondence of Philip Yorke Earl of Hardwicke: Lord High Chancellor of Great Britain* (Cambridge, 1913), vol. II, p. 114.
[2] Gipson, *The Great War for the Empire*, vol. VIII, p. 185.
[3] Gertrude Selwyne Kimball, ed., *Correspondence of William Pitt when Secratary of State with Colonial Governors and Military and Naval Commissioners in America* (New York, 1906), vol. II, pp. 370, 384.
[4] Gipson, *The Great War for the Empire*, vol. VIII, pp. 189–91.
[5] *Marlborough, Vanguard, Modeste, Nottingham, Foudroyant, Dragon*, and *Thunder* and *Granado* bomb vessels.

in conjunction with Major General Hon. Robert Monckton, to mount the assault on the island of Martinique.[1]

Rodney arrived at Barbados on 23 November 1761. A few days after he had departed from the Western Approaches of the English Channel a strong gale of wind forced Rodney, in HMS *Marlborough*, to part company with the other ships of the squadron. However, over the next several days the missing ships of his force also successfully arrived at Barbados as did a convoy carrying British troops from Belle Isle on the coast of France. On 24 December a large convoy carrying troops and Monckton also arrived at Barbados from North America. After taking on board water, and making arrangements for carrying out landing operations, Rodney together with Monckton sailed from Barbados, on 5 January 1762, with a force consisting of almost 14,000 troops and a fleet consisting of 13 ships of the line[2] and 24 smaller warships. On 7 January the British force arrived off the east coast of Martinique.[3]

In a triumph of maritime strategic mobility the British had managed to deploy off Martinique an overpowering force of ships and troops. However, because of the island's foliage and mountainous terrain, it still presented an attacker with huge problems and formidable challenges for it was almost impossible for an army, with heavy equipment, to manoeuvre in such territory. These difficulties, and others, were not fully appreciated when it was decided to land the army at St Ann's Bay, on the southern end of Martinique, and then to march overland to the French stronghold of Fort Royal. On 8 January, the British began landing operations at St Ann's Bay which, from the beginning, went wrong. HMS *Raisonnable*, a 64-gun ship of the line, was lost by being run on a rock, owing to the ignorance of her pilot, and the army, once ashore, found that, because of difficult terrain, it just could not move on to Fort Royal. After re-embarking the troops the British force proceeded northward to Fort Royal Bay.

On the morning of 16 January British troops made a fresh attempt at landing at Case des Navières on the north shore of Fort Royal Bay; this time they succeeded.[4] The distance from the landing site to Fort Royal was only about five miles, but the terrain was very difficult especially as the French defended every gully and ravine. Nevertheless, the necessary guns, men, and supplies were finally landed and then moved overland eastward, by British soldiers and seamen, to prepare for an

---

[1] Nos. 847 and 848.
[2] *Marlborough, Dublin, Foudroyant, Dragon, Téméraire, Temple, Vanguard, Modeste, Sterling Castle, Devonshire, Raisonnable, Alcide* and *Nottingham*.
[3] No. 857.
[4] No. 857.

attack on Morne Tortensen. On 25 January the necessary batteries were completed and the next day British troops attacked. And after two days of heavy fighting the French abandoned Morne Tortensen, as well as the adjacent Morne Garnier, and retreated inside the citadel of Fort Royal. After a siege, which lasted until 3 February, the French troops guarding the citadel of Fort Royal finally surrendered. On 16 February all organised resistance on the island of Martinique had ceased.[1] The capture of Martinique was brought about not only by the superiority of British military power and martial skill of the British seamen and soldiers, but also by the considerable tactical abilities and leadership skills of Monckton and Rodney.

The capture of Martinique was a great British victory for, as it was expected, it led to the collapse of the French position in the Leeward Islands and paved the way for further captures. On 26 February the French island of St Lucia surrendered to a squadron under Captain Hon. Augustus Hervey. On 5 March the island of Grenada passed into British hands and next St Vincent surrendered to the British.[2] Within weeks of the surrender of Martinique the British were in possession of all the French islands in the Lesser Antilles and all that remained of the French empire in America were St Domingo and Louisiana.

Despite such victories all strategic calculations and considerations were turned upside down several days after the surrender of Martinique with the arrival in the West Indies of news that Britain was at war with Spain and with the appearance, in the Leeward Islands, of a squadron of French warships. On 28 February Rodney learned of the start of the fighting between the British and Spanish and on 5 March government dispatches arrived in the Leeward Islands officially proclaiming Britain's declaration of war against Spain. On the same day that the official notice of war with Spain had arrived in the Leeward Islands Rodney, who was at Antigua, received further information concerning French manoeuvres. He learned that, on 23 January, a French squadron, said to consist of seven ships of the line and seven frigates, had evaded the British blockade and had escaped out into the Atlantic from Brest.[3]

Upon learning of the escape of the French squadron from Brest, Rodney immediately concluded that the enemy force was sailing to the West Indies. Orders were given to frigates, stationed to the windward of the Lesser Antilles, to watch for the approach of the French. Further orders were issued instructing the British ships of the line at St Lucia

---

[1] Nos. 858, 860, 861, 863 and 864; *London Gazette Extraordinary*, 23 March 1762.
[2] Nos. 865, 866 and 870.
[3] Nos. 864 and 867.

and Grenada to immediately rejoin Rodney at Antigua. At 4 pm on 9 March Rodney learned from HMS *Aquilon* and HMS *Woolwich*, frigates stationed to windward of Antigua, that, at about 8 am, eight French ships of the line and five smaller warships had been sighted to windward of the island standing to the south. However, before Rodney and his squadron could depart from Antigua, the French ships turned to leeward and disappeared heading in the direction of St Domingo.[1] Shortly after the disappearance to leeward of the French squadron, Rodney received dispatches from Jamaica saying that the island was under threat of attack by the French and Spanish. Upon receipt of this intelligence, Rodney decided to immediately reinforce the island in question, which was weakly defended, by sailing to Jamaica with the bulk of his squadron.[2]

Before Rodney could put into effect his intentions to sail for Jamaica with reinforcements, however, he received new orders from England. The new directive called for Rodney, in conjunction with Monckton, to prepare ships and troops to take part in an expedition to the Spanish island of Cuba to capture the city of Havana. The expedition to attack Havana, which was to be led by Vice Admiral Sir George Pocock and Lieutenant General, the Earl of Albemarle, was to have priority over all other operations. As Pocock and Albemarle would soon arrive from England in the Leeward Islands, Rodney and Monckton were directed to forthwith ready for service a majority of the warships and troops in the Lesser Antilles to take part in this operation.[3]

Upon receipt from England of the orders to prepare for the forthcoming attack on Havana, Rodney abandoned his intention of accompanying the reinforcements to Jamaica. Instead Commodore Sir James Douglas, Rodney's second in command, was dispatched to that island with a squadron consisting of eight ships of the line[4] and a number of smaller warships, while Rodney remained in the Leeward Islands to prepare for the arrival of Pocock and Albemarle. With the departure of the squadron for Jamaica, under the command of Douglas, Rodney went himself to Martinique to make preparations for the embarkation there of the troops of Monckton's army on board of transports for the operation against Havana.[5]

---

[1] No. 807.
[2] David Syrett, ed., *The Siege and Capture of Havana, 1762* (London: The Navy Records Society, 1970), pp. 63–9.
[3] No. 859.
[4] *Dragon, Temple, Devonshire, Téméraire, Alcide, Sterling Castle, Nottingham* and *Culloden*.
[5] Syrett, *Havana*, pp. 77–8, 93, 97, 99–101.

On 20 April Pocock and Albemarle arrived at Barbados and then proceeded northward to join Rodney and Monckton at Martinique. Pocock must have been suprised, and less than pleased, when he discovered that Douglas, with most of the ships of the line belonging to the squadron in the Leeward Islands, had already been sent to reinforce Jamaica. The instructions to Rodney from the Admiralty[1] had assigned overriding priority to the Havana expedition. Yet Rodney, in a decision which was probably a mistake, had dispatched to Jamaica eight ships of the line, which were to be assigned to Pocock's command. Moreover, Jamaica was so far to leeward that it was almost impossible for the ships to return to the Leeward Islands and raised the distinct possibility that these vessels could not join Pocock in time to take part in the all-important attack on Havana.

When the expedition against Havana finally sailed on 6 May from Martinique the British forces in the Leeward Islands were left in a greatly reduced state. With the departure of the troops to Havana, the army, which had so recently conquered Martinique, was reduced to little more than a corporal's guard while Rodney's squadron was reduced to three ships of the line[2] and 11 lesser vessels.[3] With this small force Rodney not only had to protect, from French and Spanish attack, British possessions in the Leeward Islands – a string of islands running for hundreds of miles from Antigua in the north to Barbados in the south – but had also to provide warships to hunt down enemy cruisers as well as to escort trade convoys to England.

The last months of Rodney's command in the Leeward Islands were largely anticlimactic. With the departure of the expedition to Havana, the centre of the war in the West Indies moved to Cuba and naval activity in the Leeward Islands consisted, for the most part, of hunting down enemy cruisers and escorting convoys of merchant ships to England. Hunting for enemy commerce raiders was a frustrating process because the enemy ships were few in number and usually small in size, making it difficult for the British to intercept them with their large warships. As a result Rodney chartered and brought into the service several small vessels which were more suitable for hunting down small enemy cruisers.[4] Just before the end of the fighting in the West Indies HMS *Antigua* fought two enemy privateers, capturing one, off of Guadeloupe and on 12 February 1763, HMS *Ferret* captured, on the south coast of Puerto Rico, the 400-ton Spanish merchant ship *Santissimo*

[1] No. 859.
[2] *Foudroyant, Vanguard, Modeste.*
[3] TNA, ADM 1/307, f. 448.
[4] No. 893.

Trinidada carrying a cargo of cocoa.[1] These two victories were among the few encounters with enemy ships in the Leeward Islands which actually materialized in the period between the departure of the expedition to Havana and the end of the war. Rodney, who was promoted to the rank of vice admiral of the blue squadron on 21 October 1762,[2] passed the last months of the Seven Years War dealing with matters such as the administration of the dockyard at Antigua[3] and battling with the army over prize money.[4]

On 2 January 1763, while Rodney was still stationed at Martinique, he learned of the signing of the Preliminary Treaty of Peace, at Fontainebleau between Great Britain, France and Spain.[5] The Seven Years War was over and Rodney, who desired to return to England, requested permission, which was granted, to leave the Leeward Islands command.[6] Several weeks after receiving leave to return to England Rodney departed from the Lesser Antilles and on 12 August 1763 arrived at Spithead.[7] When Rodney came ashore at Spithead in the summer of 1763 his situation and prospects had been radically transformed from what they had been at the outset, when as an obscure, ambitious young man, he had entered the Royal Navy, in 1732, as a volunteer per order. After 31 years of service in the Royal Navy, Rodney had risen to the rank of vice admiral; he had amassed a fortune in prize money and had obtained an estate in Hampshire. Moreover he had become a member of the political elite of Great Britain with a seat in Parliament, the crowning of success and fortune for his time. Although his private life had been plagued by personal tragedy, with the death of a wife that he had clearly loved, his professional life, material standing and social status had been blessed with success.

Notwithstanding the prerequisite degree of patronage that he had clearly enjoyed, his successes were nevertheless the result of his skill, hard work, and ability as a commander of men and ships. It would be such skills that would come to the fore in his later life and would give him the place in British naval history that is rightly his.

---

[1] Nos. 906 and 907.
[2] Syrett and DiNardo, *Commissioned Sea Officers*, p. 384.
[3] No. 888 and 902.
[4] Nos. 884 and 886.
[5] No. 902.
[6] No. 904.
[7] No. 916.

526. *From the Lords of the Admiralty*

[TNA, ADM 2/83, p. 40] 24 May 1759

You are hereby required and directed to repair forthwith to Portsmouth and hoist your flag[1] on board such of His Majesty's ships there as you shall think proper. And you are to do whatever may be in your power to forward the King's service, and particularly to hasten the dispatch of His Majesty's ships and vessels that may fit and refit within your reach, and to quicken the execution of such orders as we shall, from time to time, send to their respective commanders.

527. *To Clevland*

[TNA, ADM 1/93] Portsmouth
27 May 1759

Sir,
Admiral Holburne set out this morning for London. The orders which he has left I shall take care to comply with.

The *Swallow* sloop is just arrived with General Bocland's[2] Regiment from Jersey which shall be disembarked as soon as possible. Captain [Francis] Banks acquaints me the sloop is very foul. I have ordered her into clean agreeable to their Lordships standing orders for that purpose.

The *Jason* sailed this morning with the convoy to the westward.

528. *To Clevland*

[TNA, ADM 1/93] Portsmouth
28 May 1759

Sir,
I received yours of the 26th instant directed to Vice Admiral Holburne with their Lordships orders for the *Levant* and *Jason*.

You will please to acquaint their Lordships the *Jason* sailed yesterday morning with the trade to the westward. I have given orders to Captain [Thomas] Tucker of the *Levant* to take the trade bound to the eastward, under his convoy, and see them safe into the Downes, and

---

[1] On 19 May 1759 Rodney was promoted to the rank of Rear Admiral of the blue and assigned to act temporarily as Commander-in-Chief at Portsmouth.

[2] Lieutenant General Maurice Bocland or Bockland, colonel of the 11th Regiment of Foot.

then to follow his former orders. The *Jason* being sailed, I desire to know if their Lordships would have the sentence on the marines belonging to her put into execution. Enclosed[1] I have sent you a list of the unserviceable men at the *Blenheim* hospital ship.

529. From Clevland

[TNA, ADM 2/525, p. 342] 29 May [1759]

Sir,

I have received and read to my Lords Commissioners of the Admiralty, your letter [No. 528] of yesterday's date giving an account of the *Jason* being sailed.

As to the marines who did belong to her who are under sentence of being whipped, their Lordships leave it to you, to order them to be punished at such time as you think proper.

Their Lordships recommend it to you to examine the men said to be unserviceable on board the *Blenheim* hospital [ship], taking to your assistance the physician of the hospital and to discharge such as shall be found really unfit for service but no others.

As any new raised men are brought to you, their Lordships would have them put on board the *Fortune* sloop till she is completed and then on board the *Aurora*.

Mr. Holburne having informed their Lordships that some foreigners, who were able seamen, were willing to enter into the service and desired to know whether they are entitled to the bounty. I am commanded by their Lordships to acquaint you therewith and that they are equally entitled to the bounty with any others.

530. To Clevland

[TNA, ADM 1/93] Portsmouth
  29 May 1759

Sir,

You will please to acquaint their Lordships the *Lightning* fireship arrived yesterday after post from Liverpool with 108 impressed men which I have ordered on board the *Royal Ann*.

The *Levant* sailed to the eastward with her convoy and was out of sight last night.

---

[1]Enclosed a list of 11 men who were judged unfit for further service.

I hope the *Aurora* will be at Spithead in a day or two, and expect to have a sufficient number of men on board the *Royal Ann* to complete her, if their Lordships shall so approve.

531. From Clevland

[TNA, ADM 2/525, p. 349] 30 May 1759

Sir,

Lieutenant [James] Burnet of His Majesty's ship the *Mars*, applying to my Lords Commissioners of the Admiralty for a passage for himself and his gang to that ship, I am commanded by their Lordships to signify their direction to you to send them out in the first ship that goes to Sir Edward Hawke.

532. From Clevland

[TNA, ADM 2/525, p. 350] 30 May 1759

Sir,

I have received and read to my Lords Commissioners of the Admiralty your letter [No. 531] of yesterday's date. And [I] am to acquaint you their Lordships approve of your manning the *Aurora* from the *Royal Ann* in the manner you propose.

533. To Clevland

[TNA, ADM 1/93] Portsmouth
30 May 1759

Sir,

I have received yours of the 28th instant, with the orders enclosed for the *Levant*, *Swallow*, and *Fortune* sloop, which I have delivered to their respective captains, the *Levant* excepted. On her return to St. Helens I shall immediately order her into harbour.

534. From Clevland

[TNA, ADM 2/525, p. 352] 31 May [1759]

Sir,

I am commanded by my Lords Commissioners of the Admiralty to signify their direction to you to stop the *Basilisk* bomb vessel and her tender at Spithead till you receive further orders from their Lordships.

535. To Clevland

[TNA, ADM 1/93] Portsmouth
 31 May 1759

Sir,

I have received yours of the 29th instant, with the orders enclosed for the *Gramont* and *Basilisk*, which I have delivered to the respective captains. The wind only prevents the *Swallow*, *Fortune*, and *Aurora* from going out of the harbour.

536. From Clevland

[TNA, ADM 2/525, p. 354] 1 June 1759

Sir,

I have received and read to my Lords Commissioners of the Admiralty your two letters [No. 533] of the 30th past with the enclosed list of unserviceable men, and am to acquaint you it is their Lordships' direction that you discharge such of them as shall be found absolutely unfit for any service, even to ships in port, and then let their Lordships know how many will remain.

537. To Clevland

[TNA, ADM 1/93] Portsmouth
 1 June 1759

Sir,

I have received yours of the 30th May [Nos. 531, 532] with the orders enclosed, which I shall take care to put in execution.

And have this moment likewise received your express of yesterday with directions to stop the *Basilisk* bomb and her tender for which I have given proper directions to her commander.

The wind still continues to keep the ships in harbour.

538. To Clevland

[TNA, ADM 1/93]

Portsmouth
2 June 1759
Wind S blows hard

Sir,

I desire you will please to acquaint their Lordships that I have examined the three men named in the enclosed list,[1] pressed by the officer employed in raising men in the *Jane and Barbary* tender at Liverpool, and find them unfit for His Majesty's services for the reasons therein mentioned.

The said men were brought here by His Majesty's ship *Lightning*, to whose captain I have given orders for to discharge them unserviceable, which I hope their Lordships will approve, as the men are really nuisances, unfit for His Majesty's service, and ought not to have been impressed.

The *Levant* is this morning arrived here with the trade from the Downes, to whose captain I have delivered their Lordships orders.

The *Swallow*, *Fortune*, and *Aurora* are all ready to go to Spithead and wait only for a wind.

539. To Clevland

[TNA, ADM 1/93]

Portsmouth
3 June 1759

Sir,

I have received yours of the 1st instant [No. 536] with their Lordships' orders enclosed for the *Furnace*, and *Firedrake* bombs which I have delivered to their respective commanders.

I shall in obedience to their Lordships' commands be very strict in surveying the men reported to be unserviceable, and discharge none but such as are really so.

Enclosed I transmit the state and condition of His Majesty's ships and vessels under my command.[2]

---

[1] John Evans lost the use of his right hand and arm.
William Rylands, landman, 56 years of age, never at sea, and almost blind.
Samuel Jackson, scald head to violent degree and very infectious.
[2] Enclosed a list of ten ships with returns of men and provisions on each vessel.

540. *To Clevland*

[TNA, ADM 1/93]
Portsmouth
4 June 1759

Sir,
Please to acquaint their Lordships His Majesty's ship *Norwich* is just arrived from convoying the East India Ships. And that the *Aurora*, *Swallow*, and *Fortune* sloop sailed out of the harbour to Spithead this morning.

541. *From Clevland*

[TNA, ADM 2/525, p. 365]
5 June 1759

Sir,
The *Furnace* and *Firedrake* bomb vessels being wanted on immediate service. I am commanded by my Lords Commissioners of the Admiralty to signify their direction to you to complete their complement from the *Royal Ann*, or in any other manner that can be done, with all the expedition possible.

542. *To Clevland*

[TNA, ADM 1/93]
Portsmouth
5 June 1759

Sir,
I desire you will please to acquaint their Lordships that upon the arrival of His Majesty's sloop the *Fortune* at Spithead, her complement was completed out of the *Royal Ann*. The remainder of the supernumeraries I have ordered on board the *Aurora*, agreeable to their Lordships' directions.

543. *To Clevland*

[TNA, ADM 1/93]
Portsmouth
1/2 past 9 AM
6 June 1759

Sir,

I received your letter of yesterday's date by express, at half past two o'clock this morning, and shall strictly keep the secret his Lordship[1] has done me the honour to repose in me.[2] Though I cannot forebear mentioning that no longer ago than yesterday morning, the conversation among the sea officers, tended towards the bombardment of the very place proposed, owing I suppose to the fitting the bombs in the harbour and stopping her at Spithead.[3] I must desire you will please to acquaint Lord Anson that I have made all the necessary enquiries, without giving the least suspicion, even to the Admiral commanding here, waiting upon him very early this morning under pretence to desire leave for this day to go to Alresford, which the very bad weather, will be sufficient reason to postpone. I observe there are here but three flat bottom boats and those in good order.

The *Basilisk* bomb and her tender are ready at Spithead.

The *Furnace* was cleaned the 12th of May, has her ground tiers in and may be ready in three days, provided Mr Holburne will supply her with men which I hear he has done by ordering fifteen from the *Lightning* fireship, but I must desire you will please to let his Lordship know that her tender was lost on the coast of Barbary.

The *Firedrake* is to be docked this evening or tomorrow at 8 in the morning, her tender in the harbour, and may be ready in a few days if supplied with men.

I think it my duty to acquaint you that Captain Banks of the *Swallow* has several times assured me that he is remarkably well manned. Twenty able seamen might be taken from him without distressing the sloop.

Whatever commands my Lord Anson is pleased to honour me with, I must beg that (with my humblest respects) you will let him know, shall be punctually obeyed with the utmost diligence and to the best of my capacity.

---

[1] Lord Anson.
[2] Placing Rodney in command of a squadron to bombard and blockade the French port of Le Havre.
[3] See Nos. 537, 539 and 541.

PS. Enclosed[1] I send you the last state and condition of the three bombs. The other has only her standing mast in and not rigged.

544. *From the Lords of the Admiralty*

[TNA, ADM 2/83, pp. 76–7] 8 June 1759

You are hereby required and directed to take His Majesty's ships and vessels named in the margin[2] under your command, their commanders being directed to follow your orders, and cause their provisions to be completed to three months of all species except beer, and of that as much as they can conveniently stow, and their stores to a proper proportion for foreign service with all the expedition that is possible. And then make the best of your way with them to Gibraltar, where you are to put yourself under the command of the Rt. Hon. Admiral Boscawen, or the commander in chief of His Majesty's ships for the time being in the Mediterranean, and follow his orders for your further proceedings.

545. *To Clevland*

[TNA, ADM 1/93] Portsmouth
10 June 1759

Sir,

By yesterday's post I received their Lordships' orders [No. 544] of the 8th instant to take a squadron of His Majesty's ships under my command and proceed with them to Gibraltar.

Their Lordships may depend upon my making the utmost dispatch possible, and shall sail with them about the middle of this week provided the *Belliqueux*, *Achilles*, and *Deptford* arrive by that time.

---

[1]Not enclosed.
[2]*Belliqueux, Achilles, Norwich, Isis, Deptford, Aurora, Vestal, Juno* and *Gramont* and bombs *Basilisk, Firedrake* and *Furnace*.

546. To Clevland

[TNA, ADM 1/93]
Portsmouth
10 June 1759

Sir,
I was favoured with your letter which accompanied the order for Gibraltar.

Lord Anson may be assured every thing shall be done to keep up the appearance of going to Gibraltar. The stock I carry with me will convince people it is designed for a distant voyage, more especially as all the captains, upon their desiring to know their destination, have been told Gibraltar.

The two bombs will be at Spithead tomorrow or Tuesday morning. You will please to recollect the *Furnace* has no tender.

The *Aurora* wants 70 men and Mr. Holburne acquaints me he knows not where to get them. If their Lordships think it proper the *Lightning* fireship should spare them, I believe she has about that number.

I must be very cautious concerning the pilots, as people here are very attentive and inquisitive about what is transacting. But I was told some time since by Captain [Edward] Wheeler in conversation that he had a pilot from this place when he cruised off Le Havre.

The *Belliqueux*, *Achilles*, and *Deptford* are not as yet arrived.

I make no doubt but the whole will be ready to sail by the middle of the week. And if any thing necessary should be wanting I will take care to acquaint you therewith by express.

547. To Clevland

[TNA, ADM 1/93]
Portsmouth
11 June 1759

Sir,
The *Furnace* bomb is this morning got to Spithead, and the *Firedrake* will be there this afternoon.

Mr. Holburne has completed the complement of the *Aurora*, and when the three ships named in the margin[1] join me I shall be ready to put in execution what orders I may receive. I must again take notice that I find it so difficult to enquire about pilots with out giving suspicion that I wish they could be ordered on board the *Chatham* who is not

---

[1]*Belliqueux*, *Deptford* and *Achilles*.

under my command. If the said ship is ordered to St. Helens, I may then take them out of her without its being known.

The master of the *Norwich* is at sick quarters and the boatswain of the *Furnace* lent to the same. But nothing shall detain me when it is their Lordships' pleasure I sail.

I must however acquaint you that during the whole time I have been at sea, I never was upon that part of the coast, which it is intended to attack and therefore I shall be under the necessity to depend upon the experience of the pilots in anchoring within a proper distance to do execution. But you may depend nothing shall be wanting in me, to forward the service when I come upon the spot.

[PS] Wind at west blows fresh.

548. To Clevland

[TNA, ADM 1/93] Portsmouth
12 June 1759

Sir,

The bombs are at Spithead and completely manned.

A large ship is turning in which I take to be the *Deptford*, and as the wind is at NW and blows fresh, I hope it will bring the *Achilles* and *Belliqueux*. When they arrive and the pilots I shall be ready to put in execution the orders I may be honoured with.

549. To Clevland

[TNA, ADM 1/93] Portsmouth
13 June 1759

Sir,

I have received your letter of the 11th instant, enclosing orders to the captains of those ships their Lordships have been pleased to add to them already under my command, and shall take care to obey the directions given in your letter.

Wind SW blows very hard.

550. To Clevland

[TNA, ADM 1/93]
Portsmouth
15 June 1759

Sir,

As my accounts are passed for the time that I commanded His Majesty's ship *Dublin*, I desire that you will pleased to move their Lordships to order that I may be paid my own and servant's pay for the said ship.

551. To Clevland

[TNA, ADM 1/93]
Portsmouth
15 June 1759

Sir,

At 7 PM I was favoured with your express with the letter and orders enclosed, which I immediately delivered to the respective captains, who this morning (at daylight) sailed, and are now out of sight.

I must take notice to you that the express was 19 hours on the road, had it been forwarded with proper dispatch, Captain [John] Hollwall and the ships under his command had sailed yesterday with a brisk northerly wind, and been on their station early this day.

As the *Blast* bomb is not as yet under my command, I must beg leave to say that I believe it will be necessary that some quickening order be sent, to hasten her being fitted and manned.

552. From Clevland

[TNA, ADM 2/525, p. 405]
16 June 1759

Sir,

I have received and read to my Lords Commissioners of the Admiralty your letter [No. 551] of yesterday's date and in regard to the tardiness of the express I am to acquaint you His Majesty's Post Master General is informed of it that the persons in fault may be punished.

As to the *Blast* bomb, I am to acquaint you Vice Admiral Holburne is directed to man and hasten her fitting with all the dispatch that is possible as you desire.

553. To Clevland

[TNA, ADM 1/93]
Portsmouth
11 PM
17 June 1759

Sir,

This moment one Robert Dorret brought me a letter directed to Captain Hollwall to receive him on board His Majesty's ship *Deptford* as a pilot, and to inform their Lordships on his return from the service he was sent on, how he found him qualified.

As the ship has been sailed these two days I have ordered the man on board the *Norwich* till I know their Lordships' pleasure.

I hope, as the weather is set in fair, the other ships will soon join me that their Lordships has been pleased to put under my command.

[PS] Wind WNW.

554. From the Lords of the Admiralty

[TNA, ADM 2/83, p. 100]
18 June 1759

You are hereby required and directed to receive on board, such ship of His Majesty' squadron put under your command as you may hoist your flag on board of, Colonel Desaguliers[1] and Captain Smith[2] with their servants and baggage. And cause them and their servants to be victualled during their continuance on board as the ship's company.

555. To Clevland

[TNA, ADM 1/93]
Portsmouth
18 June 1759

Sir,

Yesterday the *Achilles* and *Unicorn* arrived here from Plymouth. They left the *Belliqueux* off the Start with a convoy, which will delay her some time.

The weather now seems to be set in very fair, which makes me anxious to put their Lordships' orders in execution, more especially as the news papers indicate the service I am going on.

[1] Colonel Thomas Desaguliers, colonel commandant of the Royal Artillery.
[2] Captain Thomas Smith, Royal Artillery.

As Lieutenant Joseph Hunt, late of the *Dublin*, is now at this port, I should be glad their Lordships would permit me to take him with me as a volunteer lieutenant when I sail, as he is a person I can depend upon, when sent on any material service.

Give me leave Sir to remind you, that there are several cutters here. They may be of great service in sounding should the pilots prove not so good as expected.

Sir,

I beg your pardon for writing by way of postscript, but since I wrote the letter I have learned that Captain [Thomas] Saumarez is laid up with the gout, which induces me to hoist my flag on board the *Achilles*, unless their Lordships should choose that I go on board the *Belliqueux*. In which case I hope they will indulge me with Captain [Jonathan] Faulknor to command her, for the time being, he is returned from Plymouth.

556. From Clevland

[TNA, ADM 2/525, p. 432]　　　　　　　　　　　　　　　20 June 1759

Sir,

I have received and communicated to my Lords Commissioners of the Admiralty your letter [No. 555] of the 18th instant. And I am commanded by their Lordships to acquaint you that, so soon as the tenders to the bomb vessels put under your command arrive at Spithead, you may expect their Lordships' orders for your farther proceedings.

Lieutenant Hunt[1] is appointed commander of the *Mortar* bomb vessel at Deptford, and their Lordships desire you will hasten him to this office to take up his commission.

With regard to the cutters, I am to acquaint you, that their Lordships give you leave to take three of them along with you, to enable you to perform the service you mention in case of necessity.

The *Belliqueux* being ordered to join Sir Edward Hawke, their Lordships approve of your hoisting your flag on board the *Achilles*.

---

[1] See also No. 555.

557. *To Clevland*

[TNA, ADM 1/93]
Spithead
20 June 1759

Sir,

Yesterday in the evening His Majesty's ship *Belliqueux* arrived here. Captain Saumarez being at present afflicted with the gout, I could wish their Lordships would indulge me with the permission to take Captain Jonathan Faulknor as a volunteer on board the *Belliqueux* with me, and suffer the *Furnace* bomb to continue under the command their Lordships have appointed, till the present service is over.

Last post brought me their Lordships' order [No. 554] to receive Colonel Desaguliers and Captain Smith on board such ship I may hoist my flag.

As the wind is now easterly I hope it will soon bring the bomb tenders and the mortars for the *Blast*.

558. *To Clevland*

[TNA, ADM 1/93]
Portsmouth
9 o'clock AM
25 June 1759

Sir,

I am favoured with yours of yesterday's date by express and will take care to have everything in readiness against my sailing orders arrive here. But I must beg leave to take notice to you that all the men belonging to the ships that were bound to Cadiz and the Mediterranean are impressed and I presume their Lordships would not have me detained for them.

559. *To Clevland*

[TNA, ADM 1/93]
Spithead
26 June 1759

Sir,

The *Blast* bomb is finished and at Spithead. His Majesty's squadron under my command are ready to proceed whenever their Lordships are pleased to honour me with their commands, and I believe I have a sufficient number of pilots to take charge of them.

560. From the Lords of the Admiralty

[TNA, ADM 2/1331, pp. 305–06]   26 June 1759

Whereas the King has received undoubted intelligence that the enemy are making great preparations for invading these Kingdoms and particularly that 130 flat bottomed boats are building at Le Havre. And it being of the greatest consequence, that all possible means should be used to frustrate this design of the enemy, you are therefore hereby required and directed to take under your command the ships and vessels named in the margin, those of them which are marked thus * being now off Le Havre, and such as are marked thus + ordered to repair thither.[1] And you are to collect all the pilots near at hand acquainted with the said port and its road, and to distribute such flat bottomed boats as are at Portsmouth among the ships of your squadron at Spithead and apply to Vice Admiral Holburne for as many of the cutters at Portsmouth as you shall judge necessary. When this shall be done, you are so soon as the wind shall prove favourable and the weather appear settled, to repair off Le Havre and having placed the bomb vessels in the best situation, and made a proper disposition of the rest of your force, you are to endeavour as well as by a bombardment as by all other means in your power, to destroy the boats building upon the beach, and also any naval or warlike materials that may be there, or any boats, magazines, stores, provisions, and materials that may be in the basin, harbour and town of Le Havre. And you are to be particularly vigilant, whilst on this service, not to permit any ships or vessels whatsoever to enter the said port.

You are to continue your operations for the aforesaid purposes so long as you shall find the same to be attended with good effect; taking care to send a cutter daily to the nearest part of the coast with an account of your proceedings and success, which is to be forwarded to us by express.

---

[1] *Achilles, Norwich, Isis, Chatham,* *Deptford,* +*Chesterfield, Brilliant,* *Vestal,* *Juno, Boreas, Unicorn, Fly* and *Wolf* sloops, and the bomb vessels *Basilisk, Furnace, Blast,* +*Mortar,* and +*Carcass.*

561. *To Clevland*

[TNA, ADM 1/93]

Spithead
27 June 1759
9 o'clock AM

Sir,

I am this moment favoured with your letter and their Lordships' final orders [No. 560] by express. I shall use the utmost diligence in getting on board the flat bottom[ed] boats, and all the pilots I can procure, and when the weather appears settled and the wind proves favourable, not a moment shall be lost in putting their Lordships' orders into execution. And till the weather has more the appearance of being settled than it is at present, I shall repair with the squadron they have been pleased to honour me with the command of, to St. Helens, as I shall be there in constant readiness to sail when the weather proves favourable.

The wind is now at WSW, blows very fresh, and I am informed makes a sea in the road before Le Havre. I conclude their Lordships' intention is that I should not make my appearance before that place till I can put their orders in execution against it.

Since writing the former part of this letter Mr. Bucknall, an inhabitant of this town, has been with me, with information that he had received intelligence from Dartmouth, from the master of a French vessel arrived there, that he should repair to Portsmouth, to fetch the hostages belonging to Cherbourg.

I think it my duty to acquaint their Lordships that I have this moment received information from Colonel Desaguliers that [F]onntinel[?] de Postelle, one of the hostages, was at the beginning of the late peace at a Roman Catholic family (a miller) 9 mile from Portsmouth, on the sea coast towards Chichester, where he learnt English. There is a Roman Catholic chapel at Bedhampton, where they have two priests, and where he has met all the Roman Catholic families. The miller and other Roman Catholics have often come to see him since being a hostage, and the hostages themselves have often rode out [and] it is supposed are perfectly acquainted with the country. I must likewise acquaint you that there are several Roman Catholic families on the common near the dock who constantly go every Sunday to Bedhampton Romish chapel.

Their Lordships may be assured that I shall exert myself to the utmost of my ability for His Majesty's service.

562. To Clevland

[TNA, ADM 1/93]
Portsmouth
27 June 1759

Sir,

Since writing to you by the messenger, I have been at the dock and demanded all the flat bottom[ed] boats which are but three. They will be ready to be launched this evening and I hope to be able to sail tomorrow early in the morning.

563. To Clevland

[TNA, ADM 1/93]
Achilles Spithead
28 June 1759

Sir,

Please to acquaint their Lordships I am now under sail with the squadron under my command, but shall come to at St. Helens till the pilots are properly distributed and the weather quite settled and favourable, which at present has the appearance of being so in a short time. The wind is now at NW which the pilots inform me makes too great a sea on that part of the coast we are destined for. Among all the pilots I have been able to procure, only three appear to be the least acquainted with the place we are going to, but I hope with the assistance of the cutters, to be able to anchor the bombs and squadron in such a manner as to execute their Lordships orders.

I hope we shall be sailed this evening or tomorrow morning at the furthest.

Captain [Dennis] Downing of His Majesty's sloop *Fly*, being so very ill that he is obliged to go on shore, I have given orders to Lieutenant [George] Gayton of His Majesty's ship *Royal Ann* to command her during their Lordship's pleasure.

564. To Clevland

[TNA, ADM 1/93]
Achilles St. Helens
29 June 1759

Sir,

I desire you will please to acquaint their Lordships that the squadron of His Majesty's ships under my command remain at St. Helens, the wind blowing hard at WSW. As soon as it moderates or appears anyways settled I shall proceed immediately to sea.

As I have but two cutters to attend the squadron I could wish their Lordships would be pleased to order four more, as I am sure they will be very useful on the service I am ordered on.

565. To Clevland

[TNA, ADM 1/93] *Achilles* at St. Helens
30 June 1759

Sir,

The wind continuing to blow very fresh at NW, which the pilots inform me makes a very great sea upon that part of the enemy's coast we are destined for, still detains me at this place. When it moderates and there is a likelihood of executing the orders I am under, their Lordships may depend upon my seizing the first favourable opportunity.

Colonel Desaguliers having acquainted me that only one officer of the Train belonging to the bombs had ever been upon service. I hope their Lordships will approve my having ordered the captains of the bombs to exercise the mortars daily, that the artillery officers and their people may be more expert when they come upon service and confusion prevented.

I am likewise sorry to acquaint their Lordships that the bombs which are intended to join me from the River are without (even) one bombardier or an officer who has ever been upon that service, but I hope with the assistance of Colonel Desaguliers and Captain Smith their Lordships' expectations will be answered.

Two small Dutch hoys calling themselves pilot boats put in here and having reason to suspect they are employed by the enemy by the confusion they were in upon their examination, I hope their Lordships will approve of my have ordered them to remain here till I am sailed.

566. To Clevland

[TNA, ADM 1/93] *Achilles* at St. Helens
1 July 1759

Sir,

The weather still continuing very unsettled and the wind at north blowing very fresh. I have examined all the pilots who are acquainted with the coast. They are unanimously of opinion we ought not to stir till the weather is quite settled as the squadron with this wind would be greatly exposed in the Road of Le Havre, and be able to do no execution it making a great sea and being a lee shore.

I assure their Lordships this delay gives me real uneasiness, but I flatter myself they will attribute it, to its real cause (the weather being so unsettled and turbulent) but if it is their Lordships' pleasure I should sail and wait in the Channel for an opportunity to put their orders in execution, not a moment shall be lost in obeying them.

I am sorry to acquaint you that one of the Dutch hoys whom I detained on suspicion of her being employed by the enemy, took the advantage last night in a very hard squall attended with thick weather to make his escape.

567. To Clevland

[TNA, ADM 1/93]
On board the *Vestal*
in the Road of Le Havre de Grace
4 July 1759

Sir,

I have the honour to acquaint their Lordships that yesterday about three o'clock PM, I anchored with His Majesty's ships under my command in the Road of Le Havre, and immediately gave orders for placing the bomb vessels in a proper place to destroy the flat bottom boats, and the enemy's magazines, stores &c. that were in the town of Le Havre. But every pilot I had in the squadron were so totally ignorant of the place that had it not been for the captains of the *Deptford*, *Vestal*, and *Juno*, and the first lieutenant of the *Deptford*, I should have found it extremely difficult and tedious to have anchored the bombs properly, these gentlemen having exerted themselves on this occasion. And during the night had placed the *Blast* and *Furnace* in such a situation that every shell they throw either falls among the flat bottom boats or into the town, which has already been twice in a blaze.

I hope in a very few hours to have all the other bombs properly placed, but I cannot help taking notice to their Lordships that the whole weight and fatigue of the execution falls upon Colonel Desaguliers and Captain Smith, the other officers not having been acquainted with this sort of service which makes it not go on so brisk as I could wish.

The *Mortar* and *Carcass* with the *Chesterfield* joined me this morning. I have hurried them all that was possible and I hope they will be in their stations in an hour or two. As I am now on board the *Vestal* (one of the frigates that supports the bombs) I can assure you I have seen several of the shells fall among the boats and store houses.

The enemy's fire is pretty brisk from two or three bomb batteries but as yet they have done no harm.

You shall hear further from me tomorrow when I hope I shall acquaint you that the bombs have had their desired effect.

The enemy appear very numerous in troops, and have several cannon, and bomb batteries along the shore from the Cap de la Hève to the town. And a number of ships appear to be in the basin.

9 O'Clock AM. All the bombs but the *Carcass* are now in their station. She is under sail and will be so in a few minutes. The enemy's fire from their bomb batteries are very brisk indeed.

Wind NbE fresh ½ past 9 AM.

568. *From Anson*

[TNA, PRO 30/20/20/4, pp. 39–40]   Admiralty
                                              6 July 1759

My dear Rodney,

Your letter [No. 567] of the 4th instant gave great satisfaction to everybody here. I have seen the King and all his servants who are extremely pleased with your commencement and don't doubt but you will go on and prosper. I take it for granted you will throw all your shells, which will convince us of the full operation of a bombardment. If more shells should be wanted, you will send some of your bomb tenders to Portsmouth. The Duke of Newcastle desires me to send you his compliments. His Grace has secured you a sure seat in Parliament.[1] I hope your good weather will continue, which has been very fortunate.

569. *To Clevland*

[TNA, ADM 1/93]   *Achilles* off Havre de Grace
                                              6 July 1759

Sir,

His Majesty's ships and bombs under my command sailed from St. Helens in the morning of the second instant, and with a favourable

---

[1] On 24 November 1759 Rodney would be elected, with the support of the government, a member of the House of Commons for the borough of Okehampton in Devon.

wind, and moderate weather, anchored the following day in the great road off Le Havre, where having made a disposition to put their Lordships' orders in execution, the bombs proceeded to place themselves in the narrow channel of the river leading to Honfleur, it being the most proper and only place to do execution from. About seven in the evening two of the bombs were stationed, as were all the rest early the next morning, and continued to bombard for fifty two hours without intermission, with such success, that the town was several times in flames and their magazine of stores for the flat bottom boats burnt with very great fury for upwards of six hours, notwithstanding the continual efforts of several hundred men to extinguish it, many of the boats were overturned and damaged by the explosion of the shells.

During the attack the enemy's troops appeared very numerous, were continually erecting new batteries, and throwing up entrenchments. Their consternation was so great that all the inhabitants forsook the town, and not one single person appeared to be working on the flat bottom boats, the troops alone being employed in extinguishing the flames.

I judge the enemy expected a descent by their appearing continually under arms, and their marching a considerable body of troops from their encampment on the hill into the town in the afternoon of the 5th.

Notwithstanding this smart bombardment, (which only ceased from the mortars and bomb beds being rendered unserviceable) I have the pleasure to acquaint you that the damage done us by the enemy has been very inconsiderable, tho' great numbers of their shot and shells fell and burst among the bombs and boats.

I shall forthwith proceed with the squadron under my command to Spithead, taking care to leave a proper number of ships to cruise off this port with orders to stop all materials that may be useful towards their finishing the flat bottom boats, which to my appearance they stand much in need of, as they are far from being completed, great numbers of them being only in their first frames.

570. *From Clevland*

[TNA, ADM 2/525, p. 498] 7 July 1759

Sir,

I have received and read to my Lords Commissioners of the Admiralty your letter [No. 567] of the 4th instant, informing their Lordships of your proceeding before Le Havre, which having laid before His Majesty, he has been graciously pleased to approve thereof. And my

Lords have great satisfaction in your having placed the bombs in such a situation as to answer the purpose so well as they have done. The conduct of the captains of His Majesty's ships is likewise very pleasing to their Lordships as well as that of Colonel Desaguliers and Captain Smith.

Their Lordships are sorry to find those pilots so ignorant and desire the captains will be cautious in giving them certificates.

I must heartily congratulate you on this commencement of success and sincerely wish the continuance of it.

571. *To Clevland*

[TNA, ADM 1/93] *Achilles* at Spithead
8 July 1759

Sir,

I desire you will be pleased to acquaint their Lordships that I am returned with His Majesty's ships and bombs under my command to Spithead (as mentioned in the margin)[1] having left the *Isis*, *Chatham*, *Unicorn*, *Boreas*, and *Fly* sloop, with three armed cutters, off Le Havre, under the command of Captain Wheeler with orders not to suffer any materials whatever that may be necessary or useful in building or equipping the flat bottomed boats to enter the port, but to seize all such and send them to England, which I hope will meet with their Lordships' approbation. It is my opinion that it will be impossible for them to finish such as are begun without a further supply.

I must likewise take the liberty to acquaint their Lordships that it is my opinion that had the enemy proper materials the boats would take a considerable time in finishing as their Lordships may perceive by the account of their condition which I have sent them from Le Havre by express.

I must likewise desire you will acquaint their Lordships that I have brought in with me a Dean [Danish] and Swedish ship loaded with timber, sparrs, deals &c. which attempted to get into Le Havre while the place was invested and I should be glad to know their Lordships' pleasure concerning them.

As all the bombs are very much shook, I have ordered them into the harbour which I hope their Lordships will approve of.

---

[1]*Achilles, Norwich, Brilliant, Deptford, Juno, Chesterfield, Wolf, Firedrake, Furnace, Basilisk, Blast, Carcass* and *Mortar*.

572. From Clevland

[TNA, ADM 2/525, p. 502]　　　　　　　　　　　　9 July 1759

Sir,

I am commanded by my Lords Commissioners of the Admiralty to acquaint you that they give you leave to come to town. And to signify their direction to you, to bring with you the marks and bearings of every bomb vessel, at the time they were employed in bombarding Le Havre de Grace.

573. From Clevland

[TNA, ADM 2/525, p. 505]　　　　　　　　　　　　10 July 1759

Sir,

I have received and read to my Lords Commissioners of the Admiralty your letters of the 6th and 8th instant [Nos. 569, 571] giving an account of your proceedings with the squadron under your command off of Le Havre de Grace. And [I] am to acquaint you their Lordships are very well satisfied with your conduct upon that occasion.

574. To Clevland

[TNA, ADM 1/93]　　　　　　　　　　　　　　　Portsmouth
　　　　　　　　　　　　　　　　　　　　　　　10 July 1759

Sir,

I am this moment favoured with your letter [No. 572] of yesterday's date by express, and when I have collected the bearings of each bomb vessel [I] shall repair forthwith to town.

575. From Clevland

[TNA, ADM 2/526, p. 52]　　　　　　　　　　　　6 August 1759

Sir,

I am commanded by my Lords Commissioners of the Admiralty to acquaint you, that they do not think the marks and bearings you have sent[1] them, of His Majesty's bomb vessels under your command, at the

---

[1] See Nos. 572 and 573.

time they were employed in the late bombardment of Le Havre de Grace, [are] so particular as is necessary to remain in this office. Both the distance of the place and the depth of water where the bomb vessels lay, being wanting, which their Lordships command me to desire you will supply them with as soon as possible.

576. *From the Lords of the Admiralty*

[TNA, ADM 2/83, p. 298]   15 August 1759

You are hereby required and directed to proceed forthwith to Portsmouth, where you will find instructions for your further proceedings.

577. *From the Lords of the Admiralty*

[TNA, ADM 2/1331, ff. 314–15]   17 August 1759

Whereas it has been judged necessary that you shall proceed again with a squadron of the King's ships off Le Havre de Grace, in order to renew the operations on the enemy's works there. And whereas we have directed the commanders of His Majesty's ships and vessels named in the margin to put themselves under your command, the five first of which are at present off that port,[1] and the remainder at, or on their way to Portsmouth or Spithead,[2] you are hereby required and directed to take them under your command, and such four of the bomb vessels as may first get their mortars on board, and having collected all the pilots near at hand acquainted with the port of Le Havre and its road, and distributed such of the flat bottomed boats as are at Portsmouth among the ships of your squadron, you are so soon as the wind shall prove favourable and the weather appear settled, to repair with them off Le Havre, and having placed the bomb vessels in the best situation and made a proper disposition of the rest of your force, endeavour, as well by a bombardment as by all other means in your power to destroy the flat bottomed boats building on the beach and also any naval or warlike materials that may be there, or any boats, magazines, stores, provisions and materials that may be in the basin, harbour and town of Le Havre

---

[1]*Isis*, 50; *Chatham*, 50; *Boreas*, 28; *Spy* and *Fly*, sloops.
[2]*Falkland*, 50; *Deptford*, 50; *Brilliant*, 36; *Æolus*, 32; *Unicorn*, 28; *Coventry*, 28; and the bombs *Thunder*, *Blast*, *Basilisk*, *Carcass*, *Furnace*, *Firedrake* and *Mortar*.

or its neighbourhood; taking particular care not to permit any ships or vessels whatsoever to enter into the said port, or to any of the ports in the River Seine.

You are to continue your operations for the aforesaid purposes, until you receive further orders from us, taking care to send in a cutter daily to the nearest part of the coast with an account of your proceedings and success, which is to be forwarded to us by express. And when you return into port you are to leave such a force off Le Havre as may be sufficient to keep that port effectually blocked up.

578. *To Clevland*

[TNA, ADM 1/93]   Portsmouth
18 August 1759

Sir,
I have received their Lordships order [No. 567] of the 15th instant.

579. *To Clevland*

[TNA, ADM 1/93]   Portsmouth
19 August 1759

Sir,
I have the honour of your letter of the 17th instant, with their Lordships' orders [No. 577] of the same date, which I shall put in execution as soon as the squadron can be got ready which I hope will be in a few days.

580. *From Clevland*

[TNA, ADM 2/526, p. 115]   20 August 1759

Sir,
My Lords Commissioners of the Admiralty having been under a necessity to take from under your command His Majesty's ships the *Falkland* and *Coventry* to detach them on another particular and pressing service, I am commanded to acquaint you therewith.

581. *To Clevland*

[TNA, ADM 1/93]   Portsmouth
                                                                   20 August 1759

Sir,

The *Thunder* and *Mortar* bombs are at Spithead, the *Furnace* and *Firedrake* will get out of the harbour this evening or tomorrow morning. I shall likewise hasten as much as possible the *Falkland* and *Unicorn* and hope by the latter end of the week at furthest to proceed agreeable to their Lordships' orders [No. 577]. And as the *Blast* and *Basilisk* will have each one thirteen inch mortar on board I hope their Lordships will give me leave to take them with me, as more service may be expected from one thirteen inch mortar than from several ten inch.

I must beg leave to take notice to their Lordships that upon examining the stores on board the bomb tenders, I find that the carcasses lately sent from Woolwich are oblong, which are really of no use on this service they mostly splitting very soon after they are discharged, and never went home. The remaining likewise of the round carcasses that came from the late bombardment are only of one hole, having been long filled, and cannot be supposed to do that service with those of five holes. As I saw many of that specie when at Woolwich [I] imagined they were to have been sent on service, but as none are come, I humbly hope their Lordships will be pleased to give directions concerning them, as five flames emitted from a shell must of course do more execution than one, and not be so liable to be extinguished.

582. *To Clevland*

[TNA, ADM 1/93]   Portsmouth
                                                                   20 August 1759

Sir,

As I intend asking my Lord Anson to let Captain [Edward] Gascoigne be my captain whenever he is pleased to appoint any particular ship for me, I must desire you will be so obliging as to procure him leave to [go] a volunteer with me.

Your compliance with this request will very much oblige him...

583. To Clevland

[TNA, ADM 1/93] Portsmouth
21 August 1759

Sir,

Some disputes relative to command having happened among the officers of the Train belonging to the bombs under my command, who are all lieutenants and young men, I think it my duty to acquaint their Lordships thereof, and hope that a captain of the Train may be sent with me. If it could be Captain Smith it would give me great pleasure as I am convinced of his knowledge, care, and experience in this sort of service.

584. From Clevland

[TNA, ADM 2/526, p. 127] 22 August 1759

Sir,

I have received and read to my Lords Commissioners of the Admiralty your letter [No. 583] of yesterday's date representing that some disputes relative to command, have arisen among the officers of the Train, belonging to the bomb vessels under your command, who are all lieutenants and young men, and requesting that a captain may be sent with them. And in return I am commanded to acquaint you, that Mr. Secretary Pitt is made acquainted with what you write, and is desired to move His Majesty that [an] officer of the Train of a higher rank and greater experience may be sent on this service.

585. From Clevland

[TNA, ADM 2/526, p. 128] 22 August 1759

Sir,

I have received and read to my Lords Commissioners of the Admiralty your letter [No. 581] of the 20th instant, who have no objection to your taking the *Blast* and *Basilisk* bomb vessels with you to sea as you propose.

An extract of so much of your letter [No. 581] as relates to the carcasses is sent to Mr. Secretary Pitt, who is desired, as the species of shells now supplied appear to be very improper, to procure His Majesty's pleasure to the Board of Ordnance to cause others to be immediately supplied.

586. *From Clevland*

[TNA, 2/526, p. 136]   23 August 1759

Sir,

I have received and read to my Lords Commissioners of the Admiralty your letter of yesterday's date giving an account that you only wait for the *Deptford*, and in return am to acquaint you that the ship is now in the Downes, and ordered to proceed to Spithead without a moment's loss of time. I sincerely wish your success in all your undertakings.

587. *To Clevland*

[TNA, ADM 1/93]   *Unicorn* at Spithead
                                                 23 August 1759

Sir,

There are now at Spithead of His Majesty's ships under my command the *Brilliant* and *Unicorn* frigates, the *Thunder*, *Firedrake*, *Mortar*, and *Furnace* bombs. The wind at present blows hard at NW. As soon as it moderates I hope the *Deptford* will be round, when I shall immediately proceed to put their Lordships' orders [No. 577] in execution.

If there should be no mortars intended for the *Carcass* bomb, I hope their Lordships will give me leave to take her with me as a frigate, she being a ship drawing but little water and may be of great service in covering the bombs.

588. *From Clevland*

[TNA, ADM 2/526, p. 137]   24 August 1759

Sir,

I am commanded by my Lords Commissioners of the Admiralty to signify their direction to you to receive on board the ship in which your flag is flying Major [James] Pattison and Captain [Edward] Whitmore of the Train, who are to be employed in the service you are going upon, together with their servants and baggage, causing them and their servants to be victualled whilst on board as the ship's company.

589. *From Clevland*

[TNA, ADM 2/526, p. 143] 24 August 1759

Sir,

I have communicated to my Lords Commissioners of the Admiralty your letter [No. 582] of the 20th instant desiring that Captain Gascoigne may be permitted to go [as] a volunteer with you. In return I am to acquaint you their Lordships have given him leave for that purpose as you desire.

590. *From the Lords of the Admiralty*

[TNA, ADM 2/83, pp. 331–2] 24 August 1759

Whereas you have represented to us, by your letter [No. 587] of yesterday's date, that His Majesty's ship *Deptford* is not come to Spithead, you are hereby required and directed, so soon as the wind moderates and proves favourable, to proceed to sea in execution of our instructions, leaving orders for the captain of the *Deptford* to follow you.

And whereas you have desired, as no mortars are intended for the *Carcass* bomb, that you may take her with you as a frigate, as she is a ship that draws but little water, and will be of service to you in covering the bomb vessels, we do hereby signify to you our approval thereof, and require and direct you to take her with you accordingly.

591. *To Clevland*

[TNA, ADM 1/93] *Unicorn* at Spithead
25 August 1759

Sir,

I have been favoured with yours [No. 586] of the 23rd instant and shall take particular care that the coast shall be reconnoitred agreeable to their Lordships' direction.

I have likewise this moment received by express their Lordships' order [No. 590] of yesterday's date, and shall proceed to sea the moment the weather moderates, and the wind proves favourable. At present it blows very fresh at SE.

Yesterday I received a letter from Captain Wheeler, dated the 23rd instant in the evening. He acquaints me that the weather was so bad he was obliged to keep at sea. But when it proved moderate he would take care to anchor the squadron in such a manner that the bombs might at once get into their station, and be properly covered agreeable to the order I had sent him for that purpose.

592. *To Clevland*

[TNA, ADM 1/93] Spithead
26 August 1759

Sir,
The *Deptford* arrived here this morning. The wind is now favourable and the weather seems likely to continue moderate.

I hope to be able to sail this afternoon and that the *Carcass* and *Basilisk* bombs will get out of the harbour this day. I have left orders with the captain of the *Blast* to follow me as soon as he receives his mortar which I hear is coming round and may be of great service, it being one that carries a shell of thirteen inches.

As a number of cutters may be very useful on this occasion, I hope their Lordships will be pleased to order some from the Downes, Admiral Holburne being able to spare me but one from this place.

593. *From Clevland*

[TNA, ADM 2/526, p. 163] 28 August 1759

Sir,
I have read to my Lords Commissioners of the Admiralty your letter [No. 592] of the 26th instant, desiring some cutters for the service you are going upon. And I am commanded to acquaint you cutters will be sent to you.

594. To Clevland

[TNA, ADM 1/93] *Deptford* off Le Havre
29 August 1759

Sir,
Please to acquaint their Lordships that I arrived here with the squadron of His Majesty's ships and bomb vessels under my command yesterday about noon. And immediately made a disposition to put their orders [No. 577] into execution, the large frigates being placed and the

bombs ready to proceed into their station. When the wind coming to the northwest, with a large swell, obliged me to defer the bombardment till it subsided. In the evening it was moderate which gave me great hopes that the operations would have commenced this morning at daylight, everything being ready for that purpose, but the wind being strong westerly and the weather very unsettled renders it impossible for the bombs to lay in that narrow channel with any degree of safety. All the pilots concurring in this opinion.

On Sunday the enemy sent out of their harbour four vessels rigged as settees,[1] rowed with forty oars, full of men, and carrying one large gun in their prow. They got under sail yesterday in the evening, and cannonaded the large frigates, but were soon obliged to retire under the cannon of the town.

I could wish I had some more sloops, or armed cutters, as they would be most useful in protecting the bombs during the service from these sort of vessels.

There are now thirty nine flat bottomed boats building on the beach. The enemy seem much alarmed, and their troops appear numerous.

You shall hear further from me tomorrow, but unless I have more cutters sent me it will be impossible to send daily accounts.

595. *To Clevland*

[TNA, ADM 1/93] *Deptford* off Le Havre de Grace
8 o'clock AM
30 August 1759

Sir,

The weather yesterday appearing very unsettled, I ordered the four large frigates who were in their stations for covering the bombs to rejoin me in the great road. It was very lucky I did so, for last night it blew a very hard gale of wind at northwest, which must have put them in imminent danger had they continued to lay so near the sands.

I was in pain for the bombs, their tenders, and all the small craft, but thank God they are all safe, and the wind now northerly but still blows very fresh and a great sea continues. I have twice since day light sent the armed cutters with pilots and proper officers into the channel where I propose to place the bombs. Their report is that nothing can be done until the weather is more favourable.

---

[1] Single decked, two masted, latten rigged vessels.

I am very unhappy at this delay as the time I arrive here, could the bombardment have commenced, was the most proper that could possibly be, the spring tides when they set in, being so excessive rapid, as to render all attempts of this sort impracticable.

I have as yet been prevented [from] sending an officer to reconnoitre the coast, between Honfleur and the Trouville-sur-Mer, but by what I can learn from a pilot who has frequently been at Honfleur that the place is fortified with five bastions and is a large town. The country between that and Trouville-sur-Mer appears very high and woody with a steep cliffy shore. Since my being here the enemy have sent over troops from Le Havre in sailing boats, which by the rapidity of the tide were drove very near within gun shot of the frigates.

They go on briskly with their flat bottomed boats, launching some daily, and to all appearance by the great number of workmen employed, will complete them soon, there being now but thirty eight on the beach.

Since writing this letter, 12 o'clock noon, the enemy have brought down the river two floating batteries with heavy cannon, and placed them on the flats which will annoy the bombs in the most effectual manner. This with the additional preparations they have made, and are daily making, will I imagine disconcert us in a great measure. However I am determined to try the force of my small squadron when I have a favourable opportunity to make the attempt, provided I find it can be done without bringing disgrace to His Majesty's arms.

596. *To Clevland*

[TNA, ADM 1/93] *Deptford* off Le Havre de Grace
1 September 1759

Sir,

In my last letter [No. 595] to you I took notice of the enemy's bringing down the river two floating batteries. I immediately sent the four armed cutters and went myself to reconnoitre them. I found them large floats, each with four embrasures in front, and a depth sufficient to contain a mortar behind the guns, which they fired at the cutters I sent into the channel where the bombs were last placed.

They were guarded by two of the largest flat bottomed boats, rigged as hoys, filled with soldiers, and had each a tier of guns which they likewise fired at the cutters. The enemy had placed them in such a manner, as greatly to annoy the bombs, and the frigates, from the shoalness of the water, could neither cover or protect them.

The weather has been, and still continues, so very bad, that I have not the least hopes anything can be done during these nip tides, and should it prove moderate weather during the ensuing spring, the very great rapidity of these tides would render it impossible to put their Lordships' orders into execution not but I think it my duty to acquaint them, that the disposition of the enemy is such, as must render any further attempts of this nature very doubtful as to the success of it.

The officers I sent to reconnoitre the coast between Honfleur and Trouville-sur-Mer report that coast to be inaccessible, from the shoalness of the water between those places with a rocky shore, and a steep ascent covered with thick woods.

Between Trouville-sur-Mer and Dives-sur-Mer is a fine sandy shore with three fathom at low water within musket shot, where an army might be easily landed in the summer months. It's about ten or twelve miles from Honfleur, but I must beg leave to take notice to their Lordships, from the obversations I have made since being here, that was an army [to] be landed in the aforesaid bay, the enemy might reinforce Honfleur with what number of troops they pleased, before it was possible for His Majesty's to march that distance. The flat bottomed boats they send daily over to that place being generally filled with troops and are seldom longer than two hours in their passage, the shoalness of the water renders all attempts to intercept them impossible.

I have sent Captain [James] Chaplen and Lieutenant [John] Thane who reconnoitred the coast to attend their Lordships' further pleasure.

597. *From the Lords of the Admiralty*

[TNA, ADM 2/83, p. 367] 3 September 1759

You are hereby required and directed to send into Portsmouth Harbour one of the fifty gun ships of your squadron that is in the worst condition, and also the bomb vessel that has not any mortars on board in order that they may be cleaned and refitted. But as it is now too late for their receiving the benefit of the present spring, you are to take care to send them in timely enough to save the next.

598. *To Clevland*

[TNA, ADM 1/93] *Deptford* off Le Havre de Grace
3 September 1759

Sir,

Since I dispatched Captain Chaplen to give their Lordships an account of the observations made on the enemy's coast, the weather has been so excessive bad as to endanger the bombs and their tenders. It is now moderate with the wind westerly. As the spring tides are set in, I shall be obliged to anchor further off the shore till they are over.

Enclosed I transmit the state and condition of His Majesty's ships and vessels under my command,[1] as likewise the intelligence given by a Dutch hoy spoke with this morning.

Intelligence given by Dutch hoy to Lieutenant John Bensley

Anson cutter
3 September 1759

Spoke with a Dutch hoy, (called the *Tobais*) from Rouen bound to Copenhagen loaded with iron pots and bail goods. The master of which says that at Rouen they have 150 flat boats, that the number to be built at Havre de Grace is 200, and in all France 500, each of which are to carry 2 twenty four pounders. The boats that are now at Rouen came all from Havre de Grace, from whence they send them as soon as they can be got ready. In his passage down the river he stopped 4 days at Honfleur at which place there are only 2 flat boats. As to the damage we did in our last bombardment he knows nothing of, nor since that, what preparations the French have made. He was informed that they had, mounted at Havre de Grace, 12 bomb mortars. The floating batteries at the entrance of the Seine he knows no more of than a distant sight of them in his passage out. As to the sentiments of the French concerning our proceedings, he seems to be entirely ignorant and either could not or would not inform me of many questions I asked concerning them.

[1] Enclosed.

599. To Clevland

[TNA, ADM 1/93]
Deptford off Le Havre de Grace
4 September 1759
12 o'clock at noon

Sir,

Nothing particular has occured since my last [No. 598], the gale still continues to blow very hard at west, which makes a great sea, and a bad roadstead for the bombs and tenders.

I am afraid I shall be under the necessity of ordering them to the Downes, for their better security, until the weather moderates. They can soon join me again with the wind easterly, which is the only wind to do anything with on this coast.

I am at this moment favoured with yours of the first instant, and shall take all possible care to prevent any ships going in, or getting out, of this port.

600. To Clevland

[TNA, ADM 1/93]
Deptford in the offing off Cap de la Hève
7 September 1759
Friday noon, wind W blows fresh

Sir,

In the night on Wednesday the 5th instant the squadron under my command was in imminent danger of being drove on the enemy's coast, in a hard gale of wind at WNW. The ebb tide coming on with the gale was the preservation of the fleet. Had it blown as hard with the tide a flood, the bombs, their tenders, and small craft could not possibly have rode it out. This has obliged me to get under sail and keep an offing, with the three large ships and the small craft, leaving the *Brilliant*, *Unicorn*, *Æolus*, *Boreas* and the two sloops in shore, to watch the motions of the enemy, as those frigates can much easier claw off a lee shore than the three fifty guns ships who are very foul and go very ill.

When the weather permits, I shall daily show myself off the port and if a proper opportunity offers, shall go in and endeavour to annoy the enemy to the utmost of my power, but as the winds seem to be set in westerly, which always throws a great sea in here, nothing can be done by bombardment during the continuance.

These two days past the weather has been so bad I could not make any observations on the flat bottomed boats. Twenty only remained on the beach on the 4th instant, and those in such forwardness that I expect they will be all off in a few days. The enemy launching them before their upper works are complete.

Captain Chaplen has joined me this morning and brought me your letter of the 4th instant, as likewise their Lordships' order [No. 597] to send in one of the fifty gun ships to clean. As the *Chatham* has but three days beer on board, and the weather not permitting boats to carry any, I shall be under the necessity of ordering her to Spithead.

601. *To Clevland*

[TNA, ADM 1/93]   *Deptford* off Le Havre de Grace
11 September 1759
Wind NW

Sir,

Since my last dispatches [Nos. 599, 600] the weather has proved moderate, and I have again anchored the squadron under my command in the road off Le Havre, the town bearing EbS, five miles.

On the 9th instant I sent Captain Chaplen with all the pilots of the fleet, in the armed cutters (the frigates likewise keeping under sail), with orders to make their observations on the situation of the enemy's floating batteries, galleys &c. and report to me whether it was possible to attack the said floating batteries with frigates or place the bombs in such a situation to do service.

This motion drew the fire from all the enemy's batteries, both afloat and ashore, but as it was afresh of wind and the cutters keeping under sail, they received no damage. The whole fleet could plainly perceive the impossibility of the bombs being stationed in the same place they were in before, which was corroborated by the report of Captain Chaplen, and all the pilots, who were unanimously of opinion that the shoalness of the water prevented an attack upon the floating batteries, galleys &c. And the impossibility of the bombing being covered from their fire.

Their Lordships I am sure are convinced that the captains of the squadron I have the honour to command, are men of gallantry, and spirit, and would exert themselves to the utmost upon all occasions for His Majesty's service. I think it my duty to acquaint their Lordships that they are unanimously of opinion that nothing further can be done by bombardment, without risking the whole squadron against the enemy's bombs and batteries. And even then the event would be very doubtful.

At present the port is closely blocked up, the enemy ignorant of our strength, and in perpetual anxiety. To attempt to throw a few shells, which must (by the present situation of affairs) fall short of the object could tend only to convince them of their security.

Yesterday I was honoured with their Lordships' orders of the 5th instant and your letter of the same date.

The *Torrington* and the victualler have joined me. I shall dispose of the provisions on board the different ships of the squadron, and dispatch them again to England, as soon as possible.

Only ten flat bottomed boats remain on the beach.

602.   From John Milnes

[TNA, ADM 2/526, p. 247] 14 September 1759

Sir,

I have received and read to my Lords Commissioners of the Admiralty your letter [No. 601] of the 11th instant, giving an account of your proceedings with the squadron under your command. And in return am to acquaint you that their Lordships do not expect anything from a bombardment, but recommend it to you to keep the port of Le Havre as closely blocked up as possible.

603.   To Clevland

[TNA, ADM 1/93] *Deptford* off Le Havre de Grace
14 September 1759

Sir,

In obedience to their Lordships orders [No. 597] of the 3rd instant, I have sent the *Chatham* and *Carcass* bomb, into Portsmouth Harbour to be cleaned and refitted.

The enemy have now only seven boats on the beach. Yesterday they brought out and moored another floating battery. They have now between the Mole Head and the Banc D'Anfar to the south, three floating batteries, and four of the largest flat bottomed boats armed. And between the Mole Head and the Banc de la Jambe to the northwest, six galleys and two armed vessels.

I fully intended yesterday evening to have made an attack on the floating batteries, with all the cutters and boats of the fleet manned and armed, but the disposition of the enemy was such, and their guard so well kept, that I was deterred from putting my scheme into execution. My design was to have gone up on the Honfleur side of the river after dark, to have crossed over on the Banc D'Ansfer at high water, and on the beginning of the ebb have attacked the floating batteries, and the vessels that guard them in the rear, but as these are the dead of the neap tides, the enemy have been doubly diligent to prevent an attack, keeping guard boats all night in each channel, and upon the least alarm the cutters and boats must have been exposed not only to the fire of the citadel and forts but likewise to the galleys and armed vessels.

The enemy's camps are increased here lately. By the number of tents it is judged they may have six or seven thousand troops.

Yesterday a Spaniard from Bilbao with wool was permitted to go into Le Havre having nothing contraband on board.

I must beg leave to take notice to their Lordships that all the fifty gun ships are very foul and go excessive bad.

604. To Clevland

[TNA, ADM 1/93] *Deptford* off Le Havre de Grace
16 September 1759

Sir,

Enclosed I transmit the state and condition of His Majesty's ships under my command.[1]

As the weather has been such as to oblige me to keep the offing these two or three days, I did not return to an anchor here till this morning. Having ordered Captain [Hyde] Parker of the *Brilliant* to remain in the road, and likewise permitted a Spanish vessel to enter the port, the consul of that nation came on board the *Brilliant* yesterday, to return thanks for the favour, and to know if all Spanish vessels were to meet with the same indulgence. As Captain Parker could not satisfy him in that point, he referred him to me when I should arrive. The intelligence he gave was that the enemy were well prepared, had twenty two mortars, thirteen armed vessels, and floating batteries with very heavy cannon. He seemed to be entirely in the French interest and exaggerated every thing relative to the enemy. Duke de Harcourt[2] with fifteen thousand men were in the neighbourhood of the town. That all the flat bottomed boats (but the seven remaining on the beach) were completed and up the river near Rouen; that twenty were building at Caen, twelve of which were completed, and that the whole number in this river and its neighbourhood amounted to two hundred.

[1] Not enclosed.
[2] Commander-in-chief of the French army at Le Havre.

605. To Clevland

[TNA, ADM 1/93] *Deptford* off Le Havre
19 September 1759

Sir,

I am favoured with yours [No. 602] of the 14th instant, and shall take care the port of Le Havre shall be closely blocked up as possible.

The *Deptford* and *Isis* have but a very few days' water and beer on board and are in great want of other necessaries. The season of the year and the openness of this road, make it very difficult to transport provisions. I shall therefore be glad to know if their Lordships approve of those ships anchoring at St. Helens to receive provisions and other necessaries, as it can be done with much greater dispatch and certainty than sending any vessels here.

The enemy have now only five boats on the beach and the frigates in the basin are quite unrigged.

606. To Clevland

[TNA, ADM 1/93] *Deptford* off Le Havre
20 September 1759

Sir,

As the *Deptford* and *Isis* are now reduced to two days' beer, I hope their Lordships will approve of my repairing with them to St. Helens or Spithead, should not a supply arrive within that time, which there is not the least likelihood of, as the wind is at southeast.

I have wrote to Vice Admiral Holburne to desire he will please to give directions to have beer and water ready, that the ships may not be detained from their station. And shall take care to leave Captain Parker of the *Brilliant* with the *Æolus*, *Unicorn*, *Boreas*, *Fly* and *Spy* sloops, and all the bombs, with orders to keep the port closely blocked up during my absence.

607. From Milnes

[TNA, ADM 2/526, p. 280] 21 September 1759

Sir,

I have received and read to my Lords Commissioners of the Admiralty your letter [No. 605] of the 19th instant, and am commanded by their Lordships to recommend it to you to send the *Isis* in to Portsmouth to clean and refit.

Their Lordships approve of sending the ships of your squadron to St. Helens, from time to time, as they grow in want of provisions and necessaries, for the reasons you have given.

608. To Clevland

[TNA, ADM 1/93] *Deptford* off Le Havre
22 September 1759
12 o'clock noon

Sir,

Captain Wheeler of the *Isis* having acquainted me that the coppers for boiling provisions for the ship's company are unserviceable, his rudder loose, and having on board only one days, beer, wood, and coals, I have sent him to Spithead, as likewise the bomb tenders, who are of no use here at present and are in continual danger of driving from their anchors.

As the *Deptford* has but three butts of beer remaining on board, unless a supply arrives tomorrow, I shall be under the necessity of repairing to St. Helens or Spithead.

The wind being now at eastnortheast, with a great sea, will prevent the enemy's coming out while it remains in that quarter. And I make no doubt of being again upon the station before they can sail, if their Lordships should so approve.

609. To Clevland

[TNA, ADM 1/93] *Deptford* at sea
23 September 1759
at 4 PM

Sir,

Enclosed[1] I transmit to their Lordships, the intelligence given me by the master of a Spanish ship from Le Havre de Grace bound to Cadiz. His account concerning the number of boats, I believe to be true, as it corresponds exactly with the intelligence given by a fishing boat, which was taken by one of the cutters a few days since.

---

[1]Enclosed is an account of the damage sustained by Le Havre during the British bombardment and of the measures undertaken by the French to defend the city.

Yesterday in a fresh of wind at northeast the enemy exercised one of their flat bottom boats, under a press of sail, having a trysail, foresail jib, and topsail. They made several boards,[1] seemed to go very upright, and upon each tack fired their bow and stern chase, their number of guns corresponding with the intelligence given by the Spaniard. It blew so fresh and the sea so great in the road, it was with difficulty the squadron under my command rode it out. The difference yesterday between high and low water was five fathom.

The beer of the *Deptford* being all expended, I am standing over with her towards St. Helens, having left Captain Parker, with all the frigates and bombs to block up the port during my absence, as I am sure the enemy cannot sail with this wind.

Yesterday morning I dispatched Captain Wheeler of His Majesty's ship *Isis*, with the bomb tenders, to Spithead and hope you have received the dispatches I sent by him.

The *Deptford* has lost one anchor and two cables in the late bad weather: all shall be got in as fast as possible.

610. From the Lords of the Admiralty

[TNA, ADM 2/83, pp. 441–2] 25 September 1759

Whereas the three East India ships named in the margin[2] are arrived at Kinsale in Ireland, you are hereby required and directed so soon as you shall be joined by the *Portland*, *Norwich*, or any other clean fifty gun ship from Spithead, to detach the *Isis* to Kinsale, directing Captain Wheeler to take the aforesaid East India ships under his care and to proceed with them with the very first opportunity of wind and weather to the Downes, where he will receive orders for his further proceedings.

611. To Clevland

[TNA, ADM 1/93] *Deptford* at St. Helens
25 September 1759

Sir,
You will please to acquaint their Lordships that I arrived here in the *Deptford* yesterday. We are getting on board provisions, anchors and

---

[1]The distance which a sailing vessel runs between tacks when working to windward.
[2]*Ilchester, Egmont* and *London*.

cables and hope I shall be able to sail again this evening or tomorrow morning.

612. To Clevland

[TNA, ADM 1/93]

Deptford in Le Havre Road
The great church in Le Havre EbS 6 miles
29 September 1759

Sir,

Please to acquaint their Lordships I sailed in the *Deptford*, the 26th instant from St. Helens, and joined part of the squadron off this port the next day. The weather had been so bad for several days past, as to oblige them to keep the sea, during which time the *Basilisk* and *Mortar* bombs parted company, and are not as yet returned into this road.

Captain Parker acquaints me that on the 23rd instant in the morning fifteen sail of Dutch ships under convoy of a man of war of 40 guns attempted to come into this port. After a little dispute the Dutchman submitted to the necessity of returning with his convoy.

By intelligence I gained last night by a Dutch hoy from Rouen, bound to Rotterdam, this convoy has been expected by the merchants for some time, who complain bitterly and are greatly distressed at the ships not being permitted to enter the Seine. The master of the hoy likewise informed me that all the flat bottom boats are up the river at, or near Rouen, that the number of soldiers were daily arriving in this neighbourbood. But the report was, the boats waited for cannon and that the invasion was not to take place till the spring.

613. To Clevland

[TNA, ADM 1/93]

Deptford off Le Havre
30 September 1759

Sir,

I must acknowledge the receipt of your letters of the 24th and 26th instant and shall take care to comply with their contents.

I have likewise received their Lordships' orders [No. 610] of the 25th instant, commanding me to detach the *Isis* to Kinsale, to take under his convoy the three East Indiamen, who are arrived at that port, and see them in safety to the Downes. I have sent Captain Wheeler orders accordingly.

The *Basilisk* and *Mortar* bombs have rejoined me and as I shall be under the necessity of sending the *Boreas* in a few days to St. Helens to victual, I hope their Lordships will please to give directions to hasten the ships who are ordered to join me.

614. From the Lords of the Admiralty

[TNA, ADM 2/83, p. 456] 2 October 1759

You are hereby required and directed immediately to dispatch His Majesty's ship the *Glasgow* into Portsmouth Harbour, where her commander is to use the utmost dispatch in cleaning and refitting her for foreign service agreeable to the orders he will find there.

615. To Clevland

[TNA, ADM 1/93] *Deptford* off Le Havre
[4 October][1] 1759

Sir,
Please to acquaint their Lordships that the *Glasgow* joined me on the 2nd instant, and as the *Boreas* and *Unicorn* are in want of provisions owing to great quantities being condemned by survey, I am under the necessity of ordering them to St. Helens for a supply, and hope they will soon rejoin me, as I have now with me only the three large frigates beside the *Deptford* (exclusive of the bombs).

I was in hopes by their Lordships order of the 25th of September that some clean fifty gun ships were ordered to strengthen the squadron under my command, which would be absolutely necessary in case the enemy should attempt to invade His Majesty's dominions from this port, as the ships I have now with me all are very foul and the *Deptford* the only one of any weight.

The enemy are daily proving mortars, and cannon, and yesterday I observed that they had broke up their largest encampment.

I still continue with the squadron at an anchor in the road but was apprehensive the weather this morning would have obliged me to put to sea. I should be glad their Lordships would please to recall the bombs, as they sail extremely ill and could by no means be able to clear the coast in any thing of weather.

[1] This letter is in error dated 4 September.

The *Anson* cutter, Lieutenant [John] Bensley has been at Dover since the 20th of September. I should be glad their Lordships would please to hasten him to his station, as the cutters are very useful in watching the motions of the enemy in shore, and the only vessels whereby I can gain any intelligence. If it was possible, I should be glad of a few more, as they very much contribute to hinder the enemy coasting trade from the different ports on this coast.

616. *To Clevland*

[TNA, ADM 1/93] *Deptford* in Le Havre Road
8 October 1759

Sir,

Agreeable to their Lordships' order [No. 614] I have dispatched the *Glasgow* into Portsmouth Harbour, having distributed her beer and wine among the ships of the squadron who notwithstanding will soon be in want of more, as their Lordships may perceive by the state and condition herewith transmitted.[1]

By intelligence received yesterday by a Portuguese vessel who came out of Le Havre, the enemy's flat bottom boats continued up the river near Rouen, that the troops in this neighbourhood amounted to twelve battalions; some passengers on board the said vessel, who had been but ten days from Paris, reported that every day they expected to hear the news of the surrender of Quebec, that all the officers of the regiment of Auvergne had been cashiered and the men dispersed among other regiments for refusing to embark on the intended invasion against England; that an engineer was arrived at Le Havre to construct fireships on a new plan in order to destroy the squadron in this road, provided they could find men who would dare venture on the attack (which I believe will be very difficult). They have now fifteen armed vessels such as galleys, flat bottom boats &c., some of which frequently come out in order to attack the cutters, when I send them in to reconnoitre, but seldom dare to venture in deep water.

When the *Boreas* and *Unicorn* rejoin me I shall be obliged to order some others to St. Helens to victual. And as I find the cutters to be very useful in annoying the enemy, I could wish their Lordships would be pleased to order a few more on this service.

[1] Not enclosed.

617. *From Clevland*

[TNA, ADM 2/526, p. 342] 9 October 1759

Sir,
I have received and read to my Lords Commissioners of the Admiralty your letter, of the 4th instant [No. 615] (dated *September*) giving an account of your proceeding and desiring some more clean fifty gun ships may be sent to you to strengthen the squadron under your command in case the enemy should attempt to put to sea. And in return I am to acquaint you that the *Norwich* shall be sent to you with all possible expedition and that more shall follow as soon as they can be spared from other more important services.

618. *From Clevland*

[TNA, ADM 2/526, p. 354] 11 October 1759

Sir,
Herewith you will receive orders [No. 619] from my Lords Commissioners of the Admiralty for sending the *Mortar* and *Basilisk* bomb vessels to St. Helens, to complete their provisions. In addition to which, I am to acquaint you that their Lordships have also detained the *Furnace* and *Firedrake* they being all wanted to proceed on another pressing service.

619. *From the Lords of the Admiralty*

[TNA, ADM 2/83, p. 468] 11 October 1759

You are hereby required and directed to dispatch forthwith to St. Helens His Majesty's bomb vessels the *Mortar* and *Basilisk* where their commanders will find orders for their further proceedings.

620. *From Clevland*

[TNA, ADM 2/526, p. 359] 12 October 1759

Sir,
I have received and read to my Lords Commissioners of the Admiralty your letter [No. 616] of the 8th instant giving an account of your proceedings and desiring more cutters may be sent out to you. And in

return am to acquaint you that more shall be sent to you as fast as they can be procured.

621. *To Clevland*

[TNA, ADM 1/93]

Deptford off Cap d'Antifer
15 October 1759
Wind WNW blows fresh

Sir,

I have this moment received their Lordships' order [No. 619] of the 11th instant commanding me to dispatch forthwith the *Mortar* and *Basilisk* bombs to St. Helens. The *Mortar* bomb having been sent with the *Æolus* to reconnoitre the coast between Dives and Cape Barfleur, has not as yet rejoined me. And as Captain [John] Elliot parted company with me two days before the late violent gale of wind, I conclude he is at an anchor with the bomb in La Hague Road, and shall immediately send a cutter with orders to Captain Hunt to repair forthwith to St. Helens.

The *Basilisk* bomb drove to sea in the late hard gale of wind, and I conclude is under Dungeness or in the Downes. I have therefore ordered the *Thunder*, the only bomb with me, to make the utmost dispatch to Spithead, which I hope their Lordships will approve.

The twelfth, thirteenth, and fourteenth instant we had a violent hard gale of wind at southwest. With great difficulty the squadron rode it out. Had it been to the northward of the west, it had been impossible without cutting away the masts. It drove all the enemy's floating batteries, galleys &c. into their harbour. And I observed this morning that the great encampment on Cap de la Hève was broke up.

The wind coming this morning to the westnorthwest, has obliged me to put sea with the squadron under my command. Their Lordships may be assured I shall keep as close off the port as the weather will permit. The *Unicorn*, *Boreas*, *Brilliant*, and *Fly* sloop are in company with me. The other vessels of the squadron are with the *Æolus* to windward under Cape Barfleur.

I shall be obliged in a few days to send the *Brilliant* and *Æolus* to St. Helens for provisions.

622. To Clevland

[TNA, ADM 1/93] *Deptford* in the Downes
17 October 1759

Sir,
Please to acquaint their Lordships that a violent gale of wind at WbS has obliged me to bear up for the Downes, being drove to leeward of Beachy Head. The *Brilliant* and *Unicorn* are come in with me, the other ships and cutters parted company.

No time shall be lost in completing the provisions and sailing the moment the wind and weather will permit.

623. From Clevland

[TNA, ADM 2/526, p. 389] [?]¹October 1759

Sir,
I have received and read to my Lords Commissioners of the Admiralty your letter [No. 621] of the 15th instant giving an account of your proccedings with the squadron under your command.

Their Lordships are sorry to hear of the bad weather you have met with, but glad to find the ships under your command have not received any damage.

In a very few days you may expect to be joined by the *Arethusa* and *Danae*.

624. From Clevland

[TNA, ADM 2/526, p. 394] 19 October 1759

Sir,
I have received and read to my Lords Commissioners of the Admiralty your letter [No. 623] of the 17th instant, giving an account of a very hard gale of wind having obliged you to bear up for the Downes. Their Lordships are extremely glad to find the ships under your command have not met with any accident, which at this season of the year they must be always liable to. And in order to prevent it as much as possible, they recommend it to you only to cruise before Le Havre when the weather is such that you can do it without hazard, and at other

---

¹This document is dated 10 October, but it was clearly written in answer to No. 621 and should be dated 18 October.

times to repair to Spithead or the Downes, according as the winds may offer.

625. To Clevland

[TNA, ADM 1/93]

Deptford in the Downes
19 October 1759 at noon

Sir,

At two o'clock this morning I received an express, which I immediately delivered to Captain [James] Galbraith. He sailed at six AM with the *Tartar* and *Britannia*, having informed me that he could not take with him the *Dolphin*, *Woolwich*, and *Aquilon* for want of pilots.

As the weather proved moderate yesterday and the wind at NNW I ordered Captain Graves in the *Unicorn*, who is clean and sails well, to make the utmost dispatch in getting upon the station off Le Havre. The *Fly* sloop and the cutters sailed with him.

The wind is now at north and makes so great a sea that I am of opinion we shall not be able to get the beer and water onboard from Dover. Should it come to the eastward I shall make the utmost dispatch to St. Helens and have wrote to Vice Admiral Holburne to have beer ready that no time may be lost in repairing to my station.

The *Isis* is just now arrived with the East India ships from Kinsale. I must acquaint their Lordships that the *Deptford* is so very foul that it is impossible for her to get to windward in anything of weather.

626. From Clevland

[TNA, ADM 2/526, p. 400]   20 October 1759

Sir,

I have received and read to my Lords Commissioners of the Admiralty your letter [No. 625] of yesterday's date, representing that the *Dolphin*, *Woolwich*, and *Aquilon* could not proceed to sea in pursuance of their orders for the want of pilots. And in return am to acquaint you that their Lordships have wrote by this post to the master of the Fellowship of Pilots at Dover to cause them to be supplied forthwith.

Their Lordships approve of your having sent the *Unicorn*, *Fly* and cutters to the station off of Le Havre, and of your proceeding to St. Helens, as you propose to get beer and water, should the wind come to the eastward.

Their Lordships will relieve the *Deptford* which you represent to go so very bad through her foulness, as soon as ever the *Norwich* is cleaned.

627. *From the Lords of the Admiralty*

[TNA, ADM 2/83, p. 490]   20 October 1759

Whereas we have ordered the commanders of His Majesty's ships named in the margin[1] to join you forthwith and follow your orders. You are hereby required and directed, so soon as they arrive, to take them under your command accordingly, and then dispatch the *Deptford* to Portsmouth to clean and refit there agreeable to the enclosed orders.

628. *To Clevland*

[TNA, ADM 1/93]   *Deptford* in the Downes
                                                 21 October 1759

Sir,

The *Deptford* and *Brilliant* having completed their beer, I fully intended returning to my station this morning, but the wind coming to the west still detains me in the Downes.

Yesterday morning I got a pilot for the *Dolphin*, and ordered Captain Barlow to use the utmost expedition to join Commodore [William] Boys[2] agreeable to his rendezvous, he sailed accordingly. And as Mr Boys was about ten leagues ahead of the [illegible] when the *Solebay* left him, and the *Phoenix* astern of him, as likewise Captain Galbraith with his squadron, I hope their Lordships will soon have a good account of him.

P.S. Since writing the letter the cutters which I sent to look into Dunkirk are returned, and report that no ships remained in that road, and they could observe only two snows rigged in the basin.

[1] *Norwich, Danae.*
[2] Commanding a small squadron blocking Dunkirk.

629. *To Clevland*

[TNA, ADM 1/93] *Deptford* at anchor in the great road off Le Havre
24 October 1759

Sir,

This day I arrived here with the *Deptford* and *Brilliant* and have been joined by the *Unicorn*, *Boreas*, *Spy* and *Fly* sloops.

The enemy have broke up all their camps in this neighbourhood and by what I can learn by a Spaniard, who came out of Le Havre this morning, the troops that composed the camps are cantoned in Le Havre and the adjacent villages.

Thirteen of their flat bottom boats are in the basin at Le Havre, two at Honfleur, and the remainder still continue up the river near Rouen.

The Spanish captain informed me, that about four days since, the second in command to Prince Soubise[1] and an admiral arrived at Havre from Paris. As Spanish ships are daily coming out I shall make strict enquiry concerning the truth of this intelligence.

630. *From the Lords of the Admiralty*

[TNA, ADM 2/83, p. 510] 26 October 1759

Notwithstanding former orders, we do hereby signify to you that, in case you shall find it necessary for the service to keep the *Deptford* longer with you, you are at liberty to do it after the *Norwich* arrives. But if you do not find it absolutely necessary to keep her with you, you are to send her to the Downes, directing Captain Hollwall to remain there for further order, it being of great consequence at this time to have a large force in the Downes.

631. *To Clevland*

[TNA, ADM 1/93] *Deptford* off Le Havre
29 October 1759

Sir,

The carpenter of His Majesty's ship *Deptford* having absented himself from his duty, I gave Alexander McLean, carpenter of the *Grampus*

---

[1]Charles de Rohan, Prince de Soubise, second in command of the French army assigned to invade England.

sloop, an order to act in his room, whom I find to be a very deserving man and entitled to preferment in his station.

632. *To Clevland*

[TNA, ADM 1/93] *Deptford* at anchor in the great road off Le Havre
31 October 1759
Wind EbS blows fresh

Sir,

Since my last the *Norwich* has joined me with orders [No. 630] to send the *Deptford* to clean, but as the wind and thick weather have been most favourable for the enemy to make their embarkation from this port (if they intended it) I thought it best for His Majesty's service to keep all the force with me in order to frustrate their designs. But I learn by the cutters, which I stationed as near the town as possible, that they have made no motion whatever, and that the flat bottom boats still continue up the river. I am now with the squadron at anchor in the great road, and can plainly perceive that all their encampments are broke up. The floating batteries, galleys, and armed vessels retired into the harbour and by the number of small boats I saw fishing yesterday when I came into the road, I concluded they are not bringing their flat bottom boats down the river, as these men are generally employed on that service.

While the wind continues in this quarter, I shall remain with the squadron at an anchor. Should it incline to the westward of the south the *Deptford* shall be dispatched to the Downes agreeable to their Lordships' order of 26th instant, as she is so foul that it would be very dangerous for her to continue on this coast, and goes so bad at present that she would be of no service in the pursuit of an enemy.

When the wind comes to the westward I shall repair to Spithead leaving behind me some cutters, and the *Unicorn*, she being the only ship of my squadron, most likely to keep her station in any thing of weather. And I must beg leave to take notice to their Lordships that the *Spy* and *Fly* sloops are not of the least service at this season of the year, going extremely ill and are in continual danger from the remarkable indraught on this part of the coast of France.

The *Danae* has not as yet joined me.

633. *From Clevland*

[TNA, ADM 2/526, p. 471] 2 November 1759

Sir,

I have received and read to my Lords Commissioners of the Admiralty your letter [No. 632] of the 31st past, informing them of your being at an anchor, with your squadron in the great road off of Le Havre, that the enemy's floating batteries, galleys and armed vessels were returned into the harbour, that their flat bottom boats continued up the river, and that all their encampments were broke up. Also acquainting their Lordships of your intentions to send the *Deptford* to the Downes and to return yourself to Spithead when the wind comes westerly leaving the *Unicorn* with some cutters on the station.

Their Lordships very well approve of your proceedings and of what you propose to do, and they hope soon to be able to reinforce you with another good frigate or two.

634. *From Clevland*

[TNA, ADM 2/526, p. 473] 2 November 1759

Sir,

I have received and read to my Lords Commissioners of the Admiralty your letter [No. 631] of the 29th past, giving an account that the carpenter of the *Deptford* having absented himself from duty, you have appointed Alexander Mclean, carpenter of the *Grampus*, to act in his room, who is a deserving man, and worthy of preferment. And in return am to acquaint you that their Lordships have ordered a warrant to be made out for him.

635. *To Clevland*

[TNA, ADM 1/93] *Norwich* at anchor in the great road off Le Havre
3 November 1759

Sir,

Since my last dispatches I have spoke with a Spanish ship from Le Havre, bound to Bilbao, the master of which reports that the Duke de Harcourt and all the troops (except two battalions) had left the place, and marched into the country, that there was not the least appearance of an embarkation of troops, the flat bottom boats continuing up the river.

As the enemy have two frigates in the basin, one of which I hear is fitting, it would be necessary should she attempt to escape, to have some clean frigates to intercept her, those with me being too foul for that purpose, and the *Norwich* a most remarkable heavy sailor, however their Lordships may depend upon as good a look out as the season of the year will admit.

The wind for these several days past has been very fresh at southeast, during which time I have kept the squadron in sight of the town, some times at an anchor, some times under sail, and shall continue so to do while the weather is favourable.

I have sent the *Deptford* to the Downes agreeable to their Lordships orders.

636. To Clevland

[TNA, ADM 1/93] *Norwich* off Le Havre
4 November 1759

Sir,
Captain Boyle Walsingham[1] of His Majesty's ship *Boreas* having acquainted me by letter of this date, that the death of the late Sir Charles Henbury Williams,[2] renders it absolutely necessary for his being in town to settle his affairs. I hope their Lordships will not disapprove of my complying with his request, having appointed Captain Gascoigne to command the *Boreas* during the absence of Captain Walsingham, or till their Lordships' further pleasure.

637. From Philip Stephens[3]

[TNA, ADM 2/526, p. 487] 6 November 1759

Sir,
I have received and communicated to my Lords Commissioners of the Admiralty your letter [No. 635] of the 3rd instant, giving an account of the proceedings of the squadron under your command, and of the

---

[1] Captain Hon. Robert Boyle. In 1752 he assumed the name Walsingham.
[2] Captain Boyle Walsingham's father-in-law. MP for Monmouthshire, 1735–47; Leominster, 1754–2 Nov. 1759. British envoy, Dresden, 1747–49. 1751–55 and then Berlin, 1750–51. Serving as ambassador to St. Petersburg, 1755–57, Williams returned to England in a state of mental disorder and on 2 November 1759 died insane.
[3] Second Secretary to the Lords of the Admiralty, 16 Oct. 1759–18 June 1763; Secretary, 18 June 1763–13 Jan. 1783; First Secretary, 13 Jan. 1783–3 March 1795.

motions of the enemy, and requesting some clean frigates may be sent to you those now with you being very foul. In return to which I am to acquaint you the *Arethusa* is ordered immediately to join you, and enclosed I send you their Lordships orders [No. 639] for sending the *Boreas* to Spithead as soon as she does so.

638. To Clevland

[TNA, ADM 1/93]

Norwich at St. Helens
6 November 1759
Wind NW

Sir,
The wind coming to the west in the night of the 4th instant, and blowing very fresh, obliged me to stand over to the coast of England. All day yesterday we had a pretty hard gale. In the evening off the Isle of Wight, the *Norwich* carried away her main topsail yard and jib boom. The ships arrived here with me are the *Brilliant* whose coppers are worked down, the *Unicorn* and *Fly* sloops in want of beer and provisions. The *Boreas* and *Spy* are off Cap d'Antifer, and four cutters off Cap de la Hèrve. The squadron shall be got ready for sea as soon as possible, and when favourable wind and weather offers shall proceed again to their station.

639. From the Lords of the Admiralty

[TNA, ADM 2/84, p. 15]   6 November 1759

So soon as His Majesty's ship the *Arethusa*, by which you will receive this, shall join you, you are hereby required and directed to dispatch the *Boreas* to Portsmouth, where her commander is to use the utmost dispatch in refitting her agreeable to the enclosed orders.

640. From Clevland

[TNA, ADM 2/526, p. 493]   7 November 1759

Sir,
I have received and read to my Lords Commissioners of the Admiralty your letter [No. 636] of the 4th instant giving an account of your having given leave to Captain Boyle Walsingham of the *Boreas*, to come to town, to attend some private affairs of very great importance

and having appointed Captain Gascoigne to command the ship in his absence. Their Lordships very well approve of what you have done.

641. *To Clevland*

[TNA, ADM 1/93]
Spithead
8 November 1759
Wind WNW blows fresh

Sir,

The *Brilliant* being exceeding foul, I wish their Lordships would be pleased to permit her to be docked the next spring tide. The *Unicorn* being almost complete, I shall send her to relieve the *Boreas*, who is in want of sails. While the wind hangs in this quarter there will be no venturing upon the enemy's coast, the cutters being the only vessels that can look into the port without hazard.

642. *From Clevland*

[TNA, ADM 2/526, p. 508]
9 November 1759

Sir,

I have received and read to my Lords Commissioners of the Admiralty your letter [No. 641] of yesterday's date representing that the *Brilliant* is very foul, and proposing that she may be refitted. And am to acquaint you that orders will be sent by this post for that purpose.

643. *To Clevland*

[TNA, ADM 1/93]
Spithead
9 November 1759

Sir,

Yesterday in the afternoon the *Boreas* and *Spy* arrived at Spithead, it having blown very hard at west and westnorthwest, which obliged them to leave to coast. When the weather moderates I shall return again to my station with the squadron under my command. The wind is at present at westnorthwest, blows hard.

644. To Clevland

[TNA, ADM 1/93]
Spithead
10 November 1759
Wind WNW blows hard

Sir,
Please to acquaint their Lordships that His Majesty's ships of the squadron under my command, are ready to return to their station, but as it has continued to blow very hard, between the west and westnorthwest, I have deferred sailing till the weather moderates, as the consequence of sailing in this bad weather would certainly be attended with driving the ships to the Downes. And their Lordships by your letter [No. 624] of the 19th of October strongly recommending it to me only to cruise before Le Havre when the weather is such that it can be done without hazard, and at other times to repair to Spithead or the Downes as the wind may offer.

Their Lordships may be assured I shall never unnecessarily come into port, or quit the station when there is a possibility of the enemy's coming out.

645. From Clevland

[TNA, ADM 2/526, p. 517]
12 November 1759

Sir,
I have received and read to my Lords Commissioners of the Admiralty your letter [No. 644] of the 10th instant, giving an account that you are ready with the squadron under your command to proceed to sea upon your station. But that you have been detained by the wind blowing too hard at west and northwest. Their Lordships approve of your not putting to sea, for the reasons you have given.

646. To Clevland

[TNA, ADM 1/93]
Spithead
13 November 1759
Wind NW blows hard

Sir,
Please to acquaint their Lordships that yesterday I intended to return to my station with the squadron under my command, but was prevented

by a calm and fog. A hard gale at northwest coming on in the night and still continuing, obliges me to defer sailing till the weather moderates, it being too dangerous to expose the squadron on that part of the enemy's coast with this wind and weather. And I wish no accident may have happened to the *Unicorn* and cutters who are already there.

647. To Clevland

[TNA, ADM 1/93]
Spithead
14 November 1759
At 8 AM wind [at] N

Sir,

Please to acquaint their Lordships, I am now under sail with the squadron under my command, and hope to be on the coast of France some time in the evening.

As their Lordships know every captain that has been long in commission has generally some men who are their particular followers. When the *Dublin* sailed for America I would not trouble them to discharge the men who have signed the enclosed petition[1] as they were going on such pressing service, and it was not in my power to give others in lieu. But as the ship is now returned to England, I flatter myself their Lordships will indulge my request, upon giving four good and able seamen in their room, as the men have been really my followers for several years past, both in the present and late war.

648. From Clevland

[TNA, ADM 2/526, p. 543]
15 November 1759

Sir,

I have communicated to my Lords Commissioners of the Admiralty your letter [No. 647] of yesterday's date desiring that the four men named in the margin[2] belonging to the *Dublin*, may be discharged into the ship your flag is on board of, upon your giving four good and able seamen in their room, as they have been your followers both in the last and present war, and petitioned to serve with you. And I am to acquaint

---

[1] Enclosed is a petition, dated 13 November 1759, signed by Jeremiah McNamara, John Miller, John Purvis, Francis Enlington requesting that Rodney arrange their transfer into his ship.
[2] Jeremiah McNamara, John Miller, John Purvis, Francis Enlington.

you that directions will be given for their being discharged for four other men as you desire.

649. *To Clevland*

[TNA, ADM 1/93]
Norwich off Le Havre
19 November 1759
Wind SSE

Sir,

Please to acquaint their Lordships that I am close off this port with His Majesty's ships and cutters named in the margin,[1] and by the report of the masters of two Spanish vessels which I saw come out of Le Havre this morning, every thing at present is very quiet there, the frigates in the basin continuing unrigged and the troops that remain in the town being only sufficient to garrison the place, all the others having marched to the northward.

The master of a Spanish ship from Rouen likewise informed me that he counted two hundred flat bottom boats between that place and the Caudebec [en Caux] hauled up on the shore in tiers of ten or twelve, and that he judged about one hundred and fifty were hauled up on the south side [of] the said river in different places.

The weather at present is very moderate.

650. *From Clevland*

[TNA, ADM 2/527, p. 18]
22 November 1759

Sir,

I have received and read to my Lords Commissioners of the Admiralty your letter [No. 649] of the 19th instant giving an account that every thing at present is very quiet at Le Havre. And that the master of a Spanish vessel from Rouen informs you 200 flat bottomed boats are hauled upon shore between that place and Caudebec en Caux, and about 150 of them on the south side of the river in different places.

---

[1]*Norwich, Unicorn, Boreas, Arethusa,* and the cutters *King of Prussia, Anson, Hector, Hunter* and *Endeavour.*

651. To Clevland

[TNA, ADM 1/93]

Norwich at St. Helens
22 November 1759
3 o'clock PM

Sir,

I remained at an anchor with the squadron under my command in the road of Le Havre from the 17th to the 20th when I was obliged to weigh and get an offing, the wind coming to the northwest and blowing hard. Yesterday it came to the northeast blowing very hard and drove the squadron to the westward of the island.[1] As it continues I have with difficulty got to an anchor here, where I shall only stay till it moderates sufficient to return to my station. As the *Arethusa* sails remarkable well, I gave her captain orders not to drive to leeward with the ship I was on board but endeavour with the cutters to keep off Cap d'Antifer.

652. From Clevland

[TNA, ADM 2/527, pp. 25–6]   23 November 1759

Sir,

I have received and read to my Lords Commissioners of the Admiralty your letter [No. 651] of yesterday's date giving an account of your arrival at St. Helens, being blown off your station by hard gales of wind, and of your having ordered the *Arethusa* to endeavour, with the cutters to keep off Cap d'Antifer.

Their Lordships recommend it to you to return to your station again, as soon as possible.

653. To Clevland

[TNA, ADM 1/93]

Norwich at sea
27 November 1759

Sir,

Please to acquaint their Lordships that these two days past we have had an excessive hard gale at southwest with thick weather, which has drove the squadron under my command off their station. We are now about mid Channel, endeavouring to gain the enemy's coast as soon as

[1] Isle of Wight.

possible, as I find the Dutch still persist to send convoys in hopes of stealing some of their ships into Le Havre. In the late gale of wind at northeast on the 22nd instant in which none of the ships of the squadron, except the *Arethusa*, could possibly keep the station off Cap d' Antifer, a Dutch man of war of 20 guns, called the *Stat Vel Warren* of Rotterdam, on the 23rd instant endeavoured to push with her convoy into Le Havre. Upon Captain [Hon. Raby] Vane's acquainting him the port was blocked up, it was with difficulty he could prevail with him to retire. For notwithstanding the Dutchman had given him his word and honour he would leave the coast, he attempted in the night to get into the port, his excuse for such gross behaviour was that he wanted to speak with me, but on my appearance in the offing in the morning, he thought proper to make the best of his way for Holland.

I must upon this occasion take the liberty to represent to their Lordships the necessity of clean frigates to be able to keep the station off Cap d'Antifer in northeasterly winds, at which time the Dutch will ever attempt to enter the port, and none but clean frigates with that wind can possibly prevent them.

The weather has been too bad lately to gain any intelligence of the enemy's motions, the cutters I have with me are employed as near into the port as possible for that purpose.

654. *From Clevland*

[TNA, ADM 2/527, p. 57] 29 November 1759

Sir,

I have received and communicated to my Lords Commissioners of the Admiralty your letter [No. 653] of the 27th instant, giving an account of your being forced off your station by contrary winds. And of a Dutch ship having attempted to get into Le Havre with her convoy, but was prevented by the *Arethusa*, the only ship of your squadron that was able to keep on the station off Cap d'Antifer. Their Lordships approve of your proceedings.

655. To Clevland

[TNA, ADM 1/93] *Norwich* at St. Helens
29 November 1759

Sir,
Please to acquaint their Lordships that after sending my dispatches [No. 653] of the 27th instant, I stood over with the squadron under my command, and made the coast of France the same evening. In the night an excessive hard gale of wind came on at west by south, which continued all day yesterday with very thick weather in which the ships of my squadron parted company. As I was obliged to stand to the northwest under the courses, yesterday in the evening the wind coming to the westnorthwest it was with difficulty I could get to an anchor in this road. This morning the *Arethusa* and *Boreas* are likewise anchored here, the *Unicorn* and all the cutters being to leeward remaining at sea, those with their Lordships dispatches on board from the severity of the weather not having joined me. The wind is at northwest blowing hard. When it moderates I shall again put to sea with the squadron under my command.

656. From Clevland

[TNA, ADM 2/527, p. 69] 30 November 1759

Sir,
I have received and read to my Lords Commissioners of the Admiralty your letter [No. 655] of the 29th instant, which came by express giving an account of the proceedings of the squadron of His Majesty's ships under your command.

657. To Clevland

[TNA, ADM 1/93] *Norwich* at Spithead
30 November 1759

Sir,
This morning the cutter returned to Spithead and delivered your letter of the 26th instant, acquainting me with the design of the enemy to transport their flat bottom boats to Dunkirk when I should be driven off the coast by bad weather. The cutters who I ordered to cruise as near the town as possible, report that the weather has been so bad, and so

great a sea, that it would have been impossible to have laid at an anchor in the road, and it was with difficulty even the cutter could be kept above the water.

Their Lordships may be assured that all the attention that is possible shall be had towards defeating the enemy's designs, and whenever the weather will permit, I shall certainly be at anchor in the road myself, and never return to St. Helens or the Downes but when the severity of the weather obliges me.

I should be glad their Lordships would please to order some more frigates under my command, as I could then station them on such parts of the coast, as would render the enemy's attempts to transport their flat bottom boats much more difficult. And as it is likewise their Lordships' directions that I station some of the frigates in the great road, I wish one of the forty gun ships was ordered on that service, they being the best roadsters. And the *Norwich* (I am in) a remarkable bad one.

I cannot think the enemy will attempt to transport their boats at this season as I always find a remarkable heavy sea on their coast when the wind is between the NE and SW, when it casts off their shore. I shall always be (or some of the frigates) close in upon different parts of their coast – between Le Havre and Dieppe. The wind is at present at NW blows fresh. The squadron is taking in beer and provisions. The moment it moderates I shall be at sea again.

If the service will admit it, I should be much obliged to their Lordships if they would appoint a large ship for me to have my flag on board.

658. *To Clevland*

[TNA, ADM 1/93]   Spithead
1 December 1759
Wind NW blows fresh

Sir,

The ships under my command having completed their beer and water are ready to proceed again upon their station and are only detained by the wind and weather which being at NW and blowing very fresh makes it too dangerous to venture on the coast.

The *Unicorn*, *Arethusa*, and four cutters are at sea, and their Lordships may depend upon all the squadron being likewise so when the weather moderates.

659. To the Duke of Newcastle

[BL, Add. MSS 32899, ff. 266–7] Spithead
2 December 1759

My Lord,

I beg your Grace will permit me to return you my most sincere thanks for the honour you have bestowed on me in choosing me a member of Parliament for Okehampton.[1] A steady adherence to your Grace's commands shall ever distinguish me while I have a seat in the House.

Give me leave to congratulate your Grace on the glorious victory obtained over the French fleet,[2] and if the service I have been employed on has merited your Grace's attention and met with your approbation it will be to me the highest satisfaction.

660. To Clevland

[TNA, ADM 1/93] Norwich at anchor in the Great Road off Le Havre
4 December 1759 at noon

Sir,

Please to acquaint their Lordships I am at anchor with the squadron[3] under my command in the great road of Le Havre. The enemy's frigates are rigged and seem ready to sail. As they must be very clean I could wish their Lordships would please to order the *Brilliant* to rejoin me as she was under my command till ordered to be cleaned.

I shall endeavour to get all the intelligence I possibly can of the enemy's motions.

661. From Clevland

[TNA, ADM 2/527, p. 96] 7 December 1759

Sir,

I have received and read to my Lords Commissioners of the Admiralty your letter [No. 660] of the 4th instant, dated in the road of Le

---

[1] On 24 November 1759 Rodney, with the support of Newcastle, was elected unopposed to Parliament for the government controlled borough of Okehampton in Devon.
[2] On 20 November 1759 the Western Squadron under the command of Admiral Sir Edward Hawke defeated the French fleet in the Battle of Quiberon Bay.
[3] *Norwich, Arethusa* and *Unicorn*.

Havre, giving an account that the enemy's frigates are rigged and seem ready to sail, and desiring the *Brilliant* may be ordered to rejoin you. And in return I am to acquaint you, that orders are given to her captain accordingly.

662. From Clevland

[TNA, ADM 2/527, p. 102] 8 December 1759

Sir,

The *Brilliant* having sailed from Spithead before the orders for her joining you got down to Portsmouth, I am commanded by my Lords Commissioners of the Admiralty to acquaint you therewith, and that they have sent the *Niger* to you in her room.

663. To Clevland

[TNA, ADM 1/93] Norwich in the Road off Le Havre
12 December 1759

Sir,

I have received intelligence by the master of a Spanish ship I saw come out of Le Havre, and likewise by a fishing boat taken this morning that the large frigate in the basin is the *Félicité* of 36 guns, who had been waiting at St. Malo for three months' past, and took the opportunity in the last hard gales westerly, to slip into this port. The day she arrived was the 25th of November. I was then close off Fécamp, the *Boreas* and *Arethusa* off Cap d'Antifer. Before His Majesty's service obliged their Lordships to reduce the squadron under my command to four sail, I had always two frigates stationed off Cape Barfleur to intercept any of the enemy's vessels coming from the westward, but lately my whole attention has been fixed to prevent the enemy's transporting their flat bottom vessels to Dunkirk, or receiving supplies from the Dutch or other neutral powers, which has obliged me to station the remaining ships under my command off Cap d'Antifer, and Cap de la Hève, when the weather would permit them to keep those stations. Their Lordships may be assured that I shall always station two frigates (or be myself) in the road of Le Havre, when the weather is such that [I] can lay there with a degree of safety, but in westerly winds it is impossible at this season of the year to remain in the road.

Yesterday the weather permitted me to reconnoitre the port, I observe the *Félicité* frigate had unbent her sails, and struck yards and topmasts. Two other frigates of 28 and 22 guns who have been here all the summer continued dismantled, and two snows of 18 guns each appeared to be ready to sail. The flat bottomed vessels are still up the river.

In the fishing boat taken this morning was a seaman lately belonging to the *Soleil Royal*. He reports that all the men are discharged to go to their homes, that the *Soleil Royal* had 1,380 men on board, and Marshall Conflan[s][1] was in the ship. That on her striking she fell on her side, but boats coming timely to their assistance, all the men were saved except three who were sick in their hammocks, and that not one man was killed or wounded in the action. He reports that the *Juste* was lost at the mouth of the Loire, one hundred and twenty men only saved out of her, and that he met five seamen at Morlaix lately belonging to the *Northumberland*[2] who were the only surviving men of that ship's crew, they cutting the painter of the boat with one oar only on board when the ship sunk, and were taken up by a Spanish ship the day after the action. It is the common report of the people here that Sir Edward Hawke has taken or destroyed twelve sail.

I beg leave to take notice to their Lordships how necessary it is for the frigates on this station to be clean. The shortness of the days and the narrowness of the channel allowing but little time to chase and come up with an enemy, who will always take care to be near their own coast.

Yesterday the *Greyhound* joined me in lieu of the *Brilliant*. And as I have this moment received their Lordships' orders to send her to the Downes, I shall dispatch her accordingly.

664. To Clevland

[TNA, ADM 1/93] *Norwich* at anchor in the Great Road off Le Havre
17 December 1759
Wind EbS

Sir,
Since my last dispatches I have received intelligence by several Spanish vessels from Le Havre, that all the enemy's frigates in that port are dismantled by an order from Paris, that the flat bottom[ed] boats are entirely unrigged, and only four remain at Le Havre, all the others having been carried up the river. The only observations I can

---

[1] Admiral Comte de Conflans, commander of the French fleet which was defeated at Quiberon Bay.
[2] Captured from the British in 1744.

make myself, is that the *Félicité* has unbent her sails, and struck yards and topmast, [and] the other frigates now appear to be entirely unrigged.

A French passenger on board one of the Spanish ships informs me that Marshall Conflan[s] and all the captains of his fleet are gone to Paris, and that the common report concerning their squadron, was, that they had burnt themselves two of the ships in the Villane[1] and expected daily to hear that Sir Edward Hawke had destroyed the others.

Enclosed I send their Lordships intelligence received this day by a Dutch hoy from Bergen.[2]

665. From Clevland

[TNA, ADM 2/527, p. 164] 20 December 1759

Sir,

I have received and read to my Lords Commissioners of the Admiralty your letter [No. 663] of the 12th instant giving an account of what intelligence you had received, concerning the motions of the enemy at Le Havre and the information you had received from the fishing boat, and respresenting your want of frigates. I am commanded by their Lordships to acquaint you they will order another frigate to join you as soon as possible.

His Majesty's ship *Unicorn* being put into Plymouth, their Lordships have ordered her to be cleaned there and have directed the *Vestal* and *Lizard* to join you.

666. To Clevland

[TNA, ADM 1/93] *Norwich* at anchor in the Great Road off Le Havre
21 December 1759
Wind SSE

Sir,

Since my last dispatches to their Lordships the enemy continue in the same situation all seemingly very quiet.

The *Niger* was off Cap d'Antifer the 18th instant spoke to one of the cutters who acquainted Captain [John Albert] Bentinck I was at an anchor in the road, but he has not as yet joined.

[1]This intelligence was not correct.
[2]Enclosed.

I cannot refrain from acquainting their Lordships that notwithstanding Captain [George] Darby of the *Norwich* represented to the officers of the yard at Portsmouth that his ship was so leaky as to require being pumped every two hours in fine weather, and almost continually when it blowed, and that his keel was so ragged as to spoil his cables when in a roadstead, at single anchor, which greatly endangered His Majesty's ship, and desiring they would take her into the dock upon the blocks.[1] They nevertheless paid no regard to his representations, and by their neglect the ship continues in the same leaky condition, and her keel so bad that within this fortnight two new cables have been rendered unserviceable.

667.   *From Stephens*

[TNA, ADM 2/527, p. 183]   24 December 1759

Sir,

Mr. John Bradshaw,[2] who commands the *Endeavour* cutter, representing that he has been above seven years in the navy, and has passed his examination for a lieutenant, and that he was educated in the academy at Portsmouth,[3] and requesting to be made a lieutenant, my Lords Commissioners of the Admiralty desire you will please to enquire and let them know what character he bears.

668.   *To Clevland*

[TNA, ADM 1/93]   *Norwich* at Spithead
                                                      26 December 1759

Sir,

Please to acquaint their Lordships I am arrived at Spithead with His Majesty's ship *Norwich*, being in want of beer, provisions and cables, having left the *Niger* and *Arethusa* at an anchor in the great road of Le Havre. The *Boreas* parted company last night in a hard gale of wind at west.

I shall use the utmost dispatch in getting beer, provisions, and cables on board, and return to my station when the weather permits.

---

[1] A line of blocks along the bottom of a dry dock upon which the keel of a vessel can rest.
[2] Commissioned a lieutenant on 31 January 1760.
[3] An institution, opened in 1729, for training volunteers before going to sea as midshipmen.

669. *From Stephens*

[TNA, ADM 2/527, p. 211] 27 December 1759

Sir,
I am commanded by my Lords Commissioners of the Admiralty to acquaint you they have ordered the *Roast Beef* privateer to join you. And desire when you have had some experience of her qualities, you will please to report your opinion of her and whether she is fit to be continued in His Majesty's service.

670. *To Clevland*

[TNA, ADM 1/93] Spithead
31 December 1759

Sir,
Please to acquaint their Lordships the weather has been, and still continues so excessive bad, that no vessel has been able to go to Spithead with provisions and water for the *Norwich*, *Niger*, and *Arethusa*. When it moderates no time shall be lost in getting their provisions and water on board, and returning to their station.

671. *To Clevland*

[TNA, ADM 1/93] Spithead
2 January 1760

Sir,
Yesterday a master of a tobacco ship arrived here from Dieppe which he left on Saturday last. He gives me intelligence that he had learnt from people with whom he had been in company, a few days before he sailed from thence, that orders had been issued for the men to repair to the flat bottom boats at Dunkirk, that the master of one of them read the order, and that the people were actually gone from Dieppe. He likewise informed me that the flat bottom boats from Le Havre designed to go along shore to take in their oars at Dieppe where a large number had been deposited, and then repair to their general rendezvous at Dunkirk.

The weather has been so very bad since I arrived at Spithead, that till this day no provisions could be got off. I shall now use the utmost dispatch, and hope to be ready to sail tomorrow morning at furthest with the *Niger* and *Arethusa*. The *Vestal*, *Lizard*, and five cutters being at present off Le Havre.

From the danger of the coast and uncertainty of the weather I cannot think the enemy will attempt to transport their flat bottom vessels to Dunkirk at this season.

However, as good a lookout shall be kept as the nature of the service and the weather will permit.

672. From Captain Samuel Hood

[TNA, ADM 1/93] *Vestal* off Le Havre
3 January 1760

Sir,

I have the honour to acquaint you of my having been upon this station since the 30th past. Yesterday I looked into Le Havre and cannot perceive the enemy to be the least in motion. The two frigates in the basin are quite unrigged, and seem not at all disposed to put to sea. I spoke with a Dutch vessel from Le Havre two days since: the master of which informed me that the enemy had no troops in the town, but had in the neighbourhood. The mate says otherwise and from the whole of what the people in general said, the French are mighty quiet. Last night about nine as I was working out from Le Havre Road, Cap de las Hère then bearing SE, about 5 miles, I saw four sloops standing right in with all the sail they could carry, and upon seeing me tacked and stood away. I came up with them fast and tho' my shot fell amongst them, not one would bring too, but all endeavoured to get off different ways, which made me conclude they were French. I then hoisted French colours and fired at them as I came within reach. At last I spoke with the *Hunter* and *Hesther*[1] cutters who told me the others were the *Anson* and *Royal George*; both of which made sail to windward. After I brought too and I have not since seen either, I wish they may not have directed their course to England, as their account will, I am afraid, alarm you. And on that motive I send you this by the *Hesther* cutter, which wants to be victualled and cleaned. I cannot help observing to you, that the officers of the cutters have shown themselves very brave for I assure you several of my shot took place, even within the random reach of a musket and they still persevered in getting off till it fell little wind and my boat rowed to them.

---

[1] The name of this ship sometimes appears as *Esther*.

PS I have just spoke with the master of a small Dutch vessel from Caen who says all the talk with those he has been with is peace, and that they seem regardless about the flat boats.

673. To Clevland

[TNA, ADM 1/93] *Norwich* at Spithead
3 January 1760 at 6 PM

Sir,

Please to acquaint their Lordships that the *Anson* cutter is this moment arrived from off Le Havre de Grace. Lieutenant Bensley who commands her reports to me that yesterday about ten o'clock in the evening he was attacked by a frigate that he saw at an anchor the preceeding day in the road, which he concluded had been one of the squadron under my command till she fired several broadsides at the cutter and struck her with grape shot. But perceiving the *Anson* out sailed her the frigate altered her course and gave chase to the *Hesther* and *Hunter* cutters. Lieutenant Bensley made the best of his way to Spithead to acquaint me with these particulars and reports the weather had been so bad for many days past that he could not venture near the shore.

The *Royal George* cutter is likewise arrived who reports that the frigate was certainly an enemy, that the cutters saw her coming out from the road of Le Havre, and were so unguarded as to bear down at her, at ten o'clock at night, taking her for the *Vestal* by which I believe Lieutenant Wallis of the *Hunter* and Lieutenant Pinfold of the *Hesther* cutter are fallen into the enemy's hands.

On my arrival here I immediately made the proper demands for beer and water and gave the captains of the *Arethusa* and *Niger* the same orders, as the last mentioned ship had but lately joined me I desired her beer might first be completed and ordered Captain Bentinck to make the utmost dispatch and return to his station which orders have been repeated, but the ship could not be got ready. The *Arethusa* is sailed, and the *Norwich* which will have completed her beer and water this night shall sail tomorrow morning at daylight.

This affair gives me the greatest concern, as I concluded the *Vestal* and *Lizard* had been off Le Havre, but the latter is arrived this day with a jury main mast and the cutters have not seen the *Vestal* notwithstanding she sailed from Plymouth on the 27th of December, and would have been on her station some time since.

674. *From Clevland*

[TNA, ADM 2/527, pp. 244–5] 4 January 1760

Sir,

In my letter of the 24th past I acquainted you that my Lords Commissioners of the Admiralty had ordered an extract of yours of the 21st [No. 666] relating to the leakiness of His Majesty's ship *Norwich*, and the negligence of the officers of Portsmouth yard in her refitting, to be sent to the Navy Board with directions to enquire very strictly into the same. And they having, in return, transmitted to their Lordships copies of two letters, one from Commissioner Hughes, and the other from the master shipwright and his assistants, by which it appears that the ship when refitted showed no such signs of leakiness as Captain Darby represents, nor did the captain make any application to those officers to take her into the dock upon the blocks, as he sets forth. I am commanded by their Lordships to send you copies of the said two letters herewith, which you will please to communicate to Captain Darby, that he may let the officers know who it was that he applied to.

675. *From Clevland*

[TNA, ADM 2/527, pp. 252–3] 4 January 1760

Sir,

I have received and read to my Lords Commissioners of the Admiralty your letter [No. 673] of yesterday's date, by express, giving an account of the arrival of the *Anson* cutter from off Le Havre de Grace, and that her commander informs you, that about ten o'clock of the evening of the 2nd instant he was attacked by a frigate that he saw at an anchor the preceding day in the road, but upon the *Anson's* outsailing her, she altered course, and gave chase to the *Hesther* and *Hunter* cutters. In return I am commanded by their Lordships to acquaint you, that they have sent a copy of your letter to [Captain] Sir Piercy Brett[1] in the Downs with directions for sending one or two of his best sailing frigates the length of Le Havre to endeavour to intercept the ship you mention, and in case of not meeting her to cruise between that place and Boulogne for 6 days, and then return to the Downes, unless you shall think it necessary to employ them otherwise.

---

[1] Commander-in-chief in the Downes.

Their Lordships expect you should not lose a moment's time in proceeding to your station. And they also desire to be informed if there has been any remissness in the captain of the *Niger's* not getting that ship ready sooner.

676. *To Clevland*

[TNA, ADM 1/93] *Norwich* at Spithead
6 January 1760

Sir,

The *Norwich* having laid two days becalmed at St. Helens, last night a breeze coming to the northeast, I put to sea. But this morning meeting with an excessive hard gale at east, which must have drove her down Channel had she continued at sea, I thought it best for His Majesty's service to endeavour to get to an anchor again, which with difficulty we accomplished, and the moment the weather moderates the ship shall put to sea.

Enclosed I transmit their Lordships a copy of a letter [No. 672] I have just received from Captain Hood of the *Vestal* off Le Havre, who was the frigate the cutters took to be an enemy.

677. *To Clevland*

[TNA, ADM 1/93] *Norwich* at Spithead
7 January 1760

Sir,

I have been favoured with yours of the 4th instant [No. 675] in answer to mine [No. 673] by express, relative to the mistake the cutters made in taking the *Vestal* for a French frigate.

All the dispatch possible was made in getting the *Norwich's* and the frigate's provisions on board that the weather would admit. I did not mean to complain [No. 673] to their Lordships of the captain of the *Niger*, but only to let them know that notwithstanding the most pressing orders it was impossible from the badness of the weather to get her to sea sooner. The night I sent the express to their Lordships the *Norwich's* ship's company were employed in getting provisions on board. At day light (though calm) we towed down to St. Helens, from whence we put to sea as soon as any wind offered, but as it blew a storm a few hours after at east, had I not returned the consequence must have been the same as happened to the *Unicorn*, it having blown very hard ever since. Their Lordships may be assured I shall not lay idle in port, when the weather is such that I can put their orders into execution, or be able to keep my station.

678. *To Clevland*

[TNA, ADM 1/93] *Norwich* at St. Helens
12 January 1760

Sir,
I must desire you will please to acquaint their Lordships that on Thursday the 10th instant, I had a very good opportunity of looking into Le Havre, and continued in the road several hours, 'till the weather obliged me to get an offing.

I could plainly perceive the enemy had dismantled all their frigates, their standing mast[s] only being in, and those unrigged, and as I missed the masts of the flat bottom vessels which used to appear in the basin and harbour, I was in hopes of getting some intelligence concerning them. In the evening observing a Spanish brig coming out of the port, I ordered one of the cutters to bring the master on board to me, whose information corroborated with what I had observed, that the frigates were dismantled and the flat bottom boats dismasted, and all the seamen belonging to them dismissed without pay, with this addition that several of them were committed to prison for demanding it. The harbour was clear of shipping and everything very quiet.

I think it my duty to acquaint their Lordships that the officers and seamen in general of the squadron under my command have suffered much from the severity of the weather, and that it has been with difficulty the ships could be worked, the sails and rigging being so hard froze and as there is now little probability of the enemy's putting to sea, I could wish their Lordships would permit me to station only two frigates and cutters, at a time off Le Havre, as I am sure that will be a sufficient force at present. The other ships of the squadron to lay at St. Helens ready to relieve those before Le Havre every eight or ten days, or to supply their place should a gale of wind drive them from thence, which must be expected at this season. By this rotation the ships' companies will be kept in health, and spirits, and the enemy's port better blocked up than if the whole squadron were cruising on their coast, as the first gale of wind either easterly or westerly must drive them from the station, there being few days to be expected at this time of the year to trust the ships at an anchor in so dangerous a place as the great road.

All day yesterday we had a severe gale of wind at eastnortheast, which obliged me to endeavour to get to an anchor in this road, to prevent being drove down [the] Channel. When it moderates, I shall again stand over to the coast off Le Havre.

679. To Clevland

[TNA, ADM 1/93]   Norwich at St. Helens
15 January 1760

Sir,

I desire you will please to acquaint their Lordships that Mr. Thomas Pomfret, master's mate belonging to the *Norwich*, who I appointed to command the *Hector* cutter in the absence of Lieutenant [William] Lowfield, has deserted from the said cutter.

I therefore hope their Lordships will please to give directions for his being apprehended. He is to be heard of agreeable to the enclosed directions.[1]

He was recommended to Captain Darby by Sir William Rowley[2] and has been midshipman and master's mate upwards of twelve months.

680. To Clevland

[TNA, ADM 1/93]   Norwich at St. Helens
15 January 1760

Sir,

Whereas Nicholas Hudson, master at arms of His Majesty's ship *Norwich*, has been ordered to act as provost marshall over a condemned prisoner now on board the *Royal Sovereign* ever since the 28th of October last, I should be glad their Lordships would be pleased to give directions that the master at arms of the *Royal Sovereign* may take charge of the prisoner and Nicholas Hudson return to his duty on board the *Norwich*, where he is much wanted.

---

[1] 'Frequents Mr. Lawson's ship chandler near the church Rotherith in whose employ he was married and lives at Newport Pagnell, Bucks., is about 5 foot 8 inches high, 33 years of age, brown complexion, wears a dark brown cut wig, a little pitted with the small pox.

I since received the undermentioned directions where he is likely to be heard of

Thomas Pomfret at Mr. Turnpenny's at three Flower de Luces, Hounds ditch, near Bishop's Gate, London.'

[2] Admiral Sir William Rowley, Lord of the Admiralty, 22 June 1751–17 Nov. 1756; 6 April–2 July 1757; MP Taunton, 1750–54; Portsmouth, 1754–61.

I must likewise desire you will please to acquaint their Lordships that James Miller, boatswain's mate of the *Norwich*, has been acting boatswain of the *Furnace* bomb since the 19th of June last. I gave him an order to act as boatswain of the said bomb in pursuance of their Lordships' directions signified to me by you.

681. To Clevland

[TNA, ADM 1/93]

Spithead
15 January 1760

Sir,
Please to move the Right Honourable Lords Commissioners of the Admiralty to order the Commissioners of His Majesty's Navy to pay me my pay to the 31st of December last.

682. From Stephens

[TNA, ADM 2/527, p. 318]

17 January 1760

Sir,
I have received and read to my Lords Commissioners of the Admiralty your letter [No. 679] of the 15th instant giving an account that Thomas Pomfret, master's mate of the *Norwich*, whom you appointed to command the *Hector* cutter (in the absence of Lieutenant Lowfield), has deserted from her, and desiring directions may be given for apprehending him. In return I am to acquaint you that their Lordships have ordered the marshall of the admiralty to apprehend him.

683. From Stephens

[TNA, ADM 2/527, pp. 320–1]

17 January 1760

Sir,
I have read to my Lords Commissioners of the Admiralty your letter [No. 680] of the 15th instant desiring that directions may be given for Nicholas Hudson, who is master at arms of the *Norwich*, and has acted as provost marshal over a condemned prisoner on board the *Royal Sovereign*, ever since the 28th of October, returning to his ship and for the master at arms of the *Royal Sovereign* taking charge of the prisoner. And I am commanded to acquaint you that

Rear Admiral [Philip] Durell[1] is directed to cause the same to be done.

I am also to acquaint you that the Lords have appointed James Miller to be the boatswain of the *Furnace* bomb vessel.

684. To Clevland

[TNA, ADM 1/93] *Norwich* Cap d'Antifer SE 3 miles
18 January 1760
Wind E

Sir,

Yesterday I again looked into Le Havre and found the enemy in the same situation as I reported in my letter [No. 678] of the 12th instant, their ships entirely dismantled, the country covered with snow, and everything very quiet.

I desired you in my letter of the 12th instant to represent to their Lordships the impossibility of the squadrons keeping upon this station, at this season in anything of a gale, either easterly or westerly, and requesting them to permit me to order only two frigates and two cutters to cruise here at a time, the others to remain at St. Helens ready, either to relieve them every eight or ten days, or to supply their place immediately after any gale may have drove them from their station.

To convince their Lordships of the necessity of such a disposition I must acquaint them that the *Vestal* and *Arethusa*, the best sailing frigates of the squadron under my command, are drove to the westward by the late hard gale easterly and have not as yet been able to regain the coast, which must have been the fate of the whole squadron had I not anchored at St. Helens during the gale which enabled me to put to sea immediately when the weather moderated, and has prevented the enemy's port being open which it must other ways have been.

685. From Stephens

[PRP, ADM 2/257, p. 354]   24 January 1760

Sir,

My Lords Commissioners of the Admiralty having received intelligence that at Boulogne there are fitting eight cutters and a snow of 18 guns which were to have been ready the latter end of last month, and

---

[1] Commander-in-chief at Portsmouth in the absence of Vice-admiral Holburne.

that the privateers of the enemy will probably go upon the Channel station rather than the North Sea, I am commanded by their Lordships to acquaint you therewith, and that they are also informed that other privateers are fitting in the French ports in the Channel. They therefore recommend it to you to keep cruisers off the headlands adjoining to your station, to protect the trade of His Majesty's subjects as well as to take or destroy the privateers of the enemy.

686. *To Clevland*

[TNA, ADM 1/93] Spithead
24 January 1760

Sir,
Please to acquaint their Lordships that on the 22nd instant we took two fishing boats off Le Havre. As the men were young and might be serviceable to the enemy, should they attempt in the spring to transport their flat bottom boats to Dunkirk, I have detained them.

Everything was in the same situation at Le Havre as I acquainted you in my last letter [No. 684]. As the wind came to the westward with a great sea, I stood over to the English shore, and having been ill of a fever for several days past, and the weather growing tempestuous, I ordered Captain Darby to put into Spithead.

687. *To Clevland*

[TNA, ADM 1/93] *Norwich* Spithead
24 January 1760

Sir,
Having been very ill for some days' past and finding myself unable to recover on board obliges me to desire their Lordships' leave to be on shore for a fortnight or three weeks in which time I hope to recover a sufficient share of health to return to my duty.

688. *From Clevland*

[TNA, ADM 2/527, p. 359] 25 January 1760

Sir,
I have received and read to my Lords Commissioners of the Admiralty your two letters [Nos. 686, 687] of yesterday's date, one giving an

account of your having taken two fishing boats off Le Havre and detained the men, which their Lordships approve of for the reasons you have given, the other representing yourself having been ill for some days' past and desiring leave to be on shore for a fortnight or three weeks for the recovery of your health.

Their Lordships are sorry to hear of your illness, and are pleased to give you three weeks leave to be onshore, in which time they hope you will be restored to your health. They have ordered Captain Darby to take upon him the command of the squadron during your absence. And I am to signify their Lordships, directions to you, to give him attested copies of all instructions you are under for his guidance during your absence.

689. *From the Lords of the Admiralty*

[TNA, ADM 2/84, p. 521] 20 May 1760

Having ordered the commanders of His Majesty's ships and vessels named in the margin[1] to put themselves under your command and follow your orders, you are hereby required and directed to proceed immediately to Portsmouth and take upon you the command of the said ships and vessels accordingly (hoisting your flag on board such of them as you shall think fit) which you are to get ready for sea, with the utmost dispatch, and hold yourself in constant readiness for sailing. You are also to take under your command such four cutters as Vice Admiral Holburne may appoint, to whom you are to apply for the same.

690. *To Clevland*

[TNA, ADM 1/93] Hill Street
21 May 1760

Sir,

I have received their Lordships' orders [No. 689] of yesterday's date and desire you will please to make known to them that I have been confined for several days with a violent cold and bilious colic, but hope in a very few days I shall be able to proceed to Portsmouth to take upon me the command their Lordships have been pleased to honour me with.

---

[1]*Deptford*, 50; *Tweed*, 32; *Aquilon*, 28; *Rose*, 20; *Albany*, sloop; *Furnace* and *Firedrake* bombs.

691. *From Clevland*

[TNA, ADM 2/528, p. 447]	22 May 1760

Sir,
I have received and communicated to my Lords Commissioners of the Admiralty your letter [No. 690] of this date, acquainting them with your having received their order to repair to Portsmouth and take upon you the command they have assigned you, and that you hope in a few days to be able to proceed thither accordingly, but that you are at present confined with a cold and bilious colic. Their Lordships command me to acquaint you that they depend on your setting out so soon as your health will admit of it.

692. *To Clevland*

[TNA, ADM 1/93]	Portsmouth
	27 May 1760

Sir,
Please to acquaint their Lordships I have hoisted my flag on board the *Deptford* at Spithead. And shall hasten the equipment of the squadron under my command with all the dispatch possible. The *Rose* and cutters are sailed to cruise off Le Havre.

693. *To Clevland*

[TNA, ADM 1/93]	*Deptford* Spithead
	30 May 1760

Sir,
As the *Furnace* and *Firedrake* bombs under my command are fitting out with the utmost dispatch, I should be glad to know if it is their Lordships' pleasure they should take the mortars on board.

694. *From Clevland*

[TNA, ADM 2/528, p. 478]	31 May 1760

Sir,
I have received and read to my Lords Commissioners of the Admiralty your letter [No. 693] of yesterday's date desiring to know whether

the *Furnace* and *Firedrake* bomb vessels are to take their mortars on board. And in return am commanded by their Lordships to acquaint you, that they should take them.

695. *From the Lords of the Admiralty*

[TNA, ADM 2/85, p. 3]   3 June 1760

You are hereby required and directed to proceed immediately, with His Majesty's ship the *Deptford*, and such other ships of your squadron as may be ready, off Le Havre de Grace, where you are to exert your best endeavours to prevent the enemy's ships from going into or coming out of the River Seine, keeping some of your ships cruising between Cape Barfleur and Beachy Head to intercept their privateers, and you are to be particularly attentive to intercept any vessels or embarkations the enemy may send coastwise.

During the continuance on this service you are to send us frequent accounts of your proceedings and of any intelligence you may procure that shall be proper for our knowledge.

696. *To Clevland*

[TNA, ADM 1/93]   Portsmouth
                                                                            4 June 1760

Sir,

I must desire you will please to acquaint their Lordships that there are neither officers or bombardiers belonging to either of the bombs under my command. If the bombs are only intended for cruisers, I should be glad their Lordships would permit the mortars to be relanded, as they make the vessels very laboursome and sail ill with them when on board.

697. *To Clevland*

[TNA, ADM 1/93]   *Deptford* at Spithead
                                                                            5 June 1760

Sir,

Last night I received their Lordships' orders [No. 695] to proceed with what ships are ready of the squadron under my command off Le Havre de Grace, in order to prevent the enemy's ships going into or coming out of the River Seine.

I have made the signal to unmoor and shall use the utmost dispatch in putting their Lordships' orders into execution, and propose sailing this day if the calm does not prevent me.

Yesterday the *Rose*, Captain Banks, returned from before Le Havre. He reports that the enemy have moored their floating batteries without the mole head and that ten galleys were anchored in the road.

698. To Clevland

[TNA, ADM 1/93] *Deptford* off Le Havre de Grace
11 June 1760

Sir,

The squadron of His Majesty's ships under my command arrived off this port the 8th instant. On its appearance the coast was alarmed as usual.

The same dispositions are made by the enemy as were last year, their floating batteries being moored off the pier head, and eight galleys stationed between Le Havre and Honfleur, three of which have three cannon and row with forty eight oars each. The other five have two cannon and row with thirty oars each. They are intended to protect the navigation of the river, never venturing into deep water, or any distance from their batteries.

The enemy have no ships fitting at this port, their trade at present (coasters excepted) being carried on in foreign bottoms, numbers of which daily arrive here. And as I have no orders to the contrary permit them to enter, except those who may have contraband goods on board.

This day I received a letter from the Spanish consul residing here, desiring my permission to let him send some small craft on board a large Spanish ship in the road, in order to take out part of her lading, that she might be capable of entering the port.

I acquainted him in my answer, that it was not His Majesty's intention the subjects of his Catholic Majesty should be molested in carrying on a legal commerce, and that he might send vessels on board the said ship in order to lighten her. I hope this will meet with their Lordships' approbation.

I must now beg leave to recommend to them Mr. Philip Walsh,[1] who has commanded the *Hunter* cutter by order almost a year. Yesterday he drove ashore a coasting vessel under Cap d' Antifer, and notwithstanding numbers of the enemy kept a continual fire from the cliffs he

---

[1] Philip Walsh was commissioned a lieutenant on 16 June 1760.

brought her off. As he has been remarkably diligent, undergone a great deal of fatigue since commanding the said cutter, and passed his examination for a lieutenant, I hope their Lordships will be pleased to grant him a commission.

Agreeable to their Lordships' commands I have stationed the *Aquilon* between Cape Barfleur and Dunnose with orders to her captain to be particularly attentive to intercept the enemy's privateers. The *Albany* sloop I have likewise stationed between Cap d' Antifer and Beachy Head, and shall dispose of the rest of my squadron when they join me so as to intercept any vessels or embarkations the enemy may send coastways. I could wish their Lordships would indulge me with an addition of two or three small frigates the more effectually to perform this service. And should be glad the *Roast Beef* armed vessel was one.

As it was impossible to procure pilots at Portsmouth for the use of the squadron, I should be glad their Lordships would be pleased to give directions to the commanding officer in the Downes that Lieutenant [Richard] Pinfold, in the *Hesther* cutter, who served last year under my command, and is well acquainted with this coast, may join me, and have orders to bring with him Mr. Robert Heriker of Dover who was pilot with me during the time I commanded off this port.

699. From Clevland

[TNA, ADM 2/528, p. 525] 11 June 1760

Sir,

I have received and read to my Lords Commissioners of the Admiralty your letter [No. 696] of the 4th instant representing that there are neither officers nor bombardiers belonging to either of the bomb vessels under your command, and desiring if the vessels are only intended for cruisers that the mortars may be relanded as they make the vessels very laboursome and sail ill. And in return I am commanded to acquaint you that for some particular reasons their Lordships would have the mortars kept on board.

700. From Clevland

[TNA, ADM 2/528, p. 543] 16 June 1760

Sir,

I have received and read to my Lords Commissioners of the Admiralty your letter [No. 698] of ye 11th instant giving an account of your arrival upon your station and of the proceedings of the enemy in consequence thereof and in return I am to acquaint you that their Lordships approved of the disposition you have made of the ships under your command.

Their Lordships have applied to Mr. Secretary Pitt for His Majesty's pleasure with regard to neutral vessels passing in and out of the port of Le Havre. And they appointed Mr. Walsh[1] to be lieutenant of the *Ranger* sloop at Portsmouth upon your recommendation.

701. To Clevland

[TNA, ADM 1/93] *Deptford* at Spithead
24 June 1760

Sir,

From the 8th to the 20th instant I continued with part of the squadron under my command in sight of the town of Le Havre where to all appearance and according to the best intelligence I could gain from neutral vessels everything remained very quiet, the enemy keeping only two of their galleys moored off the pier head.

Having received intelligence that the enemy employed a number of their best seamen in the fishery off Dieppe, I dispatched on the 12th instant the *Albany* sloop and *Hector* cutter to cruise off that place. The *Albany* rejoined me on the 15th with three large fishing vessels having on board forty stout seamen all registered for the King's service and lately belonging to Marshal Conflan's squadron. Captain [John] Jervis informs me he fell in with near one hundred sail, but as it blew hard and they were near the shore he could take but three. Lieutenant Lowfield of the *Hector* cutter has not as yet rejoined me, but I hear he has likewise taken some of their fishing vessels.

Since the 20th we have had excessive hard gales of wind which still continue and has obliged me to put into Spithead, the *Deptford* being so

[1] See also No. 698.

very crank[1] and making so much water in her upper works she will scarce bear any sail in bad weather owing to her masts and yards being out of all proportion.

As their Lordships are sensible of the frequent necessity of ships cruising in the Channel being obliged to carry sail in order to avoid a lee shore, or to keep their station, which it is impossible for the *Deptford* to do in her present condition, being obliged in the late gale to bear up in order to free her from water. I should therefore be glad they would please to order the topmasts to be shortened about three feet, the foremast yards shifted abaft to the main mast and their place supplied with yards of less dimensions. As these alterations can be made in a very few days and will greatly contribute to make the ship more useful, I hope my request may be complied with.

Enclosed I transmit to their Lordships the present disposition of the ships under my command.[2]

PS Since writing this the *Aquilon* is arrived at Spithead.

702. From Clevland

[TNA, ADM 2/529, p. 36]   26 June 1760

Sir,

My Lords Commissioners of the Admiralty having taken into their consideration that part of your letter [No. 698] of the 11th instant wherein you acquaint them that you had received a letter from the Spanish consul at Le Havre, desiring permission to let him send some small craft on board a large Spanish ship in the road in order to take out part of her lading, that she might be capable of entering the port and that you had consented thereto, acquainting him at the same time that it was not His Majesty's intention that the subjects of His Catholic Majesty should be molested in carrying on a legal commerce. Their Lordships command me to acquaint you that they extremely well approve of what you have done, and that they expect you should on all occasions treat His Catholic Majesty's ships and subjects in the most favourable man-

---

[1] A ship that cannot bear her sails because she is built too narrow and is liable to heel over.
[2] *Aquilion* between Cape Barfleur and Dunnose.
Tweed between Cape Barfleur and Le Havre.
Rose and two cutters off Le Havre.
Two cutters between Cap d'Antifer and Fécamp.
Albany between Cap d'Antifer and Beachy Head.
Deptford and bombs at Spithead.

ner and give them the like protection and assistance as to the ships of this country, and take care that the several captains under your command avoid giving any interruption to the commerce of that nation.

703. To Clevland

[TNA, ADM 1/93]
Portsmouth
28 June 1760

Sir,

The badness of the weather has drove the squadron under my command off their station, the *Aquilon* into Spithead, the *Rose*, and *Tweed* under Dungeness, but their captains informed me they should return the moment the weather moderated.

I have revictualled the *Aquilon*, who sailed for her station last night, and shall follow myself in a very few days, as nothing remains to be done to the *Deptford*, but a new fore yard, and altering the courses, which are in hand and shall be finished with all the dispatch possible.

704. From Clevland

[TNA, ADM 2/529, p. 45]
30 June 1760

Sir,

I have received and read to my Lords Commissioners of the Admiralty your letter [No. 703] of the 28th instant giving an account that the badness of the weather has drove the squadron under your command off their station. And I am commanded by their Lordships to recommend it to you, to return to it again as soon as possible.

705. From Clevland

[TNA, ADM 2/529, p. 45]
30 June 1760

Sir,

The Navy Board having in return to the direction of my Lords Commissioners of the Admiralty for shortening the masts and yards of His Majesty's ship the *Deptford* agreeable to your proposal,[1] offered their reasons to their Lordships why the ship should remain with the masts and yards she has got, I am commanded by their

[1] Cf. No. 701.

Lordships to send you an extract of their letter on this subject herewith.[1]

706. *To Clevland*

[TNA, ADM 1/93]
Portsmouth
30 June 1760

Sir,

As the fore yard and sails of His Majesty's ship *Deptford* will be completed this evening or tomorrow, I desire you will please to acquaint their Lordships that I shall not lose a moment's time in returning to my station.

A warrant having been sent here appointing John Buckworth, boatswain of the *Seaford*, to be boatswain of the *Aquilon*, the said Buckworth declines to take up his warrant notwithstanding he has been several times sent to for that purpose. I must therefore beg leave to recommend to their Lordships, one John Miller for a boatswain's warrant. He has been a quartermaster and boatswain's mate with me upwards of twelve years and is a remarkable good man.

707. *From Clevland*

[TNA, ADM 2/529, p. 47]
1 July 1760

Sir,

I have received and read to my Lords Commissioners of the Admiralty your letter of yesterday's date, informing them that you shall not lose a moment's time in returning to your station. And recommending John Miller to be boatswain of the *Aquilon* as Buckworth, whom their Lordships had appointed to her, declines to take up his warrant. And in return I am to acquaint you that their Lordships have ordered a warrant to be made out for him.

---

[1] Not enclosed.

708. *From Clevland*

[TNA, ADM 2/529, p. 62] 4 July 1760

Sir,
The Navy Board having transmitted to my Lords Commissioners of the Admiralty a letter they had received from Lieutenant Bensley, who commands the *Anson* cutter, representing that she is in want of a repair, and of several stores, she having been more than eight months from Dover, and that she cannot be repaired at Portsmouth, where she now is, as the officers are unacquainted with the works a cutter particularly requires, I am commanded by their Lordships to send you the lieutenant's letter and desire you will report to them your opinion on it.

709. *To Clevland*

[TNA, ADM 1/93] *Deptford* at anchor in Le Havre Road
6 July 1760

Sir,
I have been favoured with your letter [No. 705] of the 30th June, enclosing to me an extract of a letter from the Navy Board with their reasons why the masts and yards of His Majesty's ship *Deptford* should remain as they were.

I have great regard for the opinion of the Navy Board, as likewise for those gentlemen who formerly commanded her, but that shall never deter me from representing to their Lordships the defects, or imperfections of any ship that may be put under my command.

I must beg leave in the first place to take notice [No. 701] to their Lordships that the said ship has generally been employed in fair weather climates, seldom or ever as a Channel cruiser. Had the latter been the case I am sure those gentlemen mentioned by the Navy Board would not have been so very favourable in their reports for notwithstanding all that can be alleged, the ship has ever been reckoned remarkably tender. Her present commander, as likewise all the captains that have been under my command, both this, and the preceeding summer, frequently taking notice to me how much she was over masted for so old and crank a ship. This observation with my own experience on board her, and knowing how ready their Lordships are to grant any reasonable request, I thought it my duty to represent to them the condition of the ship, with the proposed alterations, which by your letter of the 26th

June they were graciously pleased to comply with, provided it did not detain me too long from my station.

On the receipt of the said letter that no time might be lost I immediately altered the topmasts and yards, leaving nothing to be done by the dock people, but making a new fore yard, the order for which did not arrive from the Navy Office till three days after the receipt of your letter.

I can now assure their Lordships the alteration has had the desired effect, the ship being a better man of war, and sailing faster, even in little wind.

I have been at an anchor in this road with the squadron under my command these two days, where to all appearance everything remains very quiet, the floating batteries being hauled into the pier, and one galley only remaining in the little road. Numbers of neutral vessels are daily entering and coming out of the river. Several spoke with last night, report that intelligence arrived yesterday noon at Le Havre, that a battle had been fought between the Prussians and Russians, in which the former had received a total defeat.[1]

As the *Rose* is in want of beer I have sent her into port, ordering her commander to apply to Rear Admiral Durell that she may be cleaned, in which he is to use the utmost dispatch and then rejoin me off this port.

I take this opportunity to return their Lordship many thanks for their appointing [No. 707] John Miller boatswain of the *Aquilon*.

710. *To Clevland*

[TNA, ADM 1/93] *Deptford* off Le Havre
11 July 1760

Sir,

I have received your letters [No. 708] of the 4th and 8th instant, with a copy of Lieutenant Bensley's letter from Portsmouth to the Navy Board, setting forth that the *Anson* cutter under his command has been eight months from Dover, was in want of repairs and stores, and (as he was informed by the master of her) the defects could not be repaired at that place for the reasons as set forth in his letter.

I must acquaint their Lordships that Lieutenant Bensley made the same representation to me as mentioned in his letter to the Navy Board, but could not prevail upon me to believe the master's assertion, that

---

[1] This intelligence was apparently nothing more than a rumour.

stores necessary for cutters could not be procured at Portsmouth, or the vessels properly repaired there. Experience having convinced me that the said masters made use of every artifice in hopes of being ordered to Dover, where themselves and people getting on shore prevent the vessels returning to their station. The *Anson* when sent there last year by my order stayed three weeks before she rejoined me, as many days being sufficient to clean at Portsmouth, where they are under the eye of a commanding officer who always hastens them to their duty.

I must therefore beg leave to give it as my opinion to their Lordships, that the ordering the cutters to repair to Dover, either to clean, or take in stores, would be detrimental to His Majesty's service as I am convinced the masters of the said cutters would more frequently split their sails or lose their boats, in hopes of being ordered to that port. And if their Lordships would but be pleased to give directions that the officers of the dockyard at Portsmouth, may be ordered to caulk them when leaky, I am sure there would be no occasion to send them to Dover, as the owners have frequent opportunities of sending what stores they please for them to Portsmorth, which is wilfully neglected.

I must desire their Lordships not to look upon this report as an accusation against the lieutenants commanding the cutters, all of them have been very diligent in the execution of their duty, but have been deceived by the misrepresentation of the masters. I must likewise desire you will please to acquaint their Lordships the cutters are constantly cleaned every six weeks.

In regard to your letter of the 8th instant, wherein you are pleased to acquaint me that their Lordships observing the *Tweed* has many men less than her complement, and the *Deptford* more than hers, signifying their directions to me to cause those who are more than the *Deptford's* complement to be discharged into the *Tweed*. I must desire you will please to acquaint their Lordships that it was Captain [William] Paston's earnest request to me, not to have the said supernumeraries, as with the sick men he left at Portsmouth his complement would be complete, and as those men set down 'lent' in his weekly account, being armed and employed by him in a fishing vessel that attends the ship, and frequently goes in shore in order to deceive the enemy; but as the bombs' complements are scare sufficient to work them, I propose dividing my supernumeraries between them, which I hope will meet with their Lordships' approbation. At the same time you will please to acquaint them that seventeen of the said supernumeraries are petty officers and young gentlemen followers of mine, several being recommended to me by some of their Lordships.

711. To Clevland

[TNA, ADM 1/93]　　　　　　　　　　*Deptford* at anchor off Le Havre
12 o'clock at night
12 July 1760

Sir,

Since my letter [No. 710] of yesterday's date I have received certain intelligence from the masters of several neutral vessels who came out of Le Havre this day, and in particular from a Spaniard who expressed an eager desire to speak with me, that the enemy were fitting out the *Thames*,[1] *Félicité*, and another frigate and that orders were come to Le Havre to load ninety four of their flat bottom boats with military and naval stores to be sent to Brest. That he saw seven loaded with cannon and shot, that eight thousand great shot were put on board one boat, that they were navigated with twelve men, each vessel having one gun in her prow, and another in the stern, with three months' provisions. That they were sent when loaded to Honfleur in the night, at which place seven are now ready to sail, and five at Dives. That their orders are to take the opportunity of an easterly wind and dark night to keep close in shore and to be particularly careful to destroy the vessels if in danger of the enemy. They are likewise directed to sail five or seven in company. And never to pass Cape Barfleur but in the night. The Spanish captain likewise informed me that seven flat bottom boats loaded with timber sailed from this place about the middle of May. Their getting safe to Brest he imagines has induced them to this further trial. This intelligence I believe may be depended upon its being corroborated by the master of a Portuguese brought on board me in the night.

I must acquaint their Lordships that the Spaniard's intelligence did not proceed entirely from his regard to the English but in some measure from the disappointment they have lately met with in trade, which has raised their resentment against the French and Dutch to a very high degree, as the man fairly confessed to me. Acquainting me that when the ports in the River Seine were blocked up last year, the Spaniards only being allowed to enter therein, the French contracted for forty sail of Spanish vessels to bring the King's salt to the ports of Normandy at the rate of forty two livres per ton, but since the port has been opened, the Dutch offered to be their carriers at half price and

---

[1] A British frigate which had been captured and then commissioned into the French navy.

that they would employ therein three hundred sail of vessels, to unload at any port in Normandy. The French have contracted with them accordingly. And the disappointed Spaniards are turned out of their ports in ballast.

Please to acquaint their Lordships I shall use my best endeavours to prevent the enemy designs and shall spread the small squadron under my command as much across the mouth of the river as the depth of water and the weather will permit. But as the land between Honfleur and Dives is high and the water shoal a considerable distance off, there is little probability of their being intercepted till they get fairly out of the river. But I shall continually keep cutters close into the south shore in the night; and have dispatched the *Albany* and *Furnace* with the *Anson* cutter and an armed fishing vessel, manned from the *Deptford* with orders to disguise their vessels, as much as possible, and cruise close in shore between the mouth of Caen River and the Ile St. Marcouf. I have likewise wrote to Admiral Durell to hasten the *Rose* to me as soon as possible. And desire you will please to represent to their Lordships the necessity of having more vessels under my command at this present juncture, to enable me more effectually to perform this service. The *Thames* and the frigates are intended for America. I shall easily know their forwardness, their masts being perceptible over the town, at present only their lower ones rigged.

712. *From Clevland*

[TNA, ADM 2/529, p. 91] 15 July 1760

Sir,

I have received and communicated to my Lords Commissioners of the Admiralty your letter [No. 710] of the 11th instant containing your report upon Lieutenant Bensley's letter, in relation to repairs being done to cutters at Dover instead of Portsmouth which the master of the *Anson* is desirous of, and represented that repairs to cutters cannot be done as well at the last mentioned place. Their Lordships having taken the same into consideration command me to acquaint you, that they have ordered the cutter to refit at Portsmouth.

713. From the Lords of the Admiralty

[TNA, ADM 2/85, p. 109]　　　　　　　　　　　　　　　　16 July 1760

Having ordered the captains of His Majesty's ship and sloops named in the margin[1] to proceed immediately to join you, and to put themselves under your command, you are hereby required and directed to take them under your command accordingly.

714. From Lieutenant General the Marquis de Brassac[2]

[TNA, ADM 1/93]　　　　　　　　　　　　　　　　　　　[16 July 1760]

Sir,

It is contrary to all the rules of war, that you detain those officers who very imprudently went on board your ship the last time. I never promised you to burn the five flat bottom boats that are in this port, but upon the conditions you would not accept, and lastly when one of your officers came on shore, it was by very great mistake, for on the contrary I ordered Monsieur de Beaumont to tell you, you might do what you pleased, and that I would not hear any thing more, I therefore again desire you will send back Monsieur de Beaumont, Monsieur de St. Pierre a gentleman of this country, Monsieur de Briqueval Mousquetaire, aide de camp to the Duke d'Harcourt, and Monsieur Dusaussay an officer of Montrevel, whom you detain, as I have before told you, against the rules of honour for which reason, I shall give an account of it to my royal master's minister, who will demand justice from your minister and certainly will obtain it, in regard to me, Sir, I will hear nothing further. Do your duty and I will do mine.

715. To de Brassac

[TNA, ADM 1/93]　　　　　　　　　　　　　　　　　　　17 July 1760

Sir,

I have received your letter [No. 714] of last night's date, demanding the four officers detained on board the ships of the King my master, and at the same time complaining how contrary my proceedings are to the rules of war.

---

[1]*Rose*, frigate; *Carcass*, bomb; *Pelican* and *Bonetta* sloops.
[2]The commander of the French forces at Port en Bessin. See also Nos. 715 and 716.

In my answer Sir, I shall only relate plain matters of fact, and leave the world to judge whether you or I have acted most contrary to those rules.

Part of the squadron I have the honour to command pursued and drove on shore at Port en Bessin five French vessels loaded with military stores. They immediately attacked and destroyed the battery that defended the port, when the senior officer perceiving that the destruction of the vessels would be attended with that of the town, out of compassion to the poor inhabitants caused the fire from the ships to cease, and gave the commanding officer of the French troops in the place to understand that if he would immediately burn the boats, the town would be spared. The officer desiring a truce for a few hours till he could send to you was granted. Some time after two officers from you came with a written message that you consented to burn the boats on the conditions offered, and desired an English officer might go on shore to see it executed, which officer you detained near two hours on frivolous pretences, and sent him back with another message that you would not perform the agreement, and that we might do our worst.

Such chicanery authorises the step I have taken notwithstanding the warm cannonade that succeeded has effectually destroyed the vessels, yet as a just punishment for so notorious a breach of faith, I shall persist in detaining the said officers, unless as a public atonement you cause the very remains of the said vessels to be burnt this day.

You see Sir I shall do my duty as you say you shall do yours.

716. *From Captain William Paston*

[TNA, ADM 1/93] *Tweed* off Port en Bessin
18 July 1760

Sir,

This morning at 8 o'clock Monsieur St. Pierre came on board according to promise and delivered me Monsieur Brassac's justification, which I here send you enclosed[1] together with a letter from St. Pierre by which you will find the boats are not burnt, nor intended to be so, tho' he acknowledges them all to be rendered entirely useless, every mast of them being carried away, and the boats themselves tore all to pieces, which I believe to be really the case, as I can very well see all the masts gone, and the boats to all appearance broken backed.

---

[1]Enclosed is a letter from Brassac dated 17 July 1760.

They are now hard at work erecting a battery on a rising ground to the westward of the town, and about a quarter of a mile from the beach, but for what number of cannon I cannot yet pretend to say with certainty, but if the weather continues good, I shall not fail to inform myself more particularly. And on the high land to eastward of the flag staff are encamped about two battalions of regulars. This afternoon about 2 o'clock, I sent the cutter and my own barge in chase of three coasting sloops, which they have run on shore, and are now in chase of another, which I believe will escape them being near Point Piercy. I have agreeable to your direction sent M. St. Pierre, and the other officers on shore, and Monsieur Beaumont on board the *Albany* to be brought to you.

717. *To Clevland*

[TNA, ADM 1/93] *Deptford* at anchor in the Road off Le Havre
18 July 1760

Sir,

In my last [No. 711] I sent you the disposition I had made of the ships under my command, in order to intercept the vessels transporting naval and military stores to Brest. I must now acquaint you that on the 14th at noon, the wind blowing fresh at northeast, the enemy had the confidence to send out of Honfleur five sail of flat bottom vessels convoyed by one of their galleys. Their passage down the river was close to the south shore, their colours flying, I kept my eye constantly upon them, made no signal whatever, but sent orders to the captains of *Aquilon, Tweed,* and *Firedrake* to hold themselves in constant readiness to chase the moment I made the signal, but not to loose their sails or make any motion until that time, as I knew it could answer no end until the enemy had passed the shoals at the mouth of Caen River,[1] they having it in their power to [enter the] harbour when they pleased. I observed likewise they kept a good lookout, and were continually making signals from shore. When their boats got the length of Caen (which was within an hour of sun set) they hauled their wind standing backward and forward, in the mouth of the river, which I could plainly discern till dark, and that their intention was to push for it in the night.

The moment the day closed I dispatched the *Hector* and *King of Prussia* cutters, with orders to make all the sail possible for the mouth of the river leading to Caen, and ordered the *Aquilon, Tweed,* and

---
[1] Orne River.

Firedrake to pursue and destroy the enemy, remaining myself in the road, having received intelligence that the three frigates in Havre were almost ready to sail; but in the morning, perceiving they were not so forward as reported, I got under way, soon after which I perceived five sail more of the enemy's flat bottom vessels, which I, in vain attempted to intercept, they with great difficulty getting into Caen River.

Soon after I received a message from the captain of the *Albany* acquainting me that he, in company with the *Furnace* bomb, had fell in with five flat bottom boats the preceeding night, which they had drove on shore at Port en Bessin and were preparing to destroy them. The officer in his way to me, had given the same intelligence to Captain Ogle,[1] who was making the best of his way to that place. I immediately made all the sail I could crowd, and soon heard a great firing to the westward, which continued about two hours. On my arrival off the place Captain Ogle informed me he had attacked and destroyed the fort, that protected the road, had a parley with the enemy, and a message from the Marquis de Brassac,[2] a Lieutenant General, who commanded the French troops that were encamped near that place, that he agreed to burn the boats upon condition that the town was spared, and had sent orders for that purpose, desiring an English officer to go and see it properly executed, which being accordingly complied with, they detained the said officer upwards of two hours, and then returned him on board accompanied by Monsieur Beaumont a captain in the Regiment of the Chevalier de Rohan, with another message that the General would not execute the agreement. As I judged from the beginning the enemy only wanted to gain time, and as the *Deptford* was becalmed in the offing, I ordered Captain Ogle to detain the French officers that were on board him and made the signal to renew the attack which he immediately obeyed, and most effectually destroyed the boats, the whole squadron being within a cable's length of them.

The next morning I received a letter [No. 714] from the Marquis de Brassac, which I enclose to their Lordships, with a copy [No. 715] of my answer to him.

I have left the *Tweed*, *Albany*, and *Hector* cutter off Port en Bessin, and have given Captain Paston orders to put on shore in a few days three of the French officers, who only came on board out of curiosity during the truce, but to keep on board the general's messenger, and Monsieur Beaumont unless the General complies with my demand,

---

[1] Captain Chaloner Ogle of HMS *Aquilon*.
[2] Enclosed is a translation of Brassac's letter of 16 July and Rodney's reply. See Nos. 714 and 715.

which I do not expect he will. I should therefore be glad to know their Lordships' pleasure relative to him.

718. *To Clevland*

[TNA, ADM 1/93] *Deptford* off Le Havre
18 July 1760

Sir,
At the late attack of the enemy's vessels at Port en Bessin, I perceived their troops were numerous and entrenched in such a manner as to render the attempt of landing to burn them too dangerous an undertaking.

I should therefore be glad you would be pleased to move their Lordships that the bombs under my command may take on board some shells and carcasses and a sergeant with six men to each bomb as I may have frequent occasion to make use of them on these sort of attacks. I find the enemy are more in dread of these implements of war than of cannon, even the two vessels I have now with me cause a general consternation at Havre, and on the coast.

I should likewise be glad their Lordships would be pleased to order the *Carcass* bomb Captain [Charles] Inglis to join me with his mortars on board, it being the only bomb vessel that can throw shells when under sail.

You will likewise be pleased to acquaint their Lordships the enemy had several officers and men killed at the late attack, the *Aquilon* being the only ship that received any damage and that very inconsiderable.

A Dutchman that came out of Havre this evening reports that a battle had been in Germany between the English and French troops,[1] but could tell no particulars.

719. *To Clevland*

[TNA, ADM 1/93] *Deptford* at anchor off Le Havre
20 July 1760

Sir,
Yesterday I received the enclosed letter from Monsieur Brassac, and with it transmit you a copy of Captain Paston's letter [No. 718].

I hope the intelligence I have this day received by a Dutchman from Le Havre is without foundation, but such as it is I think my duty to

---
[1] The Battle of Korbach, 10 July 1760.

transmit to their Lordships. He reports that a messenger arrived last night at Le Havre, with an account of there having been a battle[1] between the Allied army and the French, in which the former were defeated with the loss of thirty thousand men, and likewise that the Austrians had cut off eighteen thousand men of the King of Prussia's rear in his retreat.[2]

Enclosed[3] I transmit the state and condition of His Majesty's ships under my command by which their Lordships will perceive they will very soon be in want of beer.

720.   From Clevland

[TNA, ADM 2/529, p. 116]   22 July 1760

Sir,

I have received and read to my Lords Commissioners of the Admiralty your letter [No. 716] of the 18th instant informing them of the ships under your command having destroyed five of the enemy's flat bottomed boats at Port en Bessin as well as the fort that protected the road, and of the altercation that happened between yourself and the Marquis de Brassac upon that occasion, and upon the detention of some French officers who came on board the *Aquilon*.

Their Lordships command me to acquaint you that they very well approve of your conduct upon this occasion, but recommend it to you to order Monsieur de Beaumont and the other French officers to be immediately set on shore.

Enclosed I send you copies of some papers[4] received by Mr Secretary Pitt, containing intelligence of an intended invasion from Carteret and the neighbouring ports on the coast of Normandy. Their Lordships recommend it to you to keep a good lookout upon that part of the French coast, and to use your utmost endeavours to prevent any embarkation from those parts, as well as to frustrate any designs the enemy may have upon the islands of Jersey and Guernsey.

[1] Battle of Korbach, 10 July 1760.
[2] Battle of Landshut, 23 June 1760.
[3] Not enclosed.
[4] Not enclosed.

721. From Stephens

[TNA, ADM 2/529, p. 117]   22 July 1760

Sir,

I have received and read to my Lords Commissioners of the Admiralty your letter [No. 717] of the 18th instant desiring that the bomb vessels under your command may be ordered to take on board some shells and carcasses, with a sergeant and six men to each bomb, as you may have frequent occasion to make use of them, and the enemy are more afraid of them than of cannon. And in return I am commanded by their Lordships to signify their direction to you to send the bomb vessels now under your command to Spithead, that they may be supplied with shells &c., as you desire. The Board of Ordnance being desired to furnish them accordingly and to have tenders ready to accompany them.

With respect to the *Carcass*, as her bomb beds have been taken out, their Lordships do not think fit to take her from the service she is employed upon, to have them put on board again, but they will order you another bomb vessel instead of her.

722. To Clevland

[TNA, ADM 1/93]   *Deptford* off Le Havre
26 July 1760

Sir,

I have received both your letters [Nos. 720, 721] of the 22nd instant, and shall take care that Monsieur Beaumont is put on shore the first opportunity.

Upon receipt of yours [No. 720] with the enclosed intelligence from Guernsey, I completed, with the utmost dispatch the provisions of the *Aquilon*, and gave Captain Ogle orders to repair without a moment's loss of time with the ship under his command, the *Bonetta* and *King of Prussia* cutter, and cruise off the port of Carteret and the neighbouring ports on the coast of Normandy, and to use his utmost endeavours to prevent any embarkation of troops from those parts, as well as to frustrate any designs the enemy may have upon the islands of Jersey and Guernsey, and likewise to report to me the condition of the enemy on that part of the coast which I shall acquaint their Lordships with when I am better informed.

I have likewise dispatched the *Hunter* cutter to Guernsey for pilots for the use of the squadron, that no time may be lost in sending more ships on that service, or repairing there myself if necessary.

I beg leave to take notice to their Lordships that this additional service will require more cutters, which kind of vessels I find to be extremely useful in keeping close in shore in the night, which prevents the enemy from making any attempts to pass us. And whereas Lieutenant [William] Stanford of the *Endeavour* cutter was taken from this station upon the application of Captain [Edmund] Affleck of the *Launceston*, I should be glad he was ordered to rejoin me, as I have three cutters less than I had last year.

I have dispatched the *Firedrake* and *Furnace* to Spithead to take in their shells and have been joined by the *Rose* and *Pelican*.

I have spoke to numbers of neutral vessels that have come out of Le Havre. They all report that Prince Ferdinand[1] has lately gained a very great advantage over the French who have lost one hundred and fifty officers and are greatly dejected.[2]

723. From Clevland

[TNA, ADM 2/529, p. 143] 30 July 1760

Sir,

I have received and read to my Lords Commissioners of the Admiralty your letter [No. 722] of the 26th instant informing them of the proceedings of His Majesty's ships and vessels under your command and representing the want you are in of cutters. And in return I am to acquaint you that their Lordships very well approve of all you have done, and have ordered the *Roast Beef* armed vessel to proceed and join you immediately.

724. To Clevland

[TNA, ADM 1/93] *Deptford* at Spithead
7 August 1760

Sir,

Please to acquaint their Lordships that on the 4th instant, I left the *Tweed*, *Rose*, and a cutter in the road of Le Havre and proceeded myself with the bombs, close along the western shore with a design to alarm the different towns on the said coast, as likewise examining the anchorage between the islands of St. Marcouf and the main, where I had

---

[1] Prince Ferdinand of Brunswick, Commander-in-chief of the Allied army in Germany.
[2] Battle of Emsdorf, 16 July 1760.

stationed two of the vessels under my command, in order more effectively to cut off the enemy's coasting trade.

I had proceeded the length of Port en Bessin, when a most violent gale of wind which has lasted these two days, and in which the bombs were near foundering, drove me on the English coast. I must likewise acquaint their Lordships that the ships I left in Le Havre Road have been drove from their anchors, having seen them to leeward last night.

I shall make all the dispatch possible in getting on board two cables and completing the provisions of the *Deptford*.

By the best intelligence from a number of neutral vessels coming out of Le Havre the enemy, since the destruction of their five flat bottom boats at Port en Bessin, having unloaded all the others, and sent them up to Rouen, neither do they proceed in rigging their frigates.

725. From Clevland

[TNA, ADM 2/529, p. 174]   8 August 1760

Sir,

I have received and read to my Lords Commissioners of the Admiralty your letter [No. 724] of yesterday's date giving an account of your proceedings with His Majesty's ships under your command, of the bad weather you have met with, which drove you upon the English coast, and of your arrival at Portsmouth, also enclosing the state of the squadron under your command. In return I am to acquaint you their Lordships approve of your proceedings.

726. To Clevland

[TNA, ADM 1/93]   Portsmouth
                                                                     9 August 1760

Sir,

The weather has been so bad since my arrival here that the provisions and cables could not be got on board as yet. It now moderates and the utmost dispatch shall be used therein.

Two of the cutters under my command are arrived with the loss of their boltsprits, orders are given for making others as soon as possible.

Rear Admiral Durell having acquainted me that he had orders to send the bomb's tenders to Le Havre, I must desire you will please to represent to their Lordships that the bombs carry a sufficient number of shells for the service I proposed from them, which was, in case the enemy had persisted in their design of transporting naval and military stores in their flat bottom vessels to Brest, and on their being chased, had taken shelter under the cannon of the forts on the coast, near which the enemy's troops generally entrench themselves (as was the case at Port en Bessin) the bombs might then be of service, in throwing shells into the entrenchments, while the men of war were battering the fort, by which means the boats of the squadron might be enabled to burn the enemy's vessels, but as their design seems now to be at an end, I should be glad the bomb tenders were allowed to remain at Spithead as the road of Le Havre is too open and dangerous to continue at an anchor in, any time, especially to loaded vessels.

I must desire you will please to acquaint their Lordships that by the best intelligence I can get, there was not the least foundation for the report concerning the assembling of troops, and vessels, at Carteret on the coast of Normandy.[1] The *King of Prussia* cutter having looked into that port, where there is nothing but a few fishing boats, nor the least appearance of troops, that part of the coast is likewise so shoal that no pilots will take charge of any large frigates.

Captain Ogle likewise informs me that the report of the intended invasion is held very cheap in the islands, and that the States[2] were in too great a hurry in their petition. This being the case and as I find by the report of all the pilots that have been sent me from Guernsey, that the *Aquilon* draws too much water to be employed on that station, I have directed Captain Ogle to rejoin me off Le Havre, and have sent on that service the *Pelican* and *Bonetta* sloops which I hope their Lordships will approve of.

727. *To Clevland*

[TNA, ADM 1/93]
Spithead
11 August 1760

Sir,

I beg you will please to move their Lordships to order the Commissioners of His Majesty's Navy to pay me my flag pay, to the end of June 1760.

---

[1]See also No. 720.
[2]Legislative assembly.

728. *To Clevland*

[TNA, ADM 1/93] Spithead
13 August 1760

Sir,
Enclosed[1] I transmit to you a letter I have received from Captain Ogle of His Majesty's ship *Aquilon* (in Bouley Bay).[2] On the receipt of which I immediately dispatched a cutter with orders for him to remain on that station, taking the *Roast Beef* privateer under his command, in addition to the *Bonetta* sloop and *King of Prussia* cutter, already with him, employing them in the best manner for the protection of the island, and to frustrate the enemy's designs.

In the late gales of wind the *Tweed* and *Rose* lost each an anchor and cable in the road of Le Havre. The weather has been such they have not had an opportunity of looking for them since.

I am now returning to the station in the *Deptford*.

729. *From Stephens*

[TNA, ADM 2/529, p. 199] 18 August 1760

Sir,
My Lords Commissioners of the Admiralty having received information that there is fitting out at Morlaix for a privateer, a Bermudas built brig, to mount 14 carriage and twenty swivel guns, and to carry 120 men, and that it is probable she will sail early in the next month, I am commanded by their Lordships to acquaint you therewith, that you may order your cruisers to keep a good lookout for her.

730. *To Clevland*

[TNA, ADM 1/93] *Deptford* in the Road off Le Havre
19 August 1760

Sir,
Please to acquaint their Lordships that the enemy are again fitting the *Félicité* frigate of 36 guns, she being almost completely rigged. They likewise propose launching, the next spring tides, a new ship of 44 guns

---
[1] Not enclosed.
[2] Island of Jersey.

which I can plainly perceive ready in all respects to be put into the water.

The *Tweed* is remarkably foul, not having been properly docked since January last. I have sent her into Portsmouth Harbour in hopes she may get cleaned in a few days and wish their Lordships would be pleased to give directions to hasten her being docked, refitted, and rejoining me, as soon as possible, as it will be necessary to have clean frigates to intercept those of the enemy should they attempt to escape from this port.

731. *From Stephens*

[TNA, ADM 2/529, p. 216] 22 August 1760

Sir,

I have received and read to my Lords Commissioners of the Admiralty your letter [No. 730] of the 19th instant, informing them of the proceedings of the enemy at Le Havre and requesting that the *Tweed*, which you have sent in to clean, may be hastened out again with all the dispatch possible. And in return I am to acquaint you that directions are sent to Rear Admiral Durell accordingly, and that the *Tartar* is ordered forthwith to join you.

732. *To Clevland*

[TNA, ADM 1/93] *Deptford* off Le Havre
24 August 1760

Sir,

The captain of the *Bonetta* sloop having acquainted me that there is no purser belonging to her, the person appointed not having given security or made his appearance.

I must desire you will please to acquaint their Lordships that I have appointed one Mr. Lawrence Crump, a person bred in the clerk's office on board, to take charge of the provisions until their Lordships' pleasure be known.

733. From Stephens

[TNA, ADM 2/529, pp. 240–1]　　　　　　　　　　　　27 August 1760

Sir,

I have received and read to my Lords Commissioners of the Admiralty your letter [No. 732] of the 24th instant, informing their Lordships that the *Bonetta* sloop is without a purser, the person appointed not having given security or made his appearance, and that you have appointed Mr. Crump to take charge of the provisions. In return I send this to acquaint you, their Lordships have ordered a warrant appointing Mr. Crump to that sloop.

734. From Stephens

[TNA, ADM 1/529, p. 250]　　　　　　　　　　　　30 August 1760

Sir,

Captain [George] Mackenzie commander of His Majesty's sloop *Infernal* having acquainted my Lords Commissioners of the Admiralty by his letter of yesterday's date at Spithead, that on Tuesday the 26th instant he received intelligence of a French privateer that he immediately went in quest of her, and came up with her upon that same day, and engaged her an hour and a half. When she ran for it, and out sailing the *Infernal*, got into Cherbourg, or under the forts. I send this to acquaint you therewith for your information that you may take such measures for intercepting her as you may judge proper.

735. To Clevland

[TNA, ADM 1/93]　　　　　　　　　　　　*Deptford* at Spithead
　　　　　　　　　　　　　　　　　　　　2 September 1760

Sir,

Please to acquaint their Lordships I am arrived here with His Majesty's ship *Deptford*, the neap tides preventing the *Félicité* from getting out of Le Havre. I have taken this opportunity to stand over to the coast of England to complete the beer, which is near expended.

As I have just received information [No. 734] of a snow privateer putting into Cherbourg, I have dispatched the *Pelican* to cruise off that port.

The *Deptford* proving very leaky, I ordered the carpenter to examine into the cause, whose report I enclose[1] to their Lordships. And yesterday I applied to the Commissioner for proper people to be sent on board for that purpose, who acquaint me that she is in a much worse condition than reported.

736. *To Clevland*

[TNA, ADM 1/93]

Portsmouth
5 September 1760

Sir,

Upon consulting the pilots sent for the use of the squadron under my command from Guernsey, they unanimously agreed that the *Aquilon* drew too much water to be of any other use towards the protection of the island of Jersey, then by laying at an anchor in Bouley Bay. And as the *Aquilon* is a remarkable fast sailing ship and the enemy are fitting out the *Félicité* frigate with the utmost dispatch, I thought it most conducive for His Majesty's service to order Captain Ogle to rejoin me off Le Havre, the more effectually to intercept the said frigate should she attempt to sail during the dark nights and spring tides. At the same time I left for the protection of the island of Jersey the *Albany*, *Bonetta*, and *Roast Beef*, with orders for the senior officer to send me timely notice of any preparation the enemy might make on the adjacent coast. But yesterday I received the enclosed letter from Captain Ogle of the *Aquilon*, with his reason for not joining me agreeable to my orders. The States[2] of the said island notwithstanding they acknowledge there are no immediate appearances of an invasion still request that the *Aquilon* may remain at an anchor near their island; but as I think she will be better employed off Le Havre, I have sent Captain Ogle orders to obey his former orders.

If their Lordships should think it necessary that a post frigate[3] should be stationed there the *Rose* is the most proper ship as she draws the least water, and is the worst sailor, and as I have ordered Captain Paston of the *Tweed* to cruise off Cherbourg with directions to repair to the said island if necessary, I hope their Lordships will think they have a sufficient protection. More especially as the whole squadron under my command could be there in a very short time.

[1]Enclosed is an account of the structural defects of HMS *Deptford* and that the ship is making 20 inches of water an hour.
[2]Legislature.
[3]A frigate large enough to be commanded by a post captain.

737. *From Stephens*

[TNA, ADM 2/529, p. 275] 6 September 1760

Sir,

I have received and communicated to my Lords Commissioners of the Admiralty your letter [No. 736] of yesterday's date giving an account that you have ordered the *Albany, Bonetta,* and *Roast Beef* to cruise for the protection of the island of Jersey, instead of the *Aquilon* as she may be better employed being a good sailor, and I send this to acquaint you their Lordships approve thereof.

738. *From Stephens*

[TNA, ADM 2/529, p. 293] 12 September 1760

Sir,

My Lords Commissioners of the Admiralty having received information that a snow, two cutters, and a sloop whose description is herewith sent to you,[1] are ready to sail from Dunkirk, and are intended (as is supposed) to proceed to the westward, I am commanded by their Lordships, to recommend it to you, to order any cruisers that may sail from Portsmouth or that are within your reach to look out for them.

739. *From Stephens*

[TNA, ADM 2/529, p. 303] 13 September 1760

Sir,

I have received and read to my Lords Commissioners of the Admiralty your letter of yesterday's date enclosing the disposition of His Majesty's ships and vessels under your command and representing the bad condition of the *Deptford*. And in return I am to acquaint you their Lordships have ordered the *Deptford* to be taken into a dock, to be inspected and the *Nottingham*, which is just cleaned at Plymouth, to proceed and join you at Spithead, that you may hoist your flag on board her, and return to your station off Havre.

---

[1] A snow of 16 guns and 150 men.
Bermudas built sloop of 10 guns and 80 men.
Two cutters from 6 to 10 guns, and 40 to 50 men.

740. To Clevland

[TNA, ADM 1/93]
Spithead
14 September 1760

Sir,
I must acknowledge the receipt of your letter [No. 738] of the 12th instant giving me intelligence of the enemy's privateers, said to be ready to sail from Dunkirk, and enclose transmit for their Lordships' perusal the disposition[1] I have made with the ships under my command, which I hope will have the desired effect, and meet with their approbation.

As I represented the condition of the *Deptford* in my letter [No. 735] of the 2nd instant, and that the builder's assistant on examination had reported her worse then represented, and that it was absolutely necessary she should be taken into the dock, I have waited their Lordships' pleasure thereon, the ship being by no means fit to go to sea in her present condition.

I have given constant attendance and have hastened the cleaning the sloops under my command, both of which will be ready to sail tomorrow, and shall take particular care to station the ships and vessels as may best answer the ends of intercepting the enemy's privateers.

741. From the Lords of the Admiralty

[TNA, ADM 2/85, p. 238]
16 September 1760

Sir,
Having ordered Captain Smith of His Majesty's ship the *Seahorse*, who is now at Spithead, to put himself under your command and follow your orders, you are hereby required and directed to take him under your command accordingly, and employ him as you shall judge best for one month, at the expiration of which time you are to order him to return to Spithead and wait for further orders from us.

---

[1]*Albany* and a cutter between Beachy Head and Cap d'Antifer.
Aquilon, Rose, Furnance, and two cutters off Le Havre.
Tartar Cape de Le Havre and Dunnose.
Tweed and a cutter off Cherbourg.
Carcass Cape Barfleur.
Blast in quest of a privateer in the English Channel and to return off Le Havre.
Pelican, Bonetta, Roast Beef Jersey and coast of Normandy.

742. *To Clevland*

[TNA, ADM 1/93]
Spithead
19 September 1760

Sir,

Agreeable to their Lordships' order [No. 741] I have taken Captain Smith of the *Seahorse* under my command and shall employ him and the rest of my squadron in the best manner I can in order to intercept any of the enemy's privateers passing up or down Channel, and likewise to keep the port of Le Havre sufficiently blocked up.

The *Aquilon* is arrived being in want of beer, which I have ordered to be supplied him. He sails again tomorrow.

As I am in hourly expectation of seeing the *Nottingham*, their Lordships may be assured I shall not lose any time in proceeding to sea, when she arrives.

743. *To Clevland*

[TNA, ADM 1/93]
Portsmouth
23 September 1760

Sir,

The late very hard gales of wind having drove the *Tartar* and *Rose* off their stations, I must desire you will please to acquaint their Lordships therewith, and that no time shall be lost in getting their beer on board and sailing again the moment the weather moderates.

As their Lordships were pleased to appoint Captain Jervis of the *Albany* to command the *Unicorn* during the absence of Captain Graves, and no officer having appeared with their orders to command the *Albany*, I have ordered Lieutenant William Bensley of the *Deptford* to command her, till their Lordships' pleasure be known, she has been sailed several days to her station.

744. *To Clevland*

[TNA, ADM 1/93]
Portsmouth
25 September 1760

Sir,

I have received your letter of the 23rd instant acquainting me their Lordships have been pleased to appoint Josiah Marbet, purser of the

Furnace, to be purser of the *Dolphin*, and that his warrant is sent to Commissioner Hughes.

I have given directions to Captain Chaplen, to order him to take up his warrant and repair to his duty.

The weather has been so bad these three days past, that no vessels have been able to go to Spithead with provisions to the squadron under my command. The moment it moderates no time shall be lost in completing them, and returning to their station.

745. *To Stephens*

[TNA, ADM 1/93]

Portsmouth
26 September 1760

Sir,

Agreeable to their Lordships' commands, I enclosed transmit to them, the names of the cutters under my command, and how they are disposed of when the weather will permit them to keep the sea.[1] At present they are all drove into this port, the bad weather still continuing.

I must take notice to their Lordships that I find them so useful that it would be impossible effectually to block up the River Seine without them, at the same time, that they greatly distress the enemy in their coasting trade, and by keeping close in shore every night, give the ships in the road notice if the enemy's frigates should attempt to put to sea.

746. *To Clevland*

[TNA, ADM 1/93]

Portsmouth
27 September 1760

Sir,

Please to acquaint their Lordships Captain [Thomas] Willis in the *Blast* arrived here this morning. I have delivered him their order for commanding the *Rose*.

The weather still continues so bad, that no vessel can go to Spithead with provisions. The moment it moderates, no time shall be lost in completing the ships under my command.

[1] A list of armed cutters under the command of Rear Admiral Rodney.
Hector and *Anson* close in shore between Cape de Le Havre and Cap d' Antifer.
King of Prussia and *Hunter* between Trouville-sur-Mer and Dives-sur-Mer.
Royal George in the middle of the Seine River and employed in scouring the coast as far as Dieppe to the northward and Cap de le Hague to the southward.

Lieutenant [William] Brograve has not as yet made his appearance to command the *Albany*.

747. *From the Lords of the Admiralty*

[TNA, ADM 2/85, p. 278] 30 September 1760

Having ordered Captain [Paul Henry] Ourry of His Majesty's ship *Actæon* to join you, and be under your command in room of the *Rose*, which we have ordered upon other service, you are hereby required and directed to take the *Actæon* under your command accordingly.

748. *To Clevland*

[TNA, ADM 1/93] Portsmouth
2 October 1760

Sir,

I must desire you will please to acquaint their Lordships, that yesterday in the evening the *Tweed* arrived at Spithead with the *Elizabeth* privateer of Saint Malo, which Captain Paston informs me he took the day before, between Cherbourg and Portland. The privateer is a sloop, mounts six carriage and six swivel guns, with forty one men. Had been out ten days, and had taken nothing.

By the intelligence gained from him, most of the privateers from St. Malo are very small.

As the weather is now more moderate, no time shall be lost in hastening the squadron under my command to their station.

749. *To Clevland*

[TNA, ADM 1/93] Portsmouth
5 October 1760

Sir,

Please to acquaint their Lordships that the *Aquilon* and *Seahorse* are sailed for their station off Le Havre to watch the motions of the *Félicité* frigate in that port.

I had likewise given orders to Captain [John] Knight of the *Tartar*, and the *Blast* sloop to cruise between Dieppe and Cap d' Antifer to intercept the said frigate should she attempt to pass to the eastward, but I was surprised to receive a message from Captain Knight that he had orders to repair to the Nore. And from the commander of the *Blast* sloop that he was ordered to remain at Spithead; especially as I had no notice given me that their Lordships had taken the said ships from my command, which I presume has always been usual and must be owing to a mistake of your clerks.

The *Tweed* will be ready tomorrow and shall return to her station between Cherbourg and Le Havre. The *Nottingham* and *Actæon* have not as yet joined me.

750. From Clevland

[TNA, ADM 2/529, p. 372]   8 October 1760

Sir,

I have received and read to my Lords Commissioners of the Admiralty your letter [No. 749] of the 5th instant, acquainting them that you had ordered the *Tartar* and *Blast* to proceed on a cruise but was informed by Captain Knight, that he had orders to proceed to the Nore, and by the commander of the *Blast* that he was ordered to Spithead, and that you was very much surprised thereat, as you had received no notice that those ships were taken from under your command. And in return I am commanded by their Lordships to acquaint you that the orders you mention were sent open to Admiral Durell, who they concluded would have conveyed them through you to the respective captains, which is the constant method of conveying orders of this sort.

751. To Clevland

[TNA, ADM 1/93]   Spithead
                                                         9 October 1760

Sir,

You will please to acquaint their Lordships that the *Hector* cutter arrived here last night. The officer who commands her informs me that the whole squadron has been drove off their station, and separated by excessive hard gales that have lately blown and that he concludes they have been forced to the Downes.

The *Tweed* being ready, I have ordered Captain Paston to sail without loss of time to the station off Le Havre.

752. From Clevland

[TNA, ADM 2/529, p. 384] 10 October 1760

Sir,

I have received and communicated to my Lords Commissioners of the Admiralty your letter [No. 751] of yesterday's date, informing them of the arrival of the *Hector* cutter, and that the officer who commands her acquaints you the whole squadron has been blown off the station by the late hard gales, for which reason you have ordered the *Tweed* to proceed thither without loss of time.

It is their Lordships' direction that you permit Captain [Hugh] Bromedge to go on board the *Hector* cutter to search for persons supposed to be concealed there, and if he finds them, to suffer them to be taken out of her, in order to their being secured, but you will please not let this be known to anybody but Captain Bromedge.

[PS] If Captain Bromedge should have occasion to search any other cutter please to let him.

753. To Clevland

[TNA, ADM 1/93] Portsmouth
10 October 1760

Sir,

Please to acquaint their Lordships that the *Nottingham* is now turning up to Spithead. I shall shift my flag on board her as soon as possible and proceed to my station the moment the weather moderates.

754. To Clevland

[TNA, ADM 1/93] *Nottingham* at Spithead
11 October 1760

Sir,

I am sorry to acquaint their Lordships that John Miller who had been upwards of twelve years a quarter master on board the ships I commanded, and who had always behaved remarkably well, and was made a boatswain of the *Aquilon* upon my request,[1] has proved himself

---

[1] See Nos. 432, 648, 706 and 707.

unworthy [of] the preferment their Lordships were pleased to confer upon him. He has been continually drunk since being boatswain declaring that he had rather be in his former station. And when sent on shore for stores to the dock, neglected his duty and has absented himself from the service. Captain Ogle making this complaint, I have ordered one Jeremiah McNamara[1] to act as boatswain till their Lordships' pleasure be known, and am almost ashamed to ask their favour in his behalf since the behaviour of Miller, but as McNamara has been a boatswain's mate with me many years, I hope they will forgive me if I take the liberty to recommend him in lieu of Miller to be boatswain of the *Aquilon*.

755. To Clevland

[TNA, ADM 1/93]

Nottingham at Spithead
12 October 1760

Sir,

I have received your letter [No. 752] of the 10th instant and agreeable to their Lordships' directions, I shall assist Captain Bromedge in apprehending the persons said to be concealed on board the *Hector* cutter under my command.

You will please acquaint their Lordships that the *Aquilon* arrived here this morning. Captain Ogle informs me he has met with excessive bad weather, split his sails, and was near foundering upon the enemy's coast. The other ships had parted company and he was apprehensive the *Anson* cutter was lost, as he perceived the people on board her were bailing and pumping with a signal of distress out but it was impossible to give her any assistance.

It blows again very hard at SSW. When the weather moderates no time shall be lost in repairing to my station.

756. From Clevland

[TNA, ADM 2/529, p. 396]

13 October 1760

Sir,

I have received and communicated to my Lords Commissioners of the Admiralty your letter [No. 754] of the 11th instant, acquainting them that John Miller, who was appointed boatswain of the *Aquilon*, at

[1] See also No. 648.

your recommendation, has behaved very ill ever since being continually drunk, and recommending Jeremiah McNamara to succeed him. Their Lordships have ordered a warrant to be made out for him at your request.

757. To Clevland

[TNA, ADM 1/93]

Nottingham at Spithead
13 October 1760

Sir,
Please to acquaint their Lordships that yesterday evening the *Carcass* arrived in want of beer and water, which I have ordered her captain to complete as soon as possible, and shall take him to sea with me.

The *Nottingham* is now ready for sea, and I should have sailed this morning had it not blown very hard at NNW, but as Commissioner Bateman[1] has acquainted me that he has received her pay books in order to pay her company to the 31st of December 1759, and Captain [Samuel] Marshall having likewise represented to me that his men are in great want of clothes, and that their wives are all come from Plymouth, in hopes of the payment, agreeable to the late Act of Parliament,[2] the said payment will detain me for eight and forty hours longer, which will be no detriment to His Majesty's service, as there would be no venturing upon the enemy's coast with the wind as it now is.

758. To Clevland

[TNA, ADM 1/93]

Nottingham at Spithead
14 October 1760

Sir,
The *Aquilon* being very foul, and having shifted her ballast in the late hard gales, her rigging likewise being very much shattered, I hope their Lordships will approve of my having ordered her into dock to clean.

---

[1] Captain Hon. William Bateman, Extra Commissioner of the Navy, 14 June 1756–20 March 1761; Controller of Storekeepers Accounts, 20 March 1761–19 June 1783.
[2] The Grenville Act, passed in 1758, which called for seamen in the Royal Navy to receive two months' pay before proceeding to sea.

759. To Clevland

[TNA, ADM 1/93]
Nottingham at Spithead
16 October 1760

Sir,

Captain Paston in His Majesty's ship *Tweed* is this moment arrived. He acquaints me that the *Félicité* frigate of 32 guns sailed from Le Havre on the 12th instant to which ship he gave chase, and though he was many hours within point blank shot, the enemy continually firing his stern, and Captain Paston his bow chase, he never could get alongside of her. It was very unlucky that notwithstanding, I had stationed the *Seahorse*, *Albany*, and two cutters to the eastward of Cap d' Antifer, Captain Paston had not the good fortune to fall in with any of them during the chase, which continued as far to the eastward as Calais. I am convinced that Captain Paston would have given a good account if he had once got alongside her. He does justice to her commander who he says behaved like an able seaman, never once yawing his ship and giving him the least advantage.

I was in hopes the *Actæon* was on the station, as I had sent orders to her commander to hasten him off Le Havre, but Captain Paston says the weather was thick and hazey which he judges was the reason he did not see any of the other ships.

760. To Clevland

[TNA, ADM 1/93]
Nottingham at Spithead
16 October 1760

Sir,

Since acquainting you [No. 759] this morning of the arrival of the *Tweed*, the *Seahorse* is likewise returned to Spithead. Her captain informs me that she is in a shattered condition and very leaky owing to the late excessive bad weather.

As the time is near expired that she was to have continued under my command, I have agreeable to their Lordships' directions given Captain Smith orders to remain at Spithead for their further orders.

761. To Clevland

[TNA, ADM 1/93] Nottingham off Dungeness
 23 October 1760

Sir,
Please to acquaint their Lordships that an excessive hard gale of wind has forced me, and the squadron under my command, to take shelter in this road.

762. To Clevland

[TNA, ADM 1/93] Nottingham in the Downes
 27 October 1760

Sir,
Please to acquaint their Lordships that the squadron[1] under my command has been forced by continual gales of wind into the Downes, where I shall only remain till the weather moderates.

763. To Clevland

[TNA, ADM 1/93] Nottingham at St. Helens
 1 November 1760

Sir,
I acquainted you in my last [No. 762] that the continuance of very bad weather had forced me, and the squadron under my command, into the Downes, but as the wind came fair before I had an answer to that letter, and there being near four hundred sail of ships bound to the westward whose protection might be of the utmost consequence, I sailed with them keeping my squadron at a distance, between them and the enemy coast, till they were out of danger.

Off Le Havre I was joined by the *King of Prussia* cutter, the lieutenant who commanded her, acquainting me that Admiral Durell had orders to detain all the men of war at Spithead, on the late melancholy loss the nation has sustained,[2] and as every thing is quiet on the enemy's coast, I thought it my duty to repair to Spithead for their Lordships further directions, having left the *Actæon* before Le Havre, the *Tweed* between Cape Barfleur and Peveril Point, the *Car-*

---

[1]*Nottingham, Actæon, Tweed, Albany* and *Carcass*.
[2]George II died on 25 October 1760.

cass between Cap d' Antifer and the Isle of Wight, and the *Albany* between Beachy Head and Dieppe.

I presume their Lordships have been acquainted that the *Félicité* frigate was lost going into Dunkirk the very day that the *Tweed* chased her.

764. From Clevland

[TNA, ADM 2/529, p. 461] 3 November 1760

Sir,

I have received and communicated to my Lords Commissioners of the Admiralty your letter [No. 763] of the 1st instant, acquainting them, that having met the *King of Prussia* cutter in your way to your station, and having been informed by the lieutenant who commanded her, that Mr. Durell had orders to detain all ships of war at Spithead, you thought it proper to proceed thither with the squadron under your command, and wait there for further orders. And in return I am commanded to acquaint you that their Lordships expect you should return to your station whenever the weather will permit, and in the mean time they desire you will send them the name of the lieutenant who gave you such false intelligence.

765. To Clevland

[TNA, ADM 1/93] *Nottingham* at St. Helens
3 November 1760

Sir,

The wind having blown very hard at SW these two days, has obliged the *Actæon* and *Carcass* to take shelter at St. Helens. Captain Ourry reports that everything is very quiet at Le Havre and nothing fitting out there.

766. From Clevland

[TNA, ADM 2/529, p. 467] 4 November 1760

Sir,

My Lords Commissioners of the Admiralty having ordered the *Marlborough* to be fitted as a flagship for your reception. I am commanded to acquaint you therewith.

767. *To Clevland*

[TNA, ADM 1/93] Nottingham at St. Helens
4 November 1760

Sir,
Lieutenant [John] Godfrey of the *King of Prussia* cutter having been premature in the intelligence he had given me, I should have sailed again immediately, had not a hard gale from the SW prevented. It is now more moderate, and I am preparing to put to sea this night.

768. *From Clevland*

[TNA, ADM 2/529, p. 470] 5 November 1760

Sir,
My Lords Commissioners of the Admiralty having received a letter from Lieutenant Lowfield who commands the *Hector* cutter, complaining of Lieutenant [William] Maltby of the *Dorset* cutter, for not bringing to when ordered by him to do so, by which means great mischief might have ensued. I am commanded by their Lordships to send you the same herewith,[1] and to recommend it to you to enquire into the matter and report to them how you find the same to be and, with your report you will please to return the enclosed.

769. *From Clevland*

[TNA, ADM 529, p. 496] 14 November 1760

Sir,
My Lords Commissioners of the Admiralty having taken His Majesty's ship the *Actæon* from under your command, to be employed on other service and ordered the *Solebay* to be under your command in her room, I am commanded by their Lordships to acquaint you therewith.

---

[1] Not enclosed.

770. *To Clevland*

[TNA, ADM 1/93] *Nottingham* at anchor in the Road off Le Havre
14 November 1760

Sir,
As the weather is very moderate and the wind off shore, I have anchored in this road and have spoke with several neutral vessels who report that everything is very quiet at Le Havre, and that the enemy are fitting out neither frigate or privateer, which I can plainly observe myself.

They all concur that an express arrived this morning at Le Havre with an account of a general engagement between the King of Prussia and Marshal Daun[1] in which the former was defeated with the loss of twenty thousand men.[2] But as reports of this nature are often raised in order to encourage their people, I am in hopes this is without foundation.

771. *To Clevland*

[TNA, ADM 1/93] *Nottingham*
27 November 1760

Sir,
The *Nottingham* being in want of an anchor and three cables, and her beer being expended has obliged me to put in here. The *Aquilon* has likewise lost one anchor and cable and the *Carcass* expended her beer. I shall take care they are supplied as soon as possible.

As the season is so far advanced I should be glad their Lordships would approve of my keeping half the squadron on the enemy's coast at a time and relieve them every ten or twelve days. The consequence of keeping the whole squadron is a certainty of their being drove off every hard gale either easterly or westerly and the enemy's port left open. Whereas if part of the squadron should remain at St. Helens, they would be always ready after every gale to supply the place of those drove off the station.

---

[1] Field Marshall Leopold Joseph Maria Daun.
[2] An indecisive but bloody battle on 3 November 1760 at Torgau between the Austrians and Prussians.

772. *To Newcastle*

[BL, Add. MSS 32915, ff. 111–12] Portsmouth
27 November 1760

My Lord,

As I have been constantly employed on the coast of Normandy, permit me to take the opportunity of my arrival here, most sincerely to condole with your Grace on the melancholy loss the nation has sustained in the death of our late most gracious sovereign.

I must beg leave to acknowledge the very great obligations I lay under to your Grace, for all the preferments I have attained in the navy, obligations which I can never forget, and which now call upon me most humbly to offer what little interest I have in the county of Southampton, to be disposed of at your Grace's pleasure, as it is whispered in this county there is a likelihood of an opposition at the ensuing election.

In all other respects, among your Grace's many friends, you shall find none more ready to obey your commands…

773. *To Clevland*

[TNA, ADM 1/93] *Nottingham* at Spithead
29 November 1760

Sir,

As the *Marlborough* will be ready in a very few days to receive men, I hope their Lordships will be pleased to grant that the *Rainbow's* ship's company may be turned over to her, and what other men they think proper in order for her getting soon ready for sea.

774. *To Clevland*

[TNA, ADM 1/93] *Nottingham* at Spithead
2 December 1760

Sir,

As there is a vacancy for a boatswain on board the *Centaur* frigate now in ordinary at Portsmouth, and as George Harwood was made a boatswain two year[s] since by Admiral Saunders,[1] and was superceded

---

[1] Vice-admiral Charles Saunders, MP for Plymouth, 6 April 1750–54; MP Hendon, 1754–7 Dec. 1775; Commander-in-chief of the British naval forces during the attack on Quebec.

in the *Trent* by their Lordships' order at the request of Captain [John] Lindsey. As it appears by his certificate that he has always done his duty and was very diligent during the several years he served with Admiral Saunders and me, I humbly hope their Lordships will please to take his case into consideration and appoint him boatswain of the said frigate.

775. *From Clevland*

[TNA, ADM 2/530, p. 26] 4 December 1760

Sir,

I have received and communicated to my Lords Commissioners of the Admiralty your letter [No. 774] of the 2nd instant, recommending George Harwood to be boatswain of the *Centaur* frigate now l[a]ying in ordinary at Portsmouth. And in return am to acquaint you that the *Centaur* will soon be sold, otherwise their Lordships would appoint him at your request.

776. *To Clevland*

[TNA, ADM 1/93] *Nottingham* at Spithead
4 December 1760

Sir,

You will please to acquaint their Lordships that the *Actæon* and *Tweed* anchored yesterday at St. Helens, having been drove off their station by bad weather. They report that everything remained very quiet at Le Havre. They sail again this day.

The weather is now very moderate. Mr. Keppel's squadron[1] and transports are ready to take the first opportunity of sailing when the wind offers.

---

[1] The warships and shipping assembled for the attack on Belle Isle. It was at first intended to attack Belle Isle in the autumn of 1760, but owing to bad weather, the operation was postponed and did not depart from Spithead until March of 1761.

777. *To Clevland*

[TNA, ADM 1/93] *Nottingham* at Spithead
4 December 1760

Sir,
Vice Admiral Holburne having acquainted me that he had leave of absence, delivered to me the unexecuted orders that he had received from their Lordships, which I shall take care are given to the respective captains.

Yesterday in the evening the *Prince of Orange* arrived at St. Helens from Plymouth, but as it has blown very hard all night at WSW, and still continues she has not been able to get to Spithead. All the men of war and transports ride with their yards and topmast struck, to appearance no accident has happened.

778. *From Clevland*

[TNA, ADM 2/530, p. 30] 5 December 1760

Sir,
I have received and communicated to my Lords Commissioners of the Admiralty your letters [Nos. 771, 773] of the 27th and 29th past, informing them that the *Nottingham* being in want of an anchor and three cables, and her beer being expended, you was obliged to put in at Spithead to supply her as also the *Aquilon* and *Carcass*, which had both of them the same wants, and desiring to know whether, as the season is so far advanced, their Lordships would approve of your keeping half your squadron on the enemy's coast at a time, and relieve them every ten or twelve days. And in return I am commanded to acquaint you that their Lordships judge it necessary that a number of ships should appear on the coast of the enemy.

When the *Marlborough* is put into commission the *Rainbow*'s company will be turned over into her as you desire.

779. To Clevland

[TNA, ADM 1/93]

Nottingham at Spithead
Wind NNE blows very hard
5 December 1760

Sir,

Last night we had an excessive hard gale of wind at NW, most of the ships at Spithead were obliged to let go their sheet anchors, and the *Prince of Orange* (who arrived in the evening) parted two cables. I have sent her off another anchor and cable belonging to one of the ships in the harbour.

Everything at St. Helens seems safe, and the wind is now come around to the NNE, but blows too hard for Mr. Keppel to sail this day.

You will please likewise to acquaint their Lordships that I applied immediately on my arrival for the ships under my command to be supplied with beer and cables, but they have not as yet been able to procure any, all the vessels being employed in supplying Mr. Keppel's squadron and the transports.

When the service will admit, not a moment's time shall be lost in getting them ready to sail.

780. To Clevland

[TNA, ADM 1/93]

Portsmouth
6 December 1760

Sir,

The carpenter of His Majesty's sloop *Bonetta* having been left behind when the said sloop joined me in the month of July last, I appointed one Mr. John Featherstone to act as carpenter of her, who continued in that station till the 1st of December, when he was superceded by another carpenter. He is a very good man, has been bred in His Majesty's yard at Plymouth, and received certificates of his good behaviour. I must therefore take the liberty to recommend him to their Lordships' favour.

781. *To Clevland*

[TNA, ADM 1/93]
Portsmouth
Wind NNW
6 December 1760

Sir,

I have received their Lordships' order of the 4th instant and have given directions to the captains of the *Greyhound* and *Laurel* to clean and refit their ships with the utmost dispatch. I have likewise agreeable to their Lordships' directions, given Captain [John] Strachan of the *Sapphire* a weeks' leave to attend his private affairs.

The weather being now very moderate Mr. Keppel's squadron and the transports at St. Helens are getting up their yards and topmasts. I have dispatched all the vessels loaded with provisions off to them this morning and have not heard that any accident has happened.

782. *To Clevland*

[TNA, ADM 1/93]
Portsmouth
Wind WSW
7 December 1760

Sir,

I have received their Lordships' orders of the 5th instant which I have delivered to the captains of the *Pembroke* and *Sapphire*.

I have likewise received your letter [No. 778] of the same date wherein you acquaint me that at this time their Lordships judge it necessary that a number of ships should appear on the coast of the enemy.

You will please to acquaint them that when the weather permits I shall constantly endeavour to alarm the enemy as much as possible, but while the wind continues between the north and the west, it will be too dangerous to venture near their coast, more especially as the *Nottingham* is at present a remarkable bad sailor. I must therefore entreat their Lordships that they will be pleased to give directions that the *Marlborough* when commissioned may be hastened in her fitting as much as possible, as I shall be better enabled to perform the service on which I am employed in a ship of her rate than in a smaller [one].

The *Blonde* and *Speedwell* sloop is sailed.

783. To Clevland

[TNA, ADM 1/93]
Portsmouth
8 December 1760

Sir,

Yesterday in the afternoon it blew an excessive hard gale at SW, which has forced in the *Solebay*, *Actæon*, and *Tweed* with their sails spilt, and the *Solebay* very leaky. Her captain has his orders delivered to proceed to the Nore. The weather is now moderate but the wind still continues westerly.

I have received their Lordships' order, and your letter of the 6th instant which are complied with.

784. To Clevland

[TNA, ADM 1/93]
Portsmouth
8 December 1760

Sir,

Sir William Burnaby[1] of the *Royal Ann* having acquainted me he has two lieutenants and a number of men at the rendezvous in town, and as the ship is ordered to be paid off, desires to know their Lordships' pleasure relative to them.

785. From Captain Samuel Marshall

[TNA, ADM 1/93]
Nottingham at Spithead
8 December 1760

Sir,

Samuel Goff, carpenter's yeoman, and Thomas Hadley, sergeant of marines, being complained of by Lieutenant John Brown and Lieutenant [Thomas] Bradshaw of His Majesty's ship *Nottingham* under my command for selling brandy to the ship's company, for which they are now in irons on board, I desire you will please to order a court martial on them or deal with them as you shall judge proper.

---

[1] Captain Sir William Burnaby, Kt.

786. To Clevland

[TNA, ADM 1/93]
Portsmouth
8 December 1760

Sir,

Enclosed I transmit you a letter [No. 785] I received from Captain Marshall of His Majesty's ship *Nottingham*, desiring to have a court martial on Samuel Goff, carpenter's yeoman, and Thomas Hadley Sergeant of marines for selling brandy to the ship's company.

As I had no power to hold court martials, I desired him to apply to their Lordships for that purpose.

787. From Captain John Dalrymple

[TNA, ADM 1/93]
Solebay at Spithead
8 December 1760

Sir,

The carpenter of His Majesty's ship under my command having represented to me, that there is a considerable leak in the bow by which the ship makes (in a double reef topsail gale) two feet and half water in an hour, and that a large quantity of water lodges in the fore hold, which has obliged me to get down two pumps there and continually pump and bail her with buckets, I thought it my duty to represent her to you as unfit for service till she be examined by the builder and the leak aforementioned stopped.

788. To Clevland

[TNA, ADM 1/93]
Portsmouth
9 December 1760

Sir,

Since my last of yesterday nothing material has occurred.

This morning the *Prince of Orange* is come into the harbour and the *Ambuscade* arrived at Spithead from Gibraltar.

Every vessel is employed from the Victualling Office in supplying the ships at St. Helens with beer and provisions when the weather will permit them to go out of the harbour.

In obedience to their Lordships' command I ordered Captain Dalrymple of the *Solebay* to take charge of a convoy to the Downes, but this morning I received a letter [No. 787] from him a copy of which I transmit to you, and I have desired a proper officer may be sent to inspect into defects complained of.

789. From Captain Samuel Marshall

[TNA, ADM 1/93] *Nottingham* at Spithead
9 December 1760

Sir,
Mr. Bradshaw 2nd lieutenant of His Majesty's ship *Nottingham* under my command having represented to me, by the enclosed[1] complaint, that John McIntosh belonging to the said ship, drew his knife upon him. Mr. Bradshaw being then in the execution of his office, in endeavouring to send him on board, I desire you will please to order a court martial on him accordingly.

790. To Clevland

[TNA, ADM 1/93] Portsmouth
Wind NW blows hard
10 December 1760

Sir,
I have received your letter of the 8th instant and have granted leave of absence to Mr. Bradley, the purser of the *Dorsetshire* agreeable to their Lordships' directions.

I have likewise given directions for the discharge of John Morris, Robert Robinson, and Thomas Handerson, according to their Lordships' order of the same date.

Nothing has occured since mine [No. 788] of yesterday, and the *Ambusacade* who arrived is performing quarantine at the Mother Bank.

Mr. Keppel having applied to me for a number of vessels to supply his squadron and the transports with beer and water, I hope their Lordships will approve of my having given directions for every proper vessel to be employed on that service, that can be procured.

---

[1] Enclosed is a petition from J.W. Bradshaw, dated 9 December 1760.

791. *From Clevland*

[TNA, ADM 2/530, p. 52]   11 December 1760

Sir,
I have received and communicated to my Lords Commissioners of the Admiralty your letter [No. 790] of yesterday's date giving an account of the *Ambuscade* being arrived from the Mediterranean, and that she is performing quarantine at the Mother Bank. And that upon Commodore Keppel's request, you have ordered every proper vessel that can be procured to supply his squadron and the transports with beer and water, which their Lordships very well approve of.

792. *To Clevland*

[TNA, ADM 1/93]   Portsmouth
                                                        11 December 1760

Sir,
I have received their Lordships' order of the 9th instant relative to the discharge of Joseph Potts belonging to the *Vanguard*, and shall make the enquiry as directed concerning him.

The weather being now moderate Mr. Keppel has made the signal and unmoored, but as there is very little wind, I believe it will be impossible for him to sail this day.

I shall likewise put to sea with the squadron under my command the moment I can procure beer and water.

793. *To Clevland*

[TNA, ADM 1/93]   *Nottingham* at Spithead
                                                        14 December 1760
                                                              Wind WbS

Sir,
Please to acquaint their Lordships that the squadron of His Majesty's ships under my command are now unmoored, and as the beer is alongside the *Nottingham*, I propose putting to sea this day if the weather is such as to permit it.

794. To Clevland

[TNA, ADM 1/93]

Nottingham at St. Helens
19 December 1760
Wind WbN blows hard

Sir,
The weather being moderate I put to sea with the squadron under my command, but in the night of the 17th it blew so excessive hard that the *Nottingham* and most of the ships split their sails. And as the gale continued, I put back with the squadron yesterday evening to St. Helens, it being too dangerous to venture off the mouth of the Seine while it continues to blow so hard between the north and the west.
The moment the weather moderates I shall again put to sea and station the ships on the enemy's coast in the best manner the season will admit.

795. To Clevland

[TNA, ADM 1/93]

Nottingham at St. Helens
21 December 1760
Wind WNW, blows hard

Sir,
Please to acquaint their Lordships that yesterday the *Roast Beef* armed vessel rejoined me from off Le Havre. The master of her reports that he had looked into that port, where everything remained quiet, not so much as one vessel fitting out there. And as he likewise represented to me that his ship was in a shattered condition, I have ordered him into the harbour to refit which I hope their Lordships will approve of.

796. To Clevland

[TNA, ADM 1/93]

Nottingham at St. Helens
26 December 1760
Wind WbN

Sir,
Yesterday the *Royal George* cutter rejoined me, the officer of whom reports that Lieutenant Lowfield of the *Hector* and Lieutenant Godfrey of the *King of Prussia* cutters had boarded a Dutch ship that lay at an anchor under Dungeness, who came from Marseilles bound to Le Ha-

vre de Grace, by which oversight of the officer (who had particular orders to board no vessel coming from the Mediterranean) the said cutters will be obliged to perform quarantine.

The cutters report that the weather had been such they could not look into Le Havre.

The last time I put to sea I gave Captain Ourry orders to cruise between Cape La Hague and Portland, in order to protect the trade, and intercept the enemy's privateers, and conclude by his not putting back to St. Helens, as the weather has been very bad, that he is under Portland.

797. *From Clevland*

[TNA, ADM 2/530, p. 114] 27 December 1760

Sir,

I have received and communicated to my Lords Commissioners of the Admiralty your letter [No. 796] of yesterday's date informing them that Lieutenants Lowfield and Godfrey of the *Hector* and *King of Prussia* cutters, having boarded a Dutch ship that lay at anchor off Dungeness and came last from Marseilles, tho' they had particular orders not to board any vessel that came from the Mediterranean, the said cutters will be obliged to perform quarantine. And in return I am commanded to acquaint you, that their Lordships are extremely displeased at the behaviour of the lieutenants, and that it is their direction you reprimand them severely for paying so little attention to your orders by which means the service of the cutters must be lost for a considerable time.

798. *To Clevland*

[TNA, ADM 1/93] *Nottingham* at St. Helens
29 December 1760

Sir,

Their Lordships are the best judges of the expediency of the service on which I am employed, and I shall always most cheerfully obey their commands. But as at present the enemy have no ships fitting out at Le Havre and everything remains very quiet on their coast, I humbly presume my presence at this particular juncture is not essentially necessary, as there is not the least likelihood of any real service.

I must therefore desire you will please to make it my request to their Lordships to grant me leave of absence for a short time to attend my private affairs, and I shall always be ready to return on this, or go on any other service they may be pleased to command me.

799. To Clevland

[TNA, ADM 1/93]

Nottingham at St. Helens
30 December 1760
Wind SbW

Sir,

Please to acquaint their Lordships that yesterday at day light in the morning (being then about 8 leagues SW from Dunnose) I fell in with a snow privateer to which I gave chase in company with the *Carcass*, *Bonetta* and *Hunter* cutter. The *Nottingham* had the misfortune to lose her fore topmast in the chase which entirely disabled her from pursuing. But as the *Carcass*, *Bonetta* and *Hunter* continued it, I am in hopes they will give a good account of her, more especially as she stood to the eastward in the very track I had stationed the *Actæon* and *Tweed*.

The wind blew very hard at south which obliged me to bear up for St. Helens, in order to get up another topmast, and shall put to sea again the moment it moderates, but at present it blows very hard.

800. To Clevland

[TNA, ADM 1/93]

Nottingham at St. Helens
31 December 1760

Sir,

I made you acquainted in my letter [No. 799] of yesterday's date that the *Carcass* and *Bonetta* continued the chase of the snow privateer and that I was in hopes she would not escape. I have now the pleasure to tell you that the Captains Inglis and [Lancelot] Holmes had the good fortune to keep well up with her, when perceiving the *Tweed* to windward, they by signals gave Captain Paston to understand the chase was an enemy which he soon took. Her name the *Du Guay Trouin*, belonging to St. Malo, of ten guns, and fifty two men, she had been out three days and taken nothing. The *Anson* cutter likewise took yesterday in company with the said ships a cutter privateer of ten guns and fifty four men belonging to Dunkirk, had been five days from Le Havre, and taken nothing. She is a remarkable fine cutter and far preferable to any in His Majesty's service.

Another privateer is this moment come under my stern. Taken yesterday off La Hague by the *Diligence* sloop. Her name the *Favourite* of Morlaix, mounts ten guns, and sixty men, had been two days from Cherbourg.

I sincerely congratulate you on the capture of these privateers as they might have done considerable damage to the trade.

Enclosed[1] I transmit you the best intelligence I can procure from the prisoners.

801. *From Clevland*

[TNA, ADM 2/530, p. 140] 2 January 1761

Sir,

I have received and communicated to my Lords Commissioners of the Admiralty your two letters [Nos. 799, 800] of the 30th and 31st past. The former giving an account of your having lost your foretopmast in chase of a privateer and being obliged to bear up for St. Helens. The latter giving an account that the privateer had been taken by the *Tweed*, that a privateer cutter had been taken by the *Anson* cutter, and that another privateer had been taken by the *Diligence* sloop. And I am to acquaint you their Lordships are pleased with your success.

802. *To Clevland*

[TNA, ADM 1/93] London
27 January 1761

Sir,

I desire you will be pleased to move the Right Hon. Lords Commissioners of the Admiralty that they will give orders to the Commissioners of His Majesty's navy to pay me my pay to the 25th day of December last.

---

[1]Enclosed is intelligence received from the prisoners taken in the privateers, concerning the *Chevre*, several privateers, and the *Félicité* and the *Harmoine* frigates.

803. *From the Lords of the Admiralty*

[TNA, ADM 2/86, p. 51] 3 February 1761

Whereas we think fit that you shall proceed forthwith to Portsmouth and take upon you the chief command of His Majesty's ships and vessels at that port in the absence of Vice Admiral Holburne, you are hereby required and directed to repair accordingly to that place and hoist your flag on board such ship of His Majesty's there, or at Spithead, as you shall think proper. And you are to do whatever may be in your power to forward His Majesty's service and particularly to hasten the dispatch of such of His Majesty's ships and vessels as may fit and refit at that port, and quicken their commanders in the execution of such orders as they may be under, sending us frequent accounts of your proceedings.

804. *To Clevland*

[TNA, ADM 1/93] Portsmouth
6 February 1761

Sir,
Please to acquaint their Lordships I am arrived at Portsmouth and that Vice Admiral Holburne has delivered me all the unexecuted orders.

805. *To Clevland*

[TNA, ADM 1/93] Portsmouth
7 February 1761

Sir,
I have received all your letters of the 5th instant and have given orders agreeable to their Lordship's directions.

Yesterday the *Dragon* and *Garland* went out of the harbour to Spithead and the *Sandwich* this day.

The *Tweed* is sailed to the westward and the *Cormorant* is preparing to take the convoy for Plymouth.

806. To Clevland

[TNA, ADM 1/93]
Portsmouth
8 February 1761

Sir,

As His Majesty's ship *Marlborough* has been out of the dock since the 24th of November 1760 and to appearance is now very foul, I should be glad their Lordships would permit her to be taken into the dock to be washed down as it will be of no hindrance to her fitting.

807. To Clevland

[TNA, ADM 1/93]
Portsmouth
8 February 1761

Sir,

I have received their Lordship's orders and your letters of the 6th instant and shall forthwith make the enquiries as directed. And when the *Osterly* Indiaman arrives at Spithead I shall send for, and strictly examine the six men said to have been enlisted as marines at Birmingham.

The *Raven* sloop is arrived at Spithead with a convoy from Guernsey and the *Téméraire* is gone out of the harbour.

808. To Clevland

[TNA, ADM 1/93]
Portsmouth
8 February 1761

Sir,

Agreeable to your letter of the 5th instant concerning George Ross, son to John Ross merchant of Aberdeen, who was impressed and now on board the *Royal Sovereign*, I find upon enquiry that the said George Ross was impressed out of the *Augustus Caesar*, John Duffell master from Jamaica for London, by the officers of the *Princess Royal* at the Nore. He was in the quality of a foremastman, has been at sea six years, and very fit to serve His Majesty.

809. To Clevland

[TNA, ADM 1/93] Portsmouth
9 February 1761

Sir,
I have received your letter of the 7th instant enclosing their Lordships' orders of the same date to Captain [John] Macartney of the *Race Horse*, which I have delivered to him.

Yesterday the *Jason* arrived with a convoy from Plymouth and is to proceed with the trade bound to the eastward, as this day.

810. To Clevland

[TNA, ADM 1/93] Portsmouth
9 February 1761

Sir,
Enclosed[1] I return to you the petition of the two men named in the margin,[2] and must inform their Lordships that George Dixon is unserviceable as represented, but Owen Lynch's case has been misrepresented, the man being in good health and very fit for service.

811. To Clevland

[TNA, ADM 1/93] Portsmouth
9 February 1761

Sir,
Agreeable to their Lordships' commands of the 6th instant directing me to order the discharge of John Peterson belonging to the *Téméréire* and Cornelius Jacobson belonging to the *Royal Sovereign* (Danes) provided they were not married or settled in England and have not received the bounty money.

I must desire you will please to acquaint their Lordships that upon enquiry, I find that John Peterson has received the bounty money, and that Cornelius Jacobson entered [as a] volunteer about three years since on board the *St. Albans*.

[1] Not enclosed.
[2] George Dixon and Owen Lynch.

812. To Clevland

[TNA, ADM 1/93]
Portsmouth
10 February 1761

Sir,

I must desire you will please to acquaint their Lordships that yesterday after post His Majesty's ship *Success* arrived at Spithead from Plymouth, and the *Carcass* sloop from her cruise at St. Helens.

I have this moment received your letter of yesterday's date by express, signifying their Lordships' directions to give Captain Keppel of His Majesty's ship *Valiant* leave to go to town, which I have done accordingly.

813. To Clevland

[TNA, ADM 1/93]
Portsmouth
11 February 1761

Sir,

Agreeable to their Lordships' directions signified to me in your letter of the 9th instant I have enquired into the complaint of the *Laurel* sloop's company, which I find to be true in every respect, and the vessel so very bad that I think it a duty incumbent upon me to represent her as unfit for a sloop of war, from her inability to stow her men, carry sail, or fight her guns, even in moderate weather.

Enclosed[1] I return you the petition.

814. To Clevland

[TNA, ADM 1/93]
Portsmouth
11 February 1761

Sir,

I have received and delivered to the commanders of His Majesty's ships *Pembroke* and *Marlborough*, their Lordships' orders of the 9th instant, as likewise their orders of the same date directing the trial of Mr. Patherick Lukey, Lieutenant of His Majesty' ship *Superb*.[2]

Yesterday in the afternoon, I received intelligence of a small privateer being off Arundel. I immediately dispatched the *Carcass* sloop,

---

[1] Not enclosed.
[2] See also Nos. 821 and 832.

Anson and *Tartuff* cutters in quest of her, which I hope will meet with their Lordships' approbation.

The *Jason* is sailed with the trade to the eastward and the *Pelican* sloop is arrived here from a cruise.

815. To Clevland

[TNA, ADM 1/93]
Portsmouth
12 February 1761

Sir,

I have received your letters of the 10th instant and their Lordships, order of the same date, directed to Captain Marshall of His Majesty's ship *Nottingham*, which I have delivered to him.

His Majesty's ship *Dover* is come into the harbour.

The *Flamborough* attempted to sail with the transports under her care this morning, but the wind coming to the southsoutheast, with snow and thick weather, has obliged her to come to an anchor again. The *Alarm* is likewise arrived from the Downes.

816. To Clevland

[TNA, ADM 1/93]
Portsmouth
13 February 1761

Sir,

Agreeable to their Lordships' directions I have delivered to Captain [Robert] Swanton, the senior officer here, their orders for assembling a court martial for the trial of four men belonging to the *Prince of Orange*.

Since yesterday's post are arrived at Spithead and St. Helens the *Alderney*, *Wager*, and *Superb* with the trade from the Downes, who are now turning up to Spithead.

This morning is arrived the *James* transport, William Cooper master, with three hundred and eighty four French prisoners for Le Havre de Grace. She sailed from New York the 1st of January last, in company with the *Boscawen* transport, who had two hundred and fifty French prisoners on board bound to the same place. The master of the transport reports that a few days before he left New York several transports with troops on board sailed for South Carolina. This is all the intelligence I could gain from him.

I have this moment received your letter of yesterday's date by express and have directed Captain Wallis to set out immediately for London.

817. *To Clevland*

[TNA, ADM 1/93]
Portsmouth
15 February 1761
Wind SW blows excessive hard

Sir,

I have received and delivered to the respective captains their Lordships' orders for putting themselves under the command of Admiral Pocock,[1] with their orders, and your letter of the 13th instant which I have taken care to comply with.

818. *To Clevland*

[TNA, ADM 1/93]
Portsmouth
16 February 1761
Wind WSW, blows fresh

Sir,

I have received your letters of the 14th instant, and agreeable to their Lordships' directions, I have given orders to Captain [Joshua] Rowley of the *Superb* not to lose a moment's time in bringing his ship into harbour, and getting her cleared for the dock. As yet the wind and weather will not permit her coming into the harbour. When it does I have given directions that she has the preference to all other ships.

The *Peregrine* shall be manned as this day, and will be ready to proceed to sea whenever their Lordships are pleased to send orders.

I shall cause enquiry to be made concerning the white wine on board the ships now fitting for foreign service, and shall make my report to their Lordships accordingly.[2]

---

[1] Vice-admiral George Pocock, MP Plymouth, 1760–68; knighted, 23 March 1761; Admiral, 21 October 1762. On 13 February 1761 Pocock was placed in command of a squadron at Portsmouth and Plymouth consisting of ten ships of the line and a number of smaller vessels. However, it is doubtful if this command ever became operational. In 1762 Pocock would command the naval forces during the attack on Havana.

[2] See also Nos. 822 and 831.

819. To Clevland

[TNA, ADM 1/93]
Portsmouth
17 February 1761

Sir,

I must desire you will please to acquaint their Lordships that yesterday after post His Majesty's ship the *Sapphire* arrived at Spithead with a brigantine she had taken from St. Domingo, who had sailed in company with the *Diadem* of 74 guns on the 2nd of December, bound to Brest.

This morning the *Namur*, *Superb*, and *Antelope* came into harbour, and the *Lynn*, *Torrington*, and *Peregrine* went out to Spithead.

820. To Clevland

[TNA, ADM 1/93]
Portsmouth
18 February 1761

Sir,

You will please to acquaint their Lordships that His Majesty's ship *Marlborough* is clear for the dock, and notwithstand[ing] I have represented to the officers of the yard, and showed them their Lordships orders that the said ship should be cleaned, they have refused to dock her without directions from the Navy Board.

821. To Clevland

[TNA, ADM 1/93]
Portsmouth
18 February 1761

Sir,

Captain Swanton having acquainted me he cannot try Mr Patherick Lukey, First Lieutenant of His Majesty's ship *Superb*, without the surgeons of His Majesty's ships *Maidstone*, *Biddeford*, and *Cruiser*, who surveyed the body of Henry Tilley, being personally present. As likewise Mr Joseph Garlick, surgeon of the *Princess Carolina* hospital ship, from whose letter this court martial was ordered.[1]

I should be glad to know their Lordships' pleasure thereon.

---

[1] See also Nos. 814 and 832.

822. *From Captain Richard Norbury*

[TNA, ADM 1/93]　　　　　　　　　　　　　　　　　　*Sandwich* at Spithead
18 February 1761

Sir,

Agreeable to your letter of the 16th instant, I have with the officers of His Majesty's ship under my command, examined into the condition of the white wine on board, and find it to be good at present in its kind and fit for men to drink. But it not being of a strong body, am much afraid that it will not stand the heat of a hot climate, as it will be apt to ferment and turn sour.[1]

823. *To Clevland*

[TNA, ADM 1/93]　　　　　　　　　　　　　　　　　　　　　　　Portsmouth
18 February 1761

Sir,

I have received your letters of the 16th instant, and agreeable to their Lordships' direction I have given fourteen days further leave to Captain [Arthur Tooker] Collins of the marines belonging to the *Namur*.

Yesterday in the evening Captain [Mitchell] Graham of the *Aldborough* arrived at Spithead with a convoy from Oporto.

The mainmast of the *Sapphire* being condemned as unserviceable, I have ordered her into the harbour which I hope their Lordships will approve of.

The utmost dispatch is making with the *Superb* who will be ready for the dock this spring.

---

[1] At this time captains of the *Essex*, *Launceston*, *Téméraire*, *Prince of Orange*, *Dragon*, *Flamborough*, and *Swiftsure* also submitted similar reports concerning white wine on board of their ships. See No. 831.

824. To Clevland

[TNA, ADM 1/93]
Portsmouth
19 February 1761
Wind SSW blows fresh

Sir,
I have received and delivered their Lordships' orders of the 17th instant to the captains of His Majesty's ships *Wager* and *Dover*. The latter will be docked this spring and will soon be ready for the sea.

The *Albany* sloop being gone to Spithead is ready for sea. I should be glad to know if it is their Lordships' pleasure to have her employed, agreeable to her former orders, between Beachy Head and the Isle of Wight.

825. From Clevland

[TNA, ADM 2/530, p. 335]
20 February 1761

Sir,
The Navy Board representing to my Lords Commissioners of the Admiralty that the *Plymouth* transport, lying at Spithead laden with stores for Plymouth yard, is only detained for want of a convoy, and praying one may be immediately appointed the stores being extremely wanted, I am commanded by their Lordships to recommend it to you, to hasten her away under the first convoy.

826. To Clevland

[TNA, ADM 1/93]
Portsmouth
20 February 1761
Wind WNW

Sir,
I have delivered your letter to Captain Strachan of the *Sapphire*, and have likewise given directions that the mainmast be finished without a moment's loss of time, that the said ship may return to her station.

You will please to acquaint their Lordships that His Majesty's ship *Edgar* is arrived from Plymouth in order to be docked, and that the *Torrington* will sail this day with the trade to the eastward.

827. To Clevland

[TNA, ADM 1/93]
Portsmouth
21 February 1761
Wind WSW blows hard

Sir,

I have received all your letters of the 19th instant, and shall take care to comply with their contents.

It blows so fresh that I cannot transmit to you by this post the names of the tenders that will be necessary to carry the 400 prisoners of war to France.

Yesterday the *Torrington* sailed with the trade to the eastward.

828. To Clevland

[TNA, ADM 1/93]
Portsmouth
22 February 1761

Sir,

I must desire you will please to acquaint their Lordships that the *Pembroke* came out of the dock yesterday as will the *Superb* this day. The utmost dispatch shall be used in getting the said ship to Spithead.

All the tenders at this port are mentioned in the margin.[1] They can carry only 290 prisoners. I have ordered them to be disarmed and victualled and the masters to obey the orders of the Commissioners of the Sick and Hurt.

I have delivered their Lordships' orders to Captain Macartney to complete his provisions to eight months.

829. To Clevland

[TNA, ADM 1/93]
Portsmouth
23 February 1761

Dear Sir,

The dissolution of the Parliament drawing near, and having received by the last post, very pressing letters setting forth the necessity of my appearing personally very soon at Okehampton.[2]

---

[1] *Eagle, Providence, Experiment.*
[2] Rodney represented Okehampton in the House of Commons. See also Nos. 659 and 836.

I must desire you will please to make it my humble request to Lord Anson that I may be relieved in the command at this port, the great business being now accomplished, and the ships that are to compose the squadron under the command of Admiral Pocock being docked and ready for sea.

830. To Clevland

[TNA, ADM 1/93]　　　　　　　　　　　　　　　　　　Portsmouth
23 February 1761

Sir,
　　You will please to acquaint their Lordships the *Superb* came out of the dock yesterday. The utmost dispatch is using to get her and the *Pembroke* to Spithead, which I hope will be in a few days.
　　The *Marlborough* came out of the dock this morning and the *Kingfisher* arrived at Spithead with four transports from Senegal.
　　Agreeable to their Lordships' directions signified to me by your letter of the 21st instant I have given Captain [Joseph] Norwood of the *Lightning* seven days' leave of absence.

831. To Clevland

[TNA, ADM 1/93]　　　　　　　　　　　　　　　　　　Portsmouth
24 February 1761

Sir,
　　Agreeable to their Lordships' directions signified to me in your letter of the 14th instant I have caused enquiry [No. 818] to be made into the white wine supplied to His Majesty's ships fitted for foreign service, and enclosed I transmit you the captains' letters [No. 822] to me on that head. They in general think the wine improper for a hot climate as it will be apt to give the men fluxes.

832. To Clevland

[TNA, ADM 1/93]　　　　　　　　　　　　　　　　　　Portsmouth
25 February 1761

Sir,
　　I have received your letters of the 23rd instant and agreeable to their Lordships' directions I have given ten days' leave to Captain Graham

and fourteen days' leave of absence to Lieutenant [John] Drummond of the *Namur*.

I have likewith delivered their Lordships' orders to Captain Willis of the *Blast*, and directed him to hasten and take upon him the command of the *Prince Edward* at Sheerness.

Lieutenant Lukey of His Majesty's ship *Superb* was tried yesterday and honourably acquitted.[1]

The *Albany* sloop is sailed for her station, and the *Blast* and *Pelican* are gone out of the harbour to Spithead.

833. *To Clevland*

[TNA, ADM 1/93] Portsmouth
25 February 1761

Sir,

Enclosed[2] I transmit to you complaints from the captains of His Majesty's ships *Prince* and *Téméraire*, desiring a court martial on the men named in the letters, which I desire you will please to lay before their Lordships for their directions.

834. *To Clevland*

[TNA, ADM 1/93] Portsmouth
26 February 1761

Sir,

Captain [Robert] Lambert of His Majesty's ship *Wager* having acquainted me that his boatswain has deserted, and as the ship is under orders for foreign service, I have taken the liberty to appoint one George Harwood,[3] boatswain's mate of the *Marlborough*, to take upon him the charge of the boatswain of the *Wager* till their Lordship's pleasure be known. He is a remarkable good man and worthy [of] preferment.

---

[1] See also Nos. 814 and 821.
[2] Not enclosed.
[3] See also Nos. 774 and 775.

835. To Clevland

[TNA, ADM 1/93] Portsmouth
26 February 1761

Sir,
I have received and delivered their Lordships' orders of the 24th instant to the respective captains, and have likewise received your letter of yesterday's date by express. And immediately give directions for bringing the *Valiant* into the harbour, without a moment's loss of time, where the utmost dispatch shall be used in getting her ready for the dock. I hope she will get into harbour as this day.

Yesterday the *Aldborough* came into the harbour.

836. To James West[1]

[BL, Add. MSS 32919, ff. 324–5] Portsmouth
27 February 1761

Dear Sir,
A letter I received by last night's post has given me inexpressible concern. Mr. [Robert] Andrews[2] acquaints me therein that he had received the Duke of N—s[3] commands, that Mr. Wenman Coke[4] was to be chose for Okehampton at Mr. Thomas Pitt's[5] interest.[6] For God's sake Sir what have I done to gain his Grace's displeasure. You know full well Sir that it was to serve him that I came into Parliament, and was desirous to continue on no other foundation.

I must entreat you Sir, to represent my case in the humblest manner to his Grace and beg of him not to let me suffer in the eye of the public,

---

[1] Senior Secretary to the Lords Commissioners of the Treasury, 9 April 1758–29 May 1762. West was a political manager for the Duke of Newcastle.
[2] Thomas Pitt's political agent at Okehampton.
[3] Duke of Newcastle.
[4] MP for Okehampton, 1761–68.
[5] Thomas Pitt of Boconnoc whose interest controlled the Parliamentary seat at Okehampton, occupied from 1759 to 1761, on behalf of the government by Rodney.
[6] Rodney from 1757 to 1761 was an MP representing the Borough of Okehampton. However, Rodney's seat at Okehampton was actually controlled by Thomas Pitt of Boconnoc, who being insolvent had in return for a payment from the secret service funds permitted the Duke of Newcastle to select who would represent the borough in the House of Commons. At the general election of 1761 Newcastle, at the request of the Duke of Devonshire and without informing Rodney, selected Wenman Coke to represent Okehampton in the House of Commons. Another seat in the House of Commons would be found for Rodney. See No. 841.

as a person obnoxious to him, and unworthy [of] his protection, which I shall infallibly do, unless his Grace vouchsafes to let me have a seat in Parliament, by his influence.

Your mind Sir must dictate what I at present feel, better than my words can express it, and in representing my concern to his Grace you will very much oblige him who has to the honour to be Sir with real respect.

837. *To Clevland*

[TNA, ADM 1/93] Portsmouth
27 February 1761

Sir,

Yesterday in the afternoon His Majesty's ship *Valiant* came into the harbour and will be ready to go into the dock the beginning of the ensuing spring.

This morning the *Basilisk* arrived at Spithead from a cruise and the *Kingfisher* came into the harbour.

Their Lordships' orders of the 25th instant are delivered to the Captains of the *Pembroke*, *Valiant*, and *Peregrine*.

838. *To Clevland*

[TNA, ADM 1/93] Portsmouth
1 March 1761

Sir,

I have received their Lordships' orders of the 27th instant, and have delivered them to the respective captains, as likewise your letters of the same date. And agreeable to their Lordships directions I have given ten days' leave of absence to Captain Rowley of the *Superb*, and three weeks' leave to Mr. [John] Bowen chaplain of the *Namur*, and ten days' leave to Mr. [William] Farren purser of the *Dover*.

839. To Clevland

[TNA, ADM 1/93]
Portsmouth
2 March 1761

Sir,

I have received their Lordships order of the 28th February which I have delivered to Captain [John] Wheelock of the *Pembroke*.

You will please to let their Lordships know that Thomas Atherton late carpenter's mate of the *Marlborough*, who was turned over into the *Téméraire* and could not be rated in that ship, has been discharged by order into the *Launceston*, where he is rated carpenter's mate.

Agreeable to the Lordships' directions, I have given ten days' leave of absence to Lieutenant [William] Lougten of the *Dover*.

Last night the *Edgar* came into harbour.

840. From Stephens

[TNA, ADM 2/530, p. 431]
18 March 1761

Sir,

Enclosed I send you an order from the Lords Commissioners of the Admiralty to Rear Admiral [Francis] Geary,[1] directing him to send some ship to carry you to Falmouth. And I am commanded by their Lordships to acquaint you, they have no objection to your hoisting your flag on board such ship if you shall think fit to do so.

841. To Newcastle

[BL, Add. MSS 32921, ff. 51–2]
Penryn
25 March 1761

My Lord,

I must beg leave to lay before your Grace, the present situation of affairs at this place, where I arrived on Sunday last, and have in company with Lord Falmouth[2] and Mr. Edgcumbe[3] canvassed the town.[4]

---

[1]Commander-in-chief, Portsmouth.
[2]Hugh Boscawen, 2nd Earl Falmouth.
[3]Richard Edgcumbe, 2nd Baron Edgcumbe. Falmouth and Edgcumbe were Newcastle's election managers at Penryn in Cornwall.
[4]Penryn.

We find at present but a small majority owing to the defection, of several officers in the Customs and Salt Office, both here and at Falmouth, as likewise two men belonging to the packets, who are all obstinate in the opposition. The agents of the other party having had the presumption to read a letter as from your Grace, which has deluded these people so much, that Mr. West's letter signifying your Grace's pleasure, had not the least effect. I must therefore join with Lord Falmouth and Mr. Edgcumbe, for the dismission of one Charles Robbins, a tidesman at Falmouth, which may have the desired effect on the other officers.

I must now take the liberty to point out to your Grace a measure which I am sure will infallibly secure the election, and which I most earnestly entreat may take place immediately, as it will convince the people in general (whose minds have been poisoned with different notions) that I have the honour to be nominated by your Grace as a candidate.

Captain Peard of the *Savage* sloop of war, a freeman of this town, whose friends have great influence, has been offered by the adversaries a bond of one thousand pound, and that they will procure him a post ship. He has resisted the temptation and continues firm.

If your Grace will make it a point, that it may appear here, before the election that Captain Peard has post[1] I am sure all difficulties will be removed. My ship the *Marlborough* has no captain appointed yet.

From your Grace's firm friendship to me I cannot doubt but you will grant me this further mark of your favour, as I shall always continue to be with the utmost gratitude and respect your Grace's most obedient and humble servant.[2]

842. To Clevland

[TNA, ADM 1/93]

London
26 May 1761

Sir,

In obedience to their Lordships' commands, I must desire that you will please to acquaint them, that Mr. Ferall de Bellcombe, who has served as pilot on board the squadron under my command is a useful good pilot, and proved himself well acquainted with the coast of France in general. Captain [Thomas] Francis of the *Greyhound*, whose ship I ordered him on board, to pilot her to Quebec, gives him the best of

---

[1] Captain George Peard never did achieve post rank.
[2] Rodney was elected an MP for Penryn on 4 April with the support of Newcastle and the votes of government employees.

characters and declares that without his assistance, he should not have been able to have conducted His Majesty's ship under his command, into the Gulf of St. Lawrence at that advanced season of the year.

843. To Clevland

[TNA, ADM 1/93]　　　　　　　　　　　　　　　　　　4 July 1761

Sir,
　I desire your will please to move the Right Hon. Lords Commissioners of the Admiralty, that they will please to give orders to the Commissioners of His Majesty's Navy, to make out a bill for my pay to the 30th of June last.

844. To Stephens

[TNA, ADM 1/307, f 415]　　　　　　　　　　　　　　　Hill Street
　　　　　　　　　　　　　　　　　　　　　　　　26 September 1761

Sir,
　His Majesty's ship *Marlborough* being ordered for foreign service, and the people named in the margin[1] being old followers of mine, and at present disrated, I beg you will please to lay the same before their Lordships who I hope will indulge me with their discharge into the *Royal Sovereign*, till such time their Lordships please to command me on service.

845. From Stephens

[TNA, ADM 2/532, p. 25]　　　　　　　　　　　　　　28 September 1761

Sir,
　I have received and communicated to my Lords Commissioners of the Admiralty your letter [No. 844] of the 26th instant desiring that 16 of your followers therein named now in the *Marlborough* may be discharged into the *Royal Sovereign* till such time as you may be employed. And in return I am to acquaint you, their Lordships have ordered them to be discharged before the ship proceeds on foreign service.

---

[1]Edward Winnet, Joseph Brown, George Peate, William Forster, Robert Smith, Thomas Farley, George Surtes, Charles Mills, Robert Stephens, [—] Matthews, John Bradley, Edward Ellerker, James Pollard, John Purvis, Francis Emlington, Thomas Pearce.

The Leeward Islands

846. *From Stephens*

[TNA, PRO 30/20/20/14] Admiralty Office
5 October 1761

Dear Sir,

I am commanded by my Lord Anson to acquaint you that the King hath signified his pleasure that you should command in chief at the Leeward Islands, and proceed thither immediately with the reinforcement of ships that are now very near ready to sail. His Lordship therefore desires you will come to town as soon as you [can], as you cannot stay more than 24 hours after your arrival, and that you will give all necessary orders to your servants preparatory to your embarking on board the *Marlborough* at Spithead.

PS
Lord Anson desires you won't fail to be in town tomorrow.

847. *From the Lords of the Admiralty*

[TNA, ADM 2/1331, pp. 413–16] 7 October 1761

Whereas His Majesty was pleased to order a considerable body of His land forces to be sent from North America to the Leeward Islands, to be employed in the reduction of the island of Martinique; which forces, so soon as embarked, are to proceed under proper convoy, off Carlisle Bay in the island of Barbados, to enquire for orders. And, not finding any there, to make the best of their way to the island of Guadeloupe; where they might expect to find orders for their further proceedings. And where they might probably arrive by the middle of this month. And His Majesty having been further pleased, by His orders of the 21st of last month, to cause his four regiments of foot, commanded by Colonels Rufane,[1] Gray,[2] Morgan[3] and Colville[4] to be sent from Belle Isle, under convoy of a ship of the line and a frigate, to the Leeward Islands, in order to join and assist the forces before-mentioned

---

[1] Brigadier William Rufane, colonel of the 76th Regiment of Foot.
[2] George Gray, colonel of the 61st Regiment of Foot.
[3] Lieutenant Colonel H. Morgan, colonel commandant of the 90th Regiment of Light Infantry.
[4] Major General Charles Colville, colonel of the 69th Regiment of Foot.

in the reduction of the island of Martinique; which four regiments are also to call off Carlisle Bay for orders, and, not finding any there, to make the best of their way to join the other forces, according to the best intelligence they shall be able to gain of them. We did, in consequence thereof, direct [Rear Admiral] Sir James Douglas, Commander in Chief of His Majesty's ships at Barbados and the Leeward Islands, to cause a sufficient number of ships to cruise off Martinique to prevent succours of any kind whatever being thrown into that island. And then to consult with the commanding officer of His Majesty's land forces at Guadeloupe, what might be the proper place of rendezvous for the troops coming from North America; as well as those which should be sent upon this expedition from the Leeward Islands; to the end that they might proceed together, or separately, with as little loss of time as possible, to the attack of Martinique. And having so done, that he should send necessary directions, in consequence, for the commanding officer of the convoy, either to Barbados or Guadeloupe as should be agreed upon; and make such disposition of the ships under his command, as should be most conducive to the reduction of the island; co-operating with the land forces in whatever might be determined for that purpose, and assisting them, with marines, seamen, boats, stores or provisions, wherever it should be necessary and they could be spared from the service of the fleet.

But whereas we have thought fit to appoint you to be Commander in Chief of His Majesty's ships and vessels employed and to be employed at and about the Leeward Islands; and that you should immediately proceed thither and carry into execution the said orders, or such part of them, as well as any others that Sir James Douglas has received for the King's service, as are not already executed, you are hereby required and directed to repair forthwith to Spithead. And hoisting your flag on board His Majesty's ship the *Marlborough* and taking under your command such ships and bomb vessels named in the margin[1] as may be ready to accompany you (leaving the rest to follow the orders they have received from us), you are to proceed, with all possible expedition, to Carlisle Bay in the island of Barbados. And, having informed yourself where Sir James Douglas is and what operations he is employed on, you are to take him and all His Majesty's ships and vessels employed at and about the Leeward Islands under your command and carry into execution the above recited orders, or such part of them as remain to be executed accordingly.

If you should fall in with the transports, having on board the four regiments before mentioned, in your way to Carlisle Bay, or find them

---

[1] *Vanguard, Modeste, Nottingham; Thunder* and *Granado* bombs.

on your arrival there, you are to open the dispatches which the commanding officer of the convoy is charged with for Sir James Douglas (a copy of which is enclosed[1] for your previous information) and give such orders, in consequence, as you may judge necessary.

The *Foudroyant* and *Dragon* being under secret orders to proceed to the Leeward Islands, you are to call off Plymouth Sound; and, in case they are ready, to take them with you; otherwise leave them also to follow the orders they received from us.

848. *From the Lords of the Admiralty*

[TNA, ADM 2/87, pp. 114–22]   7 October 1761

You are constantly to give timely notice as well to our secretary, as to the office immediately concerned, of any supplies of stores and provisions that may be wanting for the use of your squadron, and also by every opportunity to transmit to our secretary an exact account of the state of your squadron as to men, stores, provisions, and all other particulars. And you are at the same time to send duplicates of those accounts so far as they relate to stores and the condition of the ships' hulls, masts and yards to the Navy Board, and so far as they relate to the musters and provisions to the Commissioners for Victualling. And you are upon no account to have naval or ordnance stores or provisions of any kind purchased without an absolute necessity, and if you shall be under such necessity, you are always to cause them to be purchased by the proper officers, and to take all possible care that the purchase be made on the best and cheapest terms for His Majesty and that the officers employed therein do not make any advantage to themselves. And you are to attest the bills drawn upon the Navy, Ordnance, or Victualling Boards, for what may be so purchased and to see that the reasons for the purchase be mentioned in the said bills, and to cause all possible care to be taken that the ordnance, as well as the other stores be expended with the best frugality.

In any orders that you may have occasion to give, and in all your proceedings relative to the service, you are to conform yourself to the established rules and customs of the navy, and never to deviate therefrom, or to cause any extraordinary expense of any kind whatsoever unless His Majesty's service shall absolutely require the same, nor are you to interfere with the instructions and orders which any naval or other officers may be under from the boards to which they

[1]Not enclosed.

respectively are subordinate, otherwise than to see that they pay due obedience thereto.

You are never to purchase or cause to be purchased for His Majesty any ship or vessel whatsoever, nor to cause any wharfs, storehouses, magazines, fortifications, or other buildings of any kind to be erected without first representing the want thereof to us, and sending home plans thereof with estimates of the expense and receiving our directions thereupon, but you are to cause the careening wharf with the naval buildings already erected, to be kept in repair, and to cause the naval officer to be assisted from His Majesty's ships, which may at any time be in port, with as many men as can be spared or may be wanted for those purposes or for converting old or decayed stores which may be convertible to any use of His Majesty' service. And when any ships return to England you are to cause them to receive on board such of the old stores not fit for any use in His Majesty's service abroad, as they can conveniently take in.

You are not to appoint any muster master, storekeeper, naval officer, or agent victualler to the squadron, or at any port on shore, but if the service should require any of those officers, you are to represent the same to us for our determination, and in case of the death of any navy or victualling officer on shore, you are to empower some person best qualified with respect to abilities and service to act in the vacancy until we shall appoint a successor to the deceased.

You are to cause the ships and vessels of your squadron to be supplied with what provisions they may want by such persons as may be under contract with the Commissioners of the Victualling for furnishing His Majesty's ships at Barbados and the Leeward Islands therewith, taking care that timely application be always made to the said contractors, or their agent for the same, but you are not to suffer more provisions to be at any time taken on board a ship than shall be necessary for the service whereon she shall be employed, nor are you to suffer any ship which may be on her return to England, to complete to more than three months' provisions at whole allowance upon penalty of making good what damage His Majesty may sustain by you not acting agreeable thereto.

Great liberty having been sometimes taken in supplying owners or masters of merchant ships with naval stores from His Majesty's magazines or ships abroad, upon slight occasions, which is a proceeding that may be attended with inconvenience and prejudice to the service, you are hereby strictly charged not to suffer any of His Majesty's stores to be spared for the use of any merchant ship or vessel whatsoever, unless it shall evidently appear to you, that the ship or vessel is in the utmost distress for want thereof, that the same cannot possibly be otherwise procured, and that His Majesty's stores can spare the same, without prejudice or inconvenience. And in such case you are not to take bond for the delivery of the like specie, but to take care that the same be either paid for on the spot to the naval officer, or sufficient security given that the payment shall be punctually made to the Treasurer of the Navy here at home. And you are by the first opportunity to transmit an account to us and to the Navy Board of any stores which you shall so cause to be spared out of His Majesty's stores, to whom, and the particular reasons which induced you thereto.

In case of the death of any officers of the ships or vessels of your squadron, or the dismission of any of them by a court martial, you are hereby empowered to appoint such other persons to the vacancy as by their qualifications and the nature of the their employments ought to succeed therein, particularly observing to appoint commanders to post ships in preference to lieutenants, and to take notice that we will not confirm any officers appointed to vacancies arising in any other manner; in all other cases whatsoever you are only to give an order to another person to act until the cause of suspension shall be removed.

If any of His Majesty's ships shall join you from the coast of Africa, and between the time of her departure from England and arrival under your orders, the command shall have devolved upon a lieutenant, or any officers shall have been regularly appointed to act in vacancies occasioned by death, you are not to displace such lieutenant from the command, nor such officers from their respective stations without our directions for your so doing.

You are to visit the ships under your command as often as you shall judge requisite, and to see their men mustered, and examine them as you shall think fitting, and to cause any whom you may find improperly rated or unfit for service, to be disrated or discharged taking care that the methods prescribed in an Act of Parliament of the thirty first year of his late Majesty entituled an Act for the Encouragement of Seamen employed in the Royal Navy &c.[1] (abstracts of which have been sent to you) be strictly complied with. You are to enquire into and observe the economy and order observed on board the ships, and examine to whether cleanliness (so essential to the health of their companies) be duly attended to, and you are in general to take care that all established regulations as well as all temporary orders be punctually complied with, as well by yourself, as by all persons under your command,

---

[1] 29 Geo. II c. 34. An Act for the Encouragement of Seamen and the more speedy and effectual manning of His Majesty's Navy.

unless in any extraordinary conjuncture where the King's service may render it absolutely necessary to dispense therewith, and in cases where there may be no regulations or orders for your guidance, you are to act in the best manner in your power for His Majesty's service and the good of the public.

If it shall be found necessary for the health of the companies of the ships and vessels under your command, you are at liberty to cause them to be victualled twice a week when they shall be in port with fresh provisions.

The better to enable you to keep the complement of the squadron complete, you are at liberty to pay a reward of two pistoles for every straggling seamen who shall be taken up and delivered on board any ship or vessel under your command, and one pistole for every deserter from any of the squadron who shall in like manner be secured and delivered, taking care that what shall be paid for deserters be charged against their names upon the books of the ships they shall serve in.

You are to keep a journal of your proceedings with the squadron under your command, or any part thereof, and of the services on which you send any of the ships with the reasons for the same, and also to note therein all other remarkable occurrences and particulars. And you are not to fail to send a copy thereof, to our secretary for our information by the first opportunity after the expiration of every six months. And you are also by every opportunity to acquaint him for our information with all your proceedings relating to the service and with any intelligence you may receive proper for our knowledge.

For the better maintaining a proper governance and good discipline in the squadron under your command, we do hereby authorize and empower you to call and assemble courts martial in foreign parts as often as you shall see occasion.

Whereas His Majesty has been pleased to direct by his Order in Council of the 25th March last, that for the future the exchanges of prisoners of war in the West India islands be carried on under the direction of the respective commanders in chief of His Majesty's ships for the time being in those islands, you are hereby required and directed to take upon you the care and management of the said exchange at Barbados and the Leeward Islands accordingly. We having directed the Commissioners for taking care of the Sick and Wounded Seamen and for exchanging prisoners of war to correspond with you in relation thereto and to give you such information as you may desire and shall appear necessary for forwarding that part of the service.

The merchants trading to the Leeward Islands having represented to us the great detriment it is to their trade that the homeward bound convoys do not depart punctually on the days appointed for that purpose, you are therefore to take care to fix the departure of the said convoys for England on such days as the concerned in general shall desire, appointing such force as shall appear to you necessary for the protection thereof, and to be very careful that they do leave the islands the first fair wind after the time so fixed, without showing the least regard to any private application that may be made to you for delaying their departure.

849. *To Stephens*

[TNA, ADM 1/307, f. 416] Portsmouth
9 October 1761

Sir,

You will please to acquaint their Lordships that I am arrived here, and agreeable to their instructions have taken His Majesty's ships named in the margin[1] under my command who are at Spithead and ready to sail.

As the *Granado* bomb is not yet out of the harbour, [I] have not delivered their Lordships' orders.

If the wind and weather permits their Lordships may depend upon my proceeding to sea tomorrow.

850. *To Stephens*

[TNA, ADM 1/307, f. 417] *Marlborough* at Spithead
10 October 1761

Sir,

You will please to acquaint their Lordships that this morning I made the signal, unmoored, and prepared to sail, but finding the *Marlborough* would be detained some hours, being in want of beer, water, wood, pursers necessaries, and no coals on board, I gave orders to the captains of the *Vanguard* and *Modeste* not to wait for me, but [to] proceed immediately to sea, the wind veering to the SEbE and blowing very hard prevented those ships weighing. But if it moderates ever so little, their Lordships may depend that not one moment's time shall be lost in putting their orders into execution. I am sorry to say that notwithstanding Vice Admiral Holburne has done every thing in his power towards

---

[1]*Marlborough, Vanguard, Nottingham, Modeste,* and *Thunder* bomb.

hastening the *Marlborough*, that the pursers' absence has been a very great hindrance to the service.

I must acknowledge the receipt of your packet by the Admiralty messenger, who arrived here at noon. I have detained him till this moment that their Lordships might be certainly informed if any of the ships could sail this day. They all now remain at single anchor and I hope by noon tomorrow that all of them will be at sea; tho' at present it blows very fresh at ESE.

The *Thunder* bomb has got her mortars on board and will sail out of the harbour the moment the weather moderates.

I beg you will assure their Lordships that I am as eager and desirous to proceed with dispatch on the service they have commanded me, as they can possibly be themselves.

851. *To Stephens*

[TNA, ADM 1/307, f. 418] *Marlborough* at Spithead
12 October 1761 at noon
Wind SW

Sir,

You will please to acquaint their Lordships that the weather proved so bad yesterday, and the wind so unfavourable that I could not possibly put to sea with the squadron of His Majesty's ships under my command. It has blown very hard all last night, and continues to do so, which prevents my falling down to St. Helens in order to take the first favourable opportunity that offers to proceed agreeable to their orders I have received.

I have been favoured with your letter of the 10th instant acquainting me that their Lordships had ordered another bomb vessel to be got ready, in addition to the two already with me at Spithead.

You may assure their Lordships that not a moment's time shall be lost whenever the weather will permit me to proceed.

852. To Stephens

[TNA, ADM 1/307, ff. 419–20] *Marlborough* between the buoys
14 October 1761
At noon calm

Sir,
You will please to let their Lordships know that yesterday morning at day light, and likewise this morning I made an attempt to put to sea with the squadron under my command having weighed for that purpose, but it proving calm soon after, has obliged me to anchor again.

I must likewise acquaint their Lordships that the whole squadron has been at single anchor since Saturday waiting in momentary expectation of a favourable opportunity to proceed to sea, which has not (as yet) offered since I have taken upon me the command they have been pleased to honour me with.

Their Lordships may be assured that I shall lose not a moment's time in putting to sea when the wind permits.

[PS]
Since writing this letter the wind has permitted me to get to St. Helens.

853. To Stephens

[TNA, ADM 1/307, f. 421] *Marlborough* off Plymouth
20 October 1761
At noon wind NE

Sir,
You will please to acquaint their Lordships that the squadron of His Majesty's ships under my command are now off Plymouth.

At day light this morning I ordered the *Vanguard* to make sail ahead and sent orders by her for the *Foudroyant* and *Dragon* to join me, if those ships were ready.

I can now plainly perceive that the *Foudroyant* is preparing to get under sail, but by the *Essex's* boat that is come on board me, I find the *Dragon* is still in Hamoaze.

As the wind (tho' little) is favourable, their Lordships may depend upon my making the best use of it, and I hope tomorrow to be clear of the Channel.

854. To Stephens

[TNA, ADM 1/307, f. 423]

Marlborough at sea
14 November 1761 at 4 AM
Latitude 18° 20' [N]
Longitude from the Lizard 35° 00'

Sir,

Speaking this moment with a Portuguese ship from the Brazils bound to Lisbon gives me an opportunity to acquaint their Lordships that I am thus far advanced in my passage, and hope in eight days to be at Barbados.

The *Neptune*, one of the bomb tenders, is the only vessel with me, all the other ships of the squadron having parted company in a very hard gale of wind a few days after I sailed from England.

855. From the Lords of the Admiralty

[TNA, ADM 2/1331, pp. 447–8]   5 December 1761

Whereas you will receive herewith a letter from Captain [Matthew] Buckle, commanding a squadron of His Majesty's ships cruising off Ushant, with an account of a squadron of the enemy's ships being sailed from Brest, and the best information he may be able to give of their destination. And as it is probable they may be designed to protect their colonies in the West Indies or possibly to attack those belonging to His Majesty, particularly the island of Jamaica, you are hereby required and directed to station a frigate to look out for them off the island of Désirade or any other of the Windward Islands which the enemy most frequently make when they are bound to St. Domingo, that in case of their coming into those seas, the captain of the said frigate may, without loss of time, repair to, and inform you thereof; when you are to use your utmost endeavours to take or destroy them. But, should the enemy pass by the Windward Islands and proceed towards St. Domingo or Jamaica, you are to detach Sir James Douglas with six ships of the line at least, or more if they can be spared, to join Rear Admiral Holmes[1] at Jamaica. And on the other hand, if you find the enemy are come to any of their colonies within the limits of your command and there should be a necessity for your squadron to be

---

[1] Rear Admiral Charles Holmes, Commander-in-chief of the squadron at Jamaica. On 21 November 1761 Holmes died and was succeeded as Commander-in-chief by Captain Arthur Forrest.

reinforced either to defeat their designs or forward your own, you are to apply to the commander in chief of His Majesty's ships at Jamaica for assistance, he having orders to send you such additional strength on your applying for it as you may have occasion for and he can spare without manifest hazard to the service particularly entrusted to your care.

The frigate by which you will receive this, being charged with dispatches for Mr Holmes at Jamaica, you are not to detain her on any account, but let her proceed on with them without a moment's loss of time.

856. *From the Lords of the Admiralty*

[TNA, ADM 2/87, pp. 339–40]   26 December 1761

Whereas the Earl of Egremont, one of His Majesty's principal Secretaries of State has informed us that the King some time since received undoubted intelligence of certain engagements having been contracted between the courts of Madrid and Versailles which His Catholic Majesty did not disavow, and that the Earl of Bristol, His Majesty's ambassador in Spain having desired to be informed of the nature and extent of such suspicious engagements as far as might concern the interests of Great Britain was refused all just satisfaction on that head, whereupon His Majesty judging it highly expedient to give peremptory directions to His ambassador to renew his instances with the Spanish minister to demand a categorical and satisfactory answer with regard to any articles in the above mentioned engagements which might be hostile to Great Britain, and in case the Court of Madrid should refuse to disavow any intentions to take part with our declared enemies in the present war, His Majesty's ambassador was directed to declare that the King could not look upon such a refusal in any other light than as an aggression on the part of Spain, and as an absolute declaration of war in which case he was ordered to leave the court of Madrid and his Excellency having been absolutely refused this just and reasonable satisfaction has left the court of Madrid accordingly.

And the Earl of Egremont having signified His Majesty's pleasure that we should forthwith cause hostilities of all sorts to commence against the Spaniards by endeavouring to seize and take by all possible means their ships of war and merchant ships and to annoy and distress them in the most effectual manner, and if any Spanish ships are taken to bring them into the nearest port of His Majesty's dominions there to be kept without plunder or embezzlement until His Majesty's pleasure shall be known concerning them unless in case of perishable goods which are to be sold reserving the money arising therefrom for His Majesty's future disposition.

These are in pursuance of His Majesty's aforesaid pleasure to require and direct you forthwith with the *ships and vessels* under your command to commence hostilities against His Catholic Majesty, and his subjects by taking, sinking, burning, or destroying their ships and effects, and to take the most effectual means to annoy and distress them as well as to protect His Majesty's trading subjects taking care to send into the nearest port of His Majesty's dominions such Spanish ships as may be taken there to be kept without plunder or embezzlement, till His Majesty's pleasure shall be known concerning them unless in case of perishable goods which if taken in foreign parts you are to cause to be sold to the best advantage reserving the money arising therefrom for His Majesty's future disposition, and in the meantime you will be answerable for the same.

857. To Clevland

[*London Gazette*, 6–9 March 1762] *Marlborough*
Cas des Navières Bay
19 January 1762

Sir,

I desire you will acquaint their Lordships, that I arrived at Barbados on the 22nd of November, having parted company with the squadron under my command in a hard gale of wind, a few days after we left the Channel.

The *Foudroyant, Modeste*, and *Basilisk*, joined me the 27th, the *Nottingham* and *Thunder* the 1st of December, and the *Vanguard* with the remainder of the squadron on the 9th. The *Téméraire* and *Actæon* with the troops from Belle Isle, arrived the 14th of December, and Major General Monckton,[1] with the forces from North America, on the 24th; and having remained a few days to water the ships, refresh the men, and make the necessary dispositions for our enterprise, we arrived off Martinique the 7th of January; and on the 8th we all anchored in St. Ann's Bay, the ships I had appointed (under Sir James Douglas) having silenced the forts of that coast; in performing which, we had the misfortune to lose the *Raisonable*, as she was leading in for one of the

---

[1]Commander-in-chief of the British army in Leeward Islands attacking Martinique and then later governor of New York.

enemy's batteries, owing to the pilots being ignorant of a little reef of rocks, which took her up. We have saved all her people, all her stores, and I hope soon to get all her guns.

Having, by this motion of the fleet and army, taken possession of an excellent harbour, and secured a landing on the weathermost part of the island, which might be made tenable at any time, as likewise thereby greatly alarmed the enemy, at General Monckton's request, I dispatched Commodore Swanton, with a squadron of ships and two brigades, to the Bay of Petite Ance, in order to take post there. Captain [Hon. Augustus] Hervey of the *Dragon*, having silenced the battery of the Grand Ance, landed his marines and seamen, who attacked it also from the shore, and took possession of the fort; and, on the 14th, I followed with the whole fleet and army, after destroying the enemy's batteries at St. Ann's Bay, when (having reconnoitred the coast with the General) we came to a resolution to make an attempt between Point Negroe and Cas de Pilotte, which I ordered to be attacked on the 16th; and having very successfully and with little loss silenced the batteries, I landed General Monckton with the greatest part of his force by sunset; and the whole army was on shore a little after day light next morning, without the loss of a man (the boats being commanded by Commodore Swanton in the centre, Captain [Molyneux] Shuldham on the right wing, and Captain Hervey on the left) with such neccessaries as they were most immediately in want of, and had all the ships and transports anchored as much in safety, as this coast will admit.

I also landed two battalions of marines, consisting of 450 men each.

The army are now carrying on their approaches to the heights of Mount Grenie and Mount Tortneson, which the enemy have made as art can do, and from whence the General proposes to lay seige to Fort Royal.

I have the happiness to add, that the army and navy continue in perfect health; and carry on the service with the greatest spirit and harmony.

858. *To Newcastle*

[BL, Add. MSS 32933, ff. 430–2]　　　Cas des Navières, Martinique
21 January 1762

My Lord,

By Captain Walsingham whom I send express to the Admiralty, your Grace will receive this letter as I cannot longer defer giving your Grace the satisfaction of knowing that I landed His Majesty's forces on the island of Martinique the 16th instant, after having silenced all the enemy's batteries and cleared the coast so as to prevent any opposition. For particulars I beg leave to refer your Grace to my letter [No. 857] to the Admiralty, as also to a plan of the island and coast which I send by this opportunity to Lord Anson.

I have waited five days since the landing in expectation of the Generals making an attack upon the enemy's works on the Mounts Grenie and Tortneson, but as it has been deferred from day to day and remains still uncertain, I could not defer longer giving His Majesty and the nation the satisfaction of knowing that an army of fourteen thousand effective men were landed at Martinique at a place where the enemy boasted to be impregnable against ships. Fifteen hundred Blacks from the different islands are likewise landed to assist in any laborious work.

I have likewise the additional satisfaction to acquaint your Grace that the enemy have received no succours and that all the regular troops in this island are not more than six hundred. I have put off the departure of the ship which brings this news for five days at the General's request, but receiving this day a message from him that he had no dispatches as yet to send, and likewise receiving last night an express from Lisbon with a printed copy of the Spanish manifesto dated the 15th of December at Madrid,[1] I thought it absolutely my duty not to defer a moment longer, making the administration acquainted with these important events, as I am sure it must give your Grace real satisfaction to know that I am so early acquainted with the intentions of the court of Spain, and from which I shall take such measures as will prevent any detriment arising to His Majesty's service from the situation of affairs with that court.

859. *From the Lords of the Admiralty*

[TNA, ADM 2/1332, ff. 9–11]   5 February 1762

Whereas it is hoped, from the vigour and activity which will have been exerted by His Majesty's sea and land forces, that, before this reaches you, the operations against Martinique will have been finished, by the entire conquest of that island, particularly Fort Royal and St. Pierre.

And the King judging, in this great crisis of an additional war with Spain, which the haughty and imperious conduct of that court has at last obliged His Majesty to declare, notwithstanding the moderation

---
[1] Spain's declaration of war against Great Britain.

with which His Majesty has invariably endeavoured to avoid that extremity, that nothing can so essentially contribute to his service, or so soon reduce the enemy to listen to equitable and reasonable terms of accommodation, as the making some signal and effectual impression on the Spanish colonies in the West Indies. In this view His Majesty has thought proper to appoint Admiral Sir George Pocock to be commander in chief of His Majesty's ships to be employed on this expedition, not from having conceived the least diffidence of your abilities, but the largeness of the force destined on this important expedition, and the urgency of the present crisis requiring an officer of high rank, and one, who by being on the spot to receive the necessary instructions, could be fully apprised of the present views and intentions.

And, as the various and extensive services to be supported in such distant parts of the world will not admit of an adequate force for this great and important enterprise, without employing thereon a great part of the ships under your command, as well as the land forces with Major General Monckton, for which purpose it is necessary the said ships, and at least sixteen thousand tons of the transports should be put into condition for further service, and it being expected that the fleet and land forces which will soon sail from hence under the respective commands of Sir George Pocock and the Earl of Albemarle[1] may arrive at Barbados by the middle of April.

And His Majesty's pleasure being signified by the Earl of Egremont, one of his principal Secretaries of State, to Major General Monckton, that, in case he shall be in possession of the whole of the island of Martinique he takes the proper measures for settling a garrison there sufficient to enable them to defend that conquest and that the residue of the troops under his command, with artillery and stores, should be held in readiness to embark on board the transports to be fitted by you for that purpose, in order to follow such directions as shall be given by Admiral Sir George Pocock and Lord Albemarle; and also that in case, contrary to expectation, the operations against Martinique should have been drawn to such a length that, on receipt of His Majesty's aforesaid pleasure, His Troops shall only be in possession of some principal fortress or fortresses on the said island, and shall still be pursuing the entire reduction thereof, it is his pleasure that they should immediately desist from any further operations that can, in any shape, prevent the troops being ready to embark under the command of Lord Albemarle, the moment his Lordship shall arrive or send orders for that purpose.

[1]George Keppel, 3rd Earl of Albemarle, the Commander-in-chief of the British land forces during the attack on Cuba in 1762.

And the success of this intended expedition being of such high importance to the King's service that His Majesty has judged it most indispensably necessary all other enterprises should yield to this one object, and therefore signified his pleasure likewise to General Monckton, that, in case such insuperable difficulties shall have been found, as not to be able to make himself master of any such principal fortress or fortresses at Martinique as shall be, by any means tenable by the garrison he is directed to leave, he is to withdraw from the further prosecution of any operations against the said island, which can any ways obstruct or interfere with having the troops in readiness to proceed with Lord Albemarle; for which purpose the troops &c. are to be immediately embarked, and to proceed to Prince Ruperts Bay in the island of Dominica.

And the King's pleasure having been equally signified that should his forces be employed in operations against any other island or place whatsoever they do desist from such operations and repair to Prince Rupert Bay.

We do therefore hereby require and direct you to consult and cooperate with Major General Monckton in carrying His Majesty's pleasure, signified as aforesaid, most effectually into execution for which purpose you are to assist with the ships of war and transports under your command, and to cause sixteen thousand tons of the latter to be provided and fitted for eight thousand men, and victualled for three months with all species of provisions, if that quantity remains, otherwise to be made up out of what shall be sent from hence with Sir George Pocock.

You are also to provide transports for the artillery, ordnance stores &c. And to cause such ten ships of the line, whose captains may be junior to Captain Swanton, with three or four frigates and the bomb vessels to be likewise victualled and stored, and put into condition ready to proceed upon further service by the middle of April as beforementioned.

And as the further progress of the squadron and troops expected to arrive at Barbados from England by the middle of April will be determined by the accounts Admiral Pocock and Lord Albemarle will receive on their arrival there from you and General Monckton.

You are to consult and advise with the General, whether, in case His Majesty's troops should be in possession of Martinique, that will be an eligible rendezvous and convenient for watering so large a fleet, or if St. Lucia should be in possession of that island will be more eligible and convenient, or if Prince Ruperts Bay in the island of Dominica may be thought more proper. And you are immediately after coming to a determination upon that matter, to dispatch a frigate or sloop to Barbados with an account of your proceedings, situation, and opinion concerning the rendezvous, to Sir George Pocock; sending at the same time, an intelligent sea officer, who may be able to give Sir George Pocock satisfaction with regard to any questions he may find it necessary to put, for his more particular information in those matters. As General Monckton is directed to send, by the same conveyance, an intelligent land officer who may be able to give Lord Albemarle like satisfaction. You are to observe the most scrupulous exactness and precision in the report which you shall, in concert with General Monckton, send to Barbados, marking every circumstance of time and place, which may be necessary to fix (beyond all possibility of mistake) the rendezvous at one of the three places abovementioned as shall appear most expedient. And to prevent accidents, you are to take care to send duplicates of the said report by another safe conveyance in a day or two after the departure of the orginal.

If, after making provision for embarking the troops, there shall be sufficient quantity of the transports remaining, you are to send about fifteen or sixteen thousand tons down to Jamaica under convoy of one of the frigates of your squadron to be disposed of there as the commander in chief of His Majesty's ships upon that station shall direct. But, in case there should not be that quantity of tonnage remaining, you are to send so much as may be left, letting Admiral Holmes know by the *Richmond*, as near as you can, how much it will be. And, as that ship is charged with dispatches of importance to Admiral Holmes, you are not to detain her a moment longer than may be necessary for giving such information.

As you must be sensible of the great importance of these orders it is unnecessary for us to add any motives to enforce the most punctual and expeditious obedience thereto. We therefore rely upon your hearty concurrence with His Majesty's land and sea officers employed on this important occasion; not doubting the exertion of your utmost efforts and abilities to forward the service.

And when this business is dispatched and the fleet and troops under the command of Sir George Pocock and Lord Albemarle shall be sailed, you are to use your best endeavours with the force that shall then remain with you, not only to protect and defend His Majesty's island and conquests within the limits of your command, but to annoy and distress the enemy as much as lies in your power.

860. To Newcastle

[BL, Add. MSS 32934, ff. 255–7] Fort Royal Bay, Martinique
10 February 1762

My Lord,

I hope Captain Walsingham had the honour to deliver your Grace my letter [No. 588] of the 21st January giving your Grace an account of my landing His Majesty's troops on this island.

I have now the additional satisfaction most sincerely to congratulate your Grace upon the reduction of the most important and strong citadel of Fort Royal, which has added to His Majesty's dominions the noblest and best harbour in the West Indies, as likewise induced the inhabitants of this rich and fertile island to submit to such laws as His Majesty shall please to direct for their government.

If the articles granted the troops and inhabitants are such, as your Grace approves, I shall be extremely happy. One thing I am sure of, that it will add to the Treasury a very considerable sum annually and make the inhabitants wish to continue British subjects.

I have likewise great satisfaction when I consider that this conquest puts it into your Grace's power to oblige many of your friends by the posts and employment in your Grace's gift and which are very lucrative in this island particularly those relative to the customs and Secretary of the island. This I thought my duty to represent to your Grace that you might not be deceived in their value which are computed at four thousand pound a year each.

If I have the good fortune to continue in your Grace's esteem, and that my conduct on this expedition, meets with your Grace's approbation I shall be extremely happy, as among your Grace's many friends none is more truly so than him who has the honour to be with most profound respect and gratitude.

861. To Clevland

[BL, Add. MSS 32934, f. 259] *Marlborough* in Fort Royal Bay
Martinique
10 February 1762

Sir,

Since my letter [No. 857] of the 19th January, sent express by Captain Walsingham acquainting their Lordships with my arrival, and landing the army at Cas Navières, I have the honour to congratulate them on the surrender of the most important citadel of Fort Royal and Pigeon Island; which has given His Majesty's forces possession of the noblest and best harbour in these parts of the West Indies.

The almost insurmountable difficulties the troops had to struggle with, and the surprising strength of the country, improved by all that art could add, will be best explained by General Monckton. But this I must say, in justice to those I have the honour to command, that the intrepidity and gallant behaviour of the officers and troops employed on this expedition could be equalled only by the eager and cheerful activity of the officers and seamen who contributed every thing in their power towards the reduction of the place; and made no difficulties in transporting numbers of the heaviest mortars and ship's cannon, up the steepest mountains at a very considerable distance from the sea, and across the enemy's line of fire.

I have the pleasure to acquaint their Lordships, that we have taken in this port fourteen of the enemy's best privateers, and many more which are in the other ports of the island will be immediately delivered into my hands, agreeable to the capitulation with the inhabitants; which capitulation, as likewise that of the Citadel and Pigeon Island, I have the honour to enclose to them. And for all further particulars I must refer their Lordships to Captain Darby, who is charged with these dispatches.

It give me the sincerest satisfaction, that I can assure their Lordships the most perfect harmony had subsisted between the navy and the army, each vying in the most friendly manner which should serve His Majesty and their country best.

862. *From Clevland*

[TNA, ADM 2/533, pp. 13–14]　　　　　　　　　　19 February 1762

Sir,

Sir James Douglas having acquainted my Lords Commissioners of the Admiralty in his letter of the 15th of November last, of several promotions he had made in consequence of the death of Captain [James] Doake of the *Lizard*, I am commanded by their Lordships to acquaint you, that they have thought proper to appoint Captain [John] Lendrick to the *Echo*, and therefore it is their direction that you cause Captain Banks to return to the *Rose*, Captain [John Neal Pleydell] Nott to the command of the *Antigua*, and Lieutenant [Lemuel] Shuldham who now commands that ship to return to the lieutenancy of the *Dublin*.

I am also to acquaint you that Captain [John] Brisbane, who was appointed by Sir James Douglas to the *Lizard*, will be confirmed captain of her, and paid for the time he commanded the *Echo* by order, and that Lieutenant [Charles] Buckner will be paid for the time he commanded the *Virgin* preceding the date of the commission which their Lordships have now ordered him for her.

863. To Newcastle

[BL, Add. MSS 32935, ff. 95–6] St. Pierre, Martinique
27 February 1762

Sir,
Give me leave most sincerely to congratulate your Grace on the total reduction of the isle of Martinique, the defection of the inhabitants, which Monsieur [de] la Touche[1] the General stilled rebellion [*sic*], obliged him to capitulate in order to save the town of St. Pierre, the largest and best built town in all the West Indies, it being two miles in length, a quarter of a mile in breadth, the streets regular and abounding in large commodious houses, most of which have been erected at the expense of the English commerce.

If your Grace will please to cast your eye over the map of the West Indies, you will perceive that His Majesty by the possession of the Caribbean Islands is as much a master of the key to the West Indies, as Gibraltar is to the Mediterranean, all the enemy's supplies to their colonies being obliged to take this track, as your Grace may perceive by a large Spanish ship which I took on the 4th instant loaded with powder, cannon and all sorts of ammunition designed for the Spanish forts at La Guaira.[2] This capture, though of small value to His Majesty, is a very great detriment to his enemies.

If my conduct during the time I have commanded in these seas meets with your Grace's approbation I shall be extremely happy, as the height of my ambition is to prove myself worthy of the patronage your Grace has always bestowed upon me.

---

[1]Le Vasser de la Touche, governor of the French Windward Islands.
[2]See also No. 863.

864. *To Clevland*

[TNA, ADM 1/307, ff. 433–4] *Marlborough* St. Pierre Harbour
Martinique
28 February 1762

Sir,

Since my dispatches of the 10th instant [No. 861] by Captain Darby, acquainting their Lordships with the surrender of Fort Royal and the capitulation of the greatest part of the inhabitants, I have the additional pleasure to congratulate their Lordships on the conquest of the whole island of Martinique, M. de la Touche having thought proper to send his brother on board the *Marlborough* with articles of capitulation, just in time to save the town of St. Pierre from destruction. A copy of which capitulation I have the honour to enclose for their inspection, and flatter myself it is such as will meet with their Lordships' approbation.

As this great island is now entirely subjected to His Majesty's obedience, I can only repeat in this public manner my entire approbation of the conduct of all the officers and seamen of that part of His Majesty's fleet which I have the honour to command, all having exerted themselves in their proper stations with an ardour and resolution becoming British seamen.

Immediately on the surrender of St. Pierre I dispatched Commodore Swanton with a squadron of His Majesty's ships to join those already before the island of Grenada and block up that port as close as possible. The islands of St. Vincent and St. Lucia are likewise very closely blockaded, and I make not the least doubt, but all the Caribbean Islands will in a very short time be subjected to His Majesty.

I have this moment received an express from Antigua acquainting me with the arrival of His Majesty's ship *Épreuve*, Captain [Peter] Blake, at that island in eight weeks from England, going express to Virginia, but having sprung his mainmast and bowsprit, was obliged to put into English Harbour. I have ordered His Majesty's sloop the *Guadeloupe* to proceed instantly to English Harbour and, in case the *Épreuve* is not refitted for sea, to receive the dispatches from Captain Blake and proceed with them without a moment's loss of time to Virginia. Captain Blake has transmitted to me a copy of their Lordship's orders of the 26th December commanding him to commence hostilities against His Catholic Majesty and his subjects. And as I had before acquainted their Lordships by Captain Walsingham, that I had received an express from Lisbon sent by Captain [George] Johnstone of His Majesty's sloop the *Hornet*, with the declaration of the Court of Madrid of the 15th December, last and of the British ships being seized in the ports of Spain; which was confirmed by the *Hargrove* transport, that has joined me since with two companies of Gray's[1] Regiment on board from Port Antonio on the coast of Spain, where they attempted to stop her and fired many shots, the master and several of his men having been seized and detained on shore; I therefore thought it highly necessary for His Majesty's service to station ships in proper tracts to intercept the Spanish ships coming from Europe, and [I] have the pleasure to acquaint their Lordships that on the 4th instant Captain Ourry of His Majesty's ships the *Actæon*, cruising off Tobago, fell in with and took a large Spanish register[2] ship laden with cannon, powder, small arms and ordnance stores bound to La Guaira. I have ordered her to be secured in Fort Royal Harbour until I shall be informed of His Majesty's pleasure relative thereto, and have given orders to all ships under my command to take, sink, burn, and destroy all ships belonging to His Catholic Majesty or his subjects.

Most of the ships that have been seized in the ports of this island are British property and have been claimed by the owners, only there is one remarkably fine vessel, quite new, mounting 16 guns, which will make an excellent cruiser, and is fit for a man of war sloop. I shall hire and man her until I know their Lordships' pleasure. But should be glad they would order her to be bought and commissioned as she by far exceeds any man of war sloops in these seas, and I shall discharge all the other hired armed vessels upon the expedition being over.

865. *To Clevland*

[TNA, ADM 1/307, f. 443]

Marlborough
St. Pierre Road, Martinique
1 March 1762

Sir,

I have this moment received an express from Captain Hervey that the island of St. Lucia is surrendered at discretion.

---

[1] George Gray, colonel of the 61st Regiment of Foot.
[2] A term originally used to describe a Spanish treasure galleon, but by the mid 18th century it was used by the British to denote any large and valuable Spanish vessel.

866. *To Clevland*

[TNA, ADM 1/307, f. 446]
Marlborough
St. John's Road, Antigua
24 March 1762

Sir,

Having ordered Captain Hervey in the *Dragon*, with the *Norwich*, *Penzance*, *Dover*, *Levant*, and *Basilisk*, to repair to the island of St. Lucia and summon the governor thereof to surrender the said island with its forts and garrisons to His Britannic Majesty, which if immediately complied with, he was to allow the troops of His Most Christian Majesty to be transported to France, but that I expected all the inhabitants should surrender at discretion and submit themselves to His Majesty's pleasure.

On the 26th of February Captain Hervey having summoned Mons. Longueville, governor of the said island, to surrender, and the inhabitants refusing to take arms in its defence, he thought proper to accept of the terms offered, and immediately capitulated for himself, and the troops to be sent to France, and the island surrendered at discretion. The ships immediately entered the harbour and took possession of all the forts and batteries, which were remarkably strong, had forty pieces of cannon mounted, and were capable of making a long defence.

The inhabitants are all disarmed, and I most sincerely congratulate their Lordships on His Majesty being in peaceable possession of an island, near sixty miles long, twenty broad, and abounding in good ports.

I likewise most sincerely congratulate them on the conquest of the most important island of Grenada which surrendered without opposition on the fifth instant to Commodore Swanton and Brigadier [Robert] Walch, upon the same terms as those granted to Martinique. Its port is very safe during the hurricane months and the citadel, which commands it, remarkably strong.

Enclosed I have the honour to transmit to their Lordships plans of the ports of Grenada and St. Lucia.[1]

[1] Not enclosed.

867. *To Clevland*

[TNA, ADM 1/307, ff. 450–2] *Marlborough*
St. John's Road, Antigua
24 March 1762

Sir,
I hope my last dispatches sent express by the *Zephyr* on the first of March, giving an account of the total reduction of Martinique, arrived safe. And must desire you will please to acquaint their Lordships that on the fifth instant arrived at St. Pierre's Road, Martinique, His Majesty's frigate *Sardoine*, with their Lordships' dispatches [No. 856] of the 26th December, commanding me to commence hostilities against the King of Spain and his subjects. On the same day likewise joined me the *Cygnet*, dispatched from Gibraltar (by Vice Admiral Saunders)[1] with the same orders, and the *Aquilon* sent express by Captain [Richard] Spry, on the 24th January, from off Brest, giving me an account that the French squadron, consisting of seven sail of the line and five frigates, with 2000 troops on board, had escaped from Brest on the 23rd of the same month.

As I made no doubt but they were destined to these parts, I immediately repeated my orders to all the frigates stationed to windward along the whole chain of the Caribbean islands to be very vigilant in keeping a good look out, that I might have timely notice of the enemy's approach. And as there was a real uncertainty at which of the islands the enemy would first touch for intelligence, I immediately gave Mr. Swanton (who with seven sail of the line, two bombs, and three frigates was blocking up the island of Grenada) notice of their approach and positive orders to attack them, if they appeared on his station. In which case he would certainly be joined by the *Falkland* and *Actæon*, who were cruising to windward of the said island, on purpose to look out for the enemy's squadron. I have likewise gave directions to Mr. Swanton (in case the said island had surrendered), to join me without a moment's loss of time with five sail of the line, the better to enable me to make two squadrons sufficiently strong to engage the enemy, should they appear either to the northward or to the southward of Martinique.

I likewise immediately withdrew the squadron employed in the reduction of St. Lucia, (whose inhabitants were all disarmed) and held myself in constant readiness to put to sea the moment I should receive any intelligence of the enemy.

[19]Vice-admiral Sir Charles Saunders, Commander-in-chief in the Mediterranean.

On the ninth instant about four o'clock in the afternoon the *Woolwich* and *Aquilon* appeared off the Pearl Rock, and made the signal of seeing the enemy; on which I instantly made the signal for the squadron under my command, consisting of six ships of the line and two frigates of forty guns, and got under sail. But it proving calm Captain Ogle and Captain Bayne of the *Aquilon* and *Woolwich* came on board me, the latter of whom acquainted me that at 8 o'clock that morning, being off Trinity, he had discovered thirteen sail of ships, eight of which were of the line, that they were standing to the southward, and were about five leagues to windward of the island.

I immediately made all the sail possible in quest of the enemy, and went round the island, but had not the good fortune to get sight of them, they having made all the sail possible for St. Domingo on hearing the island of Martinique was taken, as I learned afterwards by intelligence I received from Guadeloupe from which island they had been discovered steering west with all the sail they could crowd.

As it was impossible to intercept the enemy before their arrival at St. Domingo, I have not lost a moment's time in victualling and watering, and getting every ship ready with the utmost dispatch, in order to succour the island of Jamaica, having received an express from the governor and council of that island, as likewise from Captain Forrest, senior officer of His Majesty's ships employed on that station, that His Majesty's said island of Jamaica was under imminent danger and was certainly to be attacked by the united forces of France and Spain (as appeared by authentic copies of intercepted letters) wherein M. Belsunce[1] and St. Croix[2] are mentioned as intended to command that expedition, and which are now made more authentic by those officers being on board the French squadron, and requesting that Mr Monckton and myself would endeavour to prevent the said island from falling into the enemy's hands by sending them speedy and timely succours.

Immediately on the receipt of the said express, I laid the governor's letter before Mr. Monckton and proposed his having a considerable body of troops ready to embark for the relief of Jamaica, the moment we should receive intelligence that the Brest squadron had passed these seas, acquainting him at the same time that I certainly should assist them with all the naval force that could possibly be spared from the immediate protection of His Majesty's Caribbean Islands. I have again solicited the General for a body of troops since the enemy left these seas. And must do Mr. Monckton the justice to say that he seems much concerned at the

---

[1] Lieutenant General Marquis de Belsunce.
[1] Chevalier de St. Croix, the former French governor of Belle Isle.

present distress of Jamaica, but does not think himself sufficiently authorised to detach a body of troops without orders from England.

I flatter myself their Lordships will not be displeased with me, if I take the liberty to construe my instructions in such a manner as to think myself authorised and obliged to succour any of His Majesty's colonies that may be in danger.

And shall therefore without a moment's loss of time hasten to the succour of Jamaica with ten sail of the line, four frigates, and three bombs. I shall think myself happy if their Lordships approve the step I have taken in hastening to the relief of Jamaica and can assure them I have no other view in going there, but His Majesty's service, and propose (unless I receive orders to the contrary) to return to my station at the Leeward Islands, on the approach of the hurricane months, leaving such a force at Jamaica as shall then appear necessary for the protection of that island.

868. *To Clevland*

[TNA, ADM 1/307, f. 454]

Marlborough
St. Christopher's
26 March 1762

Sir,

Having acquainted you in my letter [No. 867] of the 24th from St. John's Road, Antigua, that I should hasten with the utmost dispatch to the assistance of Jamaica, I put to sea with the squadron under my command accordingly. And off this island, received their Lordship's dispatches [No. 858] of the 5th February by the *Richmond*, Captain [John] Elphinston, and as I am thereby strictly commanded, to desist from any enterprise I might have in hand, and that it was indispensably necessary that all other operations should yield to this one object of the secret expedition under the command of Sir George Pocock and Lord Albemarle, I shall hasten with the utmost dispatch to put their Lordships' said orders into execution, and beg you will assure them that every thing shall be ready to proceed at a moment's warning.

I have already dispatched a frigate to Barbados, acquainting Sir George Pocock, that the most proper place in all these parts of the West Indies for a rendezvous is Fort Royal Bay, Martinique.

I shall instantly dispatch ten sail of the line to Jamaica, which with the number already there, will make seventeen sail of the line and thirteen frigates. A force, I hope, sufficient to protect that island from any insult.

I have likewise given Sir James Douglas orders on his arrival at Jamaica, to dispatch his best sailing frigate to Martinique with all the intelligence he can possibly procure for Sir George Pocock's information, giving the captain the strictest orders to keep in the proper track of ships going down from Martinique to Jamaica; and likewise to have two other frigates, cruising in the same track, and to windward in order to meet Sir George Pocock in his passage down.

As I have acted to the best of my judgement in the steps I have taken, I hope it will meet with their Lordships' approbation.

869. *From Stephens*

[TNA, ADM 2/533, pp. 222–3] 5 April 1762

Sir,

I have received and communicated to my Lords Commissioners of the Admiralty your letters of the 19th of January [No. 857], 10th [No. 861] and 28th [No. 864] of February, and 1st of March, giving an account of the important conquest of the islands of Martinique and St. Lucia. And it is with great pleasure I receive their Lordships' commands to acquaint you with their entire approbation of your conduct and the great satisfaction they have received in the behaviour of the squadron under your command in the reduction of those islands.

I send this by the packet, being unwilling to withold from you one moment their Lordships' sentiments upon this happy event, and shall send you a more particular answer [No. 871] to your several letters above mentioned by the convoy which will sail with the West India trade from Spithead about a fortnight hence.

870. *To Clevland*

[TNA, ADM 1/307, f. 456] Martinique
10 April 1762

Sir,

With greatest pleasure I have the honour to congratulate their Lordships on the entire conquest of all the French Caribbean Islands, the inhabitants of St. Vincents having sent their deputies imploring His Majesty's protection and humbly submitting themselves to his mercy.

I take this opportunity to beg Sir, you will please to lay before their Lordships, my most humble thanks for the great honour they have done me, by appointing and supporting me in so conspicuous a command, whereby they made me the happy instrument in executing their orders to gain such signal advantages to the nation.

871. From Clevland

[TNA, ADM 2/533, pp. 343–4] 30 April 1762

Sir,

I have received your several letters of the 19th of January [No. 857], 10th [No. 861] and 28th [No. 864] of February and 1st, 24th [Nos. 866, 867] and 26th [No. 868] of last month, with the papers enclosed therein, giving an account of the success of His Majesty's arms, in the reduction of the islands of Martinique, St. Lucia, and Grenada, all which as they came to hand, I communicated to my Lords Commissioners of the Admiralty.

It is with a singular satisfaction I received their Lordships commands to acquaint you that your proceedings have met with the King's entire approbation, and that the harmony subsisting between the fleet and the army has added greatly to His Majesty's satisfaction in the courage and conduct of both. Their Lordships command me to congratulate you, in their name, on the importance of your conquest and you cannot doubt but your behaviour which has received His Majesty's particular approbation, must be equally satisfactory and pleasing to their Lordships.

Captains Walsingham and Darby whom you sent home with your letters on this occasion, not being in a state of health fit to return to their ships, their Lordships have removed Captain Hollwell from the *Marlborough* into the *Modeste*, and appointed Captain Shuldham to the *Marlborough* in his room, which they make no doubt will be agreeable to you, as you had before given them orders to command those ships. Their commissions you will receive herewith, by Captain [Richard] Bickerton, whom their Lordships have sent out to command the *Devonshire* in the room of Captain Darby.

Captain [John] Botterell being preferred to command of the *Success* at home, their Lordships leave it to you to fill up the vacancy in the sloop he commanded as they also do that in the *Stag*, in the room of Captain [Henry] Angel, whom you permitted to resign on account of his bad health. Whatever vacancies may be occasioned by these removals, you will please to fill up. And the Lordships command me to acquaint you, they will confirm your appointments.

When the several services enjoined by your instructions shall be performed, it is their Lordships' directions that you send home as convoys, those ships that shall be in the worst condition and unfit to remain abroad, and they will be replaced by other from hence as occasion shall require.

872. *To Clevland*

[TNA, ADM 1/307, f. 457] *Rochester*
Martinique
7 May 1762

Sir,
I must desire you will please to acquaint their Lordships that Mr Alexander Brown, lieutenant of marines on board the *Lizard*, was sent on shore at Barbados by an order from Sir James Douglas at the request of the governor and legislature of that island, to discipline a regiment of volunteers raised by them (to be employed in conjunction with His Majesty's forces in the reduction of the island of Martinique), which he effected with indefatigable assiduity and pains, and afterwards commanded them as major commandant during the whole time the operations were carrying on against that island, greatly to the satisfaction of General Monckton. In consequence of whose recommendations and those of the governor and legislature of Barbados, joined to his having now no proper ship, (it having been necessary for the service to order another officer in his room on board the *Lizard*). I have given him permission to go to England, and must beg leave to represent him to their Lordships as having behaved during the whole of this affair in a manner deserving their notice, and of this recommendation which I think myself obliged to make to their Lordships in his favour.

873. *To Clevland*

[TNA, ADM 1/307, f. 460] *Rochester* at St. Pierre
8 May 1762

Sir,
Lieutenant [George] Farmer who came out of England recommended to be one of my lieutenants, not caring to stay till vacancies happen, has requested leave to return to England, to which I can make no objection as he is a half pay officer, and takes the opportunity of returning in a cartel ship, which is charged to land Monsieur Rouillé and one hundred and thirty French men, late inhabitants of this island, at Le Havre de Grace. I have not the least objection to Mr. Farmer and it is at his own request that he returns.

874. To Clevland

[TNA, ADM 1/307, f. 458] *Rochester* at St. Pierre
8 May 1762

Sir,
I take this opportunity by Lieutenant Farmer (who goes to England in a transport that carries Monsieur Rouillé, late governor of Martinique to Havre de Grace) to acquaint their Lordships that Sir George Pocock and Lord Albemarle sailed from hence on the 6th instant with everything complete for their intended expedition. As a letter by this conveyance may not be the securest I shall only say that every island now owns His Majesty for their sovereign, St. Vincent having made their submission and surrendered at discretion, a full account of which their Lordships shall have by a safer conveyance.

875. To Clevland

[TNA, ADM 1/307, f. 462] *Rochester*
St. Pierre Road, Martinique
19 May 1762

Sir,
Yesterday the packet arrived here from England by which I was favoured with your letter of the 3rd of April.[1]

I beg Sir you will please to present my humblest respects to their Lordships, acquainting them at the same time, that I shall ever esteem their approbation of my conduct, as the greatest honour I can possibly receive.

I must likewise, Sir take this opportunity to return you many thanks for the most obliging manner in which you were pleased to transmit their Lordships' commands.

---

[1]Apparently No. 868 which is dated 5 April.

876. *To Clevland*

[TNA, ADM 1/307, ff. 464–7]

Rochester
St. Pierre, Martinique
27 May 1762

Sir,

Having acquainted their Lordships in my letter [No. 867] of the 26th of March from St. Christopher's that I should hasten with the utmost dispatch to execute their orders, and get everything in readiness against the arrival of Sir George Pocock and Lord Albemarle in these seas.

Immediately on Sir James Douglas' sailing, with the squadron under his command for Jamaica, I made all the haste possible to Martinique, where I had got the transports ready, and the troops embarked several days before the arrival of the squadron from England. But as many of the remaining transports wanted much repair, it was impossible to dispatch the sixteen hundred ton ordered by their Lordships to Jamaica, till the whole was surveyed and I had an exact account of the spare tonnage remaining fit for service. Nevertheless, I ordered two very large transports that were at St. Christopher amounting to seven hundred ton, to proceed directly with Sir James Douglas.

When I had got everything ready and had embarked all such troops as General Monckton thought proper should be sent with Lord Albemarle, I had the misfortune to be taken extremely ill with a bilious fever, and was obliged to be carried on shore to St. Pierres, which prevented me from paying my respects to Sir George Pocock during his stay at Cas des Navières where he arrived with the forces from England on the 26th of April.

My Lord Albemarle having found it necessary to make several alterations relative to the distribution of the troops already embarked, and sending for others from Dominica, these operations together with fitting many of the spare transports for horses, loading others with fascines, and watering the fleet &c. detained them till the 6th of May when Sir George Pocock sailed from hence with the men of war and transports under his command and proposed calling off St. Christophers for the *Edgar* and the Jamaica convoy, which were detained there by order, and the *Culloden* and *Echo* who were there with the transports of Negroes supplied by the islands for the service of the expedition; the former having been detained by defects in her lower masts which had been repaired and she was ready to sail before Sir George's arrival at St. Christophers.

As I had dispatched with Sir James Douglas ten sail of the line (including the *Culloden*) the number commanded by their Lordships orders to be ready, and intending to send the *Marlborough* home with the second convoy, I reserved only the *Foudroyant* (on board which ship I intended to hoist my flag) the *Vanguard*, and *Modeste* the condition of the three fifty gun ships rendering it necessary for them to return to England this season, by which their Lordships will perceive that only three ships of the line would remain upon this station.

Sir George Pocock thought it absolutely necessary for His Majesty's service to take the *Marlborough* with him, removing my captain and officers into the *Rochester* and the *Falkland*, and appointing Captain [Thomas] Burnet to command the *Marlborough*. And as the carrying on His Majesty's service with success so much depends upon the commander in chief having those officers about him whom he most approves, I intend hoisting my flag on board the *Foudroyant* the moment she joins me, taking Captain Shuldham with me into the said ship, removing Captain [Robert] Duff into the *Modeste*, and Captain Hollwall into the *Rochester*, which I flatter myself their Lordships will approve, more especially as it is agreeable to their seniority.

The *Alarm* with the convoy from Cork arrived here the 12th instant, having taken a French ship bound from Marseilles to St. Domingo on her passage.

The *Orford* and *Edgar* arrived at Barbados the 9th instant with the convoy from England, the latter having taken a transport from Bordeaux, with the intendant, his lady, the commandant of the troops, and one hundred and sixty soldiers, bound to Louisania being part of the regiment commanded by Count De Fremeur.

I have likewise the pleasure to acquaint their Lordships that another of the said transports with two hundred troops on board belonging to the same regiment has been taken by His Majesty's ship the *Falkland*; and as the troops are a great expense to His Majesty, and the governor and inhabitants of Barbados have made strong remonstrances against their remaining on that island, I hope their Lordships will approve of my intention to send the officers and troops to France agreeable to the cartel settled by the two nations; as I shall take particular care to have them convoyed to such a distance as to put it out of their power to carry the ship anywhere but to France.

As the first convoy will sail from St. Christopher's for Europe on the 6th of June, under the protection of His Majesty's ships *Norwich* and *Actæon*, both of which ships are represented to me by the builder and officers at English Harbour, to be in so very bad a condition as to render it absolutely necessary that they should take advantage of this season to return to England, I shall by the said ships transmit to their Lordships an exact state and condition of the squadron I have the honour to command in these seas.

I have received certain intelligence that the French squadron arrived at the Cape[1] on the 15th March, that the *Hector* of 74 guns was lost upon the rocks at the entrance of the port, and many of her people perished; another of their line of battle ships was likewise on shore and was obliged to cut all her masts away.

I take the opportunity to send this letter by a privateer of force belonging to Liverpool, and in charge of Captain Benson belonging to the army, who takes his passage on her.

877. *To Clevland*[2]

[TNA, ADM 1/307, ff 471–3]

Rochester
St. Pierre Road, Martinique
31 May 1762

Sir,

As Major General Monckton is sailed in His Majesty's ship the *Lizard* for his government of New York, and has left Brigadier General [William] Rufane, commander in chief of His Majesty's troops remaining in this island, whose numbers are scarce sufficient to garrison it, and in all probability will be considerable diminished in the rainy season, I therefore propose to take the marines from those ships bound to Europe in order to strengthen the said garrison (if necessary) which I hope their Lordships will approve; more especially as the islands of St. Luica and St. Vincent have no garrison; neither can any troops be spared from this place for that service.

Their Lordships will best judge what number of ships will be sufficient to guard the extensive tract of islands now belonging to His Majesty, and as I have already experienced their very great attention towards the completion of these conquests, I have not the least reason to doubt but they will (when more material affairs do not interfere) continue to support me in such a manner as may enable me, not only to defend and protect all these islands against any power whatever, but likewise to annoy His Majesty's enemies on their own coasts, which I shall take every opportunity of doing with the squadron now remaining under my command.

[1]Cape François.
[2]The first nine paragraphs of this letter have been omitted being the same as in No. 876.

The Spaniards continue very quiet in their ports, seem afraid to venture out, and by the best intelligence I can gain have armed only one privateer from Puerto Rico, who has very narrowly escaped my cruisers, and is drove out of these seas.

Mr. Swanton has rejoined me from the Spanish Main, where I had sent him to cruise for some time, but without success. And as I constantly keep a rotation of frigates round the Caribbean Islands and down the enemy's coast, I believe it will be difficult for their ships coming to these seas, to escape the vigilance of the cruisers or the inhabitants to receive any succours from Europe.

The *Marlborough* in her return from St. Christopher's, took, off St. Lucia, a French ship from Bordeaux bound to Louisiana. The *Modeste* on the 27th April off Tobago took a Spanish ship from St. Sebastian bound to Carthagena. The *Foudroyant*, a French ship from Marseilles bound to St. Dominigo. And enclosed I have the honour to transmit to their Lordships a list of all ships and vessels taken at or brought into Martinique since I have commanded in these seas; and shall likewise transmit to them a list of the captures carried into the other islands the moment I receive a return from the agents.

I must beg you will please to acquaint their Lordships, that His Majesty's order in council of the 25th of March 1761, relative to the prisoners of war being under the direction of the commanding sea officer has not as yet been transmitted to the governors of Barbados and the Leeward Islands.

878. *To Clevland*

[TNA, ADM 1/307, ff.474–5]   *Rochester*
                                     St. Pierre Road, Martinique
                                               31 May 1762

Sir,

I must desire you will please to acquaint their Lordships, that upon the division of the squadron under my command and the dispatching so many ships to Jamaica, I found it necessary to fill up the vacancies in the commands of the respective ships. In order to prevent confusion, and at the earnest request of all the captains concerned, all the removes being made at their own desire, and each satisfied with the ship he was appointed to. All of them being told my reasons for granting commissions and referring them to their Lordships' pleasure for their approbation.

Your letter [No. 862] of the 19th February by the *Orford* signifying their Lordships' pleasure, relative to Captain Nott's returning to the

Antigua, was prevented from being put into execution, by the *Rose's* arrival at Martinique, the very day with Sir George Pocock, who dispatched Captain Nott instantly to Jamaica before I knew of his arrival, and Lieutenant Shuldham late captain of the *Antigua* having changed command with Captain Douglas of the *Sardoine*, and being gone with my express to England with an account of the conquest of the Grenades.

I am sure it was not their Lordships' intention that any of my officers should suffer for the steps taken by Sir James Douglas during his command, and as many removes were made at the request of the respective captains, and the *Echo* during the course of the expedition having had several commanders. On the arrival of Captain Lendrick with their Lordships' commission to command the said ship, Captain [John] Boyd was superceded, and as the ship he lately commanded was gone to Jamaica he returns to England by the convoy.

As he was remarkably active and diligent during the whole expedition, is a brave and good officer, I think it a duty incumbent upon me, in justice to him, to recommend him as such to their Lordships favour.

As I have no view on the commissions I have granted, but the public service, and all removes having been agreeable to seniority, I hope to be honoured with their Lordships' approbation as I am sure whatever their pleasure is relative to the officers appointed, will be most agreeable to me.

Enclosed[1] I send their Lordships a particular list of the appointments, removes, and exchanges hitherto made in the fleet under my command.

879. *To Newcastle*

[BL, Add. MSS 32939, ff. 134–5] Martinique
1 June 1762

My Lord,

I take the opportunity by the convoy bound to England, most sincerely to congratulate your Grace on His Majesty being in the entire possession of all the French Caribbean and Neutral Islands (not one excepted). And as I am sure no person whatever more sincerely rejoices at the success of His Majesty's arms than your Grace, I have the pleasure to acquaint you that Sir George Pocock and Lord Albemarle sailed from hence on the 6th of May, and I make no doubt but they are arrived at the place of their destination by this time, and have convinced

---

[1] Not enclosed.

the Spaniards that His Majesty's arms will conquer wherever they appear.

I must beg your Grace will still continue me in your favour and protection and believe me to be with the greatest respect.

880. To Clevland

[TNA, ADM 1/307, f. 476]
Rochester
St. Pierre Road, Martinique
1 June 1762

Sir,

You will please to inform their Lordships that since my dispatches [Nos. 877, 878] of yesterday, I have had information of the death of Captain [Roger] Williams of His Majesty's ship *Crescent*, to whom I shall appoint Captain [Robert] Brice the senior master and commander on this station, and supply the vacancy occasioned thereby on board the *Guadeloupe* by the appointment of Lieutenant [James] Dalrymple, at present my first lieutenant, in his room.

I ought before this time to have informed their Lordships that the inhabitants of the island of Tobago (which indeed consist only of Indians) have some time since made their submission and possession has been taken of the island in the name of His Majesty.

881. To Captain Robert Duff

[TNA, ADM 1/307, ff. 480–1]
Rochester
St. Pierre Road
3 June 1762

Sir,

It having been judged absolutely necessary for His Majesty's service that the *Marlborough*, (on board which ship I had my flag), should proceed with Sir George Pocock on the secret expedition, I am under the necessity to make choice of the *Foudroyant*, that ship being the most proper of any remaining in these seas for a flag officer commanding in chief.

And though my Lord Anson told me in conversation that he expected I should hoist my flag on board the said ship, which supposition was very natural from her being the ship of the greatest force of all those I had the honour to command. Yet I never intended to remove into her while the *Marlborough* was in a condition to remain in the

West Indies, purely out of the personal regard I had for you, who had expressed your very great dislike to be an admiral's captain upon my mentioning to you the intention of the Admiralty at our first arrival in these seas: to which you was pleased to add that you was too old an officer to be an admiral's captain and had any admiral whatever in England hoisted his flag on board the *Foudroyant*, you would have commanded her no longer than until an express could have gone to the Admiralty.

This open declaration of yours made me conclude that whenever His Majesty's service made it necessary for me to remove into the *Foudroyant*, I could not flatter myself of it's being agreeable to you to remain in that ship as my captain. I had therefore provided myself with a captain willing and desirous to go with me in whatever ship I should be looked upon as destined for me and my officers.

And agreeable to the custom practised by all flag officers in foreign parts and generally indulged to them by the Admiralty at home, I shall appoint Captain Shuldham to command the *Foudroyant*, on board which ship I shall continue to have my flag during the time I command in these seas. Not from the least disregard to Captain Duff who I know to be as deserving an officer as any in the navy, and for whom I have the highest esteem and regard, but from the declaration you was pleased to make to me at Barbados and having it in my power to offer you the *Modeste*; a ship of equal rate (though not of equal force) with the *Foudroyant*, which ship would be ready to proceed to sea in a few days in order to cruise against His Majesty's enemies and into which you might remove what officers and followers you thought proper while the *Foudroyant*, by your account delivered to me, can be in no condition to cruise or proceed to sea, until her powder room is raised and the leak that damaged the powder has been examined into.

Judge, Sir, how much I was surprised this morning at the warmth where with you expressed your unwillingness to command the *Modeste*, declaring to me that you would except no commission whatever, to command any ship in these seas, but that granted you by the Admiralty to command the *Foudroyant* desiring to remain my captain in her. A declaration so repugnant to the conversation that passed between us on our first arrival in these seas, much astonishes me, as it is impossible you could serve with any satisfaction to yourself after the declaration you had made.

I shall therefore proceed agreeable to the known custom of the service to appoint my captain and officers into the *Foudroyant*, and shall cause a commission to be made out for you to command the *Modeste* and for such officers you may choose to take with you.

But if you persist in your determination not to command the *Modeste* and as I have all the deference imaginable for your services to the public, which I acknowledge to be great, I am glad [I] have it in my power to make you another offer (which nothing but the personal regard I bear you should induce me to) of commanding the *Falkland* bound home with the July convoy.

I therefore hope you will think coolly and deliberately before you finally resolve upon declining to accept a commission and give a real friend leave to tell you, that when you dispassionately reflect upon the occasion that has made these removes necessary, you will own it has always been the custom of the commanders in chief to take with them all their officers and if you think yourself injured, it is better you should return to England as commander of one of His Majesty's ships, than as a passenger as you will have same opportunity and with a better grace may lay your complaints before the Admiralty who are ever ready to redress real grievances, which I cannot look upon yours to be.

You will therefore, sir, let me have your answer tomorrow morning, as I shall no longer defer making those removes I think necessary for His Majesty's service. And unless I had had a particular regard for you, I should not have condescended to have given you my reasons for the steps I think proper to take on this occasion.

882. *From Duff*

[TNA, ADM 1/307, f. 479]

Foudroyant
St. Pierre Road
4 June 1762

Sir,

In your letter [No. 881] of yesterdays date, (with which I am honoured), you are pleased to acquaint me that by the *Marlborough* being carried on the secret expedition by Sir George Pocock, you are under the necessity of hoisting your flag on board the *Foudroyant* and that from my expressing a great dislike to be an admiral's captain at your first arrival in these seas, you conclude it will not be agreeable to me to serve as your captain. What I said to Admiral Rodney then, I again repeat, that was I in England, I would not serve any longer as an admiral's captain than an express could go to the Admiralty and return, being well convinced from the justice of the Lords Commissioners of the Admiralty (which I have been so happy as to experience) and the gracious manner they were pleased to honour me with the command of the *Foudroyant*, that if they judged it necessary for the service to make her a flag ship they would appoint me to command another ship equally as good as the *Foudroyant*.

But however disagreeable and inconvenient it may be to me to serve as an admiral's captain, I have the honour to acquaint Admiral Rodney, that, as captain of the *Foudroyant*, I am on all occasions ready to accomodate the service, and as ready to obey any orders he may please to send me with his flag, but that I cannot accept of a commission from Admiral Rodney, for any other ship, as there is none here under his command equal to the ship which their Lordships did me the honour to appoint me.

I cannot conclude without returning Admiral Rodney my thanks for the high opinion he is pleased to express of me as an officer, and assuring him, it would give me the greatest concern to be laid under the necessity to complain of one who does me such much honour and has always professed a sincere regard for me.

883. *From the Lords of the Admiralty*

[TNA, ADM 2/88, p. 320]　　　　　　　　　　　　　　　　　10 June 1762

Whereas the merchants trading to the Leeward Islands have represented to us that the considerable increase of that trade, by the acquisition of Martinique and its dependencies, and the backwardness of the crops, owing to the siege, renders it of great consequence that another convoy should be appointed after that of the 26th of July, and that the most convenient time for the said additional convoy to sail for Europe will be about the middle of October next, you are hereby required and directed to appoint a proper convoy to sail with the trade to Europe at the time the merchants have desired, provided it can be done consistent with the other services entrusted to your care, taking care to give the concerned timely notice of your intention.

884. *To Brigadier Rufane*

[TNA, PRO 30/20/14]　　　　　　　　　　　　　　　　　　　*Foudroyant*
　　　　　　　　　　　　　　　　　　　　　　　St. Pierre Road, Martinique
　　　　　　　　　　　　　　　　　　　　　　　　　　　　19 June 1762

Sir,

My agent having this day laid before me the account of the sale of such captors as have been taken by His Majesty's ships under my command, and sold at this place, I was astonished to find a very considerable sum of money charged, as paid, to a person calling himself a vendue master. As this charge was unusual, I demanded to know what he meant by it. He informed me that he was an officer appointed by Major General Monckton, who had obliged Mr Udney, my agent for the captors, to employ him, and pay him one per cent.

The forcing an agent for the captors to pay such an unreasonable and unjust demand, directly in contradiction to the engagement given by His Majesty and the nation, to the seamen, is but a bad return for the share they had in the reduction of this island, and the laying a duty of one per cent without legal authority of Parliament, would sound but ill at home, and is what I can not submit to, and have therefore ordered the agent to sue the vendue master for such monies belonging to the captors as they have detained in their hands. And I flatter myself you will not suffer any imposition to be laid upon such prizes as may be brought in here, but, that an entire and full liberty may be granted to our agents to employ those who will serve the captors in the best and cheapest manner.

This demand I make, sir, in the name of all the officers and seamen under my command, and in conformity of the Act of Parliament for the Encouragement of Seamen.[1] I make not the least doubt, but you will cause justice to be done in this affair, and remedy the evil I have complained of.

885. *To Clevland*

[TNA, ADM 1/307, ff. 477–8]

Foudroyant
Martinique
1 July 1762

Sir,

It is with concern I am obliged to acquaint their Lordships that Captain Duff has refused to take a commission for the *Modeste*, a ship of equal rate with the *Foudroyant*, or to command the *Falkland* going home with the convoy. The enclosed letters, [Nos. 881, 882] which I beg you will lay before their Lordships, will best explain his reasons for not accepting a commission, and my motive for refusing to accept him as my captain.

I should be sorry their Lordships should think me capable of doing an injustice, to the meanest seamen under my command, much more to an officer of distinguished rank; and as the invariable rule of service

---

[1] 29 Geo. c. 34. An Act for the Encouragement of Seamen, and the more speedy and effectual manning of His Majesty's Navy.

(ever since I have been in the navy) has been observed on this occasion, I flatter myself their Lordships will support me in the dignity of that command they have been pleased to honour me with.

I cannot conclude this letter without acquainting their Lordships that Captain Duff diligently executed the duty of his station during the time he was under my command, and am sorry he has chose to return to England a passenger rather than a command[er] of one of His Majesty's ships. And to convince their Lordships that I desire no vacancies of this sort, I have only given Captain Buckner of His Majesty's sloop *Virgin*, an order to command the *Falkland* home, and Lieutenant [Patrick] Drummond, a very old officer who was lately sent out of England in the *Danae*, an order to command the *Virgin* by which their Lordships will perceive that neither lieutenant nor midshipman belonging to me, has received promotion on this occasion, and Captain [Francis Samuel] Drake late of the *Falkland* choosing to remain in this county is removed into the *Rochester*.

886. *To Anson*

[TNA, PRO 30/20/26/5, ff. 71–9]　　　　　　　　　　　　　　Antigua
　　　　　　　　　　　　　　　　　　　　　　　　　　　　22 July 1762

My Lord,

It was with infinite concern I heard of your Lordship's bad state of health and I most sincerely hope long 'eer this, it is perfectly restored, to have a confirmation of it, will be the most pleasing news that can be brought to me.

As I presume your Lordship will be glad to know the state of the conquered islands, I must acquaint you that everything remains in the same situation as when first taken possession of, there being only a garrison in Martinique and Grenada, the Islands of St. Lucia and St. Vincent remaining as they were inhabited by the French, who lately submitted.

I cannot help again pressing your Lordship that orders may be given relative to the careenage[1] and the ports. Mr. Monckton having thought proper at the instigation of his North America followers to appoint a number of officers, such as naval officers, to the different ports, in direct contradiction to the usage of the English islands, and who think they have nothing to do but impose arbitrary fines upon all merchant ships anchoring in the ports. In short my Lord the whole is a scramble

---

[1] Careening wharf.

who shall cheat His Majesty and the nation most, not one of the persons appointed to office, belonging to the army, or even gentlemen, and so much had these sort of people imposed upon Mr. Monckton's understanding, that during my absence, and when they imagined I had quitted these seas, to protect Jamaica, they had induced him to appoint two of them vendue masters, by commission, with an arbitrary power to sell all such prizes as were brought into Martinique, and to detain one percent of all such prizes. The agent for the naval officers on this station disputing to pay their unjust demand was sent for, to Mr. Monckton, by a file of muskets and threatened to be sent to prison if he dared to sell any of the prizes, in any other manner than through the vendue masters. Thus my Lord, in violation of the Act for the Encouragement of Seamen[1] and directly contrary to the express words of the said act, have the officers and seamen of His Majesty's fleet been obliged to pay a considerable sum by an arbitrary act, imposed upon them by the very person who is most obliged to them for the conquest of Martinique, hard return for the part they had taken in the said conquest.

Your Lordship may be sure I did not submit to this arbitrary proceeding upon my return to Martinique, but as Mr. Monckton was gone before this affair came to my knowledge, I had not an opportunity to point out to him his unlawful proceedings against the navy. I have acquainted [No. 884] the commanding officer left at Martinique that I will not suffer any impositions to be laid on the sea service and that I expect full liberty for my agent to dispose of all captures in such a manner as he shall think most beneficial for the captors. His answer is he found things in such a situation and should continue them as Mr. Monckton left them. The person who was Mr. Monckton's chief adviser in this affair, is one Mr. [Lauchlan] Macklane, an apothecray of New York who is appointed collector of the customs at Martinique, and who during my illness suffered a prodigious quantity of the produce commodities of Martinique to be cleared out for St. Christophers, though he knew it was in plain contradiction to the capitulation, and that such a clearance was only a blind to carry the sugar and coffee to St. Eustatius. The moment I heard of this iniquitous proceeding which, if continued would have deprived England of the benefit of her conquests, and enriched Holland, I sent notice to the custom house and acquainted General Monckton that I insisted upon no clearances being allowed to any ship or vessel whatever loaded with commodities of the Conquered

---

[1] 29 Geo. II c. 34. An Act for the Encouragement of Seamen, and the more effectual manning of His Majesty's Navy.

Islands bound to any place but Great Britain, agreeable to the spirit and intention of the capitulation, and that I had given orders to the captains of the ships under my command to seize all vessels cleared out for any other place till His Majesty's pleasure was known.[1]

887. *To Clevland*

[TNA, ADM 1/307, f. 484] Antigua
22 July 1762

Sir,
Captain [Lucius] O'Brien's ill state of health obliging him to change into the *Woolwich* going home with the convoy. It would be doing him the greatest injustice if I did not take this opportunity to acquaint their Lordships, that his indefatigable industry in getting the cannon up the mountains during the attack on Martinique on which service he had the chief command during the whole operations, and the continued service he has since been employed on, has been the occasion of his sickness, and I beg leave to recommend him to their Lordships as an officer conspicuously active on all the services he has been employed and worthy [of] their Lordships' favour and protection.

888. *To Clevland*

[TNA, ADM 1/307, ff. 486–7] *Foudroyant*
Antigua
23 July 1762

Sir,
I have been favoured with your letter of the 30th of April by His Majesty's ship *Danae,* who arrived at Martinique on the 22nd of June, and proceeded directly with the convoy for the other islands and Jamaica.

You may be sure, Sir, it was with the highest satisfaction that I received His Majesty's and their Lordships' approbation [No. 871] of my conduct, and with my humblest thanks to their Lordships, I beg you will assure them that I shall endeavour to deserve the honour they have done me, by a steady adherence in strictly obeying their commands.

Settling the affairs in the island of Martinique and my late illness detained me there a considerable time, but as every thing now is in

---

[1] The last pages of this letter are missing.

perfect tranquillity, none remaining but those who have taken the oath of allegiance, and submitted to His Majesty's government, I thought it necessary to visit His Majesty's yard in this island, in order to hasten the fitting of such ships as were in English Harbour, and to enquire into the cause of the delay in refitting them. Accordingly on my arrival here, I found the *Woolwich* condemned as unserviceable to remain in these seas any longer, and fitting to proceed with the convoy on the 26th instant. The *Repulse* and *Stag*, who had been here near two months, almost ready for sea, but half their ship's companies sick on shore with the yellow fever. However, since my being here a sufficient number have recovered, and both ships are gone to sea. The *Virgin* who I had sent in two months ago for a new bottom, remained in the same situation as when she came into the harbour. As such a vessel is the most proper to go in quest of the enemy's small privateers, I have ordered her to be refitted with the utmost dispatch, and hope in a few days to get her to sea.

I think it my indispensable duty to represent to their Lordships how very detrimental it is to His Majesty's service, to refit all the ships in English Harbour, the time they take in going from Martinique to Antigua, being almost sufficient to careen them at the former island, whose careenage is capable to receive ships of the greatest draft of water, which might be hove down by their own guns and at a cheap a rate, as a frigate can be in English Harbour, more especially as it will be done under the eye of the commanding officer, whose principal rendezvous it must be, owing to the goodness of its port, and the happy situation of the island, which is the centre of all the Caribbean, and from whence His Majesty's ships can with much greater ease protect all the islands to the southward or northward, than can be done from Antigua, which is at the northern extreme of all the Caribbean, and without wood or water. I have therefore given directions that two sets of out riggers[1] be forthwith sent to Martinique, in order to careen such large ships as may be in want thereof; and hope their Lordships will please to give directions that a storeship with a large quantity of cordage, sails and topmasts be sent to Fort Royal, which will be a very great saving to His Majesty, as I shall be a check upon the issuing the stores, and prevent a very considerable sum being expended by the storekeeper in purchasing cordage, which I find has been a constant practice at English Harbour, owing to the impossibility of the commanding officer being constantly at that island to be a check upon him, and the other officers of His Majesty's yard.

---

[1] The projecting beams rigged on the sides of a ship to which additional shrouds are attached for the support of the masts when the vessel is careened.

As His Majesty's ships *Woolwich*, *Falkland*, and *Crescent* will sail on the 26th instant from St. Christophers with the convoy for England, their Lordships will perceive the number of ships remaining with me for the protection of this great range of islands; and as Sir George Pocock thought proper to take the *Barbadoes* and *Caesar* hired armed sloop with him, and the *Virgin* having been unserviceable for more than two months' past, I have been under the necessity to hire into His Majesty's service two vessels armed with fourteen guns each, and manned from His Majesty's ships on this station, in order to cruise against the enemy's small privateers, who have lately very much infested the islands lately conquered, and being well acquainted with every creek, can with ease elude the vigilance of the large frigates. However, since these vessels have been taken into His Majesty's service, two of the enemy's privateers have been destroyed and the islands protected from the insolence of the others.

Since their Lordships' orders signified to me, relative to the protection of the Virgin Islands, agreeable to the petition of the merchants at Liverpool, two small frigates have been constantly cruising for the protection of those islands, and one large frigate off the east end of Puerto Rico, in order to intercept the enemy's privateers fitted out from that island, as likewise to be a check upon such as take shelter in the Danish island of St. Thomas, whose governor, not only permits them to sell what few prizes they take and carry into that island, without condemnation, but likewise permits them to careen and be supplied with military stores in order to cruise against His Majesty's subjects. This I thought proper their Lordships should be acquainted with, as I have wrote to the governor on that head, who has not vouchsafed to return me an answer.

889. From Clevland

[TNA, ADM 2/534, p. 152]   28 July 1762

Sir,

I have received and communicated to my Lords Commissioners of the Admiralty your letter [No. 875] of 19th of May last, owning the receipt of mine[1] of the 3rd of April, wherein I signified to you their Lordships' entire approbation of your conduct. I think myself happy in having conveyed to you so agreeable an information.

---

[1] Cf. No. 869.

890. *From Clevland*

[TNA, ADM 2/534, p. 159]   30 July 1762

Sir,

I have received and communicated to my Lords Commissioners of the Admiralty your letter [No. 877] of the 31st of May last, enclosing a list of officers appointed, removed, and exchanged by you, during the time you have commanded at Martinique.

891. *From Colonel Gedney Clarke*

[TNA, ADM 1/307, f. 490]   Barbados
30 August 1762

Sir,

According to your and General Monckton's desire, I hired and fitted out four vessels, which I sent over to Orinoco, under convoy of the *Barbados* sloop of war, for live cattle for the use of His Majesty's army and navy.

When they arrived there, war was declared between Great Britain and Spain, so that they were glad to come away without a single bullock.

Enclosed are the charges and expenses on the said voyage, sworn before the governor of this island, which amounts to seven hundred and fifty seven pounds five shillings sterling.

As it was not owing to any neglect or fault in me that we were thus disappointed, I hope Sir, you will not let me suffer, but that you will be pleased to order me to be reimbursed and paid.

892. *To Clevland*

[TNA, ADM 1/307, ff. 494–5]   Barbados
24 September 1762

Sir,

I must desire you will please to acquaint their Lordships that on the fleet and army rendezvousing at Barbados in order to proceed on their operations against the French islands; with a view to the preservation of the health of the seamen on board His Majesty's ships under my command, I made it my business to enquire if fresh provisions could not possibly be procured from the Spanish Main. And General Monckton actuated by the same principle for the army under his command joined with me in the enquiry.

Colonel Clarke of this island from public spirited motive of forwarding the service and preserving the lives of the sailors and soldiers employed on the expedition, undertook the affair, hired, equipped, and sent out several vessels under convoy of a sloop of war I had appointed to sail with them for better effecting their beneficial attempt; which from the prudent steps that were taken would have been soon accomplished, and the desired refreshments obtained. But the news of the war arriving while they were on the coast and in the river Orinoco, the vessels were glad to get away without waiting for their lading and the whole design rendered abortive.

He has made application to me in writing [No. 891] for a reimbursement of the expenses he has incurred in endeavouring to serve the public (a copy of which I have enclosed for their Lordship's inspection) and delivered me an account of the charges he has been at in the affair, sworn to before the governor of this island, amounting to ye sum of seven hundred and fifty seven pounds five shillings sterling as set forth in the said letter.

But as it is out of my power without particular directions to order the payment thereof, I beg leave to recommend the case to their Lordships' consideration and am humbly of opinion they will concur with me in thinking that it deserves redress. Especially when they consider the motives on which he acted were disinterested, the means by which the design miscarried, accidental, and that he undertook it at General Monckton's and my own request – founded on the desire of contributing all in our power towards the preservation of the lives and health of the men under our respective commands.

893. *To Clevland*

[TNA, ADM 1/307, ff. 496–7]　　　　　　　　　　　　　　　　Antigua
3 November 1762

Sir,

I desire you will please to acquaint their Lordships that His Majesty's ship *Greyhound*, Captain [Thomas] Francis with the fleet from Cork, arrived at Barbados on the 7th of September, and that by her I received their orders of the 18th of June[1] to appoint a proper convoy to sail from these islands to Europe about the middle of October.

[1]Cf. No. 883.

In consequence of the said order I gave as early intelligence as possible that a convoy would sail from Barbados on the 20th of October and call off Martinique (waiting forty eight hours for such ships as intended taking the benefit thereof) and the other islands in the way to St. Christopher's, the place of general rendezvous, to sail from thence as soon as the trade from all the islands should be assembled. But the tempestuous weather which had for some days preceding, prevented the ships at Barbados and probably at the islands to leeward, from getting their lading on board, occasioned me to put off the day for sailing till the 24th, when His Majesty's ship *Greyhound* proceeded in consequence of the orders I had given, with the trade under convoy.

The number of ships and frigates on this station, already unequal to the service of defending this long range of islands from the insults of the enemy's small privateers, who greatly annoyed them, especially those newly conquered; joined to Captain Francis having been brought on shore so extremely ill as not to be able to proceed on the voyage,[1] and the arrival of the *Lyon* armed transport a few days before at Martinique, with several victuallers from New York for the army under the command of Lord Albemarle at the Havana, determined me to detain the *Greyhound* as a proper ship (particularly at this season) to put their Lordships' last orders in execution, and as I could ill spare any other from the service they were employed on – especially as I had just learnt that Captain Banks of the *Lizard*, who I had sent with General Monckton to his government at New York under orders to return as expeditiously as possible to this station, was gone with the troops from thence to the Havana, in pursuance of orders he received there from their Lordships, as he acquaints me by letter.

As the arrival of the victuallers which came from North America, under the protection of the *Lyon* armed transport, Captain Shakerly, might be a seasonable supply to the troops on the island of Cuba, I dispatched her, being a stout vessel with eighteen six pounders on board, and an additional number of hands, with the victuallers and ships bound to Jamaica, directly from Martinique to that island; whilst a sloop of war proceeded with the remaining ships to the islands of their destination.

You will please further to inform their Lordships that His Majesty's ship *St. Anne*, Captain [William] Harman, arrived likewise at Barbados on the 30th of September with two storeships under convoy, and having left one, which is now unloading in English Harbour for the service of

---

[1] Captain Thomas Francis died on 21 October 1762.

His Majesty's ships on this station, proceeded in consequence of the orders he was under from their Lordships.

We have had very threatening and tempestuous weather, tho' it has never amounted to a hurricane, particularly about the 16th and 17th of last month when the *Providence*, a very fine hired armed brigantine, that has been the scourge of the privateers in these seas, was drove on shore in Carlisle Bay, but has since been got off again and is almost refitted and in readiness to proceed to sea. This vessel would have been a great loss, as she sails the best of anything in these seas, and with the *Pompey* hired armed brig, are the only vessels capable of following the small privateers, who lurk in every creek among the conquered islands, and are too much assisted by the inhabitants thereof. However I have the pleasure to acquaint their Lordships that several have been taken or destroyed.

And as the *Guadeloupe* sloop on her heaving down in this harbour a few days' since, has been found entirely unfit for service and condemned by the strictest survey, I have caused her to be put out of commission and her men distributed among the ships of the squadron, whose complements have been greatly decreased by sickness, which has raged much during the rainy season.

The *Pompey* armed vessel, which I have hired is quite new, and a remarkable good sailor. I could wish (if the war continues) their Lordships would order her to be purchased and commissioned, in lieu of the *Guadeloupe*. This sort of vessel being found by experience to be the best, for scouring these seas of the enemy's privateers, and her value amounting only to sixteen hundred pounds sterling.

You will please to acquaint their Lordships that Captain [Henry] Scott of the *Antigua* died at Guadeloupe on the 23rd of September and Captain Francis of the *Greyhound* at Barbados on the 21st of October.

I have appointed Captain Drummond to command the *Greyhound* and the other removes according to seniority.

894. *From Stephens*

[TNA, ADM 2/534, p. 504]   3 November 1762

Sir,

In addition to the orders you will herewith receive from my Lords Commissioners of the Admiralty, I am commanded by their Lordships to signify their direction to you to employ the best qualified persons in your squadron to make surveys and plans of the coasts of the islands of Martinique, St. Lucia, Guadeloupe, and Marie-Galante, and of the harbours, bays, anchoring places, soundings, and quality of the ground belonging to the same. Also to describe the fortifications and their situations, and whether, and in what manner, they may be attacked by shipping, and to point out the strong and weak parts of those several islands, and the places where troops, artillery &c. can be best landed for the purposes of attacking them.

Their Lordships recommend it to you to be as full as you possibly can, in the accounts of these several particulars, in order that when they shall be added to the plans and surveys which the several governors are ordered to make of the internal parts of these islands a thorough knowledge may be had of them.

Their Lordships would have you communicate this to the governor of the island, that you may concert together such measures as may be most effectual for carrying their intentions in this matter into execution.

895. *From the Lords of the Admiralty*

[TNA, ADM 2/89, f. 229]   5 November 1762

Having ordered Robert Swanton Esq., whom we have appointed Rear Admiral of the blue squadron of His Majesty's fleet, to put himself under your command and to follow your orders, you are hereby required and directed to take him under your command.

896. *From Stephens*

[TNA, ADM 2/534, pp. 514–15]   5 November 1762

Sir,

By His Majesty's sloop the *Barbados*, which brings dispatches to you from my Lords Commissioners of the Admiralty, you will also receive packets from the Earl of Egremont, for the governors of the islands named in the margin[1] and also for the governor of Barbados, in case the sloop shall find him there. And I am commanded by their Lordships to signify their direction to you to cause them to be delivered to these governors as soon as possible, and to permit the *Barbados* sloop to go on to Jamaica, without a moment's loss of time, agreeable to her commander's orders, unless you choose to keep her with you, and to send another vessel with the dispatches to Jamaica, in which

---

[1] Leeward Islands, Martinique, Guadeloupe, Grenada.

case, their Lordships leave it to you, to do so, but recommend it to you to see that no time be lost in her proceeding.

897. From the Lords of the Admiralty

[TNA, ADM 2/1332, ff. 41–2] 5 November 1762

Whereas we have received repeated intelligence that the enemy's ships of war named in the margin are at Brest,[1] in readiness to proceed to sea, and that a very considerable body of land forces is embarked, or intended to embark, on board those ships for some expedition. And there being reason to believe that this armament may be designed against some of His Majesty's colonies or possessions in the West Indies. And that notwithstanding Vice Admiral Sir Charles Hardy[2] is cruising off the port of Brest in order to block up the enemy or intercept them if they should sail, they may, from various accidents in this advanced season of the year, elude his utmost vigilance and find an opportunity of pushing out to sea. And we having therefore, in case the enemy's said ships should put to sea and have the good fortune to escape Sir Charles Hardy, directed him to detach, with the utmost expedition, four ships of the line to reinforce you at Barbados or wherever you may be unless he shall have received intelligence or have sufficient reason to believe that the enemy are not gone to the West Indies. We have thought fit to apprise you, as soon as possible, of the said armament and the directions we have thereupon given to Sir Charles Hardy, in order that you may be upon your guard against any sudden attempt of the enemy upon His Majesty's islands within the limits of your command. And you are hereby required and directed to be constantly watchful so as not to be liable to any surprise and to take every measure that may be necessary and dispose of the squadron under your command in such manner as shall be most likely to defeat any designs the enemy may have meditated against the said islands. And, with this view, you are to concert with their respective governors (who will have been apprised of this armament by the Earl of Egremont) and to co-operate with them in whatever may be most proper for the defence of the governments committed to their care.

If Sir Charles Hardy shall receive no intelligence that shall prevent him from detaching to you the four ships before mentioned agreeable to the orders he has received, you are, upon their arrival, to take them

---

[1] Not listed in the margin.
[2] Vice-admiral Sir Charles Hardy (c.1714–80), the commander of a squadron blockading Brest.

under your command and immediately to send advice to Rear Admiral Keppel[1] of the reinforcement as well as the intelligence you shall have received. And also that it is your intention to send that reinforcement to strengthen him at Jamaica, if you shall have received any certain intelligence that the enemy have slipped by you and have formed any designs against the island of Jamaica or the Havana. And you are upon receiving such intelligence to detach the said reinforcement of four ships to Rear Admiral Keppel accordingly, with as much expedition as possible. But in case they shall not have joined you when the French squadron shall have passed you with such designs as aforesaid, you are then to detach only such ships as the situation and strength of your squadron will admit of, which we cannot specify more particularly, as, in the last dispatch from Sir George Pocock, he doubts how far he shall be able, from the state of his squadron, to complete your ships to ten sail of the line agreeably to our orders.

As it is not improbable that the armament above mentioned may be destined for St. Domingo and it is of consequence that you should have as early notice as possible of the approach and motions of the enemy, you are to keep frigates constantly cruising on the most likely stations for discovering and giving you notice thereof accordingly.

And whereas we have ordered Commodore [Richard] Spry, commander in chief of His Majesty's ships in North America, to proceed without loss of time to reinforce you with all the ships of the line under his command during the winter months when they can be of no use to the northward; you are, upon his arrival, to take him and the ships which shall accompany him, under your command, also to employ them and your whole force as you shall judge best for carrying these orders into execution. But, as it is intended that Commodore Spry should return to Halifax with the ships which came from thence, so soon as the season will admit of his employing those ships upon the North American station, you are to direct him to return thither accordingly, unless you shall find it absolutely necessary to keep him longer in the West Indies. In which case you are at liberty to detain him as long as there shall be an absolute necessity for it; permitting him, in all events, to return to his command in North America whenever the service which occasioned your detaining him will admit of it. And you are to give us the earliest and most speedy notice of your detaining him with your reasons for so doing and the time you shall judge it will be necessary to continue him on that service in order that we may send

---

[1] Rear-admiral Hon. Augustus Keppel, Commander-in-chief of the squadrons at Jamaica and Havana.

other ships to North America for the protection of the commerce of His Majesty's subjects and the security of His Majesty's dominions in those parts.

898. *From Stephens*

[TNA, ADM 2/535, p. 4] 15 November 1762

Sir,

I am commanded by my Lords Commissioners of the Admiralty to acquaint you that the preliminary articles towards a peace were signed at Fontainebleau on the 3rd instant, between the King's ministers and those of their Most Christian and Catholic Majesties. And that as soon as ratification shall be exchanged you will receive orders in form [*sic*] for a cessation of arms. But in the mean time their Lordships make no doubt but that you will exert your usual vigilance for the protection of the trade of His Majesty's subjects and for checking the privateers of the enemy.

899. *From Hon. George Grenville*[1]

[TNA, PRO 30/20/20/4, ff. 43–4] Admiralty Office
2 December 1762

Sir,

Admiral Cotes[2] having earnestly applied to me for a promotion of his son in law Mr. Charles Kendall[3] to the rank of lieutenant, which in the present situation after the rule made by the Admiralty upon the first account of the signature of the preliminaries not to make any more lieutenants till the present number is diminished, it was impossible for me to comply with. He has requested me to recommend him to your favour and protection, which I do with the greater pleasure as I am convinced that you will be glad to give any mark of your regard to an officer of Admiral Cotes' rank and merit in the service as far as is in your power. At the same time I am glad to embrace this opportunity of wishing you joy of your late promotion to the rank of Vice Admiral.[4]

---

[1]MP for Buckingham, 1741–70; Lord of the Admiralty, 1744–47; Lord of the Treasury, 1747–54; Secretary of State (North), 5 June–14 Oct. 1762; First Lord of the Admiralty, 18 Oct. 1762–20 April 1762; First Lord of the Treasury, 15 April 1762–13 July 1765.
[2]Vice-admiral Thomas Cotes, MP Great Bedwyn, 1766–67.
[3]Charles Kendall was commissioned a lieutenant on 1 February 1763.
[4]Rodney was promoted to Vice-admiral on 21 October 1762.

900. *To Clevland*

[TNA, ADM 1/307, ff. 500–503]
Foudroyant
St. Pierre Road, Martinique
11 December 1762

Sir,
You will please to acquaint their Lordships that since the sailing of His Majesty's ship *Greyhound* for England, the *Ferret* sloop of war, Captain [Peter] Clarke has joined me with dispatches from Sir George Pocock at the Havana, by which I have been informed of his being soon to sail for England with such ships of war as should not be judged immediately necessary to be left on that station, under the command of Commodore Keppel, so that I have no longer room to hope for any reinforcements of ships from thence, which I had always depended on, when the expedition should be over.

My stay at the island of Antigua was not so long as I intended, or indeed was necessary, to settle the affairs of English Harbour occasioned by an express from General Rufane, giving me an account of a conspiracy and intended insurrection at this island. In which the surprise of the troops at St. Pierre and the poisoning the cisterns at Fort Royal were designed. However, on my arrival here, which was as expeditious as possible, I found every thing quiet, as it has continued ever since, and whatever design was entertained, it seems to have been confined to the lowest class of people; encouraged thereto by the reduced state of the garrison, from which it is impossible to exclude them the knowledge of.

From information (given by the principal inhabitants) and the weak condition of the garrison, the General found it necessary to contract his quarters to St. Pierre and Fort Royal. Many batteries on the coast became thereby forsaken, and the trade more exposed to the insolence of the enemy's small privateers.

This has induced me likewise to order the other ships under my command to rendezvous here, in order to assist this island (being of the greatest consequence of all the Caribbean) as well against intestine broils as any force of the enemy that may escape from Europe during the winter months, and I shall thereby be at hand to frustrate any attempt to retake any of the other conquered islands. But their Lordships must know how inadequate the force at present under my command is, to the great extent of islands entrusted to my care.

As these islands are certainly the key to the enemy's, as well as our own possessions to leeward, and all squadrons bound there must somewhere pass the limits of these islands, the expediency of a superior fleet to windward is too plain to need pointing out to their Lordships.

With twelve ships of the line, and as many frigates on this station, no attempt with the least prospect of success can be made on any of these islands; and it would be extremely difficult for ships of the enemy to pass unnoticed. In which case, should His Majesty's fleet in the West Indies be inferior, proper detachments might be made from hence; whilst it is utterly impracticable in case of an attack at these islands, to detach a timely reinforcement from Jamaica, as ships from England for that purpose would arrive here in less time and with greater certainty.

But a number of smaller vessels would still be necessary to ferret out the small privateers of the enemy from the numberless creeks and petty bays with which this chain of islands abounds. The properest vessels for this service, are sloops from ten to fourteen guns, or brigs from twelve to sixteen, some of which I would recommend to their Lordships to purchase (on a supposition that the war continues), as the hire of them soon amounts to their value, and they may always be sold without any considerable loss. Their Lordships will do me the justice to believe, that I do not point out this method in preference to hiring, from a design to make captains; as I would recommend their being commanded by lieutenants only.

Without more vessels of this sort, it will be impossible entirely to extirpate this nest of vermin who, notwithstanding the vigilance of the few cruisers I have, and five of them being taken since my last, continue still greatly to annoy the trade of His Majesty's subjects, harbouring a great deal about the bays and creeks of this island, St. Lucia, and St. Vincent, where no garrison has yet been established.

At St. Vincent several of them have lately careened and the inhabitants have strongly remonstrated against the English colours being hoisted there, which I have ordered all ships on that station constantly to see performed.

Their letter to Captain Hollwall, as he was putting those orders in execution, I have transmitted for their Lordships' inspection, and if no new arrangement of the islands in consequence of a peace should prevent it, I intend chastising the insolence of such as signed it, by turning them off the island, as soon as the important service of protecting this island will permit me, but there are many, and those of the principal inhabitants well and loyally affected to His Majesty's government.

The attention I have been obliged to pay to that part of their Lordships' orders, which enjoins the protection of the Conquered Islands, has so taken up the force I have, that I am sorry to inform them, it has been out of my power to carry the other part of their instructions relative to the annoyance of the enemy's coasts into execution.

901. *To Clevland*

[TNA, ADM 1/307, f. 504] *Foudroyant*
St. Pierre Road, Martinique
2 January 1763

Sir,

I take the opportunity by a merchant ship who sails for England this day, to acquaint their Lordships that His Majesty's ship the *Renown* arrived here on the 23rd December, by whom I received their orders [No. 895, 897] of the 4th and 5th of November, as likewise your letters of the 3rd [No. 894], 4th, and 15th [No. 898] of the said month, with the commissions for the different officers enclosed, and they may be sure I will take care that their Lordships' orders shall be put in execution.

I take this opportunity to desire you will please to return my humblest thanks to their Lordships for the honour they have done me, in promoting me to the rank of Vice Admiral.

The *Renown* proceeded instantly with the dispatches for Rear Admiral Keppel, but none of the ships from North America or the Havana have joined me.

902. *To Clevland*

[TNA, ADM 1/307, ff. 505–07] *Foudroyant*
St. Pierre Road, Martinique
22 January 1763

Sir,

His Majesty's ship the *Renown* arrived here on the 23rd of December, by whom I received their Lordships' orders of the 5th [Nos. 895, 897] of November and your letters of the 3rd [No. 894], 4th, 5th and 15th [No. 898] of the said month, with the commissions enclosed, and take this first opportunity to return their Lordships my humblest thanks for the honour they have done me in promoting me to the rank of Vice Admiral.

The *Renown* proceeded instantly with the dispatches for Rear Admiral Keppel, and I have in the best manner I am able (with the force entrusted to my command) stationed the ships for the protection of the trade of His Majesty's subjects and destroying the enemy's privateers, who, notwithstanding the numbers that have lately been taken continue to swarm about the conquered islands, and the loss of his Majesty's hired armed sloop the *Catharine* [*sic*], on the Saints, who had been the scourge of them, and taken three within seven days, is much to be regretted. However I shall use every endeavour to protect the commerce, and immediately after the cessation of arms takes place, I shall discharge the two other hired armed vessels and likewise give directions, that no ship whatever under my command bears supernumeraries.

I have likewise given orders to the officers of His Majesty's yard at Antigua, to discharge all Black artificers whatever, and their Lordships may depend that I will cause all the economy possible to be used at that yard and the expense thereof curtailed.

On the 23rd of December Captain [John] Stott in His Majesty's ship *Scarborough* arrived here with a transport, having two hundred recovered men on board belonging to the troops of this garrison and those at the Havana. The weakness of this garrison at that time and the situation of affairs, induced General Rufane and myself to detain the said transport, until there was a certainty of a cessation of arms, more especially as the Brest squadron was ready to sail, and by many letters received by the inhabitants of this island, was certainly destined for Martinique.

I shall send the transport with another ship of war to the Havana, it being necessary to detain Captain Stott in order to execute their Lordships' commands [No. 894] relative to the taking plans of the ports and of those islands ceded to the enemy; he being recommended to me as an officer very capable of that service.

I am sorry to acquaint their Lordships that I have great reason to imagine the *Duke* packet is lost, or taken. I cannot think the latter as the *Levant* was cruising to windward of Martinique, and His Majesty's hired armed brig the *Providence*, between her and Barbados at the time the said packet sailed from that island which was on the first instant.

On the 17th of this month His Majesty's sloop the *Lynx* arrived here with dispatches for the different governments, and their Lordships' orders [No. 898] to me relative to a cessation of arms which I shall deliver to the captains of His Majesty's ships under my command. [Captain] Sir Alexander Holburne in his passage met with such severe weather as obliged him to throw his guns over board.

Rear Admiral Swanton, and the Captains [Francis Samuel] Drake and [John Carter] Allen have received their commissions.

903. *From the Lords of the Admiralty*

[TNA, ADM 2/1332, f. 47] 8 February 1763

Whereas we observe by the account of the state and condition of His Majesty's squadron under your command on the 2nd November last, that there were then on board the *Foudroyant* two hundred and fifty five supernumeraries who belonged to no particular ship. And whereas hostilities will have ceased in the West Indies before you can possibly receive this and there will not therefore be any further occasion for the King's ships there to be completed to their highest complements of men, you are hereby required and directed to send the aforementioned supernumeraries with as many more seamen from the ships under your command as will make them up three hundred, without a moment's loss of time, in the *Modeste* or *Pembroke* to the Havana, directing the captain of such ship to dispose of them there as Rear Admiral Keppel shall direct and follow the said Rear Admiral's orders for his further proceedings.

If the *Mars* shall have joined you when you receive this or should soon afterwards arrive from North America, you are to direct Commodore Spry to proceed also in her to the Havana and to follow the abovementioned Rear Admiral's orders.

904. *From Grenville*

[TNA, PRO 30/20/20/4, ff. 47–51] Admiralty Office
10 February 1763

Dear Sir,

Tho' I have but just time to acknowledge the favour of your two letters dated the 4th of December last, before the express which is to carry this letter to the captain of the *Syren* at Portsmouth sets out, yet I cannot omit writing these few lines to thank you for the many expressions of your friendship and regard to me of which I am extremely sensible, and at the same time to convince you how desirous I am to do everything you ask by informing you that I immediately laid before the King your request for leave to return to England with the summer convoy if your health or situation shall be such as to make you wish it. His Majesty was pleased to consent to it and to leave that to your own choice as the signature of the preliminaries which we hope will now soon be followed by the definitive treaty, makes your stay at the Leeward Islands of much less consequence to His Majesty's service, which you have carried on with so much advantage to the public and so much honour to yourself, than it would have been if the war had continued. I have directed Mr. Clevland to signify it to you officially and to send it by an express tonight to Portsmouth in order that it may be go by the *Syren* who is already ordered to go to you in her way to Jamaica with directions for you to send such men as you can spare to Rear Admiral Keppel to assist him in bringing home the Spanish men of war from the Havana which we fear he will scarce be able to do without them considering the number of seamen that were lost there and the sickly state of the squadron. Had the war continued I was determined to have added as much strength as we possibly could to the squadron under your command for the reasons you mention in your letter, the cogency and good sense of which I was thoroughly sensible of. With this view all the ships of the line in North America were ordered before the preliminaries to join you, and remain with you till the summer months, and a reinforcement was also destined to be sent to you from hence, but the latter of these measures is stopped by the pacification, and with respect to the former they are ordered to be sent to assist in getting home the Spanish ships from the Havana, as there is now no use of them at the Leeward Islands. I mention these things to you now the object of them is over only to show you how much I approve of what you suggested and to give you a proof that your situation and the part I take in every thing that can contribute to your reputation was early in my thoughts after my coming to this Board, to which the King from his goodness has been pleased to call me. I sincerely wish that I may be able to do my duty in it, to the advantage of this branch of the public service to which you know I have always been so warmly attached, from a full conviction that the safety and honour of the kingdom is more immediately concerned in it than in any other. Whatever, a conviction which if it had needed any confirmation would have received it from the events of this war. I will only add that if in the course of my office here, it is in my power to express my regard and friendship to you, consistently with those rules which I have laid down for my conduct in it, and which I flatter myself you will approve, it will be a very great and real pleasure to me.

[PS] I am much obliged to you for your information and observations contained in your letter which seem to me very important.

905. *To Clevland*

[TNA, ADM 1/307, ff. 508–09]

Foudroyant
St. Pierre Road, Martinique
11 February 1763

Sir,
Since my dispatches [No. 902] of the 22nd of January, I have received certain intelligence that the *Duke* packet was taken by a French frigate about twelve leagues to windward of Martinique, and the mails fell into the enemy's hand; notwithstanding the master of the packet declares he was chased six hours before he struck. The enemy ship was in her passage from Bordeaux to St. Domingo, and tho' I had a chain of frigates to windward of the islands, none of them had the fortune to fall in with the enemy's ship.

I acquainted you in my last [No. 902] with the arrival here of the *Lynx*. She proved so leaky I was obliged to order her to be careened and it being necessary that their Lordships' dispatches should be forwarded to Rear Admiral Keppel, and the transport with two hundred recovered soldiers sent to the Havana, and His Majesty's ship the *Repulse* being of no further use in these seas, as she was in no condition to cruise against the privateers who are very numerous, I have thought it proper to dispatch her to Rear Admiral Keppel, and have sent him likewise a number of seamen as I hear they were much wanted, and may not only be useful in completing the ships of his squadron, but likewise assist in navigating to Europe the Spanish ships of war lately taken at the Havana. As it was necessary to appoint a commander to the *Repulse*, Captain [Hon. Peregrine Francis] Bertie not having appeared, though two ships of war arrived express from England, and Sir Alexander Holburne having earnestly desired to command her, I have complied with his request. Had not all the other ships and frigates been employed in protecting the trade of His Majesty's subjects against the enemy's privateers, who are very numerous, and on which service the *Repulse* was in no condition to be employed, I should not have sent her, but I thought it better for His Majesty's service that she should proceed with the dispatches to leeward, than remain idle in English Harbour.

I have the pleasure to acquaint their Lordships that several of the enemy's privateers have been taken or destroyed within these few days, and as I never suffer any of the frigates to continue in port, I flatter myself the commerce will suffer very little.

The *Vanguard* being extremely leaky, I was obliged to order her to English Harbour. Rear Admiral Swanton is at that port with my directions to refit her, or any other of His Majesty's ships, and to carry on the duty of that port with as little expense as possible, and upon no account to suffer any extraordinary expense, the ships only to be fitted with stores barely necessary to carry them to England; and likewise to discharge all such artificers from His Majesty's yard, but such as are absolutely necessary to carry on the immediate service.

I hope these directions will meet with their Lordships' approbation.

906. *To Clevland*

[TNA, ADM 1/307, f. 510]

Martinique
2 March 1763

Sir,

Notwithstanding hostilities are now ceased I flatter myself their Lordships will not be displeased to be assured of the good behaviour of the officers and men I have the honour to command during the utmost continuance of them, of which I cannot omit desiring you will please to inform them; and particularly that (a short time before they did expire) Captain [Samuel] Marshall in His Majesty's ship the *Antigua*, cruising off the island of Guadeloupe was boarded in the night by two privateers, one of which of twelve guns and eighty men he carried, the enemy having 34 men killed and wounded in the action, and the *Antigua* seven. The other, by favour of the night making her escape, which from the vigilance and good behaviour of Captain Marshall and his people, there is reason to imagine he would not otherwise have been able to do, notwithstanding each of the privateers was of force little inferior to the *Antigua*.

You will likewise please to inform their Lordships that most of the ships under my command are in consequence of their orders [No. 894] employed in taking surveys of the coasts of the islands which are to be ceded, and the remainder in quest of a few little piratical privateers, who continue to commit outrages on the shore, and annoy the trade (having taken some small vessels) of the Conquered Islands, tho' the time for the cessation [of hostilities] has taken place, and they have been shown the proclamation for that purpose.

907. To Clevland

[TNA, ADM 1/307, ff. 512–14]

Barbados
8 May 1763

Sir,

You will please to inform their Lordships, that by His Majesty's ship *Syren*, Captain Paston, who arrived at Martinique the 1st of April, I received their orders [No. 903] of 8th February and that I immediately sent him on with 150 additional seamen on board, to join Rear Admiral Keppel. The *Pembroke* being at that time at this island, I immediately repaired here, and with as much expedition as possible have since detached her likewise to Mr. Keppel with more men, making in the whole above the number mentioned in their Lordships' order.

On my arrival in Carlisle Bay, I found there a Spanish ship, prize to the *Ferret* sloop of war Captain Clarke, which he had some time before brought in, and informed me by the *Syren* of, and that he had taken her out of a harbour on the SW side of the island of Puerto Rico, on the 12th of February after an engagement of three hours. When she proved to be a ship called the *Santissimo Trinidada*, laden with cocoa, bound from La Guaira to Cadiz, of about 400 tons, and 20 guns, six and nine pounders, and full of men, tho' their number could not be ascertained, as she was so close to the shore that they all made their escape after the ship struck, except one, who died of his wounds a few minutes after the prize was taken possession of.

The ship being of a force so superior to the *Ferret*, and the place where she lay, on account of the reefs and shoals which extended many leagues, of so difficult access, that they were three days in warping up to her – are circumstances, which I cannot without injustice to the perseverance and intrepidity which Captain Clarke, his officers and men exerted on the occasion, help informing their Lordships of.

I likewise found here His Majesty's ship *Melampe*, who had arrived a few days before from the coast of Africa, in so leaky a condition as to be scarcely able to swim; which will make it absolutely necessary for her to be hove down before she can proceed for England. Her commander Captain [Edward] Clarke having been in so bad a state of health on, and ever since he left the coast, as to be chiefly confined to his bed and more than once given over; and the physicians at this island assuring me, that the only chance he has for recovery will be from a speedy return to England, I have on that account put him into the *Ferret*, who I have ordered to convoy the prize to England, and appointed Captain Peter Clarke in his room to the *Melampe*.

You will please further to inform their Lordships, that neither the *Mars* nor *Wager* have appeared in these seas, tho' several ships that sailed from Cork under convoy of the latter are arrived at the different islands, and likewise, that the Spanish launches, said to be from Trinidad and Marguerita still infest the seas, notwithstanding I have wrote to the governors of Puerto Rico and Marguerita on that head. The cruisers I have sent after them have not been so lucky as to bring in any of them, tho' by the description I transmitted of one to the governor of St. Eustatius, he has been seized on putting into that port, and the principals met with codign punishment.

I should likewise have informed their Lordships that some time before I left Martinique Mr. Macdonald, boatswain of His Majesty's ship *Foudroyant* having unluckily killed a soldier on shore, I have with the advice of the Attorney General of Antigua whose opinion I first took in regard to the manner of his trial, delivered him to be tried by a court martial of land officers on shore, which I hope their Lordships will approve, especially as he was not on duty when the accident happened. However, I must do him the justice to observe to their Lordships that he has always borne a good character, and General Rufane has informed me that several circumstances appeared in his favour on his trial.

All the merchant ships that have lately arrived having brought repeated advises of the definitive treaty being signed, I remain here in hourly expectation of their Lordships' orders for the disposal of His Majesty's ships on this station.

908. *From the Lords of the Admiralty*

[TNA, ADM 2/90, pp. 210–14] 11 May 1763

Whereas the Earl of Egremont,[1] one of His Majesty's principal Secretaries of State, has acquainted us that there are two thousand four hundred and sixty five men of the King's troops to be brought from Martinique, and six hundred and seventy seven from Guadeloupe, to Great Britain; and also three hundred and twenty seven from Guadeloupe to Ireland. And whereas the transport vessels named in the annexed list[2] have been provided for conveying the said troops as well as for bringing from Martinique and Guadeloupe the detachments of artillery and

---

[1] Charles Wyndham, 2nd Earl of Egremont; Secretary of State (South), 9 Oct. 1761–21 Aug. 1763.
[2] Not enclosed.

stores, and will shortly sail from Spithead under convoy of His Majesty's sloop the *Beaver*. And whereas you will receive herewith three packets from Lord Egremont, for Governor Rufane at Martinique, Governor [Campbell] Dalrymple at Guadeloupe, and Governor [Charles] Pinfold at Barbados, or the commanding officer at St. Lucia, containing the King's orders for evacuating those places. You are to transmit the same agreeable to their address, as soon as possible, and then adjust with those governors, or the commanders in chief, all measures relative to embarking the troops, artillery and stores, and cause the same to be accordingly done at such time as shall be agreed upon, on board the aforementioned transport vessels.

And whereas the King's forces now at the Havana, which were to have assisted in navigating to England the Spanish ships of war taken at that place, are assigned some to Lousiana, others to Florida, and the rest to different parts of North America whereby Rear Admiral Keppel will be in want of men to enable him to navigate the said Spanish ships to England. And the Earl of Egremont having therefore signified to us that we may appoint any number out of the troops which are to be brought to Europe from Martinique and Guadeloupe that we shall judge sufficient to pass to the Havana, in order to be employed to assist in navigating those ships home. You are hereby required and directed to cause so many of the transport vessels as shall have on board about two thousand five hundred of the above mentioned troops, to proceed without loss of time under proper convoy to the Havana, in order to be disposed of for the purpose aforesaid, as Rear Admiral Keppel, or the commander in chief of His Majesty's ships there shall see occasion.

The rest of the transports having taken on board the remainder of the troops, with the detachments of artillery and stores, are to proceed without loss of time for Great Britain and repair directly to Spithead, excepting such of them as shall have on board Malpas's[1] Regiment which are to repair to Cork in Ireland, where that regiment is to be landed, and then those transports are also to make the best of their way to Spithead.

And whereas we intend that the four ships of the line named in the margin[2] (or if either the *Modeste* or *Pembroke* is gone to the Havana, then one of the 50 gun ships in her room) together with two frigates, and two sloops which are in the best condition, shall remain until

---

[1] George Cholmondeley, 3rd Earl of Cholmondeley, styled Viscount Malpas, colonel of the 56th Regiment of Foot.
[2] *Foudroyant, Vanguard, Modeste, Pembroke.*

further order at the Leeward Islands and Barbados, under the command of Rear Admiral Swanton. You are accordingly to put the said ships, frigates, and sloops under Mr. Swanton's orders, and give him such instructions for his guidance as shall appear best for the King's service. And you are then to return to England with all the rest of the ships and vessels now under your command in company with the transports, or if they shall not all be ready, you are to accompany the transports with such as shall be so leaving orders for the rest to follow as soon as possible.

But whereas Lord Egremont has acquainted us, that in case the transports sent from hence shall arrive at any of the places of their destination before those with the new garrisons from France, the King is pleased to leave it to the governors of the respective places, and the commanding officer of His ships, to determine, whether it shall be most advisable to wait for the arrival of the French troops, or to leave an officer with a small detachment, to give up the place, and to come away with the rest of His Majesty's troops, appointing sufficient shipping to bring away the said detachment. In case therefore the transports with the *Beaver* sloop shall arrive at Martinique and Guadaloupe before the French troops which are to take possession of those islands, you are to concert with the governors of the said islands such measures as may be proper to be taken thereupon, and to proceed in the embarking of His Majesty's forces, artillery, and stores as shall be determined by the said governors and yourself to be most advisable.

909.   *From Stephens*

[TNA, ADM 2/535, pp. 464–5]   11 May 1763

Sir,

I have received and communicated to my Lords Commissioners of the Admiralty your letters dated the 11th of December 1762 [No. 900] and 22nd of January [No. 902] and 11 February 1763 [No. 905] with the several papers enclosed therein, informing them of your proceedings with the squadron of His Majesty's ships under your command. And I am to acquaint you their Lordships very well approve of your proceedings.

Their Lordships also approve of your having ordered the Black artificers to be discharged from the yard at Antigua, and the ships to be fitted with as little expense as possible, and supplied only with stores sufficient to bring them home to England.

Enclosed[1] I send you a copy of the definitive treaty of peace, concluded at Paris the 10th day of February last, for your information and guidance.

910. *From Stephens*

[TNA, ADM 2/535, p. 467]   11 May 1763

Sir,

I am commanded by my Lords Commissioners of the Admiralty to send you the enclosed packets from His Majesty's Secretary at War, some of which are relative to the evacuation of the islands to be ceded to the French, and the others are upon public services. And it is their Lordships' directions that you cause them to be forwarded agreeable to their several addresses.

911. *From Stephens*

[TNA, ADM 2/535, p. 470]   12 May 1763

Sir,

By the *Beaver* sloop which brings this, and convoys the transports that are to receive on board His Majesty's troops now in garrison upon the islands to be restored to the French you will receive duplicates of all the dispatches lately sent for you by the *Swift* sloop. You will likewise receive a packet addressed to Rear Admiral Keppel, or the commander in chief of His Majesty's ships at the Havana, which contains duplicates of the dispatches sent also for him by the *Swift*. And I am to recommend it to you to forward the same by such convoy, as you shall send with the transports, that are to carry the troops from Martinique and Guadeloupe to the Havana.

[1] Not enclosed.

912. *From Admiral Charles Knowles*

[TNA, PRO 30/20/14] Windsor Great Lodge
12 May 1763

Sir,

Understanding from Lord Carysford[1] that you are ordered home directly, I cannot avoid repeating my request that you will not forget my friend Garnier,[2] for if he don't get post before he comes away from the West Indies, he may lose his rank for many years. I most heartily wish he had sent his commission home that we might have got it confirmed, as the vacancy seemed to appear doubtful; and more especially as the Admiralty Board is so frequently changing that the opportunity of one's friends being in, should not be lost. If his sloop is in a condition to be left abroad and you should not have it in your power to give his post before you come away may I beg you to leave him with Mr. Swanton (who I hear is to stay some little time longer) as his friends will get him recommended to Mr. Swanton.

As you have much abler correspondents than I am, and having been lately at Bath for my health, must refer you to them for news, only shall tell you the scene is shifted and the changes have been numerous. Lord Sandwich at present is at our head.[3] Mr. G. Grenville at the head of the Treasury.[4] Lord Egremont[5] and Lord Halifax[6] Secretaries of State. Mr. Ellis[7] Secretary at War, and Lord Shelbourne[8] First Lord of Trade. These being the principals. You know now the geography of the carte de politics.

PS I am to tell you the Duke expects the Barbados citron water as I showed him the paragraph of your letter promising to bring it.

---

[1]John Proby, 1st Lord Carysford, Lord of the Admiralty, 6 April–2 July 1757; 1 Jan. 1763–31 July 1763.
[2]Sometimes spelled as Garner. William Garnier was not promoted to the rank of post captain until 3 August 1768.
[3]Sandwich was appointed First Lord of the Admiralty on 20 April 1763.
[4]Appointed First Lord of the Treasury, 15 April 1763.
[5]Appointed Secretary of State (South), 9 Oct. 1761.
[6]George Dunk Montagu, 2nd Earl of Halifax; Secretary of State (North), 14 Oct. 1762–Aug. 1763; Secretary of State (South), Aug. 1762–10 July 1765.
[7]Welbore Ellis, MP for Cricklade, 1741–47; Weymouth and Melcombe Regis, 1747–61; Aylesbury, 1761–68; Secretary at War Dec.1762–July 1763.
[8]William Petty, 2nd Earl of Shelburne, First Lord of the Council of Trade and Plantations, 23 April–17 Sept. 1763.

913. To Clevland

[TNA, ADM 1/307, f. 516] Antigua
30 June 1763

Sir,
You will please to inform the Lords Commissioners of the Admiralty that His Majesty's brig the *Antigua*, having been condemned at a survey held on her by my order at English Harbour, as utterly incapable of proceeding to sea, without the expense of a repair greatly exceeding her present value.

In consequence thereof have ordered her to be put out of commission and the hull (her sails, rigging, and stores of all kind that remained serviceable being returned into store) to be put up to sale to the highest bidder; tho' from her extreme bad condition there is great reason to question whether anybody will purchase her.

914. From Stephens

[TNA, ADM 2/536, p. 66] 4 July 1763

Sir,
I have received and communicated to my Lords Commissioners of the Admiralty, your letter [No. 906] of the 2nd of March last, from Martinique, informing them of the proceedings of His Majesty's ships and vessels under your command and that a short time before the cessation of hostilities, Captain Marshall of the *Antigua* had been boarded in the night by two of the enemy's privateers, one of which he took, and the other escaped under favour of the night, tho' they were each of them of force little inferior to his own ship. Their Lordships are extremely well pleased with the account you have given of Captain Marshall's behaviour on that occasion.

915. From Stephens

[TNA, ADM 2/536, pp. 66–7] 4 July 1763

Sir,
I have received and communicated to my Lords Commissioners of the Admiralty, your letter [No. 907] of the 8th of May last, brought by His Majesty's sloop the *Ferret*, informing them of your having been joined by the *Syren*, and forwarded, by her and *Pembroke*, 300 seamen

to Rear Admiral Keppel; of Captain Clarke in the *Ferret* having taken a Spanish ship out of a harbour on the southwest side of Puerto Rico; of your having, by the advice of the Attorney General of Antigua delivered up Mr. Macdonal[d], boatswain of the *Foudroyant* to be tried by a court martial of land officers, for having unluckily killed a soldier on shore, and of other naval matters.

Their Lordships are well pleased with the account you have given of the behaviour of Captain Clarke, his officers and men, in the action with the Spanish ship they took at Puerto Rico; but they cannot conceive upon what foundation the Attorney General of Antigua could give his opinion that a person in sea pay could be tried by a court martial of land officers; and their Lordships do not therefore approve of your having delivered up the boatswain to that jurisdiction.

Their Lordships command me to acquaint you, that they expected to have received with your dispatches, an account of the state and condition of the ships under your command.

916. To Clevland

[TNA, ADM 1/307, f. 517] *Foudroyant* at Spithead
12 August 1763

Sir,

You will please to acquaint their Lordships with my arrival at Spithead with His Majesty's ships *Foudroyant*, *Levant*, and *Amazon*, in forty days from the Leeward Islands.

My extreme bad state of health obliging me to deliver the command of the squadron to Rear Admiral Swanton, and the leaky condition of the three ships I have brought home with me making their immediate departure from the West Indies absolutely necessary could not be of the least prejudice to His Majesty's service, as Mr. Swanton has a sufficient number of ships to execute their Lordships' commands.

A few days before I left Antigua Mr. Swanton acquainted me by letter that the French squadron consisting of four ships of the line, viz. *Royal Louis*, 100 guns; *Septre* [sic], *Minatour* [sic], and *Active* of 74 [guns] each, arrived at Martinique on the 15th June. That the Marquis de Fenelon was very pressing to be put in possession of Fort Royal, but as General Rufane had received no orders to evacuate that island until the arrival of His Majesty's sloop the *Swift* on the 21st June, he could not comply with the French Governor's request.

Mr. Swanton likewise acquainted me that he was hiring vessels to carry the garrisons of Martinique and Guadeloupe to Prince Ruperts

Bay, Dominica, the place he had appointed for a rendezvous until the transports arrived from England.

Enclosed[1] I transmit to their Lordships, a list of the squadron left at the Leeward Islands under the command of Rear Admiral Swanton.

917. *From Stephens*

[TNA, ADM 2/536, pp. 175–6] 13 August 1763

Sir,

I have communicated to my Lords Commissioners of the Admiralty your letter [No. 916] of yesterday's date, giving an account of your arrival at Spithead in His Majesty's ship *Foudroyant*, with the *Levant* and *Amazon*, and that the French squadron arrived at Martinique the 15th of June and His Majesty's sloop *Swift* on the 24th. And I have their Lordships' directions to desire you will please to let me know, by express, when the *Swift* sailed from Martinique, with the dispatches for Rear Admiral Keppel, and every other particular relating to that sloop, which may have come to your knowledge, as she had not reached the Havana on the 9th of July when the *Trent* sailed from thence.

918. *From the Lords of the Admiralty*

[TNA, ADM 2/90, p. 520] 13 August 1763

Whereas the service [upon] which you have been employed at the Leeward Islands, is now at an end, you are hereby required and directed to strike your flag, and come on shore.

---

[1]*Vanguard, Modeste, Rochester, Winchester, Scarborough, Aquilon, Melampe, Stag, Virgin, Lynx.*

APPENDIX

LIST OF DOCUMENTS AND SOURCES

The documents in this volume come from the collections of manuscripts in the British Library and The National Archives of the United Kingdom.

British Library

Add. MSS 15956	Anson Papers
Add. MSS 32867, 32890, 32899, 32915, 32919, 32933, 32934, 32935, 32939.	Newcastle Papers

The National Archives of the United Kingdom

ADM 1/87, 91, Admiral's Dispatches, English Channel.

ADM 1/307, Admiral's Dispatches, Leeward Islands.

ADM 1/2380–86, Captain's Letters.

ADM 2/59–63, 65–7, 70, 72–5, 78–90, Admiralty Orders.

ADM 2/526–36, 690–3, 695, 697–704, 707–10, Secretary's Letters.

ADM 2/1331–2, Secret Orders and Instructions.

PRO 30/20/4, 6, 14, Rodney Papers.

PRO 30/20/20/2, 4, 5, Rodney Papers.

PRO 30/20/26/5, Rodney Papers.

Numerical list of documents used in this volume

All references are to documents in The National Archives except those cited as Add. MSS which are in the British Library.

No.	Description	Date	Reference
1	From Mathews	31 Dec. 1742	ADM 1/2380
2	To Corbett	15 Feb. 1743	ADM 1/2380
3	To Corbett	31 March 1743	ADM 1/2380
4	To Corbett	2 April 1743	ADM 1/2380
5	From the Lords of the Admiralty	2 April 1743	ADM 2/59, p. 419
6	To Corbett	22 April 1743	ADM 1/2380
7	From the Lords of the Admiralty	10 Aug. 1743	ADM 2/60, pp. 270–71
8	To Corbett	1 Oct. 1743	ADM 1/2380
9	To Corbet	5 Oct. 1743	ADM 1/2380
10	To Corbett	9 Oct. 1743	ADM 1/2380
11	To Corbett	12 Oct. 1743	ADM 1/2380
12	To Corbett	19 Oct. [1743]	ADM 1/2380
13	To Corbett	29 Oct. 1743	ADM 1/2380
14	To Corbett	2 Nov. 1743	ADM 1/2380
15	To Corbett	9 Nov. 1743	ADM 1/2380
16	From the Lords of the Admiralty	16 Nov. 1743	ADM 2/60, p. 381
17	To Corbett	18 Nov. 1743	ADM 1/2380
18	To Corbett	Friday noon	ADM 1/2380
19	To Corbett	19 Nov. 1743	ADM 1/2380
20	To Corbett	23 Nov. 1743	ADM 1/2380
21	From the Lords of the Admiralty	2 Dec. 1743	ADM 2/60, pp. 414–15
22	To Corbett	4 Dec. 1743	ADM 1/2380
23	To Corbett	9 Dec. 1743	ADM 1/2380
24	To Corbett	11 Dec. 1743	ADM 1/2380
25	To Corbett	11 Dec. 1743	ADM 1/2380
26	From the Lords of the Admiralty	14 Dec. 1743	ADM 2/60, p. 437
27	To Corbett	15 Dec. 1743	ADM 1/2380
28	To Corbett	18 Dec. 1743	ADM 1/2380
29	To Corbett	19 Dec. 1743	ADM 1/2380
30	To Corbett	23 Dec. 1743	ADM 1/2380
31	From the Lords of the Admiralty	23 Dec. 1743	ADM 2/60, pp. 458–9
32	From the Lords of the Admiralty	26 Dec. 1743	ADM 2/60, p. 469
33	To Corbett	26 Dec. 1743	ADM 1/2380
34	From the Lords of the Admiralty	2 Jan. 1744	ADM 2/60, p. 492
35	To Corbett	5 Jan. 1744	ADM 1/2380
36	From the Lords of the Admiralty	13 Jan. 1744	ADM 2/60, pp. 522–3
37	To Corbett	24 Jan. 1744	ADM 1/2380
38	To Corbett	11 Feb. 1744	ADM 1/2380
39	From Devonshire	16 Feb. 1744	ADM 1/2380
40	To Corbett	19 Feb. 1744	ADM 1/2380
41	To Corbett	8 March 1744	ADM 1/2380
42	To Corbett	18 March 1744	ADM 1/2380
43	To Corbett	23 March 1744	ADM 1/2380
44	To Corbett	26 March 1744	ADM 1/2381

LIST OF DOCUMENTS AND SOURCES 495

45	From the Lords of the Admiralty	27 March 1744	ADM 2/61, pp. 116–17
46	To Corbett	30 March 1744	ADM 1/2381
47	To Corbett	3 April 1744	ADM 1/2381
48	From the Lords of the Admiralty	4 April 1744	ADM 2/61, p. 151
49	To Corbett	6 April 1744	ADM 1/2381
50	To Corbett	7 April 1744	ADM 1/2381
51	To Corbett	9 April 1744	ADM 1/2381
52	To Corbett	13 April 1744	ADM 1/2381
53	From the Lords of the Admiralty	13 April 1744	ADM 2/61, pp. 187–9
54	To Corbett	21 April 1744	ADM 1/2381
55	From the Lords of the Admiralty	23 April 1744	ADM 2/61, pp. 210–11
56	To Corbett	23 April 1744	ADM 1/2381
57	From the Lords of the Admiralty	23 April 1744	ADM 2/61, pp. 211–12
58	From the Lords of the Admiralty	26 April 1744	ADM 2/61, p. 227
59	To Corbett	3 May 1744	ADM 1/2381
60	To Corbett	11 May 1744	ADM 1/2381
61	To Corbett	23 May 1744	ADM 1/2381
62	To Corbett	6 June 1744	ADM 1/2381
63	To Corbett	20 June 1744	ADM 1/2381
64	From the Lords of the Admiralty	6 Aug. 1744	ADM 2/62, pp. 54–5
65	To Corbett	12 Sept. 1744	ADM 1/2381
66	To Corbett	17 Sept. 1744	ADM 1/2381
67	To Corbett	20 Sept. 1744	ADM 1/2381
68	From the Lords of the Admiralty	22 Sept. 1744	ADM 2/62, p. 205
69	To Corbett	23 Sept. 1744	ADM 1/2381
70	To Corbett	25 Sept. 1744	ADM 1/2381
71	From the Lords of the Admiralty	25 Sept. 1744	ADM 2/62, p. 211
72	To Corbett	28 Sept. 1744	ADM 1/2381
73	To Corbett	4 Oct. 1744	ADM 1/2381
74	From the Lords of the Admiralty	5 Oct. 1744	ADM 2/62, p. 252
75	To Corbett	8 Oct. 1744	ADM 1/2381
76	From the Lords of the Admiralty	9 Oct. 1744	ADM 2/62, p. 265
77	To Corbett	17 Oct. 1744	ADM 1/2381
78	To Corbett	22 Oct. 1744	ADM 1/2381
79	From the Lords of the Admiralty	23 Oct. 1744	ADM 2/62, pp. 318–19
80	To Corbett	25 Oct. 1744	ADM 1/2381
81	To Corbett	26 Oct. 1744	ADM 1/2381
82	To Corbett	28 Oct. 1744	ADM 1/2381
83	From the Lords of the Admiralty	29 Oct. 1744	ADM 2/62, pp. 334–5
84	To Corbett	31 Oct. 1744	ADM 1/2381
85	From the Lords of the Admiralty	31 Oct. 1744	ADM 2/62, p. 352
86	From the Lords of the Admiralty	1 Nov. 1744	ADM 2/62, pp. 345–7

87	To Corbett	4 Nov. 1744	ADM 1/2381
88	From the Lords of the Admiralty	7 Nov. 1744	ADM 2/62, pp. 367–8
89	From the Lords of the Admiralty	7 Nov. 1744	ADM 2/62, p. 368
90	To Corbett	8 Nov. 1744	ADM 1/2381
91	From the Lords of the Admiralty	8 Nov. 1744	ADM 2/62, p. 370
92	From the Lords of the Admiralty	8 Nov. 1744	ADM 2/62, pp. 378–9
93	To Corbett	10 Nov. 1744	ADM 1/2381
94	To Corbett	24 Nov. 1744	ADM 1/2381
95	To Corbett	27 Nov. 1744	ADM 1/2381
96	From the Lords of the Admiralty	27 Nov. 1744	ADM 2/62, p. 441
97	To Corbett	1 Dec. 1744	ADM 1/2381
98	To Corbett	10 Dec. 1744	ADM 1/2381
99	To Corbett	10 Dec. 1744	ADM 1/2381
100	To Corbett	18 Dec. 1744	ADM 1/2381
101	To Corbett	29 Dec. 1744	ADM 1/2381
102	To Corbett	4 Jan. 1745	ADM 1/2381
103	To Corbett	7 Jan. 1745	ADM 1/2381
104	From the Lords of the Admiralty	11 Jan. 1745	ADM 2/63, pp. 81–2
105	From the Lords of the Admiralty	11 Jan. 1745	ADM 2/63, p. 82
106	From the Lords of the Admiralty	14 Jan. 1745	ADM 2/63, p. 95
107	From the Lords of the Admiralty	14 Jan. 1745	ADM 2/63, p. 97
108	To Corbett	16 Jan. 1745	ADM 1/2381
109	From the Lords of the Admiralty	16 Jan. 1745	ADM 2/63, p. 104
110	To Corbett	18 Jan. 1745	ADM 1/2381
111	From the Lords of the Admiralty	21 Jan. 1745	ADM 2/63, p. 113
112	To Corbett	22 Jan. 1745	ADM 1/2381
113	To Corbett	5 Feb. 1745	ADM 1/2381
114	From the Lords of the Admiralty	9 Feb. 1745	ADM 2/63, pp. 184–5
115	To Corbett	9 Feb. 1745	ADM 1/2381
116	To Corbett	14 Feb. 1745	ADM 1/2381
117	From the Lords of the Admiralty	15 Feb. 1745	ADM 2/63, p. 217
118	To Corbett	16 Feb. 1745	ADM 1/2381
119	To Corbett	2 April 1745	ADM 1/2381
120	To Corbett	29 April 1745	ADM 1/2381
121	To Corbett	28 May 1745	ADM 1/2381
122	To Corbett	5 July 1745	ADM 1/2381
123	To Corbett	16 July 1745	ADM 1/2381
124	To Corbett	18 July 1745	ADM 1/2381
125	To Corbett	25 July 1745	ADM 1/2381
126	To Corbett	30 July 1745	ADM 1/2381
127	From Smith	31 July 1745	ADM 1/2381
128	To Corbett	1 Aug. 1745	ADM 1/2381
129	To Corbett	4 Aug. 1745	ADM 1/2381
130	To Corbett	4 Aug. 1745	ADM 1/2381
131	From the Lords of the Admiralty	12 Aug. 1745	ADM 2/65, p. 1

LIST OF DOCUMENTS AND SOURCES 497

132	From the Lords of the Admiralty	22 Aug. 1745	ADM 2/65, p. 48
133	To Corbett	15 Sept. 1745	ADM 1/2381
134	To Corbett	17 Sept. 1745	ADM 1/2381
135	To Corbett	17 Sept. 1745	ADM 1/2381
136	To Corbett	18 Sept. 1745	ADM 1/2381
137	From the Lords of the Admiralty	18 Sept. 1745	ADM 2/65, p. 156
138	From the Lords of the Admiralty	1 Oct. 1745	ADM 2/65, pp. 205–06
139	To Corbett	2 Oct. 1745	ADM 1/2381
140	To Corbett	3 Oct. 1745	ADM 1/2381
141	To Corbett	8 Oct. 1745	ADM 1/2381
142	From the Lords of the Admiralty	8 Oct. 1745	ADM 2/65, pp. 224–5
143	To Corbett	9 Oct. 1745	ADM 1/2381
144	To Corbett	10 Oct. 1745	ADM 1/2381
145	To Corbett	11 Oct. 1745	ADM 1/2381
146	To Corbett	18 Oct. 1745	ADM 1/2381
147	To Corbett	Nov. 1745	ADM 1/2381
148	To Corbett	25 Nov. 1745	ADM 1/2381
149	From the Lords of the Admiralty	26 Nov. 1745	ADM 2/65, pp. 431–2
150	To Corbett	30 Nov. 1745	ADM 1/2381
151	From the Lords of the Admiralty	2 Dec. 1745	ADM 2/65, p. 445
152	To Corbett	3 Dec. 1745	ADM 1/2381
153	From the Lords of the Admiralty	3 Dec. 1745	ADM 2/65, p. 449
154	To Corbett	5 Dec. 1745	ADM 1/2381
155	To Corbett	7 Dec. 1745	ADM 1/2381
156	To Corbett	11 Dec. 1745	ADM 1/2381
157	To Corbett	14 Dec. 1745	ADM 1/2381
158	To Corbett	15 Dec. 1745	ADM 1/2381
159	To Corbett	22 Dec. 1745	ADM 1/2381
160	To Corbett	28 Dec. 1745	ADM 1/2381
161	To Corbett	29 Dec. 1745	ADM 1/2381
162	From the Lords of the Admiralty	31 Dec. 1745	ADM 2/65, pp. 566–7
163	To Corbett	1 Jan. 1746	ADM 1/2381
164	To Corbett	7 Jan. 1746	ADM 1/2381
165	To Corbett	9 Jan. 1746	ADM 1/2381
166	To Corbett	11 Jan. 1746	ADM 1/2381
167	To Corbett	18 Jan. 1746	ADM 1/2381
168	To Corbett	20 Jan. 1746	ADM 1/2381
169	From the Lords of the Admiralty	20 Jan. 1746	ADM 2/66, p. 44
170	To Corbett	23 Jan. 1746	ADM 1/2381
171	To Corbett	29 Jan. 1746	ADM 1/2381
172	To Corbett	1 Feb. 1746	ADM 1/2381
173	To Corbett	2 Feb. 1746	ADM 1/2381
174	To Corbett	4 Feb. 1746	ADM 1/2381
175	To Corbett	15 Feb. 1746	ADM 1/2381
176	To Corbett	20 Feb. [1746]	ADM 1/2381
177	To Corbett	22 Feb. 1746	ADM 1/2381

178	To Corbett	21 March 1746	ADM 1/2381
179	To Corbett	23 March 1746	ADM 1/2381
180	From the Lords of the Admiralty	24 March 1746	ADM 2/66, pp. 402–03
181	From the Lords of the Admiralty	1 April 1746	ADM 2/66, pp. 451–2
182	To Corbett	19 April 1746	ADM 1/2381
183	To Corbett	6 May 1746	ADM 1/2381
184	To Corbett	10 May 1746	ADM 1/2381
185	From the Lords of the Admiralty	15 May 1746	ADM 2/67, pp. 140–41
186	From the Lords of the Admiralty	19 May 1746	ADM 2/67, p. 158
187	To Corbett	27 May 1746	ADM 1/2381
188	To Corbett	14 July 1746	ADM 1/2381
189	From the Lords of the Admiralty	21 July 1746	ADM 2/67, p. 495
190	To Corbett	8 Aug. 1746	ADM 1/2381
191	To Corbett	10 Aug. 1746	ADM 1/2381
192	To Corbett	3 Nov.1746	ADM 1/2381
193	From Anson	8 Nov. 1746	ADM 1/87
194	To Corbett	10 Nov. 1746	ADM 1/2381
195	To Corbett	16 Nov. 1746	ADM 1/2381
196	From Corbett	21 Nov. 1746	ADM 2/689, p. 59
197	From Corbett	25 Nov. 1746	ADM 2/689, p. 76
198	To Corbett	7 Dec. 1746	ADM 1/2381
199	From Corbett	11 Dec. 1746	ADM 2/693, p. 206
200	To Corbett	16 Dec. 1746	ADM 1/2381
201	To Corbett	20 Dec. 1746	ADM 1/2381
202	From Corbett	9 Jan. 1747	ADM 2/693, p. 339
203	To Corbett	19 Jan. 1747	ADM 1/2382
204	From Clevland	30 Jan. 1747	ADM 2/963, p. 443
205	To Corbett	5 Feb. 1747	ADM 1/2381
206	To Corbett	7 April 1747	ADM 1/2382
207	From Clevland	11 April 1747	ADM 2/690, pp. 354–5
208	From Anson	20 April 1747	ADM 1/87
209	To Corbett	5 May 1747	ADM 1/2382
210	From Anson	15 May 1747	ADM 1/87
211	To Corbett	30 June 1747	ADM 1/2382
212	From the Lords of the Admiralty	1 July 1747	ADM 2/70, p. 70
213	From Corbett	1 July 1747	ADM 2/691, p. 334
214	From Corbett	1 July 1747	ADM 2/691, p. 334
215	To Corbett	3 July 1747	ADM 1/2382
216	From Clevland	4 July 1747	ADM 2/692, p. 1
217	To Corbett	4 July 1747	ADM 1/2382
218	To Corbett	4 July 1747	ADM 1/2382
219	From Corbett	6 July 1747	ADM 2/692, p. 7
220	To Corbett	11 July 1747	ADM 1/2382
221	From Corbett	13 July 1747	ADM 2/962, p. 28
222	To Corbett	17 July 1747	ADM 1/2382
223	From Corbett	20 July 1747	ADM 2/692, p. 60

LIST OF DOCUMENTS AND SOURCES

224	To Corbett	24 July 1747	ADM 1/2382
225	To Corbett	28 July 1747	ADM 1/2382
226	From Clevland	15 Aug. 1747	ADM 2/692, p. 181
227	To Corbett	30 Aug. 1747	ADM 1/2382
228	From Anson	10 Nov. 1747	PRO 30/20/20/4, pp. 1–3
229	To Corbett	19 Nov. 1747	ADM 1/2382
230	To Corbett	1 July 1748	ADM 1/2382
231	From the Lords of the Admiralty	12 July 1748	ADM 2/72, p. 119
232	To Corbett	1 Oct. 1748	ADM 1/2382
233	From Corbett	3 Oct. 1748	ADM 2/695, pp. 452–3
234	To Corbett	23 Nov. 1748	ADM 1/2382
235	To Corbett	18 Jan. 1749	ADM 1/2382
236	To Corbett	9 Feb. 1749	ADM 1/2382
237	To Corbett	17 March 1749	ADM 1/2382
238	To Clevland	15 April 1749	ADM 1/2382
239	To Corbett	4 May 1749	ADM 1/2382
240	To Corbett	21 May 1749	ADM 1/2382
241	To Corbett	30 May 1749	ADM 1/2382
242	From the Lords of the Admiralty	30 May 1749	ADM 2/73, p. 10
243	From the Lords of the Admiralty	2 June 1749	ADM 2/73, p. 12
244	To Clevland	2 June 1749	ADM 1/2382
245	To Clevland	5 June 1749	ADM 1/2382
246	To Corbett	6 June 1749	ADM 1/2382
247	To Clevland	4 Aug. 1749	ADM 1/2382
248	To Clevland	7 Sept. 1749	ADM 1/2382
249	To Clevland	7 Nov. 1749	ADM 1/2382
250	To Clevland	14 Dec. 1749	ADM 1/2382
251	From the Lords of the Admiralty	15 Dec. 1749	ADM 2/73, p. 139
252	To Clevland	21 Dec. 1749	ADM 1/2382
253	To Clevland	23 Dec. 1749	ADM 1/2382
254	To Clevland	24 Dec. 1749	ADM 1/2382
255	From Clevland	27 March 1750	ADM 2/697, p. 289
256	From the Lords of the Admiralty	30 March 1750	ADM 2/73, p. 235
257	To Clevland	1 April 1750	ADM 1/2382
258	From the Lords of the Admiralty	19 April 1750	ADM 2/73, pp. 251–2
259	To Clevland	22 April 1750	ADM 1/2382
260	From the Lords of the Admiralty	24 April 1750	ADM 2/73, pp. 254–5
261	To Clevland	26 April 1750	ADM 1/2382
262	From the Lords of the Admiralty	30 April 1750	ADM 2/73, p. 261
263	To Clevland	4 May 1750	ADM 1/2382
264	From Bedford	5 May 1750	PRO 30/20/20/4, p. 5
265	From the Lords of the Admiralty	11 May 1750	ADM 2/73, pp. 272–8
266	From the Lords of the Admiralty	11 May 1750	ADM 2/73, p. 278
267	To Clevland	18 May 1750	ADM 1/2382

268	To Clevland	22 May 1750	ADM 1/2382
269	From the Lords of the Admiralty	24 May 1750	ADM 2/73, pp. 297–8
270	From Bedford	26 May 1750	PRO 30/20/20/4, p. 9
271	From Mount Edgecumbe	27 May 1750	PRO 30/20/20/4, p. 11
272	To Clevland	6 June 1750	ADM 1/2382
273	To Clevland	25 July 1750	ADM 1/2382
274	To Clevland	7 Aug. 1750	ADM 1/2382
275	To Clevland	25 Sept. 1750	ADM 1/2382
276	To Clevland	27 Oct. 1750	ADM 1/2382
277	To Anson	27 Oct. 1750	Add. MSS 15956, ff. 323–4
278	To Clevland	28 Dec. 1750	ADM 1/2382
279	From the Lords of the Admiralty	3 Jan. 1751	ADM 2/73, pp. 403–04
280	To Corbett	8 Jan. 1751	ADM 1/2382
281	To Corbett	13 Jan. 1751	ADM 1/2382
282	To Corbett	15 Jan. 1751	ADM 1/2382
283	From the Lords of the Admiralty	16 Jan. 1751	ADM 2/73, p. 410
284	To Corbett	18 Jan. 1751	ADM 1/2382
285	From the Lords of the Admiralty	18 Jan. 1751	ADM 2/73, pp. 415–16
286	To Corbett	27 March 1751	ADM 1/2383
287	To Corbett	5 April 1751	ADM 1/2383
288	From the Lords of the Admiralty	6 April 1751	ADM 2/73, p. 443
289	To Corbett	10 April 1751	ADM 1/2383
290	From Corbett	11 April 1751	ADM 2/697, p. 529
291	From the Lords of the Admiralty	11 April 1751	ADM 2/73, p. 449
292	To Corbett	12 April 1751	ADM 1/2383
293	From the Lords of the Admiralty	16 April 1751	ADM 2/73, pp. 450–51
294	From Clevland	22 April 1751	ADM 2/697, p. 539
295	From the Lords of the Admiralty	24 April 1751	ADM 2/73, p. 461
296	To Corbett	28 April 1751	ADM 1/2383
297	To Clevland	2 May 1751	ADM 1/2383
298	From Egremont	20 May 1751	PRO 30/20/20/4, p. 15
299	To Clevland	8 June 1751	ADM 1/2383
300	To Clevland	16 June 1751	ADM 1/2383
301	To Clevland	14 Aug. 1751	ADM 1/2383
302	To Bentinck	24 Sept. 1751	PRO 30/20/20/4, pp. 17–20
303	From Harrison	12 Oct. 1751	ADM 1/2383
304	To Clevland	15 Oct. 1751	ADM 1/2383
305	To Clevland	9 Nov. 1751	ADM 1/2383
306	To Clevland	13 Jan. 1752	ADM 1/2383
307	To Clevland	22 Jan. 1752	ADM 1/2383
308	From Clevland	20 Feb. 1752	ADM 2/698, p. 225

309	To Clevland	18 March 1752	ADM 1/2383
310	From Clevland	20 March 1752	ADM 2/698, p. 247
311	From the Lords of the Admiralty	20 March 1752	ADM 2/74, p. 89
312	To Clevland	23 March 1752	ADM 1/2383
313	To Clevland	25 March 1752	ADM 1/2383
314	To Clevland	26 March 1752	ADM 1/2383
315	From Clevland	27 March 1752	ADM 2/698, p. 252
316	To Clevland	23 April 1752	ADM 1/2383
317	To Clevland	23 April 1752	ADM 1/2383
318	To Clevland	24 April 1752	ADM 1/2383
319	To Clevland	7 May 1752	ADM 1/2383
320	To Clevland	31 May 1752	ADM 1/2383
321	To Clevland	28 Dec. 1752	ADM 1/2383
322	From the Lords of the Admiralty	16 Jan. 1753	ADM 2/74, p. 209
323	To Clevland	19 Jan. 1753	ADM 1/2383
324	To Clevland	2 May 1753	ADM 1/2383
325	To Clevland	30 June 1753	ADM 1/2383
326	To Clevland	10 July 1753	ADM 1/2383
327	To Clevland	3 Nov. 1753	ADM 1/2383
328	From the Lords of the Admiralty	3 Jan. 1754	ADM 2/74, p. 367
329	To Clevland	22 Jan. 1754	ADM 1/2384
330	From Clevland	28 Feb. 1754	ADM 2/699, p. 383
331	From Clevland	6 April 1754	ADM 2/699, p. 432
332	To Clevland	6 May 1754	ADM 1/2384
333	To Clevland	25 Oct. 1754	ADM 1/2384
334	To Clevland	3 Dec. 1754	ADM 1/2384
335	From the Lords of the Admiralty	16 Jan. 1755	ADM 2/75, p. 16
336	From the Lords of the Admiralty	18 Jan. 1755	ADM 2/75, p. 21
337	To Clevland	28 Jan. 1755	ADM 1/2384
338	To Clevland	28 Jan. 1755	ADM 1/2384
339	To Jane Rodney	30 Jan. 1755	PRO 30/20/20/2, pp. 9–10
340	To Jane Rodney	1 Feb. 1755	PRO 30/20/20/2, pp. 13–14
341	To Clevland	5 Feb. 1755	ADM 1/2384
342	To Jane Rodney	8 Feb. 1755	PRO 30/20/20/2, pp. 25–6
343	To Clevland	9 Feb. 1755	ADM 1/2384
344	To Jane Rodney	9 Feb. 1755	PRO 30/20/20/2, pp. 29–30
345	To Clevland	10 Feb. 1755	ADM 1/2384
346	To Clevland	11 Feb. 1755	ADM 1/2384
347	To Jane Rodney	14 Feb. 1755	PRO 30/20/20/2, pp. 37–8
348	To Clevland	16 Feb. 1755	ADM 1/2384
349	From Clevland	18 Feb. 1755	ADM 2/700, p. 245
350	To Jane Rodney	18 Feb. 1755	PRO 30/20/20/2, pp. 41–2
351	To Clevland	25 Feb. 1755	ADM 1/2384
352	To Clevland	20 March 1755	ADM 1/2384

353	From Clevland	21 March 1755	ADM 2/700, pp. 516–17
354	To Clevland	27 March 1755	ADM 1/2384
355	From Clevland	29 March 1755	ADM 2/701, p. 41
356	To Clevland	31 March 1755	ADM 1/2384
357	From Clevland	1 April 1755	ADM 2/701, p. 56
358	To Clevland	8 April 1755	ADM 1/2384
359	From Clevland	19 April 1755	ADM 2/701, p. 151
360	From Clevland	21 April 1755	ADM 2/701, p. 157
361	To Clevland	28 April 1755	ADM 1/2384
362	To Clevland	30 April 1755	ADM 1/2384
363	From Clevland	22 May 1755	ADM 2/701, p. 302
364	To Clevland	26 May 1755	ADM 1/2384
365	From Clevland	3 June 1755	ADM 2/701, p. 347
366	To Clevland	7 July 1755	ADM 1/2384
367	To Clevland	10 July 1755	ADM 1/2384
368	From Clevland	15 July 1755	ADM 2/701, p. 496
369	From the Lords of the Admiralty	16 July 1755	ADM 2/75, p. 287
370	To Jane Rodney	3 Aug. 1755	PRO 30/20/20/2, pp. 65–8
371	To Jane Rodney	3 Aug. 1755	PRO 30/20/20/2, pp. 67–71
372	From Hawke	4 Aug. 1755	PRO 30/20/6
373	To Jane Rodney	28 Aug. 1755	PRO 30/20/20/2, pp. 73–4
374	To Jane Rodney	8 Sept. 1755	PRO 30/20/20/2, pp. 77–9
375	To Jane Rodney	14 Sept. 1755	PRO 30/20/20/2, pp. 81–4
376	To Clevland	20 Oct. 1755	ADM 1/2384
377	From Clevland	21 Oct. 1755	ADM 2/702, p. 333
378	To Clevland	13 Nov. 1755	ADM 1/2384
379	To Clevland	1 Dec. 1755	ADM 1/2384
380	To Clevland	2 Jan. 1756	ADM 1/2385
381	From Clevland	7 Jan. 1756	ADM 2/703, p. 153
382	To Clevland	[13 Jan. 1756]	ADM 1/2385
383	To Clevland	13 Jan. 1756	ADM 1/2385
384	To Clevland	16 Jan. 1756	ADM 1/2385
385	From Clevland	16 Jan. 1756	ADM 2/703, p. 206
386	From Clevland	30 Jan. 1756	ADM 2/703, p. 272
387	From Clevland	31 Jan. 1756	ADM 2/703, p. 276
388	From Clevland	7 Feb. 1756	ADM 2/703, p. 306
389	To Newcastle	12 Feb. 1756	ADM 1/2385
390	From Newcastle	13 Feb. 1756	PRO 30/20/20/4, p. 23
391	From Clevland	14 Feb. 1756	ADM 2/703, pp. 330–31
392	To Clevland	14 March 1756	ADM 1/2385
393	To Clevland	3 April 1756	ADM 1/2385
394	From Clevland	6 April 1756	ADM 2/704, p. 126

LIST OF DOCUMENTS AND SOURCES

395	From Clevland	6 April 1756	ADM 2/704, p. 128
396	From Anson	30 April 1756	PRO 30/20/4, pp. 27–8
397	To Clevland	3 May 1756	ADM 1/2385
398	From Clevland	8 May 1756	ADM 2/704, pp. 331–2
399	To Clevland	17 May 1756	ADM 1/2385
400	To Clevland	26 May 1756	ADM 1/2385
401	To Jane Rodney	1 June 1756	PRO 30/20/20/2, pp. 99–101
402	To Clevland	1 June 1756	ADM 1/2385
403	From Angel	3 June 1756	ADM 1/2385
404	To Clevland	4 June 1756	ADM 1/2385
405	To Jane Rodney	6 June 1756	PRO 30/20/20/2, pp. 103–04
406	To Clevland	6 June 1756	ADM 1/2385
407	To Edgcumbe	6 June 1756	ADM 1/2385
408	To Clevland	8 June 1756	ADM 1/2385
409	To Clevland	11 June 1756	ADM 1/2385
410	To Clevland	13 June 1756	ADM 1/2385
411	To Jane Rodney	15 June 1756	PRO 30/20/20/2, pp. 107–09
412	To Clevland	15 June 1756	ADM 1/2385
413	To Jane Rodney	18 June 1756	PRO 30/20/20/2, pp. 111–14
414	To Clevland	18 June 1756	ADM 1/2385
415	To Clevland	20 June 1756	ADM 1/2385
416	To Jane Rodney	22 June 1756	PRO 30/20/20/2, pp. 115–18
417	To Clevland	22 June 1756	ADM 1/2385
418	To Clevland	25 June 1756	ADM 1/2385
419	To Jane Rodney	29 June 1756	PRO 30/20/20/2, pp. 119–22
420	To Clevland	4 July 1756	ADM 1/2385
421	To Jane Rodney	6 July 1756	PRO 30/20/20/2, pp. 123–6
422	To Clevland	8 July 1756	ADM 1/2385
423	To Jane Rodney	30 July 1756	PRO 30/20/20/2, pp. 127–30
424	From Sandwich	1 Aug. 1756	PRO 30/20/20/5, pp. 1–3
425	To Clevland	12 Aug. 1756	ADM 1/2385
426	To Clevland	16 Aug. 1756	ADM 1/2385
427	To Clevland	26 Aug. 1756	ADM 1/2385
428	To Clevland	27 Aug. 1756	ADM 1/2385
429	From Fox	2 Sept. 1756	PRO 30/20/20/4, pp. 31–2
430	From Ilchester	5 Sept. 1756	PRO 30/20/20/4, pp. 35–7
431	To Clevland	10 Sept. 1756	ADM 1/2385

504   THE RODNEY PAPERS

432	To Clevland	13 Sept. 1756	ADM 1/2385
433	To Newcastle	19 Sept. 1756	Add. MSS 32867, f. 343
434	To Clevland	29 Oct. 1756	ADM 1/2385
435	To Jane Rodney	4 Nov. 1756	PRO 30/20/20/2, pp. 131–3
436	To Clevland	8 Nov. 1756	ADM 1/2385
437	To Clevland	12 Dec. 1756	ADM 1/2385
438	To Clevland	24 Dec. 1756	ADM 1/2385
439	From the Lords of the Admiralty	6 April 1757	ADM 2/78, pp. 280–81
440	To Clevland	27 April 1757	ADM 1/2385
441	From Milnes	27 April 1757	ADM 2/707, p. 259
442	From Clevland	10 May 1757	ADM 2/707, p. 323
443	To Boscawen	[13 May 1757]	ADM 1/2385
444	To Clevland	13 May 1757	ADM 1/2385
445	From Clevland	13 May 1757	ADM 2/707, p. 339
446	From Clevland	18 May 1757	ADM 2/707, p. 364
447	From the Lords of the Admiralty	26 May 1757	ADM 2/78, p. 458
448	To Clevland	27 May 1757	ADM 1/2385
449	To Clevland	3 June 1757	ADM 1/2385
450	From Clevland	6 June 1757	ADM 2/707, p. 452
451	To Clevland	8 June 1757	ADM 1/2385
452	To Clevland	10 June 1757	ADM 1/2385
453	From Clevland	10 June 1757	ADM 2/707, p. 476
454	To Clevland	16 June 1757	ADM 1/2385
455	To Clevland	19 June 1757	ADM 1/2385
456	From Clevland	20 June 1757	ADM 2/707, p. 520
457	To Clevland	21 June 1757	ADM 1/2385
458	From Clevland	22 June 1757	ADM 2/707, p. 533
459	To Clevland	28 June 1757	ADM 1/2385
460	From Clevland	28 June 1757	ADM 2/708, p. 6
461	To Clevland	7 July 1757	ADM 1/2385
462	From Clevland	7 July 1757	ADM 2/708, p. 37
463	From Clevland	11 July 1757	ADM 2/708, p. 52
464	To Clevland	13 July 1757	ADM 1/2385
465	To Clevland	14 July 1757	ADM 1/2385
466	From Clevland	18 July 1757	ADM 2/708, p. 83
467	From Kennedy and Surtes	18 July 1757	ADM 1/2385
468	From the Lords of the Admiralty	19 July 1757	ADM 2/79, p. 81
469	To Clevland	19 July 1757	ADM 1/2385
470	To Clevland	20 July 1757	ADM 1/2385
471	From Clevland	20 July 1757	ADM 2/708, p. 90
472	From Clevland	20 July 1757	ADM 2/708, p. 91
473	To Clevland	20 July 1757	ADM 1/2385
474	From the Lords of the Admiralty	21 July 1757	ADM 2/79, p. 86
475	From the Lords of the Admiralty	21 July 1757	ADM 2/79, p. 87
476	From Clevland	22 July 1757	ADM 2/708, p. 97
477	To Clevland	24 July 1757	ADM 1/2385
478	From Clevland	25 July 1757	ADM 2/708, p. 115

… LIST OF DOCUMENTS AND SOURCES

479	To Clevland	27 July 1757	ADM 1/2385
480	To Clevland	28 July 1757	ADM 1/2385
481	To Clevland	29 July 1757	ADM 1/2385
482	To Clevland	30 July 1757	ADM 1/2385
483	To Clevland	3 Aug. 1757	ADM 1/2385
484	From the Lords of the Admiralty	5 Aug. 1757	ADM 2/79, p. 138
485	To Clevland	28 Nov. 1757	ADM 1/2385
486	From the Lords of the Admiralty	30 Nov. 1757	ADM 2/79, pp. 448–9
487	From Clevland	6 Dec. 1757	ADM 2/709, p. 77
488	To Clevland	9 Dec. 1957	ADM 1/2385
489	From Clevland	28 Dec. 1757	ADM 2/709, p. 148
490	To Clevland	30 Dec. 1757	ADM 1/2385
491	To Clevland	9 Jan. 1758	ADM 1/2386
492	From Clevland	10 Jan. 1758	ADM 2/709, pp. 186–7
493	To Clevland	14 Jan. 1758	ADM 1/2386
494	To Clevland	26 Jan. 1758	ADM 1/2386
495	From the Lords of the Admiralty	27 Jan. 1758	ADM 2/80, p. 66
496	To Clevland	18 Feb. 1758	ADM 1/2386
497	From the Lords of the Admiralty	23 Feb. 1758	ADM 2/80, p. 142
498	From Clevland	27 Feb. 1758	ADM 2/709, p. 377
499	To Clevland	27 Feb. 1758	ADM 1/2386
500	From Clevland	28 Feb. 1758	ADM 2/709, p. 383
501	To Clevland	1 March 1758	ADM 1/2386
502	From the Lords of the Admiralty	2 March 1758	ADM 2/80, p. 160
503	To Clevland	5 March 1758	ADM 1/2386
504	To Clevland	6 March 1758	ADM 1/2386
505	From Clevland	6 March 1758	ADM 2/709, p. 405
506	From Clevland	7 March 1758	ADM 2/709, p. 411
507	To Clevland	29 March 1758	ADM 1/2386
508	To Clevland	31 March 1758	ADM 1/2386
509	To Clevland	7 May 1758	ADM 1/2386
510	To Clevland	14 Sept. 1758	ADM 1/2386
511	To Clevland	17 Sept. 1758	ADM 1/2386
512	From Clevland	18 Sept. 1758	ADM 2/710, p. 374
513	To Clevland	18 Sept. 1758	ADM 1/2386
514	From the Lords of the Admiralty	19 Sept. 1758	ADM 2/81, pp. 112–13
515	From Clevland	19 Sept. 1758	ADM 2/710, p. 381
516	To Clevland	21 Sept. 1758	ADM 1/2386
517	To Clevland	25 Sept. 1758	ADM 1/2386
518	From Clevland	26 Sept. 1758	ADM 2/710, p. 397
519	To Clevland	27 Sept. 1758	ADM 1/2386
520	From Clevland	28 Sept. 1758	ADM 2/710, p. 404
521	To Clevland	1 Oct. 1758	ADM 1/2386
522	To Clevland	19 Oct. 1758	ADM 1/2386
523	To Clevland	21 Oct. 1758	ADM 1/2386
524	From Clevland	21 Oct. 1758	ADM 2/710, p. 493

525	To Newcastle	24 April 1759	Add. MSS 32890, f. 330
526	From the Lords of the Admiralty	24 May 1759	ADM 2/83, p. 40
527	To Clevland	27 May 1759	ADM 1/93
528	To Clevland	28 May 1759	ADM 1/93
529	From Clevland	29 May [1759]	ADM 2/525, p. 342
530	To Clevland	29 May 1759	ADM 1/93
531	From Clevland	30 May 1759	ADM 2/525, p. 349
532	From Clevland	30 May 1759	ADM 2/525, p. 350
533	To Clevland	30 May 1759	ADM 1/93
534	From Clevland	31 May [1759]	ADM 2/525, p. 352
535	To Clevland	31 May 1759	ADM 1/93
536	From Clevland	1 June 1759	ADM 2/525, p. 354
537	To Clevland	1 June 1759	ADM 1/93
538	To Clevland	2 June 1759	ADM 1/93
539	To Clevland	3 June 1759	ADM 1/93
540	To Clevland	4 June 1759	ADM 1/93
541	From Clevland	5 June 1759	ADM 2/525, p. 365
542	To Clevland	5 June 1759	ADM 1/93
543	To Clevland	6 June 1759	ADM 1/93
544	From the Lords of the Admiralty	8 June 1759	ADM 2/83, pp. 76–7
545	To Clevland	10 June 1759	ADM 1/93
546	To Clevland	10 June 1759	ADM 1/93
547	To Clevland	11 June 1759	ADM 1/93
548	To Clevland	12 June 1759	ADM 1/93
549	To Clevland	13 June 1759	ADM 1/93
550	To Clevland	15 June 1759	ADM 1/93
551	To Clevland	15 June 1759	ADM 1/93
552	From Clevland	16 June 1759	ADM 2/525, p. 405
553	To Clevland	17 June 1759	ADM 1/93
554	From the Lords of the Admiralty	18 June 1759	ADM 2/83, p. 100
555	To Clevland	18 June 1759	ADM 1/93
556	From Clevland	20 June 1759	ADM 2/525, p. 432
557	To Clevland	20 June 1759	ADM 1/93
558	To Clevland	25 June 1759	ADM 1/93
559	To Clevland	26 June 1759	ADM 1/93
560	From the Lords of the Admiralty	26 June 1759	ADM 2/1331, pp. 305–06
561	To Clevland	27 June 1759	ADM 1/93
562	To Clevland	27 June 1759	ADM 1/93
563	To Clevland	28 June 1759	ADM 1/93
564	To Clevland	29 June 1759	ADM 1/93
565	To Clevland	30 June 1759	ADM 1/93
566	To Clevland	1 July 1759	ADM 1/93
567	To Clevland	4 July 1759	ADM 1/93
568	From Anson	6 July 1759	PRO 30/20/20/4, pp. 39–40
569	To Clevland	6 July 1759	ADM 1/93
570	From Clevland	7 July 1759	ADM 2/525, p. 498

LIST OF DOCUMENTS AND SOURCES

571	To Clevland	8 July 1759	ADM 1/93
572	From Clevland	9 July 1759	ADM 2/525, p. 502
573	From Clevland	10 July 1759	ADM 2/525, p. 505
574	To Clevland	10 July 1759	ADM 1/93
575	From Clevland	6 Aug. 1759	ADM 2/526, p. 52
576	From the Lords of the Admiralty	15 Aug. 1759	ADM 2/83, p. 298
577	From the Lords of the Admiralty	17 Aug. 1759	ADM 2/1331, pp. 314–15
578	To Clevland	18 Aug. 1759	ADM 1/93
579	To Clevland	19 Aug. 1759	ADM 1/93
580	From Clevland	20 Aug. 1759	ADM 2/526, p. 115
581	To Clevland	20 Aug. 1759	ADM 1/93
582	To Clevland	20 Aug. 1759	ADM 1/93
583	To Clevland	21 Aug. 1759	ADM 1/93
584	From Clevland	22 Aug. 1759	ADM 2/526, p. 127
585	From Clevland	22 Aug. 1759	ADM 2/526, p. 128
586	From Clevland	23 Aug. 1759	ADM 2/526, p. 136
587	To Clevland	23 Aug. 1759	ADM 1/93
588	From Clevland	24 Aug. 1759	ADM 2/526, p. 137
589	From Clevland	24 Aug. 1759	ADM 2/526, p. 143
590	From the Lords of the Admiralty	24 Aug. 1759	ADM 2/83, pp. 331–2
591	To Clevland	25 Aug. 1759	ADM 1/93
592	To Clevland	26 Aug. 1759	ADM 1/93
593	From Clevland	28 Aug. 1759	ADM 2/526, p. 163
594	To Clevland	29 Aug. 1759	ADM 1/93
595	To Clevland	30 Aug. 1759	ADM 1/93
596	To Clevland	1 Sept. 1759	ADM 1/93
597	From the Lords of the Admiralty	3 Sept. 1759	ADM 2/83, p. 367
598	To Clevland	3 Sept. 1759	ADM 1/93
599	To Clevland	4 Sept. 1759	ADM 1/93
600	To Clevland	7 Sept. 1759	ADM 1/93
601	To Clevland	11 Sept. 1759	ADM 1/93
602	From Milnes	14 Sept. 1759	ADM 2/526, p. 247
603	To Clevland	14 Sept. 1759	ADM 1/93
604	To Clevland	16 Sept. 1759	ADM 1/93
605	To Clevland	19 Sept. 1759	ADM 1/93
606	To Clevland	20 Sept. 1759	ADM 1/93
607	From Milnes	21 Sept. 1759	ADM 2/526, p. 280
608	To Clevland	22 Sept. 1759	ADM 1/93
609	To Clevland	23 Sept. 1759	ADM 1/93
610	From the Lords of the Admiralty	25 Sept. 1759	ADM 2/83, pp. 441–2
611	To Clevland	25 Sept. 1759	ADM 1/93
612	To Clevland	29 Sept. 1759	ADM 1/93
613	To Clevland	30 Sept. 1759	ADM 1/93
614	From the Lords of the Admiralty	2 Oct. 1759	ADM 2/83, p. 456
615	To Clevland	[4 Oct.] 1759	ADM 1/93
616	To Clevland	8 Oct. 1759	ADM 1/93
617	From Clevland	9 Oct. 1759	ADM 2/526, p. 342

618	From Clevland	11 Oct. 1759	ADM 2/526, p. 354
619	From the Lords of the Admiralty	11 Oct. 1759	ADM 2/83, p. 468
620	From Clevland	12 Oct. 1759	ADM 2/526, p. 359
621	To Clevland	15 Oct. 1759	ADM 1/93
622	To Clevland	17 Oct.1759	ADM 1/93
623	From Clevland	[?] Oct. 1759	ADM 2/526, p. 389
624	From Clevland	19 Oct. 1759	ADM 2/526, p. 394
625	To Clevland	19 Oct. 1759	ADM 1/93
626	From Clevland	20 Oct. 1759	ADM 2/526, p. 400
627	From the Lords of the Admiralty	20 Oct. 1759	ADM 2/83, p. 490
628	To Clevland	21 Oct. 1759	ADM 1/93
629	To Clevland	24 Oct. 1759	ADM 1/93
630	From the Lords of the Admiralty	26 Oct. 1759	ADM 2/83, p. 510
631	To Clevland	29 Oct. 1759	ADM 1/93
632	To Clevland	31 Oct. 1759	ADM 1/93
633	From Clevland	2 Nov. 1759	ADM 2/526, p. 471
634	From Clevland	2 Nov. 1759	ADM 2/526, 473
635	To Clevland	3 Nov. 1759	ADM 1/93
636	To Clevland	4 Nov. 1759	ADM 1/93
637	From Stephens	6 Nov. 1759	ADM 2/526, p. 487
638	To Clevland	6 Nov. 1759	ADM 1/93
639	From the Lords of the Admiralty	6 Nov. 1759	ADM 2/84, p. 15
640	From Clevland	7 Nov. 1759	ADM 2/526, p. 493
641	To Clevland	8 Nov. 1759	ADM 1/93
642	From Clevland	9 Nov. 1759	ADM 2/526, p. 508
643	To Clevland	9 Nov. 1759	ADM 1/93
644	To Clevland	10 Nov. 1759	ADM 1/93
645	From Clevland	12 Nov. 1759	ADM 2/526, p. 517
646	To Clevland	13 Nov. 1759	ADM 1/93
647	To Clevland	14 Nov. 1759	ADM 1/93
648	From Clevland	15 Nov. 1759	ADM 2/526, p. 543
649	To Clevland	19 Nov. 1759	ADM 1/93
650	From Clevland	22 Nov. 1759	ADM 2/257, p. 18
651	To Clevland	22 Nov. 1759	ADM 1/93
652	From Clevland	23 Nov. 1759	ADM 2/527, pp. 25–6
653	To Clevland	27 Nov. 1759	ADM 1/93
654	From Clevland	29 Nov. 1759	ADM 2/527, p. 57
655	To Clevland	29 Nov. 1759	ADM 1/93
656	From Clevland	30 Nov. 1759	ADM 2/527, p. 69
657	To Clevland	30 Nov. 1759	ADM 1/93
658	To Clevland	1 Dec. 1759	ADM 1/93
659	To Newcastle	2 Dec. 1759	Add. MSS 32899, ff. 266–7
660	To Clevland	4 Dec. 1759	ADM 1/93
661	From Clevland	7 Dec. 1759	ADM 2/527, p. 96
662	From Clevland	8 Dec. 1759	ADM 2/527, p. 102
663	To Clevland	12 Dec. 1759	ADM 1/93
664	To Clevland	17 Dec. 1759	ADM 1/93
665	From Clevland	20 Dec. 1759	ADM 2/527, p. 164

LIST OF DOCUMENTS AND SOURCES 509

666	To Clevland	21 Dec. 1759	ADM 1/93
667	From Stephens	24 Dec. 1759	ADM 2/257, p. 183
668	To Clevland	26 Dec. 1759	ADM 1/93
669	From Stephens	27 Dec. 1759	ADM 2/527, p. 211
670	To Clevland	31 Dec. 1759	ADM 1/93
671	To Clevland	2 Jan. 1760	ADM 1/93
672	From Hood	3 Jan. 1760	ADM 1/93
673	To Clevland	3 Jan. 1760	ADM 1/93
674	From Clevland	4 Jan. 1760	ADM 2/527, pp. 244–5
675	From Clevland	4 Jan. 1760	ADM 2/527, pp. 252–3
676	To Clevland	6 Jan. 1760	ADM 1/93
677	To Clevland	7 Jan. 1760	ADM 1/93
678	To Clevland	12 Jan. 1760	ADM 1/93
679	To Clevland	15 Jan. 1760	ADM 1/93
680	To Clevland	15 Jan. 1760	ADM 1/93
681	To Clevland	15 Jan. 1760	ADM 1/93
682	From Stephens	17 Jan. 1760	ADM 2/527, p. 318
683	From Stephens	17 Jan. 1760	ADM 2/527, pp. 320–21
684	To Clevland	18 Jan. 1760	ADM 1/93
685	From Stephens	24 Jan. 1760	ADM 2/527, p. 354
686	To Clevland	24 Jan. 1760	ADM 1/93
687	To Clevland	24 Jan. 1760	ADM 1/93
688	From Clevland	25 Jan. 1760	ADM 2/527, p. 359
689	From the Lords of the Admiralty	20 May 1760	ADM 2/84, p. 521
690	To Clevland	21 May 1760	ADM 1/93
691	From Clevland	22 May 1760	ADM 2/528, p. 447
692	To Clevland	27 May 1760	ADM 1/93
693	To Clevland	30 May 1760	ADM 1/93
694	From Clevland	31 May 1760	ADM 2/528, p. 478
695	From the Lords of the Admiralty	3 June 1760	ADM 2/85, p. 3
696	To Clevland	4 June 1760	ADM 1/93
697	To Clevland	5 June 1760	ADM 1/93
698	To Clevland	11 June 1760	ADM 1/93
699	From Clevland	11 June 1760	ADM 2/528, p. 525
700	From Clevland	16 June 1760	ADM 2/528, p. 543
701	To Clevland	24 June 1760	ADM 1/93
702	From Clevland	26 June 1760	ADM 2/529, p. 36
703	To Clevland	28 June 1760	ADM 1/93
704	From Clevland	30 June 1760	ADM 2/529, p. 45
705	From Clevland	30 June 1760	ADM 2/529, p. 45
706	To Clevland	30 June 1760	ADM 1/93
707	From Clevland	1 July 1760	ADM 2/529, p. 47
708	From Clevland	4 July 1760	ADM 2/529, p. 62
709	To Clevland	6 July 1760	ADM 1/93
710	To Clevland	11 July 1760	ADM 1/93
711	To Clevland	12 July 1760	ADM 1/93
712	From Clevland	15 July 1760	ADM 2/529, p. 91

713	From the Lords of the Admiralty	16 July 1760	ADM 2/85, p. 109
714	From de Brassac	[16 July 1760]	ADM 1/93
715	To de Brassac	17 July 1760	ADM 1/93
716	From Paston	18 July 1760	ADM 1/93
717	To Clevland	18 July 1760	ADM 1/93
718	To Clevland	18 July 1760	ADM 1/93
719	To Clevland	20 July 1760	ADM 1/93
720	From Clevland	22 July 1760	ADM 2/529, p. 116
721	From Stephens	22 July 1760	ADM 2/529, p. 117
722	To Clevland	26 July 1760	ADM 1/93
723	From Clevland	30 July 1760	ADM 2/529, p. 143
724	To Clevland	7 Aug. 1760	ADM 1/93
725	From Clevland	8 Aug. 1760	ADM 2/529, p. 174
726	To Clevland	9 Aug. 1760	ADM 1/93
727	To Clevland	11 Aug. 1760	ADM 1/93
728	To Clevland	13 Aug. 1760	ADM 1/93
729	From Stephens	18 Aug. 1760	ADM 2/529, p. 199
730	To Clevland	19 Aug. 1760	ADM 1/93
731	From Stephens	22 Aug. 1760	ADM 2/529, p. 216
732	To Clevland	24 Aug. 1760	ADM 1/93
733	From Stephens	27 Aug. 1760	ADM 2/529, pp. 240–41
734	From Stephens	30 Aug. 1760	ADM 2/529, p. 250
735	To Clevland	2 Sept. 1760	ADM 1/93
736	To Clevland	5 Sept. 1760	ADM 1/93
737	From Stephens	6 Sept. 1760	ADM 2/529, p. 275
738	From Stephens	12 Sept. 1760	ADM 2/529, p. 293
739	From Stephens	13 Sept. 1760	ADM 2/529, p. 303
740	To Clevland	14 Sept. 1760	ADM 1/93
741	From the Lords of the Admiralty	16 Sept. 1760	ADM 2/85, p. 238
742	To Clevland	19 Sept. 1760	ADM 1/93
743	To Clevland	23 Sept. 1760	ADM 1/93
744	To Clevland	25 Sept. 1760	ADM 1/93
745	To Stephens	26 Sept. 1760	ADM 1/93
746	To Clevland	27 Sept. 1760	ADM 1/93
747	From the Lords of the Admiralty	30 Sept. 1760	ADM 2/85, p. 278
748	To Clevland	2 Oct. 1760	ADM 1/93
749	To Clevland	5 Oct. 1760	ADM 1/93
750	From Clevland	8 Oct. 1760	ADM 2/529, p. 372
751	To Clevland	9 Oct. 1760	ADM 1/93
752	From Clevland	10 Oct. 1760	ADM 2/529, p. 384
753	To Clevland	10 Oct. 1760	ADM 1/93
754	To Clevland	11 Oct. 1760	ADM 1/93
755	To Clevland	12 Oct. 1760	ADM 1/93
756	From Clevland	13 Oct. 1760	ADM 2/529, p. 396
757	To Clevland	13 Oct. 1760	ADM 1/93
758	To Clevland	14 Oct. 1760	ADM 1/93
759	To Clevland	16 Oct. 1760	ADM 1/93
760	To Clevland	16 Oct. 1760	ADM 1/93
761	To Clevland	23 Oct. 1760	ADM 1/93

LIST OF DOCUMENTS AND SOURCES 511

762	To Clevland	27 Oct. 1760	ADM 1/93
763	To Clevland	1 Nov. 1760	ADM 1/93
764	From Clevland	3 Nov. 1760	ADM 2/529, p. 461
765	To Clevland	3 Nov. 1760	ADM 1/93
766	From Clevland	4 Nov. 1760	ADM 2/529, p. 467
767	To Clevland	4 Nov. 1760	ADM 1/93
768	From Clevland	5 Nov. 1760	ADM 2/529, p 470
769	From Clevland	14 Nov. 1760	ADM 2/529, p. 496
770	To Clevland	14 Nov. 1760	ADM 1/93
771	To Clevland	27 Nov. 1760	ADM 1/93
772	To Newcastle	27 Nov. 1760	Add. MSS 32915, ff. 111–12
773	To Clevland	29 Nov. 1760	ADM 1/93
774	To Clevland	2 Dec. 1760	ADM 1/93
775	From Clevland	4 Dec. 1760	ADM 2/530, p. 26
776	To Clevland	4 Dec. 1760	ADM 1/93
777	To Clevland	4 Dec. 1760	ADM 1/93
778	From Clevland	5 Dec. 1760	ADM 2/530, p. 30
779	To Clevland	5 Dec. 1760	ADM 1/93
780	To Clevland	6 Dec. 1760	ADM 1/93
781	To Clevland	6 Dec. 1760	ADM 1/93
782	To Clevland	7 Dec. 1760	ADM 1/93
783	To Clevland	8 Dec. 1760	ADM 1/93
784	To Clevland	8 Dec. 1760	ADM 1/93
785	From Marshall	8 Dec. 1760	ADM 1/93
786	To Clevland	8 Dec. 1760	ADM 1/93
787	From Dalrymple	8 Dec. 1760	ADM 1/93
788	To Clevland	9 Dec. 1760	ADM 1/93
789	From Marshall	9 Dec. 1760	ADM 1/93
790	To Clevland	10 Dec. 1760	ADM 1/93
791	From Clevland	11 Dec. 1760	ADM 2/530, p. 52
792	To Clevland	11 Dec. 1760	ADM 1/93
793	To Clevland	14 Dec. 1760	ADM 1/93
794	To Clevland	19 Dec. 1760	ADM 1/93
795	To Clevland	21 Dec. 1760	ADM 1/93
796	To Clevland	26 Dec. 1760	ADM 1/93
797	From Clevland	27 Dec. 1760	ADM 2/530, p. 114
798	To Clevland	29 Dec. 1760	ADM 1/93
799	To Clevland	30 Dec. 1760	ADM 1/93
800	To Clevland	31 Dec. 1760	ADM 1/93
801	From Clevland	2 Jan. 1761	ADM 2/530, p. 140
802	To Clevland	27 Jan. 1761	ADM 1/93
803	From the Lords of the Admiralty	3 Feb. 1761	ADM 2/86, p. 51
804	To Clevland	6 Feb. 1761	ADM 1/93
805	To Clevland	7 Feb. 1761	ADM 1/93
806	To Clevland	8 Feb. 1761	ADM 1/93
807	To Clevland	8 Feb. 1761	ADM 1/93
808	To Clevland	8 Feb. 1761	ADM 1/93
809	To Clevland	9 Feb. 1761	ADM 1/93
810	To Clevland	9 Feb. 1761	ADM 1/93

811	To Clevland	9 Feb. 1761	ADM 1/93
812	To Clevland	10 Feb. 1761	ADM 1/93
813	To Clevland	11 Feb. 1761	ADM 1/93
814	To Clevland	11 Feb. 1761	ADM 1/93
815	To Clevland	12 Feb. 1761	ADM 1/93
816	To Clevland	13 Feb. 1761	ADM 1/93
817	To Clevland	15 Feb. 1761	ADM 1/93
818	To Clevland	16 Feb. 1761	ADM 1/93
819	To Clevland	17 Feb. 1761	ADM 1/93
820	To Clevland	18 Feb. 1761	ADM 1/93
821	To Clevland	18 Feb. 1761	ADM 1/93
822	From Norbury	18 Feb. 1761	ADM 1/93
823	To Clevland	18 Feb. 1761	ADM 1/93
824	To Clevland	19 Feb. 1761	ADM 1/93
825	From Clevland	20 Feb. 1761	ADM 2/530, p. 335
826	To Clevland	20 Feb. 1761	ADM 1/93
827	To Clevland	21 Feb. 1761	ADM 1/93
828	To Clevland	22 Feb. 1761	ADM 1/93
829	To Clevland	23 Feb. 1761	ADM 1/93
830	To Clevland	23 Feb. 1761	ADM 1/93
831	To Clevland	24 Feb. 1761	ADM 1/93
832	To Clevland	25 Feb. 1761	ADM 1/93
833	To Clevland	25 Feb. 1761	ADM 1/93
834	To Clevland	26 Feb. 1761	ADM 1/93
835	To Clevland	26 Feb. 1761	ADM 1/93
836	To West	27 Feb. 1761	Add. MSS 32919, ff. 324–5
837	To Clevland	27 Feb. 1761	ADM 1/93
838	To Clevland	1 March 1761	ADM 1/93
839	To Clevland	2 March 1761	ADN 1/93
840	From Stephens	18 March 1761	ADM 2/530, p. 431
841	To Newcastle	25 March 1761	Add. MSS 32921, ff. 51–2
842	To Clevland	26 May 1761	ADM 1/93
843	To Clevland	4 July 1761	ADM 1/93
844	To Stephens	26 Sept. 1761	ADM 1/307, f. 415
845	From Stephens	28 Sept. 1761	ADM 2/530, p. 25
846	From Stephens	5 Oct. 1761	PRO 30/20/14
847	From the Lords of the Admiralty	7 Oct. 1761	ADM 2/1331, pp. 413–16
848	From the Lords of the Admiralty	7 Oct. 1761	ADM 2/87, pp. 114–22
849	To Stephens	9 Oct. 1761	ADM 1/307, f. 416
850	To Stephens	10 Oct. 1761	ADM 1/307, f. 417
851	To Stephens	12 Oct. 1761	ADM 1/307, f. 418
852	To Stephens	14 Oct. 1761	ADM 1/307, ff. 419–20
853	To Stephens	20 Oct. 1761	ADM 1/307, f. 421
854	To Stephens	14 Nov. 1761	ADM 1/307, f. 423

LIST OF DOCUMENTS AND SOURCES 513

855	From the Lords of the Admiralty	5 Dec. 1761	ADM 2/1331, pp. 447–8
856	From the Lords of the Admiralty	26 Dec. 1761	ADM 2/87, pp. 339–40
857	To Clevland	19 Jan. 1762	*London Gazette* 6–9 March 1762
858	To Newcastle	21 Jan.1762	Add. MSS 32933, ff. 430–32
859	From the Lords of the Admiralty	5 Feb. 1762	ADM 2/1332, ff. 9–11
860	To Newcastle	10 Feb. 1762	Add. MSS 32934, ff. 255–7
861	To Clevland	10 Feb. 1762	Add. MSS 32934, f. 259
862	From Clevland	19 Feb. 1762	ADM 2/533, pp. 13–14
863	To Newcastle	27 Feb. 1762	Add. MSS 32935, ff. 95–6
864	To Clevland	28 Feb. 1762	ADM 1/307, ff. 433–4
865	To Clevland	1 March 1762	ADM 1/307, f. 443
866	To Clevland	24 March 1762	ADM 1/307, f. 446
867	To Clevland	24 March 1762	ADM 1/307, ff. 450–52
868	To Clevland	26 March 1762	ADM 1/307, f. 454
869	From Stephens	5 April 1762	ADM 2/533, pp. 222–3
870	To Clevland	10 April 1762	ADM 1/307, f. 456
871	From Clevland	30 April 1762	ADM 2/533, pp. 343–4
872	To Clevland	7 May 1762	ADM 1/307, f. 457
873	To Clevland	8 May 1762	ADM 1/307, f. 460
874	To Clevland	8 May 1762	ADM 1/307, f. 458
875	To Clevland	19 May 1762	ADM 1/307, f. 462
876	To Clevland	27 May 1762	ADM 1/307, ff. 464–7
877	To Clevland	31 May 1762	ADM 1/307, ff. 471–3
878	To Clevland	31 May 1762	ADM 1/307, ff. 474–5
879	To Newcastle	1 June 1762	Add. MSS 32939, ff. 134–5
880	To Clevland	1 June 1762	ADM 1/307, f. 476
881	To Duff	3 June 1762	ADM 1/307, ff. 480–81
882	From Duff	4 June 1762	ADM 1/307, f. 479
883	From the Lords of the Admiralty	10 June 1762	ADM 2/88, p. 320
884	To Rufane	19 June 1762	PRO, 30/20/14
885	To Clevland	1 July 1762	ADM 1/307, ff. 477–8

886	To Anson	22 July 1762	PRO 30/20/26/5, ff. 71–9
887	To Clevland	22 July 1762	ADM 1/307, f. 484
888	To Clevland	23 July 1762	ADM 1/307, ff. 486–7
889	From Clevland	28 July 1762	ADM 2/534, p. 152
890	From Clevland	30 July 1762	ADM 2/534, p. 159
891	From Clarke	30 Aug. 1762	ADM 1/307, f. 490
892	To Clevland	24 Sept. 1762	ADM 1/307, ff. 494–5
893	To Clevland	3 Nov. 1762	ADM 1/307, ff. 496–7
894	From Stephens	3 Nov. 1762	ADM 2/534, p. 504
895	From the Lords of the Admiralty	5 Nov. 1762	ADM 2/89, f. 229
896	From Stephens	5 Nov. 1762	ADM 2/534, pp. 514–15
897	From the Lords of the Admiralty	5 Nov. 1762	ADM 2/1332, ff. 41–2
898	From Stephens	15 Nov. 1762	ADM 2/535, p. 4
899	From Grenville	2 Dec. 1762	PRO 30/20/20/4, ff. 43–4
900	To Clevland	11 Dec. 1762	ADM 1/307, ff. 500–03
901	To Clevland	2 Jan. 1763	ADM 1/307, f. 504
902	To Clevland	22 Jan. 1763	ADM 1/307, ff. 505–07
903	From the Lords of the Admiralty	8 Feb. 1763	ADM 2/1332, f. 47
904	From Grenville	10 Feb. 1763	PRO 30/20/20/4, ff. 47–51
905	To Clevland	11 Feb. 1763	ADM 1/307, ff. 508–09
906	To Clevland	2 March 1763	ADM 1/307, f. 510
907	To Clevland	8 May 1763	ADM 1/307, ff. 512–14
908	From the Lords of the Admiralty	11 May 1763	ADM 2/90, pp. 210–14
909	From Stephens	11 May 1763	ADM 2/535, pp. 464–5
910	From Stephens	11 May 1763	ADM 2/535, p. 467
911	From Stephens	12 May 1763	ADM 2/535, p. 470
912	From Knowles	12 May 1763	PRO 30/20/14
913	To Clevland	30 June 1763	ADM 1/307, f. 516
914	From Stephens	4 July 1763	ADM 2/536, p. 66
915	From Stephens	4 July 1763	ADM 2/536, pp. 66–7
916	To Clevland	12 Aug. 1763	ADM 1/307, f. 517
917	From Stephens	13 Aug. 1763	ADM 2/536, pp. 175–6
918	From the Lords of the Admiralty	13 Aug. 1763	ADM 2/90, p. 520

INDEX

Aberdeen, 406
Acapulco, 20n
Achmuty, Lt. Thomas, 26
Adams, Richard, 30, 42
Adams, Lt. Thomas, 163
Admiralty, High Court of, 44
Admiralty, Lords Commissioners of, 21, 22, 26, 27, 28, 29, 31, 32, 33, 34, 36, 38, 39, 40, 41, 42, 43, 46, 48, 49, 50, 51, 52, 53–8, 60, 64–8, 69, 76, 78–9, 80–82, 85, 86, 87, 90, 94, 99, 101–2, 103, 106, 107, 108, 113, 114, 119, 121, 136–7, 140, 141, 142–7, 149, 154, 155–7, 158, 159, 166, 171, 173, 174–5, 187, 227, 230, 236–7, 238, 239, 242, 243–4, 246, 247, 249, 254, 280, 284, 301, 305, 313, 315, 317, 321, 322, 326, 364, 379, 380, 479
   declaration of war against Spain, 432–3
   orders to prepare for attack on Havana, 435–8
   orders to send trade convoys to England, 460
   orders to survey and map the coasts of captured French islands, 470–71
   orders to haul down his flag, 491
   orders
      for Leeward Islands command, 422–8
      in case of departure of French ships from Brest, 431–2, 472–3
      to pay off *Plymouth*, 21
      to take command of *Sheerness*, 22
      to sail in search of privateer, 31–2
      to escort convoy to the northward, 40–41
      to escort convoy to Holland and Germany, 54–5
      to cruise off Flamborough Head, 58
      to escort trade to Portugal, 67–8
      to escort convoy to Scotland, 80–81
      to cruise off Cape Clear, 101
      to bombard Le Havre, 287, 296–7
      to blockade Le Havre, 350, 352
      to take command at Portsmouth, 405
Affleck, Capt. Edmund, 371
Affleck, Capt. Philip, 9
Africa, 426, 483
Agua Fort, 161
Albemarle, Lt. Gen. Earl of, 270, 271, 436, 438, 447, 451, 452, 456, 469
Aldeburgh, 42, 45
Algiers, 156n, 164, 165n
Alicante, 147
Allan, Lt. James, 76, 182, 185, 186
Allen, John, 182
Allen, John Bridgar, 199
Allen, Capt. John Carter, 478
Allen, Joseph, 134, 135
Alresford, 127, 178, 189, 191, 192, 202, 210, 211, 214, 216, 219, 256, 279
Amherst, Maj. Gen. Jeffery, 132, 250
Amsterdam, 54, 57
Andrews, Robert, 197, 212, 417
Angel, Thomas, 203
Angel, Capt. Henry 54, 449
Anson, Admiral Lord, 20, 76, 104, 107, 11, 119, 130, 141, 142, 177, 198, 200, 209, 220, 224, 225, 226, 253, 255, 267, 279, 281, 298, 422, 435, 457, 462
Anstruther, Lt. Gen. Philip, 207
Antigua, 444, 445, 456, 462, 464, 465, 468, 475, 478, 484, 486, 489
Arrowsmith, Lt. Joseph, 184
Arundel, 408
Atherton, Thomas, 419
Aubrey, Capt. Lord, 7
Austrian Succession, War of, 125, 127
Avington, 3

Baird, Capt. Patrick, 134
Banc D'Anfar, 309
Banc de la Jambe, 309

Banks, Capt. Francis, 273, 279, 440
Banks off Newfoundland, 146
Barbados, 110, 267, 268, 271, 422, 423, 425, 427, 431, 433, 437, 438, 447, 450, 453, 455, 458, 467, 468, 469, 470, 471, 472, 478, 483, 485, 486, 488
Barbary corsairs, 148n
Barcelona, 147
Barlow, Capt. John, 321
Barrington, Capt. Hon. Samuel, 9
Basque Road, 132
Bateman, Capt. Hon. William 386
Bath, 121, 193, 488
Bayne, Capt. William, 446
Bayonne, 112
Bay of Biscay, 8, 15, 16, 17, 130, 131, 132
Bay of Bulls, 138
Bay of Hyères, 19
Bay of Petite Ance, 434
Bay of Seine, 261, 262, 263, 264, 265, 266
Beachy Head, 319, 352, 354, 356n, 379n, 389, 413
Bearl's Wharf, 141
Beaumont, Monsieur, 364, 366, 367, 369, 370
Bedford, Duke of, 125, 128, 131, 144, 149, 225, 288
Belgium, 13
Bell, William, 97
Bellcombe, Ferall de, 420
Belle Isle, 268, 393n, 422, 446n
Belsunce, Lt. Gen. Marquis de, 446
Bensley, Lt. John, 316, 342, 359, 360, 363
Bensley, Lt. William, 380
Bentinck, Capt. John Albert, 162n, 338, 342
Bentinck, Count William, 162
Bentley, Capt. Sir John, 247
Bergen, 338
Berlenga, 213n
Bertie, Capt. Hon. Peregrine Francis, 481
Berwick, 79
Bickerton, Capt. Richard, 449
Biddiford, 56
Bilbao, 310, 324
Birmingham, 406
Bisbane, Capt. John, 440

Bispham, John, 103
Blackstake, 155
Blake, Capt. Peter, 442
Blunt, Mr., 202, 218
Board of Ordnance, 80, 299, 370, 424
Board of Trade, 127
Bocland, Lt. Gen. Maurice, 273
Bordeaux, 453, 455, 481
Boscawen, Admiral Hon. Edward, 98, 99, 131, 208, 216, 217, 218, 220, 221, 228, 247, 250, 280
Boston, 109, 162, 164
Botterell, Capt. John, 449
Bouley Bay, 374, 377
Boulogne, 200, 343, 348
Bourbon, Isle of, 251
Bowen, John, 418
Boyd, Capt. John, 456
Boyle, see Walsingham, Capt. Hon Robert Boyle
Boys, Commodore William, 321
Bradley, John, 237n, 399, 421n
Bradshaw, Lt. John 339
Bradshaw, Lt. Thomas, 397, 399
Brassac, Lt. Gen. Marquis de, 364, 367, 368, 369
Bray, Mr., 247, 249
Brazil, 431
Breeze, Sidney, 151
Bremen, 54, 55, 57
Brest, 75, 219, 262, 266, 269, 373, 411, 431, 445, 446, 472, 478
Brett, Capt. John, 210, 215
Brett, Capt. Sir Piercy, 343
Brett, Capt. William, 206, 214
Brice, Capt. Robert, 457
Brielle, 45n
Brill, The, 45
Bristol, 35, 36, 109, 223, 252
Bristol, Earl of, 222, 223, 432
British Channel, see English Channel
Broderick, Rear Admiral Thomas, 246
Brodnick, Commodore Robert, 213
Brograve, Lt. William, 382
Bromedge, Capt. Hugh, 384
Brooks, John, 241n
Brown, Capt., 72
Brown, Lt. Alexander, 450
Brown Lt. John, 397
Brown, Joseph, 421n

INDEX 517

Browne, John, 224n
Bruges, 71, 73
Brydges, George Rodney, 3
Buchanan, John, 68n
Buchan Ness, 84
Buckle, Capt. Matthew 431
Bucknall, Mr. 288
Buckner, Capt. Charles, 441, 462
Buckworth, John, 358
Bulley, Capt. William, 90, 91, 95, 101, 122
Burlington Bay, 44
Burlings, 213
Burnaby, Capt. Sir William, 397
Burne, Richard, 68n
Burnet, Lt. James, 275
Burnett, Capt. Thomas, 453
Burnside, Robert, 241n
Byng, Vice Admiral Hon. John, 84, 85, 205, 207, 209, 212, 213n, 214, 219
Byron, Capt. Hon. John, 204, 206, 233

Calais, 387
Camelford, 128, 200n
Canterbury, 100
Cap d'Antifer, 326, 331, 332, 336, 338, 348, 353, 354, 356n, 379n, 381n, 382, 387, 389
Cap de la Hague, 381n, 402
Cap de la Hève, 292, 307, 318, 326, 336, 341, 379n, 381
Cape Barfleur, 318, 336, 352, 354, 356n, 362, 379n, 388
Cape Bonavista, 138, 146n
Cape Clear, 11, 31, 33, 101, 104, 112
Cape Finisterre, 17, 152, 188, 189
Cape Finisterre, battle of, 17–18, 104, 119n, 129, 130
Cape François, 454n
Cape Horn, 20n
Cape Sable, 252n
Cape St. Vincent, 70, 152, 164
Cape Sambrough [Sable], 252
Carbery, Lady, 178
Carlisle Bay, 267, 422, 423, 470, 483
Carpenter, Edward, 237n
Carr, John, 51
Carter, Richard, 95, 122
Carter, Robert, 215
Carter, Thomas, 224n

Carteret (Normandy), 369, 370, 373
Carteret, Philip, 41, 44
Carthagena, 455
Carysford, Lord, 488
Caudebec en Caux, 330
Cas de Pilotte, 434
Cas des Navières, 268, 433, 434, 439, 452
Caster, Robert, 206
Castres, Abraham, 140
Castill, Moses, 237n
Chandos, Duke of, 3, 6, 8
Channel, *see* English Channel
Chaplen, Capt. James, 305, 306, 308, 381
Charente River, 132
Chatham, 4, 30, 31, 65, 82, 83, 95, 98, 155, 156, 281
Chatham Chest, 5, 223
Cherbourg, 288, 376, 377, 379n, 382, 383, 404
Chester, 35, 36
Chichester, 288
Clarke, Capt. Edward, 187, 483
Clarke, Capt. Peter, 475, 483, 490
Clarke, Col. Gedney, 467, 468
Clevland, John, 108, 111, 115, 117, 118, 135, 137, 138, 139, 140, 141, 142, 144, 148, 150, 151, 153, 159, 160, 161, 163, 164, 165, 166, 167, 168, 169, 170, 171, 172, 173, 174, 175, 177, 178, 179, 180, 181, 182, 183, 184, 185, 186, 187, 193, 194, 195, 196, 197, 198, 199, 200, 201, 202, 203, 205, 207, 208, 210, 212, 213, 215, 216, 217, 218, 220, 221, 222, 224, 225, 226, 227, 228, 229, 231, 232, 233, 234, 235, 236, 237, 238, 239, 240, 241, 242, 244, 245, 246, 247, 248, 249, 250, 251, 252, 253, 254, 255, 256, 258, 273, 274, 275, 276, 277, 278, 279, 280, 281, 282, 283, 284, 285, 286, 288, 289, 290, 291, 292n, 293, 294, 295, 297, 298, 299, 300, 301, 302, 303, 304, 396, 307, 308, 309, 310, 311, 312, 314, 315, 317, 318, 319, 320, 321, 322, 323, 324, 225, 326, 327, 328, 329, 330, 331, 332, 333, 334, 335, 337, 338, 339, 340, 342, 343, 344, 345, 346, 347, 348, 349, 350, 351, 352, 353, 354, 355, 357, 358, 359, 360, 362, 363, 366, 368, 369, 370, 371, 372, 373, 374, 375, 376, 377, 379, 380, 381, 382,

Clevland, John, (contd.)
383, 384, 385, 386, 387, 388, 389, 390,
391, 392, 393, 394, 395, 396, 397, 398,
399, 400, 401, 402, 403, 404, 405, 406,
407, 408, 409, 410, 411, 412, 413, 414,
415, 416, 417, 418, 419, 420, 421, 423,
439, 440, 442, 443, 444, 445, 447, 448,
449, 450, 451, 452, 454, 455, 457, 461,
464, 466, 467, 468, 475, 477, 480, 481,
482, 483, 489, 490
Cobey, Thomas, 107, 108
Cockran, Col. James, 46
Coke, Wenman, 417
Collins, Capt. Arthur Tooker, 412
Collins, Capt. Richard, 47
Colville, Maj. Gen. Charles, 422
Commissioners of the Navy, see Navy Board
Commissioners of Sick and Wounded Seamen, 55, 414, 427
Commissioners of Trade and Plantations, 145
Commissioners of Victualling, see Victualling Board
Compton, Catherine, 176n, 212n
Compton, Charles, 131, 194n, 197n, 198, 218, 222, 223, 225, 258
Compton, Hon. Charles, 129, 131, 176n, 189n, 194n, 195, 197, 258
Compton, Elizabeth, 211n
Compton, George, 129, 258n
Compton, Jane, 129, 176n
Compton, Spencer, 129, 131, 194n
Conflans, Admiral Comte de, 337, 338, 355
Conway, Capt., 34, 35
Cooper, William, 409
Cope, James, 55
Copenhagen, 39, 306
Corbett, Thomas, 19, 20, 22, 24, 25, 27, 28, 29, 30, 31, 32, 33, 34, 35, 36, 37, 38, 40, 41, 42, 44, 45, 46, 47, 48, 49, 50, 51, 52, 53, 56, 57, 59, 60, 61, 62, 63, 65, 66, 67, 68, 69, 70, 71, 72, 74, 75, 76, 77, 78, 80, 82, 83, 84, 85, 86, 88, 89, 90, 91, 92, 94, 95, 96, 97, 98, 100, 101, 102, 103, 104, 105, 106, 107, 108, 109, 110, 112, 113, 114, 115, 116, 117, 118, 119, 120, 121, 122, 133, 134, 136, 154, 155, 156, 157, 158

Cork, 11, 34, 35, 204, 453, 468, 484, 485
Cornwall, 128, 144n
Cornwallis, Col. Edward, 142, 151
Cotes, Capt. Thomas, 168, 474
Cotterell, Col. John, 80
Cromarty, 81
Crookhaven, 104, 106
Crowley, Ambrose, 43
Crowley, John, 43
Crump, Lawrence, 375, 376
Cuba, 271, 436n, 469
Culloden, battle of, 109
Cumberland, Duke of, 72, 109n

Dalrymple, Governor Campbell, 485
Dalrymple, Lt. James, 457
Dalrymple, Capt. John, 398
Darby, Capt. George, 265, 339, 343, 346, 349, 350, 440, 442, 449
Dartmouth, 137, 288
Daun, Field Marshall Leopold Joseph Maria, 391
Davers, Vice Admiral Thomas, 48, 49
Deal, 76, 100
Deptford, 10, 12, 13, 23, 24, 25, 26, 27, 46, 50, 56, 131, 135, 227, 229, 230, 231, 232, 233, 234, 236, 285
Desaguliers, Col. Thomas, 284, 286, 288, 290, 291, 294
Désirade, 431
Devonshire, Duke of, 31, 32, 33, 34, 35, 36, 37, 417n
Dieppe, 334, 340, 355, 381n, 382, 389
Digby, Lord, 223
Dives-sur-Mer, 305, 318, 362, 381n
Dixon, George, 407
Doake, Capt. James, 440
Dodd, Capt. Edward, 71
Dominica, 437, 452, 491
Don Navarro, First Admiral, 153
Doran, John, 180n
Dorret, Robert, 284
Douglas, Rear Admiral Sir James, 181, 219, 270, 271, 423, 424, 431, 433, 440, 448, 450, 452, 453, 456
Dover, 74, 75, 76, 320, 354, 359, 360, 361, 363
Downes, 8, 13, 15, 17, 30, 32, 64, 66, 68, 71, 74, 76, 85, 96, 97, 98, 99, 100, 113, 114, 115, 116, 140, 142, 147, 153, 154,

INDEX

240, 273, 300, 302, 307, 313, 314, 318, 320, 321, 322, 323, 325, 328, 334, 353, 383, 388, 409
Downing, Capt. Dennis, 289
Drake, Capt. Francis William, 137, 161
Drake, Capt. Francis Samuel, 462, 478
Drummond, Henry, 129
Drummond, Lt. John, 416
Drummond, Lt. Patrick, 462
Dublin, 11, 32, 33, 34, 35, 36, 37, 39
Duff, Capt. Robert, 213, 453, 457, 458, 459, 461, 462
Duffell, John, 406
Duncan, George, 204
Duncannon, Lord, 31
Dundee, 85
Dungeness, 318, 357, 388, 401, 402
Dunkirk, 262, 266, 321, 333, 336, 340, 341, 349, 378, 379, 389, 403
Dunnose, 354, 356n, 379n, 403
Durell, Rear Admiral Philip, 348, 360, 363, 372, 375, 383, 388, 389
Dusaussay, Monsieur, 364
Duthy, Mr., 202, 212, 218

Eastbourne, 188n
Edgcumbe, Hon. Richard, 206, 419, 420
Effingham, Earl of, 243n
Egmont, Earl of, 129, 212n
Egmont, Lady, 212
Egremont, Earl of, 160, 432, 436, 471, 472, 484, 485, 486, 488
Elbe River, 53, 55
Elcho, Lord, 109
Ellerker, Edward, 421n
Elliot, Capt. John, 318
Ellis, Welborne, 488
Elphinston, Capt. John, 447
Elton, Capt. Jacob, 45
Emlington, Francis, 421n
Emsdorf, battle of, 371n
England, 13, 14, 17, 18, 19, 33, 47, 55, 56, 70, 72, 74, 92, 139, 163, 165, 192, 253, 257, 264, 270, 271, 272, 309, 329, 376, 407, 425, 426, 428, 431, 437, 442, 447, 450, 452, 453, 454, 456, 459, 463, 466, 475, 476, 477, 481, 485, 486
English Channel, 7, 8, 11, 15, 16, 17, 20, 68, 132, 264, 266, 268, 346, 349, 356, 379n, 380, 430

Enlington, Francis, 329n
Evans, John 277n
Exeter, 99, 100

Fabin, Joseph, 206
Falmouth, 7, 145, 209, 419, 420
Falmouth, Lord, 419, 420
Farley, Thomas, 421n
Farmer, Lt. George, 450, 451
Farren, William, 418
Faulknor, Capt. Jonathan, 285, 286
Featherstone, John, 395
Fécamp, 336, 356n
Fenelon, Marquis de, 490
Ferrol, 252
Firth of Cromarty, 81
Firth of Edinburgh, 8, 81, 84
Fitzwalter, Lord, 97
Flanders, 34, 35, 56n, 102
Flamborough Head, 58, 59
Florida, 485
Flushing, 72
Fontainebleau, 272
Forbes, Duncan, 81
Forrest, Capt. Arthur, 431n, 446
Forster, William, 421n
Fort Royal, 268, 269, 434, 435, 440, 442, 443, 465, 475, 490
Fort Royal Bay, 268, 439, 447
Fowke, Capt. Thorpe, 94
Fox, Lady Georgiana Caroline Lennox, 222
Fox, Henry, 222, 223n
Fox, Commodore Thomas, 16, 17, 18, 129
France, 16, 146, 190, 219, 253, 254, 323, 329, 333, 362, 263, 444, 446, 453, 486
Francis, Capt. Thomas, 420, 468, 469, 470
Fremeur, Count de, 453

Galbraith, Capt. James, 320, 321
Galicia, 252
Galleons Reach, 236, 239
Gardner, Charles, 102
Garnier, William, 488
Garlick, Joseph, 411
Gascoigne, Capt. Edward, 298, 301, 325, 327
Gayton, Lt. George, 289

Geary, Rear Admiral Francis, 419
Geddes, Capt. Alexander, 5
Genoa, 6
George II, 10, 13, 142n
Germany, 13, 54
Ghent, 73
Gibraltar, 6, 7, 8, 10, 19, 59, 205n, 214, 280, 281, 398, 441, 445
Glass, Christopher, 136
Godfrey, Lt. John, 390, 401, 402
Goff, Samuel, 397, 398
Goodwin, John, 120
Goodwin Sands, 116
Gordon, Capt. William, 48, 49
Goree, 59
Graham, Capt. Lord George, 101
Graham, Capt. Mitchell, 412, 415
Graham, Robert, 135
Grand Ance, 434
Grand Banks, 125, 126
Grange, Robert, 29
Graves, Capt. Thomas, 207, 320, 381
Gravesend, 77
Gray, Col. George, 422, 443n
Gray, Thomas, 83n
Greenland, 40, 41
Greenwich Hospital, 5
Grenada, 269, 270, 442, 444, 445, 449, 456, 462, 471n
Grenville Act, 386n
Grenville, Hon. George, 474, 479, 488
Grey, Robert, 224n
Grime, William, 239n
Guadeloupe, 422, 446, 470, 471n, 482, 484, 485, 490
Guernsey, 210, 215, 369, 370, 373, 377, 406
Gulf of St. Lawrence, 421
Gunfleet, 87, 88
Guy, John, 180n

Haddock, Admiral Nicholas, 6, 7
Haddock, Capt. Richard, 129
Hadly, Sergeant Thomas, 397, 398
Hague, 162
Halifax, Earl of, 488
Halifax, N.S., 132, 133, 151, 249, 250, 252, 473
Hall, Ezekiel, 44
Hall, James, 20

Handerson, Thomas, 399
Hanway, Mrs, 217
Hanway, Capt. Thomas, 57, 204
Hamburg, 54, 55, 57
Hamilton, Capt. Claud, 195
Hamoaze, 99, 100, 101, 108, 117, 118, 202, 203, 204, 205, 206, 207, 208, 210, 212, 213, 215, 216, 217, 430
Harcourt, Duke de, 310, 324, 364
Harding, Ichabod, 185
Hardy, Vice Admiral Sir Charles, 22, 37, 40, 472
Harman, Capt. William, 469
Harper, John, 141
Harrison, Capt. Henry, 21, 101, 102
Harrison, John, 257
Harrison, Capt. John, 118, 163, 164, 215
Harrow School, 3, 4
Harsel, Sergeant William, 98
Harwich, 14, 89, 90, 91, 92, 93, 94, 95, 96, 97, 122
Harwood, George, 392, 393, 416
Haslar Hospital, 244
Haswell, Lt. Robert, 232, 234, 237
Hatch, Lt. John, 187
Havana, 270, 271, 272, 469, 473, 475, 477, 478, 479, 480, 481, 485, 487
Hawke, Admiral Sir Edward, 17, 130, 132, 178, 187, 190, 214, 220, 242, 248, 250, 262, 275, 285, 337
Hayward, Lt. Thomas, 196, 201, 220
Hawford, Lt. John, 187
Heard, William, 240
Hellevoetsluis, 41, 44
Heriker, Robert, 354
Hervey, Capt. Hon. Augustus, 269, 434, 443, 444
Holburne, Capt. Sir Alexander, 478, 481
Holburne, Vice Admiral Francis, 199, 254, 255, 256, 261, 273, 274, 279, 281, 283, 287, 302, 311, 320, 348n, 394, 405, 428
Holland, 12, 13, 14, 42, 74, 142, 332
Holwall, Capt. John, 283, 284, 322, 449, 453
Holmes, Rear Admiral Charles, 431, 432, 438
Holmes, Capt. Lancelot, 403
Honfleur, 293, 304, 305, 309, 322, 353, 362, 363, 366

INDEX

Hood, Capt. Samuel, 13, 341, 344
Horn, James, 246
Howe, Capt. Hon. Richard, 215
Hoyle Lake, 36
Hoyle Road, 36
Hudson, Nicholas, 346, 347
Hughes, Capt. Richard, 9, 215, 343, 381
Hull, 25, 58
Hull, Philip, 224
Humber, 58, 244
Hunter, Capt. Joseph, 256, 285, 318
Hunter, Dr, 176

Iceland, 40, 41, 43
Ilchester, Lord, 223
Ile St. Marcouf, 363
Inglis, Capt. Charles, 368, 403
Innes, Capt. Alexander, 204, 210, 215
Inverness, 81, 83
Ireland, 11, 13, 15, 31, 33, 42, 44, 71, 109
Isle of Wight, 331n, 389
Israel, David, 164, 165n
Italy, 152, 164

Jackson, Samuel, 277n
Jacobs, James, 180n
Jacobson, Cornelius, 407
Jamaica, 48n, 270, 271, 406, 431, 432, 438, 441, 446, 447, 448, 452, 455, 463, 469, 471, 473, 476
Jersey, 210, 215, 273, 369, 370, 374n, 377
Jervis, Capt. John, 355, 380
John's Haven, 85
Johnson, Richard, 241
Johnson, William, 241
Johnstone, Capt. George, 442
Joyce, Lewis, 117, 137, 138

Kendall, Lt. Charles, 474
Keinsham, 3
Kennedy, John, 236, 239n
Kenny Peter, 109
Keppel, Rear Admiral Hon. Augustus, 9, 120, 156, 161, 219, 224, 393, 395, 396, 399, 400, 408, 473, 475, 477, 479, 480, 481, 483, 485, 487, 490, 491
King Road, 35
King's Letter Boy, 4

Kinsale, 15, 16, 101, 102, 103, 104, 105, 106, 112, 313, 314, 320
Knowles, Vice Admiral Charles, 244, 488
Knight, Dr. Gowin, 127, 158, 166
Knight, Capt. John, 151, 162, 163, 201, 382, 383
Korbach, battle of, 368n, 369n

Lagos, 19, 20, 70
La Guaira, 441, 443, 483
La Hague, 318, 404
Lambert, Capt. Robert, 416
Landshut, battle of, 369n
Launceston, 128, 144
Leaver, Lt. William, 27, 28
Ledger, Lewis, 20n
Leeward Islands, 265, 266, 267, 269, 270, 271, 272, 422, 423, 424, 427, 455, 471, 480, 486, 490, 491
Legge, Capt. Edward, 106
Le Havre, 281, 287, 288, 295, 302, 306, 307, 308, 309, 310, 311, 312, 314, 315, 316, 319, 320, 322, 323, 324, 325, 328, 330, 332, 334, 335, 336, 337, 338, 340, 341, 342, 343, 344, 345, 346, 348, 349, 350, 351, 352, 353, 355, 356, 359, 360, 362, 366, 367, 368, 369, 370, 371, 372, 373, 374, 375, 376, 377, 378, 379, 380, 382, 383, 387, 388, 389, 391, 393, 401, 402, 403, 409, 450, 451; attack on and blockade of, 291–9; failure of second bombardment of, 303–5; blockade of, 309–405
Le Havre de Grace, *see* Le Havre
Leith, 41, 43, 84
Lendrick, Capt. John, 440, 456
Leonard, Richard, 237n, 245
Lesser Antilles, 267, 269
Lindsay, Capt. John, 238, 239
Lisbon, 6, 10, 13, 19, 67, 68, 69, 70, 71, 120, 126, 139, 140, 151, 152, 163, 164, 165, 431, 435
Liverpool, 274, 454, 466
Livorno, 174
Lizard, 35, 338, 431
Lochiel, 109
Loftin, Capt. Samuel, 20, 58
Logie, Capt. James, 198, 199n, 251, 252

London, 20, 23, 41, 61, 110, 115, 134, 144, 149, 170, 173, 174, 194, 195, 209, 215, 227, 237, 261, 404, 406, 409
Longreach, 10, 26, 27, 28, 50, 51, 132, 135, 140, 153, 155, 157, 160, 166, 227, 230, 231, 232, 233, 234, 235, 237, 238, 239
Longueville, Monsieur, 444
Lorema, John, 117
Lory, Claud, 109
Lotherington, Benjamin, 75
Lougten, Lt. William, 419
Louisiana, 267, 269, 453, 455, 489
Louisburg, 133, 249n, 151, 254, 256
Lowestoft, 42, 45
Lowfield, Lt. William, 346, 347, 355, 390, 401, 402
Lukey, Lt. Patherick, 408, 411, 416
Lynch, Owen, 407
Lyon, Boswell, 70

Macartney, Capt. John, 407, 414
Macdonald, Mr., 484, 490
MacDonald, Thomas, 204
McIntosh, John, 399
Mackay, Lt. Hugh, 219
Mackay, John, 120, 180
Mackenzie, Capt. George, 376
Macklane, Lauchlan, 463
McLean, Alexander, 322, 324
McNamara, Jeremiah, 329n, 385, 386
Mace, Mr., 247, 249
Madrid, 252, 432, 435, 442
Madson, Peter, 108
Magnus, Francis, 217
Mahon, 19
Maidstone, 67
Majorca, 147
Malpas, Viscount, 485n
Maltby, Lt. William, 390
Marbet, Josiah, 380
Marguerita, 484
Marie-Galante, 470
Marseilles, 401, 402, 453, 455
Marshall, Capt. Samuel, 386, 397, 398, 399, 409, 482, 489
Marshall, William, 241
Martin, George, 56, 61
Martinique, 203n, 271, 272, 422, 423, 433, 434, 435, 436, 437, 439, 441, 442, 443, 444, 445, 446, 447, 448, 449, 450, 451, 452, 454, 455, 456, 457, 460, 461, 462, 463, 464, 465, 467, 469, 470, 471n, 475, 477, 478, 481, 482, 484, 486, 487, 489, 490, 491
  attack on, 267–9
Masson, Henry, 93
Mathews, Vice Admiral Thomas, 8, 19, 20, 21, 22
Mearns, John, 100
Mearns, Robert, 100
Meather, James, 180n
Mediterranean, 8, 68, 156n, 214, 219, 220, 280, 286, 400, 402, 441
Mediterranean passes, 148, 150, 152, 153, 159, 165n, 169
Medley, George, 181
Medley, Rear Admiral Henry, 5, 63, 68
Meuse River, 41, 45, 56, 58
Michell, Commodore, Matthew, 15, 98
Middlesborough, 72
Middleton, Capt. Charles, 9
Milbank, Lt. Mark, 76
Miller, James, 347, 348
Miller, John, 224n, 329n, 358, 360, 384, 385
Mills, Charles, 421n
Milnes, John, 228, 311
Minorca, 147, 205n
Molloy, Capt. Sir Charles, 27, 28
Monckton, Maj. Gen. Hon. Robert, 268, 269, 270, 271, 433, 434, 436, 437, 438, 440, 446, 450, 452, 454, 461, 462, 463, 467, 468, 469
Montagu, Capt. John, 140
Montrevel, 364
Montrose, 84, 85, 100
Moore, Capt. John, 35, 36
Morgan, Lt. Col. H., 422
Morlaix, 15, 337, 374, 404
Morne Garnier, 269
Morne Tortensen, 269, 434, 435
Morris, John, 399
Moss, John G., 241n
Mossom, William, 63
Mostyn, Rear Admiral Savage, 202, 203, 204, 205
Mother Bank, 399, 400
Mount Edgecumbe, Lord, 149
Mount Grenie, 434, 435

INDEX

Mundy, G.B.M., ix
Myer, Court, 74

Navy Board, 22, 23, 43, 46, 51, 53, 55, 86, 107, 108, 109, 119, 121, 143, 152, 155, 156, 166, 169, 170, 182, 183, 185, 186, 231, 232, 238, 244, 245, 246, 343, 359, 360, 373, 411, 421, 424, 426
  Rodney disagrees with, 169, 229, 359–60
Navy Office, *see* Navy Board
Nelson, Horatio, 4n
Netherlands, *see* Holland
Newcastle, 41, 42, 43, 44, 79, 80, 81, 439
Newcastle, Duke of, 131, 197, 214n, 225, 255, 265, 292, 335, 392, 417, 419, 420n, 434, 441, 456
Newfoundland, 6, 125, 126, 127, 134, 135, 136, 137, 139, 142, 144, 145, 146, 147, 148, 149, 150, 152, 155, 157, 158, 159, 160, 161, 164, 169, 170
New Spain, 19
New York, 149n, 409, 433n, 454, 463, 469
Norbury, Capt. Coningsby, 57
Norbury, Capt. Richard, 412
Nore, 10, 12, 26, 27, 28, 29, 30, 39, 40, 41, 42, 43, 45, 46, 47, 48, 51, 52, 53, 55, 56, 57, 58, 59, 60, 63, 64, 65, 66, 76, 77, 78, 79, 81, 82, 90, 93, 96, 135, 136, 153, 154, 227, 229, 230, 237, 238, 239, 240, 241, 242, 246, 383
Norgate, John, 103
Normandy, 369, 370, 373, 379n, 392
Norris, Capt. Harry, 21
North America, 248, 249, 267, 268, 329, 363, 422, 423, 433, 462, 469, 473, 474, 477, 480, 485
Northampton, Earls of, *see* Compton
North Sea, 8, 11, 12, 59, 92, 349
Norway, 12
Norwood, Capt. Joseph, 236, 415
Nott, Capt. John Neal Pleydell, 440, 455, 456
Nova Scotia, 132, 133, 142, 151

Oakley, John, 83n
O'Brien, Capt. Christopher, 25, 27
O'Brien, Capt. Lucius, 464

Ogle, Admiral Sir Chaloner, 79
Ogle, Capt. Chaloner, 367, 370, 373, 374, 377, 385, 446
Old Alresford, *see* Alresford
Okehampton, 265, 292n, 335, 414, 417
Oporto, 67, 69, 71, 147, 412
Ordnance, *see* Board of Ordnance
Orfordness, 14, 59, 77, 89
Orinoco River, 467, 468
Osborn, Sir Danvers, 149, 150
Osborn, Vice Admiral Henry, 70, 200, 205, 224
Ostend, 13, 15, 34, 35, 36, 56, 71, 72, 73, 74, 75, 76, 98, 100, 209, 215
Ourry, Capt. Paul Henry, 382, 384, 404, 443

Pain, Samuel, 241n
Palmer, Robert, 151
Paris, 316, 322, 487
Parker, Capt. Hyde, 310, 311, 313, 314
Parry, Capt. William, 253, 255
Paston, Capt. William, 361, 365, 367, 368, 377, 382, 383, 387, 403, 483
Patterson, Alexander, 239
Patterson, Col. James, 204
Pattison, Maj. James, 300
Patton, Andrew, 224n
Pawlett, Col. Charles, 92, 100
Pearce, Thomas, 421n
Peard, Capt. George, 420
Pearl Rock, 446
Peate, George, 421n
Penryn, 265, 420n, 419n
Peterson, John, 407
Peveril Point, 388
Philips, Alexander, 82, 83, 95, 122
Philips, Lt. Gen. Richard, 136
Pigeon Island, 440
Pinfold, Lt. Richard, 342, 354
Pinfold, Governor Charles, 485
Pitman, Capt. John, 81
Pitt, Thomas, 417
Pitt, William, 247, 250, 261, 264, 299, 355, 369
Placentia, 138, 145
Plymouth, 10, 11, 15, 18, 21, 35, 98, 100, 102, 103, 104, 105, 106, 109, 110, 112, 113, 115, 117n, 119, 121, 126, 128, 131, 137, 143, 144, 145, 161, 188, 189, 201,

Plymouth, (contd.)
  209, 211, 218, 253, 284, 285, 338, 378,
  386, 395, 405, 407, 413, 430
Plymouth Sound, 37, 70, 99, 104, 107,
  120, 137, 148, 150, 153, 161, 424
Pocock, Vice Admiral Sir George, 270,
  271, 410, 415, 417, 418, 436, 437, 438,
  447, 448, 451, 452, 453, 456, 457, 459,
  466, 473, 475
Point Negroe, 434
Point Piercy, 366
Ponte Riche, 146n
Pole, John, 204
Pollard, James, 421n
Pomfret, Thomas, 346, 347
Port Antonio, 443
Port en Bessin, 364n, 365, 367, 368, 369,
  372, 373
Portland, 382, 402
Portland, Earl of, 162n
Port Mahon, 209
Portsmouth, 6, 8, 11, 12, 28, 34, 38, 39,
  40, 119, 129, 130, 131, 136, 143, 167,
  171, 172, 174, 175, 176, 177, 178, 179,
  180, 182, 193, 197, 203, 209, 221, 222,
  224, 225, 227, 228, 229, 243, 244, 245,
  253, 254, 261, 262, 264, 273, 274, 275,
  277, 278, 279, 280, 281, 282, 283, 284,
  286, 287, 288, 289, 292, 296, 297, 298,
  299, 309, 312, 315, 316, 326, 336, 339,
  343, 348n, 351, 352, 354, 355, 357, 358,
  359, 360, 361, 363, 372, 375, 377, 381,
  382, 384, 392, 393, 395, 396, 397, 398,
  399, 400, 405, 406, 407, 408, 409, 410,
  411, 412, 414, 415, 416, 419, 428, 479,
  480
Portugal, 8, 13, 18, 64, 67, 68, 69, 126,
  147, 184
Postelle, Fonntinel de, 288
Potter, Thomas, 180n
Potts, Joseph, 400
Powell, Edward, 203
Powlett, Capt. Charles, 19
Powlett, Rear Admiral Lord Harry, 214,
  241
Pretender, 16, 109. *See also* Stuart,
  Charles Edward
Priest, Serjeant, 207
Prince Ferdinand, 371
Prince Royal of Denmark, 13, 53, 54

Prince Rupert's Bay, 437, 490, 491
Prust, David, 241n
Puerto Rico, 271, 455, 466, 483, 490
Punton, Robert, 81
Purvis, John, 329n, 421n

Quebec, 316, 420

Rainier, Lt. Daniel, 95
Ramsgate, 116
Regiments
  11th, 273n
  26th, 207
  34th, 243n
  40th, 136
  56th, 485
  61st, 267, 422, 443
  69th, 267, 442
  76th, 267, 422
  90th, 267, 422
Reunion, 251n
Robbins, Charles, 420
Robinson, Robert, 399
Rochfort, 132, 204
Rodney, Vice Admiral George, ix, 19,
  20n, 21, 22, 29, 76, 103, 110n, 120, 125,
  128, 129, 130, 131, 173, 174, 176n, 242,
  243, 244, 247, 254, 258, 263, 266, 267–
  9, 270, 271, 272, 273, 272–8, 279, 349,
  350, 417, 422, 435–8, 459, 460, 490;
  birth and background, 3; early career,
  5–8; promoted to post captain, 8–9;
  assumes command of *Plymouth* and
  sails for England, 19; appointed to
  command *Sheerness*, 22; order to refit
  Sheerness, 38; ordered to escort convoy
  to the northward, 40–41; assumes
  command of *Ludlow Castle*, 50; ordered
  to escort trade to Portugal, 67–8;
  ordered to escort shipping to northward,
  80–81; ordered to repair on board *Eagle*,
  90; ordered to cruise off Cape Clear,
  101; captures enemy ships, 102, 104,
  109; ordered to cruise to the westward
  of Scilly, 111; captures enemy ship, 112;
  intercepts French convoy, 113;
  appointed governor of Newfoundland,
  125, 127, 134; anti-Catholicism of, 139,
  288; instructions as governor of
  Newfoundland, 144–7; elected to the

INDEX

House of Commons, 172; appointed to command *Fougeux*, 173; letters to Jane Rodney, 176–80; appointed to command *Prince George*, 180; letters to Jane Rodney, 181, 188–92; assumes command of *Monarch*, 201; letters to Jane Rodney, 202, 204–5, 209–12, 214–19, 225–6; assumes command of *Dublin*, 227; disagreements with Navy Board, 229, 359–60; ordered to cruise to the westward of Scilly, 246; order to convey Amherst to North America, 249; returns to England, 254; promoted to rear admiral, 261; ordered to bombard Le Havre, 287; elected to House of Commons, 292; bombards Le Havre, 291–7, 303, 305; blockades Le Havre, 309–91; acting commander-in-chief at Portsmouth, 405–19; instructions as commander-in-chief of the squadron in the Leeward Islands, 422–8; attacks Martinique, 433–5; prepares for expedition to Havana, 435–8; sends reinforcements to Jamaica, 447–8; ordered to survey coast of captured French islands, 470–71; promoted to vice admiral, 474; ordered to haul down flag and come ashore, 491
Rodney, George, 129, 179, 188, 189, 192, 209, 211, 219
Rodney, Henry, 3
Rodney, James, 129, 211, 219
Rodney, Jane, 129, 131, 222, 223, 227
  death of 130, 227n
  letters to 176–9, 181, 188–92, 202, 204–5, 209–10, 211–12, 214–17, 218, 219, 225–6
  married, 176n
Rohan, Charles de, Prince of Soubise, 322, 367
Rose, Lt. Henry, 96
Ross, George, 406
Rotherhithe, 10
Rotterdam, 56, 58, 59, 88, 314
Rouen, 264, 306, 310, 314, 316, 330, 372
Rouillé, Monsieur, 450, 451
Rous, Capt. John, 151
Rowley, Capt. Joshua, 410, 418
Rowzier, Lt. John, 89

Rufane, Brig. William, 422, 454, 460, 475, 478, 484, 485, 490
Russell, William, 193, 199
Rye, 99, 100
Rylands, William, 277n

St. Ann's Bay, 434
St. Christopher's, 447, 452, 453, 455, 469
St. Croix, Chevalier de, 446
St. Domingo, 17, 113, 114, 267, 269, 270, 411, 431, 448, 453, 455, 473, 481
St. Eustatius, 463, 484
St. George's Channel, 34, 68
St. Helens, 48, 49, 209, 265, 275, 282, 288, 289, 290, 311, 312, 313, 314, 315, 316, 318, 320, 326, 331, 333, 334, 344, 345, 346, 348, 388, 389, 390, 391, 393, 394, 395, 396, 398, 400, 401, 402, 403, 404, 408, 409, 429
St. John's, Antigua, 444, 445, 447
St. John's, Newfoundland, 126, 127, 138, 139, 146, 148, 150, 152, 161, 162, 168
St. Lucia, 442, 443, 444, 445, 448, 449, 454, 455, 462, 469, 470, 476, 485
St. Malo, 111, 336, 382, 403
St. Pierre, 441, 442, 443, 445, 450, 451, 452, 454, 455, 457, 459, 460, 475, 477, 481
St. Pierre, Monsieur, 365
St. Philips, 219
St. Thomas, 466
St. Thomas Hospital, 107, 118
St. Vincent, 269, 442, 448, 451, 454, 462, 476
Saltash, 128, 172n
Sandwich, Earl of, 220, 488
San Sebastian, 15, 102, 455
Saul, Samuel, 242
Saumarez, Capt. Philip, 16, 105, 110n, 111, 198
Saumarez, Capt. Thomas, 285
Saunders, Vice Admiral Sir Charles, 392, 393, 445
Scilly Isles, 16, 102, 104, 111, 112, 119, 127, 246, 247
Scotland, 8, 12, 15, 16, 81, 109
Scott, Capt. Henry, 470
Seine River, 264, 297, 314, 352, 362, 381, 401

Senegal, 415
Seymour, Lt. Bowles, 62
Shakerly, Capt., 469
Sheerness, 7, 13, 14, 29, 44, 60, 61, 62, 53, 79, 80, 82, 83, 90, 122, 236, 238, 416
Shelburne, Lord, 488
Shetland Islands, 46
Shields, 11, 25, 43, 236

ships:
BRITISH MERCHANT SHIPS

Augustus Ceasar, 406
Duke packet, 478, 481
Egmont, 313n
Elenor, 110, 111
Greyhound, 241
Ilchester, 313n
Levant, 65, 66
London, 313n
Mars, 252
Mary, 43
Mary & Martha, 99n
Montfort, 12, 46
Osterly, 406
Prince Frederick packet, 164n, 165n, 246, 247
Prince of Wales, 77
Providence, 99n
Robert & Jane, 80, 81, 83
Robert and Mary, 99
Rover, 109
St. George, 75
Salisbury, 47
Theodosia, 43

BRITISH TRANSPORTS

Boscawen, 409
Dolphin, 253n
Elizabeth, 250
Hargrove, 443
Hope, 75
Hopeful Success, 253n
James, 409
Juno, 253n
Lark, 253n
Lyon, 469
Maria Theresa, 253n
Mary, 253n
Plymouth, 413
Samuel and Mary, 253n

Samuel and Robert, 253n
Two Brothers, 253n
Wallington, 253n

BRITISH WARSHIPS

Achilles, 262n, 280, 281, 282, 284, 285, 287n, 289, 290, 292, 294
Actæon, 382, 383, 387, 388, 389, 390, 393, 397, 403, 433, 443, 445, 453
Adventure armed vessel, 241
Æolus, 296n, 307, 311, 318
Alarm, 409, 453
Albany, 136, 265n, 266, 350n, 354, 355, 356n, 363, 366, 367, 377, 378, 379n, 380, 387, 388n, 389, 413, 416
Alcide, 242, 268n, 416
Aldborough, 46
Alderney, 70, 409, 412, 417
Amazon, 490, 491
Ambuscade, 398, 400
America, 232, 233
Anglesea, 12, 45, 215
Anson, 246, 306, 363
Anson cutter, 316, 330n, 341, 342, 343, 359, 360, 361, 381n, 385, 403, 404, 409
Antelope, 411
Antigua, 271, 440, 470, 482, 489
Aquilion, 265n, 270, 320, 350n, 354, 356, 357, 358, 360, 366, 367n, 368, 369, 370, 373, 374, 377, 378, 379, 380, 382, 384, 385, 386, 391, 394, 445, 446, 491n
Arundel, 206, 207, 208, 209, 211, 212
Aurora, 274, 275, 276, 277, 278, 280n, 281
Barbados, 467, 471
Barbados hired armed sloop, 466
Basilisk, 262n, 263, 276, 279, 287, 280n, 292n, 296n, 299, 302, 314, 315, 317, 318, 418, 433, 444
Beaver, 485, 486, 487
Bedford, 219
Beliqueux, 280, 281, 282, 284, 285, 286
Berwick, 6
Betsey tender, 80, 81, 83
Biddeford, 411
Bird in Hand cutter, 76
Blenheim hospital ship, 274n
Blast, 262n, 283, 286, 287n, 291, 294n, 296n, 298, 299, 302, 379n, 381, 382, 383, 416

INDEX 527

Blonde, 396
Bonetta, 364n, 370, 373, 374, 375, 376, 377, 378, 379, 395, 403
Boreas, 262n, 263n, 287n, 296n, 307, 311, 315, 316, 318, 322, 325, 326, 327, 330n, 333, 336, 339
Boston, 161, 163
Bridgewater, 73, 76n
Brilliant, 262n, 287n, 294n, 296n, 300, 307, 310, 311, 318, 319, 321, 322, 326, 327, 335, 336, 337
Burford, 27, 28, 253
Caesar hired armed sloop, 466
Carcass, 262n, 291, 292, 294n, 296n, 300, 301, 302, 309, 364n, 368, 370, 379n, 386, 287n, 388, 389, 391, 394, 403, 408
Catherine yacht, 237, 244
Catherine, armed sloop, 478
Centaur, 392, 393
Charlotte yacht, 55, 56, 58, 59
Chatham, 262n, 263n, 287n, 294, 296n, 308, 309
Chester, 16n, 116, 143, 144
Chesterfield, 262n, 287n, 291, 294
Chichester, 213, 214
Colchester, 53, 63
Convenor tender, 96
Cormorant, 405
Coventry, 296n, 297
Cruiser, 411, 457, 466
Culloden, 270n, 452, 453
Cygnet, 445
Danae, 319, 321n, 323, 464, 466
Defiance, 17n, 49, 51, 63, 79
Deptford, 262n, 265, 280, 281, 282, 284, 287n, 291, 294n, 296n, 300, 301, 302, 303, 304, 306, 307, 308, 309, 310, 311, 312, 313, 314, 315, 318, 319, 320, 321, 322, 323, 324, 325, 350n, 351, 352, 353, 355, 356, 357, 358, 359, 360, 361, 362, 363, 366, 367, 368, 370, 371, 372, 374, 375, 376, 377, 378, 379, 380
Devonshire, 17n, 268n, 270n, 449
Diligence, 404
Dolphin, 7, 16n, 320, 321, 381
Dorset cutter, 390
Dorsetshire, 399
Dover, 58, 316, 409, 413, 418, 419, 444
Dragon, 93, 95, 97, 267n, 268n, 405, 412n, 424, 430, 434, 444

Dreadnought, 5, 6
Dublin, 131, 132, 133, 227, 228, 229, 230, 233, 234, 235, 236, 237, 238, 239, 240, 241, 242, 244, 245, 246, 247, 248, 250, 251, 252, 253, 254, 255, 257, 268n, 283, 285, 329, 440
Dublin yacht, 36
Duke, 74, 76, 205, 210, 214, 215
Eagle, 14, 15, 16, 17, 18, 90, 91, 93, 94, 95, 96, 97, 98, 99, 100, 101, 103, 104, 105, 106, 108, 109, 110, 112, 113, 114, 115, 116, 117, 118, 119, 120, 122, 125, 137, 204, 206, 207, 208, 209, 211, 212, 214
Eagle tender, 414n
Echo, 440, 441, 452, 456
Edgar, 413, 419, 452, 453
Edinburgh, 16, 17n, 109, 110
Eltham, 40, 143, 144
Endeavour cutter, 330n, 339, 371
Épreuve, 442
Essex, 8, 155, 236, 412n, 300
Esther, see *Hesther*
Experiment tender, 414n
Falcon, 15, 101n, 103
Falkland, 6, 7, 296n, 297n, 458
Falmouth, 204, 205, 206, 208, 213, 214, 215
Ferret, 34, 271, 475, 483, 489, 490
Firedrake, 235, 241, 245, 262n, 265n, 266, 277, 278, 279, 280n, 281, 294n, 296n, 300, 317, 350n, 351, 352, 367, 371
Flamborough, 409, 412n
Fly, 262n, 263n, 287n, 289, 294, 296n, 311, 318, 320, 322, 323, 326
Fox, 84
Fortune, 274, 276
Foudroyant, 267n, 268, 275, 277, 278, 279, 424, 430, 433, 447, 453, 457, 458, 459, 460, 461, 464, 475, 479, 481, 484, 490, 491
Fougeux, 130, 173, 174, 175, 177, 178, 179, 180, 181, 186, 187, 195
Furnace, 43, 57, 58, 264n, 266, 277, 278, 280n, 281, 282, 286, 287n, 291, 294n, 296n, 298, 300, 317, 347, 348, 350n, 351, 352, 363, 367, 371, 381
Garland, 164, 404
Gibraltar, 47, 55, 57, 58

ships: BRITISH WARSHIPS (contd.)
Glasgow, 315, 316
Gloucester, 17n
Gosport, 56, 215
Gramont, 276, 280n
Granado, 267n, 423n, 428
Grampus, 23n, 322, 324
Greyhound, 31, 109, 211, 212, 214, 337, 396, 420, 468, 469, 470, 475
Guadeloupe, 442, 457
Hampton Court, 16n, 113, 115, 116
Hampshire, 40
Harwich, 40
Hawke, 33, 47
Hazards Prize, 236
Hector, 114, 115, 116
Hector cutter, 330n, 346, 347, 355, 366, 367, 381n, 383, 384, 385, 401, 402
Hesther cutter, 341, 342, 343, 354
Hind, 42
Hornet, 442
Hound, 56
Hunter cutter, 330n, 341, 342, 343, 353, 370, 381n, 403
Infernal, 376
Invincible, 218, 247, 248
Ipswich, 65, 68n
Isis, 262n, 263n, 280n, 287n, 294, 296n, 311, 312, 313, 314, 320
Jamaica, 58
Jane and Barbary tender, 277
Jason, 184, 273, 274, 407, 409
Jersey, 21, 68n, 215
Juno, 246, 247, 262n, 280n, 287n, 294n
Kennington, 117, 138
Kent, 16n, 17n, 51, 53, 54, 63, 68, 113, 130, 171, 172, 173
Kingfisher, 415, 418
King of Prussia cutter, 330n, 336, 367, 373, 374, 381n, 388, 389, 390, 401, 402
Kingston, 253, 255
Kinsale, 76n
Lancaster, 198
Launceston, 371, 412n, 419
Laurel, 396, 408
Levant, 273, 274, 275, 277, 478, 444, 490, 491
Lion, 16n, 17n
Lizard, 341, 342, 450, 454, 469

London, 82
Ludlow Castle, 12, 13, 14, 46, 48, 49, 50, 51, 52, 53, 56, 57, 59, 60, 61, 62, 63, 65, 66, 67, 68, 69, 70, 71, 72, 74, 75, 76, 77, 78, 79, 80, 82, 83, 84, 85, 87, 88, 89, 90, 91, 92, 93, 95, 98, 101, 102, 121, 122, 206, 208, 209, 210, 213, 215
Lyme, 139, 205, 206, 208, 209, 211, 212
Lynn, 411
Lynx, 478n, 491n
Maidstone, 51, 101, 103, 103, 411
Marlborough, 267n, 268, 389, 392, 394, 396, 406, 408, 411, 415, 416, 419, 420, 421, 422, 423, 428, 429, 430, 431, 433, 439, 442, 443, 444, 445, 447, 449, 453, 455, 457, 459
Mars, 484, 475, 479
Mary, 26n
Mediator, 72
Medway, 203
Melampe, *483*, *491n*
Mercury, 126, 136, 138, 139
Mermaid, 139, 140
Midford, 84
Modeste, 267n, 268n, 428, 432n, 433, 449, 453, 455, 458, 459, 461, 479, 485, 491n
Monarch, 131, 200, 201, 202, 203, 205, 206, 207, 208, 209, 210, 212, 213, 214, 215, 216, 217, 220, 221, 222, 224, 225, 227, 231, 232, 237
Monmouth, 17n, 101, 102, 215
Mortar, 262n, 285, 287n, 291, 294n, 296n, 289, 300, 314, 315, 317, 318
Namur, 8, 19, 411, 416, 418
New Britain tender, 236
New Britannia tender, 237, 239
Neptune tender, 431
Newcastle, 206, 215
Nightingale, 166
Northumberland, 205
Niger, 336, 337, 338, 340, 341, 342, 344
Nottingham, 15, 16, 17n, 101n, 195, 107, 109, 110, 120, 198, 267n, 268n, 270n, 278, 380, 383, 384, 385, 386, 387, 388, 389, 390, 391, 392, 393, 394, 395, 396, 397, 399, 400, 402, 403, 409, 423n, 428, 433
Norwich, 262n, 278, 280n, 282, 284,

INDEX

287n, 294n, 313, 317, 321, 322, 323, 324, 325, 326, 330, 331, 333, 334, 335, 336, 337, 338, 339, 340, 342, 343, 344, 345, 346, 347, 348, 349, 444, 453
Orford, 453, 455
Otter, 204, 207, 209, 210, 213, 215
Oxford, 19
Pelican, 364n, 371, 373, 376, 379n, 416
Pembroke, 396, 408, 414, 415, 418, 419, 479, 483, 485, 489
Penzance, 444
Peregrine, 215, 251, 252, 410, 411, 418
Phoenix, 321
Plymouth, 8, 9, 10, 19, 20, 21, 143
Pluto, 16n, 238
Pompey hired armed brig, 470
Poole, 76
Portland, 17n, 236
Portland's Prize, 101
Prince, 205, 210, 213, 214, 216
Prince Edward, 416
Prince George, 130, 131, 179, 180, 181, 182, 183, 184, 185, 187, 188, 190, 191, 192, 193, 197, 198, 199, 200, 201, 206, 224, 394, 395, 398, 409, 412n
Prince of Orange, 93, 95, 394, 395, 398, 409, 412n
Princess Amelia, 236
Princess Carolina, 411
Princess Louisa, 17n
Princess Mary, 62
Princess Royal, 25, 28, 406
Providence hired armed brigantine, 470, 478
Providence tender, 414n
Race Horse, 407
Rainbow, 126, 127, 134, 135, 136, 137, 138, 139, 140, 141, 142, 143, 144, 148, 150, 151, 152, 153, 154, 155, 156, 157, 158, 159, 160, 161, 163, 164, 165, 166, 167, 168, 169, 170, 392, 394
Raisonable, 268n, 433
Ranger, 355
Raven, 209, 213, 214, 406
Renown, 477
Repulse, 465, 481
Reynolds, 239
Richard & Thomas tender, 40
Rich Charlot tender, 25, 28
Richmond, 236, 438, 447

Roast Beef privateer and hired armed vessel, 340, 354, 371, 374, 377, 378, 379n, 401
Rochester, 203, 213, 450, 451, 452, 453, 454, 455, 457, 462, 491n
Roebuck, 245
Romney, 6
Rose, 350n, 351, 353, 356n, 357, 360, 363, 364n, 365n, 371, 374, 377, 379n, 380, 381, 440, 456
Royal Ann, 224, 274, 275, 289, 397
Royal Caroline, 27, 28, 50n, 96
Royal George, 218, 401
Royal George cutter, 381n, 341, 342
Royal Sovereign, 48, 49, 52, 53, 57, 62, 64, 65, 83, 93, 98, 248, 346, 347, 406, 407, 421
Ruby, 22, 23, 24, 28, 29, 31, 32, 38, 39
Rupert hospital ship, 212
St. Albans, 407
St. Anne, 469
St. George, 190
Salamander, 239
Saltash, 80, 81, 83, 126, 138, 144, 145, 147, 151, 162, 163, 164
Sandwich, 405, 412
Sapphire, 94, 96, 97, 98, 369, 411, 412
Sardoine, 445
Savage, 420
Savoy, 142
Scarborough, 478, 491n
Seaford, 358
Seahorse, 379, 380, 382, 387
Sea Nymphe tender, 213
Severn, 168
Sheerness, 10, 11, 12, 22, 23, 24, 25, 26, 27, 28, 30, 31, 32, 33, 34, 35, 37, 38, 39, 40, 41, 42, 45, 47, 48, 49, 63, 76n, 91, 121, 206, 207, 208, 209, 212
Solebay, 321, 390, 397, 398
Somerset, 7, 213, 214
Spy, 311, 322, 323, 326, 327, 396
Squirrel, 35, 36, 42, 43
Stag, 449, 465, 491n
Sterling Castle, 214, 268n, 270n
Strombolo, 236
Success, 135, 408, 449
Sunderland, 4, 5, 101n
Superb, 21, 408, 409, 410, 411, 412, 414, 415, 418, 446

ships: BRITISH WARSHIPS (contd.)
Swallow, 273, 275, 276, 277, 278, 279, 412n, 487, 490, 491
Syren, 479, 480, 483, 489
Tarter, 320, 375, 379, 380, 382, 383
Tartuff cutter, 409
Téméraire, 268n, 270n, 406, 407, 412n, 416, 433
Temple, 268n, 270n
Terrible, 179, 223, 253
Thunder, 267n, 296n, 298, 300, 318, 423n, 428n, 429, 433
Tilbury, 17n, 213, 248
Torrington, 68n, 69, 309, 411, 413, 414
Trent, 393, 491
Triumph, 4n
Tubbs, 26n
Tweed, 265n, 356n, 357, 361, 365, 366, 367, 371, 374, 375, 377, 379n, 382, 383, 388, 389, 393, 397, 403, 404, 405
Unicorn, 166, 263n, 284, 287n, 294, 296n, 298, 300, 301, 307, 311, 315, 316, 318, 319, 320, 322, 323, 324, 326, 327, 329, 330n, 333, 334, 335n, 338, 344, 380
Valiant, 408, 417, 418
Vanguard, 204, 205, 206, 207, 208, 210, 247, 250, 267n, 268n, 400, 432n, 428, 430, 437, 453, 481, 481n
Vestal, 262n, 287n, 291, 338, 341, 342, 344, 348
Virgin, 441, 462, 465, 466, 491n
Wager, 58, 409, 413, 416, 484
Warwick, 203
Weymouth, 204
William and Mary, 50
Winchester, 491n
Windsor, 17n, 204, 206, 208, 209, 211, 212
Wolf, 40, 41, 42, 43, 44, 200, 262n, 278n
Woolwich, 270, 320, 440, 464, 465, 466
Yarmouth, 17n, 104
York, 209, 214
Zephyr, 445

FRENCH MERCHANT SHIPS

Bellona, 16, 109, 110, 111
Charlotta, 17n
Du Guay Trouin, 403
Elizabeth, 382
Espérance, 17n

Favourite, 404
Foudroyant, 455
Europa, 17n
Grand Comte, 15
Joseph Lewis, 15
L'Austrée, 193
Marshal de Saxe, 16, 17n, 112
Mary Magdalene, 16
Ponte Quarré, 15
Prudent, 44
St. Claire, 17n
St. Esprit, 116
St. Malo, 17n
Shoreham, 15

FRENCH WARSHIPS

Active, 490
Chevre, 404n
Content, 17
Diadem, 411
Félicité, 266, 336, 338, 362, 374, 376, 377, 382, 387, 389, 404n
Fougeux, 17n, 18
Harmoine, 404n
Hector, 454
Intrépide, 17n, 18n
Juste, 337
L'Atlante, 203n
Minatour, 490
Monarque, 17n
Neptune, 17n, 18
Northumberland, 337
Royal Lewis, 490
Severn, 17n
Soleil Royal, 337
Septre, 490
Thames, 362, 363
Tonnant, 17n, 18
Trident, 17n

DUTCH MERCHANT SHIP

Tobais, 306

DUTCH WARSHIP

Stat Vel Warren, 332

SPANISH MERCHANT SHIPS

Experance, 15, 102
Nuestra Señora de Carmen, 15
Princessa, 20

INDEX

Prudent Sarah, 15
Santissimo Trinidada, 271–2, 483

SPANISH WARSHIPS

America, 164
Dragon, 164

Shuldham, Lt. Lemuel, 440
Shuldham, Capt. Molyneux, 434, 449, 453, 458
Shute, Jacob, 241n
Simpson, John, 232
Slade, William, 229
Smith, Capt. James, 236
Smith, Jeremiah, 156
Smith, Robert, 421n
Smith, Thomas, 157, 169
Smith, Vice Admiral Thomas, 62, 74, 75, 83, 87, 89, 93, 95, 103, 146, 148, 149, 284, 286, 291, 294, 299, 379, 380, 387
Snow, John, 206
Somersetshire, 212
Soubise, *see* Rohan
Sound, 60
Soundings, 101
Southampton, 99, 100, 392
South Carolina, 409
South Sea Company, 3
Spain, 68, 126, 189, 432, 435, 443, 446, 467
Spanish Main, 455, 467
Spinney, David, ix
Spithead, 4, 5, 6, 7, 8, 11, 12, 13, 19, 20, 30, 31, 32, 34, 36, 37, 38, 39, 48, 64, 65, 66, 67, 68, 69, 109, 113, 116, 126, 130, 131, 132, 133, 136, 137, 142, 144, 161, 166, 167, 177, 179, 183, 184, 185, 186, 192, 199, 200, 201, 210, 220, 221, 244, 246, 247, 248, 250, 253, 254, 255, 261, 272, 277, 278, 279, 281, 282, 285, 287, 288, 289, 294, 296, 298, 300, 301, 302, 308, 312, 313, 318, 320, 323, 326, 327, 328, 329, 334, 336, 339, 340, 342, 344, 347, 349, 351, 352, 355, 356, 357, 365, 373, 374, 376, 378, 380, 381, 383, 384, 385, 386, 487, 389, 392, 393, 394, 395, 398, 399, 400, 405, 496, 498, 409, 412, 413, 414, 415, 416, 418, 422, 423, 428, 429, 448, 485, 490
Spry, Commodore Richard, 116, 445, 447

Stanford Shoal, 13, 60, 61, 88
Standgate Creek, 62
Standford, Lt. William, 371
Stanhope, Capt. Thomas, 73
Start, 252, 254, 284
Stephens, Philip, 325, 339, 347, 348, 370, 374, 375, 376, 378, 381, 419, 421, 422, 428, 429, 430, 431, 448, 479, 474, 486, 487, 489, 491
Stephens, Robert, 421n
Steuart, Don Pedro, 164
Stewart, Vice Admiral James, 67, 68, 69
Stonehaven, 100
Stott, Capt. John, 478
Strachan, Capt. John, 396, 413
Stuart, Charles Edward, 109n
Suckling, Capt. Maurice, 9
Sulivan, Tomothy, 224n
Surtes, George, 236, 239n, 421n
Sussex, 160
Swanton, Rear Admiral Robert, 247, 409, 411, 434, 437, 442, 444, 445, 447, 471, 478, 481, 486, 488, 490, 491
Swynn, 59

Taunton, 160
Tavistock, 144
Temple, Lord, 227
Texel, 54
Thames River, 10, 40
Thane, Lt. John, 305
Thompson, Capt. Bradshaw, 76
Tilley, Henry 411
Titley, Walter, 39
Tobago, 443, 445, 457
Topsham, 99, 100, 137
Torgau, battle of, 391n
Touche, Le Vasser de la, 441, 442
Toulon, 79n
Townsend, Rear Admiral Isaac, 57
Trentham, Lord, 144
Trepassey, 145, 162
Trinidad, 484
Trinity, 446
Trouville-sur-Mer, 304, 305, 381n
Tucker, Capt. Thomas, 273
Tunbridge, 172
Turin, 222, 223
Turkey, 65,66
Tynemouth, 40, 43, 44, 83

Tynemouth Haven, 44
Tyrawley, Lord, 165
Tyrone county, 109

Udney, Mr., 461
Ushant, 112, 131, 132, 242, 251, 253, 431
Utrecht, Treaty of, 146n

Vanbrugh, Capt. Philip, 117, 137, 151
Vane, Capt. Hon. Raby, 332
Vernon, Admiral Edward, 84n
Versailles, 432
Victualling Board, 45, 92, 151, 156, 158, 170, 177, 221, 398, 424, 425
Vigo, 132, 133, 251
Villane, 338
Villa Franca, 8, 10
Vincent, Capt. Nicholas, 211
Virginia, 85, 442
Virgin Islands, 466

Wade, Maj. Gen. George, 56
Walch, Brig. Robert, 444
Wake, Cuthert, 92
Wallis, Capt., 409
Walpole, Horace, 125
Walsh, Lt. Philip, 353, 355
Walsingham, Capt. Hon. Robert Boyle, 325, 326, 434, 439, 442, 449
Walter, Mrs., 177
Ware, 241
Wareham, John, 168, 237
Webb, Capt., 204
Weller, Capt. John, 36, 168, 237

Wellhalm, John Frederick, 241n
Wells, William, 180n
Wemyss, David, 109n
Weser, River, 54
Wesledge, John, 180n
West, James, 417, 420
West, Rear Admiral Temple, 178
West Indies, 54, 112, 267, 430, 431, 441
Westminster, 144n
Weymouth, 137
Wheeler, Capt. Edward, 281, 294, 301, 312, 313, 314
Wheelock, Capt. John, 419
Whitby, 241
Whiting Sands, 14, 89, 92
Witmore, Capt. Edward, 300
Wild Road, 36
William, Sir Charles Henbury, 325
Williams, Capt. Roger, 457
Willis, Capt. Thomas, 381, 416
Wilson, Edward, 224n
Windward Islands, 431
Winnet, Edward, 421n
Wood, Moses, 29
Woolwich, 6, 126, 127, 140, 141, 142, 153, 154, 155, 156, 157, 158, 159, 166, 167, 170, 234, 236, 298
Woburn Abbey, 225
Wright, Henry, 215
Wynne, Mr., 144

Yarmouth, 12, 28, 41, 42, 43, 47, 59, 60, 61, 84, 85, 86, 87, 88, 241
Young Pretender, *see* Stuart, Charles Edward

NAVY RECORDS SOCIETY
(FOUNDED 1893)

The Navy Records Society was established for the purpose of printing unpublished manuscripts and rare works of naval interest. Membership of the Society is open to all who are interested in naval history, and any person wishing to become a member should apply to the Hon. Secretary, Professor A. D. Lambert, Department of War Studies, King's College London, Strand, London WC2R 2LS, United Kingdom. The annual subscription is £30, which entitles the member to receive one free copy of each work issued by the Society in that year, and to buy earlier issues at reduced prices.

A list of works, available to members only, is shown below; very few copies are left of those marked with an asterisk. Volumes out of print are indicated by **OP**. Prices for works in print are available on application to Mrs Annette Gould, 5 Goodwood Close, Midhurst, West Sussex GU29 9JG, United Kingdom, to whom all enquiries concerning works in print should be sent. Those marked 'TS', 'SP' and 'A' are published for the Society by Temple Smith, Scolar Press and Ashgate, and are available to non-members from the Ashgate Publishing Group, Gower House, Croft Road, Aldershot, Hampshire GU11 3HR. Those marked 'A & U' are published by George Allen & Unwin, and are available to non-members only through bookshops.

Vol. 1. *State papers relating to the Defeat of the Spanish Armada, Anno 1588*, Vol. I, ed. Professor J. K. Laughton. **TS**.

Vol. 2. *State papers relating to the Defeat of the Spanish Armada, Anno 1588*, Vol. II, ed. Professor J. K. Laughton. **TS**.

Vol. 3. *Letters of Lord Hood, 1781–1783*, ed. D. Hannay. **OP**.

Vol. 4. *Index to James's Naval History*, by C. G. Toogood, ed. by the Hon. T. A. Brassey. **OP**.

Vol. 5. *Life of Captain Stephen Martin, 1666–1740*, ed. Sir Clements R. Markham. **OP**.

Vol. 6. *Journal of Rear Admiral Bartholomew James, 1752–1828*, ed. Professor J. K. Laughton & Cdr. J. Y. F. Sullivan. **OP**.

Vol. 7. *Hollond's Discourses of the Navy, 1638 and 1659*, ed. J. R. Tanner. **OP**.

Vol. 8. *Naval Accounts and Inventories in the Reign of Henry VII*, ed. M. Oppenheim. **OP**.

Vol. 9. *Journal of Sir George Rooke*, ed. O. Browning. **OP**.

Vol. 10. *Letters and Papers relating to the War with France 1512–1513*, ed. M. Alfred Spont. **OP**.

Vol. 11. *Papers relating to the Spanish War 1585–1587*, ed. Julian S. Corbett. TS.

Vol. 12. *Journals and Letters of Admiral of the Fleet Sir Thomas Byam Martin, 1773–1854*, Vol. II (see No. 24), ed. Admiral Sir R. Vesey Hamilton. **OP**.

Vol. 13. *Papers relating to the First Dutch War, 1652–1654*, Vol. I, ed. Dr S. R. Gardiner. **OP**.

Vol. 14. *Papers relating to the Blockade of Brest, 1803–1805*, Vol. I, ed. J. Leyland. **OP**.

Vol. 15. *History of the Russian Fleet during the Reign of Peter the Great, by a Contemporary Englishman*, ed. Admiral Sir Cyprian Bridge. **OP**.

Vol. 16. *Logs of the Great Sea Fights, 1794–1805*, Vol. I, ed. Vice Admiral Sir T. Sturges Jackson. **OP**.

Vol. 17. *Papers relating to the First Dutch War, 1652–1654*, ed. Dr S. R. Gardiner. **OP**.

*Vol. 18. *Logs of the Great Sea Fights*, Vol. II, ed. Vice Admiral Sir T. Sturges Jackson.

Vol. 19. *Journals and Letters of Admiral of the Fleet Sir Thomas Byam Martin*, Vol. II (see No. 24), ed. Admiral Sir R. Vesey Hamilton. **OP**.

Vol. 20. *The Naval Miscellany*, Vol. I, ed. Professor J. K. Laughton.

Vol. 21. *Papers relating to the Blockade of Brest, 1803–1805*, Vol. II, ed. J. Leyland. **OP**.

Vol. 22. *The Naval Tracts of Sir William Monson*, Vol. I, ed. M. Oppenheim. **OP**.

Vol. 23. *The Naval Tracts of Sir William Monson*, Vol. II, ed. M. Oppenheim. **OP**.

Vol. 24. *The Journals and Letters of Admiral of the Fleet Sir Thomas Byam Martin*, Vol. I, ed. Admiral Sir R. Vesey Hamilton. **OP**.

Vol. 25. *Nelson and the Neapolitan Jacobins*, ed. H. C. Gutteridge. **OP**.

Vol. 26. *A Descriptive Catalogue of the Naval MSS in the Pepysian Library*, Vol. I, ed. J. R. Tanner. **OP**.

Vol. 27. *A Descriptive Catalogue of the Naval MSS in the Pepysian Library*, Vol. II, ed. J. R. Tanner. **OP**.

Vol. 28. *The Correspondence of Admiral John Markham, 1801–1807*, ed. Sir Clements R. Markham. **OP**.

Vol. 29. *Fighting Instructions, 1530–1816*, ed. Julian S. Corbett. **OP**.

Vol. 30. *Papers relating to the First Dutch War, 1652–1654*, Vol. III, ed. Dr S. R. Gardiner & C. T. Atkinson. **OP**.

Vol. 31. *The Recollections of Commander James Anthony Gardner, 1775–1814*, ed. Admiral Sir R. Vesey Hamilton & Professor J. K. Laughton.

Vol. 32. *Letters and Papers of Charles, Lord Barham, 1758–1813*, ed. Professor Sir John Laughton.

Vol. 33. *Naval Songs and Ballads*, ed. Professor C. H. Firth. **OP**.

Vol. 34. *Views of the Battles of the Third Dutch War*, ed. by Julian S. Corbett. **OP**.

Vol. 35. *Signals and Instructions, 1776–1794*, ed. Julian S. Corbett. **OP**.

Vol. 36. *A Descriptive Catalogue of the Naval MSS in the Pepysian Library*, Vol III, ed. J. R. Tanner. **OP**.

Vol. 37. *Papers relating to the First Dutch War, 1652–1654*, Vol. IV, ed. C. T. Atkinson. **OP**.

Vol. 38. *Letters and Papers of Charles, Lord Barham, 1758–1813*, Vol. II, ed. Professor Sir John Laughton. **OP**.

Vol. 39. *Letters and Papers of Charles, Lord Barham, 1758–1813*, Vol. III, ed. Professor Sir John Laughton. **OP**.

Vol. 40. *The Naval Miscellany*, Vol. II, ed. Professor Sir John Laughton.

*Vol. 41. *Papers relating to the First Dutch War, 1652–1654*, Vol. V, ed. C. T. Atkinson.

Vol. 42. *Papers relating to the Loss of Minorca in 1756*, ed. Captain H. W. Richmond, R.N. **OP**.

*Vol. 43. *The Naval Tracts of Sir William Monson*, Vol. III, ed. M. Oppenheim.

Vol. 44. *The Old Scots Navy 1689–1710*, ed. James Grant. **OP**.

Vol. 45. *The Naval Tracts of Sir William Monson*, Vol. IV, ed. M. Oppenheim.

Vol. 46. *The Private Papers of George, 2nd Earl Spencer*, Vol. I, ed. Julian S. Corbett. **OP**.

Vol. 47. *The Naval Tracts of Sir William Monson*, Vol. V, ed. M. Oppenheim.

Vol. 48. *The Private Papers of George, 2nd Earl Spencer*, Vol. II, ed. Julian S. Corbett. **OP**.

Vol. 49. *Documents relating to Law and Custom of the Sea*, Vol. I, ed. R. G. Marsden. **OP**.

*Vol. 50. *Documents relating to Law and Custom of the Sea*, Vol. II, ed. R. G. Marsden.

Vol. 51. *Autobiography of Phineas Pett*, ed. W. G. Perrin. **OP**.

Vol. 52. *The Life of Admiral Sir John Leake*, Vol. I, ed. Geoffrey Callender.

Vol. 53. *The Life of Admiral Sir John Leake*, Vol. II, ed. Geoffrey Callender.

Vol. 54. *The Life and Works of Sir Henry Mainwaring*, Vol. I, ed. G. E. Manwaring.

Vol. 55. *The Letters of Lord St Vincent, 1801–1804*, Vol. I, ed. D. B. Smith. **OP**.

Vol. 56. *The Life and Works of Sir Henry Mainwaring*, Vol. II, ed. G. E. Manwaring & W. G. Perrin. **OP**.

Vol. 57. *A Descriptive Catalogue of the Naval MSS in the Pepysian Library*, Vol. IV, ed. Dr J. R. Tanner. **OP**.

Vol. 58. *The Private Papers of George, 2nd Earl Spencer*, Vol. III, ed. Rear Admiral H. W. Richmond. **OP**.

Vol. 59. *The Private Papers of George, 2nd Earl Spencer*, Vol. IV, ed. Rear Admiral H. W. Richmond. **OP**.

Vol. 60. *Samuel Pepys's Naval Minutes*, ed. Dr J. R. Tanner.

Vol. 61. *The Letters of Lord St Vincent, 1801–1804*, Vol. II, ed. D. B. Smith. **OP**.

Vol. 62. *Letters and Papers of Admiral Viscount Keith*, Vol. I, ed. W. G. Perrin. **OP**.

Vol. 63. *The Naval Miscellany*, Vol. III, ed. W. G. Perrin. **OP**.

Vol. 64. *The Journal of the 1st Earl of Sandwich*, ed. R. C. Anderson. **OP**.

*Vol. 65. *Boteler's Dialogues*, ed. W. G. Perrin.

Vol. 66. *Papers relating to the First Dutch War, 1652–1654*, Vol. VI (with index), ed. C. T. Atkinson.

*Vol. 67. *The Byng Papers*, Vol. I, ed. W. C. B. Tunstall.

*Vol. 68. *The Byng Papers*, Vol. II, ed. W. C. B. Tunstall.

Vol. 69. *The Private Papers of John, Earl of Sandwich*, Vol. I, ed. G. R. Barnes & Lt. Cdr. J. H. Owen, R.N. Corrigenda to *Papers relating to the First Dutch War, 1652–1654, Vols I–VI*, ed. Captain A. C. Dewar, R.N. **OP**.

Vol. 70. *The Byng Papers*, Vol. III, ed. W. C. B. Tunstall.

Vol. 71. *The Private Papers of John, Earl of Sandwich*, Vol. II, ed. G. R. Barnes & Lt. Cdr. J. H. Owen, R.N. **OP**.

Vol. 72. *Piracy in the Levant, 1827–1828*, ed. Lt. Cdr. C. G. Pitcairn Jones, R.N. **OP**.

Vol. 73. *The Tangier Papers of Samuel Pepys*, ed. Edwin Chappell.

Vol. 74. *The Tomlinson Papers*, ed. J. G. Bullocke.

Vol. 75. *The Private Papers of John, Earl of Sandwich*, Vol. III, ed. G. R. Barnes & Cdr. J. H. Owen, R.N. **OP**.

Vol. 76. *The Letters of Robert Blake*, ed. the Rev. J. R. Powell. **OP**.

*Vol. 77. *Letters and Papers of Admiral the Hon. Samuel Barrington*, Vol. I, ed. D. Bonner-Smith.

Vol. 78. *The Private Papers of John, Earl of Sandwich*, Vol. IV, ed. G. R. Barnes & Cdr. J. H. Owen, R.N. **OP**.

*Vol. 79. *The Journals of Sir Thomas Allin, 1660–1678*, Vol. I *1660–1666*, ed. R. C. Anderson.

Vol. 80. *The Journals of Sir Thomas Allin, 1660–1678*, Vol. II *1667–1678*, ed. R. C. Anderson.

Vol. 81. *Letters and Papers of Admiral the Hon. Samuel Barrington*, Vol. II, ed. D. Bonner-Smith. **OP**.

Vol. 82. *Captain Boteler's Recollections, 1808–1830*, ed. D. Bonner-Smith. **OP**.

Vol. 83. *Russian War, 1854. Baltic and Black Sea: Official Correspondence*, ed. D. Bonner-Smith & Captain A. C. Dewar, R.N. **OP**.

Vol. 84. *Russian War, 1855. Baltic: Official Correspondence*, ed. D. Bonner-Smith. **OP**.

Vol. 85. *Russian War, 1855. Black Sea: Official Correspondence*, ed. Captain A.C. Dewar, R.N. **OP**.

Vol. 86. *Journals and Narratives of the Third Dutch War*, ed. R. C. Anderson. **OP**.

Vol. 87. *The Naval Brigades in the Indian Mutiny, 1857–1858*, ed. Cdr. W. B. Rowbotham, R.N. **OP**.

Vol. 88. *Patee Byng's Journal*, ed. J. L. Cranmer-Byng. **OP**.

*Vol. 89. *The Sergison Papers, 1688–1702*, ed. Cdr. R. D. Merriman, R.I.N.

Vol. 90. *The Keith Papers*, Vol. II, ed. Christopher Lloyd. **OP**.

Vol. 91. *Five Naval Journals, 1789–1817*, ed. Rear Admiral H. G. Thursfield. **OP**.

Vol. 92. *The Naval Miscellany*, Vol. IV, ed. Christopher Lloyd. **OP**.

Vol. 93. *Sir William Dillon's Narrative of Professional Adventures, 1790–1839*, Vol. I *1790–1802*, ed. Professor Michael Lewis. **OP**.

Vol. 94. *The Walker Expedition to Quebec, 1711*, ed. Professor Gerald S. Graham. **OP**.

Vol. 95. *The Second China War, 1856–1860*, ed. D. Bonner-Smith & E. W. R. Lumby. **OP**.

Vol. 96. *The Keith Papers, 1803–1815*, Vol. III, ed. Professor Christopher Lloyd.

Vol. 97. *Sir William Dillon's Narrative of Professional Adventures, 1790–1839*, Vol. II *1802–1839*, ed. Professor Michael Lewis. **OP**.

Vol. 98. *The Private Correspondence of Admiral Lord Collingwood*, ed. Professor Edward Hughes. **OP**.

Vol. 99. *The Vernon Papers, 1739–1745*, ed. B. McL. Ranft. **OP**.

Vol. 100. *Nelson's Letters to his Wife and Other Documents*, ed. Lt. Cdr. G. P. B. Naish, R.N.V.R. **OP**.

Vol. 101. *A Memoir of James Trevenen, 1760–1790*, ed. Professor Christopher Lloyd & R. C. Anderson. **OP**.

Vol. 102. *The Papers of Admiral Sir John Fisher*, Vol. I, ed. Lt. Cdr. P. K. Kemp, R.N. **OP**.

Vol. 103. *Queen Anne's Navy*, ed. Cdr. R. D. Merriman, R.I.N. **OP**.

Vol. 104. *The Navy and South America, 1807–1823*, ed. Professor Gerald S. Graham & Professor R. A. Humphreys.

Vol. 105. *Documents relating to the Civil War, 1642–1648*, ed. The Rev. J. R. Powell & E. K. Timings. **OP**.

Vol. 106. *The Papers of Admiral Sir John Fisher*, Vol. II, ed. Lt. Cdr. P. K. Kemp, R.N. **OP**.

Vol. 107. *The Health of Seamen*, ed. Professor Christopher Lloyd.

Vol. 108. *The Jellicoe Papers*, Vol. I *1893–1916*, ed. A. Temple Patterson.

Vol. 109. *Documents relating to Anson's Voyage round the World, 1740–1744*, ed. Dr Glyndwr Williams. **OP**.

Vol. 110. *The Saumarez Papers: The Baltic, 1808–1812*, ed. A. N. Ryan. **OP**.

Vol. 111. *The Jellicoe Papers*, Vol. II *1916–1925*, ed. Professor A. Temple Patterson.

Vol. 112. *The Rupert and Monck Letterbook, 1666*, ed. The Rev. J. R. Powell & E. K. Timings.

Vol. 113. *Documents relating to the Royal Naval Air Service*, Vol. I (*1908–1918*), ed. Captain S. W. Roskill, R.N.

*Vol. 114. *The Siege and Capture of Havana, 1762*, ed. Professor David Syrett.

Vol. 115. *Policy and Operations in the Mediterranean, 1912–1914*, ed. E. W. R. Lumby. **OP**.

Vol. 116. *The Jacobean Commissions of Enquiry, 1608 and 1618*, ed. Dr A. P. McGowan.

Vol. 117. *The Keyes Papers*, Vol. I *1914–1918*, ed. Professor Paul Halpern.

Vol. 118. *The Royal Navy and North America: The Warren Papers, 1736–1752*, ed. Dr Julian Gwyn. **OP**.

Vol. 119. *The Manning of the Royal Navy: Selected Public Pamphlets, 1693–1873*, ed. Professor John Bromley.

Vol. 120. *Naval Administration, 1715–1750*, ed. Professor D. A. Baugh.

Vol. 121. *The Keyes Papers*, Vol. II *1919–1938*, ed. Professor Paul Halpern.

Vol. 122. *The Keyes Papers*, Vol. III *1939–1945*, ed. Professor Paul Halpern.

Vol. 123. *The Navy of the Lancastrian Kings: Accounts and Inventories of William Soper, Keeper of the King's Ships, 1422–1427*, ed. Dr Susan Rose.

Vol. 124. *The Pollen Papers: the Privately Circulated Printed Works of Arthur Hungerford Pollen, 1901–1916*, ed. Professor Jon T. Sumida. A. & U.

Vol. 125. *The Naval Miscellany*, Vol. V, ed. Dr N. A. M. Rodger. A & U.

Vol. 126. *The Royal Navy in the Mediterranean, 1915–1918*, ed. Professor Paul Halpern. TS.

Vol. 127. *The Expedition of Sir John Norris and Sir Francis Drake to Spain and Portugal, 1589*, ed. Professor R. B. Wernham. TS.

Vol. 128. *The Beatty Papers*, Vol. I *1902–1918*, ed. Professor B. McL. Ranft. SP.

Vol. 129. *The Hawke Papers: A Selection, 1743–1771*, ed. Dr R. F. Mackay. SP.

Vol. 130. *Anglo-American Naval Relations, 1917–1919*, ed. Michael Simpson. SP.

Vol. 131. *British Naval Documents, 1204–1960*, ed. Professor John B. Hattendorf, Dr Roger Knight, Alan Pearsall, Dr Nicholas Rodger & Professor Geoffrey Till. SP.

Vol. 132. *The Beatty Papers*, Vol. II *1916–1927*, ed. Professor B. McL. Ranft. SP

Vol. 133. *Samuel Pepys and the Second Dutch War*, transcribed by Professor William Matthews & Dr Charles Knighton; ed. Robert Latham. SP.

Vol. 134. *The Somerville Papers*, ed. Michael Simpson, with the assistance of John Somerville. SP.

Vol. 135. *The Royal Navy in the River Plate, 1806–1807*, ed. John D. Grainger. SP.

Vol. 136. *The Collective Naval Defence of the Empire, 1900–1940*, ed. Nicholas Tracy. A.

Vol. 137. *The Defeat of the Enemy Attack on Shipping, 1939–1945*, ed. Eric Grove. A.

Vol. 138. *Shipboard Life and Organisation, 1731–1815*, ed. Brian Lavery. A.

Vol. 139. *The Battle of the Atlantic and Signals Intelligence: U-boat Situations and Trends, 1941–1945*, ed. Professor David Syrett. A.

Vol. 140. *The Cunningham Papers*, Vol. I: *The Mediterranean Fleet, 1939–1942*, ed. Michael Simpson. A.

Vol. 141. *The Channel Fleet and the Blockade of Brest, 1793–1801*, ed. Roger Morriss. A.
Vol. 142. *The Submarine Service, 1900–1918*, ed. Nicholas Lambert. A.
Vol. 143. *Letters and Papers of Professor Sir John Knox Laughton (1830–1915)*, ed. Andrew Lambert. A.
Vol. 144. *The Battle of the Atlantic and Signals Intelligence: U-Boat Tracking Papers 1941–1947*, ed. Professor David Syrett. A.
Vol. 145. *The Maritime Blockade of Germany in the Great War: The Northern Patrol, 1914–1918*, ed. John D. Grainger. A.
Vol. 146. *The Naval Miscellany: Volume VI*, ed. Michael Duffy. A.
Vol. 147. *The Milne Papers: Volume I*, ed. Professor John Beeler. A.

Occasional Publications:

Vol. 1. *The Commissioned Sea Officers of the Royal Navy, 1660–1815*, ed. Professor David Syrett & Professor R. L. DiNardo. SP.
Vol. 2. *The Anthony Roll of Henry VIII's Navy*, ed. C. S. Knighton and D. M. Loades. A.